# VIETNAM

# VIETNAM

## A CHRONICLE OF THE WAR

TEXT BY MICHAEL MACLEAR

PHOTOGRAPHY EDITED BY HAL BUELL

Tess
Press

NEW YORK

Illustration sources: AP Wide World Photos,
The Requiem Collection

Published by Tess Press an imprint of
Black Dog & Leventhal Publishers
151 West 19th Street
New York, NY 10011

Manufactured in  China

Jacket and interior design by Liz Trovato

Library of Congress Cataloguing in Publication Data
Available on file

ISBN-13: 978-1-57912-407-6

n m l k j i h g f

Above: January, 1945 -- U.S. Avenger warplanes return to their carrier after a strike on Saigon as the Third Fleet struck shipping and land targets along the southeast coast of Indochina.

# CONTENTS

Above: A rifle company composed of locally hired recruits pose with their French colonial officers around the turn of the century in Indochina.

Left: These are leaders of a bandit gang captured by French colonial soldiers prior to 1910. One prisoner has already been executed by strangulation. The other stands awaiting his fate. His crime and punishment is inscribed on the white card around his neck. Journals of the time said these prisoners did not request pity, and remained impassive as the execution was carried out.

# PREFACE

Above: French colonial soldiers pose with a small Chinese boy who is pretending to smoke a long stemmed pipe. Date unknown.

Above: A French fort in Song Ha was typical of the outposts in colonial Indochina. The camp is surrounded by spiked, tightly woven stakes, sometimes laced with thorns and other obstacles designed to cut invaders. These posts were commanded by French army non-commissioned officers and were manned by rather small contingents of local recruits. Lookout towers were at the corners of the walls. In many ways they resembled the protected hamlets of the mid-20th century.

What lured the French to Indochina can be summed up in one word—trade. And with trade came missionaries.

Some came as early as the 17th century. One monk created a western alphabet for the Vietnamese language thereby improving and formalizing agreements.

French and Vietnamese relations—both business and religious—were uneasy from the start. The Vietnamese were aware of the encroaching western influence in Asia—British, Dutch, Portuguese—that swirled around them. They noted, also, the powerful military machines the Europeans brought to bear upon those who resisted western influence.

The French moved forcefully into the area then known in the west as Tonkin, Annam and Cochin China. These names, all but lost now, were used as late as the end of World War II. Tonkin in the north came to be known as North Vietnam. Cochin China became South Vietnam. Annam was in the central part of the long Vietnam coastline. The Vietnamese were known generally as Annamites in the west.

French tradesmen and missionaries ingratiated themselves with the Vietnamese with promises to help local groups in their battles with other groups. These squabbles and sometimes outright wars consisted mostly of north and south Vietnamese who battled over ancient differences. The missionaries, virtually all Catholic, succeeded with their conversions with the result that anti-missionary attitudes developed within the Vietnamese leadership. Missionary executions and imprisonments were frequent. The French seized upon these troubles and, claiming protection of their citizens, moved more aggressively. In 1857 French war ships and soldiers, under orders of Napoleon III, invaded Vietnam. Soon 14 ships and 5,000 men were at Danang, then moved south to the Mekong Delta and Saigon to look after French missionary and business interests there. In future years French troops would enter Tonkin to ensure safe passage of traders to China via the Red River.

In an interesting historical footnote, American Marines from the USS Constitution landed at Tourane (later known as Danang) in 1845 and responded to French missionary requests for protection and escort. Marines aboard the vessel went as far up the coast as Hue to assist French missionaries. The effort was short lived and only mildly successful, and soon the Constitution moved on to other assignments. Some 120 years later U.S. Marines landed once again at Danang.

Affairs in Europe slowed the French advance in the 1870s but a decade later French ships bombarded Hue as they fought secret societies, many of them outright bandits but some ardent nationalists. In panic the mandarins of Hue, the ancient capital of Vietnam, surrendered the whole country to the French. By the turn of the century all of Indochina—Tonkin, Annam, Cochin China, Cambodia and Laos—was under French control.

The uneasiness remained however. French troops regularly fought bandit groups in many of the Indochina states. Nationalist uprisings also picked away at French control, even as Vietnamese were educated in France and gained substantive assignments in the French colonial bureaucracy. In Paris a Vietnamese community was integrated into society and the colony bore fruit that enriched the empire.

The French recruited locals and created an army of Vietnamese regulars who fought side by side with French troops under the command of French officers to pacify the countryside and the smaller villages. French control was harsh, even brutal, as troops confronted an enemy of long historical mix—bandits, warlords, nationalists and those reluctant to accept western rule.

Throughout the period the Vietnamese emperor remained on the throne, a monarchy that lasted until the removal of Bao Dai, the last emperor, in 1955.

In 1890 Ho Chi Minh was born into this scene. By 1912 he had left Vietnam a devoted Nationalist. Ho traveled extensively, spent World War I in France and by 1920 was active in communist circles. He lived in Russia, in China, visited world capitals including New York. Throughout his extensive travels his connections to affairs in Vietnam remained intact. As World War II expanded Ho returned to Vietnam where he began development of the Viet Minh. During the war he resisted the Japanese conquerors of Indochina, even assisted U.S. and British forces likewise battling the Japanese.

The smoke of World War II drifted away. Ho Chi Minh was ready.

Above: A member of the local colonial force prepares to decapitate a captured bandit in Indochina. Frequently the machete used the by executioner was blunt and several blows were required to complete the execution. Date unkown.

Below: French soldiers pose in Indochina in their battle gear. The wear small back packs, and are equipped with bayonets for their rifles. These men were typical of the French colonial army enlisted man.  Date unknown.

Above: May 1941 - Bao Dai, emperor of Annam, appears in the doorway of his palace in Hue, the capital of the French protectorate.

Below: Annamite soldiers march in a parade in Paris on July 14, 1913.  Local recruits were sometimes taken to the French capital for training and to celebrate expanse of the French Empire.

Above: Annamite soldiers of the French colonial army pose in uniform and with weapons prior to a review of troops in Indochina in 1891.

Right: 1940 - French and government forces handle an uprising in Indochina.

Below: September 26, 1940 - French colonial troops move out of Haiphong as Japanese occupied the port city under a Franco-Japanese agreement. Only a small French garrison remained.

Above: 1940 - Marchers protest in Indochina.

Right: 1940 - Bystanders run from the scene of an uprising in Indochina.

Above: January 11, 1945 - Precious Japanese fuel burns at a Saigon depot after an air raid by U.S. carrier-based planes.

Below: January 12, 1945 - Avenger torpedo-bombers of the U.S. Navy 3rd Fleet cross the coast of Indochina en route to Saigon on a bombing run of Japanese shipping and military installations. Hundreds of Japanese ships and planes were reported destroyed during a two-week sweep of the South China Sea.

# ACKNOWLEDGEMENTS

This book was made possible in large measure by the extensive contribution of Peter Arnett to the television history series of the same title. Arnett's Vietnam reports for the Associated Press over thirteen years won him the Pulitzer Prize, and the AP, in graciously granting Arnett several months leave to help counsel and write the first such history series, greatly ensured its authenticity. Peter's knowledge and reportorial skills resulted in the important, pungent and vividly fresh accounts by the principal figures in the Vietnam war who were mostly interviewed by Arnett – and this book is based on those interviews.

The author is equally indebted to senior researcher Oleh J. Rumak, whose painstaking pursuit of the facts—and the interviewees—was the foundation of both the series and the book; and in the preparation of this manuscript is indebted above all to researcher and associate writer Shelley Saywell. In terms of effort, ideas and enthusiasm this book is as much hers as mine.

Admiration as well as gratitude is felt for the senior producer of the series, Ian McLeod, and for its director, Mike Feheley, whose encouragement took the noble form of relieving me of other pressures; my special thanks to Julie Smith-Eddy for her tireless help on the typing of the manuscript; to Nicholas Jones of Thames Television who first suggested making a book from the series; to Ann Wilson of Methuen for her wise counsel and revisions, and to Leslie M. Pockell of St Martin's Press for his sage suggestions; to film producer Paul Lang who shared the history-making visit to Vietnam; to Yasuo Yanagisawa and the staff of Nihon Denpa News who made the arrangements, and my thanks to so many helpful people in both Vietnam and the United States. Yet the book would still not have been possible without the patience and extra care of my wife, Mariko, and daughter Kyo.

This book is dedicated also to the cameramen whose lens saw the battle clearest—especially to the late Kimbei Nakai who first took me to Vietnam, to Ryoko Fujii, Misao Ishigaki and Phillip Pendry who shared the tight corners in North and South, and to a dear friend, Yoshihiko Waku, who went with me but did not return.

—MICHAEL MACLEAR

The following people were invaluable — many thanks for expert help to: Grant Lamos V, Lotus Photography, and Richard Horwitz, PhotoIdeas, for digital photography; Chuck Zoeller, Associated Press, and Richard Hortwitz, PhotoIdeas, for captions; Horst Faas, Associated Press for antique picture research; Chuck Zoeller, Associated Press and Jorge Jaramillo, AP/Wide World Photos for photo research assistance; thanks to Horst Faas, Malcome Browne, Nick Ut and Eddie Adams for telling their stories; Richard Pyle, Associated Press for work on the chronology.

—HAL BUELL, NEW YORK, 2003

Above: November, 1941- During the buildup to war in the Pacific, Japanese tanks enter a town in Indochina.

Left: March 1937 - French officers and native troops practice war maneuvers in a rice field in Cochin China which later became South Vietnam.

Right: February 1937 - Vietnamese peasants with full field equipment are trained by the French at a camp at St. Jacques, in the French province of Cochin China, to defend France's far eastern empire.

Above: Members of an infantry regiment of the French colonial army work with a machine gun while on maneuvers in Indochina. French soldier mans the trigger as Annamite troops feed the belt. Date unknown.

Right: Locally recruited troops of the French colonial army stand in a fort captured from the enemy during a battle in Tonkin shortly after the turn of the century.

# INTRODUCTION

Above: A prisoner in Indochina wears the wooden stockade device used to prevent escape. He is guarded by a local recruit of the French colonial army. Picture circa 1900.

Above: Pirates captured in 1885 are shown wearing the stockade like device around their neck to prevent escape. The group was later decapitated.

The main events of the Vietnam war are familiar reading and many of the principal figures have written their own accounts of it. Vietnam: The Ten Thousand Day War attempts to provide what has been missing: a compilation of first-hand testimony, the collective findings of those who planned and fought this century's longest and most controversial war, covering the entire period of both the French and American involvement from 1945 to 1975. It draws on scores of interviews with French and American, South and North Vietnamese participants recorded recently for the television series of the same title and which are original to the series and this book. The television account, however, could only present a fraction of the interview material contained here.

The book is primarily concerned with America's Vietnam policy and its present-day implications. It is by no means a definitive record of all the events, policies and personalities of those thirty years, although every effort has been made to update statistics and verify or correct previously published facts. The linking narrative provides the reader with background information on the people interviewed and the events they describe; it aims to clarify, not judge, the statements made. Some of the accounts are no doubt self-serving, others are remarkably self-critical; some regret the war, others regret only that it was militarily 'limited'; but taken as a whole they amount to the first tentative effort at national debate on the war.

Vietnam is unique as the first television war, and for the passions and opposition which the living-room images aroused. Quite simply, the cameras revealed nothing of purpose. A war longer than all previous major wars of the century combined, bloodier than any in terms of the small arena involved, is all the more haunting for its apparent lack of meaning, a war for which the answers are still sought in the field of psychiatry because there were none on the field of battle. A decade after the United States had ceased combat in Vietnam, almost two-thirds of the Americans who served there, or 1,750,000 soldiers, are officially described as in need of psychiatric counseling. The world's most advanced nation became a social casualty of the first television war in which, relatively, only the commercials made sense.

It is Vietnam's uniqueness as a case-study of future war – how it should be fought, *if* it should be fought, whether even democracies might opt for all-out war rather than its drawn-out images – which provides an immediacy to those who people these pages. There is the sense of a war still being lived rather than just remembered. Vietnam is a continuing urgency, petrifying the future. Some Americans feel its heat re-erupting in every brushfire. Some, conversely, fear a war-seared pacifist America inviting its own ashes.

What emerges from these recorded interviews is an extraordinary profile of democracy's super-power at war, disturbing for the confusion, indecision and deception which is clearly documented and admitted; extraordinary in its parallel struggle to distinguish right from wrong, for few of those involved can be wholly cast as hero or villain: just all too sadly human, flawed by the collective impulse to action, minds immobilized by the sheer speed of modern war.

For the tens of millions directly touched by the war, there is little comfort in these recollections. The interviews with the senior policy-makers reveal an ignorance of, or a withholding of facts that were always available. Motives and objectives are no clearer now than at the time: indeed, they are often shown as non-existent. And so the rationale for the sacrifice thins. Historian Arthur Schlesinger Jr calls it 'the most useless, most mysterious war' but he is only partly right. The only mystery is that the facts were withheld so long, preventing corrective action. The flaw was more of the mind than of the soul, for the public could only judge the war as it slowly revealed itself in their living-rooms. They had *seen* the facts. But the facts had in reality never been given to them. That was the essential flaw, the extent of the mystery.

—MICHAEL MACLEAR
TORONTO

# VIETNAM CHRONOLOGY

Left: 1940 - Saigon, principal city of southern French Indochina, is a tranquil scene before it was occupied by Japanese naval and land forces.

**September, 1945**—Japanese surrender to British troops at conclusion of World War II. Ho Chi Minh declares Vietnam an independent state.

**September, 1945**—Reclaiming Indochina colonies after World War II, France rebuffs demands for independent Vietnam but allows Democratic Republic of Vietnam, founded by revolutionary leader Ho Chi Minh, to become "free state" within French Union.

**September, 1945**—French troops return to Vietnam; battles break out between French and Communist Viet Minh and Nationalist forces.

**March 1946**—France formally recognizes the free state, Democratic Republic of Vietnam, within the French Union and as part of the French IndoChina Union.

**December, 1946**—Communist Viet Minh launches war for independence against France thus rejecting France's "free state" offer.

**March, 1949**—France establishes an independent Vietnam and names Emperor Bao Dai as its leader.

**July, 1949**—Laos is recognized as an independent state but with special ties to France.

**November. 1949**—Cambodia follows the Laos pattern.

**January, 1950**—China recognizes the Republic of Vietnam with Ho Chi Minh as its leader.

**February, 1950**—The United States recognizes the Vietnams.

**March, 1950**—The U.S. makes its first financial aid to pro-French Vietnam; aid is channeled through France.

**June, 1950**—The first U.S. military advisors are sent to Vietnam. They are called MAAG (Military Assistance Advisory Group).

**September, 1951**—U.S. aid to France for Vietnam is increased substantially and includes military equipment.

**1952/1953**—French troops, equipped with U.S. materiel, fight an increasing aggressive Viet Minh. The period is marked by terrorists attacks in various cities, including Hanoi and Saigon.

**March, 1954**—The critical battle at Dien Bien Phu begins.

**May, 1954**—The French garrison at Dien Bien Phu surrenders to Viet Minh forces.

**May, 1954**—Geneva Conference on Vietnam convenes.

**June, 1954**—Ngo Dinh Diem, appointed Prime Minister by Bao Dai, arrives in Vietnam.

**July, 1954**—Geneva agreements completed, dividing Vietnam at the 17th parallel, into two separate states, the Democratic Republic of Vietnam (DRV) and the Republic of South Vietnam. The U.S. and South Vietnam do not sign the agreements. Elections within two years are to unite North and South Vietnam.

**July, 1954**—The ICC (International Control Commission) is appointed to oversee compliance.

**August, 1954**—Refugees, estimated at more than 1,000,000, leave North Vietnam for the South.

**September, 1954**—SEATO (Southeast Asia Treaty Organization) is formed to contain Communist expansion in the area.

**October, 1954**—President Eisenhower gives aid directly to South Vietnam, bypassing the French channel.

**October, 1954**—French military forces depart Hanoi and the Viet Minh control North Vietnam.

**February, 1955**—U.S. advisors begin direct training of South Vietnamese military, though French advisors are also involved.

**March, 1955**—Diem confronts Binh Xuyen, certain religious sects and other secret societies. Hundreds are killed but Diem's forces, by mid-year, defeat the opposition.

**July, 1955**—Diem refuses to participate in all-Vietnam elections, saying free elections in the north are not possible.

**October, 1955**—Diem, in a referendum, deposes Emperor Bao Dai and becomes unchallenged President of South Vietnam.

**March, 1956**—General Assembly elections are held in South Vietnam with a major victory for Diem party members as the result.

**April, 1956**—U.S. advisors take over full training duties of Vietnamese army. The last French troops depart Vietnam.

**July 1956**—U.S. Vice President Richard Nixon visits South Vietnam.

**October, 1956**—Three U.S. installations in Saigon are bombed.

**January, 1957**—ICC complains that neither North or South Vietnam is complying with Geneva accords.

**May, 1957**—Diem visits the U.S., addresses Congress.

**June, 1957**—Last French military advisors leave South Vietnam.

**November, 1957**—Ho Chi Minh visits USSR and Europe.

**January, 1958**—Communist forces attack plantation near Saigon, the latest in an increasing level of insurgency in the South.

**December, 1958**—Message exchanges are intercepted in which North Vietnam says it will undertake overt insurgency in the South.

**May, 1959**—North Vietnamese central committee resolution calls for ``armed struggle" to reunite Vietnam, codifying Hanoi's support for overthrow of Saigon regime by National Liberation Front (NLF), or Viet Cong.

**July, 1959**—Viet Cong attacks U.S. military installation at Bien Hoa, killing and wounding U.S. advisors. These are the first U.S. casualties in the area.

**October, 1959**—Heavy communist casualties are reported after Government military campaign in Camau peninsula.

**January, 1960**—Largest communist insurgency operation overthrows a Vietnamese army installation Tay Ninh province, captures weapons and ammunition.

**November, 1960**—John F. Kennedy is elected President of U.S.

**November, 1960**—Diem's Presidential Palace is surrounded by South Vietnamese paratroops demanding reforms, but the coup attempt is put down.

**December, 1960**—Hanoi forms National Liberation Front. Diem calls them Viet Cong, pejorative shorthand for Vietnamese Communists.

**April, 1961**—Diem elected as President by overwhelming majority.

**May, 1961**—Vice President Lyndon Johnson visits South Vietnam.

**May, 1961**—President Kennedy, in a press conference, says use of American troops in Vietnam is under consideration.

# CHRONOLOGY

**June, 1961**—President Kennedy and Premier Khrushchev meet in Vienna.

**September, 1961**—A Viet Cong force seizes a provincial capital only 50 miles from Saigon.

**October, 1961**—President Kennedy sends Maxwell Taylor to Vietnam.

**November, 1961**—Maxwell Taylor's report on Vietnam results in President Kennedy sending more advisors.

**January, 1962**—Defoliation begins.

**February, 1962**—Strategic Hamlet program is inaugurated.

**February, 1962**—South Vietnamese aircraft bomb and strafe Presidential Palace in Saigon. Diem escapes injury.

**August, 1962**—Troops from Australia are assigned to Vietnam.

**October, 1962**—Cuban missile crisis.

**December, 1962**—U.S. troops in Vietnam number some 11,000.

**May, 1963**—Government forces fire on Buddhists flying the Buddhist flag in Hue. Nine die in riots which continue nationwide through the summer.

**June, 1963**—Monk commits public suicide by setting himself afire.

**June, 1963**—Kennedy names Henry Cabot Lodge as ambassador to South Vietnam.

**August, 1963**—President de Gaulle of France says Vietnamese must free themselves from foreign influence. His remarks are interpreted as an attempt to get France back into Vietnam.

**September,1963**—Kennedy sends Defense Secretary McNamara and Maxwell Taylor to Vietnam. Visit lasts until October, 10.

**October, 1963**—Seventh Buddhist monk burns himself since June 11.

**November, 1963**—Diem assassinated in military coup. His brother, Ngo Dinh Nhu, also assassinated. Council of Generals, headed by Gen. Duong Van Minh, assumes power.

**November, 1963**—President Kennedy assassinated. Lyndon Johnson sworn in as President.

**December, 1963**—McNamara visit Saigon to check progress in war under South Vietnam's new leadership.

**December, 1963**—U.S. troops in Vietnam number 15,000.

**January, 1964**—Military coup led by Gen. Nguyen Khanh ousts government of Gen. Duong Van Minh after three months in power.

**April, 1964**—Gen. William Westmoreland succeeds Gen. Paul Harkins as U.S. commander in Vietnam.

**June, 1964**—Johnson names Maxwell Taylor as ambassador to Vietnam.

**July, 1964**—New Zealand sends troops to Vietnam.

**August, 1964**—North Vietnamese torpedo boats attack U.S. destroyers Maddox and C. Turner Joy in the Gulf of Tonkin.

**August, 1964**—U.S. congress passes Gulf of Tonkin resolution, giving Johnson wide military power.

**November, 1964**—Johnson re-elected.

**December, 1964**—Terrorist bombings in Saigon kill Americans.

**December, 1964**—Bombing of the Ho Chi Minh trail in Laos begins.

**December, 1964**—U.S. troops in Vietnam number 23,000.

**January, 1965**—South Korean troops arrive in Vietnam.

**January,1965**—Buddhist demonstrations disrupt life in major cities. A Buddhist nun commits fiery suicide, first since 1963.

**February, 1965**—Gen. Khanh ousted as head of government.

**February, 1965**—USSR's Premier Kosygin meets with Ho Chi Minh in Hanoi.

**March, 1965**—U.S. Marine infantry, first American combat forces, arrive in Vietnam at Danang.

**March, 1965**—Terrorist bomb explodes at U.S. embassy. Two killed, many injured.

**March, 1965**—Operation Rolling Thunder begins sustained bombing of North Vietnamese targets.

**April, 1965**—Johnson offers aid to North Vietnam if peace is secured, but is rebuffed by the North.

**June, 1965**—Gen. Nguyen Cao Ky is named as new head of the South Vietnamese government.

**July, 1965**—Ambassador Lodge returns to Vietnam as ambassador.

**November, 1965**—U.S. troops and North Vietnamese troops meet for the first time at Ia Drang. Losses are heavy on both sides.

**December, 1965**—U.S. troops in Vietnam number 181,000

**January, 1966**—U.S. bombing of North Vietnam resumes after a month- long pause.

**February, 1966**—Johnson and Ky confer in Hawaii.

**May, 1966**—Thousands in Washington, DC, demonstrate against the war.

**May, 1966**—Government troops recapture Danang from government troops that were pro-Buddhist.

**June, 1966**—Oil refineries in North Vietnam bombed for the first time.

**October, 1966**—Johnson visits Vietnam.

**December, 1966**—U.S. troops in Vietnam number some 400,000.

**February, 1967**—Operation Junction City begins in Tay Ninh province. It is the largest operation of the war to this date.

**March, 1967**—Ellsworth Bunker is named successor to Lodge as U.S. ambassador to Vietnam.

**June, 1967**—Johnson and Kosygin meet to discuss Vietnam peace. No progress made.

**September, 1967**—Gen. Nguyen van Thieu elected President of South Vietnam. Ky becomes vice-president.

**September, 1967**—Troops from Thailand arrive in Vietnam.

**December, 1967**—U.S. troops in Vietnam number nearly, 500,000.

**January, 1968**—Marine combat base at Khe Sanh comes under siege by North Vietnamese regulars. The struggle becomes symbolic, is compared to Dien Bien Phu.

**January, 1968**—The Tet Offensive begins, with most major cities under attack.

**January, 1968**—U.S. embassy in Saigon is attacked by enemy sappers. Invaders are slain, but damage is heavy.

**January, 1968**—Hue becomes major Tet battleground. Military and civilian casualties are heavy.

**January, 1968**—Heavy fighting begins in Saigon as part of Tet Offensive.

**March, 1968**—The battle for Hue ends with North Vietnamese repulsed.

**March, 1968**—My Lai massacre.

**March, 1968**—Johnson announces he will not seek re-election.

**March, 1968**—The Tet Offensive battle for Saigon ends.

**April, 1968**—Khe Sanh siege lifted.

**April, 1968**—Gen. Creighton W. Abrams named to succeed Gen. Westmoreland in Vietnam.

**April, 1968**—Letter exchanges between Hanoi and Washington indicate possibility for peace talks.

**May, 1968**—Participants agree on Paris as the site for peace talks and negotiators arrive for preliminary discussions.

**May, 1968**—New, sharp fighting breaks out on the outskirts of Saigon. North Vietnamese troops fight inside Saigon for the first time.

**June 4, 1968**—Heaviest rocket attack during the war hits Saigon.

**June, 1968**—In late June Le Duc Tho, chief North Vietnamese negotiator, leaves Paris talks and returns to Hanoi.

**July, 1968**—Johnson and Thieu meet in Honolulu.

**August, 1968**—Chicago Democratic Convention is the scene of heavy anti-war demonstrations that lead to riots.

**October, 1968**—Johnson says bombing of North Vietnam will end. His statement angers South Vietnamese government.

**November, 1968**—Richard Nixon is elected U.S. president.

**November, 1968**—Le Duc Tho returns to Paris for peace talks.

**December, 1968**—Paris peace negotiators squabble over the shape of the talk tables.

**December, 1968**—U.S. troops in Vietnam number 536,000.

**January, 1969**—Formal truce negotiations open in Paris.

**February, 1969**—Communist troops launch rocket attacks against more than 100 cities in South Vietnam.

**March, 1969**—Mass graves of hundreds of civilians executed by Viet Cong uncovered in Hue.

**June, 1969**—Bombing of North Vietnam resumes briefly in retaliation for the loss of a U.S. reconnaissance plane.

**June, 1969**—Nixon and Thieu meet at Midway Island where Nixon says he plans withdrawal of 25,000 American troops as part of his Vietnamization program.

**July, 1969**—Secret letters between Nixon and Ho Chi Minh are exchanged, in which agreement is reached to work for peace.

**September, 1969**—U.S. troops in Vietnam are reduced by 25,000 per Nixon's earlier announcement. Nixon says 35,000 more troops will depart.

**September, 1969**—Ho Chi Minh dies.

**November, 1969**—My Lai massacre revealed.

**November, 1969**—Some 250,000 protestors gather in Washington for the largest anti-war demonstration in the nation's history.

**December, 1969**—Nixon says 75,000 more troops will be withdrawn from South Vietnam by Spring, 1970.

**December, 1969**—U.S. troops in Vietnam number 475,000.

**February, 1970**—Henry Kissinger begins secret talks with North Vietnam in Paris.

**March, 1970**—Prince Sihanouk of Cambodia is ousted as head of state by Gen. Lon Nol.

**March, 1970**—South Vietnamese launch a major assault into Cambodia to attack North Vietnamese camps. U.S. provides support.

**April, 1970**—Some 50,000 demonstrate in Washington to support Nixon's handling of the war.

**May, 1970**—Campus anti-war demonstrations are wide spread in the U.S. At Kent State four students are killed by National Guard gunfire.

**June, 1970**—The U.S. Senate repeals the Gulf of Tonkin resolution.

**June, 1970**—Congress Cooper-Church Amendment bars future Cambodian incursions by U.S. troops.

**October, 1970**—Nixon announces a withdrawal of another 40,000 U.S. troops.

**December, 1970**—Congress repeals Gulf of Tonkin resolution.

**December, 1970**—U.S. troops in Vietnam number 334,000.

**February, 1971**—South Vietnamese troops, with U.S. air support, enter Laos to cut the Ho Chi Minh trail in an operation called Lam Son 719.

**March, 1971**—Operation Lam Son 719 concludes after U.S. loses 100 helicopters.

**March, 1971**—Lt. William Calley found guilty of the My Lai massacre and sentenced to life imprisonment.

**April, 1971**—Nixon announces 100,000 troops to be withdrawn by the end of 1971.

**April, 1971**—Some 500,000 anti-war demonstrators rally in Washington, DC. Demonstrators in San Francisco number 150,000.

**May, 1971**—Paris peace talks enter their fourth year still in deadlock.

**June, 1971**—The Pentagon Papers published by the New York Times.

**July, 1971**—The final U.S. Marine infantry unit departs South Vietnam.

**October, 1971**—Thieu is re-elected President of South Vietnam.

**December, 1971**—The first bombing of North Vietnam since 1968 takes place north of the 20th parallel in response to the buildup of North Vietnamese forces.

**January, 1972**—Nixon announces troop withdrawals that will reduce U.S. strength to 70,000 by early spring.

**February, 1972**—Nixon visits China.

**March, 1972**—Large North Vietnamese force moves southward with artillery, rockets and tanks.

**April, 1972**—The North Vietnamese offensive heads for Quang Tri, a major city near the northern border of South Vietnam. Thousands of refugees flood south toward Hue. Quang Tri falls.

**April, 1972**—Heavy fighting pits South Vietnamese against North Vietnamese at An Loc and Khe Sanh.

**April, 1972**—U.S. bombers attack Hanoi and Haiphong.

**May, 1972**—Nixon announces the mining of Haiphong harbor.

**May, 1972**—Secret meetings between Kissinger and Le Duc Tho resume.

**June, 1972**—Five men are arrested in the break-in of Democratic Party offices at the Watergate Hotel in Washington.

**July, 1972**—The siege of An Loc is broken and the North Vietnamese army retreats into Laos.

**August, 1972**—The last American combat unit departs South Vietnam.

**September, 1972**—Quang Tri is recaptured by South Vietnamese troops, but the countryside remains in North Vietnamese control.

**November, 1972**—Nixon re-elected.

**December, 1972**—Paris peace talks collapse.

**December, 1972**—Bombing, some of it the heaviest of the war, is resumed with Hanoi the target. Bombing is limited to below the 20th parallel when Hanoi agrees to continue talks.

**December, 1972**—U.S. troops in Vietnam number 24,000.

**January, 1973**—Kissinger and La Duc Tho resume talks in Paris.

**January, 1973**—A peace agreement is signed. The last American to die in the war is killed by artillery at An Loc in late January. Nixon suspends military action against North Vietnam.

**February, 1973**—Last military forces of the U.S. leave Vietnam and final POWs arrive in the Philippines.

**June, 1973**—Graham Martin arrives as the new U.S. ambassador to Vietnam.

**October, 1973**—Kissinger and La Duc Tho are awarded the Nobel Peace prize, but La Duc Tho refuses his award saying there is no peace.

**January, 1974**—The war continues; Thieu says 55 Vietnamese soldiers have died in two clashes.

**August, 1974**—Nixon resigns over Watergate scandal. Gerald Ford becomes U.S. president.

**December, 1974**—The North Vietnamese attack Phuoc Long to see what U.S. reaction will be. There is none.

**January, 1975**—Phuoc Long falls to North Vietnamese. Hanoi prepares a general offensive.

**March, 1975**—The North Vietnamese find success in attacking Central Highlands towns; Thieu calls his troops back and abandons the Highlands, withdrawing from Pleiku and Kontum. Refugees clog the roads and North Vietnamese attack, killing thousands.

**March, 1975**—Refugees flee Hue. Quang Tri is captured by the North.

**March, 1975**—The success spurs the North to escalate a plan to conquer the South in 1976, and try for a final campaign before May when spring rains slow movement of troops. Hue is abandoned. Danang falls.

**April, 1975**—The U.S. embassy in Cambodia is evacuated and the government surrenders to Communist Khmer Rouge.

**April, 1975**—President Thieu resigns and flees Vietnam. Gen Duong Van Minh takes over.

**April, 1975**—On the last day of April North Vietnamese tanks crash through the gates of the Presidential Palace, and Saigon falls. Minh surrenders.

Later in the year the Pathet Lao capture Vientiane, capital of Laos. All of French Indochina is part of the communist world.

# THE FIRST REVERSAL

Seen from the beginning there is nothing mysterious about America's lost third of a century in Vietnam.

The clock of those thirty years begins in April 1945 when Major Archimedes Patti of the American OSS – Office of Strategic Services – agreed to a secret rendezvous on China's southern border with a man who used many aliases – so many that even his followers found it simpler just to call him 'the General'. The 'General' led a ragtag army of exiles from an obscure part of Asia known as French Indo-China in which America had taken a sudden interest. Major Patti had just arrived in neighboring China to head a new World War II mission for the OSS – the forerunner of the CIA. He was to establish an intelligence network

## 'We want America's moral support. We ask for nothing else.'

### – HO CHI MINH, 1945

behind the lines in Indo-China, which had been occupied by the Japanese since 1940. As a new American authority, Patti had been immediately approached by the exile group which told him that the General 'needed American recognition'. Patti needed contacts and information. 'It began just as a feeler,' says Patti.

When the two men met, in a dusty village 'tea shop' in a corner of the world as remote as any, Patti found himself facing an improbable figure: a frail, stooped old man with a wispy beard who wore rice-mat sandals and baggy trousers held up by string. The guerrilla general disdained his military title. 'Welcome, my good friend,' he said to the American in perfect English. He then introduced himself by a name which would become a

North Vietnamese leader Ho Chi Minh.

1945—A commander of the Japanese secret police bows as he surrenders his sword to Allied forces in Saigon.

legendary one – though it was just another alias. He called himself Ho Chi Minh.

Despite their physical differences, the frail Asian and the khaki-clean American found they had much in common. Both men had endured a lifetime's hard journey when their paths converged. Patti judged Ho to look 'about sixty', though he knew him to be fifty-four. As they talked into the late evening, Ho Chi Minh confirmed what Patti already knew of him from the OSS files. For thirty-four years – slightly longer than Patti's age – Ho Chi Minh had wandered the world as an exile seeking support for the independence of a country known centuries earlier as Vietnam. For almost a hundred years his country had been occupied by the French and amalgamated as part of their Indo-China colony, and now events had assumed a new urgency for both Ho and Patti. A French quisling regime had continued to rule Indo-China under Japanese authority until a few days earlier, when the French colonial garrison had tried to regain control. The Japanese had quickly crushed the attempt and now ruled directly – which made Patti's task more difficult.

At the same time, unknown to the world, the Vietnamese were enduring a terrible fate, Ho Chi Minh told Patti. In recent months between 1.5 and 2 million Vietnamese had died of starvation because of wartime conditions and unprecedented floods, but, said Ho emotionally, as quoted by Patti in *Why Vietnam?* written thirty-five years later, none of Vietnam's foreign rulers had gone hungry. Patti, a New Yorker born to poor Italian immigrants, was 'indelibly' impressed by Ho Chi Minh's compassion and lifetime patriotism. Ho was frank as to his political intentions – he was determined to drive out both the Japanese and the French. Patti cautioned that his strict objective was to harass the Japanese – and they agreed on this common aim.

Over the teacups, with Ho Chi Minh gratefully smoking Patti's Chesterfields, the two men discussed 'pragmatic' means of co-operation. Neither could foresee the role history would accord them, nor the significance of the moment for millions of their countrymen as yet unborn. The future first president of Vietnam and the first American soldier to be specifically assigned to Vietnam had met and agreed on mutual interests, and Patti felt that 'much good' would come from this meeting. The might-have-been destiny of this initial encounter would be part of the agony decades later.

Patti, interviewed for this history, remembers that he met Ho Chi Minh 'on the last day of April 1945' – and it was on the same day thirty years later, 30 April 1975, when the last American soldiers left Vietnam. Between those dates 2.8 million US troops would have followed Major Patti to Vietnam – and 57,000 Americans and at least two million Vietnamese would die in this sliver of a land during 10,000 days of war and 'mystery'. From the start Patti provided a 'voluminous record' on Ho Chi Minh and his 'philosophy and activities'. Much later Patti's successors in the CIA would describe Vietnam as a massive failure throughout of available intelligence.

Major Archimedes L.A. Patti came highly trained to his Vietnam mission. He had just spent three years fighting fascism in his ancestral land. From 1941 to 1943 he led covert operations in North Africa, Sicily and Salerno, and when he first heard of his new assignment to Asia he was

1950—The name of Ho Chi Minh, leader of Indochina's Vietminh, appears on a cable that offers to discuss a possible armistice for ending the seven-war in Indochina with the French.

actually with the invading force nearing the Anzio beaches in Italy. It was 21 January 1944, the start of the Allied counter-offensive in World War II. Operation Overlord – the main thrust at Germany through France – was in the final planning stage, and now the prior invasion of Italy was beginning. Patti and others were huddled in the midnight cold aboard a pitching landing craft talking with Major General William J. ('Wild Bill') Donovan as they closed in on the Italian coastline, and Donovan – the head of the OSS – was already planning his moves on the other side of the world. The days of clandestine operations in Europe were almost over, he was saying, and the greater drama would soon be in Asia. He needed experienced men in a place called Indo-China. Patti then 'knew nothing about Indo-China. I remembered it was somewhere in Asia – that was all.' Who would like to go? Donovan asked. When? said Patti. Oh, after Rome, said the nonchalant Donovan. As they waded ashore Rome was only twenty-five miles away, but it took five exceptionally bloody months to reach. The Allies entered the city on 4 June, two days before the landings in France, but Patti had meantime set out for the war in Asia – a war which he considers went on for another thirty years.

Patti's specific instructions were to 'establish an intelligence network in the entire peninsula of Indo-China'. He was to assist all the Allied forces –

British, French, Chinese and Americans – in 'combating the Japanese'. It was a high priority assignment: Indo-China was strategically centered between the three vast war theaters of mainland China, the South Pacific and Burma to the far west. Patti first spent several months in Washington receiving State Department and White House briefings. His preparations were intensive 'because we all anticipated that the war [in Asia] would go on until 1947, or even 1948'.

Since 1940, helped by a French collaborationist government in Indo-China and a co-operative one in adjacent Thailand, the Imperial Japanese Army had swept through South-East Asia, occupying the Dutch East Indies and a collection of Europe's minor colonies, had then struck west taking the British 'fortress' of Singapore in February 1942 and had advanced on British Burma, seeking to complete a huge circle into the south-west of China where the Japanese already held the industrial north and the coast. In the vast rural center of China the Japanese were being engaged separately by two rival Chinese armies, those of Mao Tse-tung's Communists and Chiang Kai-shek's 'Nationalists' – with the US aiding both armies against the common enemy. This was the primary intelligence mission of the OSS at Kunming in the center of China's southern border when Major Patti arrived there in early April 1945

2

to expand the operations into Indo-China. The Japanese had then imprisoned the 8500-man French colonial garrison after its bungled uprising, and this left Patti without any potential ally – until Ho Chi Minh approached him.

Patti had a particular problem: apart from harassing the Japanese he was concerned with the fate of American flyers who might be shot down in the region. He needed reliable contacts and escape routes in Indo-China. It was clear from the OSS files that Ho Chi Minh's exile organization had developed an extensive underground network during many years of resisting first the French and then the Japanese. Patti's Washington briefings had fully dealt with Indo-China's social history and it seemed to him that Ho Chi Minh's actions fitted ancient nationalist tradition. Even in the dryly worded OSS files Ho Chi Minh came across as the embodiment of his nation: a poor but culturally proud figure whose very age expressed the native resilience.

Although his country was only a slight tuft on the chin of China, as sparse and straggling as Ho's beard, he and his people had the reputation of an Asian Samson, again and again displaying leg-endary strength. The Vietnamese had a recorded history of more than two thousand years – and it had been an almost continuous chronicle of resist-ance against the feudal Chinese. Endless war, rebellion and privation had become the perma-nent subculture of a people who were as tough and durable as the mountainous jungles and trackless mangrove swamps where they had so often gath-ered to wage guerrilla war – and where Patti's mis-sion was to prevent or limit American casualties in this harsh, alien terrain. Patti knew that the upris-ings against the colonial French had been just as constant and fierce, and he was aware of Ho Chi Minh's extraordinary personal struggle against America's wartime ally, France. As he set out to meet the Vietnamese leader Patti again carefully read the detailed OSS file on Ho. It alerted Patti that his journey might be as contentious as Ho Chi Minh's own strange route.

Ho Chi Minh's real name was Nguyen That Thanh, the youngest of three children all jailed by the French for preaching the nationalism taught to them by their father, a middle-level civil ser-vant dismissed for his views. In 1911, at the age of twenty-one, Ho had left his country as a galley-hand on a French merchant ship bound for Britain. There, while serving as an apprentice chef at the aristocratic Carlton Hotel in London, he helped organize an anti-colonial group called the Overseas Workers' Association, championing among other things independence for Ireland. He briefly visited the United States, shoveling snow for a living in black Harlem, then as a sailor again he journeyed to France during World War I, set-tling in Paris as a gardener and laundryman, and describing the poor of his colonial master as 'oppressed as our own people'.

In 1919 he joined the French Socialist Party and when it split ranks he became a co-founder in 1920 of the Communist Party of France. He became editor of an exile newspaper Le Paria – The Outcast – and his articles under the alias Nguyen Ai Quoc (Nguyen the Patriot) began to find their way back to Indo-China. Helped by Jean Longuet, the son-in-law of Karl Marx, he traveled across Europe as the Party's expert on colonial issues, then in 1922 went as its delegate to the Communist International in Moscow. He stayed two years studying Marxist doctrine, and personal-ly met Lenin. He left the Soviet Union in 1925 to become an aide at its consulate in Canton, then director of the Communist International Bureau in Shanghai – its headquarters for Asia.

Over a period of twenty years, shifting his base between China, Hong Kong and Thailand, con-stantly in and out of jail, he built up a corps of Vietnamese guerrillas who, led by a history teacher called Vo Nguyen Giap, infiltrated Tonkin, or North Vietnam. On 19 May 1941, Ho and his fel-low exiles felt strong enough to declare openly their political objectives. They gathered in south-ern China at the village of Chingsi and formed the Vietnam Doc Lap Dong Minh, or League for the Independence of Vietnam, which became known by its abbreviation, the Viet Minh.

Ho's name 'first popped up in State Department files in 1942,' says Major Patti. This was after the Nationalist Chinese had jailed Ho Chi Minh as a suspected Communist. On hearing of this 'Washington blew the roof', reveals Patti, and US diplomats in China were ordered to obtain Ho's release. As Patti explains the irony, the Americans had then established 'a so-called obser-vation mission' with the Chinese Communists – a war liaison group 'including OSS people who were in contact with Mao Tse-tung personally'. The Americans 'in those days were doing things that perhaps [Nationalist leader] Chiang Kai-shek wasn't too aware of' – that is, they were secretly aiding both rivals in the immediate fight against the Japanese, and Ho Chi Minh was a friend of Mao's. In asking for Ho's release 'the Chinese Communists actually were the ones who provided the OSS with all the information on Ho Chi Minh – where he was, what he was doing, his background, and what he was hoping to achieve in the long run'. In a fur-ther irony, Mao suggested that the Viet Minh might eventually prove useful to the Americans in Indo-China, where the French collaborators were a suspect source of information.

In fact, Ho Chi Minh quickly proved grate-ful – and useful. After the Americans obtained his release in early 1943, he went to the wartime cap-ital of Chungking and provided intelligence and translation services for the US Office of War Information there. He now used his prison alias, Mr C.M. Hoo. Periodically he would disappear.

September 1945—Ho Chi Minh, *right*, poses with Vo Nguyen Giap, minister of the Interior in Ho Chi Minh's provisional gov-ernment. Giap went on to lead the Vietminh and North Vietnamese military through the fall of Saigon.

January 1945—A geyser of water erupts as an American bomb misses two Japanese ships, one of them already burning heavily during a carrier-based air attack near the entrance to Quinhon Harbor in French Indochina.

January 1945—As a Curtiss Helldiver flies overhead, a Japanese tanker burns heavily after a U.S. Navy bombing run in the South China Sea. The Navy announced the destruction of three enemy convoys during two days of strikes by the Third Fleet.

number of years.' At successive Great Power conferences at Cairo, Teheran and Yalta, Roosevelt had 'pressed the question of trusteeship' but his wartime allies adamantly opposed it. The result had been an inconsistency between Roosevelt's personal views and his publicized foreign policy. Then on 12 April 1945, as Major Patti arrived in Kunming on his Vietnam mission, Roosevelt died.

'I personally admired Roosevelt,' says Patti. 'I was in full agreement with his philosophy of relieving the subject people of South-East Asia from the previous history of colonial burden.' As Patti saw it the US had firmly intended self-determination for the Vietnamese, and he fully advised Washington on the relations that he continued to develop with Ho Chi Minh: 'I did pass all this information through normal channels, which were the American Embassy in Chungking.' Patti stressed that Ho was not 'a hardened Communist' but foremost a nationalist – a conclusion fully supported in field reports by others in the OSS, reports which would only become public at Senate hearings twenty-seven years later. Patti says that he heard nothing back: 'All the information that people in the field passed to Washington ended in a dry well.'

Patti's instructions on leaving Washington had been very specific on one point: 'They came from the White House through General Donovan [head of the OSS]. My instructions were not to assist the French in re-occupying Indo-China in any way whatsoever.'

An insight on the policy confusion of this period comes from a principal figure who as Secretary of State in the 1960s would find himself prosecuting a war in a region for which he could not get a clear policy position in the 1940s. In early 1945, as Major Patti prepared to head for Indo-China with 'specific' instructions. Dean Rusk was a deputy Chief of Staff with the Allied Command in Asia. He recalls that the French were pressing for American military support for clandestine operations in Indo-China. 'So we at headquarters', says Rusk, 'sent a message to our own Chiefs of Staff saying, "Request guidance on American policy toward Indo-China". And for months and months nothing happened. Finally a paper arrived headed "US Policy Toward Indo-China". And it said, when asked by the Joint Chiefs of Staff for a statement on US policy in Indo-China, President Roosevelt replied, "I don't want to hear any more about Indo-China." '

Rusk, like Patti, is clear on the initial policy: Roosevelt 'did try to plan' for the independence of Europe's former colonies but 'tired of banging his head against Winston Churchill on this matter', and by the time of his death had 'abandoned' his anti-colonial policy. Another interpretation is that Roosevelt was privately biding his time. A young career officer then in Asia, William H. Sullivan who would also rise high in the State Department, recalls that 'after World War II most of us who had been junior officers came out of it with an appreciation of the postwar objectives that Roosevelt had set'. Sullivan asserts that Roosevelt 'would have been quite stern in his insistence that there be a withdrawal of French colonial control from Indo-China'. But, says Dean Rusk, both Roosevelt and then President Harry Truman failed to 'press that policy; it was possible but they simply didn't do it'. This meant that 'the British went back to India and Burma, the Dutch

Occasionally during 1944 he would show up at the OSS in Kunming to provide 'target information' on Japanese bases and troop movements and to request weapons and ammunition. These were denied: the OSS was not yet active in Indo-China; it was under orders to avoid local political involvement, and the French intelligence mission in Kunming insisted that the Viet Minh was a militant arm of distrusted Soviet foreign policy. Major Patti's actions on his arrival in Kunming in April 1945 therefore marked a controversial change.

'I was aware', says Patti, 'that Ho Chi Minh was a Communist, or had been in Moscow and had some training there and that his Viet Minh had a party line.' But Patti was 'interested' in the Viet Minh 'strictly from the viewpoint that would actually be of assistance to my intelligence mission'. Patti would later write, in *Why Vietnam?*, his own exceptionally detailed account of the historic meeting, that 'from a practical viewpoint, Ho and the Viet Minh appeared to be the answer to my immediate problem of establishing relations in Indo-China'. Ho Chi Minh, wrote Patti, 'did not strike me as a starry-eyed revolutionary or a flam-

ing radical, given to clichés, mouthing a party line. . . . I saw that his ultimate goal was to attain American support for the cause of a free Vietnam and felt that desire presented no conflict with American policy.'

In Washington Patti had been briefed on US political intentions for the postwar world, in which President Franklin D. Roosevelt envisaged an end to colonialism. An internal memorandum from Roosevelt on Indo-China had stated: 'France has had the country, thirty million inhabitants, for nearly one hundred years, and the people are worse off than they were at the beginning.' The memorandum called for an international trusteeship to administer Indo-China once the war was over. 'Don't think for a moment', Patti cites Roosevelt as saying in January 1943, 'that Americans would be dying in the Pacific tonight if it hadn't been for the short-sighted greed of the French and the British and the Dutch. Shall we allow them to do it all, all over again? . . . The United Nations – when they're organized – they could take over these colonies, couldn't they? Under a mandate, or as trustee – for a certain

1945—Members of the Japanese secret police in Vietnam put down their swords as they surrender to Allied Forces in Saigon.

back to Indonesia, and the French back to Indo-China, and we reverted to the pre-war situation. History could have been very different.' Rusk concludes.

That was the first reversal.

Rusk at the Allied Command in Asia had been left with a memorandum suggesting that America's anti-colonial policy had been abandoned. Major Patti had been left alone in charge of US affairs in Indo-China with quite contrary instructions, never exactly rescinded. Roosevelt had left a dilemma that would plague six successive American presidents.

The first of these, President Truman, who was preoccupied with the occupation of Germany and the US advance in the Pacific, simply shelved the issue of self-determination. An early Truman directive to the field offices in China stated that it was the President's 'intention at some appropriate time' to ask France for 'some positive indication' on future self-government in Indo-China. In fact, as Washington was well aware, France was already providing positive indication that it would not set Indo-China free.

Major Patti had reported that in May 1945 a French major, Jean Sainteny, had arrived in Kunming to reorganize a French counterpart Indo-China operation called M-5 or Mission-5. Sainteny's arrival was clearly a response to Patti's – though the French had prepared well before revealing their move. Sainteny, who would have a principal role in political events for many years, called on Patti and revealed that unknown to the OSS the French had for some time been establishing a sizeable intelligence network along the Indo-China border, but M-5 now needed American help. The loss of the French colonial garrison had left France without any military forces in place and the Japanese take-over had resulted in another serious embarrassment for the French. Japan had declared that the Indo-China states were henceforth inde-

pendent – albeit under the Greater East Asia imperial aegis – and had even restored their former names: Cambodia, Laos and Vietnam. The former Vietnamese Emperor Bao Dai, who had nominally ruled under the French, had agreed to be Head of State of the 'new' Vietnam.

Compounding Sainteny's problem the Japanese now had a fight on their hands – not from the Allies but from Ho Chi Minh's independence movement, the Viet Minh. In May, Ho's guerrillas had begun sustained attacks on Japanese positions, and the Viet Minh was rapidly establishing its authority in the countryside. A French military reoccupation had become far more difficult and Sainteny now appealed to Patti: the French had prepared clandestine units, but needed weapons.

'What he wanted from us, from the Americans and from me particularly because I was his contact,' says Patti, 'were planes, ships and communications to pursue their objective of re-establishing themselves in Indo-China. I told him point blank that we just couldn't do anything along those lines of trying to reconquer the colony.'

Like Patti, Sainteny was in his early thirties and a veteran of the French equivalent of the OSS, the Deuxième Bureau. The two majors now began a battle of wits in executing their respective orders. Patti's primary mission was to obstruct the Japanese: he announced that he would assist any force, including the French, who could do this. Sainteny was quick to respond. In mid-June he presented a detailed plan for extensive commando landings involving a thousand-man force, mainly French-trained Vietnamese. Patti records that he was impressed and recommended the plan to his seniors, but on certain conditions: American officers would be in charge and only OSS radio codes would be used to ensure US control of the action. Sainteny rejected this and Patti then became distrustful of the French, whose clandestine efforts – he later wrote – were 'cluttering' the Allied intel-

ligence effort and at times amounted to 'juvenile melodramatics'.

In contrast, Patti had established 'a certain rapport' with members of the Viet Minh in Kunming, with whom he conversed in their colonial language – French. Ho Chi Minh now sought to outmaneuver the French. In June – concurrent with the French plan – he let Patti know that the Viet Minh would make available an equal force of 1000 guerrillas to assist any American operation in Indo-China. Patti was then planning the first US armed action in Vietnam. Its code name was Deer Team and it called for a small joint American-French drop behind Japanese lines at an important communications center close to the China border; the Deer Team would organize resistance and facilitate the eventual entry of Allied Forces from China. But this still seemed two or three years away; it was urgent to disrupt and stretch Japanese lines and Patti worried about delays in this. On other proposed operations the French, says Patti, suddenly 'staged a couple of sit-down strikes on me'. The American OSS leader says he had 'a tremendous débâcle with Major Sainteny' and says that Sainteny then ordered a complete end 'to collaboration'. At this point Major Patti came to an historic decision which he felt was in America's direct military interest. He would rely not on the French but on the Viet Minh.

'I had no one to turn to but the Viet Minh,' says Patti. 'I started to work with them very, very closely.' He requested Ho Chi Minh to assist an American-only Deer Team operation and by 30 June Patti and Ho had agreed on the revised plan: 'He offered to provide guides and give protection and shelter.'

Major Sainteny had flown to Paris, arriving for Bastille Day, 14 July, to make urgent warnings of revolution in France's most prized colonial possession. Sainteny wanted his government immediately to pressure the United States to prevent any further spread of Viet Minh authority. He was aware of the terms that the Great Powers were drawing up for the eventual Japanese surrender. These provided that when the time came British troops would occupy Cochin-China and Annam (South and Central Vietnam) and Chiang Kai-shek's Nationalist Chinese would occupy Tonkin, or North Vietnam. There was no active French army in the area to provide a French role in the formal surrender. Although the Japanese had kept Saigon as the capital, the Japanese surrender was to be taken in Hanoi in the North – which thus became the main prize in the race to establish political power. But Sainteny was now far behind in the race. General de Gaulle, about to set off for the Allied summit at Potsdam which would redraw the postwar map, was too busy to see him. With the US needing Western solidarity against Soviet territorial demands in Europe, the anti-colonial pressure had ceased. Paris considered that the Viet Minh was without support. Sainteny, who knew otherwise, returned to match wits with Major Patti. He was now well behind. The Americans and the Viet Minh had joined forces.

On 16 July, a fifty-man 'OSS guerrilla group' led by Patti's deputy, Major Allison Thomas, had parachuted into a small village in a mountainous triangle only seventy-five miles north-west of Hanoi. The Deer Team, says Patti, then 'spread out with troops under Giap'.

The Viet Minh commander, Vo Nguyen Giap, had earlier impressed Major Patti as an extremely able tactician. Giap had been Ho Chi Minh's military strategist since the early 1940s and would remain the military mastermind for thirty years. Appropriately, he was a former history teacher who had made a special study of French wars. Giap's early activism had been limited to political speeches for which he was jailed by the French, and though he escaped his family had been cruelly persecuted. Giap, in Patti's view, was more militant than Ho Chi Minh: 'He was hoping really to avoid the United States, or any of these imperial powers as he liked to call them.' But Giap 'was a realist; he couldn't go it alone. He did need help – American help. Anything he could get.'

Patti in turn felt that realistically he, or his fifty-man commando force, could not go it alone for very long. The Viet Minh were providing shelter and advice: they could do more. Patti decided to train and arm them with modern American weapons for joint combat operations: 'We gave them some machine-guns, Browning automatic rifles, hand grenades. We parachuted them in.'

'Giap,' says Patti, 'attacked several Japanese outposts with our men – after they had been trained by the Americans in the use of grenade launchers and flame-throwers, rifles, machine-guns and so on. It was combat. It was a very small operation as far as a war is concerned, but nevertheless it is true that we did work with the Viet Minh against the Japanese.' The Deer Team remained with the Viet Minh, securing a wide area. In his book, *Why Vietnam?*, Patti writes: 'Some of us may have suspected that in the future the weapons and training might be used against the French, but no one dreamed that they would ever be used against Americans.' In retrospect he realizes that in just one month the OSS trained 'about 200 hand-picked future leaders' of the Viet Minh.

According to Vo Nguyen Giap, soon to become Commander of the People's Army, the village region which the Deer Team helped him secure was named Tan Trao. It would shortly enter the history records as the site where Ho Chi Minh established his provisional government. In quick succession the American OSS had trained Ho's men, armed them and fought alongside them – and subsequent events, in the light of history, would seem even more implausible.

After Ho Chi Minh had journeyed from China to Tan Trao in July 1945 – his first return to his country after almost thirty-five years – the Americans saved his life, according to an OSS account. Ho was then extremely ill from malaria, but recovered – it was said – after receiving quinine and sulfa drugs from OSS personnel. In an otherwise detailed account the Viet Minh commander, Giap, makes no reference to the OSS claim but recalls how he 'sat up all night beside Uncle Ho's bed in a small bamboo hut when he was seriously ill in Tan Trao'.

Giap provides a vivid portrayal of the events of 1945-46 in a publication only issued in Hanoi in 1979, titled *Unforgettable Days*. Giap graphically describes Ho Chi Minh after his recovery: 'He was quite at ease in his brown peasant pajamas. He still looked rather thin. His cheek-bones were protruding. Blue veins were clearly visible on his forehead and temples. But with hislarge forehead, his black beard, and especially his bright eyes, a surprising moral strength seemed to radiate from his slender body.'

Ho's hypnotic quality and oratory had mes-

merized and deceived the OSS and in particular Major Patti, the French would bitterly contend. The OSS would later blame the French for exaggerating Ho's Communist allegiance in order to provoke a colonizing war. Giap makes only casual reference to the OSS – and if he felt that the Americans had been easily deceived he might have been expected to pronounce as much in his account rendered long after the war. 'While the French were desperate to return to Indo-China,' says Giap, 'the American officer by the name of Patty [sic], for some reason not clear to us, showed sympathy for the Viet Minh's *anti-Japanese struggle* [author's italics].' Giap did not describe the OSS as siding against the French, as they maintained.

The French would accuse Major Patti of being too free-wheeling in his interpretation of US government policy, but the Potsdam Agreement signed on 24 July defined only the future Allied military arrangements – and rule – in Indo-China. There was an unwritten understanding that France might later act as 'trustee' for Indo-China's political future, but no date or details had been settled and even this seemed of dubious legality. Japan had declared the independence of Vietnam – and the law of the occupying power was perhaps as valid, or more so, than that of the previous colonizer. Certainly the French major, Jean Sainteny, had no higher authority or official case to use against the American major, Archimedes Patti, and the two intelligence chiefs appeared set on a prolonged rivalry, but then, as Patti records, 'the abrupt end of the war took everyone by surprise'. After the use of atomic bombs on Hiroshima on 6 August and Nagasaki on 9 August, Japan surrendered a day later – and then, says Patti, 'On August 10th Sainteny for the first time wanted a conference.'

The French desperation to reach Hanoi ahead of the Viet Minh now took an extraordinary form: 'Sainteny and several others wanted to go into Indo-China before the actual Japanese surrender, before Ho Chi Minh got to Hanoi, in order to be able to have an organization of government in being. He wanted air transport. And he wanted American protection – he wanted to use the American flag. He wanted', discloses Patti, 'to use American uniforms for his men until they got in and over the Japanese hurdle, because the Japanese were still in command, and they were armed.' As Patti explains, 'Americans were the victors. They were acceptable to the Vietnamese and to the Japanese. They had to be acceptable.'

Patti had fought for years in Europe alongside agents of the British MI-5 and the French Deuxième Bureau, and 'I still felt a certain amount of allegiance'. The Japanese were holding some 4000 French prisoners of war in Hanoi. On 22 August Patti flew to Hanoi and took Sainteny and four other French officers as his 'guests'. Ho Chi Minh was still in Tan Trao. But Sainteny had not won the race. He had virtually flown into a cage: La Cage Dorée – The Golden Cage – as the Vietnamese called the Governor-General's palace. Viet Minh cadres had already – to Patti's surprise – 'taken over the city', and Sainteny and his colleagues were courteously housed in the French-built palace and kept there under armed guard.

La Cage Dorée contrasted with the outer ambience. An OSS agent gave an account of Hanoi in those days – entered in Senate records: 'Hanoi was a strange and stricken town, restive, covered

with a film of red dust raised, more often than not, by crowds of tense demonstrators moving in the streets. Most of the demonstrators carried streamers identifying them as Viet Minh, but there was also a profusion of non-Communist groups, less numerous and less well-organized, marching in counter-demonstrations. Whatever their political identification, the processions invariably headed for a dark red building then called Le Palais du Gouvernement inside of which lived a frail lonely man named Ho Chi Minh.'

Giap describes Hanoi as his Viet Minh troops took over: 'Life was precarious; there were not enough dust-carts to carry those who had died from starvation to the outskirts of the city where they were thrown into common graves. At the city gates, large numbers of starving people were pouring in from the countryside. They staggered about as lifeless as withered leaves in winter – a light push by a policeman might send someone down never to rise again.'

Giap again vividly conveys Ho Chi Minh's life to the moment he arrived in Hanoi on 26 August 1945: 'It was the first time he had been to Hanoi. It had taken him thirty-five years to reach the capital from the small thatched house in Kim Lien village where he was born 300 kilometres to the south. . . . On that day his name was still unfamiliar to his own people.' To the Viet Minh he was the 'General', to the Vietnamese public he was Nguyen Ai Quoc, to the Chinese he was Mr C.M. Hoo, and to the Americans he was Ho Chi Minh and it was this name that the fifty-six-year-old Nguyen That Thanh decided to keep. Ho Chi Minh means 'He who enlightens'.

A day earlier, the 25th, in the hills of Tan Trao, Ho – still accompanied by the American Deer Team – had proclaimed independence for what he named the Democratic Republic of Vietnam (DRV), but with a concession to the French. It would be a republic 'within the French Union' with future relations to be negotiated. Ho chose 2 September as Independence Day and then, says Giap, 'Red flags grew in number and splendor, fluttering in the wind and splashing the houses and streets like a festival for the oppressed.'

In preparing for independence Ho on his arrival in Hanoi had immediately sought American support. 'Ho called for me to see him urgently,' relates Patti. 'He presented me with these sheets of paper. I looked at them and I said "What do I do with them? I can't read them". He started to translate. So I just listened carefully and I was shocked. I was shocked to hear the first few words of our own Declaration of Independence, especially it making reference to the Creator. He had the words life and liberty kind of transposed and I worked it out for him a little bit and I said "I think this is the way it should be." '

The first paragraph as publicly pronounced in Hanoi on 2 September 1945, and thereafter etched in bronze in Hanoi's Museum of History, read: 'All men are created equal. They are endowed by their Creator with certain inalienable rights, among these are Life, Liberty and the pursuit of Happiness.'

'He meant it – definitely,' says Patti. 'It was also a gesture to the American government. But he meant it. This was exactly what expressed his thoughts, his views. He wanted his people to be happy, he wanted them to be free. He knew they had been in chains for a long, long time. And they – that's it.'

And with the phrasing of the Declaration completed, a delegation of the Viet Minh provisional government, led by newly promoted General Giap, called at the OSS villa. Says Patti: 'They put on quite a performance. They had bands sitting outside the villa, playing "The Star Spangled Banner" like you never heard before in the Far East – very well, a good rendition. They played "God Save The King", they played the Chinese national anthem and they played, of course, "The Soviet Worker's March".' Patti noted that at this ceremony for the first time the Viet Minh flag – a lone gold star on a field of red – had appeared in public 'together with the colors of Great Britain, China and the United States'.

He describes the general atmosphere preceding Independence Day as 'joyous, festive, though somewhat restrained on the part of the French, to say the least'. The Japanese stayed within their barracks. Within the week, says Patti, the Viet Minh provisional government had reorganized food distribution, city transportation and utilities. But no nation had recognized the self-proclaimed republic, and 'Ho was very anxious for recognition'. Patti says he and his staff were in 'daily contact' with Ho's staff, headed by Vo Nguyen Giap. The Americans were the only member of any foreign government given a place of honor when the Democratic Republic of Vietnam officially came into being on 2 September 1945. Major Patti stood next to General Giap.

'The autumn sun was bright the day Ba Dinh Square made history,' says Giap. 'Our fighters who a few days earlier had taken important towns and cities in the South now stood side by side with the self-defense units of workers, youth and laboring people. Hundreds of thousands of peasants had journeyed to Hanoi. People's militia-men came carrying quarter-staffs, swords or scimitars; some even carried old-style bronze clubs and long-handled swords taken from the armories of temples.'

'The President', says Giap, 'now appeared for the first time before his people, a thin old man with a broad forehead, bright eyes and a sparse beard, wearing an old hat, a high-collared khaki jacket and white rubber sandals.'

Ho Chi Minh arrived in a pre-war French car with outriders on bicycles. He spoke from a crude platform and read the words which every American schoolchild knows, and in this declaration to life and liberty he incorporated the past, referring to Vietnam's French colonizers as having 'built more prisons than schools'. 'It was a very touching ceremony,' as Patti recalls it. 'I could tell from the reaction of the crowd, and the crowd was fantastic. The people were responding with enthusiasm, even adulation.'

Ho declared: 'Vietnam has the right to be a free and independent country; and in fact is so already.' In fact, full independence lay 10,000 days in the future. Ho Chi Minh had spent more than thirty years seeking it; another thirty years would pass attaining it, at which time he would lie embalmed in a Leninesque mausoleum on the very spot in Hanoi's Ba Dinh Square from which he was now speaking. But General Giap and the other early Viet Minh leaders would still be there.

As Ho made his declaration the first American fighter planes came to Hanoi. A squadron flew in low, dipped their wings, and disappeared. The OSS men say they had no idea who ordered this.

1945—Maj. Gen. D. H. Gracey, chief of the allied control commission in French Indochina, at his headquarter's desk.

The French contend that the OSS played wholly into Viet Minh hands on Independence Day by their presence in uniform, saluting with Ho as his lone-star flag was raised; that by identifying with the American victors Ho assumed a legitimacy and recognition which no country had yet accorded him; that his gestures to the Americans were an interim power-play of no great significance. However, US government records, only disclosed twenty-six years later in the *Pentagon Papers,* showed that from late 1945 to the end of 1946, when Vietnamese-French hostilities degenerated into war, Ho Chi Minh repeatedly cabled or wrote to the White House requesting recognition, citing first the Atlantic Charter and then the United Nations Charter on self-determination. Ho received no response.

The French in Indo-China had been defeated by the Japanese. The Japanese had been defeated by the Americans, and the American OSS mission in Hanoi in its final report before being disbanded in late September 1945, clearly looked to Ho Chi Minh as the only legitimate national leader. The report quotes Emperor Bao Dai who had then abdicated as having told the OSS that his abdication was 'voluntary' and that he was in 'complete accord' with Ho's provisional government and its aspirations.

Ho, however, now faced the political chaos which descended with the Allied occupying forces. British troops, under the Potsdam Agreement, had taken over the country to the 16th Parallel – the southern half. In October a purely bilateral British-French agreement recognized French administration of this zone only. None of the postwar Great Powers had recognized Ho's republic, but neither had they recognized French sovereignty over Indo-China. Of the three Indo-China states, Laos had just declared itself independent – but French troops were en route there; Cambodia had been reoccupied by the French and proclaimed 'autonomous' within the

French Union; and in Vietnam Ho had cautiously linked independence with the French Union while trying to negotiate what it meant – insisting that Vietnam be fully self-governing, not merely autonomous.

Ho's Viet Minh, with their 'scimitars and bronze clubs', were hopelessly ill-equipped to deal with the situation which now prevailed, and they had hardly any armed base in the South. With the British – having released thousands of French troops – holding the South; with 60,000 Japanese troops disarmed but hostile in their barracks and 200,000 of Chiang's soldiers 'rampaging' in the North, Hanoi after its independence euphoria had become a nightmare. As Giap puts it, Chiang's troops 'swept over the North like a plague'.

At this moment the OSS mission in its collective final report was advising Washington of an extraordinary statement attributed to Ho Chi Minh. The OSS quoted Ho as saying that 'although he formerly favored Communist ideals, he now realized that such ideals were impracticable for his country, and that his policy now was one of republican nationalism'. The American public would, however, only learn of this some 10,000 days later.

Major Patti recalls his last meeting with Ho: 'He kept repeating, "Why doesn't the United States give us moral support? We don't want anything else, nothing but moral support. Look what you have done in the Philippines. You promised them a date for independence, you have given them independence. Why can't you do the same for us?" '

There now came a poignant moment. The first American military officer sent to Vietnam had just learned that a fellow officer of the OSS, Colonel Peter Dewey, had become the first American to be killed in the fighting – in a Viet Minh skirmish against a French post outside Saigon. Colonel Dewey, says Patti, had worn no insignia because the reputedly pro-colonial British Commander in Saigon, General Gracey, 'had prohibited' the display of the American flag or colors 'even on jeeps, even on the uniforms, which looked very like the French uniforms'. Ho responded that he would write a personal letter of condolence to the President of the United States, and Ho vowed, says Patti, 'that it would never happen again, except over his dead body'.

'Before I left him,' says Patti, 'Ho gave me a message to take back to the American people: that the Vietnamese loved the Americans; they had followed its history and were looking to the United States because of the history of the revolutionary war. They were looking to the Americans because they had promised so many things in World War I and again in World War II. And in World War II they had delivered. And to go back and tell the Americans that the Vietnamese would never fight the Americans."

Patti, who continued to be actively engaged in national security affairs, and spent twelve years with the Executive Office of the President until concluding his career in 1971, ends his Vietnam account by stating that everything he heard or learned was included in his despatches and these remain 'part of the official record'.

The essential issue is whether the United States, with this early intelligence, failed to recognize in Ho Chi Minh a potential Asian Tito. The tone of Patti's official despatches is corroborated by others. Major Frank M. White, who replaced the OSS mission as a political observer in Hanoi for the State Department, testified twenty-seven years later at Senate hearings on 11 May 1972, when the American combat role had all but ended, to lengthy meetings with Ho Chi Minh in December 1945.

Ho's statement then is even more significant, as quoted by White: 'Eventually he had gone to the Soviet Union, he said, and studied the teaching of Marx and Lenin. He did not dwell on this much except to say that he believed that revolution had benefited the Russian people and that he had become a believer in Communism. But he went on to say that he did not believe that the Soviet Union could or would make any kind of a real contribution to the building of what he called a new Vietnam.'

White, while in Hanoi, received a dinner invitation from Ho. The senior British, French and Chinese officers in Hanoi were present and the greetings to the American were 'glacial'. When the others were seated, White saw there was only one place remaining – next to Ho, and the invitation card there had White's name on it.

'The dinner was a horror,' recalled White. 'The French confined themselves to the barest minimum of conversation. The Chinese got drunk – really wildly drunk. I said, "I think, *Monsieur le Président*, there is some resentment over the seating arrangement." I meant my place, of course, next to him as the seat of honor. "I can see that," said Ho, "but who else would I have to talk to?"'

'I think it was a rather telling anecdote,' White told the Senate Committee on Foreign Relations.

The Committee then heard from Abbot Low Moffat, who left Hanoi to head the Division of South-East Asian Affairs at the Department of State, 1945-47. His might be considered the most authoritative testimony.

'I have never met an American,' stated Moffat, 'be he military, OSS, diplomat, or journalist, who had ever met Ho Chi Minh who did not reach the same belief: that Ho Chi Minh was *first and foremost* a Vietnamese nationalist. He was also a Communist and believed that Communism offered the best hope for the Vietnamese people. But his loyalty was to his people. When I was in Indo-China it was striking how the top echelon of competent French officials held almost exclusively the same view.

'As Department concern about the Communist domination of the Vietnam government became more apparent and more uncritical we began, I felt, to allow fears of such domination to overrule better judgement; we let the nationalist feelings of the country recede in importance and we ignored the father figure that Ho Chi Minh was becoming for most Vietnamese. The French seemed not averse to taking advantage of our increasing preoccupation with Communism.'

Moffat summarized that in the early cold-war climate with Stalin's Russia, in which the US needed its European allies, he could not get higher attention for the warnings the State Department was still receiving from its consul in Hanoi, James O'Sullivan. In urgent diplomatic cables O'Sullivan pointed out that the French had always known Ho's background, were prepared to negotiate with him, but were also 'preparing to force the Vietnam government to collaborate on French terms or to establish a puppet government in its place'.

'French concern over Communism,' as Moffat quoted from his dead-letter file, 'may well be devised to divert the Department's attention from French policy in Indo-China.' There was a silence at the Senate hearings when those words registered twenty-seven years later. Then Committee Chairman Senator William Fulbright exploded: 'So we have been had, as the slang goes, by our allies influencing our judgement. . . . It is just incredible that a great nation could be so misguided.'

US Defense Department records are equally revealing as to what was occurring in late 1945 in Hanoi, where Ho Chi Minh had agreed to an Allied compromise that the 200,000 Chinese troops in the North would withdraw if 15,000 French troops replaced them to help keep order. Ho is quoted as angrily rounding on pro-Chinese elements in his government who opposed this, telling them: 'You fools! Don't you realize what it means if the Chinese stay? Don't you remember your history? The last time the Chinese came they stayed one thousand years. The French are foreigners. They are weak. Colonialism is dying out. Nothing will be able to withstand world pressure for independence.'

Giap in his account substantiates the sentiment, if not the actual words, saying: 'We agreed to let French troops into the North for a specified time in order to drive out the Chiang troops who would otherwise stay on indefinitely.' In other words, there was no reliance on Mao Tse-tung to drive out Chiang's forces, and no approach at that time for Chinese Communist aid. The Soviet Union did not recognize Ho Chi Minh's government until 1950 – five years after he had pleaded for US recognition.

In what Ho saw as an unavoidable deal with the French, the two sides settled on a measure or definition of independence pending the fine print. France agreed to recognize Vietnam as 'a free state' – which Giap defines as meaning a republic 'with its own government, parliament, army and finances, within the French Union' – and France further agreed to withdraw her 15,000 troops from the North in five annual installments, or by 1952. The Viet Minh pledged to end guerrilla activity in the South. This compromise meant there would be two power bases, in Saigon and Hanoi, but there were to be negotiations in Paris to reconcile this.

The signing of the agreement would only take place when all but a token force of Chinese had withdrawn and the months of waiting are described in the Senate record by the American observer in Hanoi, Major White: 'The overall scene remains as vivid as a flash of lightning against a towering storm. There were mobs in the streets. Chinese troops continued to file out of Hanoi, carrying their loot in bullock carts, captured Japanese trucks and even on their backs. They took everything – plumbing fixtures, tiles off the roofs, even the pipes of buildings.'

The Viet Minh now showed its discipline. They did not fire on the pillaging Chinese. The people of Hanoi and its twin port-city, Haiphong, were ordered not to react – and they did not – as French warships and soldiers returned and paraded. White recounts that 'at the epicenter of all this sat Ho Chi Minh . . . his beard was then wispy and his manner curiously detached. The United States, Ho said, was in the best position to aid Vietnam in the postwar years. He dwelled at some length on the disposition of Americans as a people to be sympathetic to self-determination. But he said he felt the US government would find more urgent things to do . . . that, after all, Vietnam is a small country and far away.'

Only the American consul was present as a courtesy when the French-Vietnam agreement was signed at 4 pm on 6 March 1946. By then all American military personnel had left. They had been in Vietnam less than a year. Only one had been killed – inadvertently. Major Patti was back in cold-war Europe, heading a new mission in Trieste where the US was interested in a guerrilla father-figure named Tito who seemed a Communist of independent mind. In Hanoi, as Giap records it, 'a slender old man in a faded khaki suit' signed the agreement, then looked up to the Frenchman facing him. It was the man whom Major Patti had flown to Hanoi out of a sense of loyalty. Major Sainteny signed last.

Sainteny raised his glass and, Giap recalls, 'expressed his joy at having driven away the specter of armed conflict'. Ho Chi Minh responded in French saying, 'We are not yet satisfied because we have not yet won complete independence.' He paused, then in a 'calm firm voice' said, 'but we will achieve it'.

# FRANCE IN VIETNAM

Within a year of the signing of the French-Vietnam agreement Ho Chi Minh was driven back to the guerrilla sanctuary of Tan Trao which the Americans had helped him to secure, there to conduct eight years of unremitting war against the French whom the United States now militarily supported for reasons of wider geopolitics. Vietnam, even then, was labeled a 'sideshow'. The subsequent eight years of direct American engagement are remarkable for the many political and military parallels with the previous eight French war years. The first parallel is of leaders beset by rival political advisors, while the military initially tried to exercise restraint.

The political terms of the 6 March 1946 agreement had pleased neither the pro-Chinese Mao faction in the Viet Minh, nor the new French High Commissioner in Saigon, Admiral d'Argenlieu, who – like the American Ambassadors years later –

> '**We didn't press the French to withdraw. We didn't want Indo-China on our hands.**'
>
> — DEAN RUSK, SECRETARY OF STATE

had overall command. D'Argenlieu had been appointed directly by de Gaulle after the Japanese surrender and had received instructions direct from him during the negotiations for the return of French troops to the North. The statements of both men suggest that the French public – like the American public in its turn – were deceived by political moves which disguised military preparations. When de Gaulle abdicated power in late 1945 his successors (the first of fifteen French governments during the Indo-China years) were too weak to contend with the High Commissioner of France's most prized overseas possession. The occasional pronouncements of the retired de Gaulle, who for so long personified the spirit of France, had the force of religious commandments, and d'Argenlieu, a one-time priest and monk, shared this mystical authority by association.

Some of the character of d'Argenlieu and of

March 1947—The port of Saigon, capital of the French colony of Cochin China, is considered one of the finest cities in the Far East. Modernized since the French arrived in 1861, it has new quays for its large rice trade.

Left: July 1946—Ho Chi Minh, *center*, president of Vietnam, leaves the French Foreign Ministry during his visit to Paris. At right is Marius Moutet, French minister of colonies.

Below: July 4, 1946—Ho Chi Minh, president of the Republic of Vietnam, signs the guest book during an official visit to City Hall in Paris.

the French political-military command is revealed in anecdotes told by the Viet Minh commander, General Giap. With French troops in place in Hanoi in March 1946, d'Argenlieu – says Giap – decided to demonstrate French power, and his own. He sailed into Haiphong from Saigon with every French warship in the region, then peremptorily invited Ho Chi Minh to review the fleet – and to come by himself.

Aboard d'Argenlieu's flagship, Ho watched in drawn-out silence as gunship after gunship slowly cruised past. In Giap's account Ho had come conveniently equipped with a broad-brimmed hat. This he pulled well down while 'leaning on a bamboo stick' on the Admiral's deck. Ho on returning to Hanoi related all this to Giap, then added: 'D'Argenlieu has made a big mistake. Those ships can't sail up our rivers.'

Giap goes on to chart, perhaps unintentionally, the minutiae of individual hostility that can contribute to great human conflict. In April he met with d'Argenlieu personally during a month-long conference arranged to discuss the political relationship of South and North. Both sides had set what would become the future pattern for negotiations – days of intensive fighting beforehand which continued during negotiations – and from the start the meeting seemed doomed by the characters of the two principals.

Giap related that d'Argenlieu began by 'boasting that he knew a lot about me. He inquired after my family.' If d'Argenlieu did know a lot about Giap, he would have known that he was a man hardened by the bitter experiences of his youth,

July 4, 1946—Ho Chi Minh speaks as president of the new Communist-dominated independence movement, popularly known as the Vietminh, before beginning an eight-year fight with the French, who were unwilling to grant independence to their colonies.

and the death of his wife only three years earlier. He was born in 1912 in the village of An-Xa in Quang-Bing Province, just north of the 17th Parallel (to become the Partition Line), where life was always hardest. He was the product of a poor but scholarly father who had participated in the last major rebellion of 1888 – and of the hard rice-lands he tilled in his determination to pay his way to the distant university of Hanoi. But he practiced history long before he taught it there. At fourteen he joined an anticolonial party. At eighteen he was jailed for three years for political activity. At twenty-four he organized national student strikes, and then went underground. At thirty-one he was a widower – his young wife had died while in jail serving a life-sentence for 'conspiracy'. He had then joined Ho Chi Minh and Pham Van Dong in China as a co-founder of the Viet Minh.

Giap bitterly remembers France's first postwar proconsul in Indo-China. He describes his first meeting with d'Argenlieu: 'This defrocked priest had small, wily eyes under a wrinkled forehead, and thin lips. My impression after spending a moment with him was that he was a cunning, arrogant, mean man.'

Giap wanted a referendum in the South on the issue of one Vietnam. D'Argenlieu refused. They agreed only that Ho Chi Minh would negotiate further in Paris in late June. But on 1 June d'Argenlieu announced that the South had been accorded the status of a 'free republic' under its old name, Cochin China. D'Argenlieu himself records that he then told the new French commander, General Valluy: 'I am amazed, mon Général, yes amazed, that France should have such a fine expeditionary corps in Indo-China and that its leaders should prefer to negotiate rather than fight.'

As fighting spread, French Premier Bidault had to choose between conflicting advice from his senior fieldmen – as Presidents Kennedy and Johnson later had to do. D'Argenlieu had hurried to Paris, where the previous political head of mis-

sion, Major Sainteny, had been pleading for a return to a moderate policy and good-faith negotiations. However, for Bidault, heading a fractious coalition, any policy or government could well be shattered by a stentorian word from the brooding de Gaulle.

When negotiations finally began in Paris on 6 July 1946 – ten days after Ho Chi Minh's arrival – Ho was dismayed, according to Giap, to discover that the head of the French delegation was d'Argenlieu's senior aide from Saigon. As the talks dragged on into August, d'Argenlieu returned to Indo-China and defiantly convened a 'federal conference' of Indo-China states. D'Argenlieu was recalled and reprimanded, but not relieved of his post – and the first Paris peace talks broke down, to be resumed twenty-two years later.

Ho Chi Minh and Premier Bidault now at last began personal talks, and it was then that de Gaulle broke his silence. He chose 27 August 1946 – the day when a new Franco-Laotian agreement was signed after the reoccupation of Laos by French troops. De Gaulle – as quoted by Le Monde – declared: 'United with the overseas territories which she opened to civilization, France is a great power. Without these territories she would be in danger of no longer being one.' Giap suggests that de Gaulle's pronouncement was fatal to any remaining chance for a political settlement, and after that 'all the meetings and discussions were of no avail'.

As Ho Chi Minh sailed from France empty-handed, General Giap was observing the first anniversary of Independence Day, 2 September, in Hanoi with a calculated show of defiance. It showed the Viet Minh's extraordinary development in just six months. As Giap describes his new army: 'A regiment of the national army of Vietnam, properly equipped, clad in green uniforms, gold-starred caps and leather boots and carrying rifles, were proudly parading before the stand to the stirring music of the military band. Preceding each unit was the commanding officer

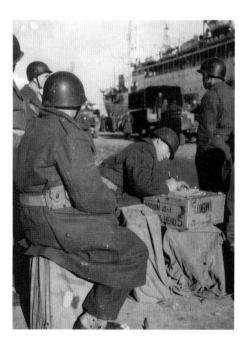

January 14, 1947—A French soldier writes a letter home from Marseille port before shipping out to Indochina that night aboard the troop ship Athos II.

armed with a long sword and with the political commissar marching beside him. This was a highly significant event at a time when red-bereted French paratroopers were tramping the pavements and vehicles of the [French] Second Armored Division were roaring up and down the streets of Hanoi.'

Ho Chi Minh returned aboard a French warship which, in Giap's words, 'sailed rather slowly'. This might also describe the French-Viet Minh political negotiations – they were to be resumed in the New Year. However, the military clashes were now seriously escalating. On 20 November fighting between French and Viet Minh troops broke out in the port city of Haiphong over who should control the customs house – and therefore the flow of arms. As Giap describes it, the days alternated between cease-fires, ultimatums, and fierce unpredictable fights over 'the control of a street, a lane or a house'. At this moment France was without a government.

On 23 November the French bombarded and occupied Haiphong. By early December the fighting had spread to Hanoi and for the last time Ho Chi Minh appealed to the United States to support independence. He now received what would be his last French visitor for eight years, press attaché Jean Lacouture, and even then, with the gunfire closing in, Ho 'was smiling, was very gentle'.

Ho seemed to be reaching for days and ideals he knew were passing forever, reminiscing yet resigned, as Lacouture remembers: 'We talked about French civilization, about the French Revolution, about the books we liked. It was so strange. We were at war – and he was speaking as a friend. He was so charming. I can never forget this old gentleman of Asia. I tried asking questions – about negotiations, about the chance for peace. And he said, "Ask my friend Giap. He is better informed." '

Vo Nguyen Giap recounts that in mid-December, as news came through of French troop ships sailing from Marseilles, Ho Chi Minh summoned him and they had this brief historic exchange: ' "How long can Hanoi be held if the enemy extends the war in the North?" "Possibly for a month." "What about the other towns?" "We can hold them more easily." "And the countryside?" "There's no doubt that we can hold the countryside." Ho pondered for a while and said, "We shall return to Tan Trao." '

Giap provides an exact date for the start of a war that would last, in its different phases, for 10,360 days! 'It was on a winter evening that President Ho's call for the national resistance war – 20 December 1946 – was broadcast by the Voice of Vietnam radio from a place not far from Hanoi as we moved to a base camp.' In his broadcast Ho recalled the line of a poem from his prison days: 'If we endure through this cold winter, we shall see spring.' Then, says Giap, Ho 'at fifty-six years, with a bamboo walking stick and a pair of rubber sandals' led the Viet Minh back to Tan Trao.

Giap's forces put up a rear-guard action in Hanoi, then evacuated the city in early January 1947. Later, 15,000 French troops were sent into the China border mountains where Ho and the Viet Minh leaders constantly shifted headquarters. At one place French paratroopers found Ho's mail ready for signature, but the Viet Minh were as elusive as eagles in this high eyrie.

Ho and his lieutenants had come to know this

almost inaccessible terrain during twenty years of infiltrating back and forth from China. From the northern border jungles around Lang Son westward to the Truong Son ('Long Mountains') they had charted bases and hideouts, and now along hundreds of miles of indefinable front line, the guerrillas emerged, attacked, and then vanished back into the Truong Son, which the Americans would later call the Ho Chi Minh Trail.

The French, from the outset, were fighting not just the Viet Minh but history. The Truong Son, separating Vietnam and Laos, curved physically like a spinal cord and had been the nerve center of Vietnamese nationalism for 2000 years. Its caves and redoubts were as familiar as birthmarks from countless ancestral wars. Here, highland tribes like the Moi, Muong, Miao Mongol extraction had settled in the lowlands.

The recorded history of the Vietnam nation dates from 207 BC when a Chinese warlord established his own kingdom and called it Nam Viet. Chinese rule lasted until the tenth century when after a series of risings the Vietnamese drove out the Chinese and established their own dynasty in the year 939. There were another ten centuries of alternating invasion and independence before the mid-nineteenth-century arrival of the French Catholic missionary, Bishop de Behaine, followed by the landing of French troops on 2 September 1858, on the shores of Da Nang – where a century later the first American combat troops would wade into the quagmire.

To the Viet Minh the monk d'Argenlieu was only the ghost of the Bishop – and no more intimidating. As Roosevelt had remarked, the French had ruled Vietnam for a century and the people were 'worse off than at the beginning'. The bitterness that motivated the Viet Minh, and the peasantry that supported them, is conveyed by one of the movement's young officers, Ha Van Lau, who would eventually become Vietnam's first Ambassador to the United Nations.

'The Vietnamese', he says, 'had been submitted to the double burden of colonialism and feudalism. The peasantry were vassals of the farmers and landlords. When they died their bodies served as manure in the plantations. Our history is one of many thousands of years, but in colonial days Vietnam didn't even appear on the world map. The country was divided into three parts. That was the politics of divide and rule.'

Vietnam had still to appear on the map, and now in March 1947, in the heightening East-West cold war, Roosevelt's aspirations were overtaken by the Truman Doctrine which linked the defense of Europe with collective security in Asia. Truman stated: 'It must be the policy of the United States to support free peoples who are resisting attempted subjugation by armed minorities.'

Though the Doctrine could be read both ways, the French interpreted it as support for them – and a State Department analyst at that time, William Bundy, who would become a senior policy-maker, confirms that this was Truman's intent. This new tolerance of colonialism, says Bundy, was 'justified on the basis of the way the French government and people felt at that time. They were not prepared to withdraw. If we had said we won't help you in Indo-China, I think it would have seriously reduced the chances of the effective organization and rearming of the NATO countries. So it tied in to Europe. In that direct way.'

January 12, 1947—Some of the 8,000 French troops aboard the *Ile de France* jam stern section prior to departure from Toulon Harbor for duty in Indochina.

Above: December 1946— Vietnamese insurgents jump from trenches they are digging in a Hanoi street. Heavy fighting took place in Hanoi as the French removed street barricades erected near the capital's airfield.

Right: January 1947—With a building burning in the background, French soldiers patrol the streets of Hanoi during fighting with Vietnamese insurgents.

How France felt about the war in Indo-China was now, ironically, in conflict with what the United States officially felt. There was clear and open division among public and policy advisors. Ho Chi Minh had proposed negotiations, cabling the new French government this message: 'When France recognizes the independence and unity of Vietnam we will retire to our villages, for we are not ambitious for power or honor.'

Socialist Premier Ramadier then sent a three-man mission to Hanoi to evaluate the situation, which reported its findings at the same as the Truman Doctrine was stated. It reached no consensus – a dilemma which Washington would experience again and again. One member, d'Argenlieu, emphasized 'the security of strategic bases within the framework of the French Union'. The military fact-finder, General Leclerc, made a diametrically opposite recommendation, stating: 'In 1947 France can no longer put down by force a grouping of people which is assuming unity and in which there exists a xenophobic and perhaps a national ideal.'

The third member, Socialist Party representative Marius Moutet, who had been instructed to assess only political prospects, decided that it was Ho Chi Minh's armed resistance rather than his ideology that was unacceptable. Moutet reported: 'Before any negotiations it is necessary to have a military decision. I am sorry, but one cannot commit such madness as the Vietnamese have done with impunity.'

The French public had already voted on the issue. The results of an opinion poll, as reported in the *New York Times* of 4 February 1947, showed that thirty-six per cent of those questioned favoured force; forty-two per cent favoured negotiations and another eight per cent thought France should leave Indo-China altogether. The remaining fourteen per cent had no opinion.

France was now a nation divided over Vietnam, as in time America would be. In the first two years of combat France had sent or had readied 150,000 troops, as America would. The first wounded veterans were returning – to averted eyes. In words descriptive of a later generation from another land, a French captain quoted by *Le Courrier de la Nation* told of the soldier's malaise: 'We turned in upon ourselves, we lived among ourselves, and we became as touchy and sensitive as men flayed alive. But how great was the despair we felt at being rejected by our country – and how great was our need of fraternity.'

Americans who would be able to shape later history were paying close attention at the time. Graham Martin was a counselor at the US Embassy in Paris in 1947; he states: 'It was a fascinating sort of lesson. . .on the nature of guerrilla war in the middle of the twentieth century. And whether or not modern armies – trained for conventional combat – could be sort of geared down to handle guerrilla combat.' Martin would be the last senior American in Vietnam to seek the answer, as Ambassador to Saigon in 1975.

Ambassador Ha Van Lau describes the pattern that would prevail throughout: 'The Viet Minh were like fish in water. That was our slogan. Our fighters moved and worked among the people like fish in water.'

For the French command, random action became the substitute for actual battle. The French now began punitive raids on villages assist-

Left: January 1947—French troops man a rooftop machine gun against the Vietminh during fighting in Hanoi.

Right: January 1947—A French soldier searches for snipers during fighting in Hanoi.

ing the Viet Minh. They forcibly evacuated entire regions, creating a vast refugee problem – and more Viet Minh supporters. The French did not – and could not – hold the countryside. They were safe only in the cities.

Essentially it was a question of whether a strong military force could defeat a strong political organization. And it was the infrastructure of the Viet Minh, rather than its mixed results in battle, which sustained Giap's strategy of protracted war – and which warrants attention. Ha Van Lau, then a guerrilla fighter in the South, points out that the Viet Minh was not, as popularly imagined, the army: the soldiers were only a part of it. 'The Viet Minh, for example, brought together organizations of peasants, workers, the youth, the women, even the Buddhists. It included urban groups, cultural associations, intellectuals, artists, elements of the national bourgeoisie. The Viet Minh constituted one of the principal factors assuring victory.'

General Giap, who had fused the popular militia with the regular People's Army which he now commanded, claims that by 1947 this combined force numbered one million men. This force had evolved within just two years from the Viet Minh political grouping. Though Giap reveals nothing of his personal life, this one-time history teacher provides a concise, terse account of 'how it was done' – and presents the greater objective as uncompromisingly ideological. However, he reveals that intensive organization had only begun 'toward the end of 1945' when the North was obliged to accept French troops.

'At this time', says Giap, 'self-defense units were organized in almost every hamlet, village, street and factory; one or two companies in some places, at least one platoon in others. They were put under the close leadership of the Party and given assistance in military training by government authorities, but were wholly self-supporting in food and equipment. In areas not yet at war, they proved an efficient instrument of dictatorship for the revolutionary power, ensuring security for Party, State and [Viet Minh] Front offices, main-social system the North Vietnamese openly criticized as culturally sterile and thus motiveless.

Giap's military model was Napoleon. Indeed, the impression on meeting Giap was of a man Napoleonic in stature, nature and knowledge. He dominated any assembly without seeking to – his mere presence imperious, seemingly aloof and never quite present. He was the master strategist with a mind that raced time, one hand reaching now for a pawn, the other biding the years for the queen. He could recite all Napoleon's campaigns, but Giap was different: he lost many battles, but never a war. His comrades called him Nui Lua – 'ice-covered volcano'.

Yet it was tremors from outside Vietnam that now brought dramatic eruption of battle. In January 1950 the new People's Republic of China formally recognized Ho Chi Minh as leader of all Vietnam. The Soviet Union quickly did the same. In February the United States recognized the newly installed Saigon government of Bao Dai, the former Emperor who had once more changed sides to become head of state of the Republic of Vietnam 'within the French Union'. The political lines had finally been drawn, but the military odds had changed. In the North, with easier access to Communist Chinese supplies, General Giap pronounced that the guerrilla phase of the war was over: the counter-offensive had begun.

taining peace and order, and suppressing the reactionaries. The Hanoi city self-defense corps included practically all young men and numbered tens of thousands. They managed to procure various sorts of weapons for themselves from daggers and shotguns to anti-tank mines and Japanese machine-guns.

'The core of this force was made up of self-defense shock units. They included workers, poor laborers, schoolboys and students. They were armed and equipped by the Ministry of National Defense and mostly quartered together in barracks because of the situation. Their daily needs were supplied by the people. Along with the task of defending the revolutionary power against the reactionaries, they also took part in propaganda work and helped train the other self-defense units.'

Giap stresses that the development of this political militia largely preceded 'the building of a *regular army* [Giap's italics]. Then, with the establishment of base areas, 'Party committees for the various military zones were formed. Cadres from the Party were assigned to work in the army. The system of commander and political officer sharing the leadership of the unit was applied throughout the army. There was a political commissar for every military zone, and a political officer for every unit from regiment down to platoon level.'

This grass-roots discipline, both voluntary and imposed, this million-man army that was everywhere but nowhere, is what the French tried to counter with conventional regiments. Though the French could at any time and any place deploy far superior fire-power, they were in fact outgunned and hopelessly outnumbered, their entire army effectively besieged. Historian Lacouture would rate Giap's organizational 'genius' as comparable with Mao's. In fact Vo Nguyen Giap, who would retain overall military command for the next thirty years, would probably disdain the comparison. His political guide was Marx not Mao; he leaned ideologically towards Moscow not China – whose

Above left: April 28, 1949—Bao Dai, emperor of the French protectorate of Annam, is welcomed to Dalat in the central highlands of Vietnam, after signing an agreement in Paris which the French hope will end the war in Indochina. Pham Van Gia, governor of central Vietnam, at microphone, speaks to, *from left*, Leon Pignon, French high commissioner; Bao Dai; Gen. Nguyen Xuan, president of Vietnam, Central Government; and Tran Ven Huu, president of Vietnam, Southern Government.

Left: Indochina of 1950 still carried its historic names. The northern area of Vietnam was called Tonkin. The central area was called Annam and the south was known as Cochin China. Cambodia and Laos, part of the French Indochina empire, were to the west. Siam, still further to the west, became in later days known as Thailand. Ho Chi Minh and his Vietminh army had been active for some five years, harassing the French and steadily increasing its influence in the countryside.

**14**

This – and French requests for US military aid – still received little attention in Washington. Then, in June the Korean war broke out as the Communist North Korean army crossed the 38th Parallel – the postwar partition line between the Communist North and the non-Communist South – after years of border tension. The United Nations Security Council, on US recommendation, obtained the agreement of member nations for immediate armed support of South Korea. Fearing wider Communist expansion, the US administration announced a program of military aid for Indo-China. It was modest – $10 million worth of equipment in 1950 – but US military involvement had begun.

Previously the policy switch had been 'tied in to Europe' – as State Department official William Bundy defined it. Now the US, says Bundy, 'had a true commitment situation in Indo-China. In particular [Secretary of State] Dulles believed it was the only way to hold the line – to contain China. He didn't use that word but that is what he was doing.' Bundy stresses how costly that $10 million decision would prove: 'Obviously it got us in very much deeper, and I think to a very large extent made the decisions of the late 1960s almost inevitable.'

Dulles, announcing that military aid would be ongoing, now imposed terms that shaped the 1960s. He called for the formation of a Vietnamese National Army in the South, with the implication that the US would then arm it. One Secretary of State had conceived 'Vietnamization' as a doorway to the region; other Secretaries, including Dean Rusk, would continually enlarge it as the exit from a trap.

Somehow, as Rusk explains it, the US rationalized that by aiding the French in Vietnam it could itself avoid involvement. 'On the one hand', says Rusk, 'we were giving France assistance for postwar construction. On the other hand we pressed them very hard to make a political settlement with Indo-China – to work it out on the same basis on which the British were working out their relations with India and Burma. We did not press the French to the point where they would simply withdraw and say, Okay, it is yours, you worry about it. We didn't want to push them that far because we didn't want Indo-China on our hands.'

Rusk says in effect that, given American concern at the time over the Sino-Soviet alliance, France had more leverage than the US in Vietnam. From November 1950, when 180,000 Chinese troops entered the Korean War, the price of French co-operation rose one-hundredfold. The initial $10 million leapt annually by hundreds of millions, exceeding $1000 million by 1954 – seventy-eight per cent of the French war bill – even though all concerned conceded that the war could not be won.

This Asian investment on behalf of a European ally would cost the US $140 billion – and much else – by the time its last Ambassador to Saigon pulled out. Even in the 1950s, as a counselor in Paris, Graham Martin could see the dimension of the cost for the French alone: 'It was enormous. The French spent, in effect, in Indo-China, about what we had given them through the Marshall Plan for aid and reconstruction. And

in one way you could say that we paid for the French experience in Indo-China. But if they had not had that [aid] what might have happened to the French economy could have paralleled the record in Germany'.

On the question of whether the US at the time thought the expenditure had any appreciable effect on the war, Senator William Fulbright of the Finance Committee states that Vietnam even then was 'a side issue – we did it only to please the French'.

In his book *The Two Vietnams* the late French historian Bernard Fall, who observed the war at first hand over many years, writes that American military aid 'was to make no difference whatever in the eventual outcome of the war'. He notes that General Giap had launched his first major counteroffensive in October 1950, prior to the widening of the Korean War and the US aid build-up, and that 'the Indo-China war was lost then and there'.

Giap, equipped with new heavy mortars from China, targeted a string of French forts in the far North, and one by one they were overwhelmed. Giap then switched to a premature general offensive and sustained severe defeats – a setback lasting two years – but the French losses that October (6000 troops killed or captured) were described by Bernard Fall as France's 'greatest colonial defeat since Montcalm died at Quebec'.

As another French historian, Jean Lacouture, puts it: 'That was the first disaster of the war, and that gave the idea that the war was nearly impossible to win because the Viet Minh, with China behind it, had a great enormous sanctuary. So the ar became more and more unpopular from 1950 – and very expensive, though of course the United States paid.'

Two future US presidents visited Vietnam during the French years to pronounce on cost and cause. On his return in November 1951, Senator John F. Kennedy declared that 'in Indo-China we have allied ourselves to the desperate effort of the French regime to hang on to the remnants of an empire'.

Nine years later Kennedy would send the first US military advisors. Nine years after that President Nixon would begin troop withdrawals, but as Vice-President in late 1953 Nixon arrived in Hanoi and told the French that a peace settlement would place the people under Communist bondage, and he stated: 'It is impossible to lay down arms until victory is won.'

A few weeks earlier, after joining a presidential mission to Vietnam, America's foremost counter-insurgency expert, General Edward Lansdale, had come to a quite different conclusion, which the American public did not hear. Lansdale says he then had 'very strong feelings that a colonial power – which the French were – couldn't win the people's war that was being waged. Only the Vietnamese themselves could win in such a war.'

Lansdale had been asked to assess the plans of the new French commander in Vietnam. General Henri Navarre. Although he had no experience of Indo-China, or of guerrilla warfare, Navarre as the French Chief of Staff with the Allied command in Europe had been chosen to bring 'a new objectivity' to the situation. He had been sent in May

1953 by Premier René Mayer with orders to return within a month and report 'what was possible'.

'It struck me immediately', says Navarre, 'that there was no possibility of winning the war in Indo-China. The Viet Minh had gained a considerable advantage over us in mobile forces. The situation had deteriorated the previous year. We had to evacuate all the upper region and a good part of Laos. The military situation was very bad.'

Navarre's reasoning was the same as General William Westmoreland's fifteen years later – the changed political climate would not allow an all-out military effort: 'If we had wanted to win the war, France would have had to make a great effort in Indo-China, and the French political situation would absolutely not have allowed this. France was tired of the war.'

Navarre returned to Paris to find that the Mayer government had been defeated in parliament. There was a new government headed by Premier Laniel 'who gave me hardly any mission at all'. Navarre's recommendation would be repeated twenty years later by American leaders in almost identical words: 'I proposed that we find an honorable exit from the war, creating a military situation that would allow an honorable political solution.'

In July 1953 the Korean armistice was signed. It was seen as a model – negotiate from maximum strength. Navarre formulated a plan, and the US backed it with a massive airlift of equipment. Using new American helicopters and paratroop aircraft, supported by carrier-launched fighter planes, Navarre's plan relied on rapid mobility to search out the enemy, 'harry him and destroy him' – the 'Search and Destroy' strategy the US would adopt twelve years later. After months of effort and failure, bringing mounting doubts at home, Navarre criticized 'sensational' press reporting of the war. Again presaging the future. Navarre's forces were openly resentful. In one published account, a battalion commander asked, 'What is our goal? *Mon commandant*, give me a moral reason, even if it is only for my men.'

By this time, after seven years of war, France had lost 74,000 troops in Vietnam, with another 190,000 bogged down. The basic problem persisted: as an occupying power France lacked the popular support to make American aid effective.

The corollary problem was an outmoded military force trained and equipped for the large conventional confrontations of World War II. Navarre decided that his only hope was to maneuver the Viet Minh into a set-piece battle, confident that French infantry experience would then prove decisive. Navarre was certain that a large blocking of the Viet Minh supply route to Laos would force them to respond. He decided to occupy a small crossroads town in a distant valley in the extreme north-west.

This remote outpost in an obscure Asian war would indeed prove decisive. It had a falsely melodic name, unknown to the outside world, with no meaning for France which had occupied it sixty-five years before and forgotten it. But the name went far back in the battle roster of Asian history, and the local people knew it as a place better to let sleep. They called it the 'arena of the gods'.

The world was now to hear of Dien Bien Phu.

January 1947—French troops maneuver through Hanoi in armored vehicles while fighting Vietnamese guerrillas.

Right: January 1947—French soldiers man a sandbagged bunker on a Hanoi street during fighting with the communist-led Vietminh.

October 1948—Workers salvage scorched rice at a fire-damaged mill in Cholon, Saigon's Chinatown. The mill's Chinese owners were hoping to sell the rice as cattle feed.

Above: January 1947—Refugees search for shelter near Hanoi after the fighting between French troops and Vietnamese insurgents drove them from their home.

Right: January 1947—A French soldier receives first aid for wounds suffered during fighting with Vietminh forces on the outskirts of Hanoi.

Left: January 1947—A disabled French tank lies near Hanoi during fighting between the French Union and communist-led Vietminh forces. The Vietminh uprising is reported to be spreading beyond northern Indochina.

Below: November 1948—Vietnamese soldiers train in high grass as they prepare to join French Union troops fighting the Communist-led Vietminh.

February 13, 1949—Pro-French Vietnamese peasants demonstrate in Hanoi for the return of Bao Dai, the last emperor of Vietnam, who had abdicated in 1945.

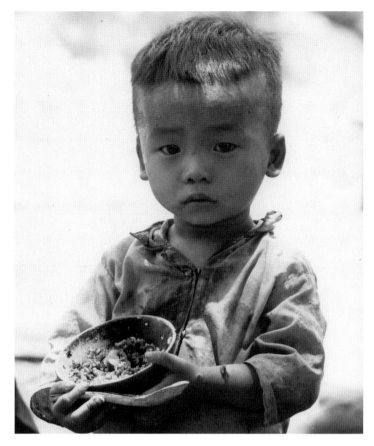

Vietnamese boy with a bowl of rice.

Left: March 19, 1950—A French army jeep burns in front of Saigon's city hall after it was overturned and set afire by rioters.

Below: May 26, 1950—The Vietnamese National Army's first paratrooper unit parades through Saigon as the French try to organize and expand the army for the fight against the Communist-led Vietminh. The Vietnamese government hopes to build an army of 100,000, anticipating aid from the U.S.

Left: March 1950—French Foreign Legionnaires advance across a flooded rice paddy in Cochin China.

Below: March 1950—Wrecked buildings and debris litter Market Square in Saigon after rioting during the visit by American warships to demonstrate U.S. backing of Emperor Bao Dai, head of the French-sponsored government in Indochina.

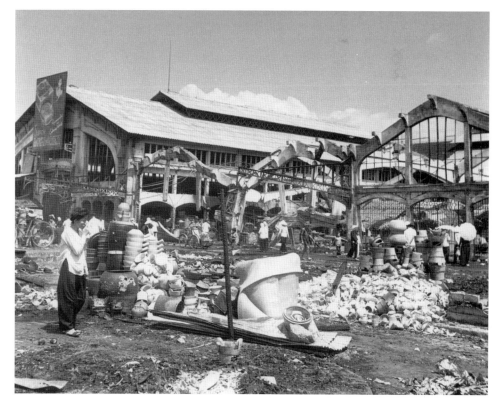

Left: February 3, 1950—Former Emperor Bao Dai, chief executive of the Vietnam state in Indochina, reviews troops of the Thai tribe at Lai Chau northwest of Hanoi. Between the Thai troops are French paratroopers. The Thais have pledged loyalty to the French but want an autonomous organization within Vietnam.

Above left: July 1950—French Marine commandos wade ashore from a landing craft off the Annam coast of Indochina.

Above right: October 1950—French Legionnaires hold a Vietminh prisoner near Thainguyen, which was described as the base for a network of French fortifications in the heart of northern Vietnam.

Left: October 1950—The French defense line encompassing Hanoi includes this post at Phu Langthuoung. The French had lost eight such posts to the Vietminh in the previous month.

October 1950—The French post of Dam-Ha lies on the highway between Moncay and Tienyen, part of the French defense line. Vietminh forces had been attacking in the Tienyen area.

Left: October 1950—A Vietnamese peasant family huddles in an area north of Hanoi as French forces advanced against Vietminh troops.

Above: By late 1950 the Soviet Union recognized the anti-French government of Ho Chi Minh, whose Vietminh army battled the French. The United States and Great Britain supported the Vietnam headed by Emperor Bao Dai, who was also supported by the French. Area A in the map is where most of the military action took place. Hanoi was the French bastion city, while Thai Nguyen, 45 miles to the north was the Vietminh military center. In Cochin China, marked B, French troops said they cleared the Vietminh forces from the region north of Saigon.

Right: November 1950—French Foreign Legionnaires use amphibious 'crabs' against Vietminh forces in the marshes south of Saigon.

Above: November 1950—French Legionnaires patrol rice paddies in their search for Vietminh south of Saigon.

Left: November 1950—French Foreign Legion troops hold a Vietminh guerrilla suspect south of Saigon. A hammer-and-sickle flag was found with the suspect.

Below: November 1950—A Moroccan, *bottom*, fighting for the French Union forces, lies dead alongside a member of the Vietminh after hand-to-hand fighting in Cochin China province.

Above: November 1950—A Moroccan soldier wounded fighting the Vietminh in Cochin China, southern Indochina, receives a drink from a native orderly as he awaits evacuation.

Left: December 1950—Vietminh prisoners are held by French forces after fighting at Vinh Yen and Phuc Yen.

Above: November 1950—A French Union soldier displays one of the improvised missiles being lobbed against the French by the communist-led Vietminh at a base in the Tonkin Delta defense zone.

Below: February 5, 1951—French troops aboard an armored vehicle patrol the country side on the lookout for signs of Vietminh rebels.

Above: December 8, 1950—Ex-emperor Bao Dai and Gen. Marcel Carpentier, commander in chief of French forces in the Far East, enjoy refreshment in the presidential palace in Saigon after signing the Franco-Vietnam military pact creating a pro-French Vietnam army under Vietnam command, though it remains under French command in tactical matters.

Left: December 1950—Dead French and Vietminh troops line the road leading to the Da Phuc fortress.

February 1951—Temporary repairs to a bridge partially blown up by the Vietminh allow convoys to pass between Saigon and Dalat. Towers at intervals along the road, such as the one at far right, serve as shelters in case of attack.

Right: February 1951—French soldiers guard a guerrilla suspect captured overnight with a sampan full of weapons on the Saigon River delta. Three of his companions escaped.

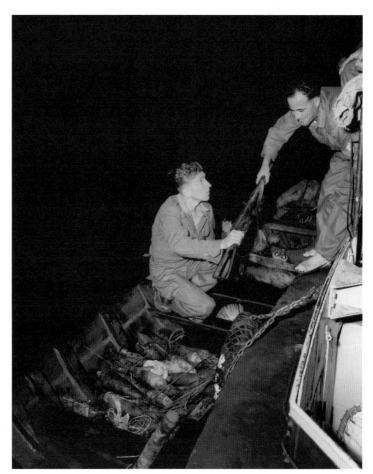

Above: February 20, 1951—During a lull in ground fighting, two members of the French Army's waterborne cavalry keep watch at the start of a night patrol in the Saigon River delta. The armored boats operate in pairs, waiting in ambush for Vietminh watercraft.

Right: February 1951—Cavalrymen of the French army collect weapons from a captured sampan during a night ambush operation of the Saigon River delta. The cavalry patrols the delta for guerrilla activity during lulls in ground fighting.

Above: February 3, 1951—With a population of 124,000 and as the capital of Cochin China, Saigon is crowded with sampans on the Saigon river.

Right: February 5, 1951—Vietnamese peasants pull a cart carrying a French sergeant after he was wounded by a Vietminh grenade 30 miles northeast of Saigon.

February 1951—A deep trench and spiked slopes protect this watchtower on the Michelin rubber plantation near Saigon, where Vietminh attacks were common.

Above: February 1951—Guards stand the watch on a Michelin rubber plantation 50 miles north of Saigon. Workers at the plantation were kidnapped by Vietminh in their effort to disrupt production.

Right: February 1951—French military guide an armored boat as they escort a supply ship in the Saigon River headed to the Michelin rubber plantation north of the capital. Supply boats were a target of Vietminh units in the area.

February 1951—Youngsters bathe their water buffalo in a flooded rice paddy on the outskirts of Saigon. In rural areas, boys are often charged with the responsibility of watching over the buffalo.

February 1951—French troops from Algeria disembark from a LCT as they arrive to reinforce local troops guarding a Michelin rubber plantation north of Saigon. Work on the plantation was seriously disrupted by intense Vietminh activity in the area.

February 1951—A French column crosses the Thi Ninh River by boat bridge during a patrol of rebel territory about 60 miles north of Saigon. The 43rd Colonial Regiment was destroying Vietminh facilities, equipment, and supplies, while also seizing prisoners and weapons.

Above: March 1951—Soldiers of France's 43rd Colonial Infantry Regiment fill their water cans during a five-day patrol in Vietminh-held territory 60 miles north of Saigon. The patrol's mission is to destroy or recover anything useful to the enemy, including housing, equipment, weapons, and food.

Right: March 1951—A Montagnard tribesman guards the gate to a rubber plantation 50 miles from Saigon. Fortifications against Vietminh attack consists, in part, of sharpened bamboo stakes mounted in the walls and gates of the compound.

Above: March 4, 1951—Vietnamese pass the time in Bac Minh, a town 30 miles northeast of Hanoi. Bac Minh was largely destroyed in 1947 during fighting between French troops and the retreating Vietminh.

Above right: March 1951—A driver, seated on his pedicab, has his fortune told in a Saigon street. Fortune-telling is big business in Vietnam.

Above: March 6, 1951—Thai soldiers with packhorses disembark from a Black River ferry at Laichu.

Left: March 4, 1951—Vietnamese porters pass ruins in Bac Minh, 30 miles northeast of Hanoi. The church in background was one of the few parts of the town spared during fighting between the French and the Vietminh in 1947.

Above: March 1951—Stone is unloaded from barges on the Clear River for the building of defense blockhouses at Viet Trih, the most remote French outpost northwest of Hanoi. The workers include French Foreign Legionnaires and native adults and youngsters.

Right: March 1951—As smoke rises from earlier bombing, a French Air Force Junkers 52 drops 100-pound bombs on Vietminh strongholds 100 miles north of Hanoi.

Above: March 1951—A French soldier, exhausted by a five-day patrol in Vietminh-held jungle, is carried over a boat bridge crossing the Thi Tinh River 60 miles north of Saigon.

Right: March 1951—The commander of the French outpost at Dinh Quan, on the route between Saigon and Dalat, lives in this native-style villa built by Moi tribesmen in his regiment.

Above: March 1951—Cambodian soldiers of the French Union's 43rd Colonial Infantry Regiment patrol a muddy rice paddy about 60 miles north of Saigon.

Above: June 1951—Two teenage boys raise their arms in surrender. They were among 65 suspected guerrillas captured by French forces in a four-day sweep of the Plaine des Joncs, southwest of Saigon.

Left: April 1951—From a high point overlooking the Thai country of Indochina, Thai partisans loyal to the French stand guard over an outpost of Phong Tho on the Clear River. The area was populated by some 300,000 mountain tribesmen who did not support the communist-led Vietminh.

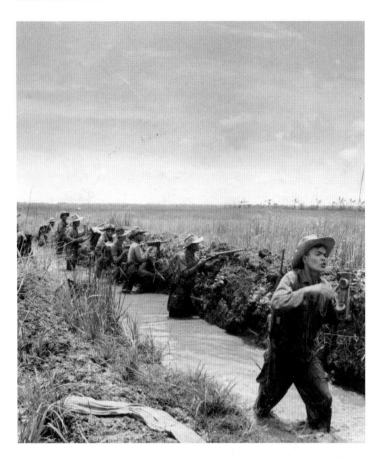

Above: June 1951—Vietnamese troops deployed along a canal wait for strafing attack to end before advancing in an area of Vietminh concentration south of Saigon.

Above: September 18, 1951—Gen. John de Lattre de Tassigny, high commissioner of France in Indochina and commander in chief of French forces in the Far East, holds a news conference at the Pentagon. He was in Washington to ask for U.S. equipment for his troops in Vietnam.

Above: July 1951—A French officer radios his position to his unit commander during a patrol of guerrilla territory about 25 miles northeast of Saigon. Joint French and Vietnamese forces were searching for Vietminh armament works and supplies.

Above: October 1951—A French lieutenant radios artillery instructions from a tree in the Thai Binh area of northern Indochina, about 30 miles west of Haiphong. Vietminh forces were infiltrating the area, threatening the route between Hanoi and the coast.

Above: September 14, 1951—Gen. Jeane de Lattre de Tassigny (*center*), commander of French forces in Indochina, is welcomed to Washington by Gen. Joseph Collins, U.S. Army chief of staff, and French ambassador Henri Bonnet. He was in Washington to confer with American officials on the situation in Indochina.

Right: December 12, 1951—Vietnamese infantrymen make their way across a narrow ledge as they occupy a former Vietminh village about 60 miles south of Hanoi.

Below: November 10, 1951—French paratroopers, dropped near Cho Ben (about 30 miles south of Hanoi), cross a wooden bridge during a surprise attack supported by French Union ground forces and artillery.

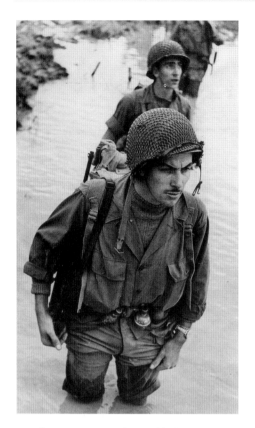

November 10, 1951—A French corporal leads his men through water in the Cho Ben area, about 30 miles south of Hanoi, during a surprise attack by paratroopers and ground forces supported by artillery. The government forces reported that they trapped pockets of retreating Vietminh.

January 1952—A victim is carried from the Place de Theatre in Saigon after a series of explosions.

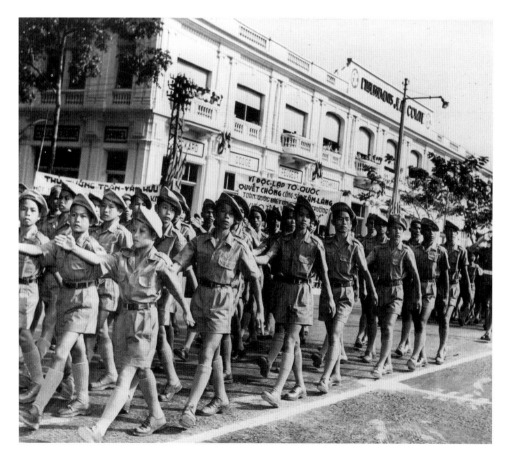

March 8, 1952—Vietnamese youth parade through the streets of Saigon to celebrate Independence Day.

1952—Ho Chi Minh is leader of the Vietminh against the French and Vietnamese forces in Indochina.

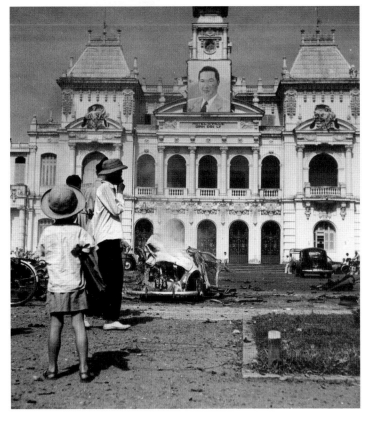

March 1952—A French column advances to the southeast of Ninh Giang during a week of bitter fighting to reclaim territory from the Vietminh.

Above: July 1952—French Union troops try to maneuver a patrol boat through flooded rice paddies in a remote district southeast of Hai Duong. The objective in these isolated districts was reinstallation of local Vietnamese administrators.

Left: January 9, 1952—The wreckage of a car bomb smolders outside Saigon's Hotel de Ville moments after two Vietminh-planted bombs exploded, killing four people, including two French citizens. A portrait of Chief of State Bao Dai hangs in the background.

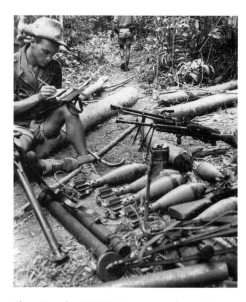

Above: November 9, 1952—Enemy arms and ammunition are inspected at Phu Doan after French Union forces captured the Vietminh base.

Above: October 1952—French paratroopers, dropped 100 miles northwest of Hanoi, hold a trench against possible attack during the Vietminh advance from the Red River to the Black River in northwestern Indochina. Paratroopers—French and Vietnamese—saw heavy fighting during the communist advance in mountainous terrain.

Above: November 1952—The Nasam base on Thai territory in northern Indochina is reinforced in anticipation of communist-led Vietminh attacks.

Right: December 1952—French troops search a swamp for hidden Vietminh weapons in the area south of the Tonkin Delta.

Left: November 24, 1952—Repelled by French Foreign Legionnaires, Vietminh dead lie at the barbed wire defenses of the Na San airbase, 117 miles west of Hanoi.

Above: December 21, 1952—Bao Dai, former emperor of Annam, walks under a welcome arch at Hoa Binh, in Tonkin, northern Indochina. He is accompanied by Gen. Raoul Salan. The village was retrieved from the Vietminh rebels.

Right: December 1, 1952—After reoccupying a strategic hill at Na San, northern Indochina, French Union paratroopers examine Vietminh casualties.

Left: December 1, 1952—French Union paratroopers storm the top of the hill at Na San, eventually recapturing the strategic position from Vietminh forces in hand-to-hand fighting.

# DIEN BIEN PHU

At 0630 hours on 20 November 1953, a single American C-47 scout plane began banking between the peaks of the hills that encircle Dien Bien Phu. Fog that sometimes covered the place for days on end clung tightly to the valley floor. In Hanoi, 170 miles away, an air armada of paratroops was waiting. Months of logistics and secrecy dictated that the mission was now or never. An hour passed, then another. The C-47 had enough fuel for only two hours over the drop zone. The pilot was about to turn back when the fog suddenly lifted. He made a last turn over the now clear valley, seeing the narrow six-mile road from the Laotian border leading like a handle to the main basin almost seven miles around and banked by high wooded hills. It was shaped – as the waiting Viet Minh described it – like a frying pan.

On the ground at Hanoi, Major Marcel Maurice ('Bruno') Bigeard and 800 men of the 1st Colonial

> ‘I kept telling my men, “We must hold on one more day. The Americans will come.”’
>
> – GENERAL MARCEL BIGEARD

Paratroop Battalion were already aboard sixty-four silver-new American C-47s when the ‘go’ signal came through to the squadron leader, whose code name was ‘Texas’. The battalion had been due to return to France when suddenly given new orders the night before. Only its commander, Bigeard, knew the destination, but he had been told that if the weather was unfavorable, if there was fog or heavy rain, the operation would be permanently canceled because secrecy could not be kept. As he now says: ‘I have often asked myself, why did it not rain that day and we would have avoided Dien Bien Phu?’

Bigeard was the son of a railway worker, a one-time clerk and French resistance fighter, with nine years of combat experience in Indo-China. He was known for his mystical view of comradery and death, and would often tell his men: ‘Learn to look death in the face. You're going where men die.’ He describes that first drop:

Above: November 20, 1953—French paratroopers *(foreground)* cover the landings of their comrades at Dien Bien Phu on the first day of Operation Castor. Thousands of paratroopers were dropped in to occupy the garrison at Dien Bien Phu.

'When we came down on November 20 we were told there would be no Vietnamese. But there were two companies exactly where we jumped. Some of my men were killed before they even touched the ground, others were stabbed where they landed. The combat lasted all day, with forty men killed on our side and the two Viet Minh companies almost totally destroyed. It was a hard day – but Dien Bien Phu had been taken.'

A week later General Henri Navarre personally visited Dien Bien Phu. With 10,000 French troops in place, and another 5000 in reserve, Navarre deemed the situation 'excellent'. There had been no further opposition from the Viet Minh, but Navarre confidently expected it. The main route to Laos, and the linking supply route from China, had now been blocked. The village of Dien Bien Phu – 'seat of the border county prefecture' – seemed grandly named for a collection of a hundred stilt houses, but its strategic importance had been realized for centuries. The trade caravans from China, Laos, Siam and distant Burma had converged here since earliest times, and the great powers of the day had constantly fought to control the valley. Only a century earlier the King of Laos had sent 10,000 men and ninety elephants to chase out the Siamese. In 1887 it had been the last area of Indo-China to be subjugated by the French – after a period of Vietnamese resistance led by a man called Nguyen Van Giap!

Navarre did not expect Vo Nguyen Giap to do any better this time. At Dien Bien Phu, Navarre found everything according to plan. The old Meo houses in the valley center were being pulled down to help build ounkers and command posts. A central airstrip was taking shape; the five low hills around it, and seven outer bastions, would form a chain of strongholds, each with artillery

and infantry battalions. With these, and with air supremacy, Navarre's forces would move out to destroy Viet Minh supply lines, forcing – he believed – a set-piece battle and negotiations.

Navarre had no illusions that he could win the war: the French had lost overall mobility, but he knew that a victory in this remote valley had huge political and ideological importance for France and the Alliance. France could provide no more troops; America wanted results for its aid. Navarre knew this had to be his last stand: 'I chose the solution of the Dien Bien Phu entrenched camp because with the state of my forces, which were inferior to those of the Viet Minh in terms of mobile forces, this

solution was the only one which seemed to be reasonable. I am still certain that it was the only one.'

Historian Lacouture explains that the French command 'thought that the Viet Minh had no trucks, no means for bringing weapons, food and so on for a battle fought so far from its rear. It was not stupid at all – it was a very sensible idea.'

There was one serious concern: the total reliance on air support. The supply planes in Hanoi could just make the 340-mile return trip. But, weather permitting, it was accepted that the planes could land unchallenged. The Viet Minh lines were stretched even more – across 500 miles of mountain and jungle to the supply depots inside

Above: November 20, 1953—The first French paratroopers to land at Dien Bien Phu watch fellow troops landing during Operation Castor. Six battalions were dropped in to occupy and fortify the fortress at Dien Bien Phu, about 180 miles west of Hanoi.

Left: November 1953— French paratroopers orient themselves in Operation Castor, during which thousands of paratroopers began the occupation and fortification of Dien Bien Phu.

Above: November 20, 1953—A helicopter hovers over French paratroopers during Operation Castor, in which the French occupied the garrison at Dien Bien Phu.

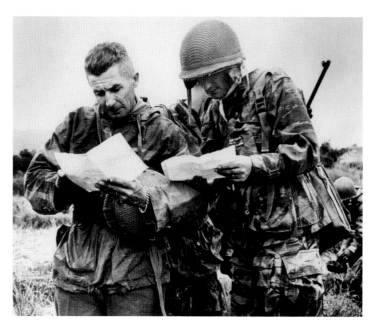

Above: November 20, 1953—French colonel Fourcade (*left*), one of the ground commanders of Operation Castor, studies plans with an officer at Dien Bien Phu. Six battalions of paratroopers manned this fortress, about 180 miles west of Hanoi.

China. The high rim ten miles beyond the French camp seemed safely distant – and silent.

Far to the north-east, at a base sixty miles from the China border, Ho Chi Minh studied reports of Dien Bien Phu, then in early December 1953 he summoned General Vo Nguyen Giap, who relates: 'We talked all night. He asked me, "Our forces grow stronger day by day, but we must not let the enemy destroy our strength – can you do it?" I thought for a while and answered, "The enemy won't be able to destroy our strength. The difficult thing will be to take the initiative." '

The Viet Minh commander told Ho he could put 50,000 troops around Dien Bien Phu; but to gain the initiative he had to overcome the French air advantage. He had a plan, but it would take months. 'We would have to count every bullet. But we were inspired because we never before had been able to gather such a force.'

Giap's orders were to mobilize two armies. One, a peasant force of 20,000 men, women and youths, would hack new jungle routes for weapons and supplies, and the other, the regular army, would then force march twenty miles a day. Throughout the North, thousands more civilians would bring in enough rice to last the army for several months. The mobilization reached as far as Thanh Hoa province, 200 kilometers south-west of Hanoi, where the political commissar at Pho Moi village explained the orders. A hundred men were to form a 'brigade of iron horses' – bicycles – to carry the rice. In this typical village Dinh Van Ty was appointed brigade leader, and he later wrote of those days. He felt he was a natural choice – he was the village bicycle-repair man.

'We had one day to make preparations,' Dinh recalls. 'First our bicycles had to be turned into *xe tho* [pack bikes], with the crossbar capable of carrying 200 kilos or more. We had to strengthen all the parts. We had to fix two hard bamboo sticks – one to form a long handlebar for easier steering, the other to extend the seat to act as balance and as a brake. We camouflaged everything with leaves and moved at night.

'The first night the tires kept bursting. I pondered the matter, then tore the legs of my khaki trousers into long bands which I wound around the inner tubes before filling them with air at high pressure. It was successful – no tires burst. But now instead of trousers the entire company were wearing shorts.'

In the far north-west Ha Van Lau, then a young officer, was on the forced march with Giap. The future UN Ambassador recalls: 'We had to move through the jungle. We couldn't take the main roads because of the bombing. And then to transport one kilo of rice to the front we had to bring four kilos to feed the transporters, who carried it on their backs or on bicycles. At first at the front we lived on cold food. We couldn't heat the rice because that would give out smoke and attract planes. At first we just dug in. We dug and dug around the enemy fortifications.'

Every available Viet Minh soldier was converging on one remote valley, and behind them came hundreds of civilian brigades – People's Porters – with thousands of hand-pushed bicycles and pack animals somehow inching across the rivers and mountains. And Giap, orchestrating it all from Dien Bien Phu, told his staff there, 'We will take the French by the throat.'

The French soon felt the pressure. The commander of the airborne forces at Dien Bien Phu was the fierce Breton aristocrat, Colonel Pierre Langlais. He describes the situation after only six weeks: 'As of 1 January 1954, movement in or out of Dien Bien Phu had become impossible'. Langlais and the 10,000 French force did not know that the encircling Viet

November 20, 1953—A French Union paratrooper, his parachute still lying at his side, aims his automatic weapon during an operation to secure the fortress at Dien Bien Phu. Within months, the French garrison would become the scene of the pivotal battle of the war, leading directly to the French withdrawal from Indochina.

Above: February 1954—French officers review the troops at an inspection of the camp at Dien Bien Phu. From left are Gen. Henri Navarre, commander of French forces in Indochina; Col. Christian de Castries, commander of the camp; and Gen. René Cogny, commander of forces in North Vietnam.

Minh were far stronger than expected – but it was known in Hanoi.

"I only learned through my intelligence service gradually,' says General Navarre. 'When I occupied Dien Bien Phu I expected to have to deal with two divisions, then eventually two and a half, three. . . . It was not until 20 December that I learned we would actually be dealing with four divisions. At that point it was much too late to evacuate Dien Bien Phu because the first division had arrived at the edge of the entrenched camp, and if I had withdrawn I would have lost all our men and supplies. And if I had abandoned Dien Bien Phu we would certainly have lost the war.'

Giap had rushed in enough troops to prevent a French withdrawal, but his plan of offensive was far from ready. He had defined his strategy – 'Strike to win, strike only when success is certain, or do not strike at all.' And week after week he held his fire. But he now faced a deadline. In mid-February the 'Big Four' powers – the United States, the Soviet Union, Great Britain and France – had agreed to meet in Geneva in late April to discuss cold-war issues, including Indo-China. Giap had only ten more weeks in which to achieve a military *fait accompli*.

'The Viet Minh', says Navarre, 'understood that if the French command could be seriously defeated at Dien Bien Phu, this would allow them, politically, to win the war. Then they decided to take all the risks, increase their manpower and accept even greater losses than before, and China granted massive assistance.' This assistance included 600 Russian-built Molotova trucks, packed with weapons. The French ceaselessly bombed the huge convoy along the 450 kilometers of semi-passable road to the front, but without detecting its surprise content of heavy guns.

Traveling from China on one truck as far as Ho Chi Minh's headquarters, Wilfred Burchett of the London *Daily Express* found Ho Chi Minh unusually euphoric, though otherwise unchanged. 'When I met him he was walking up a jungle path with a wind-breaker across his shoulders, with a bamboo walking stick, a sun-helmet on his head, rubber-tire sandals and a bit of rope around his waist to keep his trousers up.'

Burchett, the only Western journalist to report from the Viet Minh side (which he would continue to do), found Ho's headquarters after several miles walk through the jungle: 'It was completely safe from air observation. There was a thick ceiling of branches and practically no light at all. Virtually the moment I saw Ho I said "I hear on Hanoi radio – three or four times a day – about a place called Dien Bien Phu. Something's happening: what is it?" '

Ho Chi Minh took off his sun helmet. 'He turned this upside down on the table and he felt around in the bottom of it, and he said "Dien Bien Phu is a valley, and it's completely surrounded by mountains. The cream of the French expeditionary corps are down there, and we (feeling the brim of his helmet) are around the mountains. And they'll never get out." '

The French force in the valley had been strengthened to 15,000, half of them Algerians, Vietnamese and Legionnaires. They knew they were outnumbered three to one. On 4 March General Navarre paid his last visit to Dien Bien Phu to confer with the base commander, Colonel Christian de Castries, on whether reinforcements were needed.

'I was much less confident than the local commandant,' Navarre remembers. 'I thought of suddenly bringing in three additional battalions – and since the Viet Minh were very methodical I thought they would then think twice.' Navarre says de Castries told him to keep the battalions in reserve, and 'that is what I did – I was probably wrong'.

By now the French knew that Giap had heavy guns, but underestimated their caliber and numbers. Historian Jean Lacouture, then with the Hanoi command, states: 'The fact that Giap had very strong artillery was not known at all. It was Chinese and Russian artillery and Giap had organized it in a way impossible to destroy.' Giap, in his official despatches, said that 'Navarre was not in the least worried about our artillery, which he thought weak and not transportable to the approaches of Dien Bien Phu'.

The French believed their main artillery to be the most powerful available – American 105mm. They had twenty-eight of these. Giap was about to reveal that he had forty-eight of this caliber and more than 150 lighter artillery pieces. Two hundred 'steel elephants' had been hauled through the last fifty miles of mountain jungle – in Giap's words – 'by a superhuman effort, by nothing but sweat and muscle'. Relay teams roped to the artillery, in constant danger from bombing and napalm, had moved the guns an inch at a time, half a mile a day. It had taken three months.

Giap now had at least three-to-one superiority in both fire-power and manpower. His artillery overlooked the French but was virtually undetectable, secreted in caves and dugouts on the dense wooded slopes. Hiding all activity, deep trenches ringed the hilltops. In contrast, the French had stripped the land of wood and scrub to build their entrenched camp, revealing their every movement.

On the eve of battle, Giap – as he records it – surveyed the valley arena and counted 'forty-nine strong-posts, grouped into three main sectors capable of supporting each other'. These were Huguette to the west, Dominique to the northeast and Claudine to the south. Beyond this triangle were four other isolated hill bastions, Anne-Marie, Gabrielle, Beatrice and – six miles to the south – Isabelle. Within the triangle, buffered by five low hills called Eliane, lay the airstrip and command center. There on 12 March 1954, Colonel de Castries summoned his senior officers to alert them to urgent intelligence: Giap's offensive would begin at 1700 hours the following day.

The French officers felt, if anything, relieved. They were well provisioned, including 49,000 bottles of wine. The battle would lift the siege mentality which seemed to beset Hanoi more than them, reflected in press reports that the situation was 'desperate'. At this moment infantry commander Colonel Pierre Langlais was angrily preoccupied with a headline in Le Figaro – 'Ils sont foutus' ('They are finished'). Langlais, who had survived the Sahara campaigns with only camels and rifles, was not a man to consider defeat. He was on his third tour of duty in Indo-China; he could hardly count all the battles.

In Hanoi, Commander-in-Chief General Navarre had a wider political perspective. 'The military conditions,' he says, 'were completely changed because of the acceptance of the Geneva conference.' To the world at large Dien Bien Phu might seem as remote as the Sahara, but to Navarre it was no longer a messy local war – it had become a crucial proxy conflict of global ideologies, and in the circumstances he did not like the provisioning.

US military aid had mainly comprised 1400 tanks (only 10 of them at Dien Bien Phu), 340 planes, 350 patrol boats, 240,000 rounds of small arms and 15 million bullets – with only the air force and ammunition of much use to Navarre now. From China alone the Viet Minh had received up to the end of 1953, in addition to heavy artillery, an estimated 800 recoilless cannon and machine-guns, 6000 submachine-guns and automatic pistols and 6 million rounds of small arms. Giap no longer had to count every bullet.

And Navarre had to count on a numerically inferior force: 'I thought of giving up my command several times. I believe I would have done so if I faced an absolute refusal of any reinforcements. But I was told, yes, perhaps we'll give you a portion of it – they were promised on a certain date. Two months later they had still not arrived.

'And then the battle of Dien Bien Phu commenced, and it is contrary to military honor for a leader to think of resigning in the midst of battle, just saying to his men "Manage on your own". So I stayed. I was wrong, perhaps, but that's how it happened.'

The predicted moment of Giap's offensive, 1700 hours on 12 March, had arrived. Says Colonel Langlais: 'Nothing happened at 5 pm as we were expecting – so I went to take a shower.' He lowered his eyes as he remembered the moments that followed. All at once Giap's 200 artillery pieces were sight-shooting at the airstrip

and central entrenchments on an exposed flat plain in a five-mile triangle. The barrage lasted an hour until sunset – an eternity. 'It was a massacre,' states Langlais.

The first rounds killed the commander of the central section. Langlais was now put in charge of it. He found that the French artillery could not locate Giap's guns even when they were firing. The commander in Hanoi, Navarre, asserts that everyone was surprised: 'All the French and American artillerymen who had visited Dien Bien Phu – and there were many Americans – thought that the Viet Minh would have to stay behind the ridges to fire on the entrenched camp. The surprise was that they managed to bring their artillery much closer than we had thought possible. This obviously indicated an error in reasoning on the part of the artillerymen, for which I was responsible, of course, because I was in charge.'

In the first hours 500 French troops died on one hill alone. At sunset the Viet Minh had thrown an entire infantry division against outpost Beatrice – the closest to the central section. By midnight Beatrice was a grave. Only 200 of its 700-man garrison escaped, and after the first massacre the garrison artillery commander, Colonel Charles Piroth, committed suicide.

In successive days, by 15 March, two other strongholds – Gabrielle and Anne-Marie – were silenced, and what Giap called his 'death-braving' volunteers – or suicide squads – were poised close to the center encampment, reaching for the throat of Eliane.

In Hanoi, where he had returned with his battalion, Lieutenant-Colonel Bigeard was once more packing to leave Indo-China for France. On 16 March he was summoned to Navarre's headquarters and told, ' "Bigeard, you must go to Dien Bien Phu once again." "General, I am ready, but my men have almost come to the end of their term. Give me another battalion." "No, that battalion is trained and it must stay with you and go with you."'

Bigeard was told: 'Everything is going badly. We don't know who is in command there – but the impression is of complete chaos.'

On 16 March 1954 Bigeard and his battalion jumped again.

Piroth's fate had altered Bigeard's own. He judged the dead man heroically. 'I had known him as a man of duty and heart who had said that as soon as a Vietnamese cannon was found he would overpower it. But they were invulnerable. We could fire 100 shots on their positions and still be incapable of destroying their cannon. Giap had

Right: March 14, 1954—A French hospital helicopter hovers near allied forces dug in at a perimeter post of the besieged French fortress at Dien Bien Phu.

Below: April 1954—French defenders of Dien Bien Phu return enemy fire on the shell-blasted battlefield around the besieged Indochina fortress.

Above: March 1954—Col. Christian de Castries, commander of French forces at Dien Bien Phu, studies a map in his underground command post during fighting against communist-led Vietminh rebels.

Below: March 13, 1954—French Union soldiers leave their foxhole during a counterattack in the first days of the Vietminh siege of the French fortress at Dien Bien Phu.

March 1954—French and Moroccan officers dine at their base in Gia Loc. Although far from the besieged fortress at Dien Bien Phu, the Gia Loc garrison was responsible for protecting the vital Hanoi-Haiphong supply line from nightly Vietminh raids.

March 1954—Helmeted French Union troops guard wounded Vietminh prisoners after fighting south of Dien Bien Phu. The French command claimed some 1,400 enemy soldiers killed in the first major counterattack since the communist-led Vietminh stormed the French fortress about two weeks earlier.

attacked only when he felt that everything was just right. Piroth, who was an honest man, killed himself. He took the pin out of a grenade and died on the spot.'

At Dien Bien Phu Bigeard 'found a colonel in command who did not dare come out of the shelter, Colonel de Castries – he was not yet a general at that time. He was always clean-shaven, tidy and impeccable. I found my friend, Langlais, commanding the intervention units. The units under him were tired – they had made counter-attacks. But Langlais, a very dynamic man, always ready to attack, had the mentality of a lieutenant although he was a colonel.'

The deeds of Langlais were as legendary as Bigeard's own and the two men could relate despite their very different backgrounds. Langlais and de Castries were both brothers of the military college of Saint-Cyr; between them there would not be a word of recrimination. The three men now effectively agreed on a pact of command and tolerance, for the sake of the 15,000 men besieged. 'In fact', says Bigeard, 'it was Langlais who was commanding with me – and de Castries, so as to give the impression that he was keeping his command, had told me, "Bruno, you look after contacts and Langlais will be defending the fort." '

The Viet Minh were heavily entrenched immediately east of the command center. Bigeard got orders to clear the area, with infantry, artillery and air force under his command: 'I thank de Castries for having had confidence in me – that is why I keep a good memory of de Castries.'

But it was a one-time operation. Bigeard co-ordinated the attack in four hours: 'I had all the artillery firing at once. Two thousand shots fired on one position. As soon as this was over the air force arrived and attacked the same positions, then we started the assault. The combat lasted all day. It was really tough. But we destroyed the equivalent of a battalion. It was the first victory of

Dien Bien Phu. The Vietnamese were shattered.

'So de Castries said to me, "Bruno, only you could have pulled this one through." I said, "Yes, Colonel, but operations like this cannot be carried out every day because I just lost my best officers, both senior and junior. It would be possible if you gave me the men to start all over, but we cannot play this game very long." '

But there could be no more reinforcements. On 27 March, with the closest strongholds broken and Eliane-I captured, Viet Minh fire closed the central airstrip, and the French at Dien Bien Phu were now cut off from the world except for uncertain parachute supplies. But morale was undiminished says de facto commander, Colonel Langlais: 'That did not spell the end for me, or for my comrades. It did not mean the end of fighting since if the planes could not land they could still carry out parachuting operations. I did not consider the closing of the airfield to be a catastrophe in terms of further combat.'

It was, however, in terms of suffering. The wounded could no longer be evacuated. The most serious cases had been stranded when the hospital plane caught fire on the runway – and stranded with them was the only French woman at Dien Bien Phu, air force nurse Genevieve de Galard: 'The wounded had been so full of hope because they thought it was the last day for them in Dien Bien Phu – that it was the end of this hell place for them. And it wasn't.'

The worst hell now began. The French underground hospital had facilities for only forty beds. There were only four surgeons for the 12,000 who had so far survived, most with wounds. The French began digging hospital tunnels, placing the wounded on ledges carved in the clay. For three weeks of the coming slaughter Genevieve de Galard never left the hell underground. 'I slept on a stretcher that I folded in the morning. I opened it every night and folded it every day.'

March 1954—French Union troops man a trench surrounding the airstrip at Dien Bien Phu. Reinforcements parachuted in as the besieged fortress survived intense Vietminh assaults in mid-March.

This daughter of Vicomte Oger de Galard Terraube, who could trace her lineage back five centuries to a crusader who served with Joan of Arc, insisted that the soldiers call her just Genevieve – 'or if they didn't know me well, Mademoiselle. But they never called me "Angel". I think that name [the Angel of Dien Bien Phu] was invented by American journalists.'

Genevieve inspired them – but Beatrice, Gabrielle, Anne-Marie and Dominique were gone, and the defenders clung to part of Huguette and Eliane with only Claudine and Isabelle to the south still secured. For four days from 1 April, Giap had launched his second-wave offensive and the French main force was now surrounded on Eliane-IV. As the French territory diminished, so did supplies. The C-47s had to fly high above Giap's guns, and their parachute loads landed

March 1954—A wounded French Union soldier is loaded aboard an evacuation helicopter at the French fortress of Dien Bien Phu, under siege by the communist-led Vietminh. As a stretcher-bearer runs off for another wounded soldier, a flag with a red cross is waved to discourage enemy fire.

increasingly in Viet Minh hands. The French had at any cost to recapture Eliane-I to the east and re-secure the airstrip drop zone.

Once more Major Bigeard coordinated a desperate counter-attack: 'We started shooting and we fired 3 or 4000 shots and all the cannon of Dien Bien Phu, all 120 mortars, were aimed at the one position. My men got out of the trenches and went to the attack. But the Viet Minh were also entrenched – maybe half of them had been killed, but there still remained the other half and they fought like the great fighters that they are.

'They fought man-to-man with daggers, but my own men put up such a fight that after one whole day we had recaptured Eliane-I. Then my men had to occupy the trenches but they were digging upon fallen bodies. The soil was covered with dead bodies, French and Vietnamese. The smell was horrible.'

As Colonel Langlais grimly describes it: 'The dead were buried where it was possible to do so. From mid-April on, they were just left behind.'

The terrible bloodshed of early April, at least 2000 dead on each side, now caused General Giap to pause. The Viet Minh were believed to have only one surgeon, in addition to medical orderlies, for a force now reduced to some 40,000 men. Giap subsequently admitted to what he called 'negative thoughts' affecting troop performance. He now decided on a radical change of tactics – an underground offensive. He deployed tens of thousands of troops and civilians to dig a 100-mile network of trenches right to the valley center.

In the French medical catacombs the scene was nightmarish. The underground hospital had been extended until it reached close to the now disused graveyard. There came a day when the wounded found large white worms from the graves crawling amid their bandages. 'We could see legs with maggots', says Bigeard, 'but the doctor left them on because he said, "I think it prevents gangrene." So those maggots were moving around on the patients' legs. It was terrible.'

Colonel Langlais was forced to move the able-bodied out of their bunkers to take their chances on the open plain in order to accommodate the wounded. It allowed the French soldiers a moment of collective chivalry. Genevieve, who had been stranded with one blouse, a pair of trousers 'and a lipstick', was given her own small shelter under-

Above: March 1954—French Union soldiers in the besieged fortress at Dien Bien Phu load wounded comrades aboard an evacuation helicopter. The French accused the Vietminh of firing on hospital flights and evacuation airstrips during the siege.

Right: March 1954—Allied soldiers reinforce defenses near the airfield at Dien Bien Phu as the French garrison came under heavy attack in mid-March.

ground. Langlais had put in a bed and his own armchair from the command post. Officers and troops had stitched parachutes to drape over the damp clay walls. It was 13 April and Genevieve's twenty-ninth birthday. 'It was a very small home', Genevieve recalls, 'but a great joy because they made it a surprise for me.'

Above ground, French aerial photos revealed the rapid spread of Giap's trenches, and the Hanoi command, in radioing this information, proposed a parachute-load of sound detectors. The Dien Bien Phu command responded, 'No need, we can hear them digging'.

From his mountain top Giap was reporting that 'our fighters have dug hundreds of kilometers of trenches. Now we can move in open country despite enemy napalm and artillery.'

On the few low hills which they still held, the French were made more brutally conscious of each day. 'I saw my men disappear one after the other,' says Bigeard. 'This battalion of 800 men with whom I had jumped had become a force of 700 men, then 600, then 400, then 300 and then I had perhaps 180 troops left with 80 survivors at the end.'

Across the world, the fury, folly, valor and dilemma of Dien Bien Phu filled the front pages. Under the heading 'Cold War', *Time* magazine of 3 May 1954, began its cover story: 'The long night of defeat is closing down inexorably on the gallant

garrison of Dien Bien Phu. In Paris, where the trees burgeoned in gracious spring, the mood is as dark as the lengthening shadows in the Indo-China valley 6000 miles away.'

*Le Monde* wrote: 'The surgeons at Dien Bien Phu are reaching the limit of their endurance, and the overflow of wounded are waiting on the ground for their dressings to be changed. The water of the river in which bodies float can be filtered only in eyedrop amounts. There is just enough water to give the men when they get delirious from thirst.'

And there was the political pain. The Geneva Conference had just convened. *Time* reported: 'The men of Communism arrived smiling smugly and talking of peace. "They come here all dripping with blood and mouthing these pious statements," raged one US delegate.'

President Eisenhower, who had taken office on 20 January 1953, had earlier memoed British Prime Minister Winston Churchill, stating: 'If I may refer again to history, we failed to halt Hirohito, Mussolini and Hitler by not acting in unity and in time. That marked the beginning of many years of stark tragedy and desperate peril.' Eisenhower wanted Allied participation – especially active British support – in any military intervention.

Washington meantime drew up a bombing scenario. Historian Lacouture, then in Hanoi, says that under the code name 'Operation Vulture' the US was prepared 'to send from Manila 200 bombers to destroy Giap's positions, artillery and infantry'.

Although the *Pentagon Papers* uncovered no official record of the Operation, Vice-President Nixon contends that the scenario went further. Nixon states in his *Memoirs*: 'In Washington the Joint Chiefs of Staff devised a plan, known as Operation Vulture, for using three small tactical atomic bombs to destroy Viet Minh positions and relieve the [French] garrison.' Nixon does not say what action he supported but – in his own words – told Eisenhower that the President should not 'underestimate his ability to get the Congress and the country to follow his leadership'.

'The bombing', says Lacouture, 'was stopped by leaders of the Congress – above all by [House Leader] Lyndon Johnson. Churchill, who was a fighting man, thought it was impossible, extremely dangerous.'

Among those who opposed any US intervention was John F. Kennedy. The young Senator then stated: 'No amount of American military assistance in Indo-China can conquer an enemy which is everywhere and at the same time nowhere, "an enemy of the people" which has the sympathy and covert support of the people.'

In the first days of May, Eisenhower became the first American President who had to decide whether or not to argue for war in Vietnam. *Time*, in its old inimitable style, concluded its report of 3 May: 'Was there a chance of relief? Was Red General Giap's army as worn out as the garrison? Or would the outcome be the simple probability – death or Red captivity in one of three bitter ways: a sudden, crushing onset in the dark, or death by the thousand cuts of a siege, or surrender with the honors of war? There were lurking uncertainties in the dusk of Dien Bien Phu.'

In the valley itself at this time the protagonists were strangely close. Giap's trenches had reached to within 400 yards of the French command post, but there was little shooting and there were moments when the two sides communicated their feelings and view of history. Over a loudspeaker from the Viet Minh trenches came the World War II song of the French Resistance, with its haunting line, 'Companions, freedom is listening to us in the night'. And from their last redoubt on Eliane, French troops would ease the nights singing *La Marseillaise*.

'I kept telling my men', says Bigeard, 'we must hold on one more day. The Americans will not let us down; the free world will not let us down. They may come. That is why we saw this thing through.'

The French government had now made de Castries a general and had cited every man for the *croix de guerre*. Bigeard wryly commented: 'They thought we would die in combat, so they may as well decorate us.'

The officers decided on a greater honor for Genevieve. She was summoned to the command post: 'And when I arrived they said, We have something for you. And General de Castries gave me an envelope. When I opened it I saw a medal – the Legion of Honor.' 'I can still see that scene,' says Colonel Langlais, 'Genevieve walking in unsuspectingly and de Castries pinning the award on her.' As the French later said, the only meaning left was to demonstrate their own honor.

Langlais recounts that 'the final attack lasted two days, from the night of the 5th, all day on the

April 1954—French Union troops board a U.S. Air Force C-124 Globemaster at Orly Field, Paris, for transport to Indochina. The troops were reinforcements for the beleaguered French base at Dien Bien Phu, under siege for more than a month.

6th, and ending on the morning of the 7th. The positions around us fell one after the other.' And Bigeard evokes the final scene: 'So some got up, one who had lost an eye, one who had lost an arm – "One-Arm" we called him – and said, "We are going back". And they were still asking for a weapon to continue the combat. It was remarkable; there was a great spirit.

'On May 6th we went to see Langlais, and everybody was exhausted – completely exhausted. We knew we could not go further. There was no more ammunition and the men could not take it anymore. So when the Viet Minh attacked on May 7th it was really the end.'

The French had planned an almost certain suicidal break-out. Two columns would dash toward Laos and each would take its chance. Early on the 7th Langlais called the surviving officers together to commence the attempt. 'But', says Langlais, 'they reported that the men could no longer hold on. I then told General de Castries what the situation was. He phoned Hanoi and informed them that combat had to cease.'

Bigeard continues: 'We gathered the few chiefs of battalion still on their feet and said we would try the breakthrough. They said, "No, it is not worth it. . . . We might as well die. We could not go 100 meters without passing out." So de Castries said to Hanoi, "It is over." Navarre said on the radio, "Do not raise the white flag, but stop fighting."'

Colonel Langlais confirms that Hanoi agreed to the surrender 'provided the white flag of capitulation was not hoisted. By then it was 1 pm on the 7th.'

The officers gathered with Genevieve in the command post – to wait. It was just after 5 pm, fifty-five days to the minute from when the battle began, that they heard the Viet Minh all around them. 'We heard something rolling over the roof,' says Langlais. 'I was seated in my chair – not thinking of anything in particular. The stairs leading to the outside were in front of me, and we could see a patch of sky there. We all thought, a grenade – God – a grenade would be thrown down the stairs and explode, but that wasn't the case. We saw a victorious Viet soldier in a cork helmet carrying a

bayonet on his gun, who said only "Get out".'

The empty French command post still remains as it was at that moment on the plains of Dien Bien Phu. Twisted pieces of artillery still lie all around it. Only a small bronze plaque has been added. It records simply the moment of the end: '1730 hours, 7 May 1954'.

Even in recent times there had been longer sieges. The British held Tobruk for 241 days. The Germans held Stalingrad – involving a million men – for sixty-seven days. The Americans held Bataan for sixty-six days. But the French defeat was greater than the scale of battle. In the fifty-five days they had lost 3000 men and an equal number were permanently disabled – with Viet Minh losses estimated at 8000 dead – but France had also lost Indo-China, except that now, in the cold-war minds, Indo-China was no longer seen as the loss of a colony: it belonged to the Western cause. One decade of war would merely be the seeds of another.

General Navarre, who from the start considered that France could not win the war, concluded that the United States could and should have done so: 'There is no doubt that if the American air force had been heavily involved, as was proposed to me by the Pentagon, and as President Eisenhower had not dared to do, Dien Bien Phu would certainly have been saved. The US would not have had to become involved later as it was obliged to do.

'We used our soldiers, but our adversaries were fighting a complete war in which all the disciplines – politics, the economy, propaganda – were involved. That is my opinion as to the reason for the French defeat and ultimately what can be called the American defeat, since even though it didn't happen in the same way it was an incontestable defeat.

'I accept full blame for Dien Bien Phu. But . . . if it had not been decided to hold the Geneva conference without my having been consulted Dien Bien Phu would have ended not in a victory as I wished but by a type of victory. Therefore I accept full responsibility, but not any guilt.'

The Geneva conference had begun on 8 May 1954 and in July the Geneva powers agreed to a temporary partition of Vietnam. The United States, however, would not sign the Geneva Accords, and historians therefore concluded that it was at Geneva, not Dien Bien Phu, that the political dilemma of Vietnam went unsolved.

As the Geneva conference had opened, the 8000 survivors of Dien Bien Phu began a sixty-day march to prison camps in the Red River delta 500 miles away. The Viet Minh had left Genevieve de Galard to tend the most seriously wounded until French hospital planes could evacuate them. De Castries, Langlais and Bigeard joined the march – and three months of internment – which only one in two of the French force would survive.

'Half of the survivors of Dien Bien Phu died in captivity,' claims Bigeard. 'Worn out and aban-

doned they lay on the roadside and we were forbidden to help them.' The Viet Minh were without doctors. Those captives who weakened died where they fell. Says Bigeard: 'The Viet Minh would leave them to their fate, feeding them a handful of uncooked rice. The poor fellows died along the roadside.'

The most respected French journalist of the time, Robert Guillain of *Le Monde*, believed that the war had no meaning for the French soldiers, or a very different meaning: that nothing had been lost – except lives. As the survivors marched and fell, he cabled to his newspaper from Hanoi a bitter valedictory in the name of the dead: 'We'll show the people, the people of France above all. They have to be shown what their neglect, their incredible indifference, their illusions, their dirty

politics have led to. And how best may we show them? By dying, so that honor at least may be saved. Our dead of Dien Bien Phy died, I claim, protesting, appealing against today's France in the name of another France for which they had respect. The only victory that remains is the victory of our honor.'

The one-time clerk, 'Bruno' Bigeard, had a respect for the Viet Minh, and a perception of them, which few then seemed to share. 'I saw them', he says, 'start out with haphazard weapons, such as hunting guns, and then from month to month they were able to get organized to go from small groups to sections, and from sections to companies. And then on to battalions and brigades and finally to full divisions.

'I saw all this and I can tell you they became the greatest infantry in the world: these enduring men, capable of covering fifty kilometers in the night on the strength of a bowl of rice, with running shoes, and then singing their way into battle. In my opinion they turned out to be exceptional infantry and they managed to defeat us. Now, we were not that many, we were far from France, but we have to admit they also beat the Americans. So they were exceptional.'

*Time* magazine presented a different view after the battle. 'The Viet Minh are not as strong as we have pretended they are,' it reported in quoting a 'gallant' opponent. And it concluded on the domino theme of the day: 'Hanoi lies and awaits its end with the gunfire rustling the tamarind leaves, and dogs barking through the night. Nanking fell to the sound of gunfire and the barking dogs upon such a quiet night one April, Shanghai one May, Pyongyang one December. No one knows when Hanoi will go too, but no one doubts that it will.'

Right: March 1954—A French soldier bandages a wounded Vietnamese ally after a skirmish to reestablish a link between the besieged French garrison of Dien Bien Phu and one of its southern defense outposts.

Below: April 20, 1954— French paratroopers in civilian clothes arrive with their gear at Paris's Orly Airport for their flight to Indochina. The U.S. announced that it was carrying French reinforcements to Indochina at the request of the French government.

Above: April 1953—Trees are cut down and trenches dug out as a defense zone is readied against a Vietminh attack in Xieng Khouang, Laos.

Below: January 1954—Vietnamese paratroopers, one of them wounded, take trench positions against communist-led Vietminh forces near Seno, Laos. French Union troops fought to contain communist forces that had cut across Indochina to the Mekong River border of Thailand.

Above: September 1953—A young Private Tuat of Hanoi fights with the French Union forces against the communist-led Vietminh.

Right: April 1953—French Union reinforcements disembark at the Plain of Jars in Laos. With several French garrisons effectively cut off from ground supply, air transport was becoming a vital link, and France asked Britain for aircraft.

Map indicates Dien Bien Phu in northwestern Indochina's mountainous area near the border of Laos. Qui Nhon was the site of a major French victory over the Vietminh about the time the battle for Dien Bien Phu began.

Map shows how Vietminh forces gradually squeezed the French base of Dien Bien Phu during the weeks long siege of the French outpost. Dotted lines indicate Vietminh control in March at the start of the siege and in May, days before the base fell to the enemy and after the air strip was captured.

Maps locate Dien Bien Phu fortress in three perspectives.

Left: January 1953—French troops guide pack animals through a river during an operation against the Vietminh.

Right: January 1953—Captured Vietminh weapons are displayed by French Union forces in the Van Cu area, about 10 miles south of Nam Dinh..

Above: July 17, 1953—French paratroopers land in the Langson area during a raid by 5,000 paratroopers on a Vietminh base six miles from the Chinese border. The French troops spent 12 hours removing or destroying about 5,000 tons of Vietminh supplies before making a 48-hour march deep into rebel territory, where they linked up with a relief column sent from Hanoi.

Left: July 17, 1953—French Union paratroopers drop near the communist-held town of Langson on the Indochina border.

Above: July 1953—Vietnamese fighters, loyal to the French, defend the village of Hung Yen from communist-led Vietminh forces. Hung Yen, the war capital for the French about 35 miles southeast of Hanoi, was also called the 'ambush capital' for its frequent Vietminh assaults.

Above: July 17, 1953—A French Union paratrooper examines a Vietminh propaganda poster found near the communist-held town of Langson. About 5,000 tons of enemy supplies were reported destroyed by the paratroopers before they linked up with a relief column from the Hanoi area.

September 24, 1953—French Foreign Legion paratroopers coordinate a sweep of suspected guerilla positions in the Hung Yen district during Operation Brochet.

Below: September 1953—A young Private Tuat of Hanoi fights with the French Union forces against the communist-led Vietminh.

Left: September 1953—French Union troops advance through rivers and mines in the district north of the Bamboo Canal in northern Indochina during Operation Brochet. The French encountered the communist-led Vietminh with violent results.

Above: September 1953—Canon fires on Vietminh positions as French step up military pressure on the enemy.

Above right: December 31, 1953—A wounded Vietminh soldier is discovered in a stack of straw by French troops during Operation Gerfaut in Tonkin, northern Indochina.

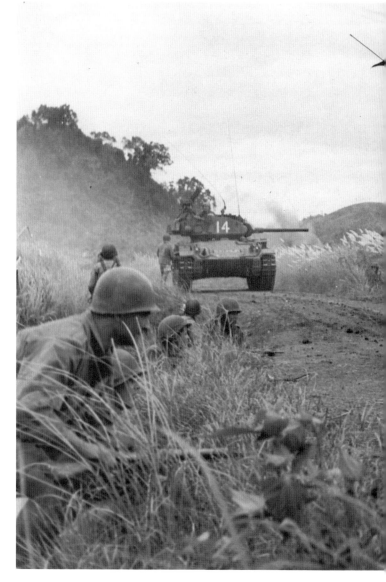

Above: December 31, 1953—With a pagoda in the background, French Union troops cross a river near Song Tra Ly in the Tonkin region.

Right: October 22, 1953—French Union infantry and armor advance through the limestone hills surrounding Phu Nho Quan during Operation Mouette.

Left: March 13, 1954—French Union soldiers sweep for mines at Qui Nhon in central Vietnam during Operation Atlante. The landing at Qui Nhon was intended to secure the coastal position, and establish contact with troops inland.

Right: January 9, 1954—A wounded Vietnamese paratrooper is carried to aid during operations against the Vietminh near Seno, Laos.

Above: April 1954—On the rail line between Hanoi and Haiphong, a crew arrives by train to repair a section of track blown up by Vietnamese rebels. The frequent attacks to the rail line were usually repaired quickly.

Above: March 1954—Christian de Castries, commanding colonel of French Union troops, looks out over the area at Dien Bien Phu during a calm period in the battle.

Above left: February 2, 1954—Vietnamese troops fighting with the French Union forces advance through jungle north of Dien Bien Phu.

Above: April 1954—U.S. Air Force personnel line up for a meal at their Haiphong base in northern Indochina. They were providing support for French forces defending the garrison at Dien Bien Phu from the Vietminh.

Right: April 1954—U.S. Air Force technicians relax at their quarters in Haiphong, northern Indochina. They were assigned to maintain the U.S. planes used by the French in their war against communist-led Vietminh forces.

Above: March 1954—The besieged French fortress at Dien Bien Phu takes fire from Vietminh forces in the surrounding hills.

Right: March 1954—French defenders of Dien Bien Phu man an underground command post in the battered northwest bastion of the beleaguered garrison.

Below: March 1954—A French stretcher-bearer looks out over the besieged fortress at Dien Bien Phu as soldiers take cover in a trench. Casualties were high on both sides as the Vietminh launched multiple assaults on the garrison.

Above: March 1954—French Union troops carry a wounded comrade during intense fighting at the besieged mountain outpost at Dien Bien Phu.

Above right: March 1954—Reinforcements parachute into the surrounded French fortress at Dien Bien Phu.

Right: March 1954—As French Union forces watch from trenches in foreground, napalm bursts over Vietminh positions surrounding the French fortress at Dien Bien Phu. The costly French defeat at Dien Bien Phu led directly to the end of French colonial rule in Indochina.

Right: March 25, 1954—A wounded soldier is carried to an aid station by a French Union comrade. The outnumbered allied forces were surrounded by the communist-led Vietminh.

Below: March 23, 1954—French and Vietnamese infantrymen advance with automatic weapons against communist-led Vietminh troops surrounding the besieged French fortress at Dien Bien Phu.

Above: March 23, 1954—French Union soldiers, supported by a tank, patrol a battered outpost of the surrounded garrison.

Left: March 25, 1954—Wounded Vietnamese soldiers at Dien Bien Phu wait for aid after an intense Vietminh attack.

Above: April 1954—Smoke and flames erupt from a plane destroyed on the ground by Vietminh shelling of the garrison at Dien Bien Phu.

Above: April 1954—A Corsican machine gunner with French Union forces watches for Vietminh raiders from a blockhouse at Gia Loc, on the supply route between Hanoi and the port of Haiphong. Vietminh raiders were attacking the area each night, trying to disrupt the flow of supplies to the fortress at Dien Bien Phu.

Below: April 1954—Light bombers aboard the French carrier *Arromanches* are checked before missions defending the French fortress at Dien Bien Phu.

Above: March 1954—Wounded French Union soldiers, including two Vietnamese, leave a first-aid station at the garrison at Dien Bien Phu.

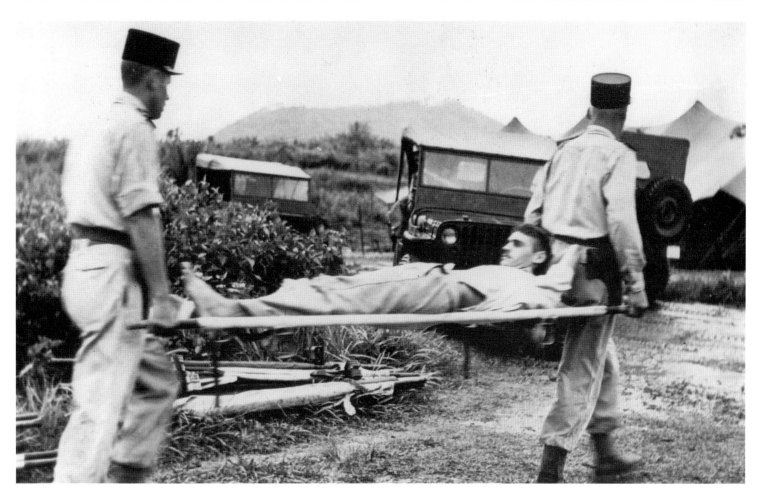

Above: May 14, 1954—With hospital tents in the background, two French Foreign Legion soldiers carry a wounded French paratrooper evacuated to Luang Parabang from the fallen fortress of Dien Bien Phu.

Left: May 1954—Wounded French Union soldiers rest at Lanessan Hospital in Hanoi after evacuation from Dien Bien Phu.

Above: May 1954—French and Vietnamese troops take a break during a three-week trek through the jungle to a point about 18 miles south of the French fortress at Dien Bien Phu. The column was intended to distract communist forces from the southern outpost of the garrison, but the column retreated as the fortress was captured by the Vietminh.

Above: May 1954—Ho Chi Minh, at 64.

Right: June 1954—Vietnamese natives, pressed into service by the French, fortify the bunkers of the Phu Ly garrison, in the delta south of Hanoi. Communist-led Vietminh troops had recently been stationed in the hills across the nearby Day River.

Left: June 1954—A truck carrying French and Vietnamese troops to the garrison at Phu Ly passes a French blockhouse on the road south of Hanoi. Such outposts in the area were under constant threat of night assaults by the communist-led Vietminh.

Above: June 1954—Hoping for any type of transportation north, Vietnamese women and children wait with their few belongings in Nam Dinh, 45 miles south of Hanoi. With Vietminh forces advancing, Nam Dinh was one of two major French outposts evacuated starting June 28.

Above: June 1954—French artillerymen reload at Nai Tuu, a newly fortified base, while firing on Vietminh positions near the abandoned Red River delta communications center in Phu Ly, about six miles south.

Below: July 1954—French Union troops guard a vital supply route between Hanoi and the port of Haiphong.

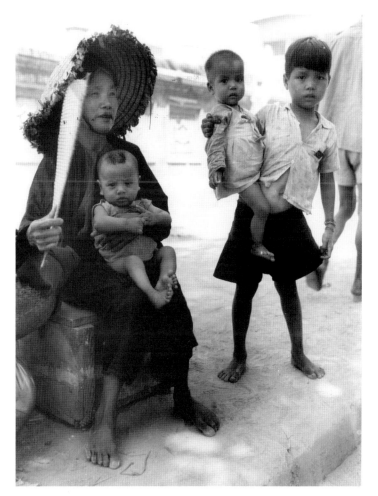

Above: June 1954—Refugees wait for transportation out of Nam Dinh during the French withdrawal from the southern Red River area. Fearing reprisals from the communist-led Vietminh, many refugees fled north to Hanoi and Haiphong, still within the French defenses.

Above: June 1954—Shortly after the French port of Nam Dinh was abandoned to the Vietminh, a Vietnamese woman shades her children while waiting for any type of transportation to Hanoi, about 45 miles away.

Above: July 26, 1954—French Union troops gather around a field radio at an outpost just north of Hanoi, waiting for the cease-fire order ending the Indochina War. The order goes into effect the following day, although some sporadic fighting is reported.

Left: July 1954—A French guard and his Vietminh counterpart carry identical American-made carbines at the heavily-secured cease-fire talks in Trung Gia, north of Hanoi. The communist-led Vietminh made a point of displaying U.S.-made military equipment that they said was captured in the fall of Dien Bien Phu two months earlier.

Above: July 1954—Senior Vietminh delegate Gen. Van Tien Dung *(left)* addresses cease-fire talks between the Vietminh and French Union forces in the village of Trung Gia, 25 miles north of Hanoi. Photographers were excluded from the hut after the opening day of talks.

Above and below: July 4, 1954—Cease-fire meetings open at Trung Gia, 25 miles north of Hanoi. In the top photo, Gen. Van Tien Dung *(seated left)* head of the Vietminh delegation, meets with his delegates in their quarters, decorated with a photo of Ho Chi Minh, a Vietminh flag, and a parachute they said was taken at Dien Bien Phu. In the bottom photo, the French Union delegation listens as Gen. Dung makes his opening speech at the far end of the table.

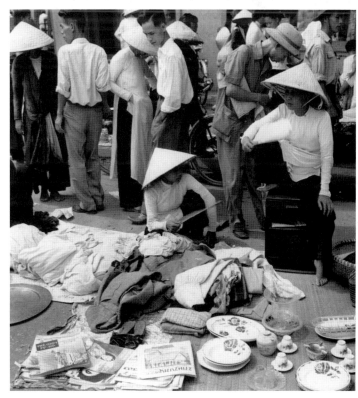

Above: July 1954—Northern Indochina villagers, many of them Catholics, sleep on straw mats in a Hanoi street as they flee to the south in advance of the communist takeover of the north under terms of the Geneva Conference.

Right: July 1954—A woman displays her possessions for sale on a Hanoi street, as civilians waiting for evacuation to the south disposed of many personal items. The French had promised to remove anyone who wanted to leave Hanoi before the communist takeover.

Above: August 29, 1954—French Union prisoners are released by the communist-led Vietminh at the Vietri exchange point.

Above: August 1954—French prisoner Rene Alexander, released in the prisoner exchange at Viet Tri, awaits transportation to freedom in Hanoi, but unlike many of his French Union comrades, he avoided shaking hands with his former captors.

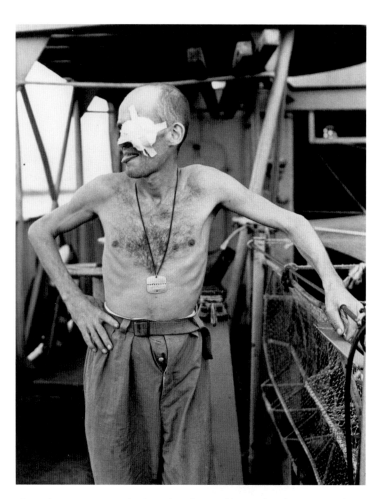

Above: July 19, 1954—Crowds gather near Hanoi's opera house during a peaceful demonstration against the partition of Indochina.

Above: July 1954—An emaciated and injured French Union soldier was released in a prisoner exchange with the Vietminh. Some French prisoners described mistreatment at the hands of their captors.

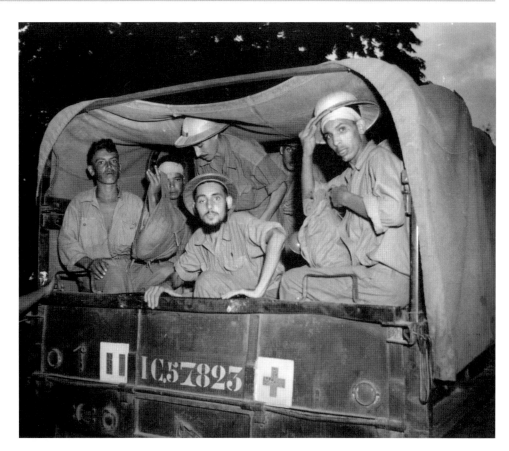

Above: August 24, 1954—Brigadier Gen. Jon Masson, deputy French commander in Indochina, greets released French Union prisoners returning to a Hanoi hospital. The 500 troops released at the Vietri exchange point were all North African or German members of the French Foreign Legion.

Right: August 24, 1954—French Union prisoners arrive at Hanoi after their release by the communist-led Vietminh at the Vietri exchange point. Some 500 North African and German members of the French Foreign Legion were released.

Left: August 24, 1954—North African and German members of the French Union arrive at Lanessan Hospital in Hanoi after their release by the Vietminh at the Vietri Exchange Point, about 40 miles from Hanoi.

Right: August 18, 1954—
Released French Union
troops sing and clap hands
after the first mass prisoner
exchange with the Vietminh
at Viet Tri, Indochina. The
French released 1,000 Vietminh and the Vietminh freed
350 French Union troops.
The sign in background
means 'Long Live Peace in
Indochina.'

Below: September 3, 1954—
Gen. Christian de Castries,
commander of the fallen
fortress of Dien Bien Phu,
weeps as he hears the French
national anthem at Hanoi
following his release by Vietminh forces.

Above: September 1954—Commander J. G. Wells supervises the distribution of rice to Vietnamese refugees aboard the carrier H.M.S. Warrior. The Warrior transferred thousands of refugees from Haiphong to St. Jacques.

Left: September 1954—U.S. seamen carry an elderly man, unable to walk, aboard the attack transport U.S.S. Menard off the coast of Vietnam. Civilians fleeing northern Indochina before the negotiated communist takeover were transported to southern Indochina in the operation known as 'Passage to Freedom.'

Above: October 9, 1954—Vietminh parade victoriously into Hanoi as they take control of the capital under the terms of the Geneva Conference. About 5,000 troops were welcomed by civilians at the same time that the French were evacuating the city.

Right: October 10, 1954—A smiling Vietminh stands with a French officer on a rainy Hanoi street as the communist-led Vietminh assumed control of northern Indochina under the terms of the armistice negotiated in Geneva.

Left: October 9, 1954—Children parade beside the first Vietminh troops marching into Hanoi, while elsewhere in the capital the French were withdrawing under the terms of the Geneva Conference. Hanoi's citizens appeared to welcome the Vietminh takeover.

Left: October 1954—A portrait of Ho Chi Minh, communist leader of the Vietminh forces, hangs over a Hanoi street several weeks after the Vietminh assumed control of Hanoi from the departing French, under terms of the Geneva agreements.

Below: October 10, 1954—North African troops of the French Union leave Hanoi as Vietminh forces took control of the city following the agreements of the Geneva Conference.

# EARLY HOPES

The curtain fall of Dien Bien Phu ending the first act of Vietnam's three-decade drama merely cleared the stage for a reversal of roles. The second act – and decade – had the Americans replacing the French as supporting cast in their own script which presented a new leading man, South Vietnam's President Ngo Dinh Diem, on the world's center-stage.

Well before Ho Chi Minh's troops entered Hanoi five months after Dien Bien Phu, the new Saigon-Washington alliance was taking shape. Initially it centered on two men: one was Ngo Dinh Diem, the other was the senior US military advisor in Vietnam, Colonel Edward Lansdale, formerly of the OSS. Like his predecessor, Major Patti, who nine years earlier had been drawn to Ho Chi Minh, Lansdale's official assignment 'very shortly became a personal friendship'. He extolled Diem for much the same qualities as Patti had found in Ho – 'a very warm-hearted man' with 'sides to his character I hadn't heard from others'. This question of character judgement would again beset the US for another nine years. Diem's long tenure was remarkable in that he was a mandarin upheld as an answer to Marx, a devout Catholic in a country ninety-five per cent Buddhist, and within a short time the despair of the democracy which kept on

> '**I cautioned Diem against rigging the election. I said, "All you need is a fairly large majority—not 99.99 per cent of the vote."**'
>
> – EDWARD LANSDALE,
> CHIEF US MILITARY ADVISOR

backing him because 'if we can't win with him – who else?'

Whether America's early hope was also its hand-picked choice, or whether Diem's emergence was a chance which the US took, is part of the 1950s puzzle. Known as a nationalist who opposed both the French and the Viet Minh, Diem had been a high-ranking civil servant for some twenty years when he chose voluntary exile after the French reoccupation. He settled first in Belgium, then in the US, where Arthur Schlesinger Jr, one of Senator Kennedy's aides, recalls meeting him: 'When Diem was in exile in the United States, he came to us. He was sponsored by such exemplary figures as Bill Douglas of the Supreme Court and Mike Mansfield of the Senate. And Kennedy met him then, and when Diem went back to Vietnam Kennedy was among his supporters.'

On 7 July 1954, South Vietnam's Head of State Bao Dai, unpopular because of his perennial absence in Paris and his softness towards corruption, suddenly appointed Diem as his Prime Minister. The Geneva Accords, partitioning Vietnam but calling for joint elections on reunification within two years, were concluded two weeks later – 21 July. The United States and the

1939—Family of South Vietnam's leader, Ngo Dinh Diem, surrounds matriarch Madame Ngo Dinh Kha, seated under the portrait of her husband, Ngo Dinh Kha. Standing from left are Ngo Dinh Nhu, President Ngo Dinh Diem, Archbishop of Hue Ngo Dinh Thuc, Mrs. Nguyen Van Am, Mrs. Ngo Dinh Nhu, Ngo Dinh Cam, Ngo Dinh Luyen and Nguyen Van Am. Children are Ngo Dinh Trac, 14, Ngo Dinh Quynh, 9, Ngo Dinh Le Quyen, 2, and Ngo Dinh Le Thuy, 16.

Saigon government were not signatories to the agreement, but the US declared at Geneva 'its traditional position that peoples are entitled to determine their own future and that the United States will not join in an arrangement which would hinder this'. But in June, according to the *Pentagon Papers*, the US had decided on measures to train and finance a 234,000-man Vietnamese National Army and to 'work through the French only insofar as necessary'.

Colonel Lansdale had by then arrived in Saigon as Chief of the Military Advisory and Assistance Group (MAAG). All this suggests that the US conspired against the Geneva terms, but Lansdale denies any such knowledge: 'People have felt that this was a conspiracy, that Americans had hand-picked Diem to go out there and be Prime Minister and that I had been picked to coach him along and to make him into a power. I myself was completely unaware of any conspiracy at all.'

Lansdale says he 'had never heard' of Diem before his appointment, but 'every Vietnamese I talked to knew a great deal about him. Some of them liked him very much, and some of them hated him.' He found general agreement that Diem was personally honest.

Lansdale had previously led the OSS counterinsurgency which helped achieve independence for the Philippines – prompting Ho Chi Minh's praise of America – and Secretary of State Dulles had told Lansdale 'to go to Vietnam and do what you did in the Philippines. I said that I didn't want to go there to work with the French but to help the Vietnamese. He [Dulles] told me to go and help the Vietnamese.'

In the Philippines Lansdale had helped shape 'not only military affairs but some social, political and economic matters as well.' In Vietnam his role supposedly inspired Graham Greene's *The Quiet American*, in which a young idealist believed he could create a third force to thwart both the French and the Communists. 'So when I met Diem I hoped that he would be a power himself,' explains Lansdale. 'I felt that it was time to fix on

Above: 1955—South Vietnam Premier Ngo Dinh Diem *(right)* walks with two of his brothers, Catholic bishop Ngo Dinh Thuc and Ngo Dinh Nhu.

Above left: June 1955—South Vietnamese Premier Ngo Dinh Diem, fresh from victory in his struggle for power, greets villagers during a visit to the coastal town of Binh Dinh.

Left: August 1954—Vietnamese refugees are transported from Haiphong to a U.S. Navy ship for evacuation to Saigon in 'Passage to Freedom,' a mass evacuation before the communist takeover of northern Indochina.

Right: August 1954—Some of the 300 women prisoners released by the French Union to the Vietminh wade ashore from a landing craft at the Vietri exchange point.

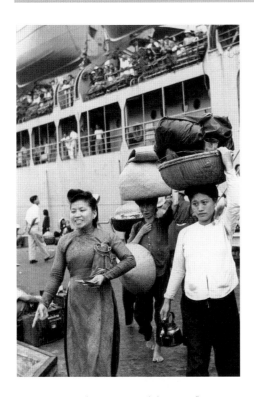

one person, and get some stabilizing influence at work among the Vietnamese.'

France had already fixed on Ho Chi Minh as the certain victor in future national elections. After almost a century in Vietnam, France had agreed at Geneva to withdraw all its troops within one year. The Viet Minh had agreed to a three-month period of legal migration between North and South before the formal partitioning at the 17th Parallel on 11 October. French historian Jean Lacouture says the sentiment at Geneva was that the Communists had made 'a large concession to the French and to the West. Almost everybody thought that the elections would end in a victory for the North and the reunification of the country. That was said in the memoirs of Eisenhower and it was the opinion of ninety per cent of the people after the Geneva conference.'

While the US recognized that Ho Chi Minh would be the certain victor in elections, President Eisenhower and particularly Secretary of State Dulles were determined to prevent this. Hanoi, they believed, would become Communist China's gateway to South-east Asia, and South Vietnam had to be given every chance to develop independently or the small nations would 'topple like dominoes.' The French, as Dulles saw it, had 'given in' at Geneva and, even worse, were accelerating Ho Chi Minh's hegemony by actively befriending Hanoi. Premier Mendes-France had immediately sought reconciliation, sending Major Jean Sainteny from Geneva to Hanoi to establish new cultural and economic relations. The US could not understand this drastic French turnabout after nine years of bitter war, and the French could not make the US understand that the very scale of the conflict now warranted that the huge cost and sacrifice not be totally in vain. The French, deeply torn by the long war, had foremost to heal the wounds at home, and a coming to terms with Vietnam was a way to do it. France did not wish defeat at Dien Bien Phu to be followed by dishonor at Geneva: it was guarantor of the peace and must demonstrate goodwill.

Left: May 1955—Vietnamese refugees carry their possessions as they arrive at port in Saigon after evacuation from Haiphong in 'Passage to Freedom.' The refugees were relocated to the south under terms of the Geneva cease-fire agreement dividing North and South Vietnam.

Above: May 9, 1963—Ngo Dinh Nhu, brother and advisor to South Vietnamese President Ngo Dinh Diem, sits in front of a map of Southeast Asia in his study in the presidential palace in Saigon.

Above: Madame Ngo Dinh Nhu, wife of Ngo Dinh Nhu, brother and close advisor to President Diem. She was officially the first lady of Vietnam and an active leader in anti-Buddhist government actions.

This policy of reconciliation was presented as realistic and pragmatic. Vietnam could still express French global influence. France had a vast investment in coal, cement and heavy industry in the North, as well as in the rubber and other plantations of the South. These were not yet economically profitable but might be in a unified, peaceful Vietnam, and anyhow Ho Chi Minh was pledging economic compensation, if political association failed, provided that France meantime maintained the industry and expertise which the North needed for postwar reconstruction. More than 6500 French businessmen and technicians were then in Hanoi. Major Sainteny was urgently instructed to negotiate with Ho's government and to keep the French presence intact during the three-month transitional period.

In the twist of events, Sainteny once again found himself desperately trying to counteract the US intelligence chief in Hanoi – only now their positions were reversed, with the French opposing further American operations against the Viet Minh. After Geneva, Dulles had reassigned Colonel Lansdale from Saigon to Hanoi with orders to initiate 'psychological operations' before the Viet Minh take-over in October. The OSS had now become the CIA – with Lansdale in the dual role of senior military advisor and CIA chief in Vietnam. His new mission was to stimulate a refugee exodus to the South.

The CIA concentrated on the large Catholic population in the Hanoi delta, where the Church and its parishioners owned an estimated thirty per cent of the land. Catholic Ngo Dinh Diem, anxious to broaden his power base, promised grants of land in the South which the French were conveniently leaving. The Diem-inspired slogan was 'God has gone South'.

To persuade those who might not have been moved by faith alone, the CIA adopted scare tactics, inciting dissent and predicting disaster. In perhaps the first CIA exercise in disinformation it exploited traditional Vietnamese belief in fortune telling. 'We put out a book', recounts Lansdale, 'that told the fortunes of Communist leaders and what would happen to a Communist society eventually in Vietnam. It was a very unhappy ending for all of the leaders.' The book, Lansdale says, was very effective – 'We didn't know what to do with the profits' – but it would prove ironic in what lay ahead. Of all the Vietnamese leaders only Ngo Dinh Diem would meet a bloody end.

Within a few weeks, 850,000 people migrated South, most of them Catholics and small landowners. Some 80,000 Vietnamese went North, almost all of them guerrilla cadres who had resisted the French. During the same period the US had quietly made it known that it would blacklist French businesses which retained operations in the North. The result was a huge setback for both Paris and Hanoi: only 114 French businessmen remained in Hanoi on 11 October as the two Vietnams came into being.

France considered that its postwar policy of reconciliation had been severely sabotaged as it continued to implement the Geneva provisions, withdrawing its last troops from the North without incident. The occasion was one of friendly ceremonial, as recalled by left-wing journalist Wilfred Burchett: 'It was to be a block by block withdrawal by the French, and one block behind the French came the Viet Minh taking over. At times you could see both forces – the French waving, and the Vietnamese waving. Then the streets burst into life and color, block by block, as the French withdrew.'

The French withdrawal was followed, as previously agreed, by an economic and cultural pact signed in November by Ho Chi Minh and Major Sainteny. Although the treaty's practical value had been largely diminished along with the French presence, Ho still regarded French ties as his best guarantee of the Geneva terms and France was still trying to persuade the US that its involvement in Vietnam was 'naive', that Ngo Dinh Diem was an unrepresentative figure in the South and that if Ho could not look to France and the West he would be forced to turn to the Communist bloc. The French briefly tried supporting the many sects in the South which opposed Diem, hoping that a coup would put an end to both Diem and American interest, and the result of all this Allied backstabbing was a mutual recrimination and suspicion that would linger for decades. A US State Department memorandum, as quoted in the *Pentagon Papers*, bluntly summarized the opposing positions: 'France objected to anything which could possibly delay or destroy [the Geneva agreed] elections in 1956', and now Dulles decided

'to take the plunge.' The US announced that henceforth American aid would be given not through the French but directly to Diem's Saigon government.

France itself, with a new struggle on its hands in Algeria, was equally dependent on the US purse strings. Under economic pressure, France agreed to forgo all political authority in the South as well – and on 1 January 1955, it dissolved Indo-China's status within the French Union, turning over sovereignty in South Vietnam to Ngo Dinh Diem. In a complete reversal, France continued to develop diplomatic ties in the North, hoping these might avert a new war in Vietnam, while in the South US advisors took over the training of Dien's forces – as Washington had planned six months earlier.

The first year's military cost was budgeted at $214 million, with an equal amount in economic aid after Diem had promised to initiate social reforms. This million dollar a day commitment went almost unnoticed in Congress, relates William Fulbright, then on the Senate Finance Committee. 'Indo-China was just an expression,' he says. 'I had never been there, and no one on the Committee had ever been there. The truth of the matter is that we didn't know anything about it.'

Nor did the US military, according to future

Saigon Ambassador Graham Martin who from 1955 spent two years as a State Department liaison officer during Pentagon studies on combating guerrilla warfare. Martin states that the air force argument was 'you simply used your overwhelming air power to obliterate the enemy,' while the army argued that 'you just simply applied conventional power'. Martin found that the US 'had no acceptable doctrine on how you might conduct that kind of war'.

Even as the US announced direct military aid for Diem the first doubts about him were being voiced by the American Ambassador then in Saigon, General J. Lawton Collins. The *Pentagon Papers* show that by late 1954 General Colins was advising Washington that an alternative to Diem's government 'should be urgently considered'. Collins cited Diem's unwillingness to delegate authority, the influence of his family, and the opposition of powerful sects. In a subsequent review, Secretary of State Dulles called the 'investment in Vietnam justified if only to buy time to build up strength elsewhere in the area' – and Dulles stated: 'We have no choice but to continue our support of Diem. There is no other suitable leader known to us.'

By early 1995 both the US and Diem felt a lot

Above: 1955—A Cao Dai temple in the Mekong Delta.

Left: April 29, 1955—An aged Vietnamese woman hobbles away from the flaming Cholen area of Saigon following clashes between national army troops and the Binh Xuyen.

Below: April 29, 1955—Soldiers of the southern Vietnam National Army line Boulevard Gallieni during a two-day battle between Binh Xuyen sect and Ngo Dinh Diem's government.

Left: March 30, 1955—An injured civilian is helped by friends after violence flared between the Binh Xuyen private army and government troops.

May 15, 1955—An estimated 40,000 demonstrate in Saigon's marketplace to support South Vietnamese premier Ngo Dinh Diem, and show their disapproval of Bao Dai.

February 1956—Members of the Vietnamese Citizens Committee tote election banners through the streets of Saigon urging people to vote in the fist balloting for the Republic of Vietnam to choose an assembly to write a constitution.

more secure. In February the eight-nation South-East Asia Treaty Organization (SEATO) came into force, and a protocol guaranteeing protection for Cambodia, Laos and the 'free state' of Vietnam would henceforth become the basis for American military support of Saigon.

Then in April with CIA assistance, Diem outwitted his considerable opposition – a bizarre collection of religious and criminal sects, each with its private army. The CIA account shows that with its help Diem had planned to crush the sects as a first step towards defying the North and the Geneva elections provision. William Colby, the subsequent Saigon CIA chief, was then in Washington. Unlike the US military, the Agency throughout had a professional confidence in Diem's methods and cunning.

As Colby puts it: 'When he started he controlled very little more than his own palace. There was a bandit gang that ran the police in Saigon. There were various religious armies in the countryside. Diem however decided that he really wasn't going to be just a transition to Communist rule – and he grabbed hold of the situation and the United States decided that it would support him, but that we would not involve ourselves directly.'

For months the Prime Minister and the CIA's Lansdale plotted from the palace – outwardly an ill-matched couple: Diem so tiny that 'when he sat his feet didn't reach the ground', Lansdale like a burly Lone Ranger with charm as his gun. On one occasion Lansdale journeyed alone for several days through marsh and mountains to negotiate with the leader of the dissident Cao Dai religion and 'we hit it off right from the first moment'.

The sect leaders were a coalition of militant religious leaders and vice lords whom Emperor Bao Dai had always treated indulgently. Together they could muster 40,000 armed men who exacted tribute from their domains to buy off Bao Dai's police. In the coming ideological choice the gods of the Hoa Hao, Cao Dai and Dan Xa were unaffordable fantasy. One sect, the Cao Dai, had become living fiction, worshipping statues of Shakespeare and Victor Hugo at a temple near Tay Ninh. And there was the Binh Xuyen, a huge pirate force with a fleet of river boats controlling much of Saigon's commerce, gambling, opium dens and lavish brothels. Its leader, Bay Vien, promptly mortared

Diem's palace after a decree outlawing prostitution.

In a series of edicts, and by carefully placing his family and close friends in positions of power, Diem divided the sects and curtailed their activities. Then in March 1955, with his American-financed army committed to him, Diem attacked the Binh Xuyen-controlled Saigon police headquarters. During a brief truce, Ambassador Collins again advised Washington to consider a change of leadership. The CIA – Lansdale reveals – opposed this. In April, Diem struck again at the Binh Xuyen and in two days of fighting scattered his opposition.

Lansdale recounts that he saw Diem just before this. 'It was felt that I shouldn't be in the palace with him during this trouble. One of the stories that has come up depicts me standing there giving directions over a radio from his office. This just simply wasn't true at all.'

Head of State Bao Dai then cabled Diem from Paris accusing his Prime Minister, says Lansdale, of 'selling the blood of Vietnamese' and ordering him to resign. Diem – 'receiving lots of popular support' after his clean-up – asked Lansdale what he should do. 'I said, well, your only authority is Bao Dai. The only higher authority would be the people. The only way you could possibly stay would be to have the people ask you to stay through a plebiscite.'

Diem agreed to this and Lansdale cautioned him 'against being carried away and rigging the election. I said, all you need is a fairly large majority. I had to go to Washington for consultation at that period and I said, 'While I'm away I don't want to suddenly read that you have won by 99.99 per cent. I would know that it's rigged then."'

That conversation was in May 1955. In June Hanoi asked for formal talks to prepare for the internationally supervised elections scheduled for 1956. In October Diem held his plebiscite. He won by ninety-eight per cent. 'In that election he didn't have to cheat,' says Lansdale. 'I think his brother [Nhu] got his organization out to stuff some ballot boxes and to destroy others.'

Diem, a bachelor like Ho Chi Minh, had also spent his years in exile in contemplating methods of power. For a time he entered a monastery in Bruges, there in solitude pondering a philosophy

called 'Personalism'. Diem's family had been converted to Catholicism in the seventeenth century but had always belonged to the mandarin class at the Imperial capital of Hue. Now at the age of fifty-four, appointing himself President after a 'rigged' plebiscite, Diem implemented the rule of personalism. 'Society', he said, 'functions through personal relations among men at the top.'

He appointed his younger brother, Ngo Dinh Nhu, as chief advisor, his sister-in-law, Madame Nhu, as official hostess, her father as Ambassador to the United States, her mother as observer at the United Nations, his elder brother as Archbishop of Hue, and two other brothers as regional overlords – with various cousins and in-laws filling the Cabinet and senior provincial posts.

His senior advisor, Nhu, had formed a secret police called the Can Lao – which Lansdale suspected of fixing the plebiscite – and Diem now informed Lansdale that he would hold parliamentary elections in the South instead of joint elections with the North.

'I advised the American government what he was going to do,' reveals Lansdale. Diem 'felt very strongly that conditions in the countryside were such – and the Communist methods were such – that an election would have been rigged by the Communists and they would have won unfairly, and that his side didn't have a chance. I had to agree with that appraisal,' says Lansdale. In other words, Diem's 'side', after a rigged election, was arguing that the opposition might be as bad as him.

In Hanoi, Prime Minister Pham Van Dong viewed Diem's establishment of a National Assembly in March 1956 as a US conspiracy, calling it 'a blatant violation of the Geneva Agreements'. But Hanoi waited. As the CIA's William Colby summarizes it: 'The Communists had a full job organizing North Vietnam for the first two or three years. They went through land reform that managed to create an enormous famine. They killed a lot of landlords and things of this nature.'

The 'things of this nature' were, on a US intelligence estimate, that 30,000 landlords and dissidents had been executed in the North. (According to American historian Gareth Porter, who analyzed the war in a book *Peace Denied*, this estimate

October 26, 1955—Premier Ngo Dinh Diem proclaims free Vietnam a republic and himself as president during ceremonies in Saigon that followed his victory in a referendum.

Above: March 15, 1956—Spectators gather at Saigon's Municipal Theater as the 123 newly elected deputies of the first National Constituent Assembly pose on the steps before their inaugural session.

February 1957—Ngo Dinh Diem drinks chum-chum, a local rice beer, at an economic fair soon after an assassination attempt. A shot missed as the South Vietnamese president listened to a welcome address at the fair in Banme Thuot, 225 miles north of Saigon.

was based on the reports of a Vietnamese exile who was receiving a US government grant. Porter himself estimates that executions in the North did not exceed 2500.)

In the same three-year period Diem's effort at reforms had also brought rural upheaval and resentment. He had successfully resettled 850,000 refugees, but his plan for redistribution of land – only begun in mid-1956 – became corrupted by his system of nepotism and patronage. Often the land went only to the highest bidder. The cost of the central government's huge network of controls pushed village taxes as high as sixty per cent. The peasants increasingly found they were paying more for the same land they had tilled for the French.

The resulting dissent forced Diem to abolish traditional elections of village chiefs – replaced by Saigon appointees. Even the French colonial administration had scrupulously respected village autonomy. Diem himself was still viewed as honest but isolated. His brother Nhu's Can Lao secret police systematically purged South Vietnam's 16,000 hamlets of opposition – officially described as former Viet Minh. By one estimate, in Alexander Kendrick's *The Wound Within*, 75,000 persons were killed and more than 50,000 imprisoned.

Much later, in *Our Endless War*, Diem's last military Chief of Staff, General Tran Van Don, acknowledged the excesses of the regime, which the US said or imagined was democratic: 'They resorted to arbitrary arrests, confinement in concentration camps for undetermined periods of time without judicial guarantees or restraints, and assassinations of people suspected of Communist leanings. Their use of Gestapo-like police raids and torture were known and decried everywhere. Had they confined themselves to known Communists or proven Communist sympathizers, one could understand their methods. The repression, however, spread to people who simply opposed their regime, such as heads or spokesmen of other

political parties, and against individuals who were resisting extortion by some of the government officials.'

The destruction of village government left a visible target. The eventual Director of the CIA, William Colby, puts the date as 1957 – one year after the deadline for elections on reunification – when the North Vietnamese 'began to look South'. 'About 1957-8, the documentation shows, they began to think of re-activating their networks in the South,' says Colby. 'Now I think at that time they had a double approach. They would have been glad to kind of work their way into the political spectrum somewhere, or on the other hand they could go back to what they called People's War on which they had written the doctrine.'

The Hanoi leadership still sought a political solution, according to American historian Gareth Porter, and was 'consistently attempting to keep a lid' on former resistance people in the South who 'were eager to take up arms once again'. Porter says the round-up of suspected Communists brought 'very very strong pressure' on Hanoi. One sign of it was the increasing assassinations of Saigon-appointed village chiefs.

In January 1957 the International Control Commission (ICC), comprising observers from India, Poland and Canada, reported that neither South nor North Vietnam had honored the armistice agreement. The findings of the ICC would become ammunition for both sides. A Canadian ICC observer at that time, Christopher Dagg, says the 'absence of some spirit of detente between the two sides' rendered the Commission ineffective from the start.

Diem could now point to evidence of guerrilla activity. He already had an army of 135,000, trained by 300 American advisors, but he urgently requested Washington to accelerate the MAAG advisory program and to demonstrate US support.

In May, Diem was invited to address a joint session of Congress at which President Eisenhower declared: 'The cost of defending freedom, of defending America, must be paid in many forms and many places. Vietnam cannot at this time produce and support the military formations essential to its survival. Military as well as economic help is currently needed in Vietnam.'

Diem soon had stronger evidence for his argument. In October terrorist bombs wrecked US installations in Saigon. In January 1958 guerrilla bands attacked plantations north of Saigon. Diem now introduced the term 'Vietcong' – a pejorative abbreviation of Vietnamese Communists. It would become globally adopted, though it would finally express the same prestige as Viet Minh.

For both sides 1958 was the crunch year in judging mutual intentions. On 7 March, President Diem received a personal letter from North Vietnam's Prime Minister Pham Van Dong. It proposed discussion on troop reductions and trade relations as a renewed step towards reunification. Diem's reply of 26 April rejected any discussions until North Vietnam had established 'democratic liberties similar to those existing in the South'.

Washington's perspective of South-east Asia at that time is described by diplomat Kenneth Galbraith: 'It was, in my view, simplistic. There was the notion that this was part of the great revolution of the time, and that the revolution stemmed from a monolithic expression of the power of China and Russia, and no distinction was made between the Soviet Union and China at that time.'

Historian Gareth Porter asserts that the North Vietnamese 'were essentially following a Soviet policy as closely as they could of avoiding provoking the United States. But the pressures became stronger and stronger as time went by.' Porter's analysis is that in early 1959 Hanoi authorized cadres in the South to defend themselves if attacked in order to preserve their political base, but 'immediately the cadres in the South went beyond the authorization and began to take over whole segments of the countryside of South Vietnam'.

William Colby had now arrived in Saigon as CIA station chief, and found 'a gradual increase of Communist presence throughout the countryside'. Colby's analysis differs only slightly from Porter's. What was significant to Colby was 'the return of some of the people who had gone North in 1954'. The CIA estimated that 5000 Southern-born cadres infiltrated back in 1959, but Colby says their activity was essentially political.

'They first began the process of political organization in the villages,' says Colby, 'going through the villages, giving the arguments on behalf of the continuing revolution – now not against the French but against the Americans and Diem, who they called the American Diemist. This was the political approach: they were trying to identify the continued effort with the earlier nationalist effort. Now this struggle went on in the villages. There were speeches, recruiting, things of this nature, an occasional murder of a very vigorous village chief, an occasional murder of some corrupt official . . . this went on for a couple of years.'

Colby would later become Director of the Central Intelligence Agency. His recollections of the findings he presented at the time are in retrospect perhaps the most severe criticism of US policy by a principal advisor.

'Now at this point,' says Colby, 'I think a very critical fact of the Vietnam history arose and that is that the military there, and many of the military on our side, were of course thinking of the Korean war as a precedent for what might happen. Therefore as the tension level grew in Vietnam the tendency was to strengthen the military forces against the prospect of an attack by North Vietnam.

'Now here, I think, the Americans made a fundamental error that pursued us all the way through Vietnam, because we said "If there's a war going on it must be an affair for soldiers." '

In 1960, when as Colby notes the Sino-Soviet alliance was breaking up, the US doubled its mili-

tary advisory force in Vietnam to 685 men. Colby says that with Diem's approval he then pursued a strategy to win over the villages politically – called the Strategic Hamlet program. At this period those close to both Diem and Ho Chi Minh felt that neither regarded direct combat as necessary or unavoidable.

In Hanoi journalist Wilfred Burchett again met Ho Chi Minh after the formation by southern guerrillas of the National Liberation Front (NLF). Burchett had read the NLF program claiming a neutral foreign policy and he questioned Ho Chi Minh about this. 'Ho Chi Minh said, "It is up to them to decide. It is their problem. They know far better than we do what are the possibilities. And we think it is also an acceptable policy for them. It is one which would enable them to have the best relations with neighbors, which have chosen neutral policies – Cambodia and Laos. And one which is probably more acceptable also for the Western world in general. And so we think that this is quite a wise decision they have made – but in any case it is up to them." '

In Saigon Vietnamese officials, both pro and anti-Diem, found him anxious about US military and political intentions. Diem's press secretary at

that time, Ton That Thien, states that 'from 1960 on, the Americans started . . . stronger consultation, so they were thinking of moving into Vietnam at the time, and President Diem and especially his brother Nhu were dead set against the Americans moving in and taking over'.

A senior general, Tran Van Don, who was then losing confidence in Diem's personal rule, says there was agreement on the military objective to avoid 'a big war'. He then felt that 'we didn't need to have foreign troops. What we needed at the time was to pacify ourselves.'

But Tran Van Don also felt the dilemma which started with the 1960s: Diem had lost popular support, particularly among the peasantry which comprised eighty-five per cent of the population, and Diem 'began to be oppressive in his ambition. He would like to become King of Vietnam. He believed too much that God had ordered him to South Vietnam with a mystic mission.'

Diem's closest American friend now described the President as a 'recluse' inside his palace. Colonel Lansdale, returning to Saigon in December 1960 on a fact finding mission, found 'a very great contrast' in both guerrilla activity and

May 9, 1957—South Vietnamese President Ngo Dinh Diem addresses a joint session of Congress in Washington from the rostrum of the House of Representatives. Behind him are Vice President Richard M. Nixon and House Speaker Sam Rayburn.

May 7, 1957—President Ngo Dinh Diem of South Vietnam, on a state visit to the United States, views San Francisco from a sightseeing boat passing beneath the San Francisco–Oakland Bay Bridge. With him are Lt. Gen. John W. O'Daniel (ret.), left, chairman of the American Friends for Vietnam, and Robert Blum, head of the Asia Foundation.

May 9, 1957—President Dwight D. Eisenhower welcomes President Ngo Dinh Diem of South Vietnam to the White House for a candid talk on means of safeguarding Diem's communist-threatened country. At right is Secretary of State John Foster Dulles.

'active opposition to Diem and his measures.' Lansdale confides that 'I reported back to Washington that Diem had to be much more open in his leadership. He was depending more and more on his brother Nhu.'

Nhu and the CIA's Colby were co-ordinating the most unpopular measure – the Strategic Hamlets. In remote and guerrilla-active areas, villagers were relocated in larger 'agrovilles' or fortified camps, enclosed by ditches, barbed wire or spiked bamboo fences. Each Strategic Hamlet had a local militia guard. The program was presented as helping the villagers defend themselves. It was found that very few did, preferring to let in the guerrillas at night, then resume 'normalcy' by closing the barricades at dawn.

Such was the atmosphere – one of slow siege both in Saigon and Washington – when John F. Kennedy took office as President on 20 January 1961. Under Eisenhower the US had supported Diem as the price of 'defending freedom, of defending America', but Americans in Vietnam – and in particular the press – were reporting that there was no freedom under Diem. Two months earlier Diem's elite paratroop battalions had launched an unsuccessful coup against him. Two weeks after Kennedy's inauguration Diem was to stand for 're-election' – and the NLF had vowed a guerrilla offensive. But Kennedy, according to his aides, initially never considered cutting US losses in Vietnam, and up to then only one American advisor had been killed in guerrilla action.

Kennedy is portrayed as enormously influenced by the venerable soldier-father figure of Eisenhower, with Kennedy equating the advent of his own presidency with the need for a world police-chief to prevent what seemed the imminent threat of totalitarian terror. In the days before Kennedy's inauguration, Soviet Premier Khrushchev had made a tough speech in support of world revolutions, and in Laos the Royal Lao Army and the Communist Pathet Lao were suddenly at war.

On Inauguration Day, Eisenhower took Kennedy aside to give some urgent advice, according to Kennedy aide Roger Hilsman. The ex-President, having himself consistently avoided any US combat involvement in Southeast Asia, now pointed to Laos as justification for a much tougher policy toward Communism. 'Eisenhower said two things to him,' reveals Hilsman. 'First "Laos is your big problem" and second – and this is very important – Eisenhower said "I think you are going to have to send troops and if you do I will come up from Gettysburg and stand beside you and support you." '

Another Kennedy advisor, historian Arthur Schlesinger Jr, confirms this account, stating that Eisenhower in his briefing 'emphasized Laos'. 'He said that Laos was of very acute importance to the security of the United States. He even urged on Kennedy the notion of unilateral intervention in Laos if necessary. But Kennedy got [British Prime Minister] Macmillan to send Eisenhower a letter pointing out why this would be foolish terrain to commit white troops.'

However, Eisenhower's advice had a broad influence on Kennedy in the opinion of Clark Clifford, chief advisor in the transition period. Clifford arranged numerous formal briefings between the two men – the last on 19 January 1961, the eve of Kennedy's inauguration. Clifford was present taking notes.

Left: November 11, 1960—A wounded rebel is carried away by young spectators who watched South Vietnam paratroopers try to storm the palace of President Ngo Dinh Diem during an uprising in Saigon.

Below: November 11, 1960—A cyclist rides past a burning armored car in Saigon during an attack on the presidential palace.

'The first item on Eisenhower's agenda was South-east Asia. He attached unusual and unique importance to it. He said he had placed it first on the agenda because it offered the greatest danger to peace in the world. He ended his briefing on South-east Asia by saying that he felt the matter was so important that first we should call upon our member nations of SEATO. He said at the very end – and this is almost a quote – "If we cannot get our allies to help us, then we must do it unilaterally." '

Clark Clifford, who would later become Secretary of Defense, recalls that Eisenhower elaborated on his domino theory: 'He had in mind that if we let South Vietnam fall, the next domino Laos, Cambodia, Burma, and on down into the sub-continent would go, the Philippines would go and possibly even Australia and New Zealand. That had an enormous impact upon the thinking of President-Elect Kennedy.'

That was 19 January 1961. On 9 April President Diem was re-elected by an overwhelming majority and with little immediate guerrilla reaction. Kennedy's new Ambassador to Saigon, Frederick E. Nolting, reveals that Diem then told him that South Vietnam 'did not want combat troops' from the United States.

One month later, on 5 May, Kennedy declared at a press conference that if necessary he would consider the use of US forces 'to help South Vietnam resist Communist pressures'. Vice-President Lyndon Johnson would leave immediately for talks with Diem.

Ambassador Nolting was there during the Johnson discussions. 'The net result was a very strong communiqué giving US moral and material promises of support. There were toasts as usual, at the end of which Johnson toasted President Diem in very extravagant terms, really, as the George Washington of Vietnam. And we all rose and drank a toast in warm champagne.'

Before Johnson's return to Washington four days later a cease-fire had been announced in

Above: September 19, 1960 —The bodies of four Viet Cong guerrillas killed by civil guards are displayed for two days in the village square of Cai Lay, 50 miles southwest of Saigon. The local district leader said one of the rebels, Muoi Thau, was personally responsible for 50 terrorist killings in the area.

Right: September 19, 1960— Six Communist terrorists are in custody after they were taken prisoner by civil guards during a clash near Cay Lay, 50 miles southwest of Saigon.

Laos. On 16 May a fourteen-nation conference on Laos convened in Geneva, and following it Kennedy and Soviet Premier Khrushchev personally met in Vienna to affirm Lao neutrality. Within five months the situation which Eisenhower had cited as reason for the US to go to war had been resolved.

After leaving Khrushchev, Kennedy called on President de Gaulle in Paris. De Gaulle told him: 'The ideology that you invoke will not change anything. . . . You Americans wanted, yesterday, to take our place in Indo-China, you want to assume a succession to rekindle a war that we ended. I predict to you that you will, step by step, be sucked into a bottomless military and political quagmire.'

But Kennedy remained 'extremely sensitive' over Vietnam and, says aide Roger Hilsman, saw it in a global context with 'the world deemed to be exploding into wars of national liberation and Communist-led insurgencies'. Hilsman, a World War II OSS agent and one of Kennedy's key foreign policy planners, points to the 1961 Cuba (Bay of Pigs) invasion as Kennedy's first realization that the US should tone down its policy.

Hilsman worked with Kennedy throughout the Cuban crisis. 'Kennedy said many times, "The Bay of Pigs has taught me a number of things. One is not to trust Generals or the CIA, and the second is that if the American people do not want to use

American troops to remove a Communist regime ninety miles away from our coast, how can I ask them to use troops to remove a Communist regime 9000 miles away?" ' On the other hand, Kennedy evidently recognized the domestic political value of acting tough in foreign affairs.

One of Kennedy's special advisors, economist John Kenneth Galbraith, also listened to Kennedy react to the crises in Cuba and Laos which 'were both criticized as being in some sense a surrender'. Galbraith urged the President to consider 'the relative unimportance of Vietnam. And Kennedy said "Yes, I agree with you". But he said "There is the political problem. I can only have so many political defeats in one year." '

From late 1961 Kennedy is portrayed as torn by totally conflicting advice on both the military and political situation. The US military informed him that it estimated guerrilla strength at 17,000 men – up 300 per cent within two years but 'ninety per cent locally recruited'. Though Saigon's army had increased to 200,000 men, a guerrilla force had ransacked a provincial capital only sixty miles away without resistance. President Diem then declared a state of emergency and privately sent Kennedy an urgent letter requesting a bilateral security treaty. Kennedy now turned to General Maxwell D. Taylor, his personal military advisor.

'I met the President one morning in the

White House,' recalls Taylor. 'He was walking down the corridor and he said "I have a letter here from President Diem. Tell me how to answer it." Well I spent the next eleven years we were involved in answering the question because what it really amounted to was: would the United States favor a major increase in the military to accomplish the political objectives in Vietnam?'

In Vietnam, General Taylor consulted with Diem: 'It was always a bit of an ordeal. . . . The President insisted on going back two centuries to trace the historical background and bring it forward to the current time. The conversation was in French. He was constantly smoking a cigarette. He would get a glazy look in his eyes, as if he was dozing off himself. . . . It was hard going. But nonetheless I had a high regard for the little man. He was certainly an intense patriot.'

Taylor says he and Diem agreed that the United States and South Vietnam would 'make a new start' – meaning political reforms in return for new forms of military aid. Taylor's recommendations, delivered personally to Kennedy in November 1961, included a combat commitment.

Kennedy's political advisor, Arthur Schlesinger Jr, says a specific proposal was for 'a force of 9 or 10,000 combat troops disguised as a flood control mission'. Kennedy told Schlesinger he was 'very much opposed to this'.

But within weeks Kennedy compromised and dispatched the first American helicopter units, called 'Eagle Flights'. The 300 American pilots were ordered to lead the Vietnamese into battle but not to engage in combat – unless in self-defense. By early 1962 US military advisors in Vietnam had increased ten-fold to 4,000. These included detachments of Green Berets, or Special Forces, as the main cutting edge of a new Counter-Insurgency Council chaired by General Maxwell D. Taylor.

One of the Green Berets, Captain Brian Jenkins, stresses that Kennedy's decision was generally popular. 'One has to recall the rhetoric of the Kennedy era, whether it was in the form of the Peace Corps – this new invention of the Kennedy era – or in the form of the Army Special Forces, another symbol of willingness to become engaged. There were notions of patriotism, of serving one's country, and volunteering for even more as it were. It was always a very special relationship between Kennedy and the Special Forces. They were the closest thing in the United States to Kennedy's own. They had a specialized capability for dealing with guerrilla warfare.'

But at the same time Kennedy is pictured as wondering what he was doing. A Kennedy confidant at the State Department, Graham Martin, then liaising with the Pentagon on updating military strategy, recalls advising that the Green Berets were a mistake because they had been taught 'to be guerrillas, not anti-guerrillas'. Martin records the reaction of both Robert and John F. Kennedy: 'I know from my own personal experience how concerned they were that the Americans really were not capable of understanding and coping with this kind of war.'

Kennedy's Secretary of State Dean Rusk depicts him as bemused and burdened by the expectations of the globe: 'Vietnam posed for us a serious question about where we're going in respect of collective security', and Rusk stresses that if the US 'had done nothing about Vietnam' then its allies would have been the first to say 'You see, you cannot trust the Americans'.

America's way out of the dilemma now depended on a recluse Prime Minister of seventeen million people 9000 miles away – on Diem's promised reforms at grass roots. Kennedy got conflicting reports on the purpose of Diem and his Strategic Hamlets. In 1962 the Saigon government reported that it had built 4000 of an intended 11,000 Strategic Hamlets and that thirty-nine per cent of South Vietnam's population had been resettled in these. (When the author visited one in 1962, there was sudden guerrilla fire from nearby, and the hamlet defenders, youths hardly taller than their rifles, immediately threw open the fortified gate and threw down their guns. The pilot of the US helicopter who had flown in the author and the cameraman observed what had occurred and came back to the rescue.)

Ambassador Nolting, after 'traveling about three-quarters of the forty-four provinces', became convinced that Diem was 'most respected as a leader'. He characterized Diem as 'a very honest mandarin' and rejected criticism of Diem's family. 'The influence of his brothers was on the whole, in my opinion, certainly not bad, in many cases good,' considers Nolting. 'For example, Ngo Dinh Nhu was the inspiration for the Strategic Hamlet program which in my opinion was a successful way to protect the peasant population from the depredations of the Vietcong.'

Kennedy now had to weigh the judgement of his Ambassador against identical words used by the Prime Minister of North Vietnam and the US Assistant Secretary of State, Roger Hilsman. In Premier Pham Van Dong's words: 'They organized camouflaged concentration camps dubbed "prosperity zones", "agricultural settlements" and "Strategic Hamlets".'

In Hilsman's words: 'Diem and his brother Nhu actively resisted the counter-insurgency program. They took the so-called Strategic Hamlets which were supposed to protect the people and made concentration camps. There was just an utter complete reversal of the policy we were enunciating.'

Hilsman goes further and suggests – as the CIA's William Colby had – that the US military and 'West Pointers' considered there could only be a military solution, and that 'winning hearts and minds was somebody else's job'. Hilsman's circle became 'convinced that the military subverted the program and deliberately sabotaged it and even lied to us'.

As Hilsman says, 'I think the tragedy is greater than that. President Kennedy sent me out specifically to try to explain the theory behind this policy to [Commander in Chief] General Harkins. I don't think he misunderstood the policy. I came to the conclusion years later that he and the people under him thought that it was somebody else's business.'

Kennedy now had his personal, political and military advisors, his Ambassador and Commander in Chief in the field, the people at the State Department, Pentagon and CIA all at odds in a chain of blame. And by late 1962 he had 12,000 military 'advisors' in Vietnam to carry out the tactics no one could agree on or define. Kennedy continued to send out a succession of observers.

His Assistant Secretary of Defense, Paul Nitze, states: 'North Vietnamese infiltration had been

Above: April 29, 1961—Ngo Dinh Diem delivers his inaugural address for his second five-year term as president of the Republic of Vietnam. Behind him are members of the National Assembly.

Below: March 16, 1961—U.S. President John F. Kennedy sits in his favorite rocking chair at the White House as he meets with Defense Secretary Robert S. McNamara and Vice President Lyndon B. Johnson.

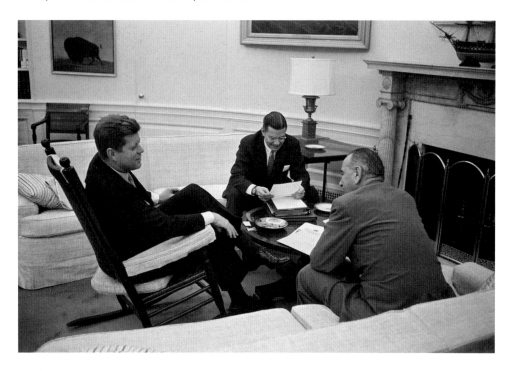

highly successful. They had achieved in part their aim of destroying the normal structure village by village. . . . It was the kind of political action that I had seen undertaken in other parts of the world. Therefore it was to my mind extremely doubtful that we could – through military action – reverse this problem.'

His personal military advisor, General Maxwell Taylor, states: 'Our civilians in the Embassy, and our military people in our mission in Saigon, were all convinced that South Vietnam could never make it against the increased

Vietcong effort without American aid and American presence.'

His special advisor, Kenneth Galbraith, states: 'One had a sense on all sides of the pathological incompetence and unpopularity of the government at the time. Here were just a few thousand Vietcong guerrillas scattered over that still quite huge country and a vast array of armed men already incapable of doing anything about them.'

His CIA station chief, William Colby, states: 'Now my argument was frankly a little in between. I disagreed that the problem was a military war, but I also disagreed that democratizing at the Saigon level wouldn't make much difference. I was convinced that sooner or later Vietnam would democratize a little bit.'

White House aide Schlesinger recounts that in early 1963 when 'Kennedy had been assailed by this conflicting advice' he sent a two-man mission to Vietnam – a counter-insurgency expert, General Victor Krulak, and State Department official Joseph A. Mendenhall, who had previous experience of Vietnam. Schlesinger says: 'The National Security Council was assembled to hear their views. Krulak said that everything in Vietnam was going fine. Diem is a much loved figure, the morale is high, and all we need do is just back him to the end and he will win the war. Then Mendenhall reported and said Diem was extremely unpopular, the regime was in a very precarious state, the Buddhists dislike him, the liberal democrats dislike him and he does not provide any kind of possible basis for a successful American policy. President Kennedy listened very carefully and said finally, "Were you two gentlemen in the same country?" '

The Vietnam morass divided Kennedy's advisors into two distinct camps. There were those who blamed his early 'simplistic' script of America the global policeman arresting Communism. The Kennedy administration had taken a decisive step away from massive retaliation when it was 'officially recognized that this was dangerous nonsense', says former Assistant Secretary of Defense Adam Yarmolinsky, but even so Kennedy believed that the Sino-Soviet alliance could be contained if 'one of their henchmen and one of our Green Berets go off in the forest and fight a duel. And when the duel is over and we win, everybody goes back to building sewage systems for the villages of the Third World.'

The other camp would insist that the scenario was right but that Ngo Dinh Diem was miscast ('a mandarin of the marshes'), a leader whose staying power was in not leaving his palace for most of nine years. This camp would now prevail as Buddhist riots over alleged religious persecution escalated through the summer of 1963. The pivotal crisis developed after the Diem government's denial of the simple right of flying a religious flag on Buddha's birthday. Diem's troops killed forty Buddhist demonstrators and arrested thousands more.

In the words of Kennedy's Assistant Secretary of State, Roger Hilsman, 'Here you had a country that's ninety-five per cent Buddhist, led by French-speaking Vietnamese who were beating up pagodas, killing nuns, killing priests. I would say

certainly by the beginning of the Buddhist crisis he [Kennedy] was already discouraged; by the middle of it I think he was totally discouraged.' President Diem himself, in conversation with the author, stubbornly insisted that the Buddhist opposition was Communist-inspired.

On 11 June, in an image that seared Kennedy and the world, a Buddhist monk (Thich Quang Duc) was drenched in gasoline on a Saigon street and then set light to himself. Diem's sister-in-law, Madame Nhu, laughed off the suicide, calling it a 'barbecue'.

The CIA's William Colby was then back in Washington: 'The thing that did as much as anything to lead to the overthrow of Ngo Dinh Diem was that photograph of the bonze burning himself. Now the fact was that the bonze did that in protest against Diem. The fact also was that his fellow bonzes had alerted the press in a rather cynical maneuver to get the maximum possible coverage.' Ambassador Nolting supported Diem's explanation: 'It was contrived in my opinion, strictly by the Vietcong. It was a political rather than religious outbreak with political rather than religious motives.'

Kennedy abruptly relieved Nolting, who heard the name of his successor 'over the public radio'; the Ambassador was now considered too

Above: May 13, 1961—Vice President Lyndon B. Johnson says good-bye to Vietnamese youth groups and children at Saigon Airport.

Left: Black areas on map locate the five main areas where, in 1961, the Viet Cong boasted centers of strength and control over parts of the countryside. Arrows and broken line show inland supply routes along jungle trails through Laos and Cambodia. Small arrows indicate coastal infiltration points used by junks and fishing craft from the north.

Above: March 1961—With a Viet Cong flag still flying in the background, South Vietnamese troops pose with the bodies of Viet Cong guerrillas in the Mekong Delta region.

Above: 1961—Ngo Dinh Diem, president of South Vietnam, rides through the streets of Saigon.

Left: April 1961—Shaven-headed Buddhist nuns walk in a solemn procession through the grounds of a pagoda at Vinh Binh as they pray for peace.

close to Diem. Nolting comments that 'quite frankly – here I'm going to be very, very frank – I think some influences in the State Department, principally, were glad to have me away . . . because they wanted to give Diem a lot of rope to hang himself. There was a dump Diem movement which I could feel in the atmosphere coming from people like [Under Secretary of State] Averell Harriman, Roger Hilsman, and others – in the White House. This was against the CIA's advice: I'd like to get that on the record.'

Hilsman says that the Geneva Accords, ignored seven years earlier, and their success in Laos, which two years earlier had been viewed as the first toppling domino perhaps warranting East-West war, now became Kennedy's model. Hilsman was informed by Kennedy that 'the time had come for us to seriously consider withdrawing. In my

office as Assistant Secretary for Far Eastern Affairs we began actively to seek ways to withdraw. We began to look for a neutralist leader in Vietnam as we had in [Premier] Souvanna Phouma in Laos around whom we could build a Geneva Accord neutralizing the country.'

William Bundy, Deputy Assistant Secretary of Defense, recounts the stages of Washington's dealings with Diem up to late August 1963, by which time six Buddhist monks had committed public suicide. 'We exerted all the private influence we could to get him [Diem] to adopt reform measures. He did not do so, but instead in August there was obviously a calculated seizure of the main [Xa Loi] Buddhist temple in Saigon, and some very nasty repressive measures followed. Kennedy had to consider whether we should seek to dissociate ourselves from him . . . to get a really truly consulta-

tive government – not a democratic one, but a consultative one.'

William Colby of the CIA recalls a year-long crisis atmosphere as 'the debate raged between the two poles of we cannot win the war with Diem and the other side saying that we have no choice but to continue to support this particular government, carrying on the struggle in basically the right direction, and we can solve these problems later after we beat down the Communist threat. And that argument raged through the year of 1963.'

By then General Maxwell D. Taylor was chairman of the Joint Chiefs of Staff. 'We saw these dramatic and terribly impressive pictures of Buddhist monks burning themselves – presumably in protest at the tyrannical rule of Diem. It resulted in really a split between Kennedy's advisors on where do we go from here – because there was a strong group that had picked up the slogan "You can't win with Diem". The other group, to which I belonged, argued maybe we can't win with Diem, but if not Diem – who? And the answer was complete silence.

'So we never really got our hands on the situation at the Washington end. President Kennedy was hoping that it would work itself out, and became sympathetic to the idea of a coup if the Americans were not responsible, and not involved in it.'

Above: The Mekong Delta area.

Above: April 29, 1955—A Vietnamese paratrooper takes cover as refugees flee the Cholen area of Saigon during fighting with rebel Binh Xuyen.

Left: April 29, 1955—Fires from heavy street fighting between rebel Binh Xuyen sect forces and government troops rage over Saigon.

Above: April 28, 1955—Refugees run for cover in Saigon during fighting between army forces and soldiers of the Binh Xuyen sect.

Above: April 6, 1955—Injured are removed from the scene of a terrorist bomb explosion in a customs building in Saigon.

Above: April 1955—Troops patrol the streets of Saigon following the attack by three of South Vietnam's numerous private armies on the residence of Premier Ngo Dinh Diem, the army headquarters, and the prefecture.

Right: April 29, 1955—Soldiers in a National Army armored car move past a bright fire in Saigon during fighting with Binh Xuyen demonstrators.

Left: April 28, 1955—Refugees, some carrying children, flee fire and fighting in Saigon. Soldiers of Ngo Dinh Diem fought with the private army of the Binh Xuyen sect.

Above: April 29, 1955—Firemen battle a blazing building on Boulevard Gallieni as fighting continues with the Binh Xuyn near the new police security building.

Right: April 28, 1955—Civilians run from a street battle in Saigon in which forces of Prime Minister Ngo Dinh Diem defeated troops of the rebel Binh Xuyen sect.

Above: April 29, 1955—National Army soldiers battle the Bink Xuyen sect as fighting raged in the center of Saigon.

Right: May 2, 1955—South Vietnamese paratroops take a break before leaving battle-scarred Cholon after defeating the private army of the Binh Xuyen Society.

Above: May 1955—After a grim battle against the Binh Xuyen Society private army, a soldier of the victorious South Vietnamese army enjoys time with his pet monkey.

Below: April 28, 1955—Terror-stricken residents of Saigon flee from burning ruins of their homes.

Right: May 1955—A child sits in a basin awaiting the return of his parents, who were nearby searching the ruins of what was their home in Cholen, the Chinese community of Saigon. The area was destroyed in fighting between government troops and the Binh Xuyen.

Above: June 1955—South Vietnamese troops train with U.S. weapons.

Above: Some 300,000 people applauded Vietnamese army troops during parade to celebrate their victory of the Binh Xuyen rebels in the swamps south of Saigon. The battle was an important victory for the Diem regime.

Above: July 28, 1955—Agricultural gifts from the United States are prepared for distribution in Cantho during Premier Ngo Dinh Diem's trip to southern South Vietnam. Included are sacks of seed, fertilizer, plows, and shovels.

Above: July 20, 1955—Student rioters do $1 million damage to the Majestic Hotel in Saigon during anti-communist protests.

Above: June 12, 1955—South Vietnamese premier waves to the crowd as he leaves a village in the Banmethuot mountain region.

Left: September 1955—Infantrymen stand at attention in water as Premier Ngo Dinh Diem makes a tour of the troops in the Rung Sat swamp to thank the men who defeated the rebel Binh Xuyen forces.

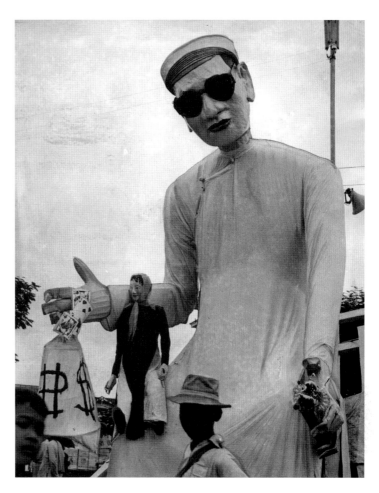

Above: December 21, 1955—For the first time, tribesmen from the mountains and plateaus of Vietnam come to Saigon to swear allegiance to the new republic and pay their respects to President Ngo Dinh Diem *(left)*.

Right: October 1955—An effigy of Vietnamese emperor Bao Dai stands outside Saigon's main marketplace before his twenty-three-year rule ended with the election of Premier Ngo Dinh Diem. Bao Dai is lampooned with playing cards, a money bag, and woman on his knee to satirize his absentee existence on the French Riviera.

Left: October 26, 1955—A crowd outside Independence Palace in Saigon listens to Ngo Dinh Diem proclaim the new Republic of South Vietnam, with himself as president and prime minister. Ngo received 98 percent of the votes in the referendum against the absentee emperor, Bao Dai.

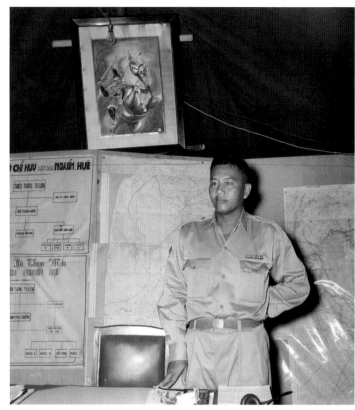

Above: April 1956—Gen. Duong Van Minh, leader of the operation to defeat the sects threatening the Diem regime. In 1963, as a leader of the coup that toppled Diem, he would briefly become head of state.

Above: January 2, 1955—Ngo Dinh Diem, the new president, makes his appearance at celebrations marking the establishment of South Vietnam as a republic.

Right: May 1956—A 500-meter-long multicolored dragon, constructed by the Chinese community of Saigon, is prepared for a parade to commemorate the first anniversary of the national police force under the direction of Gen. Nguyen Ngoc Le.

Above: 1957—Ho Chi Minh, president of North Vietnam.

Right: March 1957—A parade in Saigon celebrates the anniversary of the ancient soldiers who fought for the Trung sisters, who led the first national uprising against the Chinese in about A.D. 40.

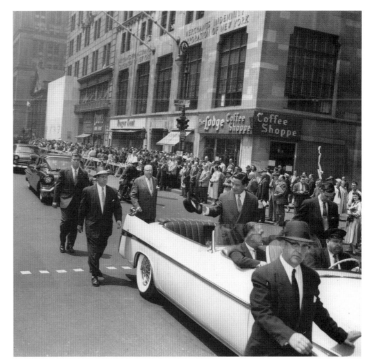

Above: May 13, 1957—President Ngo Dinh Diem of South Vietnam waves from his open car in a parade in his honor on Broadway during his three-day visit to New York following his meetings with President Dwight D. Eisenhower in Washington.

Left: May 8, 1957—U.S. President Dwight D. Eisenhower rides in an open car at National Airport in Washington with Ngo Dinh Diem, president of South Vietnam.

Above: September 1960—Some barefooted, some wearing only rubber sneakers, bootless South Vietnamese troops parade in Saigon in a training session, armed with French World War II rifles. About 30,000 troops are the mainstay of the South Vietnamese forces.

Left: Man and child in a Montagnard village.

Above: 1961—Vice President Lyndon B. Johnson inspects guard of South Vietnam's President Ngo Dinh Diem during a full military honor ceremony on his arrival in Saigon.

Above: October 28, 1960—The fifth anniversary of the Republic of South Vietnam is celebrated with a military parade on Thong Nhut Boulevard in Saigon.

June 1961—South Vietnamese militiamen, automatic weapons in hand, stand guard in My Qudi, a village about 75 miles southwest of Saigon in an area threatened by guerrilla forces.

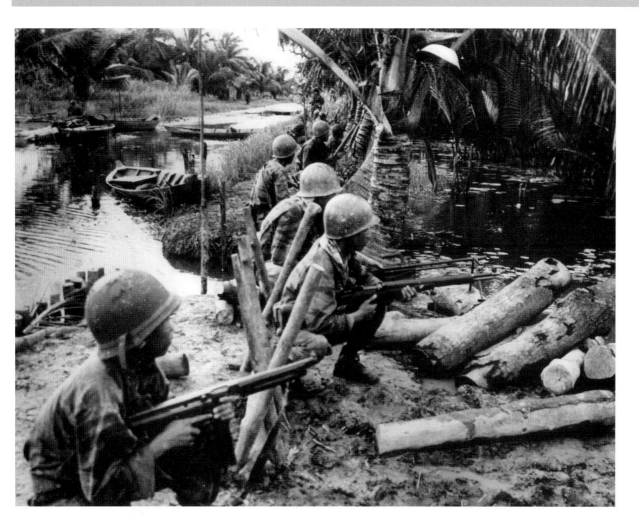

Left: January 1961—A squad of South Vietnamese marines, using American weapons, crouch on a stream bank during a hunt for guerrillas.

Below: July 1961—A South Vietnamese soldier chats with civilians in front of a typical Vietnamese military control tower, a lookout post made of brick walls and thatched roof.

Above: March 1961—Saigon citizens crowd in to look at posters of presidential candidates. Six candidates were running for Vietnam's presidency and vice presidency.

Left: October 1961—American advisor instructs Vietnamese troops in the operation of a machine gun.

Above: December 12, 1961—An elderly woman bursts into tears as she kneels in prayer at a huge container holding the ashes of 21 villagers killed by Viet Cong terrorists at her village about 140 miles southwest of Saigon. The incident took place during a rare ceremony in which mountain tribes came to Saigon to pledge fealty to President Diem and his government.

Below: December 22, 1961—The grave of U.S. Army Specialist 4 James Thomas Davis in Livingston, Tennessee, in 1985. On December 22, 1961, Davis became the first U.S. soldier killed in Vietnam when the unit he had been advising was ambushed by the Viet Cong.

Above: August 1961—Government troops line up at Moc Hoa village, about 60 miles southwest of Saigon, following victory over Viet Cong rebels during which they seized vast stores of arms and munitions.

Above: June 1961—A South Vietnamese patrol passes through a Mekong Delta village following numerous Viet Cong raids in the rice-growing region, about 115 miles southwest of Saigon.

Above: 1962—A Viet Cong bugler sounds a victory call. According to information with this photo, which was taken from the body of dead VC, Viet Cong use the bugle announcements and pictures like this to inspire confidence in their cause.

Right: Walt W. Rostow, a member of the Kennedy and Johnson administrations, was one of the 'best and brightest' who led the United States into the Vietnam War.

Left: October 10, 1961— Maxwell Taylor inspects a 105mm Howitzer during a visit to Vietnam.

Left: July 18, 1955—Ho Chi Minh *(center)*, president of North Vietnam, and A. I. Mikoyan, first deputy premier of the Soviet Union, sign a joint declaration in the Kremlin under which the Soviets agree to allocate 400 million roubles to help restore North Vietnam's economy, train Vietnamese technicians, and build 25 projects in North Vietnam.

Left: 1955—Ho Chi Minh stands with Chinese Premier Mao Tse-Tung before leaving Hong Kong for Hanoi after a tour of China and the Soviet Union. The two children had presented flowers to Ho, who praised the Soviet Union and China as 'friendly countries' that helped the Vietminh with money and materials.

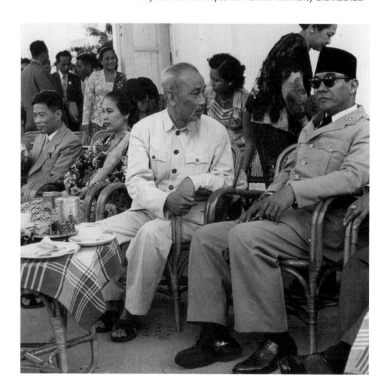

Above: March 1, 1959—North Vietnam's president Ho Chi Minh turns to speak with President Ahmed Sukarno during a meeting on arrival at Tjipans, Indonesia.

Below: August 13, 1957—Ho Chi Minh delivers an address to a gathering of thousands of Bulgarians at Ninth of September Square in Sophia. The president of North Vietnam was on a five-day visit to the Balkan state during his tour of communist countries.

Above: August 5, 1957—North Vietnamese President Ho Chi Minh, on a tour of European communist countries, receives a toast from President Joseph Broz Tito during a luncheon at the Yugoslav Federal Executive Council in Belgrade.

Left: June 1955—Ho Chi Minh (left), president of North Vietnam, and his host, Premier Chou En-lai of China, share places of honor at a banquet in Beijing.

Below: February 1962—With U.S. Army Rangers in the background acting as advisers, a South Vietnamese Ranger marches from his camp on a patrol for communist guerrillas.

Above: February 1962—South Vietnamese troops aboard a U.S. helicopter await landing near a Viet Cong stronghold at the southern tip of Vietnam. The troops reported success in driving out a strong Viet Cong force.

Left: January 25, 1962—Lights brighten the streets near Saigon's central market in preparation for Tet, the Vietnamese New Year.

Right: February 1962—South Vietnamese marines ride a small river craft looking for Viet Cong near the village of Ap Ton Long.

Left: February 1962—South Vietnamese marines cross a muddy ditch in South Vietnam's southern province of An Xuyen to look for Viet Cong rebels.

Above: February 27, 1962—One of two South Vietnamese air force planes, flown by dissident pilots, circles over President Ngo Diem's palace in Saigon. No one was injured when the planes bombed, rocketed, and strafed the palace, setting part of the building on fire.

Right: February 26, 1962—The palace in Saigon is hit by an isolated attack by two members of the South Vietnamese air force. President Ngo Dinh Diem was unhurt.

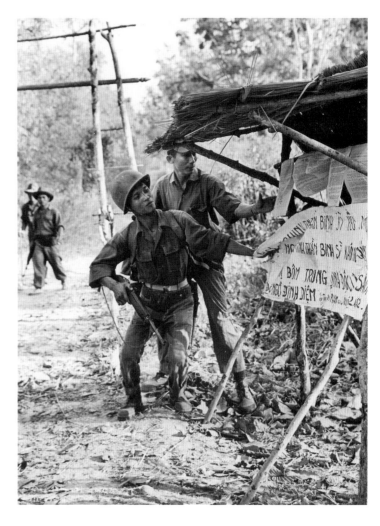

Above: March 12, 1962—A South Vietnamese militiaman holds his weapon at the ready during a training session. Armed with simple weapons, the militia is trained to hold off rebel attacks until regular military forces arrive.

Right: March 24, 1962—South Vietnamese soldiers tear down signs critical of President Ngo Dinh Diem near a Viet Cong stronghold at Tam An, 15 miles northwest of Saigon.

Left: March 1962—A peasant pushes her small boat away from the converted carrier U.S.S. *Breton*, which arrived in Saigon with a shipment of U.S. aircraft, including 30 single-engine T-28 fighters and H-21 helicopters, for the South Vietnamese air force. U.S. officials announced that American pilots were engaged in combat missions to train South Vietnamese pilots.

Above: March 1962—A government soldier checks the tall sword grass near Tourane, where it provides good hiding for enemy soldiers.

Above: March 1962—Bodies of government militiamen, killed in a Viet Cong ambush, lie on the edge of a water hole in Xuyen province.

Left: April 1962—A gunner keeps his weapon ready as his chopper, carrying South Vietnamese troops, heads for a rendezvous with other troops to undertake a cleanup operation in the Mekong Delta.

Above: April 28, 1962—With a captured Viet Cong flag in the foreground, a South Vietnamese officer looks over the bodies of Viet Cong troops killed during a sweep of Phong Dinh province, 110 miles southwest of Saigon.

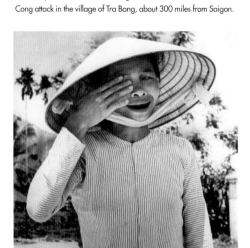

Below: April 5, 1962—A mother grieves for her son, slain in a Viet Cong attack in the village of Tra Bong, about 300 miles from Saigon.

Above: April 1, 1962—Ngo Dinh Nhu, brother and closest advisor to President Ngo Dinh Diem, reviews troops in a strategic hamlet at Cu Chi.

Below: May 18, 1962—Handcuffed Viet Cong prisoners, part of a group of 34 captured, file to a prison camp near Saigon during Operation Dan Tien. The prisoners, including a captain, were captured about 50 miles southwest of Saigon.

Above: April 5, 1962—President Ngo Dinh Diem leads a ceremony honoring soldiers and civilians who died in South Vietnam's fight against the communists.

Above: June 1962—An amphibious vehicle cruises along a river during a search for signs of Viet Cong rebels.

Below: July 1962— A South Vietnamese soldier escorts a blindfolded Viet Cong prisoner through a swamp in the Plaine de Joncs during an operation against a Viet Cong command center.

Above: June 1962—Two Viet Cong guerrillas, captured by U.S.-trained tribesmen, are held in a bamboo-covered pit under armed guard. The fortified training camp was near Ban Me Thout, in the central plateau area of South Vietnam.

Above: July 1962—South Vietnamese troops dash out of a U.S. Marine helicopter as another is about to land on a reed plain near Rach Gia on the Gulf of Siam.

Right: July 2, 1962—Special Forces advisor teaches mountain tribesmen the finer points of aiming and using a rifle at a fortified training camp near Ban Me Thout in central Vietnam. The purpose is to arm and train villagers to protect their villages against Viet Cong attack.

Above: July, 1962—South Vietnamese troops examine machine guns, ammunition and other Viet Cong supplies captured during a routine patrol in the countryside.

Right: July 1962—U.S. Special Forces personnel show Montagnard fighters the finer points of rifle handling and safety during a training session.

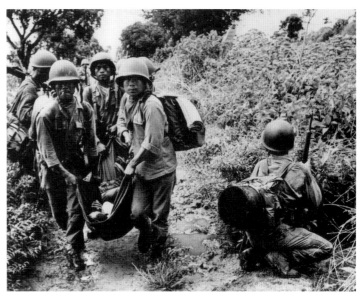

Above: August 1962—A platoon leader, seriously wounded when he stepped on a mine, is carried by Vietnamese soldiers retreating from the mountain where they unsuccessfully attacked the Viet Cong.

Above: August 24, 1962—A Vietnamese Marine threatens a captured Viet Cong guerrilla during a field interrogation in the southern delta region of South Vietnam.

Right: August 1962—As helicopter delivers supplies, soldiers take advantage of a lull in the action to improve bunker fortifications.

Above: August 24, 1962—A South Vietnamese Marine questions captured Viet Cong guerrillas in a weed-filled marsh of the southern delta region. The prisoners were searched, bound and questioned before being marched to join others captured during the raid.

Above: August 1962—A U.S. H-21 Shawnee helicopter flies over a Catholic church in Hue.

Above: August 1962—Baskets of chickens, ducks, and fruit are loaded into a helicopter at Hue for a supply flight to South Vietnamese outposts near the Laotian border.

Below: August 1962—A South Vietnamese soldier marches a Viet Cong suspect and a small boy through marshland in the southern Mekong Delta after a spotter plane called in government ground troops sweeping the area.

Above: August 18, 1962—Vietnamese soldiers pass a burning Viet Cong hut in the village of Ap Ba Nam, a communist stronghold in South Vietnam's Camau province. A watchtower was among the installations destroyed by the government force of some 4,000 troops on the five-day mission.

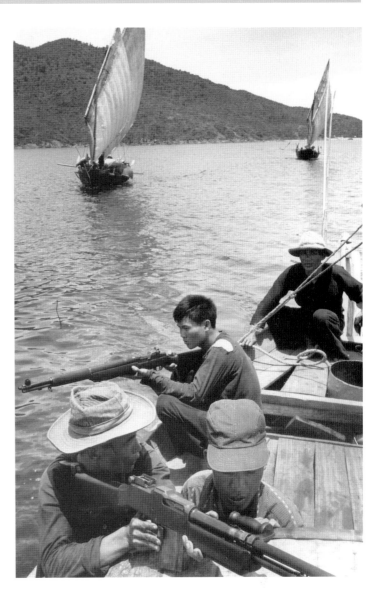

Above: August 1962—The crew of a Vietnamese junk take part in training exercises near the Danang naval base. A fleet of 40 junks patrolled the waters off South Vietnam to intercept Viet Cong forces arriving in similar vessels.

Left: August 1962—Artillery troops of the South Vietnamese 25th Division line up for a parade with their 105 and 155 Howitzers in the coastal town of Quang Nai.

Above: August 20, 1962—Fear is the telling feature on his man's face as he is interrogated by troops after a strike against the Viet Cong in the delta area.

Left: August 1962—South Vietnamese government troops from the 2nd Battalion of the 36th Infantry sleep in a U.S. Navy troop carrier on their way back to the provincial capital of Ca Mau. The soldiers were on a four-day and night operation against the Viet Cong communists in the swamplands of the southern tip of the country.

Above: August 12, 1962—South Vietnamese troops rush toward waiting helicopters and a five-day mission against the Viet Cong, part of a 4,000-man operation in southern Camau province.

Above: August 1962—A U.S. Army H-21 helicopter lands at an outpost east of Quang Nai, near the Laotian border. Remote Vietnamese observation posts such as this one near the demilitarized zone depend on supplies flown in by helicopter.

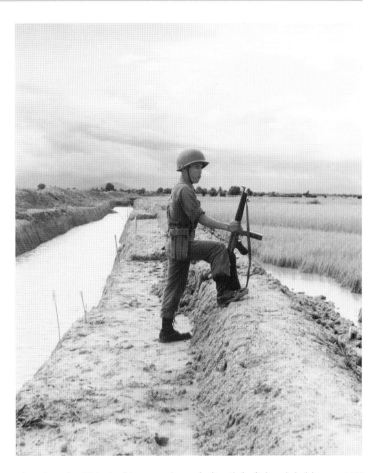

Above: September 1962—A militiaman guards part of a five-mile fortified trench, built by some 4,000 residents of Phan Thiet, that serves as a defense perimeter against the Viet Cong.

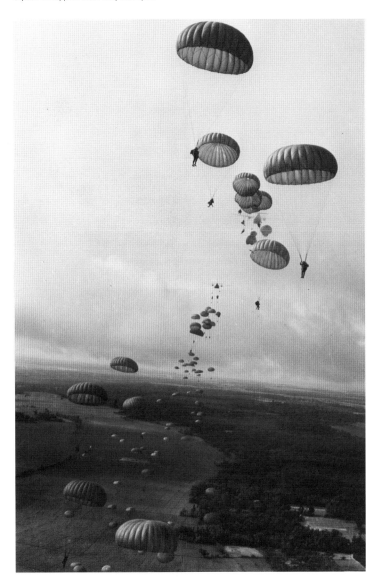

Above: September 25, 1962—Paratroopers of the 6th Vietnamese airborne battalion drift earthward in an operation northeast of Saigon.

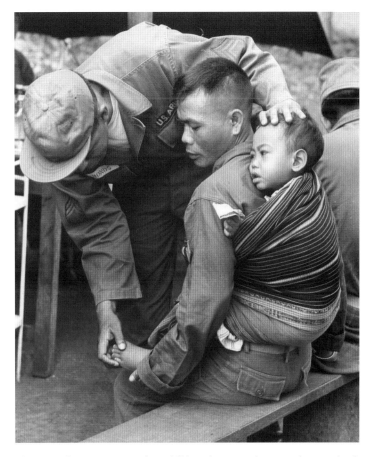

Above: September 1962—A U.S. medic at a field hospital in Ban Me Thuot treats a boy carried on the back of his uniformed father, a Radai tribesman trained in the Highlands by government Rangers.

Above: October 24, 1962—Ngo Dinh Nhu, younger brother and political advisor to South Vietnamese President Ngo Dinh Diem, parades through the National Stadium in Saigon. He took an oath before 3,000 delegates of the Cong Hoa (Republican) Youth to carry out faithfully the job of leader of the Vietnamese Youth Organization, a 1.5-million member group that helps fight Viet Cong in hamlets.

Above: October 1962—South Vietnamese troops and a U.S. adviser, far right, fan out from a U.S. Marine helicopter. The extensive use of helicopters in Vietnam was just beginning, and the combat capabilities of helicopters were expanding.

Left: October 1962—U.S. advisor trains Vietnamese troops in the use of a flame thrower.

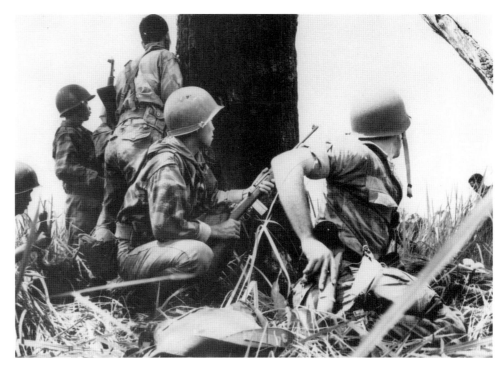

Above: October 13, 1962—From behind a big tree, South Vietnamese soldiers watch Viet Cong guerrillas move into position for an ambush on a road about 60 miles northwest of Saigon.

Above: October 1962—Two U.S. Rangers wear camouflage as they train South Vietnamese troops in a jungle clearing. Of the thousands of U.S. servicemen then in Vietnam, the Rangers reportedly did much of the dangerous jungle training.

Left: November 1962—A U.S. Army sergeant advises a group of district volunteers during an operations training mission in South Vietnam.

Above: November 16, 1962—Flying at first light, U.S. Army H-21 Shawnee helicopters carry South Vietnamese troops over rice paddies on an operation to intercept Viet Cong troops reported near Cantho, about 55 miles southwest of Saigon. No significant enemy contact was made during a day-long search.

Above: November 1962—A U.S. officer advising South Vietnamese forces poses with a group of Montagnards at a military camp in central Vietnam after government troops relocated the tribal people from a forced labor camp of the Viet Cong. South Vietnam's government hoped for the Montagnards' support in the fight against communist forces.

Below: November 17, 1962—Viet Cong prisoners carry a wounded comrade into a helicopter of the U.S. 93rd helicopter support company after being rounded up by Vietnamese troopers near Mytho, 50 miles southwest of Saigon. A U.S. advisor follows.

Above: November 1962—Peasants ferry government troops in sampans through flooded reeds in South Vietnam in a search for underwater Viet Cong hideouts. Guerrillas can stay underwater for hours by making breathing tubes out of the bamboo.

Left: December 1962—A South Vietnamese trooper, in pain after being wounded in battling the Viet Cong in the Mekong Delta, is ferried on a sampan toward an evacuation helicopter.

Above: December 1962—Their hands tied behind their backs, communist guerrilla fighters cross a creek at gunpoint of South Vietnamese soldiers. The prisoners were taken during fighting in the delta area south of Saigon.

Left: December 1962—Capt. George Ingraham, a doctor from Oakland, California, treats a wounded Vietnamese soldier aboard a U.S. helicopter after being evacuated from Pleimrong, a training center for Montagnard tribesmen, for the 25-mile trip to Pleiku.

Left: December 1962—A crewman runs through high grass near the village of Ca Mau at the southern tip of South Vietnam after a troop helicopter crashed during a government raid on the Viet Cong–infiltrated area. After transferring personnel to another helicopter, the crashed aircraft was completely destroyed to keep it out of enemy hands.

Above: December 1962—Vietnamese troops, some of them wounded, run to a waiting helicopter after another U.S. helicopter crashed near the village of Ca Mau at the southern tip of Vietnam.

Right: December 1962—A U.S. Special Forces soldier jumps from a helicopter near Tacanh, north of Kontum. U.S. Special Forces and South Vietnamese Rangers were parachuting into almost inaccessible Central Highlands, a Viet Cong stronghold, on intelligence patrols.

Right: December 16, 1962—Aerial view of a self-defense village built for Montagnard tribes to protect them from Viet Cong attack. Previously the mountain people lived in two- and three-family groups and were easy targets for the Viet Cong. The resettlement villages bring more people together and are designed as fortifications.

Below: December 12, 1962—U.S. Defense Secretary Robert McNamara inspects Vietnamese civil guards during a visit to training operations at Song Mao, 100 miles east of Saigon. McNamara is accompanied by Col. Nguyen Quoc Hoang, chief of Binh Thuan province.

Above: December 5, 1962—A Vietnamese soldier questions a woman at Ca Mau in the swampy delta area of southern Vietnam. She was asked about her husband, a suspected Viet Cong rebel.

Left: 1963—Viet Cong guerrillas move past two trussed and wounded prisoners during operations in Vinh Long province.

Above: 1963—President Ho Chi Minh is surrounded by representatives of ethnic minorities living in North Vietnam during their visit to Hanoi.

Left: 1963—Madame Ngo Dinh Nhu officiates at a construction project of a Social Welfare Center of the Vietnamese Women's Solidarity Movement of Saigon.

Below: 1963—A patient is treated in a Viet Cong aid station, according to information obtained in this picture captured by government forces.

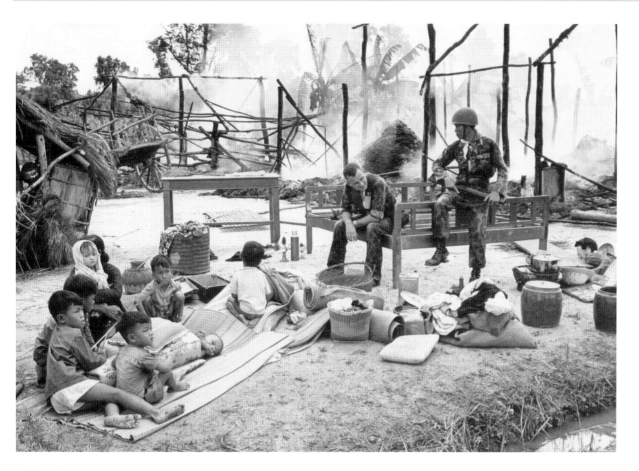

Left: January 1963—A U.S. military adviser sits in the wreckage of a village burned by South Vietnamese government troops. Soldiers discovered large quantities of supplies stored in the village, and burned about 100 houses after allowing women and children to remove personal items. Most of the adult men, suspected of being Viet Cong, had fled.

Below: February 27, 1963—Armed with U.S. rifles, women paramilitary volunteers salute as they march past first lady Madame Ngo Ding Nhu in Saigon during their graduation from military training. About 3,000 women in South Vietnam had so far been trained.

Above: January 1963—A T-28 fighter-bomber escorts a supply train through the South Vietnamese jungle about 25 miles southeast of Bien Hoa.

Right: January 1963—Members of the Dan Ve Men, South Vietnam's self-defense forces, fire American-made Tompson submachine guns as they undertake a six-week military and political training course at an outpost in the Mekong Delta.

Above: February 1963—A South Vietnamese civil guard unit passes Viet Cong suspects captured in the Mekong Delta. The suspects were brought to a secure government hamlet for interrogation.

Above: February 21, 1963—The crew chief of a heavily armed UH-1B Huey checks rockets and machine guns mounted on the helicopter during an operation in Vinh Long province. The fast, maneuverable Hueys, then relatively new to Vietnam, were often flying cover for the lumbering H-21s and other transport helicopters.

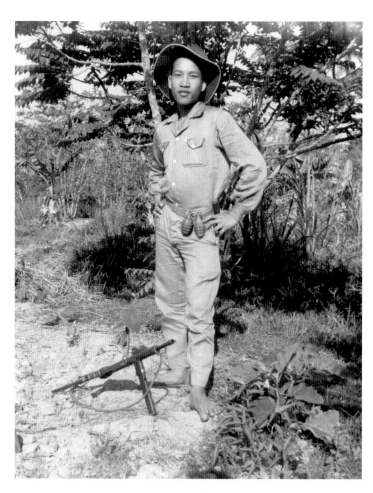

Above: February 1963— After a day working on a strategic hamlet in South Vietnam, Viet Cong prisoners return by landing craft to the Nam Can camp.

Left: February 1963—A Vietnamese soldier keeps his carbine dry in the Camau district of Vietnam, an area of saltwater swamps and rivers.

Above: February 1963—Viet Cong guerrilla Nguyen Van Ba, 19, poses with two French grenades and a Bren light machine gun at his feet a few weeks before his capture at Dinh Tuong, South Vietnam. This photo was found in his wallet when he was taken prisoner.

Above: 1963—Viet Cong soldiers walk waist deep through water as they advance to attack and eventually overrun a South Vietnamese outpost at Cai Keo in Camau province.

Right: September 9, 1963—Viet Cong guerrillas in a night attack at the South Vietnamese outpost of Dam Doi in Camau province. Some have breached the outer defensive perimeter and are about to penetrate the post which, according to the photographer's caption, fell at 3 am.

Left: September 9, 1963— Soldiers of a regular Viet Cong battalion, some of them dragging heavy equipment, mill about in a swamp as they group to attack Dam Doi in Camau province.

Above: March 1963—Stirring clouds of dust, a South Vietnamese tank passes a cluster of tombstones in a deserted village north of Saigon. The area had been under control of the Viet Cong for nearly 15 years.

Above: March 1963—Vietnamese troops sit in a crowded H-21 helicopter en route to a hunt for Viet Cong in Ling Long province, 70 miles south of Saigon.

Above: March 1963—South Vietnamese rangers scamper down a 50-foot wall during training at Duc My Ranger Station in the coastal resort area north of Saigon. They were part of a group that went through a rigorous 42-day training session.

Right: April 1963—A 13-year-old soldier of the Laotian neutralist forces stands guard near a villa at Khan Khay, Laos, where leaders were negotiating settlement of the kingdom's political crisis.

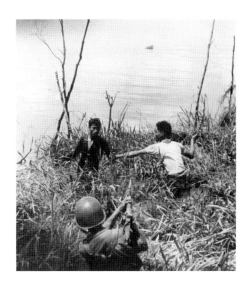

Above: May 1963—Brandishing a knife and backed up by armed troopers, a South Vietnamese soldier discovers and captures a Viet Cong rebel in the Plain of Reeds, about eight miles from the Cambodian border.

Above: April 1963—Villagers taught self-defense tactics defend government-secured areas surrounded by bamboo fences. U.S.-made weapons are rapidly replacing sticks and machetes.

Right: June 13, 1963—A Viet Cong soldier is searched by a member of the U.S. 114th Air Mobile Company before being put aboard a helicopter in Bac Lieu Province in South Vietnam.

Above: July 1, 1963—South Vietnam's President Ngo Dinh Diem reviews honor troops in Saigon, making his first appearance in public since the crisis between Diem, a Roman Catholic, and the Buddhists.

Above: July 1963—Vietnamese troops and their American adviser leap out of a hovering U.S. helicopter as they begin an attack against a village suspected of harboring Viet Cong rebels in south Vietnam. The choppers did not land because of possible guerrilla traps in the form of spikes and wires that would prevent its taking off again.

Above: June 1963—Madame Ngo Dinh Nhu visits military cadres at a training camp.

Left: July 17, 1963—Buddhist monks and women pull at a barbed wire road barricade in front of the Giac Minh Pagada set up by police to halt Buddhist demonstration in Saigon. Club-wielding police injured at least 50 persons among protesters against South Vietnam's President Ngo Dinh Diem, a Roman Catholic.

Above: July 1963—U.S. advisers and South Vietnamese troops wade across a creek during an attack on a Viet Cong village defended by snipers.

July 14, 1963—A Vietnamese woman hurries her daughter and baby from their burning home in a village near Tay Ninh, about 60 miles from Saigon. South Vietnamese soldiers raided the village, believed to be a Viet Cong supply depot, burning houses and rice stores. Soldiers found only women, children, and old men in the village.

Right: July 11, 1963—U.S. Ambassador Frederick Nolting, *right*, accompanied by charges d'affaires William Truehart, returns to Saigon after meeting with President Kennedy. Nolting was to be replaced by Henry Cabot Lodge later in the year.

Left: August 5, 1963—A severely wounded South Vietnamese soldier is comforted in a sugarcane field near Duc Hoa, 12 miles west of Saigon after a Viet Cong ambush. The one-day operation involved about 3,000 troops in tanks, armored river craft, and on foot.

Above: August 1963—A U.S. serviceman rides aboard an Eagle Flight helicopter during operation in the Mekong Delta area. The Eagle Flights, carrying a small number of troops, hovered over potential trouble spots. When a target was identified, the helicopters would quickly drop their troops for a search of the area.

Right: August 1963—U.S. C-123s spray a concentrated defoliant along power lines in the jungle-covered hills between Saigon and Dalat. The planes flew just above the terrain at dawn to ensure that the defoliant would be effective against the jungle vegetation.

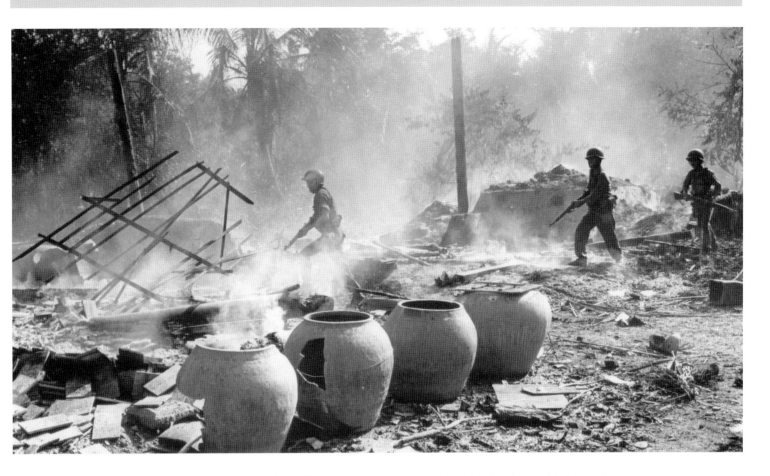

Above: July 21, 1963—South Vietnamese troops charge through smoking ruins left after a napalm attack on a Viet Cong village in the Mekong Delta.

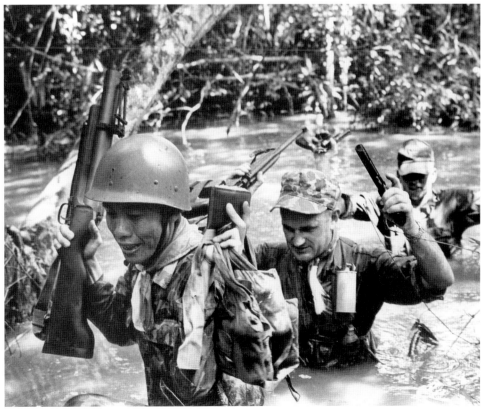

August 1963—A U.S. advisor wades through chest-deep water with South Vietnamese troops.

Above: August 1963—Ngo Dinh Nhu is chief political advisor to South Vietnamese President Ngo Dinh Diem as well as his younger brother.

Above right: August 22, 1963—Henry Cabot Lodge, newly named U.S. ambassador to South Vietnam, is welcomed to Saigon by Gen. Paul D. Harkins, commander of U.S. forces in South Vietnam.

Below right: August 24, 1963—A shouting student exhorts fellow demonstrators as they march and finally take over the South Vietnamese Information Ministry. Students play a key role in Vietnam's many street disturbances.

Above: August 1963—Policeman breaks up an advertisement for a beauty parlor because it violates laws for a 'healthier society.' Fancy hairdos and seductive smiles were outlawed in ads and other public displays.

Above left: August 26, 1963—U.S. Ambassador Henry Cabot Lodge is welcomed to the presidential palace in Saigon by President Ngo Dinh Diem for talks about South Vietnam's political and religious situation.

Left: August 28, 1963—South Vietnam's President Ngo Dinh Diem receives Buddhist monks at the Gia Long palace while soldiers patrolled Saigon to prevent further fire suicides by which Buddhist monks protest government action against their religion.

# THE ULTIMATE PROTEST

One of the iconic photographs of the Vietnam war is the picture by Malcome Browne of Associated Press showing a Buddhist monk's immolation on a Saigon street in 1963. The picture drew world wide attention and thrust the Vietnam story into the headlines. This is the story of the photo.

June 11, 1963—The story starts with a phone call to AP correspondent Malcome Browne on the night of June 10. Buddhist monks advise that they will have something important to say at 8 am in the Xa Loi pagoda, one of Saigon's important Buddhist centers.

Browne, in recent months, had received many of these calls, followed the next day by yet another small parade and another Buddhist statement protesting oppressive actions against them by the government of Ngo Dinh Diem, a Catholic.

The next morning Browne stands among some 350 monks and lay people gathered at Xa Loi. For an hour mesmerizing chants fill the room. The smoke of burning joss and the muggy heat of a late Saigon spring stifles breathing. Browne notes that several of the Buddhist nuns wear white garments, the color of mourning, and are weeping as they serve tea. Odd, he thinks, there had been no recent deaths. Browne notes another oddity as the group takes to the street: the column is led by a small gray car carrying five monks.

About 15 minutes into the parade the car stops. A monk removes a gasoline can from the car. An elderly monk, later identified as Quang Duc, gets out assisted by younger companions. The elderly man sits on a mat in the street and takes the lotus position. One monk moves forward with the can of gasoline. In that instant Browne, standing 20 feet away and slightly in front of the scene, realizes what is about to happen.

The monks exchange a few words with Quang Duc...they pour the contents of the gasoline can over him....they step back... the elderly monk strikes a match, drops it into this robes and is instantly enveloped in flames. It is 9:22 am.

The old man does not cry out though he winces as the flame envelope his body. The smell of burning flesh fills the street. In moments,

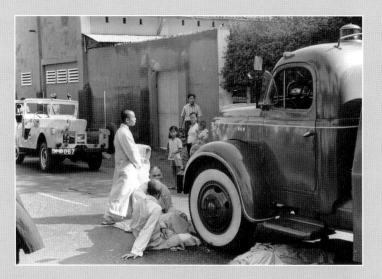

Left: Monks place themselves under the wheels of a fire truck thus preventing any possible rescue attempts or other interference in the immolation.

Left: Buddhist monks pray at the Xa Loi pagoda.

Right: Quang Duc, an elderly monk, sits on a small mat in the street as other monks pour gasoline over him. At rear, other Buddhists watch the procedure.

Above: A Buddhist column, typical of the way in which many Buddhist demonstrations start in Saigon, marches through the city's streets to a major intersection.

Right: After dropping a match into his gasoline soaked robes, Quang Duc is immediately enveloped in flames. He does not cry out, but winces ever so slightly.

Right: Finally, minutes after setting himself afire, Quang Duc's charred body topples over.

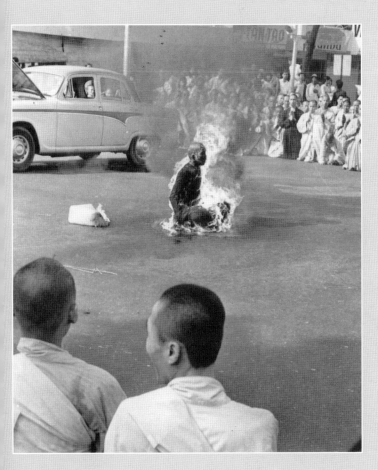

Left: The burning continues.

Quang Duc's charred body topples over. It is 9:35am. Wails of the mourners fill the street.

Browne's pictures and story leap across the world, transmitted on AP international circuits. The picture becomes the first of many photographic icons to emerge from the Vietnam war though the Vietnam saga is not, in 1963, a major news story.

The next morning Browne's pictures are on the desk of President John F. Kennedy. who utters an expletive as he exchanges views with Henry Cabot Lodge, the new ambassador to Vietnam. The sense of their conversation, Lodge later tells Browne, is that something has to be done about the situation in Vietnam where American involvement is just beginning.

Two views of the Vietnam situation come quickly into focus.

The first describes a government structure heavily Catholic that takes a vigorous stand against Buddhists who seek a greater role and a greater say in the government. This version says that the Buddhist demonstrations distract the government from the more important issue, defeat of the communists. It says also that the Buddhists, if not outright communists, aid and abet the communist cause.

The second version paints a picture of an authoritarian, Catholic government hierarchy that oppresses the Buddhists on religious grounds. Advancement in government and in the military require some officials to become Catholics. Goods and services provided by the government go to areas of the country that are predominantly Catholic.

The pictures of Quang Duc's suicide amply demonstrate the fervor of the Buddhist position. There are no comparable photographs that illustrate the government's position. And in fact, the government is disadvantaged by the pronouncements of Diem's sister-in-law who terms Quang Duc's suicide a barbeque, and who offers to pay for the fuel for anyone who wants to use it on western correspondents.

After the immolation new Buddhist demonstrations, and more fiery suicides, become central to the Vietnam story.

—Hal Buell

Above: Those monks who attended sit and observe the scene. The wails of mourners are the only sound.

Above: June 1, 1963—Vietnamese Buddhist nuns go on a hunger strike on the floor of the An Quang pagoda's nunnery in Saigon. They fasted to protest government religious policies.

Left: May 30, 1963—Buddhist monks and nuns march in front of the Vietnamese National Assembly building. The four-hour demonstrations called for a government policy of religious equality.

Above: May 1963—Daughters of a woman killed in a bloody riot in Hue view their mother's coffin during a funeral ceremony. The riots exploded in protest against President Diem's order to replace Buddhist flags with the national one.

Below: June 19, 1963—Buddhist monks march in a funeral procession in Saigon for Quang Duc, the 72-year-old monk who burned himself to death to protest government oppression of his faith.

Above: June 16, 1963—A Vietnamese girl in traditional Ao Dai dress grabs for a rock, and a policeman tries to protect himself behind a shield during a clash between Buddhist demonstrators and riot police in Saigon after Buddhist leaders called off funeral services for Quang Duc, the monk who killed himself.

Above: July 1963—Buddhist monks grasp barbed wire during an attempt to pull down barricades thrown up by police around the Buddhist pagoda in Saigon.

Above: July 7, 1963—Police in Saigon stop Buddhist monks carrying the ashes and a photo of the monk who burned himself to death. They tried to march following a memorial service for the monk.

Above: July 1963—Buddhist priests are led by elder monks in a memorial parade for Quang Duc, the monk who set himself on fire to protest the South Vietnamese government. Police stopped the parade.

Below: July 17, 1963—About 200 Buddhist monks and nuns launch a hunger strike at the Xa Loi pagoda in Saigon after a demonstration in front of the residence of the U.S. ambassador to South Vietnam.

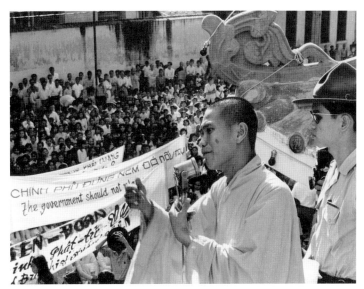

August 18, 1963—Buddhist monk Giac Duc addresses a crowd demonstrating against government policies outside the main Buddhist pagoda in Saigon.

Above: September 1963—A duck sticks its head out of a knapsack on the back of a government soldier during an operation against the Viet Cong in the Mekong Delta. It was considered the best way to carry food in the hot, humid area.

Above: September 27, 1963—Gen. Maxwell D. Taylor (left), chairman of U.S. Joint Chiefs of Staff, and U.S. Defense Secretary Robert McNamara (second from left) listen to a briefing by a captain of the Vietnamese Army's Special Forces. Taylor and McNamara, a two-man fact-finding committee in South Vietnam, were briefed at Plei Mrong as they toured the central highlands to witness the war against the Viet Cong guerrillas. Gen. Paul Harkins, commander of the U.S. forces in Vietnam, sits at McNamara's left.

Above: September 24, 1963—After arriving in Saigon on a fact-finding mission, U.S. Defense Secretary Robert McNamara (left) and Gen. Maxwell Taylor (center), chairman of the Joint Chiefs of Staff, meet with U.S. Ambassador Henry Cabot Lodge.

Right: September 15, 1963—A woman attends her daughter, wounded by machine-gun fire from a U.S. helicopter, as South Vietnamese troops pass through Ca Mau to pursue Viet Cong.

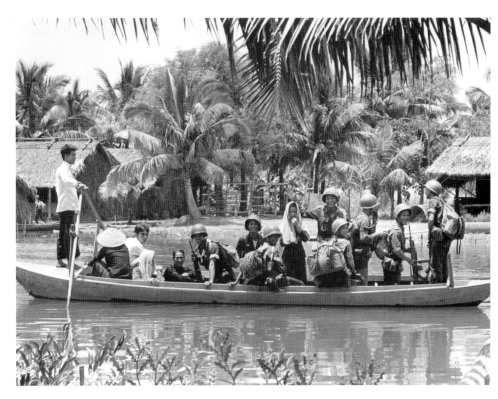

Above: September 1963—South Vietnamese troops use a river boat to transport prisoners and suspects along a canal in the Mekong Delta.

Left: September 9, 1963—Ngo Dinh Nhu, brother and trusted advisor to South Vietnamese President Diem.

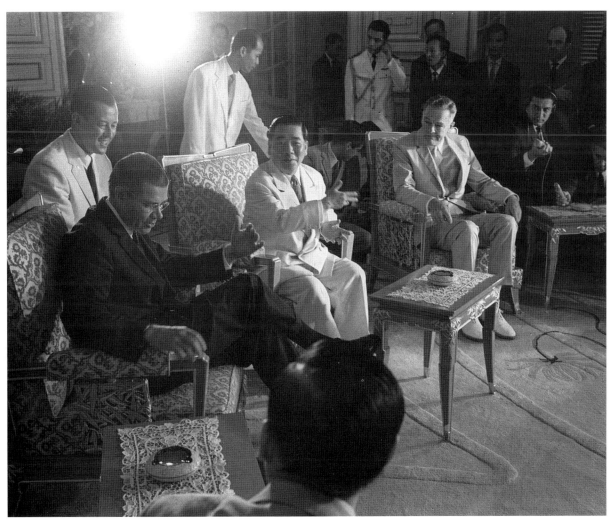

Left: September 29, 1963—Secretary of Defense Robert S. McNamara (*left*) and South Vietnamese President Ngo Dinh Diem gesture during their three-hour conference in Saigon. McNamara was ending a week-long tour of South Vietnam as personal representative of President John F. Kennedy.

Left: October 3, 1963—Wife of the brother of South Vietnam's President Ngo Dinh Diem, Mrs. Ngo Dinh Nhu, who advocates a hard line against Buddhists in her country, speaks to a news conference at the Vietnamese embassy in Paris.

Right: October 3, 1963—Secretary of Defense Robert McNamara poses with a map he used in a closed-door briefing of the Senate Armed Services Committee. He discussed a recent trip to Vietnam.

Below: October 16, 1963—Armed South Vietnamese marines march past Saigon's Xa Loi Pagoda, once headquarters of the Buddhist opposition, as they participate in National Day Thanksgiving Service.

Left: October, 1963—At a schoolhouse in the Mekong Delta, villagers line up for examination and treatment by a joint U.S.-Vietnamese medical team headed by Lt. Joseph Burn, *right*.

Above: October 26, 1963—South Vietnam's President Ngo Dinh Diem, left, reviews troops on the eighth anniversary of his regime. Gen. Doung Van Minh, presidential advisor who later led a revolution to overthrow the government, stands behind him in uniform.

Left: 1963—A woman soldier of the North Vietnamese Army shoulders an ammunition case as she wades through a river along the Ho Chi Minh trail. Crate markings are in English.

Right: 1963—Viet Cong militiamen pose atop a downed American plane in the Mekong Delta.

Right: 1963—A unit of Viet Cong militiamen travels along a French build canal.

Below: January 2, 1963—Camouflaged Viet Cong guerrillas man a machine gun during action at Ap Bac in the Mekong Delta.

# ASSASSINATION

The warmth of Honolulu did not extend to the three senior American officials who were meeting there at Pacific headquarters on 21 August 1963. Their differences over the distant war brought tension to the conference room where the outgoing Ambassador to Vietnam, Frederick E. Nolting, faced his successor, Henry Cabot Lodge. Although he was the new man, Lodge, as always, exuded certainty – and now, en route to Saigon, he had one word for the problem that lay ahead of him: Diem.

Nolting, always expressive of his feelings (his quip of the day was that he had been 'disLodged'), was saying with some passion that President Diem had promised to make concessions to the Buddhists and so the crisis was almost over. The third man, Assistant Secretary of State Roger Hilsman, kept a discreet silence. He was there to oversee formally this courtesy meeting and he could not let his scepticism show. Nolting was saying that Diem always kept his word; then the news came over the wire: the most sacred Xa Loi pagoda in Saigon and other main Buddhist temples all across the country had been raided by the special police. Thirty monks had been injured and 1400

'This was a Vietnamese generals' coup, yes, but I think the fundamentals of it were decided in our White House.'

– WILLIAM COLBY,
DIRECTOR OF THE CIA

arrested. Then, says Hilsman, 'the ticker-tape came over that they had beaten up the pagodas. I can remember Nolting in a shocked voice saying "But he promised me, he promised me".'

Hilsman and Nolting were on the next plane to Washington. Lodge reached Saigon within hours, finding 'a curfew and soldiers at all the intersections'. Even high-school students had been jailed in the widening riots. The pagoda raids had clearly been timed to the absence of an American Ambassador. The US had now to decide whether Diem was totally challenging its authority – as was feared – or merely misreading the signals. Washington had been ambiguous on the significance of the change of ambassadors, with Nolting and Lodge getting a different emphasis from President Kennedy.

Before leaving Saigon (two years earlier than expected) Nolting was asked by Diem whether US aid and support for his government would remain the same. Nolting cabled the State Department: 'I said it is very crucial and got a reply which said from the highest authority – which is the shorthand for the President – "Yo u can assure him that

Right: June 16, 1963—A Vietnamese policemen uses a tree branch to disperse stone-throwing rioters during a Buddhist demonstration in Saigon. Smoke rises from a tear-gas grenade.

June 16, 1963—A barefoot Buddhist leader stands on top of a car to address a crowd of Vietnamese Buddhists in Saigon after calling off funeral services for the monk who publicly burned himself to death to protest government restrictions.

there's no change in American policy in this respect.'" At the time Kennedy was telling Henry Cabot Lodge: 'I have confidence in you and I want you to go out there and see if we can't get the government to behave better.'

As a Republican and a 'Boston Brahmin' Lodge was anyhow viewed as very much his own man. He was given exceptional powers, including, in fact, control over the aid flow. This meant life or death leverage over South Vietnam. It could be applied against Diem – or to support him. Governing power could only lie with the recipient of the US aid.

In Saigon Lodge began with a symbolic cut-off – by delaying the usual diplomatic rounds. Having arrived at night he was on the street the next morning personally questioning people in French on their opinions of the Buddhist crisis and Diem's rule. He pointedly visited the Xa Loi pagoda. US displeasure was now very evident.

Within two days – 24 August in Washington – Lodge sent an urgent cable to his established channel, Roger Hilsman. It advised that the Embassy had been approached by 'a number of Vietnamese generals'. The generals had 'information' that the special police run by Diem's brother, Ngo Dinh Nhu, were planning a purge of the military. These generals – as Hilsman quotes Lodge – 'might take matters into their own hands and pull a coup'.

Lodge had spent a month at Pentagon briefings; he should know if developments were urgent. Hilsman regarded the cable as top priority. It was Saturday morning in Washington. President Kennedy, Secretary of State Dean Rusk and Secretary of Defense Robert McNamara were all out of town. But their deputies – Averell Harriman and James Forrestal – were available, and with their help Hilsman began to draft a 'boiler-plate' emergency response. It made clear that Washington would no longer tolerate Nhu's influence over Diem. The President was to remove his brother from power. Failing this, the generals were

to be told that all US economic and military support would be discontinued.

With the wording complete, Hilsman called both President Kennedy and Secretary of State Rusk to brief them quickly on the situation. They approved his response – and Hilsman then sent what became known as the 'green-light' cable. It did not deal with the warning about a coup and therefore seemed to countenance one.

This rushed reply, Hilsman says, 'is not as infrequent an occurrence in American foreign policy as you might think. This happens a lot of times. There is a boiler-plate reply when you're ill at ease with the country which is that we will examine any new government on its own merits.'

According to Hilsman the implications of the cable were fully grasped, and 'greatly strengthened' by Rusk, who inserted a paragraph stating that if there were problems in Saigon, then attempts would be made to deliver supplies for the war effort through Hue. This implied support for any prolonged rebellion. 'The overall gist of that cable,' admits Hilsman, 'was to say that we would prefer a government continuing under Diem, but if they – the generals – felt they had no choice, then we would examine the government that they established on its own merits. Now of course there is no question that this, with all of its hedges, does encourage them.'

Ambassador Lodge interpreted the cable as meaning 'go out and see if there is a coup' and so 'he sent out the CIA' says William Colby, then Chief of the CIA's Far East Division at Langley, Virginia. In this senior position, Colby saw all cables at the Agency's Virginia headquarters. The controversial 24 August cable told Lodge that he must press Diem to take 'prompt, dramatic action' to correct the Buddhist crisis. It instructed him that 'at the same time' he should tell 'key military leaders' that continued aid would be 'impossible' unless action was taken 'immediately'.

Lodge now called in the US Commander, General Paul Harkins, and other senior personnel. On the next day, the 25th, the Embassy sent a return cable accepting the instructions but defining them as 'a basic decision from Washington'.

In Saigon early on the 26th, a Voice of America news broadcast blamed Ngo Dinh Nhu's secret police for the pagoda raids, thus absolving the army. At the same time the semi-official radio network speculated on a suspension of US aid. On Monday the 26th, after five days in Saigon, Lodge went to present his credentials to President Diem – and to present the demand for Nhu's removal as senior advisor. But by now Nhu had become the eyes and ears – and iron hand – of the recluse President.

Diem was coldly 'unreceptive', says Lodge. In this crucial first conversation between the two men Lodge does not recall what was actually said – only what was inferred. 'He almost said to me, well, what business is it of yours whether I have my brother here to advise me or not. To which of course there was a very good answer: it's my business because the President of the United States has made it my business. I didn't say that but I thought that.'

President Kennedy himself was having Monday morning second thoughts. As Lodge faced Diem, the National Security Council was convening at the White House. Kennedy learned that a Saigon CIA agent, Colonel Lucien Conein, was even then briefing the Vietnamese generals. There was consensus that matters were proceeding too fast. Washington needed more precise information on which generals were involved, exactly what they planned, and on the possibilities of President Diem conforming. Lodge was to be asked for more details.

But the 24 August instructions had not been retracted, and in the opinion of ex-Ambassador Nolting, then back at the State Department, the green-light cable had 'prejudiced the position almost beyond Kennedy's recall'. 'The axis of Lodge and [Under Secretary of State] Harriman was too strong for President Kennedy to thwart or overcome – even if he wanted to, and I was not sure whether he wanted to.' And Nolting – who would resign from the Department over the Diem affair – says Secretary Rusk just bowed to the prevailing mood: 'Rusk was this way and that way.'

Rusk says that long before the green-light cable Washington's growing impatience with Diem was known to the generals. In Rusk's version it was the generals who dictated events: 'I supposed the South Vietnamese military came to the conclusion that if they replaced President Diem somehow we would try to live with the results.'

In the CIA version the generals were at first extremely nervous over the Agency's follow-up approach to them. As William Colby recalls: 'We frightened an awful lot of generals. They were terrified that this would get back to the government and lead to their arrest and incarceration, at least. And they said "No" at that time. But they said that if we get interested we will give you a call.'

The generals began to weigh which was the greater danger – a coup attempt, or no attempt. A US aid cut-off could mean their own demise as well as Diem's. But for them the more immediate danger was that Diem would get warning and strike first. Initially only one of them, General Khiem, met with CIA agent Lucien Conein. Although Conein was well known to him, Khiem wanted higher credentials: who in the Embassy or in Washington had authorized the approach? Conein was not at liberty to say. In an interview recorded for NBC television in December 1971, he said, 'It was quite obvious that if at any one point the American hand had shown, the whole thing would blow up and it would be an extreme embarrassment. Therefore Ambassador Lodge made it very clear to me that if something went wrong he would have to be able to have deniability that I even existed.'

After meeting Khiem on the 26th, Conein had nothing specific about a coup to report to Lodge – and Lodge now had Washington's second thoughts cable requesting more details, not least on whether President Diem might still be won over.

With little information from Conein the most hesitant general at that moment was US Commander Harkins. He doubted that the coup forces would prove strong enough. Harkins expressed this to Lodge and then cabled the Secretary of Defense urging restraint at the Department of State. Washington's response on the 27th was to request both Harkins and Lodge for a joint up-to-the-moment assessment.

On the 28th the CIA and the generals again made contact, and this time Conein found himself dealing with no less than President Diem's personal military advisor, General Duong Van Minh,

known as Big Minh because of his six-foot height and bulk. Conein learned the names of other interested generals. As well as his first contact, Tran Thien Khiem, the line-up included regimental commanders Nguyen Khanh, Le Van Kim and Nguyen Van Thieu. But the position was the same: the generals needed formal notification of US government support – meaning a direct endorsement from Ambassador Lodge.

Lodge and General Harkins again conferred, then Lodge sent Washington a strong recommendation for action. His cable (quoted from the *Pentagon Papers*) included the following points:

1) We are launched on a course from which there is no respectable turning back: the overthrow of the Diem government.

2) The chance of bringing off a generals' coup depends on them to some extent; but it depends at least as much on us.

3) We should proceed to make all-out effort to get the Generals to move promptly.

In point 8, Lodge stated that 'General Harkins thinks I should ask Diem to get rid of the Nhus before starting the generals' action. But I believe that such a step has no chance of getting the desired result and would have the very serious effect of being regarded by the Generals as a sign of American indecision and delay. . . .' Lodge concluded by saying that except for point 8 'General Harkins concurs in this telegram'.

In Washington the National Security Council hastily convened. There was intense day-long debate and the final decision was to leave Ambassador Lodge with the responsibility of determining policy. Secretary of State Dean Rusk now personally cabled Lodge. Rusk noted the different views on whether President Diem shold first be persuaded to remove his brother Nhu and the equally unpopular Madame Nhu, but Rusk said this was best coupled with sanctions on US aid when the generals were ready to move. The generals could then negotiate directly with Diem on the Nhus. Rusk cautioned against applying sanctions until the generals were ready, because – Rusk cabled – if Diem was alerted he might 'take some quite fantastic action such as calling on North Vietnam for assistance in expelling the Americans'.

President Kennedy had just publicly explained why he thought Vietnam was important, stating: 'We don't want to have a repetition of China because that was the most damaging event, certainly, that's occurred to us – perhaps in this century.' In Vietnam the denial of a religious flag three months earlier had caused the festering of a situation which if it continued might leave no flag to defend. Privately, Kennedy was studying ways of withdrawing from Vietnam – but at the same time he was taking greater risks, as he now admitted in a prophetic cable to Ambassador Lodge.

A US Senate study shows that on 29 August, when Lodge had his recommendations confirmed, Kennedy also cabled as follows: 'I have approved all the messages you are receiving from others today, and I emphasize that everything in these messages has my full support. We will do all that we can to help you conclude this operation successfully. Until the very moment of the go signal for the operation by the generals, I must reserve a contingent right to change course and reverse previous instructions. While fully aware of your assessment of the consequences of such a reversal, I know from experience that failure is more

destructive than an appearance of indecision. I would, of course, accept full responsibility for any such change as I must also bear the full responsibility for this operation and its consequences.'

With the President himself now endorsing a coup and accepting the consequences, CIA agent Conein again contacted the generals, asking their intentions. Two days later, 31 August, General Minh gave his reply – and he tactically backed off. He said his forces were not yet ready, and there was no date in sight. At this point, says Ambassador Lodge, 'The generals were very unwilling to take Americans into their confidence because they thought Americans talk too much, and it was impossible for an American to keep a secret. So that whole so-called coup . . . evaporated.'

The generals now heard the strongest yet official US criticism of the Diem government, stated by Kennedy himself. On 2 September the President said in an interview with Walter Cronkite on CBS television that the US would continue assistance to South Vietnam, but Kennedy added: 'I don't think the war can be won unless the people support the effort, and in my opinion, in the last two months the government has gotten out of touch with the people.'

Kennedy's Assistant Secretary of State, Roger Hilsman, considers this public criticism to have been the catalyst: 'We knew that there was coup plotting but we did not know when it was scheduled.' Hilsman felt 'at the time' that Kennedy's comments on television were 'our contribution' to the coup. 'Kennedy said that he was very pessimistic – this is on public television – but that perhaps with a change of policy and a change of personnel' victory was possible. What Kennedy 'had in mind', says Hilsman, was a pro-Buddhist policy and the removal of Diem's brother, Nhu. On a second national television hook-up, Kennedy was asked about continuance of aid 'and Kennedy said we will continue aid which furthers the war effort and we will stop aid which interferes with it. He meant that we were cutting off aid to brother Nhu's pet projects but we would continue aid to the army. Now in hindsight I think that encouraged it.'

Whether encouraged or not, the generals in Saigon kept silent. In early September Kennedy sent Secretary of Defense Robert Strange McNamara and a group of advisors to observe first-hand. McNamara's assistant, William Bundy, went on this ten day visit: 'The tide of opposition included not only Buddhists and students but leading members of the government who came to us quietly and told us there simply was no way for this to go on unless Diem totally reformed his administration. I think it was virtually inevitable that there was going to be a change if Diem went on as he did.'

Bundy says the American role with the generals 'was really one of saying "We won't try to stop this and we will work with you if you do it" – but we were hoping, hoping to the last, that Diem would stop the repression'.

With the return of the mission the Kennedy administration began what William Colby of the CIA recalls as 'the most agonizing and intense period of debate I've experienced inside our government'. The National Security Council was back to the drawing-board, but with no outline emerging. Nothing had been resolved. The generals remained silent, Diem obdurate. For weeks the debate raged over the unbendable and unpredictable mandarin who could not survive without the United States but – and this was the fear – who might decide to try and bid his ally to leave. Could Diem be coerced? Should aid be totally suspended? Or should the US fully back Diem, put aside the political problems and concentrate wholly on winning the war in the countryside? In Colby's words, 'There was very intense division of opinion.'

On 2 October Kennedy approved a much revised policy resulting from the intense month-long review. Diem would be given until the end of the year. The US would then announce the withdrawal of 1000 American advisors. And military aid would go only to the generals who opposed Diem. Meantime, Ambassador Lodge was instructed by Kennedy to take no further steps in support of a coup but to keep cultivating alternative leaders.

The new policy held good for one day. On 3 October General Duong Van Minh informed CIA agent Conein that a coup was being planned, and – according to Conein's eventual Senate testimony – Minh outlined various courses of action including 'assassination' of Diem's brother, Nhu.

It emerged that the generals had interpreted a much stronger 'go' signal shortly before when Washington recalled Saigon CIA Station Chief, Richardson. The significance of this was only realized much later at the State Department, says Roger Hilsman: 'Ambassador Lodge was quarrelling with Richardson. The quarrel had nothing to do with the coup, but Lodge insisted that Richardson be removed – and it's one of those happenings in Vietnamese eyes: Richardson was very close to Nhu and Diem, and so the removal of Richardson sent a signal to the Vietnamese generals that we did not intend.'

For the first time the generals had outlined actual coup plans, but the hint of assassination alarmed CIA Director McCone. He went personally to President Kennedy and, according to Senate testimony, told him: 'Mr President if I was manager of a baseball team, and I had one pitcher I'd keep him in the box whether he was a good pitcher or not.' Diem's removal, McCone argued, would merely lead to a succession of coups. McCone left Kennedy believing that the President had agreed to a 'hands-off' policy. The CIA response to Saigon on 5 October unequivocally stated: 'We certainly would not favor assassination of Diem' and concluded 'believe best approach is hands-off. However we are naturally interested in intelligence of any such [coup] plan.'

The night of the same day, the 5th, Conein was summoned to meet General Minh. Conein relayed the message that the US opposed assassination and was told, 'Alright, you don't like it, we won't talk about it any more.' But General Minh insisted that he must know the final US position in respect to a coup scheduled for the 'near future'. Conein checked back with Ambassador Lodge. 'My instructions were that I was to inform General Minh that the United States would not thwart their coup. And I conveyed this.'

From now on the CIA agent found himself dealing with a new, impressive go-between: Chief of Staff General Tran Van Don. There were several meetings during October – and another important signal to the generals. On 17 October the US informed the Saigon government that aid to Ngo

Above: November 2, 1963—Civilians take cover behind tanks near the presidential palace in Saigon during the final effort to oust President Diem from power. The coup was successful, and Diem died in the attack.

Left: November 2, 1963—Soldiers on tanks blaze away at the presidential palace and civilians duck for cover during a coup that overthrew the government of Ngo Dinh Diem.

Below: November 2, 1963—A Vietnamese soldier walks past a shattered wall during fighting around the presidential palace. A coup overthrew the regime of President Diem.

Dinh Nhu's special forces would only be continued if channelled through the army command. The generals however were still concerned that the US was notfully behind them. General Don had met Ambassador Lodge at a party and in private conversation Lodge had given no indication that he was aware of a coup.

'On the 25th of October,' says General Don, 'once again Lucien Conein came to ask me when we planned to make the coup. How to answer him I didn't know. And I asked him again "Are you authorized from the American side to talk to me and discuss with me about the coup?" And he said "Yes, by Lodge". I said "Lodge didn't tell me anything".' It was arranged that Lodge would make contact with the General at an airport function the next day.

'That day,' says Don, 'I went to the airport and met Lodge. I asked him immediately, "Is Conein with you?" He told me Conein was his representative. I said, "Now I know" and I talked to Lodge, saying the morale of the Vietnamese forces is low

Left: November 6, 1963—Maj. Gen. Duong Van Minh, *left*, one of the leaders of the coup that toppled South Vietnamese President Ngo Dinh Diem, appears at a Saigon news conference with Nguyen Ngoc Tho, the junta's choice as prime minister.

because of the Buddhist affair, and something must be changed. And Lodge said, "If you need me, we are ready to help you." And I told him, "Mr Ambassador we have enough means already – what we need is your support, the support of the United States if we would succeed." And I told him, "Please don't interfere in this case because this is a Vietnamese affair between the Vietnamese themselves." '

General Don – confident that he had direct access to Lodge – summoned agent Conein three days later, 28 October, and said 'Come over to our offices – we are having a meeting'. There Conein learned that the coup was imminent. General Don told him that the exact time would be made known to the Embassy only hours before. But he requested that Ambassador Lodge should not cancel a scheduled trip to Washington for fear of tipping off the palace. The trip had been arranged for 31 October.

As the countdown proceeded, Washington was again in turmoil. On 30 October the US Commander, General Harkins, sent a furious cable suggesting that he trusted neither the generals nor Lodge, stating 'General Don is either lying or playing both ends against the middle. He told Conein the coup will be before November 2nd. He told me he was not planning a coup.'

Harkins said that if a coup was in progress he had 'not been informed by the Ambassador that he has received any such plan'. 'We didn't know,' contends Ambassador Lodge. 'They kept a secret awfully well. And I respected them for it. I wasn't brought into the picture in a complete way until literally the night before.'

With the White House gravely concerned over the rift between the Defense and State Departments, Lodge was cabled on the same day – 30 October – and told to dissuade the generals unless he was absolutely sure the coup would succeed. A second urgent cable stated: 'We cannot accept conclusion that we have no power to delay or discourage a coup.' But Lodge replied that it was too late: it was in the hands of the Vietnamese. 'They didn't want us to interfere,' says Lodge. 'They didn't want help in the planning, let alone . . . weapons and equipment. They wanted it to take its course. They wanted the Vietnamese to run it. And

Washington said they would stay out of it and they stayed out of it.'

From his supervisory position at the CIA, William Colby saw it quite differently: 'Now this was a Vietnamese generals' coup, yes. But I think that the fundamentals of it were decided in our White House because a few weeks before the President in a press conference had said that it was essential to contemplate new people in the Vietnamese government and that could only be interpreted as Diem and his brother.

'We cut off the support the CIA was giving to a particular unit of the Vietnamese army [Nhu's Special Forces], and the interpretation of that was that if we were dissatisfied with the leadership we would cut off the assistance there. Now these were green lights to the generals to go ahead . . . reinforced by their question, Would the United States

support a successor regime? Answer from the White House – Yes.'

In Saigon, Ambassador Lodge delayed his scheduled 31 October departure. At 10.00 am on 1 November, the Ambassador called on President Diem together with General Harkins and visiting Pacific Commander Admiral Felt. The President's press secretary, Ton That Tien, was present: 'Lodge kept President Diem busy until past twelve. Each time Admiral Felt goes to leave, Lodge asks another question and we know now from the *Pentagon Papers* that Lodge knew all along that the coup would be staged and he was simply pinning down President Diem to deny him access to his staff. Downstairs Mr Nhu – this was a coincidence, a strange coincidence – was being asked all sorts of questions by [General] Thieu. Afterwards I talked to people who wanted to get in touch with either Mr Nhu or the President to tell him that there was something going on. And they couldn't get to him, they couldn't get any orders from the palace at all until the rebellious troops were on the outskirts of Saigon. You cannot say that this is sheer coincidence.'

Lodge gives his version: 'I went to see Mr Diem because I was going back to Washington for a routine report. And I was to present Admiral Felt. Diem said, "Every time the American Ambassador goes to Washington there's a rumor of a coup." He said, "I hear these rumors now, and I know there's going to be a coup, but I don't know who is going to do it or where he's going to do it" – and he said, "The coup planners are very much cleverer this time than they've ever been before because there are a number of them and I can't find out which is the real one." That's what he said. That was noon.'

At 1.30 pm while Lodge was having lunch at the Embassy he recalls '. . . this tremendous automatic fire: it sounded as though it was right in the next room – and the planes flew overhead, and that was the beginning of the overthrow'.

November 3, 1963—Jeering crowds with the head of a demolished statue move through the streets of Saigon following the fall of the Diem government. The monument was destroyed because of its resemblance to Vietnam's former first lady.

Above: November 3, 1963—Barefooted youth jumps on the head of a statue in a Saigon street after the government of Ngo Dinh Diem was overthrown in a military coup. The statue was symbolic of the influence of Madame Ngo Dinh Nhu, the president's sister-in-law.

The go-between General Tran Van Don then viewed the coup as perfect timing: 'The time was 1.30 in the afternoon. All coups everywhere in the world are made at night. We believed that the coup was a good coup and we must do it in the daytime. It surprised many people, especially the presidency and the presidential guard because we knew that at night they have to watch, to be awake, and have to sleep in the daytime. It was very good timing.'

The coup forces seized key installations, then surrounded Diem's palace. 'One division', says General Don, 'was commanded by a Colonel whose name was Nguyen Van Thieu. He was very famous after that.' Don and the other generals had summoned all senior officers to central headquarters to ask them to support the coup. Only one, Colonel Tung Do, refused – and was later executed.

CIA agent Conein joined the generals at headquarters as the coup progressed. 'I had a special radio that kept me into a special net directly to the Embassy; plus I had – with the junta's agreement – a special telephone line directly to the US Embassy.' 'I could be reached,' says Ambassador Lodge, 'whether I was in my residence or in the office. I had the equipment to reach people locally and reach Washington to some extent.'

At 3.00 pm General Don called the Embassy to ask if there was any plan to get Diem and his family out of Vietnam if they were to surrender. He was assured that a plane was ready (Lodge himself had a plane standing by for his Washington visit).

At 4.00 pm – after Diem had twice refused to surrender – the coup forces began to mortar the palace, but resistance from Diem's presidential guard prevented an assault. Diem now appealed to the American Ambassador. 'The telephone rang,' says Lodge, 'and it was President Diem saying that the coup had begun, and he wanted to know what I was going to do. And I said the obvious truth, that I had no instructions, that it was four o'clock in the morning in Washington and I'd had no opportunity to deal with it.

'He said, "Well you must know what the policy is." "Well," I said, "I don't know what the policy is for every circumstance. And", I said, "I'm worried about your safety. I've made arrangements to get you out of the country so as to protect your safety. And if you don't like to do that, I've made arrangements which would authorize your becoming titular head of state, and you can stay here in a position of honor and you'll be relatively safe." He said, "I don't want to do that. I want to restore order and I'm going back now to restore order." And he hung up.'

General Don says he tried to reason with Diem: 'During the coup, Diem called me from his palace. I said to him, "Mr President, I am sorry for what has happened but what I ask you now is be wise and understand the situation and a special plane is ready if you surrender without any conditions to carry you and your family out of Vietnam.'

Again Diem and his brother, Ngo Dinh Nhu, refused to surrender. Using a secret exit they escaped from the palace after dark, hiding at the home of a friend in Cholon, the Chinese quarter. From this base they remained in touch with the generals throughout the night – at one point defiantly calling on the generals to surrender. But at 3.30 in the morning of 2 November, after aerial and were taken from the church to an armored personnel carrier.

General Don makes this allegation: 'I can say frankly that Big Minh [General Duong Van Minh] didn't want them alive. They were killed on the way to headquarters.' (General Minh's version is unobtainable. Of all the senior plotters, only he remained in Vietnam as Saigon fell on 30 April 1975.) When the troops arrived at the Cholon house Diem and his brother were not there. They were discovered shortly after in a nearby Catholic church. The brothers surrendered unconditionally and were taken from the church to an armoured personnel carrier.

Ambassador Lodge says he was shocked: 'I had reports of him [Diem], culminating of course in the horrible tragic reports of his assassination. Terrible thing, terrible thing. And I don't believe we know now whether that assassination was private initiative, or in response to governmental initiatives.' The first report issued by the generals had stated that the brothers had committed 'accidental suicide' while trying to seize weapons. The CIA later obtained photographs of the bodies of Diem and Nhu. They had been shot with their hands tied behind their backs.

After the killings, General Don was delegated by the coup committee to explain matters to the American Embassy. 'On the 2nd of November, I was sent by the committee to the American Embassy where Ambassador Lodge was waiting for us to know more details about the results of the coup. We were very welcome at the gate of the Embassy. But in his office Lodge told us immediately that President Kennedy and the people of the United States were very shocked. I told him it was not planned to kill Diem and Nhu. . . . What can I say now? – what I have said to the family: we are very sorry.'

In Washington, President Kennedy heard of Diem's murder while in session with the National Security Council. His military advisor, General Maxwell Taylor, was present: 'The cable was brought in by one of the President's aides and put in front of him – and he read it. There was a silence around the table. The President was obviously shaken, sprang to his feet and walked out of the room saying nothing to anybody – and stayed out of the room for some minutes.'

Kennedy had now to endure the memory of his early cable to Ambassador Lodge 'accepting the consequences'. He had approved a coup, then rejected it, then permitted it again. He had taken weeks arriving at various policies, only to abandon them within days. He had endorsed a political solution – preparing plans for the withdrawal of US advisors – but at the same time he had pursued an opposite course into the unknown, pledging military support for untested generals who had begun

Above: November 3, 1963—Helmeted rebel troops and Vietnamese civilians celebrate the successful coup that ousted President Diem from office.

Above: December 20, 1968—U. S. Defense Secretary Robert S. McNamara walks with Maj. Gen. Duong Van Minh, chairman of South Vietnam's ruling junta, during their meeting in Saigon. McNamara flew in from Washington to discuss U.S. support for the war against the Viet Cong.

Right: This map, based on a official pamphlet issued in 1964 by the North Vietnamese government, showed the location of Viet Cong bases in South Vietnam, and routes used to supply them. The guerillas claimed that half of the territory and three-quarters of the people in South Vietnam were under Viet Cong control.

by bloodying their own and America's image – and this image was his reason for being in Vietnam, to uphold and guard American ideals. In this he had tried to serve America. And Diem – he had fought the Communists for nine years: he deserved a better end than assassination, Kennedy told his silent aides when he re-entered the room.

William Colby of the CIA was present: 'Kennedy was obviously upset, distraught. . . . I think that he felt a sense of personal responsibility for it. Certainly he hadn't anticipated it – whether he should have or not is another question.'

Kennedy's special advisor, Arthur Schlesinger Jr, stated: 'It was no part of our plan, or expectations, that Diem and his brother would be murdered. For reasons of their own the generals decided to kill them. The death of Diem upset Kennedy partly because he was a humane man and didn't like people being killed – particularly perhaps other heads of state – but in part because he may have feared that this was going to pull us in.'

'It was a shock to all of us,' says Kennedy's military advisor, Maxwell Taylor, 'but I think perhaps to the President more than any of us – because he didn't realize that we were all playing with fire when we were at least giving tacit encouragement to the overthrow of this man.'

'There were then', recalls Schlesinger, '16,000 American advisors attached to the army of Vietnam. [There had been only 900 American advisors in Vietnam when Kennedy took office.] The total number of Americans killed in combat in Vietnam by the end of 1963 was around seventy-five – obviously seventy-five too many but inconsiderable in comparison with the numbers that were to be killed later.'

After nearly three years of indecision Kennedy, belatedly trying to prevent the coup, had planned to give Diem a last chance. If Diem had not conformed within two months Kennedy had privately decided to withdraw 1000 troops as the beginning of America's withdrawal. But would he have done?

Assistant Secretary of State Roger Hilsman says, 'We instituted a lot of planning in the State Department about how to withdraw but we never dared send one of those pieces of paper to the Pentagon.' He states that Kennedy trusted Defense Secretary McNamara, but not the military: 'We thought that somebody on his staff might well undercut and destroy. So this whole documentary evidence of the other option – the option of withdrawal – is still not on public record.'

Could Diem have survived in this confused US policy situation? Most of Kennedy's men – who did not know of his last-minute withdrawal plans – considered Diem's downfall a Vietnamese affair. The Vietnamese generals, however, effectively regarded the coup as American-ordered, and it was staged only when the generals knew they would inherit American aid. Diem's press secretary, Thien, quotes one of the coup leaders, General Kim, on his motivations: 'I asked him afterwards because I considered him loyal to President Diem. And General Kim said "The Americans told us to choose between Diem and American aid. We had no choice." '

Washington now had no choice but to recognize the new Saigon government – a military junta headed by Generals Minh, Kim and coup go-between Tran Van Don. None of Washington's foreboding was evident in Saigon, according to Ambassador Lodge: 'There was a great joy . . . when a man has been a dictator, absolute ruler for eight or nine years he begins to do things that he wouldn't do at the end of one year. So there was a great atmosphere of joy. The American Embassy was extremely popular. People would cheer and wave flags when they went by.'

The cheers – and the junta – lasted three months. Diem would be the last civilian strong-man. In the next twenty months there would be ten changes of government, with the generals deposing each other. Major-General Edward Lansdale, the American who had advised Diem

when he was the early hope, foresaw 'a tragedy for Vietnam'. He was by this time back in Washington with the CIA and he says the Agency 'had been opposed to the way it happened. . . . With his overthrow, they overthrew a constitution, and with the constitution they waived orderly change: a way to reappoint Province Chiefs and District Chiefs. In effect the political move to knock off the Chief of State actually was dividing politically in the face of a very alert, smart, energetic enemy.'

The North Vietnamese 'were startled that we would have participated in the overthrow of President Diem and they were essentially caught by surprise,' says William Colby. As the CIA's Far East Director at that time Colby hastened to Vietnam and reported back that the war would soon be over – and lost.

'It really sounds incredible today,' says Colby, looking back, 'that we made those decisions about getting rid of Diem without really careful consideration about what kind of government would replace him. And of course we got rid of a mandarin to select some generals who would presumably bring about a more democratic government.

'The chaos and anarchy which infected the Vietnamese government at that time caused everything to fall apart. The assessments were very clear that the situation was going downhill very fast during 1964, and our assessment was that the Communists would probably win the war by about the end of 1965. They began to send their military units – not just infiltrators but military units – down the Ho Chi Minh Trail in the fall of 1964 to begin to build up the military force to administer the *coup de grâce*.

'Now President Johnson who was in charge of it at that time was of course a very tenacious Texan, a very tought fellow, and he wasn't about to have that happen.'

Left: November 3, 1963—Young demonstrators cheer the rebels who overthrew the government in a violent coup the previous day.

Below: December 20, 1963—South Vietnamese students carry placards and banners as they march near the French embassy in Saigon to protest French President Charles de Gaulle's proposals for neutralizing Vietnam.

Above: November 2, 1963—Mrs. Ngo Dinh Nhu tells a news conference in Beverly Hills, California, that the deaths of her husband and brother-in-law in South Vietnam 'were murders, either with the official or unofficial blessings of the American government.'

Above right: December 1963—U.S. Army Special Forces Staff Sgt. Howard Stevens, *right*, leads a South Vietnamese patrol deep into mountain terrain on a search for Viet Cong forces.

Right: December 1963—U.S. soldiers and the Koho tribesmen they trained crouch in underbrush to return fire against a Viet Cong ambush party in the jungles of Vietnam's central mountains.

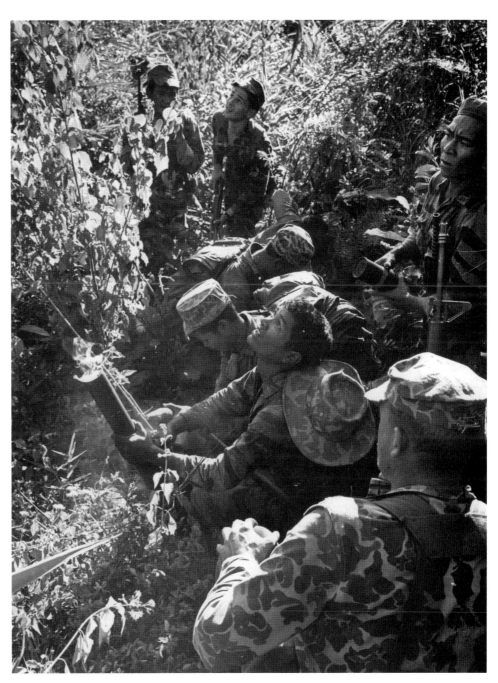

Left: December 1963—A patrol of U.S.-trained Koho tribesmen sets out from the strategic hamlet of Fillian for six days and nights of deadly hide-and-seek with the Viet Cong in rugged Montagnard country in the central mountains of South Vietnam.

Right: December 27, 1963— Gen. Duong Van Minh, South Vietnamese chief of staff, joins a dancing dragon at Cao Dai temple in Tay Ninh during a ceremony in which the religious sect officially aligned itself with the New South Vietnamese regime.

# DAYS OF DECISION

Three weeks after the bloody coup in Saigon, Kennedy's senior advisors were once again hastily abandoning a top-level conference in Honolulu. At the same time, aboard Airforce-1 en route from Dallas to Washington, Lyndon Baines Johnson was being hurriedly sworn in as the thirty-sixth President of the United States. It was 22 November 1963, and John F. Kennedy had been assassinated that afternoon.

The abrupt transition of power began America's most painful decade since the Civil War. It was the genesis of the most questionable conflict of arms in modern history, its dimension and duration seemingly inexplicable unless first examined through the combustive interaction of several factors. There were the contrary character and ideals of Kennedy and Johnson, the nature of the presidential office itself with its pressures to allow domestic considerations to influence foreign affairs, and the tragic confluence of America's presidential drama and the entrenched leadership

> '**If we get involved in that bitch of a war my Great Society will be dead.**'
>
> – LYNDON JOHNSON
> TO HIS BIOGRAPHER

and objectives of North Vietnam – portrayed here in previously unpublished 'top secret' official papers.

Vietnam plagued Johnson almost from the moment he was sworn in. It destroyed his presidency, drained his enormous vitality, aborted then reversed the fuller democracy for which he had struggled a lifetime, and finally left him – the most grass roots of Presidents – a physical and embittered wreck of a man, isolated from and doubting 'the fickle public' whom he had so long revered, and, because of Vietnam, so long deceived. From that extraordinary moment speeding to the capital aboard Airforce-1 when Johnson took the solemn oath to 'uphold the constitution' (no words could be more sacred to Johnson, judged on his record) Vietnam became a corrupting fixation, forever poignant as to purpose, irredeemable in blood and lost innocence.

Johnson's first words to the nation when he arrived in Washington were a pledge to heal the

November 22, 1963—Lyndon B. Johnson becomes president of the United States, sworn in by Judge Sarah T. Hughes aboard the presidential jet after John F. Kennedy is assassinated in Dallas. Mrs. Johnson stands to the left of her husband; Mrs. Kennedy to the right.

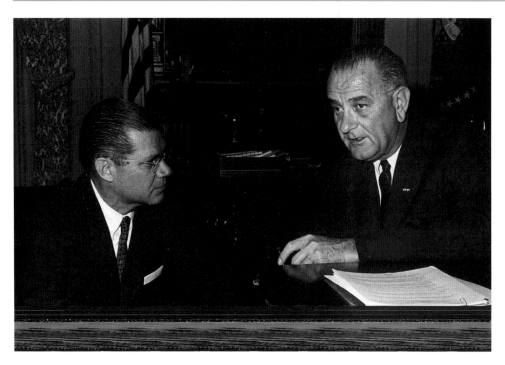

November 23, 1963—President Lyndon B. Johnson confers with Secretary of Defense Robert S. McNamara, one of many conferences by the new chief executive.

wounds of assassination inflicted in his own home State of Texas, and to build a 'Great Society' based on equitable civil rights. His dream, he would tell biographer Doris Kearns, was to be remembered as the greatest social reformer in American history. As Johnson entered the Oval Office, says Kearns, Vietnam was 'clearly not an issue that he cared very much about – not at all with the conviction that he cared about the "Great Society": black issues, the poor, feeding people, educating people. He really cared about that. Vietnam was abstract.'

Within twenty-four hours the abstraction changed as Johnson found himself 'weighed by the dynamics of military involvement'. Only one day into his presidency he was hearing Kennedy's own advisors doubting Kennedy's last course of action: to begin withdrawing American military advisors from Vietnam on 3 December. Johnson now heard from Secretary of Defense McNamara and Secretary of State Rusk that Kennedy's instructions were incompatible with his wider objectives of containing Communism.

McNamara and Rusk had been conferring in Honolulu on the phased withdrawal with Ambassador Lodge and General Harkins. They concluded that the political climate in Vietnam following the assassination of Diem was not as expected. In Saigon there was quiet but persistent 'neutralist' talk – attributed to junta leader General Duong Van Minh, who was believed to have family connections in Hanoi. Three days earlier Cambodia's Prince Sihanouk had suddenly put an end to all US military and economic aid, accusing the CIA of plotting a coup against him. The assessment was that the Communists were exploiting confusion in South-east Asia by encouraging neutralist forces which they could very soon dominate.

Like Kennedy, Johnson had repeatedly drawn a scenario of aggressive monolithic Communism on the march, with South Vietnam as a measure of the Free World's determination. Yet Johnson had passionately opposed direct US combat involve-

ment in earlier years, instead advocating third-party containment. Kennedy had clearly, if belatedly, tried to curtail the US military commitment in Vietnam. Kennedy, according to sources, had specifically instructed Defense Secretary McNamara to effect the withdrawal of American helicopter pilots who were ferrying the South Vietnamese into combat – and at times engaging in it. Johnson could therefore come to one of two

conclusions: either Kennedy considered the scenario to be wrong or South Vietnam no vital part of it. Alternatively, Kennedy would have reversed his orders had he now been listening to McNamara's urgent recommendation that the troop withdrawal should be delayed. McNamara was forceful with Johnson, declaring that Kennedy's orders would be a 'death sentence' for South Vietnam at this time.

Within forty-eight hours of taking office, President Johnson announced that US military support for the Saigon junta would continue. The first-stage withdrawal of 1000 troops was outwardly to take place, but Johnson privately agreed that this should comprise only support staff who would then be quietly replaced. There would be no actual reduction of US forces. Johnson's days – and ways – of decision had begun.

Within three months Kennedy men who had complied with his concerns would be completing detailed plans for direct American military intervention. Within nine months, without prior warning, Johnson would take America to war in Vietnam. He would eventually commit 543,000 combat troops to 'draw a line' against Communism – 9000 miles from America's shores. The ensuing tragedy, with its vast social impact on America, would seem Emersonian: as if events were in the saddle', riding Johnson. He had inherited the confusion of two assassinations, together with Kennedy's imperfect circle of domino-minded advisors. His sudden commitment of public resources and emotions to a distant war was demonstrably in conflict with his known domestic goals. Circumstances forced his decisions – *or was it the reverse?*

Perhaps the most devastating revelation of the entire war is Johnson's admission – as quoted here – that party political interests were a major

February 11, 1964—Maj. Gen. Duong Van Minh, right, greets U.S. Ambassador Henry Cabot Lodge and other members of the U.S. Mission in Saigon. At left is Gen. Paul D. Harkins.

factor in his early military decisions. Long afterwards Johnson told biographer Doris Kearns that he knew 'better than any' of his advisors the alternatives that he faced. Reveals Kearns: 'He said, "I knew from the start what the choice involved." He said if we got involved in that bitch of a war over there my Great Society was going to be dead. And yet on the other hand if he let the war go, and he let the South Vietnamese lose, then he was afraid that all of the old traditional anti-Democratic Party feeling – you lost China, you lost Vietnam – was going to come screeching at him.'

Judged by this statement Johnson's immediate motivation in Vietnam was political self-defense as much as defense of the Free World. In something akin to a test of national machismo, he had to hold Vietnam in order to hold the White House. The theoretical fear of losing the leadership if he lost Vietnam was at least as equal a determinant as the actual military situation when he took office. The intensity of Johnson's ambitions for his people would bring only vast social upheaval, but if it was an inescapable irony that the Great Society had to be won in a foreign jungle, then perhaps the essential flaw was not in Johnson's character but in that of the office itself.

The abrupt Kennedy-Johnson transition pointed to a fundamental weakness in the governing system: the successor had been kept ignorant of higher policy, had taken virtually no part in previous decision making and had no new mandate, yet he represented a radical overnight change of leadership methods and character. Johnson's actions and the origins of war can only be explained in this context. As biographer Kearns says, 'It is crazy to pretend that he went blindly into this thing happily.'

Kearns undoubtedly had a greater insight into Johnson's character and problems than anyone else outside of his family – and she became almost part of that. Probably no other presidential biographer was afforded such a candid study of the subject and the office. Johnson's revelations to Doris Kearns about his Vietnam motivations are essential to any understanding of America's sudden plunge into war.

Johnson was almost sixty, Kearns in her late twenties, when they first met in 1967. The occasion was a White House dance held to celebrate the annual Fellows program, which selects bright young academics to work as special assistants of the President and the Cabinet. Doris Kearns was then studying for a Harvard Ph.D. in government

and had just co-authored an anti-war article in the *New Republic* titled 'How to remove LBJ in 1968'. Johnson knew of this. At the White House dance Kearns was a challenge to him: he would waltz the New Left. As they danced Johnson told her: 'Come down to Washington and if I can't convince you young Harvard girls, then I am not worth anything.' Kearns did strongly believe in Johnson's social reforms. She joined the Labor Department, setting up educational projects for young urban blacks. A year or so later, after Johnson's withdrawal from office, he asked Kearns to work with him on his memoirs. She spent four years on this and produced her own study, *Lyndon Johnson And The American Dream*. She records that while working and staying at the Johnson family ranch she watched the death of his resolve, saw him 'crumpled, ragged and defenseless'.

Johnson 'slept poorly' and 'we talked mostly in the early hours of the morning'. In her account for this book Kearns describes how 'a ritual had developed'. She would rise and dress at 5 am and Johnson would arrive soon after: 'He would get into the bed – I would sit in a chair. He would pull the sheets up, almost like a little kid, and he would start talking to me then about all of his hopes and dreams and what he had wanted out of the presidency.'

March 9, 1964—Secretary of Defense Robert S. McNamara, left, and Gen. Maxwell D. Taylor, chairman of the Joint Chiefs of Staff, raise the arms of South Vietnamese Premier Nguyen Khanh in a victory salute during a visit to Bac Lieu on their tour of the Mekong Delta to gain public support.

In the months before he died (January 1973), 'he had begun to question, not so much Vietnam, but whether a life that is lived, as his was, always for public approval, is really ever going to produce satisfaction in the end'. In one such bedroom confessional the leader of the Free World admitted to his biographer that his decision to commit America to war in Asia was essentially based on maintaining public approval. Johnson felt that he was trapped from the beginning by the Eisenhower-Kennedy rhetoric of America as the global policeman, that his domestic goals and political base would be lost in any perceived failure of this foreign policy.

After the first three years of war, with his presidency destroyed by public divisions, Johnson could see the paradox but could not see that there had been any option. Johnson, wrote Kearns, believed that if he let Vietnam go 'they would all be saying he was a coward. Then the conservative uprising would be so great that he would lose the Great Society either way.' Kearns characterizes Johnson as 'a sad man, from the beginning'.

At the beginning of his presidency, therefore, Johnson was influenced towards war by his perception of his office. The old adage that the office makes the man only implies that it makes a better man. Johnson before assuming the presidency had served and mastered the political system better and longer than most public figures of his time. But the system was such that nothing in Johnson's twenty-six years of high Washington office could have prepared him for a leadership in crisis so suddenly thrust upon him. Johnson's personal position on Vietnam had been one of caution. The office would unmake the man.

In 1954, as the Senate Democratic floor leader during Eisenhower's presidency, Johnson had been largely instrumental in blocking American intervention at Dien Bien Phu. Seven years later, as Vice-President, he made his first brief visit to Saigon, declaring that 'the battle against Communism in South-east Asia must be joined with strength and determination'. But his recommendations merely reiterated administration policy, or continued aid. Vietnam was 'abstract' if only because, as Vice-President, Johnson had no direct authority – and during Kennedy's last embattled months had almost no access to the President. None of Kennedy's advisors knew his ultimate intentions on Vietnam and only a few close aides knew of his inner doubts. The Kennedy-Johnson ticket was one of party expediency, not compatibility. In background and character the two men were opposites.

Kennedy's life had been privileged and politically ordained, yet he was physically and to some critics even intellectually weak. His family power and personal charisma were popularly construed as maturity, yet he was culturally elitist, a man oversensitive and susceptible to his 'Eastern Establishment' academic circle, whose accounts portray Kennedy as in constant need of reassurance and consensus, increasingly indecisive lest his acts betray the myth.

Lyndon Johnson was the product of his impoverished boyhood on a small Texas farm: physically, mentally, he was Texas for ever – taller, tougher, rougher than the next man. He was charged with energy, impatience and arrogance, a man who rose from teacher's college to the presidency propelled by his conviction that he could change grass-roots America. Johnson and Kennedy were alike only in that grand visions possessed them, but their dreams were as separate as their characters and as far apart in plausibility. If Kennedy sought to be the world's Moses who would part the onrushing Red Sea, Johnson sought to be the home savior who would close the widening tide between black and white. Vietnam was no part of Johnson's crusade, but it now became his priority: a nightmare to be resolved before his dream could be realized. Johnson was also a man in a hurry – he had suffered two heart attacks before assuming the presidency.

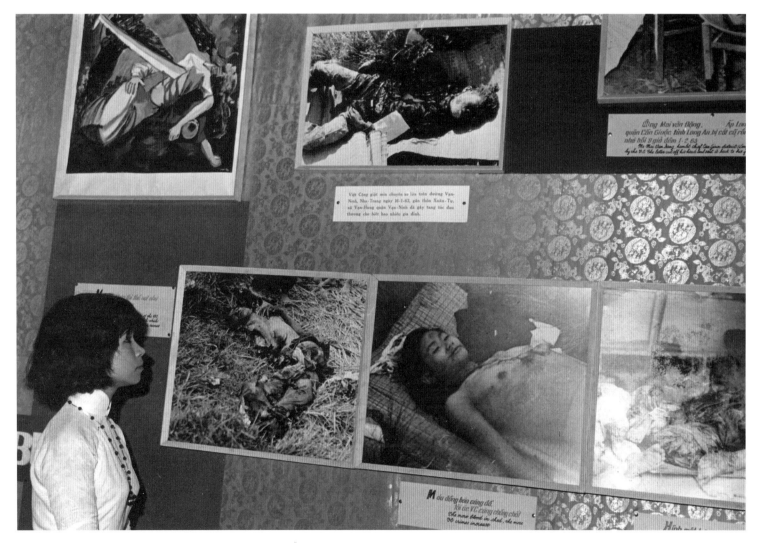

July 20, 1964—A visitor views photographs of Viet Cong atrocities posted at the Information Hall in Saigon. The exhibition was part of a National Day of Shame, held to mark the anniversary of the signing of the Geneva Accords in which Vietnam was divided into two nations.

As Vice-President Johnson's role in the system had been that of a stand-in who in reality could not understudy the principal player. He had been hardly closer than any other American to the daily pressures of the world's most powerful office which he might at any moment inherit. This aberration of government now proved a dangerous one as Johnson's urgency fused with Kennedy's legacy, or confusion of policy. Johnson managed the White House in the same domineering, manipulative way that he had controlled the factional Congress. Says biographer Kearns: 'You just have to remember Johnson's perception of his own past. Always he had been the master behind-the-door bargainer – probably the best the Senate had ever seen. And his technique had always been, "Don't let anybody really know what you are doing. If this Senator knows and that one doesn't know, all the better." Somehow he believed that as long as he kept American attention on the Great Society, on civil rights progress, and on the things he was doing at home, that war over there just wouldn't matter very much.'

Overnight the United States had a new President who on the one hand was charged with maintaining continuity without any personal knowledge of it, and who on the other hand had his own priorities and had been ceded total power of decision. As a life-long Congressman Johnson knew as well as anyone the intended constitutional limitations on presidential power, but Johnson's total command of the constitutional system demonstrated another weakness: a President who knew it well enough could avoid the checks and balances.

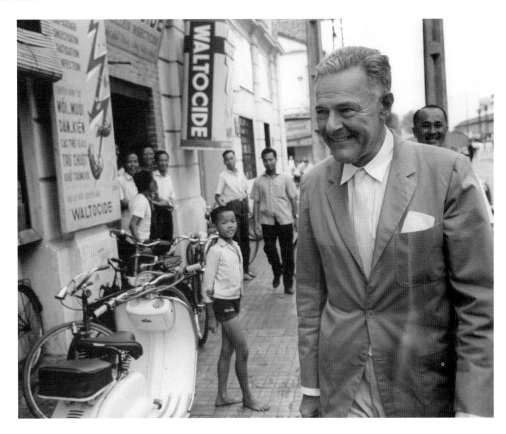

March 10, 1964—U.S. Ambassador Henry Cabot Lodge smiles on a Saigon street while spending the day with Defense Secretary Robert McNamara. On the same day, Lodge was the surprise write-in winner of the New Hampshire primary, although he had no stated plans to run for president.

January 29, 1964—A North Vietnamese farmer waits with his hands clasped over his head to be transported to a prisoner of war interrogation camp after capture by South Vietnamese government forces.

151

Kearns, paraphrasing Johnson, says: 'What happened as decisions on the war concentrated in the White House is part of what happened to American government in the twentieth century. More and more foreign policy decisions became concentrated in the White House rather than in the Congress. And his [Johnson's] power was such that dissenters had a very hard time staying within the framework of dissent – within the White House. He really didn't have to listen to anybody.'

Johnson's public position on the war was generally accepted even when his methods were condemned. Vietnam would be widely viewed as a tragic error – but, an *error*. America's intentions if not its actions would be held to be of the highest order, and this remains the assessment of many of the policy makers and text books. But the evidence of these pages is that Lyndon Johnson's conduct of the Vietnam war was the foreign policy equivalent of Richard Nixon's Watergate: the deception of the public and the Congress had – at least at the beginning – the same element of political self-preservation.

'I think the best thing that could have happened to him [Johnson]', says Kearns, 'would have been to have had a structure of government more like the British or somewhere else, where you had to *listen* to Congress. All he had to do was hear them [the dissenters] complaining, or 'bellyaching' as he called it. But he knew that he had the power of decision in his hands.'

The observations of Kearns, based on Johnson's admissions, raise profound questions for all democracies on the extent to which an American President, as the Free World leader, can arrogate power and circumvent the Congress. While this may always have been so, the implications become awesome with the documentation here of the casual origins of America's longest, most brutalizing war. As Kearns recounts Johnson's early Vietnam decisions, he thought he 'could finesse it somehow. He would send in a few people here and there. He would send a few bombs here and there. But he just could never believe at that point that it was going to turn out to be the size and commitment that it eventually became.'

As the commitment grew, Johnson and his aides had perforce to enlarge on their original rationale. They all, as Kearns notes, held a genuine fear of Communism and shared 'a simplistic sense of history' which they adjusted to their actions. Johnson, says Kearns, 'got to the point where the North Vietnamese fitted the categories of the Germans in World War I and World War II'. America had helped to end those wars 'and now here he was preventing World War III'.

But however sincere Johnson's original fears, he made it clear to Kearns that it was initially the advice at hand as much as any distant Communist action which dictated his decisions. Johnson had retained Kennedy's inner circle and, says Kearns in her biography, he felt that 'so long as his policies were approved by these men who represented the established wisdom he was, at least, insured against appearing foolish or incompetent'.

Even those Kennedy men who decided there was no longer wisdom in the White House, and who would shortly resign, assume that it was the inner circle which had Johnson besieged rather than it being the shield Johnson says it was. The historian Arthur Schlesinger Jr, a close friend of Kennedy's and his Special Assistant, who briefly

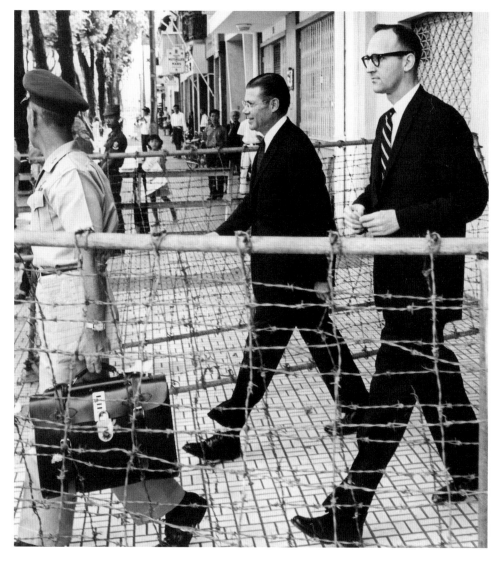

March 8, 1964—U.S. Defense Secretary Robert S. McNamara, on a fact-finding mission to assess the status of the battle against the Viet Cong, leaves the U.S. embassy in Saigon after meeting with Premier Gen. Nguyen Khanh.

remained with the new President, says that at first Johnson could certainly argue that he was 'doing what Kennedy would have done, and had reason to think this, because he kept as his advisors people like McNamara, Bundy and others who in that period, though they came to change their minds later, still thought the war might be won'.

William Bundy, then McNamara's deputy at Defense, says Johnson was 'carrying on exactly the basic policy that Kennedy had pursued regarding containment of China'. But would Kennedy have extended this to hot pursuit? Even Bundy doubts that Kennedy 'would have necessarily taken the same kinds of decisions that Johnson did. He was more sceptical. I think, than Johnson of what American military force might do. But there is no question on the basic judgements about the importance of Vietnam, and the importance of holding on.'

In fact, there was much last moment questioning by Kennedy, according to Roger Hilsman of the State Department, but it was not known to the Bundys and McNamaras. As Hilsman has noted, his group 'did not dare' advise the Defense Department of Kennedy's various troop withdrawal plans – the overall numbers and dates – and in this environment it is questionable whether Kennedy could have resisted the military dynam-

ics any more than Johnson. What is certain is that as Johnson took office neither American nor North Vietnamese forces were fighting in Vietnam. The trigger of war was the interaction in Johnson's mind of the *perceived* threats of foreign and domestic defeat, and possibly Johnson's fear of these twin specters ensured their substance. From his first days in unelected office he conveyed the impression of a man looking over both shoulders. His admirers and detractors agree that while he did not seek war he sought quick solutions. Roger Hilsman and others at the State Department – with the notable exception of Secretary Rusk – would soon resign over this approach. Rusk, too, emphasizes where Johnson's real interest lay; the war, even at its hottest, was an abstraction.

'President Johnson', says Rusk, 'was a man in a great hurry, possibly because he never knew from one day to the next whether he would still be alive. But except for the men who carried the battle, and their families, no one agonized over Vietnam more than Lyndon Johnson did. There was so much he wanted to accomplish in the time that he had, so many things were barred to him by the problems of Vietnam. So I think that this was the inherited burden which he had to carry, which he would have been glad to do without.'

January 12, 1964—U.S. Army H-21 Shawnee helicopters, "Flying Bananas," fly in tight formation while providing air support for South Vietnamese operation near Bien Hoa, north of Saigon.

Rusk's deputy, Roger Hilsman, felt that Johnson's personal predicament had led him to set a time limit. 'I stress that I don't see that Johnson was plotting to escalate the war from the moment Kennedy died. I think that if in the next six months the counter-insurgency policy of giving them aid and advisors had worked he would have been content. But I think he had already made up his mind that he would not permit the loss of Vietnam.'

Exactly six months after his first presidential act postponing Kennedy's troop withdrawal Johnson had the US on a secret war alert. The military preparations in Washington gained a velocity far beyond the existing fighting, and these became self-escalating. They had a logic of their own, or that of the American domestic political situation. In the early weeks in which Johnson reversed military gears to fast forward, there were strategically some compelling reasons and justification, counseled by some advisors and allies, for backing off. The scenario of monolithic Communism was breaking up with the Sino-Soviet rift, and while the wider ideological front was threatening in places – North Vietnam was heavily backed by China – the wisdom of making South Vietnam the battle front for defending Western values was

February 4, 1964—Former Vice President Richard Nixon visited Vietnam on a private visit. He is shown here at a reception, from left: Ambassador Henry Cabot Lodge, Nixon, Gen. Duong Van Minh, and Prime Minister Gen. Nguyen Khanh.

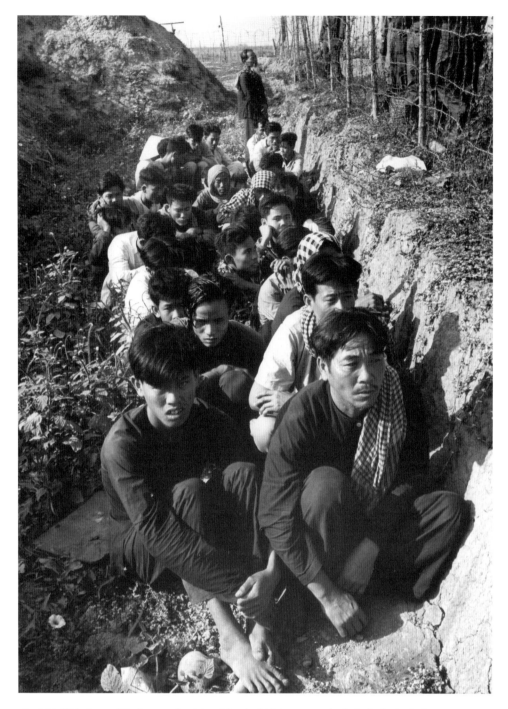

March 16, 1964—Suspected Viet Cong guerrillas sit in a ditch at the Cai Cai outpost near the Cambodian border. South Vietnamese troops reported 17 enemy dead, and 300 captured, in a victory at Cai Cai.

claimed strongman, General Nguyen Khanh, had replaced the troika. Khanh, a regimental commander and a minor ringleader in the Diem coup, was a total unknown to the Americans. Embassy officials could provide visiting newsmen with little precise biographical data of the new top dog in the junta line-up: he was 'the short, fat one in the middle'. Though Khanh would last a year his authority would be constantly challenged by fellow generals who could safely keep elbowing for power knowing that the United States could not condone any more bloody rolling of heads – a situation of impotence which left Khanh hospitalized with hypertension much of the time.

From the start the junta was a hydra, with its many heads biting at each other. The original coup leader, General Duong Van Minh, or 'Big Minh', had enough support to remain as titular Chief of State despite his suspected neutralist leanings. The new 'strongman', Khanh, acquired the semblance of popularity by simply naming himself Prime Minister, though he never held elections. He retained American support by telling the US what it least wanted to hear. He had taken command, he said, because the previous junta had 'inclinations to a neutralist solution which they wanted to impose on South Vietnam'. As Khanh put it (in an interview with the author in Saigon, February 1964) he had 'to break the bad eggs before they hatched a neutralist maneuver'.

Ultimately, eleven years later, 'bad eggs' General Minh and Chief of Staff General Tran Van Don would be urged by the US itself to seek a neutralist formula with the invading North Vietnamese, but in February 1964 General Khanh was advocating in press interviews that the South should invade the North with full US support. His statements were not repudiated in Washington. In the ensuing weeks Communist guerrillas enlarged their attacks closer to Saigon and began targeting US installations and personnel. For the first time in downtown Saigon the bar mysteries of the *Tu Do* and other places patronized by Americans were hidden behind iron grilles and steel-mesh windows as Molotov cocktails were pitted against Manhattans.

The US domino scenario was now complicated by a strong appeal from French President de Gaulle for a neutralist solution in Vietnam like that negotiated in Laos, and by Cambodia's Prince Sihanouk who announced that he would, after all, continue to accept US military and economic aid in order to stabilize the region provided Cambodia's neutrality was respected. Defense Secretary McNamara responded publicly that South Vietnam was a different case, its situation 'grave', with world freedom in the balance. South Vietnam, he told the House Armed Services Committee, 'is so important to the security of South-east Asia and to the free world that I can conceive of no alternative other than to take all necessary measures within our capability to prevent a Communist victory'. As McNamara was speaking France announced that it was establishing diplomatic relations with Communist China.

By March, McNamara was making his fifth on-the-spot survey. What he found to be the most 'grave' development, an inconceivable alternative, was talk of neutralism. From Saigon he cabled Johnson stating that 'dangerous neutralist' sentiments persisted. Johnson cabled back: 'We must stop neutralist talk wherever we can by what-

more doubtful by the week. In Saigon, government roulette among the generals meant that Washington was gambling one million dollars a day in military support for alternating, anonymous leaders who had no electoral mandate and no political solidarity. As the generals began deposing one another there was the embarrassing risk that the United States might find itself ejected in this revolving door. Had the phased troop withdrawals begun as planned weeks earlier, the US could have been seen as having decided itself to pull out. Now, as guerrilla activity increased with the political chaos in Saigon, it would appear one way or another that the United States was about to be pushed out. Whether this was of any great geopolitical consequence it would certainly have

profound American domestic impact – and perhaps in the long run this would be the same. With his first decision to stand firm, Johnson was in a quagmire.

Only six weeks into his presidency, and only nine weeks after the assassination of Ngo Dinh Diem, Johnson found himself dealing with a new Saigon government. He would do so on average once every two months for two years, and with each change in Saigon he would regard his options as less alterable. On 6 January 1964, the junta was shuffled to vest all power in a troika of generals, but the leader of the Diem coup, suspected neutralist General Minh, again emerged on top. On 30 January Saigon awoke to a new set of epaulettes; in the next of many coups a self-pro-

April 18, 1966—Vietnamese Buddhists—including soldiers, peasants, students, and businessmen—listen to a policy speech by Buddhist leader Thich Tri Quang in Da Nang.

ever means we can.' The immediate means was a planned increase in the US advisory force from 16,000 to 23,000 troops.

A neutralist solution, modeled on Laos, was what Kennedy had hoped for only a year or so earlier. Former Kennedy advisor William Bundy now considered this unreal. At this time Bundy had become Assistant Secretary of State for South-east Asia (a position which Roger Hilsman had resigned), a crucial job because it filtered field intelligence. Bundy's position-papers could greatly influence his seniors. Bundy, who had gone from Harvard to the DC bar to the CIA, would help structure Johnson's pivotal case persuading Congress to endorse military action. Bundy, says one critic, believed in covert methods because of his CIA background and believed that whatever means America employed, those of the Communists were worse. Bundy's report on Vietnam now differed significantly from that of the CIA: 'We believed,' says Bundy, 'and I think that history has tended to bear out this judgement, that North Vietnam was

implacably dedicated to establishing its control over South Vietnam initially, and eventually over the whole of Indo-China. And unless neutralization was fortified by clear resolve to prevent North Vietnam renewing military action, it would be a mirage.'

In fact, North Vietnam was not 'renewing' any military intervention because it had not yet begun any, according to the CIA's William Colby. His intelligence – and he was still Chief of the Far East Division of the CIA – shows that North Vietnamese main forces did not start moving South until late 1964, or several months after the fifty per cent increase in US troop levels. It was only then that Colby assessed that the Communists 'would probably win the war by the end of 1965'. Bundy responds that from early 1964 the North Vietnamese 'were sending arms and cadres' and 'were already clearly winning the war'. By this analogy, America was losing a war it had not yet entered.

Bundy's old chief at the Defense Department, Robert McNamara, returned from Vietnam in mid-

March and both his assessment and solution were apocalyptic. On 17 March, Johnson convened an extraordinary session of the National Security Council: it had to agree immediately on war policy measures. McNamara informed the Council that South Vietnam was on the 'verge of total collapse'. McNamara was known for his love of logistics; he would be viewed as the dispassionate architect of Vietnam's ultra-technological war, though finally he would become its foremost opponent. McNamara had gone from Harvard Business School to World War II, helping develop the logistics for mass bombing of Germany and Japan. He was President of the Ford Motor Company when Kennedy named him Secretary of Defense. Johnson, says his biographer, would come to feel 'really taken in' by McNamara's 'passion for facts'. McNamara now recommended, and it was agreed, that Kennedy's plans for phased withdrawal should be scrapped completely. He proposed, and it was agreed, that South Vietnam should begin general mobilization, with the new army receiving the

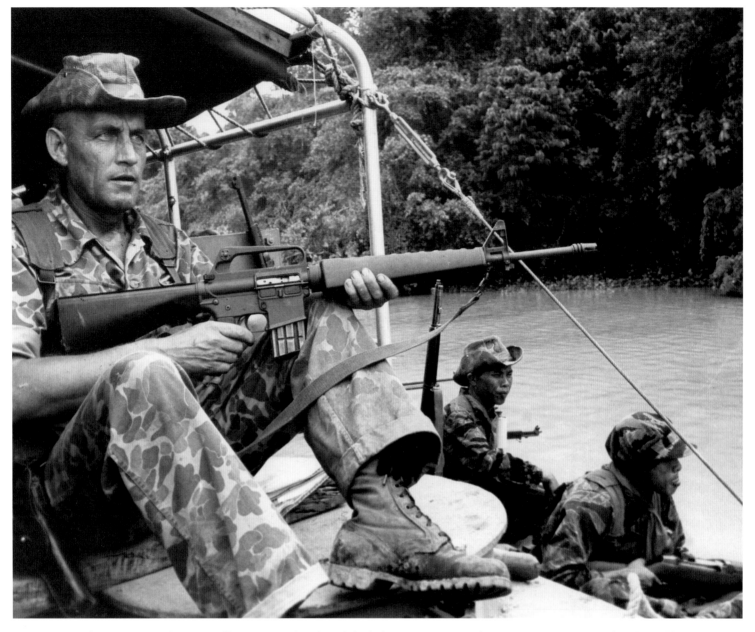

June 1964—A U.S. advisor accompanies South Vietnamese soldiers on a river patrol near the Cambodian border. Coming upon a suspected Viet Cong encampment, no men were found, but the soldiers destroyed buildings, livestock, and food after evacuating women and children.

most modern US equipment. He urged, and it was agreed, additional covert action against the North. Finally McNamara recommended exact planning for taking the war to the North, and this too was endorsed.

There would be a two-phase bombing plan. In phase one the United States Air Force would be ready at seventy-two hours notice to launch 'retaliatory' strikes against North Vietnamese military installations and against guerrilla sanctuaries inside the Laotian and Cambodian borders. In phase two, on thirty days notice, the US would start a 'program of graduated overt military pressure' – or intensified bombing against the North. Without any delay President Johnson authorized the planning stage of the bombing strategy.

In the Pentagon a young ex-Marine named Daniel Ellsberg, then described by a fellow Marine as a 'tough, hard-nosed hatchet man', was assigned to help prepare the bombing scenario. Ellsberg was also known as a Harvard thinker who practiced his

ideas. He had, ironically, achieved his Ph.D. with a paper titled 'Risk, Ambiguity and Decision', which induced the Rand Corporation to hire him as a war analyst. Ellsberg would eventually serve two years as an intelligence officer in Vietnam, having begun as a hawk, or one of 'McNamara's Boys', at the Pentagon in 1964. The 'Boys' were now asked for a bombing list. These early preparations for an escalated war only became known seven years later when Ellsberg leaked McNamara's remorseful internal study called the *Pentagon Papers*. Ellsberg asserts that in March 1964 the Pentagon chiefs were not only convinced that bombing of North Vietnam 'was essential but that it should have been done earlier'.

In analyzing this military planning in a domestic context, Ellsberg says he had 'the documents in my safe in 1964 that I later published in the *Pentagon Papers* that would have proven the degree to which the public was being lied to. . . . In other words, our democracy was being subvert-

ed in its most basic aspect of issues of war and peace. The Congress was being manipulated and the public was being manipulated. And all this was taking place, by the way, during a [presidential election] campaign.'

Within sixty days of Johnson's order, Ellsberg says, the Joint Chiefs 'had a very large target list'. It was co-ordinated with Pacific headquarters in Honolulu, which also provided separate logistical and strategic scenarios within only thirty days. Operation Plan 37-64 computerized the number of planes and tonnages needed for each phase of the bombing scenario. Operation Plan 32-64 analyzed the possible reactions of the Communist world, specifically China. It did not comment on whether this should be an influencing factor: it merely dealt with the US military requirements that might become necessary. Significantly, these requirements included the use of American ground forces. Honolulu was already one move ahead of Washington. There the Joint Chiefs finally revised the target priority to concentrate on crippling first-strikes against all installations supporting infiltration. It was calculated that with saturation bombing and bombardment by the 7th Fleet based in the Western Pacific all North Vietnamese facilities servicing the war in the South could be destroyed in just twelve days.

The completed scenario was delivered to the President in mid-May. Johnson placed it 'under consideration'. The considerations included the views or handling of Congress, public opinion in the form of the November presidential election, Allied opinion and the reaction of Hanoi to elements of the scenario already in effect. Johnson would delay full action for nine months, but the scenario for entering the war historically documents the administration's thinking, if not its leanings, within its first few months. Other negative factors influenced this thinking. In Saigon on 4 May Ambassador Lodge faced a distraught General Khanh who could not discipline the junta let alone the army. Khanh told Lodge that the war could not be won in the South. It must therefore be quickly taken to the North. He wanted immediate bombing and 10,000 American Special Forces to seal the border. Lodge countered only that bombing might be considered: Saigon knew nothing of Washington's preparations.

Only two weeks later Khanh's fears of a major border incursion seemed more rational to Washington. In Laos on 17 May Communist Pathet Lao troops launched a brief but punishing offensive against right-wing forces. It appeared that the three-year-old neutralist or coalition government could be toppled at any time. Sporadic skirmishes had never ceased, but unknown to the world the US had engaged in covert air activity in Laos – first running supplies, then bombing – for several years. Old T-28 fighter bombers – with Royal Lao markings, piloted by American and Asian mercenaries hired by the CIA – were strafing Pathet Lao positions and the border infiltration trails along which North Vietnam was sending cadres and weapons. Both sides were breaching Lao neutrality, and were silent about it. With this precedent, and with the escalating Communist attacks, Johnson decided on further secret warfare. On land, sea and air he took the first small steps toward the Pentagon war scenario.

In the field two imminent moves signified to both Hanoi and the American public a hardening of US resolve. US forces in Vietnam got a new, tough commander, General William Westmoreland, purportedly described by William Bundy as 'a blunt instrument'. And outgoing Ambassador Lodge was replaced by no less than the Chairman of the Joint Chiefs of Staff, General Maxwell D.

Taylor. In his first direct combat move, Johnson authorized US Navy and Air Force jets to fly reconnaissance support missions for the T-28s in Laos. At sea, Operation 34-A was intensified. This was the code name for clandestine raids on the North Vietnamese coast by South Vietnamese PT boats – an operation begun five months earlier coinciding with 'neutralist' talk. With these moves Johnson had a 'duress' rehearsal and the target information went to the super-secret 'Boys' at the Pentagon, among them Daniel Ellsberg: 'We were launching US-run CIA missions of torpedo boats, and other vessels, against the shores of North Vietnam, shelling, kidnapping, even assassinating, in various places.'

While Ellsberg would come to consider these commando raids as a provocation and the fuse for all-out war, William Bundy at his new State Department desk regarded them 'as a very small thing: a pin-prick'. Bundy says the Operation 34-A raids were 'directed squarely at what the North was doing in the South' or at bases from which material was being shipped to the guerrillas. Bundy says this infiltration of supplies was 'clear-cut, in international law terms, aggression' and so 'we looked hard for ways that might at least retaliate in some measure'. Bundy does not state whether he considered the US response a breach of international law. As the retaliatory measures

June 7, 1964—More than 40,000 South Vietnamese Catholics pack the Lam Son Square in Saigon to denounce the United States and Ambassador Henry Cabot Lodge.

June 20, 1964—Lt. Gen. William C. Westmoreland is shown in Saigon after taking over as commander of U.S. forces in Vietnam.

began, Bundy's new boss, Secretary of State Dean Rusk, was dispatched to Saigon for what would be the last senior field assessment before America's entry into the war. He spent three days there.

Rusk was considered a shadow Secretary of State under Kennedy, chosen say his critics for his pliability, but Johnson 'built his advisory system around Rusk'. Johnson would constantly tell biographer Doris Kearns how much he 'hated' Kennedy's Harvard circle, whom he called 'cold, purists, elitists who never understood the common people'. Rusk was merely a Rhodes Scholar who had worked his way through college; like Johnson, he was of common soil, the son of a poor Presbyterian minister, and he was much like his predecessor at State, John Foster Dulles, in his extreme visions of imminent Communist menace. Rusk would defend the US presence in Vietnam as insurance against 'a billion Chinese on the mainland, armed with nuclear weapons'. He would be Johnson's Chief Public Defender throughout and Rusk 'was the one person Johnson would never speak ill of. He would say "I love that Dean".'

Rusk was now entrusted with what amounted to Johnson's defense before the Court of History.

On 17 May 1964, the day when new fighting in Laos further weakened the pro-neutralist camps, Rusk flew into Saigon. His particular task was to rally Ambassador Lodge on the various 'retaliatory' moves being contemplated or effected. The outgoing Ambassador was being rumored as a Republican draft candidate for the Presidency. His support or his involvement was imperative. Lodge, briefed on the bombing scenario but mindful of how events had escalated since the last secret plot to overthrow Diem, strongly advised that North Vietnam should first be given a direct warning – and an inducement: 'carrot and stick', he told Rusk.

Rusk and Johnson had already agreed that concurrent with the airwar planning they must have dialogue with Hanoi. Rusk had appealed to the Canadians. In Ottawa on 30 April he had obtained Prime Minister Lester Pearson's agreement to send a Canadian emissary to Hanoi. But Rusk had proposed to Pearson only a very generalized warning.

Lodge had been advised of this approach but was dissatisfied. The US must be candid, he told Rusk. It was moving too fast, too directly. He had always felt that for as long as absolutely possible all

combat should be left to the South Vietnamese. It was a view Rusk shared. Though the Secretary would unhesitatingly defend every escalation of American combat once it had begun, his policy and belief were that global Communism could be contained through a show of force rather than the use of it. While victory in Vietnam was essential to American security it was, hopefully, a 'psychological struggle'. Rusk had supported the bombing scenario – he would later assert – believing that the threat or initial use of it would 'bring this matter to a conference table'. But, says Rusk: 'I thought we ought to try to get as much as possible of the burden carried by the South Vietnamese themselves.'

Lodge now had some specific advice on this. The 'stick' should be used immediately but lightly by the South Vietnamese before any messenger went to Hanoi. After some Communist 'terrorist act of the proper magnitude' Saigon's air force should attack a specific target in the North 'as a prelude' to the messenger, Lodge said. The Ambassador would reinforce his advice to Rusk by repeating it directly to President Johnson in an exchange of hitherto unpublished cables. Copies of these obtained by the author reveal that the Ambassador had grave concerns as he heard the Secretary of State outline the scenario for American air intervention. Lodge was blunt in his response: 'The Vietnamese Air Force must be made capable of doing this, and *they* [author's italics] should undertake this kind of action.'

'I much prefer', said Lodge, 'a selective use of Vietnamese air power to an overt US effort perhaps involving the total annihilation of all that has been built in North Vietnam since 1954, because this would surely bring in the Chinese Communists, and might well bring in the Russians. Moreover, if you lay the whole country waste, it is quite likely that you will induce a mood of fatalism in the Viet Cong.' Lodge was saying that the Pentagon scenario was risking a superpower war, and he again emphasized 'it should be covert and undertaken by the Vietnamese'.

Lodge was no ordinary Ambassador: he was not a Party man. In words of the thinnest diplomatic disguise he asked whether the administration had considered the possibility of nuclear escalation. 'It is easy for us', he said, 'to ignore our superiority as we did at the time of Berlin in 1948, when we still had sole possession of the atomic bomb. It is also a relatively simple concept to go out and destroy North Vietnam. What is complicated, but really effective, is to bring our power to bear in a precise way to get specific results.'

Rusk went over the priority bombing targets – specific military installations, specifically feeding the war in the South. These could be taken out, the North Vietnamese war effort crippled, it was calculated, in just twelve days. Lodge was clearly sceptical. The US government had to be morally accountable to the world at large. There first had to be an equivalent and demonstrable South Vietnamese effort against the North. Then, he said, 'We would be in a strong moral position with regard to US public opinion, the Congress and the United Nations.' Lodge advised that the US must 'have a record to show that we had given Ho Chi Minh fair warning' and had given 'honest and valuable inducements'. Lodge proposed that if Hanoi called off the war then the US should also help the North recover from the ravages of it with 'economic aid, notably food'.

April 18, 1964—Vietnamese Premier Nguyen Khanh, Secretary of State Dean Rusk, and U.S. Ambassador to Vietnam Henry Cabot Lodge talk politics in a meeting in Saigon.

Right: June 23, 1964—U.S. Ambassador Henry Cabot Lodge accompanies South Vietnamese Premier Maj. Gen. Nguyen Khanh to a marketplace during a speaking tour in the Mekong Delta. Hours later, Lodge's resignation was announced.

Rusk agreed that the 'carrot' should be offered. He would confer with the President. But a day after his return to Washington it was made clear to Lodge that America, if using a stick at all, would wield its own. On 22 May, having arranged a personal meeting between Canada's Prime Minister and President Johnson for the 28th, Rusk sent Lodge a top-priority coded cable headed: LITERALLY EYES ONLY FOR AMBASSADOR FROM SECRETARY.

It turned down Lodge's advice for prior covert South Vietnamese action on the grounds that 'substantial' attacks would have to be acknowledged and 'the finger would point straight at us and the President would then be put in perhaps a far more difficult position toward the American public and the Congress'. Rusk also questioned whether the warning to Hanoi should be too explicit: 'We tend to see real difficulty in approaching the Canadians at this time with any message as specific as you suggest, i.e., that Hanoi be told by the Canadians that they will be punished. But we are keeping this in mind.'

Lodge tartly responded to the effect that on an issue of war and peace the sensitivity of the messenger hardly mattered. The Ambassador cabled by return: LITERALLY EYES ONLY FOR THE SECRETARY FROM LODGE – 'It is not repeat not at all necessary that the Canadians either agree or disagree. What is important is that the Canadian transmit the message and be willing to do that and report back accurately what is said.'

Rusk now decided that the Canadian emissary to Hanoi must carry an ultimatum. But the Canadians had to be persuaded on this; the mission had to be ultra-secret yet Hanoi had to be forewarned of its importance, and finally for the public record there was the need for what might later seem 'fair warning' to explain either covert or overt action. In a speech on the day that he cabled Lodge rejecting his lighter stick, Rusk ranged over the choices in Vietnam and declared that one choice 'would be to expand the war. This can be the result if the Communists persist in their course of aggression.'

This speech and other intelligence had Canadian Prime Minister Pearson alarmed as he faced Johnson at an ostensibly casual encounter in New York on 28 May. The basics of the mission to Hanoi had been pre-agreed. Canadian members of the ICC – the International Control Commission or supposed truce supervisory group – rotated regularly between Saigon and Hanoi. Canada's new senior delegate. Commissioner James Blair Seaborn, was about to take up his post. He would make his first 'courtesy' visit to Hanoi on 18 June. A meeting with Prime Minister Pham Van Dong had been arranged. But Prime Minister 'Mike' Pearson had the feeling he was not hearing the full story from his old friend, Lyndon. How far would America go with the bombing scenario? What were the risks?

Pearson shared the same fears – and possibly information – as Ambassador Lodge. In a revealing document, the only official US reference uncovered on an unmentionable subject, the Pearson-Johnson exchange was cabled to Lodge from the State Department only minutes later: STATE 2133 TO AMEMBASSY SAIGON PRIORITY 30 MAY 10.40 AM: 'President told Pearson he wishes Hanoi to know that while he is a man of peace he does not intend to permit the North Vietnamese to take over South-east Asia. He needs a confidential and responsible interlocutor to carry the message of US attitudes to Hanoi. In outlining the US position there was some discussion of quote carrots and sticks unquote. Pearson after expressing willingness to lend Canadian good offices to this endeavor indicated some concern about this nature of the quote sticks unquote. He stipulated that he would have great reservations about the use of nuclear weapons but indicated that the punitive striking of discriminate targets by careful iron bomb attacks could be quote a different thing unquote. He said he would personally understand our resort to such measures if the messages transmitted through the Canadian channel failed to produce any alleviation of North Vietnamese aggression and that Canada would transmit messages around this framework.'

Canada's image both as a member of the ICC and as peace-keeper at large would emerge blackened after its Vietnam role, and Nobel Peace Prize winner Lester Pearson would later get a cold reception from Johnson to appeals to stop the bombing which he had seemingly so quickly endorsed. But Pearson's defenders see him as guiding Johnson to the far lesser of two evils, influ-

July 19, 1964—Effigies of Charles DeGaulle and Ho Chi Minh holding hands are displayed in Saigon during a Remembrance Day celebration. The effigies represent DeGaulle's attempt to reconcile North Vietnam and South Vietnam differences, which were interpreted by the south as favoring the north.

enced by nuclear fears. The question raised in Top Secret Deptel 2133 is whether a nuclear stick was actually under consideration and not just the personal fear of Pearson – and, for that matter, Ambassador Lodge. The Pearson-Johnson exchange with Pearson's 'stipulation' against nuclear weapons might be read as a specific reaction to options discussed in the overall scenario. Canada's 'carrot and stick' mission was known only to the senior principals and to the select Pentagon group, including Daniel Ellsberg, who had to keep refining the scenario.

'I was given to understand', says Ellsberg, that the mission 'was the most sensitive secret that I learned during that period. Canada was being used as a channel for what amounted to an ultimatum to the North.' The documentation of this mission – presented here – did not come out in the *Pentagon Papers*.

However, Ellsberg – whom, it must be pointed out, would become a foremost critic of the war – says there *was* 'discussion of the possible use of nuclear weapons in Vietnam in that very month, in May of 1964, involving Lodge, McNamara and others'. Ellsberg does not claim to have been in on such discussions but in his sensitive Pentagon post he was attuned to the options, and from this vantage point Canada was viewed 'as an ally throughout'. Ellsberg describes the mission to Hanoi of Canada's Blair Seaborn as 'a quasi-colonial inter-

June 1964—A Vietnamese woman and children walk across a field as a hut burns. The village, a suspected Viet Cong encampment near the Cambodian border, was attacked by government troops. Food was burned, livestock killed, and women and children evacuated. The men of the village disappeared before the assault.

vention in the same framework of the French re-invasion of Vietnam in 1946 in which we supported them, as Canada supported us now'. Ellsberg indicates that the Seaborn mission was a mere formality, a Johnson defense posture.

Seaborn says that both for him and the Canadian government the mission was 'an obligation' to ensure understanding between Hanoi and Washington of each other's intentions and 'help to defuse a situation which gave evidence of perhaps getting quite difficult'. Seaborn asserts that 'on the Canadian side we do not have any written record' of the Pearson-Johnson exchange and 'frankly I do not believe – I say this quite strongly – that there was any serious contemplation of the use of nuclear weapons. Nothing I ever was aware of led to that as a supposition, but I would not expect to have been taken into the inner thinking of the American military, the alternative scenarios and possibilities that they might have in mind.'

Johnson convinced Pearson that he sought to be the restraining influence. As Johnson summed up his Vietnam years to his biographer he 'was being stampeded on all sides'. Either a dramatic warning or dramatic action would end the Vietnam affair. He had confidence. He spoke in the metaphor of when he 'was a child and wanted nothing more than to be the daring cowboy, and once the cattle started stampeding whip them around and lead them to safety, because he could run faster than all of them'.

As the leaders met in New York, State Department officials were in Ottawa briefing Seaborn and Canada's External Affairs Minister, Paul Martin, whom they described as nervous about the prospect of 'expanding the war'. Seaborn was given a precise 'talking paper' on what he was to say to North Vietnam's Prime Minister Pham Van Dong. It included other instructions. The Americans were now asking for considerably more than just the delivery of a message: they wanted an intelligence assessment of North Vietnam's war capability. The US officials left Ottawa very satisfied. Seaborn, they reported, struck them as 'an alert, intelligent and steady officer' who had 'readily agreed to these conditions and has made immediate plans for an accelerated departure'.

As Seaborn set forth he knew that in his reporting role to both sides there could be 'no pulling of punches at all'. Seldom, if ever, had one man set out on a solo mission which might – just might – avert a great war. The State Department summary at this juncture noted that the messages carried by Seaborn were 'unusually substantive and dramatic' and added: 'To the extent they believed each other, the two sides were amply forewarned that a painful contest lay ahead.'

It was, if either side but knew or cared, the eleventh hour.

Map locates all the provinces of South Vietnam.

1964—Capt. Roger Donlon, of Saugerties, New York, received the Medal of Honor for his heroic actions as commanding officer of U.S. Army Special Forces at Camp Nam Dong. Under intense attack in the predawn hours of July 6, 1964, Donlon marshaled his troops, exposing himself to heavy enemy fire and receiving multiple wounds.

January 1964—A U.S. advisor, Sgt. Dwain V. Ames of Nashville, Tennessee, helps carry a wounded Vietnamese soldier after being cut off and trapped by the Viet Cong in jungle fighting at Ben Suc, 35 miles northwest of Saigon.

Above: 1964—South Vietnamese troops seeking Viet Cong drift past fishing nets set out to dry.

Left: 1964—A Montagnard village in the highlands is home to Green Beret advisors who train, equip, and lead the mountain fighters on patrols to seek out the Viet Cong.

EDITOR'S NOTE: The Vietnam war was photographed like no other war for the entire length of its long history. Horst Faas was there 10 years for Associated Press during the time of the most bitter fighting. Here is the story of his first foray into the war accompanied by the pictures that won a Pulitzer Prize in 1965.

# ASSIGNMENT VIETNAM    BY HORST FAAS

I still remember my first helicopter assault, Many similar ones would follow over the next years.

Twenty-nine years old, I had never flown in a helicopter.

Hitching a 'milk run' flight with an American lieutenant who was returning to his Vietnamese unit I had reached an unlit airstrip in the Mekong Delta in late June 1962, surrounded by flooded paddy fields, barbed wire and watchtowers

As we waited, watching the sunrise, the Vietnamese Army battalion arrived on trucks before the helicopters suddenly appeared on he horizon. They troops lined up, a group of twelve to fifteen soldiers for each helicopter, first lift ready to go, the others waiting for the second and third turn around in the grass alongside the airstrip. I introduced myself to a surprised Vietnamese battalion commander and his advisor, a US Army Captain. 'Be my guest, and take care, we expect machineguns', he said.

Flying just above ground level the swarm of about twelve helicopters landed, never shutting off their engines—the noise made by the flailing rotor blades made it impossible to understand what the American Captain and his young radio operator, who seemed wired to the Captain, tried to tell me. Then he just pointed to a helicopter, my first.

I pulled myself aboard a shaking and rattling banana-shaped U.S. Army H-21 helicopter, following a gaggle of Vietnamese soldiers, loaded down with their packs, mortar tubes, a machinegun and a lot of ammunition and a few live chicken.

I was travelling light: A plastic case with three Leica camera bodies, lenses and some ten rolls of film, canvas shoes, floppy hat, and a backpack with poncho, mosquito net and some canned food, dressed in a Saigon 'Minh the Tailor' makeshift uniform with two canteens of water dangling from the belt. On advice of the AP's Saigon bureau chief I also carried a 100-Dollar note in a waterproof wrapping. 'You may need that to bribe the Vietnamese to carry you out if you get hurt',

Malcolm Brown had said.

The helicopters spiralled upwards and then headed straight south. I looked down, past the tips of my feet on the wondrous glowing light of the first sunlight across the geometric patterns of paddy dykes. Then the helicopters took a steep, frightening dive, stopping only about hundred feet above a canal. The American machine gunner, finger on the trigger and pointing the barrel of his gun towards the rows of thatched huts alongside the canal opened up. All other machineguns joined in—they called it 'suppressing fire'—and it all seemed rather unreal on such a beautiful morning. I could see the bullets hitting the water.

My helicopter never landed—it hovered about four feet above ground and the Vietnamese jumped into the water, then racing towards the nearest paddy dike, firing from the hips. The water was quite cool at this time of the day, the gooey mud underneath pleasantly lukewarm. Leaning low behind a dyke I wiped some spray from my lenses and then started with what I had come here for: taking pictures: soldiers rushing from helicopters, running past me, hitting the ground firing or heaving grenades. The firing noise of the departing helicopters abated and all soldiers fired now at targets I could not see. By the time the second wave of the helicopter assault came in my troops had reached the canal and were poking their weapons into the huts or dropping grenades into underground shelters inside or close to the huts. Now I saw my first victims of the war: a few bedraggled old people, bleeding, and a hideously wounded woman holding up her child. The American captain tried to help. Eventually the woman and a few other injured civilians were put on a boat and pushed off down the canal towards the government controlled district town. The first fifteen minutes of my first 'operation' were the exciting ones. I was frightened, confused and exhilarated. The casualness with which the injured were treated depressed and angered me.

Three days of wading through swamps, paddies and mangrove thickets, long hot walks in the sun, followed. If there ever were any Viet Cong around they had vanished. On the third day I walked back into a government post and was trucked out with the troops, eventually reaching Saigon to tell my story and transmit the photos from day-one.

In the populated parts of South Vietnam—especially the Mekong Delta and the narrow fertile land stretching along the whole eastern coast of Viet-

November 29, 1964—In this two-picture sequence, a demonstrator is dragged away by soldiers during a Buddhist funeral that turned into a street demonstration.

nam – pictures of the innocents suffering almost always followed pictures of battle, a pattern that did not change until the last day of the war.

One or two forays into the war per week similar to my first operation became a pattern to cover the war. As the number of American helicopters increased photographers, too, became more mobile. The way into action was almost always via the helicopter assault, the way out became the 'medevac' helicopter. It became possible to switch from a unit that had not made any enemy contact to one engaged in battle by darting in with a COC (command and control) or medevac helicopter. Photographers in Vietnam mostly preferred to travel alone rather than in teams. The single photographer had the advantage over a television newsreel team of three (camera, sound and correspondent) when only one person could be squeezed in with the Rangers going out for an 'Eagle flight' (rapid raids conducted by platoon size small units) or between the wounded and dead lifted out of a battle zone.

Helicopter pilots and officers advising and accompanying Vietnamese troops got used to 'their' photographers. Vietnamese soldiers were equally happy to see the big overweight photographer again, who provided the only laughs for them, falling of every slippery bamboo pole bridge into the mud. Older Vietnamese officers and soldiers used the photographer trudging along to try their rusty French on him – and French often became the language to tell something that the American was not supposed to hear.

There were always two sides to a story in Vietnam – what reporters saw, experienced and were told in the field – and the official version or the daily briefing report put out in Saigon or Washington. The two versions rarely matched. News photos reflected the reality in the contested countryside of Vietnam and could not be denied. Soon Americans in the field were glad for a photographer or newsman to show up at their often isolated towns and outposts. Out there the true realities of Vietnam could not be hidden. Soldiers and newsmen became friend who trusted each other, friendships that lasted when the soldier would return for his second or third one-year tour of duty and find the reporter still in Vietnam. Many more friendships developed after the war, when both shared memories.

Top: 1964—Bodies of soldiers slain in an operation are taken from the battle in an ox cart.

Center: November 25, 1964—A Vietnamese soldier grimaces in pain as he is hit in the face with a rock thrown by rioting students in Saigon. A fellow soldier wears a gas mask as troops prepare an attack on the demonstrators.

Right: March 19, 1964—A child, killed when government troops and Viet Cong guerrillas battled near the Cambodian border. Vietnamese Rangers are aboard their tank.

Above: December, 1964—A single Ranger sits lonely among his dead comrades after a devastating battle near Binh Gia. Some 60 Rangers were killed in the first assault against the enemy. Hundreds died before the week long battle ended.

Right: March 19, 1964—A father holds his badly burned daughter after her rescue from a field near the Cambodian border. The child was injured when South Vietnamese aircraft dropped napalm on a village where Viet Cong had fled to hide among civilians.

Below:November 25, 1964—Saigon student demonstrators threaten an already wounded soldier during riots in the Vietnamese capital. Paratroopers used teargas to finally put down the disturbance.

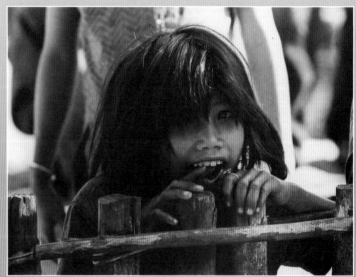

April 18, 1964—A young Vietnamese girl peers over a picket fence to watch government troops pass through her village in search of Viet Cong guerrillas. After inspection the village was set afire and the residents moved to a fortified area.

Left; March 14, 1964—A Viet Cong prisoner peers under guard's weapon through barbed wire in a compound at Cai Cai, near the Cambodian border. He was one of 300 VC captured in the operation.

Above: January 8, 1964—A South Vietnamese Ranger uses the end of a dagger to strike a farmer for providing government troops with false information about Viet Cong guerrillas in the area.

Above: January 8, 1964—A South Vietnamese Ranger stomps on a farmer as punishment for providing false information about Viet Cong guerrillas in the area.

Right: July 5, 1964—A Vietnamese Special Forces soldier carries a comrade who was wounded when a Viet Cong mine exploded under their truck near Tay Ninh. Ten were wounded in the guerrilla attack.

January 2, 1964—A Vietnamese Ranger points his rifle toward a Viet Cong guerrilla who crawls from a tunnel in the jungle some 35 miles northwest of Saigon.

November 4, 1964—Vietnamese paracommandos are dropped from U.S. helicopters on a graveyard near the Mekong Delta town of Mo Cay during a battle between government troops and a large unit of Viet Cong soldiers that tried to overrun the provincial capital.

April 18,1964—A boy smokes a cigarette, gift of a South Vietnamese soldier, during military operation. Children frequently smoke in Vietnam.

Left: January 17, 1964—U.S. gunners in H-21 Shawnee gunships fire at a Viet Cong guerrilla who ran to a foxhole from the sampan on the river bank. The U.S. provided air support during a South Vietnamese offensive in the Mekong Delta.

Below: January 12, 1964—A crewman sits in the open door of a rocket-equipped U.S. Army Huey helicopter during an assault mission in the jungle near Bien Hoa, north of Saigon.

Above: February 27, 1964—Viet Cong guerrilla fighters, captured by Vietnamese Marines in battle near Long Binh on the Mekong Delta, crouch on the ground with their hands tied. One wears a U.S. type protective helmet, which he had on when he was captured.

Right: February 27, 1964—A dying Viet Cong guerrilla raises his hands as South Vietnamese Marines search palm groves near Long Binh in the Mekong Delta. The guerrilla died in a foxhole.

Above: February. 16, 1964 - Members of the U.S. and Vietnamese bomb squad go into action within minutes of an explosion at the American movie theater in Saigon which killed two American servicemen and injured 49 others.

Above right: May 1964 - Viet Cong prisoners, bound and guarded by Vietnamese rangers, await questioning.

April 10, 1964 - Vietnamese women and children are rounded up by government troops at their hamlet in the Mekong Delta. Their husbands and fathers are always "away" when troops come — with the Viet Cong say the South Vietnamese.

Above: A U.S. adviser leads South Vietnamese troops across the Thanh River on a pontoon bridge just south of the 17th parallel. Vietnamese engineers built the bridge in Quang Tin province, long controlled by the Viet Cong.

Below: February. 6, 1964 - A soldier sifts through debris after a terrorist bomb exploded in a Saigon bar, killing five Vietnamese and injuring six U.S. servicemen.

Above: March 19, 1964 - A Vietnamese soldier carries his wounded buddy from battle after government troops clashed with the Viet Cong on the Plain of Reeds near the Cambodian border.

May 2, 1964—A military policeman goes to the aid of an American who was shot in a Saigon street, one of a series of terrorist attacks on civilians in the Vietnamese capital.

June 4, 1964—Refugees huddle around a helicopter gunner who helps them into his chopper. The refugees, mostly dependents of Viet Cong, were evacuated as military operations sought to flush the enemy out of villages.

June 1964—Soldiers of South Vietnam find a Hannibal-type carrier is more suitable to jungle warfare than modern motorized vehicles near Da Don, about 20 miles from the Cambodian border.

July 19, 1964—A Viet Cong prisoner kneels on the ground as Vietnamese rangers bind his arms during a major operation near Cai Lay, south of Saigon. Thirty Viet Cong were captured in this operation.

July 1964—A woman captured at a Viet Cong house is bound and slapped by South Vietnamese troops during an interrogation about Viet Cong operations. After refusing to talk, the woman was released and the troops moved on to another village.

**173**

July 11, 1964—Communist Viet Cong prisoners, their arms pinned to their sides, board a U.S. Army Eagle Flight helicopter in southern Delta region to be transported to a Mekong Delta prison camp.

August 12, 1964—Helicopters converge on a Viet Cong machine-gun emplacement in the jungles northwest of Saigon during a major air assault involving almost 100 U.S. and South Vietnamese helicopters.

# CARROT AND STICK

By mid-June the first dry summer heat had added to Hanoi's always somnolent atmosphere. In the noon-hour torpor the city centre seemed abandoned except for the car bearing the stranger. Even the police traffic stands were deserted. Only the occasional speeding jeep was an indication that somewhere there was war in this land. The very width of the main boulevards increased the sense of emptiness. The colonial mansions that now served as government offices were exactly as the French had left them ten years before lookalikes with a decor of dust, and these too were empty now. On the side streets homes and stores were shuttered, but against no greater enemy than the midday sun. The stranger on his urgent journey would seem to have come to the wrong place. He was looking for signs of fatigue, but the silence was only the afternoon siesta which events would never change.

The Russian-imitation Buick which delivered Blair Seaborn from the airport to the Thuong Nhat ('Reunification') Hotel was so far the only Communist trapping familiar to him. During his sixteen years with Canada's Department of

'The struggle of our people exceeds the imagination. It has astonished us, too.'

– North Vietnam's Prime Minister Pham Van Dong, June 1964

External Affairs, Seaborn had been Counsellor in Moscow from 1959 to 1962, then Head of the East European section in Ottawa until taking on his new assignment as Chief of the Canadian ICC delegation. His credentials were perfect for his secret mission as interlocutor of Hanoi-Washington intentions, and the mission was personally comforting. Seaborn wasn't overjoyed' by the ICC posting, but it had 'rather suddenly acquired far more professional interest'. The ICC peace-supervisory troika of Canada, Poland and India had been established under the Geneva Accords. It was supposedly neutral while reflecting the geopolitical make-up of the Western, Communist and Third Worlds. Its membership was too narrow and unreconcilable – no one could remember when the Commission had held its last full meeting – and as an inspection force it had been kept totally inoperative. Its field surveys were hopelessly limited or slanted.

The ICC aircraft which had brought Seaborn from Saigon headquarters to Hanoi symbolized the Commission's outmoded and bizarre existence. The twenty-six-year-old plane never seemed sure

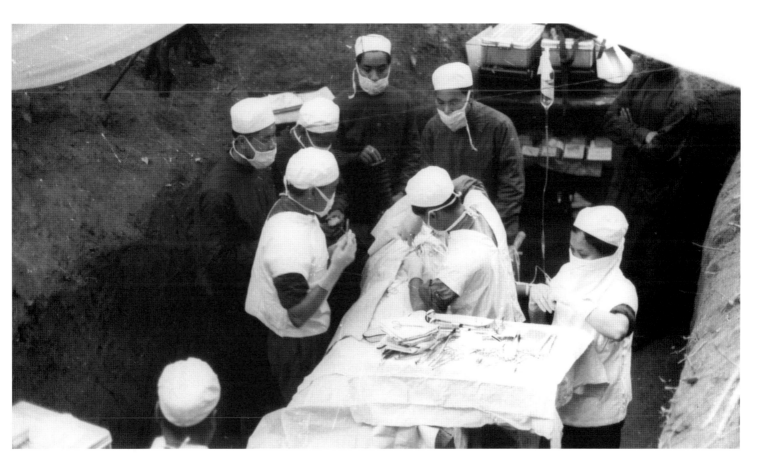

Undated—Surgeons operated on a wounded soldier in a North Vietnam open air aid station. Location of this picture is not known but is thought to be on the Ho Chi Minh Trail in North Vietnam.

of topping the monsoons or the border mountains and was therefore high among Vietnam's risks. On its regular run via Vientiane in Laos the old prop flew to a 'no photos, please' announcement over trails where US reconnaissance jets now roamed and where North Vietnamese weapons flowed South. The ICC did not operate these flights: they were serviced by Air France, the French pilots apparently being the only acceptable neutrals who knew the route, and the only distinct evidence that the year was not still 1954 was the Parisian stewardess in powder-blue mini-skirt. On the hour-leg to Hanoi she dispensed nothing more than candy; the ICC was in debt to the airline for $600,000.

Only two ICC flights a week to Hanoi were permitted, and these had to depart within one hour of arrival. ICC personnel did not even enjoy diplomatic status in the North. The Canadians, in particular, were shunned and distrusted. The ICC mission was housed in two tatty villas with a North Vietnamese soldier, bayonet fixed, always on duty, alert to who entered. Inside, among the unchanging cane furniture and ennui, the only smiles were the framed ones of the Queen and the Canadian Prime Minister of the day. A permanent staff of three, a political officer and two military men, a sergeant and a corporal, completed the pecking-order atmosphere. They met no one of consequence, and Seaborn knew that even the head of delegation on quarterly visits shared this isolation and frustration. The ICC existed only as a formality which might have its uses, as Seaborn's presence now demonstrated, but to his Canadian colleagues so desperate for news and purpose he could say nothing.

Even though he was in Hanoi in the role of America's messenger, with precise 'instructions' from the State Department, Seaborn felt that Canada had been unfairly castigated as a US dupe. He recalled that it was China's Premier Chou En-Lai who had proposed Canada as a 'good' Western nation to serve on the ICC, and Canada, says Seaborn, was 'expected to be representing the Western viewpoint'. Seaborn had anyway made a personal vow to carry out his mission 'accurately and dispassionately'.

Already, as Seaborn waited for his audience with Prime Minister Pham Van Dong, he had found Hanoi far healthier than depicted in Western press accounts. By 5 pm, as stores and market-places reopened, the city was filled with people scurrying on renewed business or idling around the sidewalk tea and fruit vendors. As he walked, Seaborn noted for his official report that there were 'some queues but no evidence of malnutrition'. The city itself 'though austere looked much less run down than I expected'. On the broad boulevard circling the central lake, shoals of cyclists glided round and round. Very soon thousands of people, often two or three to a bicycle, had joined this ritual of the long bright evenings. Seaborn had been asked to look for signs of 'war weariness' – but no matter how great the fury of war directed from here, Hanoi would always appear like the calm eye of the hurricane.

Apart from the message he was tasked with, Seaborn had been given what was essentially an intelligence or eye-spy assignment. This had been detailed in a 'top-secret' State Department thirteen-point memorandum headed 'Instructions for Canadian Interlocutor' (these papers, as well as

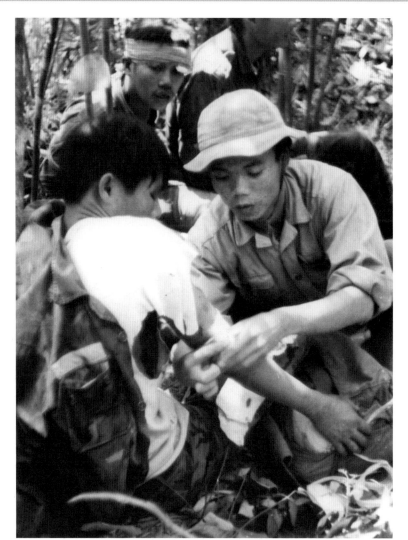

Left: Undated—A North Vietnamese medic treats the wounds of a soldier at an unknown location.

Below: Undated—Viet Cong and North Vietnamese troops engage in a game of tug-of-war during a rest day at a base of unknown location.

Seaborn's own official assessment, were obtained by the author from US sources). After advising on diplomatic niceties, point 4 of the Instructions required that: 'Mr Seaborn should also, by listening to the arguments and observing the attitudes of the North Vietnamese, form an evaluation of the mental outlook. He should be particularly alert to (a) differences with respect to the Sino-Soviet split, (b) frustration or war weariness, (c) indications of North Vietnamese desire for contacts with the West, (d) evidence of cliques or factions in the Party or Government, and (e) evidence of differences between the political and the military.'

This wording was a diplomatic refinement of an earlier draft which proposed that Seaborn 'should start out' by checking whether Ho Chi Minh (or whoever he met) 'considers himself over-extended and exposed, or whether he feels confident that his Chinese allies will back him to the hilt. We want to know whether his current zeal is being forced upon him by pro-Chinese elements in his own camp, or whether he is impelled by his own ambitions.'

The Canadian intermediary had no reservations about these instructions if only because of the greater misgivings he and his government shared. On the one hand, as he put it later, 'all of us had doubts right along the line that a large increase of American force . . . would lead to an eventual political settlement' between North and South. On the other hand 'all of us were so concerned and preoccupied with the possibilities of a great escalation of the military situation in that area and what it might lead to'. In these circumstances, says Seaborn, his assignment was 'something which no Canadian government could refuse'.

The attitude and use of the Canadian channel at the outset of the mission remain highly relevant to this history because both Ottawa and Seaborn assumed that whatever resulted Hanoi would have had every warning and option fully presented. What the Canadians did *not* know was that Seaborn was carrying only part of the message – a relatively insubstantial part. Both the exact military ultimatum and the inducements for heeding it were held back by Washington.

As Seaborn set out for his 'hopefully' historic meeting on 18 June, the content of his message differed in every essential from a second secret 'Talking Paper' which amounted to a specific peace package. This analyzed the conflict and a settlement without reference to wider East-West issues. It stated precisely what military action the United States would take against the North if the war in the South continued, and it spelled out US concessions if hostilities ceased.

By comparison, the 'carrot and stick' that Seaborn now brought was neither tempting nor intimidating. Though Seaborn presumably knew from the Pearson-Johnson talks of the bombing contingency, he was not instructed to warn specifically of this. He was to say only that US patience was 'growing extremely thin'. He could 'hint' at the economic and other benefits enjoyed by Communist countries like Yugoslavia which had 'not sought to expand into other areas', and he could 'state that the US does not seek military bases in the area and is not seeking to overthrow the Communist regime in Hanoi'.

In the old Russian car taking him to his appointment Seaborn once more reviewed the points he was to make. The strongest part of the

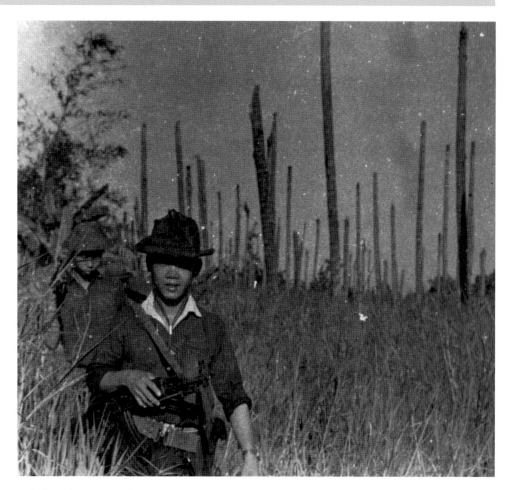

Undated—North Vietnamese and Viet Cong troops advance through a countryside stripped of greenery because defoliation spray.

message was intended as much for Moscow and Peking. The US considered the Vietnam conflict 'as part of the general Free World confrontation with this type of violent subversion in other lesser developed countries'. The US stake in Vietnam had 'a significance of world-wide proportions'. On the other hand Seaborn was to tell Pham Van Dong that the US 'holds Hanoi directly responsible' for continuation of the fighting.

Seaborn found the Prime Minister waiting for him in 'a large impressive room' of the former French Governor's palace, now used only for ceremonial occasions or for receiving foreign dignitaries. In fact, the room was the size of a Versailles ballroom, filled with Vietnamese antiques and deep armchairs. Only one other person was present, ICC deputy-liaison officer Lieutenant-Colonel Mai Lam, who took notes. Seaborn went alone because of 'the high secrecy'. He recalls that 'I tried to talk, think and do note-taking all at the same time'. The conversation was entirely in French ('the Premier's French is impeccable') without 'any use of Vietnamese'. The forty-year-old Seaborn had the stern looks and fastidiousness of a school inspector, and he immediately accorded high marks to the son of a mandarin scholar who confronted him in a Mao tunic. Pham Van Dong 'gave me a careful hearing with no attempt to interrupt, disagree, contradict or even express displeasure to assertions which were clearly unpalatable'.

Seaborn wasted little time on preliminaries, except to produce a letter of authority from

Canada's Prime Minister Pearson. Pham Van Dong read it twice. 'Canada's role is important and desirable,' he responded. 'You'll appreciate, Prime Minister,' Seaborn began, 'that our relationship with the United States is close and friendly. We feel we've an excellent insight into American thinking.' The secret papers show that Seaborn then explained how the US saw Vietnam in a global context. President Johnson was a man of peace. He sought to avoid a confrontation between major powers, but he was determined that South-east Asia should not fall under Communist control through 'subversion and guerrilla warfare'.

'American ambitions are limited', Seaborn said, 'but American patience is not limitless.' After explicitly relaying the State Department's message, Seaborn concluded on a personal note. He feared escalation. He did not think this was in anyone's interest but if it happened the North would suffer the 'greatest devastation'. 'Is there any message I can convey to the United States?' Seaborn asked.

'No,' Pham Van Dong replied, 'not at this time.' But the two men continued to converse for a further hour. Seaborn had met many high-ranking Communists while in Moscow. He would report that 'in presence and mental stature' Pham Van Dong was 'an impressive leader by any standards'. At fifty-eight, his hair was iron-gray, his eyes sunken from his youth in French jails, but a suave civility and a preference for laughter took ten years off his age. Among the Vietnamese he was known as 'Uncle Ho's favorite nephew'. He had been at Ho Chi Minh's side from the beginning,

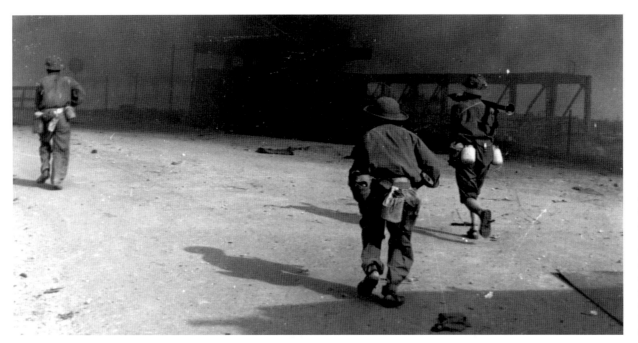

Left: Undated—North Vietnamese arm soldiers attack a military compound. Place and date are unknown.

Below: Undated—A North Vietnamese tank driver with boxes of ammunition that carry American writing. The North Vietnamese used tanks for the first time in 1969 in an attack on a Special Forces post at Ben Het.

forty years before. He had been his country's international negotiator and government spokesman for almost twenty years. He now told Seaborn that he would 'like to expound on the points raised'. It was Seaborn's turn to listen.

'We must learn to co-exist, to find a solution for this problem that has wracked us for so long, but it has to be a just solution,' the Premier said in a wide-ranging presentation of Hanoi's point of view, which the American public would never hear. 'I'll tell you what we mean by a just solution,' the Premier continued. 'First it requires an American withdrawal. Secondly it means that the affairs of the South must be arranged by the people of the South. It must provide for the participation of the Liberation Front. No other group represents the broad wishes of the people. There must be peace and neutrality for South Vietnam, neutrality in the Cambodian manner. Thirdly, a just solution means reunification of the country. This is fundamental.

'But we want peaceful reunification, without military pressures. We want round-table negotiations. There must be sincere satisfaction with the arrangement for it to be viable. We are in no hurry. We're willing to talk but we'll wait till South Vietnam is ready. I realize this won't be easy for the United States to accept,' Pham Van Dong told the Canadian emissary. 'The US can go on increasing aid to South Vietnam. It can increase its own army personnel. I suffer to see the war go on, develop, intensify. Yet our people are determined to struggle.' Pham leaned forward: 'It's impossible, quite impossible – excuse me for saying this – for you Westerners to understand the force of the people's will to resist, and to continue. The struggle of our people exceeds the imagination. It has astonished us, too.'

The premier asked Seaborn to consider recent history in South Vietnam. Since the assassination of President Diem it had been a *'cascade'*. The prospects for the US were *'sans issue'*. Reinforcing the Khanh army would not help. The people had had enough. There had to be a government of national coalition. The original coalition of Laos should serve as a model. The North was not sending units to the Pathet Lao, but the US military was interfering:

'There are daily incursions of our air space across the Laotian border and by commando units bent on sabotage.' In Vietnam, it was a question of a *'guerre à outrance'* – a war to the end – 'which the United States won't win in any event, or neutrality.'

Looking amused, Pham Van Dong said, 'Let me quote to you America's Walter Lippmann: "There's no light at the end of the tunnel." My government does not yet have concrete suggestions to put forward, but this is our thinking.'

'Thank you, Prime Minister,' Seaborn said, 'for your detailed exposé of your government's views. I'll transmit these faithfully.' 'You may not believe all I've said', Pham Van Dong replied, 'but I assure you I've spoken in all sincerity and frankness.'

Seaborn asked if he could put 'a few personal' questions. 'I'm interested in your comment', Seaborn said, 'that as a condition for restoring peace, South Vietnam should become neutral as a first step prior to reunification.' Pham Van Dong quickly interrupted. 'I didn't refer to neutrality as a first step only,' he said. 'Whether South Vietnam continues neutral would depend on the people of South Vietnam. I don't prejudge.' 'Well,' said Seaborn, 'the Liberation Front represents a certain force in South Vietnam, but not all the people, nor even a majority.' Pham Van Dong said nothing to this as Seaborn went on to say, 'I appreciate that the Front would have to participate should a coalition ever emerge. The fear however is that the coalition would soon be taken over by the Front. This has happened in other countries.' 'There's no reason to have such fears,' Pham Van Dong replied.

'Prime Minister, do you fully appreciate that the United States' obligations in South Vietnam have implications far beyond South-east Asia – it relates to guerrilla subversion in Asia, Africa and Latin America?' 'Yes, we appreciate this,' the Premier replied. 'We realize that the "loss" of South Vietnam for the Americans might well set off – what's the atomic expression – a chain reaction. But please understand that the principles and stakes involved are just as high for the Liberation Front in South Vietnam and its supporters.'

'Mr. Seaborn,' the Premier went on, in a test of the message, 'we're glad to hear that the US does not intend to attack our country.' Seaborn then 'corrected' him, saying the US 'didn't want to carry the war to the North but might be obliged to do so if pushed too far'. 'American patience isn't limitless,' Seaborn repeated.

Without any change of tone, Pham Van Dong retorted that if the war was 'pushed' to the North, then the North had friends: *"Nous sommes un pays socialiste, un des pays socialistes, vous savez, et le peuple se dressera.'* 'We will not force the United States [to such action], we will not provoke the United States,' the North Vietnamese leader concluded. And he told Seaborn: 'I look forward to further conversation. Next time you will meet Ho Chi Minh. The President is on leave at present, but has sent his greetings.'

On returning to Saigon two days later, 20 June, Seaborn transmitted to the State Department via Ottawa two lengthy cables, the first summarizing his ninety-minute conversation with Pham Van Dong and the second quoting him near-verbatim from notes. On 22 June Seaborn cabled a further report titled 'Attitudes and Outlook' in which he analyzed the mood of the North and included his personal assessment that a widening of the war would be both unsuccessful and dangerous. In his first cable Seaborn conveyed the tone as well as content of the interview, stating that Pham Van Dong 'took pains throughout to give the impression of quiet sincerity, of realization of the seriousness of what we were discussing and of lack of truculence or belligerency'. Seaborn concluded this cable: 'I would welcome comments from you [External Affairs Department] and the

State Department on any suggestions for talking points for further conversations on next visit to Hanoi.' There is no record of any substantive reply. All of Seaborn's cables were duly transmitted back to the American Embassy in Saigon in State Deptel 115 of 11 July. The State Department had therefore had almost three weeks to consider Seaborn's cables and whether, in view of them, to request 'further conversations' based on specific peace proposals which had been withheld from the Canadians. Just three weeks later the fuse of war would be ignited in much disputed circumstances.

Right: Undated—Two young boys in a Viet Cong controlled area saw off the barrel of a destroyed Russian tank. The barrel will be used for the fabrication of other weapons.

Below: Undated—Anti-government sympathizers arrive by boat for a Viet Cong rally in the Mekong Delta.

In his first cabled report on his mission Seaborn summarized that Pham Van Dong, while perhaps not yet fully believing the 'firmness' of US determination, 'could not however claim that he has not had US views and intentions conveyed to him most explicitly'. Seaborn had evidently never seen the separate instructions, prepared on the same date as his first briefing paper, headed 'Further Outline for Mr Seaborn'. In this the State Department began by stating '. . . we would probably not wish to hand this further outline to the Canadian government pending the initial soundings of the Canadian interlocutor in Hanoi'. This suggests that Washington was prepared for negotiations if Hanoi was. But the 'Further Outline' provides no guide-line as to what precisely was expected from Hanoi on the first round. The withholding of both carrot and stick in tangible form raises hard questions as to whether Hanoi had anything really firm to consider, and whether Washington really had any serious intentions, or any faith, in negotiating at this time. But if it did, then the first soundings from Hanoi and Washington's prepared terms were sufficiently conciliatory to warrant the conclusion that the climate to avert war existed but was missed or bungled despite weeks of opportunity.

The peace package that was never offered, and of which the public would never know, reveals the terms which the United States at least contemplated while also drawing up its war scenario. Equally important, the terms reveal a political-military analysis very different from Washington's public pronouncements. The linking of Vietnam to global issues, which Seaborn was required to stress, is nowhere mentioned. Not even the word 'Communist' appears.

Instead, the document proposed a withdrawal of opposing forces to ensure 'the independence and territorial integrity of South Vietnam'. Future safeguards, or Communist guarantees were not mentioned. Hanoi itself had the political power to end the war because 'the virtually complete cease-fires which have obtained at Tet [the Vietnamese New Year] for the past two years demonstrated the ability of Hanoi to control all Viet Cong operations in South Vietnam if it has the will to do so'.

On this assumption, the United States would adopt one of two courses: if Hanoi did not stop the war, 'the United States will initiate action by air and naval means against North Vietnam until Hanoi does agree to stop the war'. If hostilities ceased, the US would then undertake:

> 'To obtain the agreement of Saigon to a resumption of trade between North and South. . . .
>
> 'Initiate a program of food assistance to North Vietnam either on a relief grant basis . . . or for local currency.
>
> 'Reduce controls on US trade with North Vietnam. . . .
>
> 'Recognize North Vietnam diplomatically and, if Hanoi is interested, undertake an exchange of diplomatic representatives.
>
> 'Remove US forces from South Vietnam, on a phased basis, winding up with a reduction to the level of 350 military advisors, or trainers *as permitted under the Geneva Accords* [author's italics].'

The Johnson administration undertook in this hitherto unpublished document to adopt and accelerate the Kennedy plan. It pledged to withdraw American forces – then projected at 23,000 – within one year. The peace package guaranteed a full amnesty for all Southern guerrillas, then estimated to number 103,000, and it proposed that 'if the DRV [Democratic Republic of Vietnam] desires to repatriate Viet Cong from South Vietnam this can be done over whatever period the DRV desires'.

The US terms were a complete face-saving formula for both sides: no official announcement of a settlement need actually be made. The war would simply fade away. As the document phrased it: 'If the DRV does not desire a public announcement of its agreement to have the Viet Cong cease resistance, then the United States measures of concession to North Vietnam can be announced only over a phased period.' Conversely, if Hanoi agreed to this settlement, then Washington proposed a joint announcement within just three days of a cease-fire. The document made no mention of consultation with Saigon on a settlement.

But all these carrots were to be dangled from a very heavy stick. The timetable required that 'all hostilities must cease within one week of the approach to the authorities at Hanoi. If they have not stopped within that time, the US will immediately initiate air and naval action against North Vietnam.'

Assuming some flexibility in the timetable, the US stipulations and those of Hanoi hardly appeared irreconcilable. American and North Vietnamese forces were not in direct confrontation. Pham Van Dong had told Seaborn that Hanoi would 'not provoke the United States' – intimating that North Vietnamese troops would not directly intervene, as they had not yet done. The Soviet and Chinese commitment in Vietnam had not yet reached the point where a quiet cessation of fighting, also involving American withdrawal, could be viewed as a serious ideological defeat. Against the risk that the Communist powers might permanently withdraw their support, or that the US might renege, Hanoi would have had to consider the neutralist sentiment gaining hold in Saigon, and Pham Van Dong had repeatedly

Undated—South Vietnamese militiamen throw up their hands as they surrender to Viet Cong and North Vietnamese forces.

emphasized that neutrality and a coalition government were the immediate objective. Any such development after a US withdrawal would be a better demonstration of popular support (which Seaborn had challenged) and preferable to imposed reunification. Finally (taking the cynical approach) if the Americans were to leave, then even if the settlement broke down there was a chance that the US would never return, whereas Hanoi now recognized that it was 'difficult' for the US to withdraw. From the US point of view, if it was later obliged to intervene militarily it would then, with the peace terms, have the clear 'moral' justification that Ambassador Lodge had so strongly urged.

Having contemplated specific peace terms conditional on Seaborn's initial findings, Washington had now to evaluate or co-relate these. For the first time in almost twenty years, since before the French Indo-China war, a Washington intermediary had obtained a concise outline of what Hanoi itself termed its 'thinking'. Seaborn had observed that the mood did not appear 'belligerent'. A key consideration for Washington was whether in fact Hanoi could think for itself.

Seaborn had tapped a wide variety of opinion in Hanoi. In his evaluation titled 'Attitudes and Outlook' he stated: 'No Vietnamese with whom I spoke made even reference by name to the USSR or China.' He pointed out that Pham Van Dong had made 'only the most oblique reference' to his country's membership of the Socialist group 'in the context of possible results of the US taking the war to the North'. He quoted French contacts in Hanoi

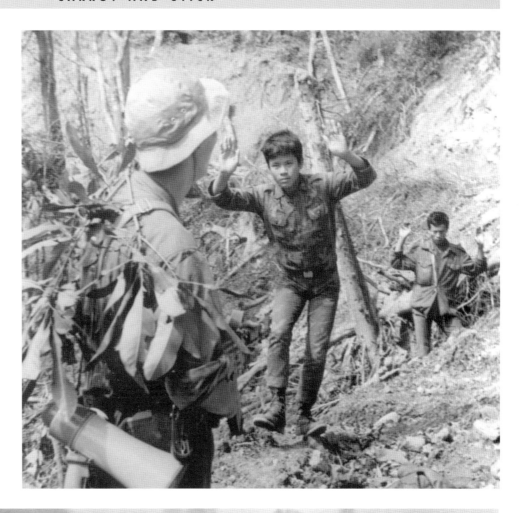

Top: Undated—A South Vietnamese soldier surrenders to North Vietnamese troops. Location unknown.

Right: Undated—A North Vietnamese artilleryman, wearing a straw helmet, prepares the next shell for firing.

as saying the leadership was 'honestly concerned by the bad effect' of the Sino-Soviet split. In the French view – and they had the closest relations with Hanoi of any Western nation – the North Vietnamese 'fear a definitive rupture which would throw them fully under Chinese control, a fate they hope to resist as long as possible.'

Seaborn visited an exhibition on ten years of North Vietnamese life since the defeat of the French and 'during a lengthy tour the guide managed to describe economic progress for at least half an hour without once mentioning aid received from other Socialist countries (though when questioned it was admitted that Soviet and Chinese aid had been a great factor)'. Seaborn spoke with the Soviet chargé in Hanoi and reported that 'Soviet aid in the form of technicians and training of students in the USSR had diminished as the DRV capacity for training their own cadres had grown. He admitted that the Chinese were still very active in the aid field.'

As to Washington's request for evidence of pro-Chinese or pro-Soviet factionalism among Hanoi's leaders. Seaborn cabled that he could add nothing to 'the commonly accepted line-up' other than 'to draw attention to the moderateness of Pham Van Dong's tone'. Seaborn observed that 'Ho Chi Minh appears still to enjoy tremendous prestige and is venerated as a demi-god, perhaps above any factional strife'. He added that 'non-Communist representatives in Hanoi warn against overemphasis on factionalism as something from which the West might derive benefit. National pride is apparent from Pham Van Dong's remarks and from his call for economic self-help.'

On US speculation about 'war weariness' Seaborn had 'no evidence that such exists, and indeed all Vietnamese emphasized quiet determination to go on struggling as long as necessary. These assertions carried a good deal of conviction as if really believed. Nor did I find people looking markedly sadder or more serious than those in the South. [ICC] Team-site officers have seen no evidence of over-discontent among the people.'

Under the heading 'Conclusions' Seaborn advised that it would be 'unwise' for the US to count on internal factors in North Vietnam to cause Hanoi to 'jump at the chance of reaching an accommodation'. Seaborn's never publicized report clearly shows that he considered an enlarged war (at that point) neither warranted nor manageable. He informed the State Department: 'The prospect of the war being carried to the North may give greater pause for thought. But I would hesitate to say that the DRV are yet convinced, despite US public statements and moves and the private message I have conveyed, that the US really would be prepared to take this step, the ultimate consequences of which could be the start of World War III.'

Seaborn would say later that he felt his account of his crucial mission was 'accurate and objective reporting of the situation as I encountered it.' Seaborn had not made further reference in his June 1964 'Conclusions' to the invitation to return and meet Ho Chi Minh, which in Hanoi's lexicon meant that further talks would be formal, nor had he personally recommended further talks in his first report.

'Canada didn't have any instant solutions, either,' Seaborn would later explain – but the United States did, as documented. The Canadians would never know whether they were used as a conscience-buffer. Asked later about Washington's

reaction to his reports. Seaborn says: 'I didn't get a great deal. I know that the messages had a rather sobering effect, particularly my analysis of the determination of the North to keep going. I think that had a sobering effect because there had been some feeling I believe in some corners of Washington that perhaps they were on the rump or close to it in North Vietnam. Everything I reported indicated quite the opposite to that: also there was disappointment, though perhaps not surprise, that Premier Pham Van Dong had not picked up this tentative offer of getting into negotiations.'

Looking back, he felt that there 'was no real expression of interest or response from the North Vietnamese side to this rather tentative sounding probe by the Americans as to their willingness to look for discussion, negotiation, accommodation. There was no such indication.' Seaborn, while feeling that Hanoi was not 'jumping' at this 'tentative sounding probe', did not have the benefit of knowing, or expounding, the specific US peace terms.

In a covering memorandum filed later with Seaborn's reports, the State Department made this contradictory observation: 'The two sides were never close in their proposals, though in both cases their initial language was sufficiently flexible to permit subsequent bargaining and compromise.' But, the memorandum noted, 'these opening positions were swamped then and subsequently by the discussion of military measures and their possible consequences'.

Either because of delay or lack of interest the details of Seaborn's historic mission would never be disclosed; for America nine years of war would ensue, and any opportunity for peace in the summer of 1964 was quickly swamped in mysterious circumstances in the Gulf of Tonkin.

Undated—North Vietnamese run to the site of downed airplane. Location unknown.

Top: August 22, 1964—A U.S. Special Forces adviser directs a helicopter to a landing zone in a jungle clearing marked by a smoke grenade.

Right: August 22, 1964—Special Forces companies and an armored vehicle move from Tay Ninh, enroute to Giang Bac to reinforce the outpost there. Such convoys were frequent targets of Viet Cong ambushes.

Below: August 27, 1964—Vietnamese troops with fixed bayonets face demonstrators in front of the building where the ruling military junta meets in Saigon.

Above: August 28, 1964—A city bus is seized by a mob of students and driven through Saigon.

Right: August 8, 1964—Recruits wait outside a military hospital in Danang for medical checkups before going into the South Vietnamese army.

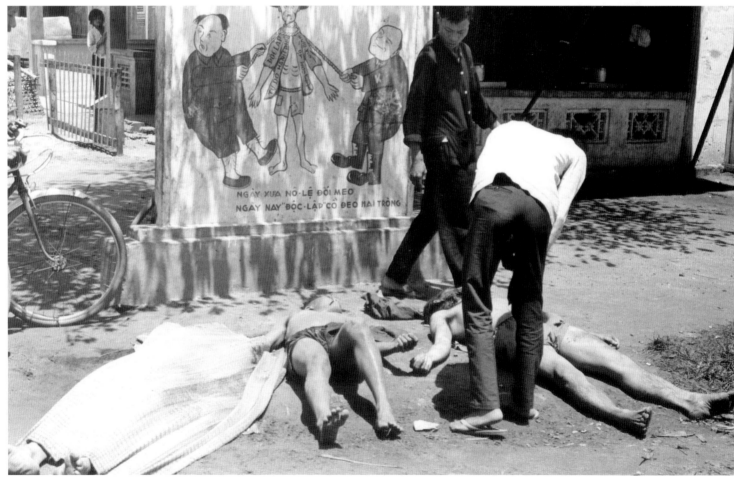

August 1, 1964—Bodies of Viet Cong guerrillas killed in a battle at a village near Saigon are displayed in the village square in front of a government propaganda poster that shows Mao Tse Tung and Nikita Khrushchev strangling a Vietnamese peasant.

August 28, 1964—Demonstrators, mostly Buddhist, advance through Saigon in a fight with Catholics barricaded in a downtown Catholic church.

August 28, 1964—Demonstrators, mostly Buddhist, advance through Saigon in a fight with Catholics barricaded in a downtown Catholic church.

Left: August 29, 1964—Catholic children wear the traditional Vietnamese white of mourning as they file through a suburb of Saigon to view the coffins of six fellow Catholics. The six victims died when government troops fired into a crowd demonstrating in front of military headquarters in Saigon.

Below: September 5, 1964—Buddhist monks pray at the graveside for two Buddhist students killed during antigovernment riots in Saigon. A funeral procession estimated at more than 100,000 stretched for miles.

Top: September 13, 1964—Heavily armed rebel troops leap from their truck during the seizure of Saigon in an ill-fated attempt to overthrow Premier Nguyen Khanh.

Right: September 13, 1964—An armored car with rebel soldiers arrives at the Saigon offices of Premier Nguyen Khanh, which were occupied by army officers blacklisted by the Buddhists. Khanh fled under protection of a loyal air force unit.

Below: September 13, 1964—Rebel troops move in armored vehicles alongside Boy Scouts on bicycles in Saigon during the coup against Vietnamese Premier Nguyen Khanh.

Above: September 16, 1964—Vietnamese marines are reflected as they patrol along the dike of a rice paddy in Long An province.

Right: September 1964—A Nung soldier removes a wooden spear that had been set to injure anyone handling the vines along the Ho Chi Minh Trail at Cam Duc.

September 22, 1964—A replica of the Statue of Liberty stands in a square of Cam Duoc, 30 miles south of Saigon in Long An province, a heavily Viet Cong–infiltrated area. The town's administrators erected the statue to show their appreciation for American values and aid.

# COUNTDOWN

Around midnight on 31 July 1964, a cluster of South Vietnamese assault boats sped out of Danang at the southern lip of the C-shaped Gulf of Tonkin. Their target was two North Vietnamese offshore islands sixty miles from the coast at the 19th Parallel. A hundred miles south-east, the destroyer USS Maddox was bearing toward the Gulf with orders to stay at least eight miles from shore. With its sophisticated radar and monitoring equipment the Maddox was the eyes of the Honolulu Pacific naval command. It was described as being on a routine mission and several hours distant when the South Vietnamese gunboats struck at the two tiny islands named Hon Me and Hon Nieu. For a few minutes an intense fire-fight seared the 3 am darkness as the swift PT boats raked the island garrisons then raced for home. This covert attack on North Vietnamese coastal facilities was also considered routine – by now, Operation 34-A had lasted six months – but this time the harassment snapped a nerve somewhere ashore.

As the USS Maddox neared the coast thirty-six hours later, 2 August, she urgently signalled Honolulu. From there a priority alert was flashed to Washington: the Maddox was exchanging fire with three North-Vietnamese torpedo boats. She gave her position as thirty miles offshore in 'international' waters. Though the time was nearing midnight in Washington, the Joint Chiefs aroused President Johnson. At the Pentagon and at the

> 'Once we brought any troops in, that was the nose of the camel. It would be difficult to know how much was enough.'
>
> – GENERAL MAXWELL D. TAYLOR, AMBASSADOR TO SAIGON, 1964–65

State Department, those involved in the contingency planning began a fateful, though brief, vigil. William Bundy, who would draft Johnson's version and verdict, had no doubt at least about this first US-North Vietnamese engagement in the Gulf: 'There was a clear-cut attack on one American destroyer on August 2nd,' says Bundy. 'There has never been any doubt of that attack. Bullet holes, all the rest.'

The Maddox now reported that she had repulsed and damaged all three raiders. Johnson ordered another destroyer, the USS C. Turner Joy, to join the Maddox and by the early hours of 4 August the two American warships resumed the intelligence mission code-named DE SOTO. Bundy says they were 'fifty to seventy-five miles off the coast' when they linked up. At the same time, as the destroyers turned back into the Gulf, more South Vietnamese 34-A ships were striking coastal installations.

It was again midnight Pacific time – twelve hours earlier in Washington – when naval command sent its next DE SOTO red alert: the North Vietnamese were attacking. Bundy says 'A destroyer reported – and it was during the night – that it had been attacked again. And it had seen torpedo wakes, and so on and so on.' Within minutes the security Chiefs had convened. With President Johnson's approval it was decided to start immediately phase one of the bombing scenario – a single 'retaliatory' strike. Fighter-

August 1964—The U.S. Navy destroyer U.S.S. Maddox was attacked by torpedoes and gunfire off Vietnam in the Gulf of Tonkin.

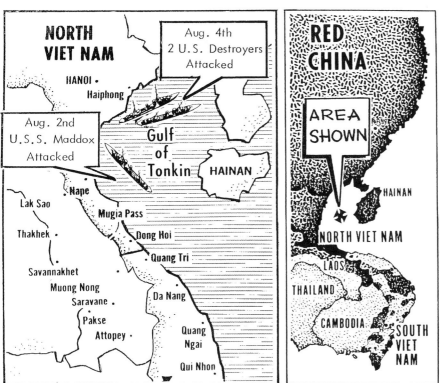

Maps locate the area where two US destroyers were attacked by North Vietnamese torpedo boats. This incident led to the Gulf of Tonkin Resolution of 1964.

'Launch Pierce Arrow.' The bombers were in the air as Johnson told the nation: 'Renewed hostile actions against United States ships on the high seas in the Gulf of Tonkin . . . have today required me to order the military forces of the United States to take action in reply.'

In the first bombing of North Vietnam, sixty-four naval aircraft struck the oil storage and port facilities at Vinh just north of the Partition line. The Pentagon estimated that ten per cent of the North's oil supply had been destroyed. It had taken ten minutes. The United States had directly entered the Vietnam war without declaration at 11 am, 5 August 1964.

It would be many years later before debate began on what really happened in the remote Pacific, and on whether Congress had been deceived into supporting the 'Gulf of Tonkin resolution' approving Johnson's action – and further actions. William Bundy, who drafted the resolution, cites the 'evidence' on which Johnson acted: 'We had intercepted North Vietnamese messages that followed in sequence on the date of August 4: get ready to attack, advance readiness, and go ahead. Well, this intelligence evidence, which in the case of the intercepts could not be disclosed at the time, seemed to all of us in the government to make it conclusive that North Vietnam had made a second attack.

'And it was on the basis of that, and the feeling that this had now turned into a challenge to

bombers of the 7th Fleet would take out the first of the preselected targets.

Washington cabled Honolulu a pre-arranged code: prepare to launch Pierce Arrow. It was 3 am in the north-west Pacific. The carrier-planes began to load up for launch at 1030 hours, 5 August.

At 4 am Pacific time Honolulu sent another urgent flash. It advised the Joint Chiefs: weather stormy – heavy seas – DE SOTO uncertain of actual attack or any damage. In the Pentagon 'War Room', Defense Secretary McNamara picked up the hot line to the President. They decided there had to be firm confirmation that the destroyers had not been attacked. The bombing countdown continued.

At dawn Pacific time Honolulu again cabled that rough seas still prevented verification of any damage. It was unclear in all the cables whether the destroyers had actually sighted North Vietnamese ships, but Washington was told to stand by for earlier radio intercepts picked up by the *Maddox*. As these were decoded, Johnson summoned Congressional leaders to the Oval Office and informed them of the attack. Four hours remained in the countdown.

The White House now alerted the national television networks to stand by for a possible presidential address to the nation. At the Pentagon McNamara's mildly named 'Study Group' – among them Daniel Ellsberg – were relaying the coordinates from their target list. Liaising at State, William Bundy evaluated the radio intercepts as the minutes ticked by without further advice from the storm-beset destroyers. With thirty minutes left in the countdown Johnson was called for make-up for the television cameras. As their red lights went on, a message went across the Pacific:

August 6, 1964—Secretary of State Dean Rusk *(foreground)*, Secretary of Defense Robert S. McNamara, and Gen. Earle Wheeler, chairman of the Joint Chiefs of Staff, examine notes before a closed-door session of the combined Senate Foreign Relations and Armed Services committees in Washington. They were there to support a resolution giving bipartisan backing of President Lyndon B. Johnson's military actions in Southeast Asia.

the United States, that President Johnson immediately after talking to Congressional leaders took the action of a small but important bombing attack. We thought it was a clear-cut case of an unprovoked attack on our destroyers in international waters, and that we had to respond.'

Says Daniel Ellsberg, 'It was not unprovoked', and the mission of the *Maddox* 'was not a routine patrol'. In his ultra-confidential Pentagon post, Ellsberg felt that the intelligence-gathering destroyers were effectively backing up the covert 34-A raids. As to the crucial 4 August incident Ellsberg says that among the Pentagon planners at the time 'there was a great uncertainty as to whether there was such an attack. Tremendous uncertainty. So much so that the Commodore on the spot had recommended delaying any retaliation at all until there could be a daytime reconnaissance to see if there had been any attack.

'In retrospect, it is unequivocally clear that there was no second attack. Very few Americans would ever come to realize that, but the evidence has been pinned down by now. But even at the time the statement that it was a clear attack to which we were justified in responding to so fast, was a lie.' Ellsberg says the 'alleged second attack' was used to get 'the functional equivalent of a declaration of war' from Congress and that Johnson did not ask for an actual declaration 'lest he raise the debate again'. In this way, Congress gave 'what amounted to a blank cheque'.

'Johnson wanted', says Ellsberg, 'to underline by bombs, by a little killing, the threats that he was already making to Hanoi. At the same time, he didn't want to reveal the threats which did indeed foreshadow an endless war of enormous proportions. So Tonkin Gulf seemed to give him the perfect opportunity to carry out a little bombing while not suggesting that it was part of a larger program of bombing – which it was.'

The man who had the responsibility of putting many of Johnson's key policies into words, Assistant Secretary of State William Bundy, discloses that the need for a Congressional resolution had been considered three months earlier. The President 'felt that if we wanted to stabilize the situation, establish a clear-cut American policy for the future that we should get a Congressional resolution. We had in the government discussions of such a resolution back in May.' It was in May that Johnson received the completed bombing scenario. But, says Bundy, these earlier discussions 'had been completely put to one side and shelved'.

As Bundy puts it, the 'expectation' within the government was that 'we would at least go through the period of the American election without any further change in policy. But we felt that these two attacks forced the issue and we had better get the Congressional resolution at that stage. And we presented what I still believe was a completely honest picture.'

The key figure in getting Congressional back-

ing was William Fulbright, Chairman of the Senate Foreign Relations Committee. Fulbright recalls that on 5 August, some four hours before the bombing began, he and other Senate and House leaders were 'briefed by the President, Secretary of State, the Chairman of the Joint Chiefs and the Secretary of Defense Mr McNamara – who played a very important part in this – about these attacks, and that these should be repulsed. It was "outrageous" – the attack upon us, upon our ships.' Fulbright then heard of the proposed resolution – 'a resolution by the administration' – drawn up, he says, by William Bundy.

Bundy claims that Fulbright and the others were told of the covert 34-A raids 'and that one of these had come only a short time before the first attack'. But, says Bundy there was 'no operational connection' between the South Vietnamese assault boats and the US destroyers and 'we said so to the Senators'.

Fulbright recalls being told that the destroyers 'were attacked while they were on the high seas, and without provocation'. Fulbright, a lawyer and 'close friend of Johnson during eighteen years shared in the Senate, had been a principal election speaker for the President in the previous months: 'I made speeches that he was a man who would keep peace around the world. And [Senator Barry Goldwater was considered the warmonger. He was going to threaten them, or use nuclear weapons and so on. And I made speeches on the Floor criticizing Goldwater and supporting Johnson.

Undated—This is an aerial view of the U.S. 7th fleet operating in the China Sea. Jet bombers from carriers in this fleet struck targets in North Vietnam.

Undated—A bridge in North Vietnam destroyed by U.S. jet bombers.

'I made speeches that there was no intention to send troops – ground troops to Vietnam. And General MacArthur, I think, had made speeches before that it would be insanity to mount a land war in Asia. And so on. I said that in the course of the debate, when the [Gulf of Tonkin] resolution came to the Senate.'

Fulbright, who told friends he could never believe LBJ would lay the wool on him, quotes Johnson as saying that if Congress would pass the resolution 'quickly, and he was most urgent about this, it would create a mood on the part of the Vietnamese to settle the war. He sold it as a means to prevent any widening of the war, that we were going to face this little country of – he said – seventeen million people with the great might of the United States; they would clearly be inclined to settle and to compromise and there wouldn't be any war. In other words, if we acted together and showed our united strength, this was the way to prevent a major war.'

Bundy counters this by stating that he and Fulbright, both one-time lawyers, 'worked over' Bundy's department draft 'so that there would be a complete understanding that this was intended to authorize responses in the future – if there should be any further repetition of this kind of attack on our destroyers'. Bundy, wrote David Halberstam in *The Best and The Brightest* 'knew something about Vietnam, and had more sophistication about the war and the enemy than most of the players. Brains were not his problem; it was a question of assumptions.'

Bundy assumed the Congress would comfortably identify sections of the resolution – 'word for

word the same', he says – with the one it had itself initiated two years earlier during the Cuban missile crisis. But he concedes that the Gulf of Tonkin resolution was 'a much broader mandate'. It authorized the President to take 'all necessary measures' to 'repel any armed attack' against US forces in South-east Asia and it approved in advance 'all necessary steps, including the use of armed force' in meeting any requests by the SEATO nations for assistance.

Bundy states: 'I would make two points – that the Congress understood what was being asked of them and participated fully in the framing of the resolution. Secondly, although there were a few marginal facts that were not known to the executive at the time, none of them affected the belief that there had been two clear-cut North Vietnamese attacks.'

'I don't think anyone considered it a declaration of war,' says Fulbright. 'I don't think anyone thought of it as an authorization to wage the kind of war that Johnson waged.' Despite the doubts about Saigon's capability, Fulbright says he and Congress believed 'that with a show of strength' the South Vietnamese would win the war. 'And that was the way it was sold to us – it was never sold as a declaration of war,' says Fulbright.

On 7 August the resolution was passed first by the House 416-0, then – introduced by Fulbright – by the Senate 88-2 (Senators Wayne Morse and Ernest Gruening were the dissenting votes). In the space of three days, the Johnson administration had implemented the two key elements of the May scenario: the initial first strike at North Vietnam and Congressional endorsement of it. The resolu-

tion, to quote the *Pentagon Papers*, 'set US public support for virtually any action'.

Fulbright made a profuse public apology a few months later for his Congressional role, charging that Johnson had misled him. But he also depicts Johnson as a product of his background and of the system: 'He was an extremely able man. Big physically, and a powerful intellect, but with no training and no experience [for the presidency]. He had hardly been out of the country before he became President. I think he had been to Mexico. In any event, he had no background in foreign relations, and I think that the Texans – and he especially – had a way of feeling that they could do anything. He believed that with the primitive society the Vietnamese had, they couldn't possibly prevail against the United States with its unlimited power.' The President, says Fulbright, could not understand the 'restraints' that went with such power: 'This was much too subtle for Johnson.'

Johnson's Secretary of State Dean Rusk disputes this, saying that Johnson 'as soon as he took office' urged restraints. 'He said: "If we stay there [Vietnam] very long, or if we have to increase our effort, we must go to the Congress." That was the basic origin of the Gulf of Tonkin resolution.' Rusk, like his deputy William Bundy, insists there was no deception. Years later when Rusk was called to give Senate testimony – or in his words 'when some dispute broke out over the facts' – he was questioned as to whether the administration had done all it might during the countdown. Why did the military or Johnson's senior people not 'call the captains of the two destroyers – they were available, why didn't they call them to see what

Above: December 1965—U.S. F-4 Phantoms bomb North Vietnam before a Christmas Eve bombing halt. Bombing resumed in January.

Left: Undated—Henry Cabot Lodge and Maxwell Taylor are photographed together in Saigon. Both men served as U.S. ambassador to Vietnam during the critical years of the war.

they thought was happening?' Rusk remembers the question as if he, subsequently, had wondered about this himself. 'But in any event', says Rusk, 'in my testimony I told them exactly what I thought was the truth.' Asked if Senator Fulbright was wrong to feel 'betrayed', Rusk replied, 'That's correct'.

Fulbright feels that after the Gulf of Tonkin 'firebreak' Johnson, like Kennedy before him, was tormented by the division among his closest advisors as to who was right or wrong on Vietnam and he 'had no basis to judge it. He was being torn by two kinds of thoughts. On the one hand mine and [Senate Majority Leader] Mike Mansfield, on the other hand Rusk, Bundy and McNamara – and above all General Taylor.'

Taylor had replaced Henry Cabot Lodge as Ambassador to Saigon three weeks earlier. He had fully concurred with the bombing strategy. 'I was convinced', says Taylor, 'that we could get at least three advantages in the use of our air-power. First, morale in South Vietnam – to give them the feeling of striking back would certainly mean a great deal to them. Secondly, of course, a great deal of war equipment and manpower was being sent in by

Above: March 16, 1965—A U.S. Navy Vigilante bomber is prepared for takeoff from the deck of the U.S.S. *Ranger*, off the coast of South Vietnam just south of the 17th Parallel.

Right: October 1964—A U.S. Marine helicopter finds a tiny landing zone to resupply troops on a 12-day patrol near the Ho Chi Minh Trail.

the North. I had no impression that we could stop that, but at least we could inflict losses; we could slow it down. Finally I felt the air-arm gave us a device by which – if used gradually and decisively – we could convince Hanoi that the price was too great to pay. We visualized a progressive movement of air strikes of increasing intensity toward Hanoi until they were faced with the obliteration of the capital if they didn't come to the negotiating table and seek a solution.'

General Maxwell Davenport Taylor, fourth in his West Point Class of 1922, was regarded as America's four-star intellectual. He had the reputation of a military 'thinker' in two previous administrations. Under Eisenhower, while Army Chief of Staff in 1955, he had argued against a policy of nuclear retaliation, instead favoring stronger conventional capability. Under Kennedy he investigated and condemned the Cuban Bay of Pigs invasion. Taylor became Kennedy's personal military advisor and was among the few who counseled against the overthrow of President Ngo Dinh Diem. In July 1962 Taylor was appointed Chairman of the Joint Chiefs of Staff, a position he retained under Johnson while arguing for a combination of civilian reforms in the South and military pressure on the North. The General was viewed as the perfect Ambassador.

With Taylor's arrival – and that of the new Field Commander, General William Westmoreland – the problems in the US command structure were presumed resolved. The previous Commander and Ambassador had become increasingly divided over policy and lines of authority. This had caused tension both in Saigon and Washington. But Taylor had made numerous missions to Vietnam. He had first-hand knowledge of the country. And it was expected that Westmoreland, with his World War II expertise in rapid infantry deployment, would quickly shake up the ARVN (Army of the Republic of Vietnam) – and the guerrillas – while deferring politically to his former Chief of Staff at the Embassy. Hanoi would feel the stick in both North and South.

But Johnson found the reports and recommendations from his new field men ever more foreboding. Taylor cabled that Communist infiltration had recently increased by an estimated 34,000 men, or thirty per cent. Westmoreland cabled that his MACV (Military Assistance Command, Vietnam) advisory force must have 4000 additional troops immediately. Westmoreland already felt that things were being politically mishandled: 'There was a tendency by Mr Johnson's administration to low-key the war. They wanted to avoid getting the American public aroused.' Westmoreland recalls that he then informed Defense Secretary McNamara that it 'was going to be a long drawn-out affair; it was going to test the patience of the American people.' Ambassador Taylor was advising that the war might prove all too short. He directly cabled the President stating that the Khanh government had only 'a fifty-fifty chance of lasting out the year'. The military outcome was still jeopardized by social and political decay. Says Taylor, 'I was not a newcomer. I knew the ambience and general problems. Ever since the overthrow of Diem we had nothing but disorder. It was perfectly apparent that we were going downhill and losing course. And if we didn't change that course we had better change our objectives.'

Taylor's cable to Johnson dated 10 August, only five days after the first bombing of the North, was a recommendation to proceed to phase two: sustained bombing. The Ambassador proposed to the President that he 'implement contingency plans against North Vietnam with optimum readiness by January 1, 1965.'

Johnson had now to decide for himself on further escalation. Among his senior advisors there was none left who counseled against it. On his Oval Office desk, alongside Taylor's cable, Johnson read and reread another dramatic opinion – that of the American public. The verdict of a Harris Poll was that the nation admired his firm handling of the Gulf of Tonkin 'crisis'. His personal popularity had soared from forty-two to seventy-two per cent overnight. The election was only three months away. But after Tonkin Johnson had pledged to 'limit American involvement if possible'. Taylor was telling him it was impossible. Taylor had called it right on Diem: was he right about Khanh? Could Vietnam – and perhaps public support – be lost at any time?

Westmoreland wanted to rally the public behind the war, and the President certainly had the public with him. But the promised mandate, Johnson knew, would also be a vote for moderation – or fear of 'hawk' Republican opponent, Senator Goldwater. Yet now Johnson's own administration had hardened in favor of Goldwater's position, had secretly planned escalation and now sought to expedite it. His inherited circle of advisors no longer shielded; it shackled. The military chiefs, McNamara, Taylor, Westmoreland, were

telling him that action – escalation – was imperative. Taylor's cable of 10 August urging a deadline for optimum action against the North perhaps had additional significance in its timing. The Ambassador knew that Canadian intermediary Blair Seaborn had left Saigon that very day on a second secret mission to Hanoi. Johnson now found no enthusiasm for bargaining with Hanoi, nor was he doing so: there was to be no hint of a carrot this time, just a heavier emphasis on the stick.

The timing of the 5 August bombing and Johnson's second use of the Canadian channel was also significantly close. Within hours of the air strike Washington had arranged with Ottawa to test Hanoi with a tougher message. It would state

flatly that both US destroyers had been attacked. Seaborn was to say that while the confrontation in the Gulf was unsought, the US was now obliged to increase its forces in South Vietnam (Hanoi was thus informed of these military moves before the American public). The June peace package, drafted as a potential follow-up to Seaborn's first visit to Hanoi, had been totally discarded. There was not now to be any ultimatum, or even a specific warning. Seaborn was not to state if or when the bombing would resume – and Ambassador Taylor's 10 August cable proposing a bombing deadline was sent after he had seen a copy of the non-specific message to be carried by Seaborn. This went to Saigon on 8 August:

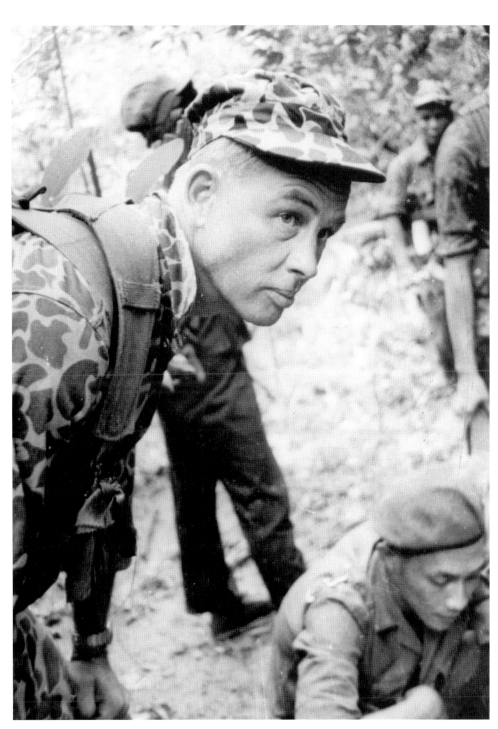

November, 1964—A U.S. advisor, Master Sgt. Fred R. Williamson, accompanies a South Vietnamese unit on a mission against a Viet Cong village near Saigon.

October 1964—Resting his rifle on his steel helmet to relieve his weary arm, a Vietnamese soldier plods through deep water of the Mekong River on a mission to ferret out bands of Viet Cong.

TOP SECRET STATE 383 TO AMEMBASSY SAIGON

Canadians are urgently asked to have Seaborn make following points as conveyed to him by us government August 6:

1. Neither the *Maddox* or any other destroyer was in any way associated with any attack on the DRV islands.
2. Regarding the Aug 4 attack by the DRV on the two US destroyers the Americans were and are at a complete loss to understand the DRV motive. About the only reasonable hypothesis was that North Vietnam was intent either upon making it appear that the United States was a 'paper tiger' or upon provoking the United States.
3. Our response for the moment will be limited and fitting.
4. In view of the uncertainty aroused by the deliberate and unprovoked DRV attacks of this character, the US has necessarily carried out precautionary deployments of additional air power to South Vietnam and Thailand.

In Hanoi, Seaborn found noticeable change: people were conducting air-raid drills and digging street trenches and brick bunkers. Evacuation of women and children was being prepared, he reported. Politically, Hanoi was also digging in. This time Seaborn waited three days before Premier Pham Van Dong would see him and, after delivering the message, 'Pham's reaction was extremely angry'. There had been 'no DRV provocation', rather the US had found 'it is necessary to carry the war to the North in order to find a way out of the impasse in the South'. And 'Johnson worries also of course about the coming electoral battle in which it is necessary to outbid the Republican candidate'.

In a furious tone, Pham told Seaborn that if the war came to the North the US would be creating 'a very dangerous situation – I repeat, very dangerous' and it would be a 'real miscalculation'. 'Up to now we have tried to avoid serious trouble', the Prime Minister said, 'but it becomes more difficult now because the war has been carried to our territory'. Pham delivered his own warning: 'If the war comes to North Vietnam it will come to the whole of South-east Asia, with unforeseeable consequences.'

As Seaborn noted in his secret report, Pham's reaction was anything but retreat. 'We don't hide the fact that the people will have to make many sacrifices', the Prime Minister said, 'but we are in a state of legitimate defense because the war is imposed on us.' He was 'visibly angry' shaking his fist as he emphasized points, and Seaborn recalls at one point 'interposing rather quickly and saying, "Mr Prime Minister, can I use the old phrase about not shooting the messenger." ' Pham then 'calmed down a bit and he laughed'. In his report at the time Seaborn stressed that Pham Van Dong had stated 'unequivocally that he wanted to keep open the channel of communication'.

Looking back to this second mission after the Gulf of Tonkin affair – 'that rather bizarre incident . . . and I'm not sure if we've still sorted out exactly how that all happened' – Seaborn says the North Vietnamese 'saw no reason to be flexible. They were quite confident if they hung tough and hung in there long enough they would eventually have things the way they wanted them . . . and history proved them right.'

Seaborn feels that the Americans had 'genuine' hopes for his mission and says they were 'almost desperately looking' for a resolution to Vietnam. In his official 13 August report Seaborn warned that Hanoi was also 'genuinely convinced' that there 'was no need to compromise'.

A subsequent secret State Department memorandum on the August mission viewed it as a second lost opportunity, stating: 'The negotiating content of this mission was totally barren as a result of its timing and its complete focus on the events immediately preceding it rather than on the broader issues as had been adumbrated at the June meeting.' Significantly, this memorandum notes that 'the first organized NVA [North Vietnamese Army] units infiltrated into SVN [South Vietnam] were dispatched from the DRV in August 1964'.

From August, in fact, events in South Vietnam had the look of a speeded-up old newsreel. Washington delegations were rushing back and forth. Once again the Ambassador and the Field Commander were finding it hard to agree. The ARVN (Army of the Republic of Vietnam) was being dubbed 'As Really Very Nervous'. The Buddhists were rioting again; coups and rumors of coups were met with almost daily indifference;

political reforms were proclaimed then jettisoned along with the generals in a dizzy gyration of governments. On 16 August General Nguyen Khanh became President, ousting General Duong Van Minh and promising a new constitution. Eleven days later the constitution was withdrawn, Minh was back as Chief of State and Khanh reverted to being Premier. Two days later Khanh was out altogether pleading 'mental breakdown'; five days later he was in again as Premier; ten days later he was out in a bloodless coup and the next day he was back in a counter-coup, and so it went on, with Ambassador Taylor trying to keep a grip on his own nerves and on the government – if any – of the day.

Says Taylor, 'In the course of my Ambassadorship which had been agreed to last just one year, I dealt with five governments, which meant five sets of senior generals, five sets of provincial chiefs governing forty-four provinces. In other words the house was cleaned – turned over – five different times with the chaos that one can imagine, and furthermore from the outset there was no one firm government at any time to build on.'

On 18 August, when Seaborn's Hanoi report was relayed from Ottawa to Washington to Saigon, Ambassador Taylor advised the White

House that bombing of the North might not be enough: General Westmoreland foresaw a need for US Marines in South Vietnam. Johnson was under different pressure from United Nations Secretary General U Thant, who proposed that direct negotiations between the US and North Vietnam be held in Rangoon. U Thant, who said he had Hanoi's agreement, was told negotiations could only be considered after the presidential election. On 27 August, as thousands of student demonstrators tried to attack ARVN headquarters in Saigon, Johnson was holding a combined birthday-political party at his Texas ranch and pledging moderation. He said: 'I've had advice to load our planes and bomb certain areas that I think would enlarge and escalate the war and result in our committing a good many American boys to fight a war I think ought to be fought by the boys of Asia.'

Three days later the Saigon government disclosed that in one week 449 people had been killed on the streets in Buddhist-Catholic clashes or by troops keeping order. At an urgent White House strategy session it was decided that intensified air attacks against North Vietnam were 'probably necessary' to retrieve the situation in the South. But Johnson would not set a date and he would tell political advisors like J. Kenneth

October 1964—A Vietnamese troop reconnaissance unit walks hip-deep in water as an armed troop-carrying U.S. helicopter skims over the high reeds on the lookout for Viet Cong guerrillas in the Mekong Delta.

Galbraith that he was 'doing the minimum necessary' and "trying to restrain the military.'

In every sense, Galbraith was a large figure on Johnson's side. The 6ft 9in former Ambassador to India, a distinguished diplomat, economist and historian, was the administration's 'giant intellect' with the heaviest credentials. Says Galbraith, 'We were the same age, came to Washington at the same time; good friends' and Johnson's liberal instincts were 'as deep as my own'. He had campaigned hard that summer for Johnson, believing him 'a safer figure' than Senator Goldwater. 'Johnson made a persuasive case', says Galbraith. 'I remember his saying once, "Ken, do you have any idea what [Air Force Chief of Staff] Curtis LeMay would be doing if I weren't here to restrain him?" . . . One always came out of the meetings with the feeling that President Johnson was trying to follow a moderate policy or mediatory policy. Or would have done so if the weight of the military and those dynamics of military involvement weren't pressing him in the other direction.'

Galbraith, who says that he remains an admirer of Johnson the man, would be the next key political defector from the administration as the war escalated. As Chairman of a liberal group called Americans for Democratic Action he turned his public oratory against the war; he was joined by Senator Fulbright and Senator Robert F. Kennedy. Even before the election the first notable protest against the war had occurred on 30 September at the University of California at Berkeley. But the polls were overwhelmingly supporting the President; the public was not his worry; nor especially the critical American press in Saigon. It was the first hints of dissent, the first signs of desertion among his 'old' circle – effectively his White House guard – that drove Johnson into deeper isolation, and deeper action. Biographer Doris Kearns says that Johnson's 'sensitivity' to criticism 'more and more walled him off from any kind of outside advice'.

As Johnson expressed it to Kearns, 'Everybody was operating for motives. If you were a journalist, you were against the war because you realized that to write good things about the war would never win you the Pulitzer Prize. If you were Fulbright, well you had to develop a constituency that would make you different from the State Department [Johnson thought Fulbright aspired to be Secretary of State]. If you were Bobby Kennedy, well you want to be President. You want to take over Johnson's job and you can't differ with him on the Great Society because he has done a wonderful job on that. Galbraith – well he had to symbolize the Harvard crowd.'

Says Galbraith, there were 'those of us who were concerned from the very beginning' who wanted to 'talk to the people about our fears as to what was happening'. But if a few were concerned, there were few yet prepared to listen. The people's fear was of Goldwater. American deaths in Vietnam were already becoming dramatic and alarming. On 1 November four Americans were killed and five B-57 bombers destroyed as guerrillas mortared the US Bien Hoa airbase close to Saigon. Two days later, Johnson won a landslide victory as the moderate candidate.

As Americans voted, Johnson met with the Joint Chiefs of Staff to consider the US response to the Bien Hoa attack. The Chiefs told the President there had been 'a Communist change in the

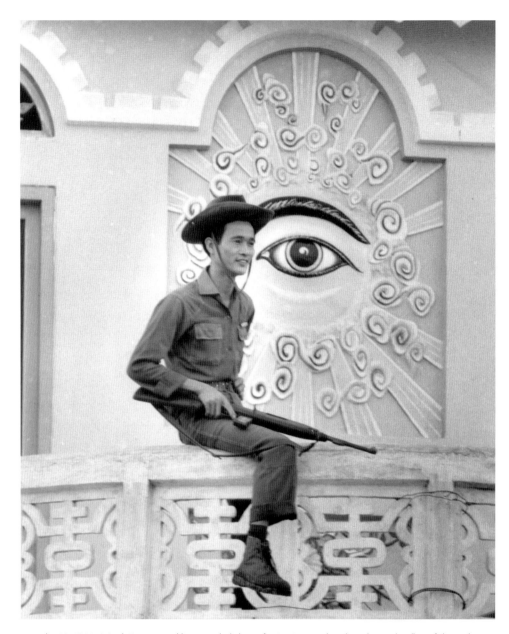

November 10, 1964—A South Vietnamese soldier sits on the balcony of a Cao Dai pagoda in the Mekong Delta village of Phu My, keeping an eye out for Viet Cong guerrillas while keeping an eye on him is the 'all-seeing eye' of the Cao Dai religion, a mixture of Christian, Buddhist, and Hindu beliefs.

ground rules' – meaning that because American troops were in Vietnam this was no reason to attack them. The Chiefs urged immediate strikes against airbases near Hanoi. Johnson instead ordered an updated bombing scenario and appointed Assistant Secretary of State William Bundy to liaise with the Pentagon. On 5 November Bundy memoed the planning group. 'Bien Hoa may be repeated at any time,' Bundy wrote. 'This would tend to force our hand but would also give us a good springboard for any decision for stronger action. The President is clearly thinking in terms of maximum use of a Gulf of Tonkin rationale.'

In this planning, awaiting a rationale, Daniel Ellsberg was summoned to assist. 'On election day I met in the office of William Bundy to look at alternative bombing options, to begin soon. We didn't wait until the day after the election: that would have wasted time. We didn't meet the day before the election on this because that might have leaked. And Goldwater who was proposing

this was in the process of being repudiated by the American people.'

In the last week of November, William Bundy presented the refined scenario to the President. It was for 'surgical' bombing – an American version of the Asian thousand cuts. Target A would be taken out; if that brought no response then Target B and so on at a quickening rate of destruction. Hanoi, despite its warning that bombing would be 'a real miscalculation', would seek peace within two to six months, Johnson was told.

At the same time thousands of Vietnamese of divergent interests were rioting in Saigon demanding reforms and elections. As the riots spread to other cities. Ambassador Taylor's prediction that the Khanh regime would not last out the year proved correct to the month: a military purge on 19 December again ousted Khanh as Premier and a few weeks later he was out of the country. Taylor, distressed at being right because it meant more was going wrong, stormed into ARVN headquarters to find out who were the coup leaders or who was his

November 12, 1964—Maj. Gen. Duong Van Minh *(left)*, former South Vietnam chief of state, gets a good-bye handshake from his one-time rival, former Premier Nguyen Khanh, as he was leaving Saigon for an extended trip abroad.

new ally. There he confronted Air Vice-Marshall Nguyen Cao Ky and General Nguyen Van Thieu and, with the South Vietnamese General Staff present and listening, America's former Chief of Staff – now Ambassador to a sovereign state – briefly lapsed into a four-star dressing down of his juniors. 'I told you all clearly', Taylor told them with disdain, 'we Americans are tired of coups. Apparently I wasted my words. . . . Now you have made a real mess.'

Marshall Ky and General Thieu, until recently commodore and colonel, who would alternatively rule South Vietnam for its remaining ten years, politely informed Ambassador Taylor to tend to his diplomatic duties. Compounding the 'mess' the new Armed Forces Council thereupon dissolved the 'civilian' High National Council, or what passed for parliament (though the army command still allowed a succession of premiers). In one sense America got its way – there would be no more coups – but this also left the US with no other way but to follow the dictates of the generals. Its last ally, General Khanh, firmly supported military rule, saying as he prepared to bow out that South Vietnam was not fighting 'to carry out the policy of any foreign country'. As the new High Command set about putting down civilian demonstrations, Johnson faced the same predicament as Kennedy had. He could either get out of Vietnam, or he could ignore the fact that the democracy 'vital' to the Free World did not exist and get on with this inherited 'bitch' of a war for which Kennedy had pledged America to 'pay any price,

November 25, 1964—A Buddhist monk tries to calm demonstrators who took refuge in the National Buddhist Headquarters in Saigon.

bear any burden, meet any hardship . . . to assure the survival of liberty'. But getting out now presented far greater difficulties.

As 1965 began, the 'Free World' was joining in – or at least those hemispheric nations heavily dependent on the US umbrella. South Korea had sent 2000 military advisors. Thailand and the Philippines were readying representative battalions, and Australia was being coerced on a contingency basis. And now, with the new year, Johnson received from his Field Commander news which left him no way out short of negotiation. North Vietnam had not retreated under the threat of bombing: it had advanced, Johnson was informed. Westmoreland's MACV command reported that North Vietnamese troops had entered the war directly: four NVA divisions had been sighted.

Their impact was swift and devastating, says Westmoreland: 'The Vietnamese ARVN were losing a battalion a week, destroyed by North Vietnamese troops or by Viet Cong main force troops operating from border base camps. That trend, if continued, would have resulted in a disastrous outcome.'

Westmoreland's MACV records reveal that on 1 January 1965 the US itself took a major preparatory step towards entering the ground war. Contingency plans for the dispatch of American combat troops were put on first-phase 'alert' coded OPLAN 32-64. That date was also the contingency deadline advocated by Ambassador Taylor for bombing the North. But Westmoreland's argument was for troops – and Taylor, while still arguing for 'gradual' bombing, had strongly opposed as overkill the Joint Chiefs' election-day recommendation to bomb Hanoi-adjacent airbases. Johnson kept the National Security Council in almost constant session as he considered the conflicting advice and which course he should proceed on – air or land war, or both. It was no longer a case of contingencies, but of choice. In effect, Washington was adopting Hanoi's analysis: the very weakness of America's ally forced a widening war. By the end of January the consensus was that air war against the North promised the most results and the least controversy – and a week later it was set in continuous motion by America's bloodiest day so far in Vietnam.

On 7 February, hours after a guerrilla blitz on the US military compound at Pleiku in which nine Americans were killed and seventy-six wounded, Johnson authorized FLAMING DART. It was a Pentagon phase one code-name for an eye for an eye response. From the 7th Fleet, forty-nine Skyhawks and Crusaders swept unopposed on the Dong Hoi barracks, North Vietnam's major troop dispersal base above the Partition line. Simultaneously across South Vietnam a pre-arranged plan for evacuating US dependents went into immediate effect. On the same day as hundreds of wives and children were airlifted out, Johnson ordered the countdown for the phase two sustained bombing. It was code-named ROLLING THUNDER.

At dawn on 2 March a hundred fighter-bombers crossed the 17th Parallel and within minutes bridges, rail-lines, port and supply facilities were devastated in a bombing plan a year in the making. On national television, Johnson told his people: 'I regret the necessities of war have compelled us to bomb North Vietnam. We have carefully limited those raids. They have been directed at concrete and steel and not at human life.'

With 'Rolling Thunder', the groundswell of world criticism and concern began. Senator William Fulbright was dismayed. Johnson had 'always maintained that his purpose was not to widen the war but to make peace'. But, says Fulbright, 'he changed his views in early 1965 with the Pleiku incident, and he began to widen the war'.

As Secretary of State Rusk saw it, there 'was no change of mind. There was a major change in the situation in Vietnam.' Rusk says that 'after our election' the entry of North Vietnamese regiments was 'threatening to cut the place in two. And the shape of the struggle became very different. We had to consider whether we got out under those circumstances or try to resist that increased force being applied by the North Vietnamese, and the decision was made to try to resist it'.

Immediate world reaction was fear of escalation to super-power confrontation. The UN Secretary-General, U Thant, again called for a peace conference – this time to include all the nuclear nations, the US, USSR, China, Britain and France, plus the two Vietnams. The US responded that North Vietnam must first 'cease aggression'. Rusk contends that it was China, not the US, which opposed negotiations throughout, saying 'it was not a matter for the United Nations'.

'There were times', says Rusk, 'when we wanted to go to the United Nations over Vietnam. When the Chinese rejected the UN we said, alright, let's use the Geneva machinery. But the Chinese prevented the use of that. It was the harsh, adamant, unyielding attitude of the Chinese that had a great deal to do with making it so difficult to bring the North Vietnamese into any kind of discussion.'

February 9, 1965—Two U.S. F-105 fighter/bombers take off together from the Danang airbase for a raid on communist bases in Laos.

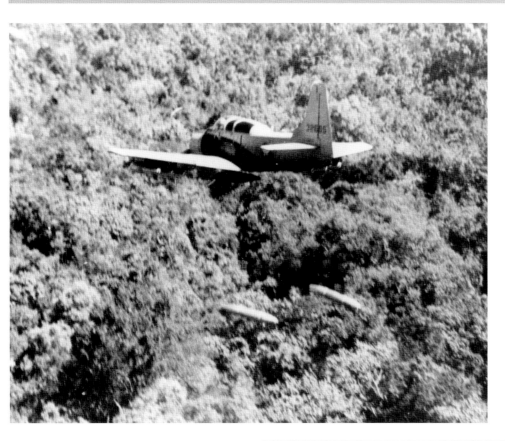

that with 'the aero-naval war against North Vietnam the occasion was lost to end the war'.

From that point on Ha Van Lau agrees that China exploited the war and in effect says China trapped the US into a prolonged war. Ha Van Lau says Peking made it known to Washington that 'China would not make war with the US if the US didn't attack China – and with that, with the Chinese card in hand, Johnson pursued the war'.

Johnson, Ha Van Lau concludes, 'was ill-advised. And he himself was responsible for that. He was responsible for his foreign policy'. Indeed, Johnson was now acutely feeling this responsibility. Having commenced 'Rolling Thunder' or 'graduated' bombing of the North on 2 March, he was under immediate pressure to adopt a similar policy in the ground war and commit large American combat forces at a publicly digestible rate. The first wave of Marines was now en route to Vietnam. The 'sighting' of North Vietnamese units had fol-

Left: March 1965—A South Vietnamese Air Force A-1 Skyraider drops bombs on suspected Viet Cong targets concealed by dense jungle.

Below: April 28, 1965—A U.S reconnaissance jet casts a shadow near a burning North Vietnamese patrol boat, one of five such boats reported destroyed by U.S. air strikes at the mouth of the Son Giang River near the Quang Khe naval base in North Vietnam.

Hanoi's version – disclosed in a special interview for this history – is a totally opposite one: it contends that the US and China came to a hands-off agreement to allow the US freedom to pursue the war. In these different versions, historians may find some insight – and contemporary meaning – on the crucial issue of why the Great Powers failed to resolve a war that first threatened world peace and then maintained world tension for an entire decade.

The US – judging from secret memoranda – did attempt new negotiations with Hanoi, believing that China might support these. This attempt was based on French contacts with the Chinese during the critical January period (when both sides made moves for a ground war). The French were optimistic that Peking would relay to Hanoi – and thus implicitly endorse – proposals for a neutral South Vietnam with wider powers accorded to the ICC, the International Control Commission. In early March, after the escalation to 'Rolling Thunder', ICC intermediary Blair Seaborn was sent back to Hanoi specifically to probe whether China was exerting any leverage. This time Seaborn failed to see Prime Minister Pham Van Dong. Instead he met with ICC liaison chief, Colonel Ha Van Lau. Seaborn went over the text of the French conversation with the Chinese. Ha Van Lau responded that it 'contained nothing new' and that Hanoi 'already had' the text from the Chinese. Seaborn was left feeling that there was no interest.

In fact, Ha Van Lau says the United States had left it too late. He says that at any time in its first year of office the Johnson administration 'could have put an end' to the war if it had accepted 'the line traced by the National Liberation Front of the South for the withdrawal of US forces and government of coalition with a foreign policy of peace and neutrality. Instead, Johnson 'sought to annihilate' the NLF. Ha Van Lau, who would become Vietnam's Ambassador to the United Nations, says lowed the phase one bombing. This had triggered phase two or 'Rolling Thunder', which then became an argument for sending in the Marines for 'base security' in case of retaliation. In late February, during the bombing countdown, the troop contingency plan had also been made operational. Johnson authorized the dispatch of two battalions of Marines to 'guard' the US air and sea base at Da Nang. They were scheduled to go ashore on 8 March. The President had not informed the public of this in his 2 March broadcast.

Within the space of a week the American people heard of this second fateful decision. Secretary of State Rusk announced that the Marines were not to engage in combat and would fire only if fired upon. But well before this announcement, Johnson – having agreed to send 'security' forces – was being asked to go the whole hawk and commit *combat* troops immediately, and thereafter as needed. Johnson now faced this paramount decision. He had to agonize alone, haggard, visibly ageing, with his casting vote. His most trusted advisors were sharply divided on whether air or land war was the most viable option, and each step Johnson took became an argument for the next. He was not at all outrunning the stampede: he was being herded along by the 'military dynamics'.

He had taken the war to the North because of the political mess in the South, or as a military cable phrased it after General Khanh's removal: 'Khanh goes abroad, Rolling Thunder rolls.' He had opted for air war to avoid a ground war. He had been told that North Vietnam would be on its knees in two months or so. Now he was told there was not that much time. Saigon's Young Turks were vocally challenging Johnson's mettle: the South was about to be 'overrun' while the US stood by. The Pentagon was telling Johnson to deploy troops 'before the tragedy'. Secretary of State Rusk thought the South might be 'cut in two' and in the North 'Rolling Thunder' showed

every sign of fizzling.

The bombing was scheduled at irregular intervals. This 'graduated' concept envisaged that after a pause there would be a response, but from the start this took the form of heavy anti-aircraft resistance. The Air Force had reported that North Vietnamese defenses were stronger than imagined, though it could not conceive just how strong they would prove. (Though 'Rolling Thunder' was essentially written off very early as an effective solution, the bombing continued for eight years. US planes struck at North Vietnam 350,000 times. In North and South Vietnam the US dropped close to eight million tons of bombs – quadruple the tonnage used throughout World War II. The US estimated its aircraft losses at about 1000 over the North, 3720 overall, plus 5000 helicopters. More than 8000 American airmen were killed.)

The CIA assessed that the bombing had 'hardened' Hanoi's resolve, and now Secretary of Defense McNamara who had promoted the bombing strategy was backing Field Commander William Westmoreland in saying it was not enough: America must enter the ground war.

Westmoreland argued from the concept stage that phased bombing 'just wouldn't work'. As he explains, 'Once the North Vietnamese realized what was taking place they dissipated the targets, and instead, for instance, of having their petroleum concentrated in one place, they moved it in little packages around the country. . . . I always considered the enemy a pretty tough group, that they would adapt themselves to a particular level of bombing, and that the message Washington was trying to submit would not get through by this off and on again bombing.'

Westmoreland argued that the bombing would logically bring retaliation against US air bases in the South, and that after the Bien Hoa and Pleiku guerrilla attacks the US could no longer rely on South Vietnamese forces to defend these bases. He

considered the main US base at Da Nang, on the coast only 100 miles south of the Partition line, especially vulnerable. In supporting Westmoreland, the Joint Chiefs initially recommended Marine units for Da Nang as a one-shot response to a particular security problem. As the Pentagon phrased it, troops were needed 'to deter overt retaliation to the air strikes'. In other words, troops were now necessary to back up an air offensive designed to avoid the use of troops.

Ambassador Taylor expressed his alarm. He cabled Johnson warning that if the Marines took over ARVN security duties it would encourage Saigon to 'shuck off greater responsibilities'. He urged reliance on the air war until more ARVN units were trained. Taylor criticized the 'unnecessarily timid' conduct of the bombing, proposing 'a more dynamic schedule of strikes'. Though the bombing schedule had been devised by the Pentagon, Taylor considered that Western peace efforts were holding up the air war. He cabled that 'current feverish diplomatic activity particularly by French and British' was confusing the chance to 'progressively turn the screws on the DRV'. Failure to do this was encouraging requests for combat troops. If these were sent, Taylor told Johnson what would happen: 'The "white-faced" soldier cannot be assimilated by the population; he cannot distinguish between friendly and unfriendly Vietnamese; the Marines are not trained or equipped for jungle guerrilla warfare.' As quoted in the *Pentagon Papers* Taylor prophesied that the US – like France – would fail to adapt to such conditions.

But the Joint Chiefs, until recently headed by Taylor, adamantly disagreed. The Marine deployment, far from being an encouragement to use US troops in combat, would free four South Vietnamese battalions for anti-guerrilla operations, it was argued. And, if it came to it, the Marines had 'a distinguished record in counter-insurgency operations'.

March 31, 1965—A Phantom II fighter-bomber takes off from the U.S.S. *Coral Sea* for a raid on radar installations in North Vietnam.

March 18, 1965—U.S. Marines wade ashore at Danang to defend the coastal airbase against Communist attack.

Johnson, having sent the Chairman of the Joint Chiefs to Saigon as his most trusted military man, had removed the main restraint from Washington, where it counted most. Taylor had been Army Chief of Staff for four years, then personal advisor to Kennedy and Johnson before becoming Chairman of the JCS in 1962. With these credentials Taylor's judgement of the military climate in the US during this period is an authoritative and disturbing one.

'Starting in 1961', he says, 'and then progressively' the right wing were 'urging' the use of 'our ground forces'. 'I personally,' says Taylor, 'realized the undesirability of this. The longer I was in Vietnam the more I felt the danger of our taking over too much of the war from the Vietnamese. Once we brought any troops in, that was the nose of the camel. It would be difficult to know how much was enough.'

Johnson had appointed a senior military man to be Ambassador to Saigon in order to end the previous friction between the Embassy and the military command. And Taylor says 'my authority as Ambassador put me in charge of the military operation'. But now Johnson's own generals in Saigon were disagreeing. Taylor had been sent to advise what the policy should be and General Westmoreland had been sent to execute it, but Johnson was now about to reverse these roles. Westmoreland says he was told by Defense Secretary McNamara to ask for whatever he wanted – and he wanted troops. He was supported at the State Department where the Assistant Secretary for South-east Asia, William Bundy, assessed that the South Vietnamese army 'might collapse'.

'It seemed at that stage', says Bundy, 'that only

an infusion of American combat units, divisions and all the rest, could stop the rot and level things off and make progress.' The new political power in Saigon, General Thieu, also supported Westmoreland. 'The Communists', says Thieu, 'controlled seventy-five per cent of the countryside. We controlled only the chief towns. We had the impression we would be overrun. There was a crucial need for American troops.'

Finally, Ambassador Taylor 'concurred' with the landing of Marines. Taylor describes Westmoreland as 'a close friend' and says 'Westy and I checked constantly on our thinking'. The two generals were veterans of Korea, both had been superintendents of West Point. Says Taylor, 'When Westy brought in evidence of the decay of the South Vietnamese forces in the Da Nang area, and the increasing threat of infiltration from the North, I eventually decided yes, Da Nang is in danger.' Taylor recommended sending me battalion. Westmoreland recommended two. The Joint Chiefs recommended two. Johnson authorized two.

Having approved the first troops without yet announcing it, Johnson, in Taylor's metaphor, had been sold the whole camel. Says Taylor, 'Very soon I saw cables going around the world that indicated that our armed forces in every place were being alerted to the possibility of getting involved in Vietnam. And that resulted in a string of complaints, as you will find in the record, against the over-rapid introduction without careful concurrence with my Embassy assuring for the readiness to receive troops. . . . Also politically from the point of view of the [Saigon] government'.

'The first troops', says Westmoreland, 'were

invited in to protect our air bases. Now once those troops were at those bases, it made no sense at all to have them dig in and go strictly on the defensive.'

In the days immediately before and after the dispatch of the first two battalions President Johnson had Pentagon requests for forty-four additional battalions. While considering these, Johnson ordered that units sent to Vietnam could be used in combat. But he ordered that this decision be kept secret. From this point, says biographer Doris Kearns, Johnson did not look back until his presidency was destroyed. 'As he became more committed to actions', says Kearns, 'he became less and less doubtful.'

Johnson was no longer alone. Though some questioned the wisdom, none seriously doubted that America would prevail. Initially hesitant, Ambassador Taylor modified his position on combat troops: 'I became for it', he says, because 'we obviously had the resources to end the thing if we followed that course vigorously'. With the imminent landing of Marines, Johnson ordered all his top men to Washington for a 'what next?' conference, and Taylor attended: 'What was our intention now? Where do we go from here? And I found that the President – and I heard no advisor who did not share his feelings – felt that we really had to lift the level of our support to include ground forces until the Field Commander reported that we had a stable situation.'

On 8 March 1965, a flotilla of landing craft thudded on to the beaches at Da Nang, where the French had re-invaded twenty years before, and the first American combat troops waded ashore. They numbered only 3500 then.

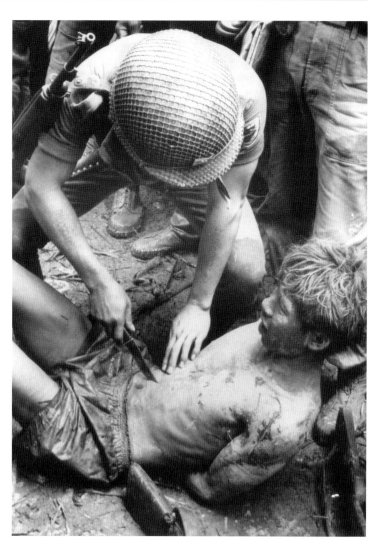

October 2, 1964—A U.S. Army helicopter flies past the bodies of Viet Cong guerrillas who were trapped by South Vietnamese forces near Tan Phu village, north of Camau in southern South Vietnam.

October, 1964—The point of a knife is pressed harder and harder against the belly of a Viet Cong prisoner, one of four captured in the Mekong Delta area. Continued interrogation eventually revealed the location of hidden weapons.

1965—A delegation of North Vietnam's elite fighters who have been fighting in South Vietnam call on President Ho Chi Minh (fourth from left) during a visit to Hanoi.

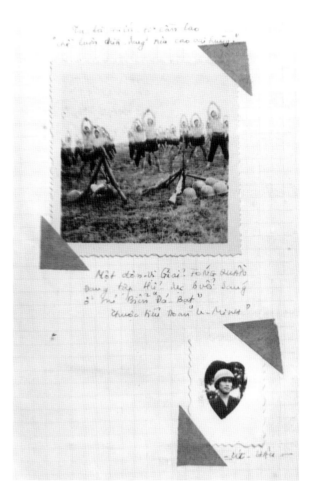

October 1964—South Vietnamese Rangers submerge the head of a bound Viet Cong in a water urn during an interrogation in the Mekong River town of Cau Ke. Ten men, including a U.S. advisor, had been killed at Cau Ke a month earlier.

1965—A page from the notebook of a slain Viet Cong soldier contained a picture of his unit workout at a beach location at Da Bat. Notations in the book read: 'We are worker fighters,' and 'We will protect our heroism,' and 'We will always be valiant.' A soldier's portrait in a heart-shaped cutout was also in the book.

November 22, 1964—Anti-government demonstrators try to defy first explosions of tear gas thrown by charging paratroopers that eventually broke up their rally in front of Saigon's Gia Long presidential palace.

Above: October 1964—A South Vietnamese patrol follows the Ho Chi Minh Trail through a mountain stream.

Right: November 1964—Supported by American 'Eagle Flight' helicopters, Vietnamese troops wade through a rice paddy in Log An province during operations against Viet Cong in the Mekong Delta.

November 22, 1964—Anti-government demonstrators face paratroopers at Gia Long palace in Saigon where tear gas was used to break up the demonstration.

November 28, 1964—Tracks of army carriers cut through flooded rice paddies after a battle near Chao Gao in the Mekong Delta, 27 miles southwest of Saigon.

Above: November 18, 1964—U.S. helicopters carrying Vietnamese marines scramble into the air from Bien Hoa during an air assault by more than 100 helicopters on suspected Viet Cong positions northwest of Saigon.

Right: December 10, 1964—U.S. military adviser Maj. David R. Pinney from Harrisville, New Hampshire, gestures as he tries to explain something to his South Vietnamese counterpart, a leader of the group of Vietnamese Nung, on the Ho Chi Minh Trail in South Vietnam.

Above: 1965—This picture shows a Viet Cong regional force platoon in the Cu Chi district 20 miles northwest of Saigon as it passes through gates of an abandoned hamlet. The gate has been smeared with VC flags.

Left: 1965—Viet Cong troops participate in training session. Location is unknown.

Below: 1965—Viet Cong troops, surprised by an unarmed U.S. reconnaissance plane, scramble for cover. The U.S. Air Force did not say exactly where or when the photo was taken.

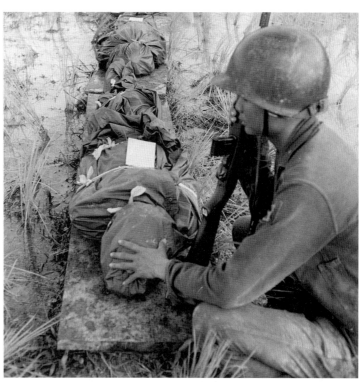

Above: A South Vietnamese soldier from the Ranger battalion kneels at the edge of a row of dead comrades in bags laid out on a paddy dike to be evacuated by helicopter on Tan Dinh Island in the Mekong Delta.

Left: December 1964—A U.S. sergeant leads a patrol of ethnic Nungs through a riverbank clearing along the Ho Chi Minh Trail.

Below: 1965—A South Vietnamese commander interrogates a Viet Cong suspect in Tan Dinh province during an operation against rebel forces.

Above: December 1964—As smoke rises from a previous bombing, an A-1 Skyraider dives low over the jungle to release twin 500-pound bombs on a Viet Cong target.

Left: December 16, 1964—Hundreds of Buddhist monks and nuns sit in the pagoda of their national headquarters in Saigon as they begin a hunger strike against the South Vietnamese government, which they feel persecutes Buddhists.

Below: A Viet Cong suspect is interrogated at knifepoint by South Vietnamese soldiers in Ap La Ghi in South Vietnam's Mekong Delta. The soldiers questioned the woman, who was thrown to the ground with her hands tied, about local Communist guerrilla strength.

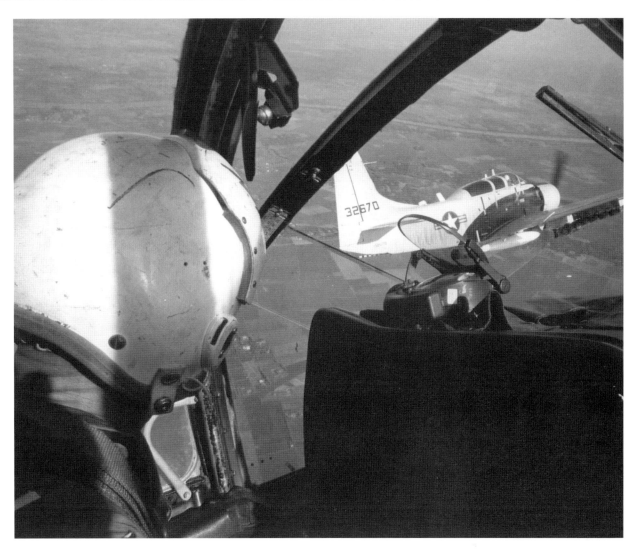

Right: December 1964—U.S. Skyraiders fall into position for an air strike against Viet Cong bases in South Vietnam. The Vietnamese pilots carry bombs, napalm, 20mm cannons, and American advisors.

Below: 1965—North Vietnamese women workers rally outside a Hanoi factory.

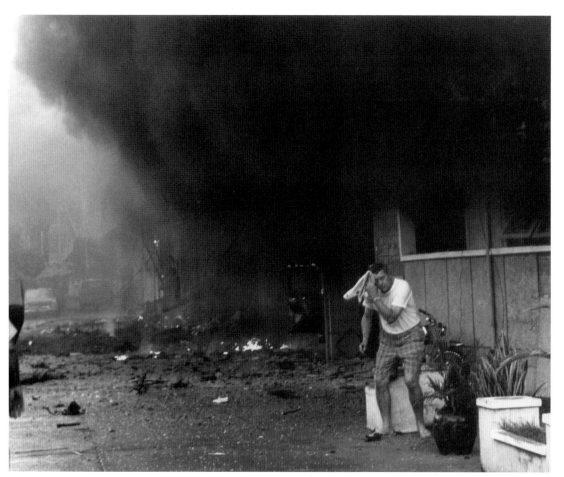

Left: December 24, 1964—Billowing black smoke fills the street after a bomb blast struck an officer's billet in Saigon. A survivor of the blast steps into the street in his underwear to escape the burning structure.

Below left: December 24, 1964—Bloodied and shocked, an officer sits on the steps of a billet hit by a terrorist bomb in Saigon.

Below: December 24, 1964—An American officer has his wounds treated after an officer's billet in central Saigon was hit by a terrorist bomb.

1965—Local residents man a light machine gun in the North Vietnamese town of Hatinh, about 250 miles south of Hanoi. The caption of this photo released in Hungary claimed 13 U.S. planes had been shot down in the area during March 1965.

Above: 1965—Viet Cong fighters march quickly on a trail in South Vietnam.

Right: 1965—Women teachers and students at Hanoi University train with dummy grenades.

Above: December 1964—The first rays of dawn break through the dense jungle around the embattled town of Binh Gia, 40 miles east of Saigon, and a group of paratroopers rest after a cold and tense night of expecting a Viet Cong ambush.

Left: January 5, 1965—Long lines of graves are dug between a cemetery and fields at the provincial capital of Baria for South Vietnamese Marines killed in action.

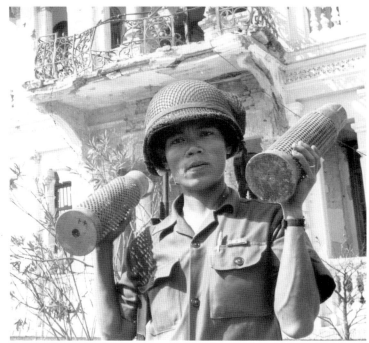

Left: January 6, 1965—A wounded soldier climbs onto the back of a Vietnamese paratrooper outside the old French fort at Dat Do for a ride to a first-aid station.

Above: January 9, 1965—A Vietnamese soldier, who survived an attack on his outpost near Saigon, displays cannon shell casings left behind by the Viet Cong. One American adviser was killed in the attack.

Below: January 17, 1965—Senior U.S. advisers sip rice wine through long straws at Banmethuot, in the Central Highlands, 150 miles northeast of Saigon. The wine was a gift of Montagnard tribesmen, presented as a token of friendship and allegiance.

Above: January 22, 1965—A club-wielding Vietnamese paratrooper wearing a gas mask tries to arrest a man on the run during Buddhist antigovernment demonstrations in front of the U.S. embassy in Saigon.

Right: January 22, 1965—Two schoolchildren, tears streaming down their faces, flee tear gas fired into their school by riot police. A melee broke out at the opening of the school day with children shouting antigovernment slogans.

Below: January 22, 1965—Buddhist monks and demonstrators are stopped as tear-gas grenades explode among them at an anti-American protest outside the U.S. embassy in Saigon.

Right: January 22, 1965—A Buddhist monk stands to ignore the tear gas used by soldiers outside the U.S. embassy in Saigon as other demonstrators kneel and squat.

Below: February 1965—Observers of the International Control Commission inspect weapons recovered from a ship sunk by bombs off South Vietnam's coast. The cache was believed destined for Viet Cong troops in the south.

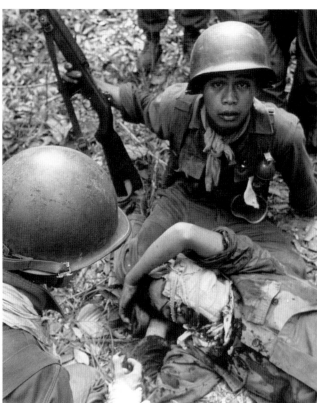

Above: March 28, 1965—Vietnamese soldiers tend to their comrades who were accidentally hurt in friendly fire when Skyraiders mistakenly bombed their position during an attack on a Viet Cong headquarters.

Left: February 16, 1965—A farm woman holds her child as she pleads with a South Vietnamese soldier whose unit was burning down a Viet Cong–controlled village near coastal Tam Ky in retaliation for enemy gunfire coming from the village.

February 20, 1965—Rebel troops sit passively in their foxholes at Tan Son Nhut airfield as government forces occupied the base, ending the coup attempt against Gen. Nguyen Khanh, who had seized power a year earlier.

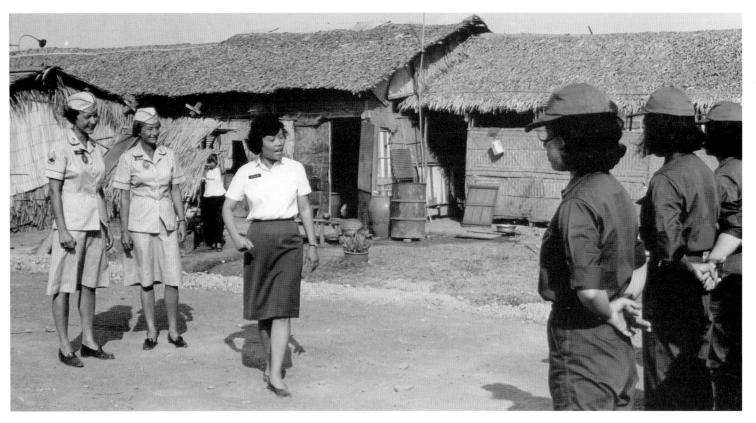

March 1965—Members of the U.S. Women's Army Corps (WACs), left, instruct a class of the South Vietnamese Women's Armed Forces Corps on marching technique.

Left: March 1, 1965—A U.S. Air Force officer (center) and his radio man run past the bodies of two South Vietnamese paratroopers while taking cover from sniper fire near Bing Gia. A helicopter also takes off under fire.

Below: March 28, 1965—A South Vietnamese soldier strikes a Viet Cong suspect during a sweep of Quang Nam province, 10 miles southwest of Danang. Two government battalions took 30 prisoners, 13 of whom were described as hard-core Viet Cong.

Above: March 30, 1965—A man searches for his child among the dead and wounded on a street near the U.S. embassy in Saigon after a bomb was exploded by Viet Cong terrorists.

Left: March 28, 1965—A South Vietnamese soldier threatens a Viet Cong guerrilla into revealing the hiding place of Chinese-made grenades. He was captured in Quang Nam province, 15 miles southwest of Da Nang.

March 3, 1965—South Vietnamese medics carry a poncho holding a wounded soldier, hit by mortar fire, through high grass to a waiting helicopter near Bing Gia, about 40 miles southeast of Saigon.

March 30, 1965—A U.S. serviceman carries the body of an elderly Vietnamese woman from the scene of an explosion outside the U.S. embassy in Saigon. The woman was a food peddler on the street corner opposite the embassy.

March 1965—South Vietnamese troops with gas masks explode phosphorous grenades at entrances to underground shelters and tunnels used by the Viet Cong near Trung Lap, northwest of Saigon.

March 22, 1965—Villagers watch as aircraft strafe and bomb Viet Cong positions only hundreds of yards away from their bunker. The local people, who live in a town just 40 miles from Saigon, are caught between oppressive actions of the Viet Cong and the military attacks of the government forces.

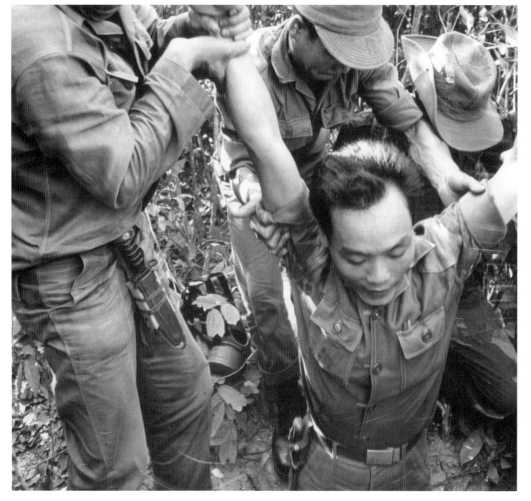

Above: March 29, 1965—A South Vietnamese infantryman camouflaged with jungle foliage sits in an ambush site near a Viet Cong trail north of Tay Ninh.

Left: March 8, 1965—An exhausted Vietnamese army engineer is pulled from the entrance of a Viet Cong tunnel north of Saigon after he helped place three tons of explosives to blow up the tunnel.

Above: March 30, 1965—Blood-covered officials leave the U.S. embassy after a bomb explosion.

Right: March 30, 1965—Blood streams from an American official as he is escorted from the U.S. Embassy in Saigon after a bomb explosion.

March 30, 1965—Bloodied U.S. embassy personnel are carried on stretchers after a bomb explosion rocked the embassy building in Saigon.

1965—The faces of U.S. servicemen fighting in South Vietnam.

# UNEASY ALLIES

On 1 March 1965, one week before US forces were to go ashore in Vietnam and exactly two months after they had been put on 'alert', Ambassador Taylor in Saigon called on interim Premier Phan Huy Quat to impart this totally surprising information: the Marines were coming. In effect, Taylor's message was that one nation had decided by itself to send troops to another country to protect it from a third. The Marines were about to embark and South Vietnam was only now hearing that foreign troops were to enter the country for its own good. The Ambassador, of course, phrased it differently, but as State Department DEPTEL 1840 of 26 February instructed Taylor: 'Approved deployment. Secure GVN [Government of South Vietnam] approval.' Three days later he was taking the routine approach through the office of the Premier with a request clearly regarded by Washington as mere formality: would the South Vietnamese government 'invite' the United States to send in the Marines?

> 'I can say that the mutual understanding was none. Zero'
>
> – PRIME MINISTER NGUYEN CAO KY

Though US military personnel in South Vietnam then exceeded 20,000 (with more committed), these were advisors whereas the Marines would have the role of a defense force, prepared to fight. Premier Quat, according to his Chief of Staff Bui Diem, was completely unaware of the American troop plan: 'He was informed at the very last stage after the decision.' Quat had only been appointed to the job by the Armed Forces Council ten days earlier. After an astonished pause he thanked Taylor and said he would consult with General Nguyen Van Thieu, the Council leader.

After Taylor had left, Quat summoned his Chief of Staff and told him the news. They agreed that it was all most embarrassing: who was running the country? Looking back, Bui Diem felt this was the point of emasculation, setting a course for defeat: the US would assume control and would tire of the burden which Saigon felt it never had a chance to share. Bui Diem would be a member of the Cabinet for the next two years, seeing US troop

April 10, 1965—U.S. Marines wade ashore at Red Beach, Danang, South Vietnam, reinforcing the Danang air base as South Vietnamese Rangers battled communist guerillas about three miles south of the beach.

April 29, 1965—U.S. Marine helicopters leave troops in a suspected Viet Cong area during full-fledged heliborne assault operation by U.S. Marines near Da Nang, South Vietnam.

commitments grow to 82,000 in the first six weeks; 120,000 within four months, 184,000 within that first year, 300,000 by mid-1966 and more than 500,000 by 1967 when Bui Diem became permanent Ambassador to Washington.

'I think', he says, 'that most of the time the Americans made the decisions and the South Vietnamese government was informed afterwards.'

After discussing Ambassador Taylor's brief announcement about the coming of the 3500 Marines, Bui Diem says he and Premier Quat still 'knew nothing about it' except that the Marines would embark on the 6th and land at Da Nang on the 8th. Quat, portrayed as a 'mild, self-effacing' man – he would last as premier for only four months – had now to obtain the formal approval of the real power, General Thieu. And then the people had to be told. The South Vietnamese and American public were to be informed as the GIS went ashore.

'The only thing we did at this time', says Bui Diem, 'was to sit down and try to draft the communiqué.' The generals, already concerned that the South might be 'overrun', unhesitatingly issued an 'invitation'. (At this time, the South Vietnamese army numbered almost 500,000. The US estimate of guerrilla strength, made public with the landing of the Marines, was 37,000 regular troops and 100,000 militia, 'an increase of thirty-three per cent over 1964'.) In approving the Marine landing, General Thieu worried about how the Buddhist and student population of Da Nang, the South's second largest city, might react. He requested that the Marines be 'brought ashore in the most inconspicuous way feasible'.

General William Westmoreland was there to greet them. In his book *A Soldier Reports*, he described the landing as 'a re-enactment of Iwo Jima'. Washington wanted the symbolism known. As in the dark days of World War II American boys were again storming the white sands of Asia to push back the unimaginable, this time with the television cameras rolling. Though the military had thus far reported only one guerrilla probe of

April 28, 1965—A Marine carries another wounded Marine on his back to stretcher bearers at the base of a hill. They were part of a large patrol several miles from Danang that moved deep into Viet Cong territory.

'unknown size' near the Da Nang base, the Marines had orders 'to occupy and defend critical terrain features in order to secure the airfield'. At exactly 0900 hours on 8 March, scores of amphibious craft hit the sands of Da Nang and Marines, in full combat gear, brandishing M-14 rifles, rushed the beaches.

In a series of troop landings the soldiers faced probably the strangest introduction to any war. There on the sands would be a stately welcoming committee beaming against the background of palms like a 'you-should-be-here' postcard, with pretty girls everywhere. They had amber skin and mischievous almond eyes and black tresses to the waist with pastel *ao dais* that split at the thigh over their rustling silk trousers. The girls moved among the young soldiers adorning them with *leis* of white and pink orchids. In their slim, tight, multi-colored tunics they floated like day-dreams, something to struggle for, ideals to be saved, as they shyly smiled at the 'round-eyes' semi-hallucinating on this paradisial beach.

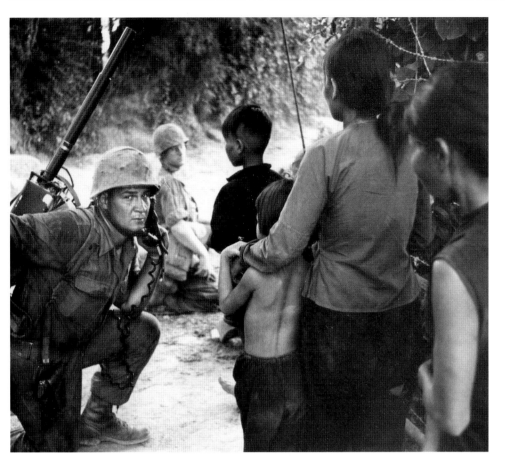

May 25, 1965—Vietnamese women and children watch U.S. Marines check a bunker in Nam Yen, 10 miles northwest of Da Nang. The Marines found 12 Viet Cong suspects along the Ca Be River.

thought, 'my God, there's the enemy, don't they know that? It really was strange.' On arrival, Santos found that lunch was ready in a prefabricated airport officers' club: 'There was this huge buffet – it was like, I don't know, like a regular club in the States, apart from the heat and the fans. . . . I was shocked. I expected war.'

'I was surprised', says Sergeant Tim O'Brien, 'when we began going out on operations . . . walking around in a kind of vacation land. It reminded me of what Miami Beach must have been like without all the hotels. Beautifully clean sand and in the distance green, sloping jungle. Beautiful.'

Most would land at these coastal 'enclaves' and find themselves initially patrolling resort-like areas with little children and ice-cream vendors chasing after them. After intensive training in the US and psychological prepping for the terrors of the interior, many GIS found their early days unreal, and for the rear-echelon majority the unreality was permanent. They would have only superficial contact with the Vietnamese, learning little if anything of local feelings or culture – yet their sheer numbers, their overwhelming presence and affluence, would fracture and corrupt this culture. Most Vietnamese, in turn, would see the GI only through the war's schizophrenic character: one moment with guns blazing satanically, the next as Santa personified.

For the GIS, whether they came in the earliest days or in the later years, civilian contact would develop strictly on a need-to-know basis. On base perimeter patrols, says Tim O'Brien, 'we would be followed by a hundred, a hundred and fifty Vietnamese. I suppose they lived in neighboring

In the years to follow almost 2.8 million GIS would rotate through 'Nam' on twelve-month duty tours which a great many of the troops would remember as 'some mad roller-coaster ride'. They would often be whirled from base-luxury to jungle action and back again in time for the nightly movie – like as not starring John Wayne in some war or other, or out 'nailing Indians'. Vietnam was 'Indian country' beyond the GI bases – and the great majority never saw much beyond the stockades. Even at peak strength of 543,400 men only one quarter of this force (at most) was on combat assignment, and by some estimates seldom more than five per cent were actually engaged in combat at any one time. Years later, despite the war's ferocity, its remorseless toll and unpopularity, the 'pinch-me' quality of the Da Nang welcome would remain the norm. 'From the start', says one soldier, 'the idea was to sanitize the war for the folks back home.' For years officers assigned to Saigon would fly in on scheduled airlines.

'One of the hardest things for me to really adjust to in my mind', recalls Marine Platoon Commander and author James Webb, 'was to step off an air-conditioned plane where I'd just watched a first-run movie and hear this stewardess say "Have a nice war".'

'I remember my first thought,' says Infantry Lieutenant Robert Santos – who did not know his destination, 'coming out the back of the plane – because you can't see where you're landing – and I had my weapons ready. But it was an airport, and a bunch of Vietnamese were walking around drinking Coca-Cola with all the Americans. And I first

May 26, 1965—A Buddhist nun prays as a U.S. sergeant of the 1st Battalion, 173rd Airborne Brigade patrols Hat Lang village. The unit had earlier come under sniper fire in the area.

May 27, 1965—An American lieutenant is wounded in an operation in the Mekong Delta, where he was adviser to a Vietnamese reconnaissance company.

villages. There were prostitutes; there were young kids; there were girls peddling cocaine at a dollar a whack. They were making a killing on us.' O'Brien would write two books on Vietnam – *If I Die In A Combat Zone* and the satirical *Going After Cacciato*. 'We had our personal "mascots" or valets,' he recalls. 'A little kid of seven or eight would hook up with a soldier and would wash his socks for him and clean his rifle for him – and sometimes carry his rifle for him if he was exceptionally tired that day. They'd dig our foxholes at night. . . . We were feeding off them, and they were feeding off us.'

Language was only a parasitical lexicon. 'I knew a little pigeon Vietnamese', says O'Brien, 'and the Vietnamese learned a strange version of English, mostly four-letter words.' Beyond the relative relaxation of the base areas, in the no man's land or rural areas that held eighty-five per cent of the population, there was even less communication and no trust at all. 'We had a few words that

we all knew', says James Webb, 'and that civilians knew too. But their main presentation to us was absolute numbness.' Webb, who would be one of the most decorated Marines, wrote *Fields of Fire*. He says that when the GIS ventured into the real Vietnam, the villages, the people would 'just squat there. They learned not to move; that's the main thing. They just froze. And then if we wanted something from them, we'd approach them.'

As their numbers increased, the new GIS would find contact and co-operation that much harder because of the build-up of resentment preceding them. Even the first arrivals found their image among the villages prejudged by the advisory troops and helicopter pilots who led the ARVN into combat. Over much of the countryside the Americans had been an unseen force except for the neucopter gunships which spewed death at people in traditional black pajamas who may or may not have been guerrilla infiltrators.

Though the pilots were supposed only to ferry

the ARVN troops into battle and not engage in combat, they frequently did – and with relish. At base-camp the pilots would openly re-fight the day's battles each night over a fifteen-cent beer. 'Quite an operation today, wasn't it?' said one, sipping his Schlitz in the officers' club of a helicopter support company. 'Yeah, good job. I saw you splatter one right in the back with a rocket,' another pilot said in a recorded chat. 'Lucky, I guess. A lucky shot. Blew the other guy about ten feet. Got two others with a machine gun. Satisfying to know that sometimes you do kill people with these things.'

From the early 1960s the Americans felt increasingly at risk, and increasingly obliged to join the fighting, because of ARVN's failure in the field. It induced a contempt and indifference in American ranks which conditioned attitudes and policy when the first ground forces arrived. Military operations in US base areas were then under ARVN control. But command sharing was considered vital only in the area of air support. Integration of units and of strategic planning was nominal, and would remain so. Even had the US military sought integration of its new ground forces and ARVN – and it clearly did not–it was boxed by its own approach. Its proclaimed role was defensive, or protection of US bases, and though this posture was soon discarded the early uneasiness between the allies quickly rendered any sharing of combat duties or command more hazardous than helpful. From the start, therefore, the military and cultural separation was acute, and the sudden doubling and redoubling of US forces would only accentuate it. The early mutual distrust, which rapidly festered beyond healing, would explain why so many American troops for so long achieved so little, and the urgency for more and more troops once the first had been deployed.

The first two Marine battalions at Da Nang were joined by two more within a month and now President Johnson authorized that their mission could be altered 'to permit their more active use'. But these orders were discretionary and secret. Within six weeks of the first Marine landing the US had drawn up plans for four brigade-size 'enclaves', or huge 'holding' positions, requiring 82,000 American troops. In addition to Da Nang, major air-infantry bases would be developed at Chu Lai, Quang Ngai, Qui Nihon, Bien Hoa and Vung Tai – all on or near the coast. Simultaneously, planning began for a giant naval base at Cam Ranh Bay.

To quieten any public doubts, Ambassador Taylor was to inform the Saigon government that the US would only gradually announce troop deployments 'at appropriate times'. Sharing this secret commitment, America's Pacific allies had pledged an additional 7250 troops, including an ANZAC [Australian-New Zealand Army Corps] battalion, for the 'enclave' strategy. Within nine weeks of Westmoreland's welcome to the first 3500 Marines, he commanded or was about to command 90,000 'Free World' troops. The *Pentagon Papers* show that on 9 May he outlined to Washington how he proposed using 'ground combat forces in support of the South Vietnamese *air force* [author's italics]'. His plan comprised three stages: first, 'security of base areas'; secondly, 'deep patrolling and offensive operations'; and finally 'Search and Destroy' (enlarged) operations.

In Washington, President Johnson's closest

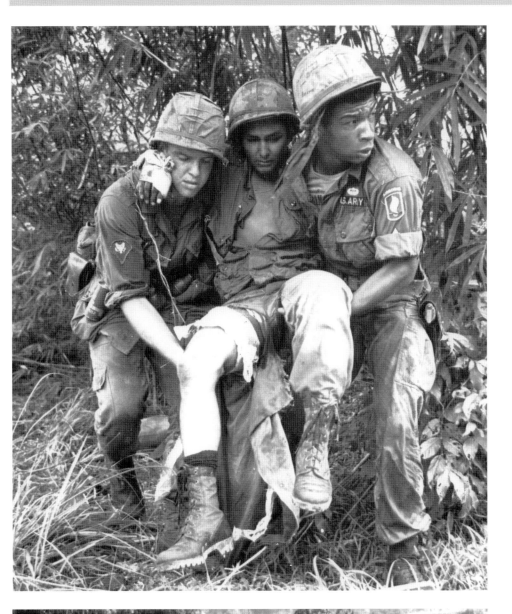

Left: June 24, 1965—Two U.S. medics, under intense sniper fire, carry a wounded paratrooper to an evacuation helicopter in the jungle near Thuong Lang. A company of U.S. paratroopers had dropped directly into a Viet Cong staging area.

Below: June 1965—A Vietnamese peasant walks down a road with a sickle over his shoulder as a U.S. armored personnel carrier passes through Bien Hoa on a reconnaissance mission.

and soon to depart White House advisor, Kenneth Galbraith, saw a radical alteration of the strategy he had advocated. He felt the enclave policy would be a 'popular' one if American forces were just to 'pull back' to these bases 'and wait and wait. And eventually some sort of a negotiated solution would emerge. In the meantime there wouldn't be very many lives lost either on our side, or Vietnam's side. Time would work its own solution.' Westmoreland bluntly rejected this. As he puts it, 'To surrender the initiative to the enemy and to dig in in enclaves on the defensive . . . in my opinion, was a self-defeating procedure'.

In Saigon, Ambassador Taylor supported Westmoreland but wanted slowed deployment because he foresaw two problems: 'boredom' among the GIS and a mutiny by the generals in Saigon, who considered even a joint command structure 'repugnant'. He needed time to sort this out, he cabled the State Department on 24 May. But less than two weeks later, on 5 June, he cabled that time had run out. According to the *Pentagon Papers* Taylor and Westmoreland now concurred that 'a series of recent ARVN defeats raised the possibility of collapse. To meet a shortage of ARVN reserves, US ground troops would probably have to be committed to action'.

In just three weeks, a 'one-shot' base security need for two battalions had changed to a situation of imminent countrywide 'collapse' requiring twenty or more combat battalions, with as many more requested. Da Nang and other bases were reported in a stage of semi-siege. President Johnson now stepped up the tempo of 'Rolling Thunder' attacks on the North while trying one last time to measure the pulse of the South. He turned to his Secretary of the Navy, Paul Henry Nitze, who also had charge of the Marines. Nitze was to begin at Da Nang. Prior to the landing of Marines there had been only one minor guerrilla probe reported by the Da Nang base: so why this dramatic reversal? Was the military exaggerating? If not, what was the bottom line – how many troops, for how long? Nitze set out immediately and by mid-June after 'a fairly detailed survey' he concluded that Da Nang's position was 'most dangerous'.

'The Viet Cong', as Nitze recalls, 'controlled the countryside right up to the fence surrounding the airfield at Da Nang. They controlled the mountains looking down over the airfield at Da Nang. You couldn't get from the airfield to the harbor at night, only during the daytime. And Monkey Mountain which is between the airfield and the ocean, was controlled by the Viet Cong. Similarly in Chu Lai. . . . Phu Bai was entirely surrounded by Viet Cong forces.'

Hurrying back to Washington, Nitze reported first to Defense Secretary McNamara. He had in mind a radical recommendation. In 1950, as head

July 16, 1965—U.S. Secretary of State Robert McNamara makes a statement on his arrival at the Saigon airport with Henry Cabot Lodge (right), who succeeded Maxwell Taylor as U.S. ambassador to Vietnam.

of policy planning at the State Department, Nitze had proposed that America should unilaterally undertake the defense of the non-Communist world. He had changed his views. In late 1967 Nitze and McNamara would join forces in trying unsuccessfully to de-escalate the air and land war. But now two years earlier the Secretary of Defense could not accept what the Secretary of the Navy was telling him. Nitze had been told that 200,000 troops might do it, but he doubted that even this number was enough. He planned to recommend getting out.

After the take-over in Saigon by the Armed Forces Council only weeks earlier, General Westmoreland had informed the Joint Chiefs that 'Vietnam's social and political institutions remained remarkably intact under the powerful disintegrating blows to which subjected. . . . We do have the very real asset of a resilient people and this gives hope that there is more time available than we might think: time in which, if properly exploited, the needed national leadership could evolve.'

Nitze now disagreed with Westmoreland on all counts: 'It seemed to me that the political structure and the rest of the country was not strong, and that the military position of our forces was dangerous indeed. Frankly, I didn't see how it would be possible with 200,000 people to turn that thing around and achieve a military success.

'I can remember Mr McNamara's reaction: "Well, Paul, if we don't reinforce there, what do we do? Do we withdraw our men?" ' Nitze said, 'That's what we would have to do.' 'If we withdraw from Vietnam', McNamara asked, 'do you think it is likely that the Communists will challenge the Western world some place else afterwards?' 'I should think it wholly likely,' Nitze told him. 'Then', said McNamara, 'do you think we would necessarily be in a better position geographically and politically to resist at this other place than we

are in South Vietnam?' 'I can't guarantee that.' 'Well then', McNamara said, 'you're really not giving me an alternative.'

Nitze says, 'I had to agree. I wasn't giving him an alternative.' He could see every reason for helping South Vietnam, 'resist subversion from the North', but 'I didn't see how it could be done within a reasonable limit of the resources we could bring to bear'.

A former presidential advisor to Kennedy and Johnson, historian Arthur Schlesinger Jr, says the error was one of assumption. 'Somehow in 1965', he says, the idea still held that 'the Viet Cong were the instruments, the spearhead of a planned system of Chinese expansionism in the Far East. You will find that said by otherwise sensible people.' For instance, liberal champion Adlai Stevenson, in a letter released after his death, argued that 'we are preventing Chinese aggression in Asia'. Yet, says Schlesinger, from what was known at the time about the centuries-old hostility between China and Vietnam 'the notion that the Viet Cong and the North Vietnamese were undergoing all this sacrifice in order to turn their country over to the Chinese was preposterous'.

(In fairness, the long-persisting domino theory was not propagated only by those in government. It was sounded with as much or more alarm by the 'sensible' press. As late as mid-1964, when Saigon correspondents of the *New York Times* were consistently questioning US values in Vietnam, a *Times* article was stating: 'The stakes in South-east Asia are huge. If Laos and South Vietnam should fall to the Communists, they would likely take with them Cambodia, Thailand, and Burma, possibly even Malaysia and the Philippines – close to 115 million people.')

The US government 'needed' to believe this because the public had been told it for so long. Johnson, in his turn, had 'to build the threat . . . save the world from the hordes of Red China'.

Schlesinger asked Johnson's people 'how in the world' they came to believe this, and was told, 'we're paying the price of the 1950s'. Washington could not just argue, says Schlesinger, 'that it was saving the world from Ho Chi Minh. No one in their senses expected that if Ho Chi Minh won in Vietnam the next week his legions would appear on Malibu Beach.'

American beach-heads in South Vietnam now seemed to spread with each tide as Johnson, unpersuaded by Nitze's doubts, ordered McNamara on 18 June to 'find more dramatic and effective actions in South Vietnam'. On the same day the Joint Chiefs recommended that US troop levels in Vietnam – then 51,000 – be immediately raised to 116,000. The arrival of the 1st Battalion, Royal Australian Regiment, with more South Korean, Thai and Philippine troops to follow would raise 'Free World' forces to 19,750.

On the next day the Saigon generals formed a new government, with an all-military cabinet. A week later William Bundy cabled from the State Department informing Ambassador Taylor that US forces could engage in combat 'in any situation in which the use of such troops is required by an appropriate GVN commander'. The very next day – 27 June – US airborne forces launched the first major American offensive in Vietnam, a 'Search and Destroy' sweep of war zone D north of Saigon. It was a full month after Americans had gone into combat – in a counter-offensive role – before the US public was told of the dimensions of it by their President.

'The really major decision', says William Bundy, 'was announced by President Johnson on 28 July 1965, when he said that we would commit 125,000 troops and that we foresaw the possibility that there would be more to come. And I regarded that as the second truly big decision [after the initial Marine deployment] that President Johnson made.'

Historians mark this point, when a 'protective' mission turned out to be full-scale combat, as the beginning of 'the credibility gap' between Johnson and the press and public. Asked if the administration had played square with the public, Secretary of State Rusk felt it had, on the argument that what happened had to be expected. 'I think that most people realized', says Rusk, 'that if you put armed Marines into a situation to protect something they were very likely going to have to shoot if somebody else wants to take away what they are protecting.'

The administration, anyhow, now felt less constricted. It had no more secrets. It would pursue the war with a 'two-fisted' strategy. One fist, the American force, would hit out at the enemy in tactical offensive operations; the other fist, ARVN, would close around military bases, towns, cities, and wherever possible, the villages. In large measure the ARVN and US forces were now reversing roles, and America's one problem – apart from the enemy – was its ally. How would the generals react?

In Saigon, Bui Diem had remained as Special Assistant to the new 'Prime Minister'. Air Force Commander Nguyen Cao Ky, member of a seventeen-man War Cabinet led by Chief of Staff General Thieu. Ky and Thieu agreed (and it was about all they did agree on) that American troops were needed, and Ky would hold to Washington's reasoning long after it – and South Vietnam – had

September 1965—Elements of the U.S. 1st Cavalry Air Mobile division in a landing craft approach the beach at Qui Nhon, 260 miles northeast of Saigon. Advance units of 20,000 new troops were being launched for a strike on the Viet Cong.

been abandoned. As Ky puts it: 'When Vietnam as part of the Free World was attacked by Communists, with the Chinese and Russia at that time behind them, I think it was the duty of America to come to the rescue.' But, says Ky's deputy, the July day when Johnson came unequivocally to the rescue was also the first day Ky heard about it.

As with the March landings, says Bui Diem, 'the same situation happened with the increase of troops in July. I remember [Deputy Ambassador] Alexis Johnson informed me on the phone about President Johnson's speech. I doubted that Prime Minister Ky was involved . . . in the final decision about the increase of American troops to such an extent.' There was again 'the urgent problem' of how to 'inform the public' and, says Diem, 'as time went on, the Vietnamese government tried to cope with the formulation of policy but the co-ordination between the Americans and the government was more on small logistical problems than on the strategic level'.

Ky is portrayed as liking the Americans to the point of imitation and General Thieu as fearing them to the point of basing every decision on whether they would approve. As Premier, Ky still preferred the uniform sported by his old officer squadron: fancy-cut silk fatigues, usually black or canary yellow, with a violet silk scarf, and legend has it that once when he entered a session of the War Cabinet dressed this way, with Coca-Cola in hand, one general remarked to another, 'At least no one can mistake him for Ho Chi Minh'. Ky personified what went wrong. He was aggressive, willing to fight, but would be shut out from US deci-

sions, unable to prove leadership and so to his critics would seem only a willing dupe because of his support of the US.

Ky and Westmoreland had perhaps the closest friendship of any in the High Command – based, it was believed, on what they regarded as common qualities. 'Ky was a man of action,' says Westmoreland. 'He was a swashbuckler, but at the same time he was highly intelligent.' Ky's deputy, Bui Diem, says there were weekly meetings with Westmoreland but 'mainly on how to cope' with the needs of American troops. 'On one side we had the Prime Minister, myself and some important ministers; on the other side the Ambassador and General Westmoreland. Every week, for instance, we tried to deal with the problem of how to prepare the Saigon Port or the Port of Da Nang for welcoming the arrival of US troops.'

It was a far different government from that of the fiercely independent and unco-operative Ngo Dinh Diem, assassinated twenty months earlier, but now the American Ambassador of that period was back. After a year's sabbatical Henry Cabot Lodge had returned despite the July developments. The war had been taken over from the South Vietnamese; the Buddhists were again rebelling over oppressive rule, freedom of assembly had been banned: all the ills that Lodge once opposed now prevailed. The new War Cabinet had proclaimed martial law, closed down most Vietnamese-language newspapers, and was soon arresting hundreds of critics. Already the war seemed to have exhausted all reasoning. Its very momentum now suggested that there was a clear purpose, and its very scale imbued confidence.

Outgoing Ambassador Maxwell D. Taylor, having strongly opposed then quietly accepted the sending of American ground forces, decided that his last official duty would be to greet the 101st Airborne Division – the 'Screaming Eagles' – which he had commanded in World War II. They would land at the new super-base at Cam Ranh Bay. Taylor's son had been assigned to the Eagles, arriving in Vietnam as his father left, and now Taylor took 'great personal pleasure' seeing his son with the Eagles 'hoping that it would make a better man out of him'. Completing the irony Taylor recalls that 'I had trouble convincing them that there was a war going on because everything was so quiet there. They said, "General, where is this war?" and I told them you wait until after dark and you go over that hill and you will find out.'

Indeed, outwardly little had changed except the rate of attrition. The war was always 'over that hill' without recognizable front or enemy, sudden ambush or contact usually lasting only minutes. It was still an unseen war for most Americans in Vietnam, apparent though from the statistics which the US began issuing in August 1965. Between then and the year's end 808 Americans were killed in Vietnam compared to 561 for the five-year period since January 1961, when the record of death was begun.

The dollar cost had risen from a mere million a day in the early 1960s to a requested $12.7 billion for 1966, a thirty-fold increase. For the average Vietnamese the cost was also greater but the results no different from when it all first happened, exactly twenty years before, with the return of the French. Saigon's leaders still bowed – and thrived –

under an alien culture as they had for a generation, and in the countryside the sound of the helicopters had never quite receded; for a lifetime, white faces in foreign uniforms had pursued zealots in black, while the peasant had bent to the rice-paddy where eking out the grains of life was struggle enough. Strategic hamlets had replaced the agrovilles; some general had replaced the emperor; the roads to the cities were again filling with refugees, fleeing taxation and the fighting. Once again rice was being sent with the gunships because of the devastation in the rice-lands, and in return the villagers had to send their sons to fight to protect all this. They died at the rate of 2000 a month or twenty for each foreigner who fell; dying as of old, deserted by their officers in the field who like as not had bled them earlier by pocketing their meager pay, and earning the contempt of an advanced civilization which could not or would not understand, but which thought it had the answers. The images had never changed, and the Americans, fighting for a world free of enforced rule or ideas, did not see that they were now imposing their own culture. An American military analyst who had extended service in Vietnam says, 'We were into every aspect of Vietnamese society.'

'The American presence was a major corrupting factor,' says Captain Brian Jenkins, a Special Forces officer who served three tours of duty. Jenkins was later with the Long Range Planning Group at MACV HQ in Saigon. He made numerous official studies of the war and its impact. 'A massive infusion of American culture came with the American military presence; also a tremendous intervention in the Vietnamese political system', says Jenkins, 'to the point that Americans – not the military advisors but American political advisors – were deciding what colors the lights in the fountains should be in downtown Saigon; whether the library and national museum in Saigon should adopt a decimal system; whether the trees in Saigon should be cut down to make way for parking meters. . . . Certainly there was a destruction of the Vietnamese identity; certainly this would have had a major adverse effect on the cause.'

While Premier Ky's deputy, Bui Diem, complained of the lack of consultation on strategy, Captain Jenkins from his observations on field missions and at HQ arrived at a simple answer: there was no strategy. Or, as he reported in an official wartime study criticizing the approach: 'It is not possible to measure progress toward an ultimate victory because that goal has never been clearly defined. The *operations are the strategy* [his italics].'

'Every instance of failure', he noted, brought requests 'for additional troops on the assumption that additional force would hasten the arrival of an inevitable victory. As long as the belief in "more" existed, the necessity for change was not considered.' By late 1965 the war had more than

Top: October 5, 1965—Wounded U.S. paratroopers are helped by fellow soldiers to a medical evacuation helicopter. Paratroopers of the 173rd Airborne Brigade's 1st Battalion suffered many casualties in the clash with Viet Cong guerrillas in the jungle of South Vietnam's "D" Zone, 25 miles northeast of Saigon.

Right: August 22, 1965—Trucks carry troops of the 173rd Airborne Brigade into Kontum after driving along Route 14 from Pleiku.

ever the dynamics of a stampede, with its logic escaping the major Free World nations whose liberty was supposedly being safeguarded by the war but whose views on it were summarily rejected. In quick succession South Vietnam broke relations with France; a United Nations proposal to convene the Great Powers was rejected as 'unrealistic' until North Vietnam ceased 'aggression'; a subsequent report that Hanoi wanted bilateral talks was confirmed by the State Department but talks were now ruled out because 'we do not believe they're serious'; and a peace plan by British Commonwealth premiers was regarded by both sides as interference bordering on impertinence. The press coverage of this war for democracy was such that the Saigon MACV command asked American journalists to practice 'voluntary censorship'.

On 2 November a Quaker named Norman Morrison committed Buddhist-style immolation by fire outside the Pentagon. On 9 November a member of the Catholic Worker movement, Roger Allen La Porte, chose the same death outside the United Nations building. On 27 November 35,000 Americans of an organization called SANE marched on the White House where on that day Johnson was hearing the Pentagon's solution to it all – 'More'. US troop levels, he was told, must be increased from 120,000 to 400,000 by the end of 1966. And with these in prospect General Westmoreland would begin 300 major sweep operations with names like Starlight, Silver Bayonet, Masher White Wing, Double Eagle, Dragon Fire, MacArthur, Shenandoah and Saratoga – and, near the end, Napoleon.

As military analyst Brian Jenkins summarized the Alice in Vietnam situation at the time, operations were the strategy and 'in the absence' of any other strategy the 'operational criteria remain valid by default, and by those criteria we are winning', and so one does not change a 'winning' strategy.

The operations necessitated that at least three out of four of this vast US force were cooks, dishwashers and mechanics living not off the land but American-style, with their every need imported. 'Where the American soldier goes, so goes the American culture', says Jenkins, 'but perhaps never before to the degree that was the case in Vietnam. The wealth of our country and our technology permitted us to carry this to absurd lengths. And the absurdities are numerous: the armed forces television station in Vietnam broadcasting daily the weather reports of the United States, that it was raining in Detroit, that there's a low pressure over Seattle, so that the American soldiers could see this.' They saw, in particular, long-legged, miniskirted, weather-girl Bobbie, – 'the bubbling bundle of barometric brilliance, Bobbie' – who on a given day would tell them, 'All you long tall Texans out there had a cool fair day of 68 [in Texas]' and who would sign off, 'Have a pleasant evening weather-wise and y'all know, of course, other wise'. With the temperature in Vietnam in the humid high 90s, Jenkins says some officer clubs found the air-conditioning so fierce they had 'to have a fireplace'. He recalls 'trailer camps for the senior officers, surrounded by white-picket fences, and barbecues on Sunday afternoons; helicopters flying in daily beer – and not only beer but ice so that the beer could be cold – to troops in battle'.

Around each American base, with its clubs and restaurants, grew a 'tinseltown' built of packing-cases and waste or pilfered material from the base. Here the GI could buy those commodities missing on his side of the high-wire: sex, drugs, valet service, and whatever was unavailable in the PX. Any GI could live like a warlord. Goods or equipment from the base sold on the black market would buy any service. As Lieutenant Robert Santos recalls '. . . the black market was incredible. Anything you want you could buy outside the base more easily than inside. It went from food to a stereo or any kind of equipment. Anything that they sold in the PX. It wasn't too hard to figure out.' Gold watches, diamonds, cars, minks, marijuana, opium, heroin ninety per cent pure – everything was available for dollars cash, and just like the days of Emperor Bao Dai's vice-lords the cash would pay off district chiefs who often used it to buy American arms to sell to the guerrillas for more cash.

Map shows the route taken by American B-52s from Guam to South Vietnam where they drop their bombs on Viet Cong positions.

October 1965—A U.S. Air Force B-52 drops 750-pound bombs near Tay Ninh, 56 miles northwest of Saigon.

The GI had only to walk outside the camp to get his uniform laundered, his shoes shone, his rifle cleaned or all thoughts of the war removed in the makeshift brothels. Saigon itself and its twin city of Cholon were soon Sodom and Gomorrah enlarged. A one-time population of half a million had become three million by 1966, a city of destitute refugees and enriched elite servicing the US effort. In the night-clubs the music was Stateside, the mood gay and abandoned: with so many Americans the war would be won, the champagne, already flowed, and the favorite song was 'Everything's Coming Up Roses'. Beyond the flower-manicured central boulevards and the encircling pastel villas, the red-light districts had industrial dimensions, employing in 1966 an estimated 30,000 war-orphaned prostitutes – who would multiply with the troop levels. Elsewhere gangs of juvenile delinquents said to number 200,000 – as numerous and menacing as the old secret sects – held sway over dark inner citadels 'off limits' even to the police. In the general crowded squalor, the fear was not of war but of disease and hunger. At different times there was every kind of epidemic, from typhoid to bubonic plague. At this time it was believed – and no one really knew – that one child in three died before the age of four. The US army had a particular health concern. That year one in four GIS had venereal disease.

'Vietnam was a poor country for a thousand years', reflects Premier Ky, but now the endemic poverty was harder amid so much unobtainable affluence. Asked if the sudden presence of so many Americans was as overwhelming as Communist fire-power, and therefore self-defeating, Ky says 'Yes, it's one reason'. The GIS were needed but not their life-style.

'The American soldiers', Ky says, 'brought a living condition, compared to Vietnamese conditions, so high, so comfortable, that in many ways it corrupted. . . . Instead of helping us it really created more problems for the Vietnamese government.' On government corruption, 'Yes there was corruption', but Ky says, 'Where did it come from? It came from the various American PX.' Says Saigon observer Brian Jenkins, 'There was no shortage of willing accomplices in this corruption.' It permeated officialdom 'economically, politically, culturally. But the net result was that the leadership could claim less and less legitimate authority.'

The situation was as always: the social and political deficiencies belied or betrayed the military objectives. President Johnson had promised to extend his 'Great Society' to Vietnam, to provide 'food', 'shelter' and 'job opportunities'. Premier Ky now pressed for massive economic aid, and on 8 February 1966 the two allies met halfway in Honolulu to plan victory in 'the other war'. Johnson agreed to commit immediately 750 million dollars (one fifteenth of the military bill) to start building an industrial base in the South. Johnson told Ky, 'We are determined to win not only military victory but victory over hunger, disease and despair.' Ky promised to bring about a social revolution.

Premier Ky was considered the exception in a generally corrupt regime. His problem was image. His personal history, flamboyance and military record did not complement his effort at reforms. Born in the North near Hanoi, he entered a French military academy aged eighteen, then in

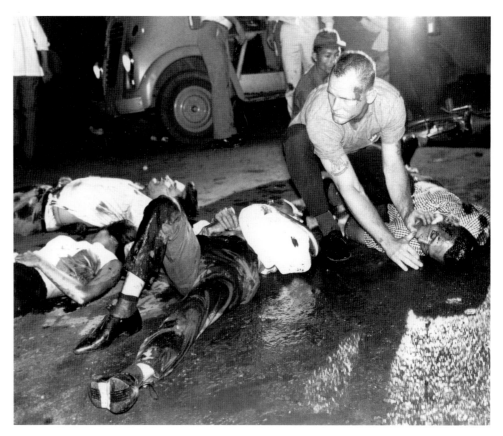

June 25, 1965—The bloody carnage spills out onto the sidewalk after two terrorist bomb exploded at a crowded restaurant on the Saigon River.

Map locates sites in Saigon hit by Viet Cong terrorist bombings between May 1, 1964 and January 1, 1965. They are: 1-Metropole Hotel, 2-Cung Hoa Stadium, 3-National Police Headquarters, 4-My Canh restaurant, 5-U.S. Embassy, 6-Brink Hotel, 7-Caravelle Hotel, 8-A U.S. naval vessel.

July 19, 1965—U.S. Secretary of Defense Robert S. McNamara talks with Prime Minister Nguyen Cao Ky (left) and Chief of State Nguyen Van Thieu during a reception at Gia Long palace in Saigon.

'For the benefit of the radio and television audience', says Lodge, 'this group took over this big city of Da Nang in the middle of the night and they proceeded to let it be known that they were going to take over all the big cities in Vietnam. Well, of course, the Viet Cong had the countryside – if you give them the cities there isn't anything left.'

With Buddhist dissent crushed, the US military commended Premier Ky (a Buddhist himself) for what it called 'a solid political victory'. In fact, it marked a distinct turning point toward defeat, the first open evidence of distrust which would dictate the course of the war and the nature of its end. The anti-American riots made visible the growing mutual uneasiness, exacerbating the clash of cultures and the clash of commands. The turnabout by the Embassy dashed hopes of reforms or any immediate prospect of – or belief in – elections. (When elections were finally held seventeen months later, on 3 September 1967, it was after months of bitter argument between Ky and General Thieu who each wanted to campaign for President. Finally they agreed to a joint ticket – Thieu for President, Ky for the Vice-Presidency. Eighty-one per cent of those eligible voted and the military again retained power though receiving only thirty-five per cent of the vote.) Corruption increased with the disillusionment, further demoralizing the ARVN and in turn the Americans, who increasingly felt that they alone were doing the fighting. In 1966, 5008 Americans died in battle, almost five times the previous year's toll.

'I remember one time going into Da Nang', says Jack McCloskey, a Marine medic who arrived a little later, 'and watching all these kids on Honda motorcycles – Vietnamese kids, eighteen or nineteen years old, and me seeing the day before my buddies getting blown away, and saying "Hey, what the hell is happening here? These guys invited me over here to fight for democracy, and these guys are running around on Honda motorcycles. What the hell is happening here?" '

The answer was lack of motivation or even economic incentive. Colonel Nguyen Be was the deputy province chief of Binh Dinh at that time. 'A colonel like myself', he says, 'got only $70 a month. An interpreter or a girl working for the Americans got at least $200 or $300 a month.' Colonel Be would later head up South Vietnam's 'Pacification' program to improve rural morale. One innovation would permit young men of draft age to stay in their villages better to assist the local economy and defense. But by then a disillusioned America would begin withdrawing, leaving the ARVN in disarray. By then, says Colonel Be, the concerns of the officer corps were other than the war: 'Most of the officers didn't want to lose their position in society, so they would ask the province chief "How can I make a living; how can my wife make a living?" '

The ordinary ARVN soldier had no opportunity for corruption. His army pay was only one sixteenth of the GI's. This disparity, seen against the American affluence and the billions it was sending at Saigon's request, was a major blunder in the view of a young officer fresh from the Pentagon. Daniel Ellsberg had been assigned to MACV intelligence with the rank of Special Liaison Officer, American Embassy, in 1965. Having once helped plan the war, he was beginning to see it differently now that he was in Vietnam.

'The burdens of the war on our Vietnamese', Ellsberg says 'were extremely bad. How did we get anyone to fight in that army at all – as little as we

1952 attended aviation courses in France and French Morocco. He joined the French Air Force, returning to Vietnam in 1954 after Partition. Later he trained in the US, then back in Vietnam flew clandestine missions with an American group known as the 'Dirty Thirty'. The Americans alternately regarded him as an asset and a liability. At first, as the aggressive air force commander in 1963, he was America's staunch 'co-pilot'. At times, wearing a pearl-handled revolver with his tailored fatigues, he was known as 'The Cowboy' who too often shot from the hip. He was quoted as saying he had only one hero, Hitler, because 'he pulled his country together'. He was then a political embarrassment who suddenly emerged as Premier. Only thirty-five, he hurriedly imposed drastic discipline, announcing that profiteers and corrupt public employees would face the firing squad, and this political morality was applauded. But when he actually ordered one execution he was damned as too extreme. Now, with the enlarged American aid effort, Ky at some risk to himself warned his fellow generals against corruption in their own families.

Within weeks vast quantities of US material arrived – and much of it just as quickly vanished. The US, while increasing food relief for the countryside, sent vehicles and machinery of every kind to build highways, steel, chemical and pharmaceutical factories: all to rebuild urban hope. A Saigon journalist, Ton That Thien, then described what happened: 'Most of the more than a thousand million dollars poured into Vietnam yearly have found their way into the pockets of this urban population in the form of buildings, bars, restaurants, nightclubs.' Saigon received forty garbage trucks; several were immediately stolen. Overnight, vehicle thefts became an industry. Companies obtained high-priced permits to order excessive stockpiles –

paid for by the US. The Americans quietly asked Ky to investigate. He reportedly found enough cement on order to turn the whole of Vietnam into a concrete platform.

'Little has changed since the overthrow of Diem,' wrote journalist Thien in an article called 'Vietnam: A Case of Social Alienation'. Thien had been press secretary to the late President and both had feared excessive American influence. Thien now saw economic aid as a form of it: 'If change has occurred, it has been for the worse.' A military leader could win more money in a poker game one night than a peasant could dream of earning in a lifetime. 'American aid simply adds to social alienation, from city to countryside.' Thien said the money should go to improve rural education and communications and to pay social workers enough to go to the countryside and stay there. But it was anyhow too late.

The misused aid quickly became a platform for renewed Buddhist dissent. The government had delayed on a promise of civilian elections, a pledge which had quietened the Buddhists. Now the most powerful Buddhist in the senior military, Lieutenant General Nguyen Chanh Thi who commanded the northern region including Hue and Da Nang, threatened that his provinces would secede unless corrupt generals were purged. Instead, Thi was dismissed and the US Embassy praised Premier Ky for thwarting 'war-lordism'. The northern cities erupted, with Buddhist rioters bearing anti-American slogans. On 4 April, Ky sent 4000 South Vietnamese Marines to Da Nang to put down the demonstrations – and he personally flew in to direct operations. Across the country thousands of Buddhists and other critics were jailed. A 'Struggle Movement' in Da Nang appealed to Ambassador Lodge, as the Buddhist leaders had done in 1963. But priorities had changed.

May 20, 1966—A government soldier mans a machine gun on a tank in Danang, where Buddhist rebels exchanged fire with the troops sent to put down the revolt.

paid them; as miserable as their shelters were in which their families would live near their posts? Their alternative in that war was to go into the jungle and join what they saw as the patriots, whether they liked them or not.'

In 1966, according to the US Department of Defense, desertions by South Vietnamese troops exceeded 124,000, or twenty-one per cent of the total ARVN ground force. It was a consistent annual average. The ARVN was without motivation, wrote journalist Ton That Thien at the time. Peasants fought in the lower ranks, while officers were drawn from urban backgrounds and richer families. 'To send these officers out into the field is to ask them to undergo hardship, perhaps to die, for what, in their eyes, is not really in their interest . . . they feel completely lost in a milieu and a life to which they have become foreign. From the point of view of the peasants, why should they die to preserve the comfort and property of the urban ruling elite, whose representatives are their commanders, rarely seen at the heads of the columns or among them in dangerous and critical situations?'

Thien was with the prestigious *Vietnam Guardian* until it and other critical newspapers were closed down by Premier Ky. Thien stresses that he was not anti-American, saying America's mistake was in permitting blatantly unrepresentative government in Saigon, epitomized for him by Premier Ky. Thien found a friend in Daniel Ellsberg: 'I remember Ton That Thien, a very respected journalist at that time, saying "It is an insult the people you have chosen for us: Prime Minister Ky – why do you have to humiliate us by hiring a man of this caliber for us? We could live with a puppet – we're on your side – we could work with you with much more self-respect if you had someone more representative of Vietnamese values." '

Premier Ky became embittered at the suggestion – fostered he says by the press, in particular the American press – that he was a puppet: 'At

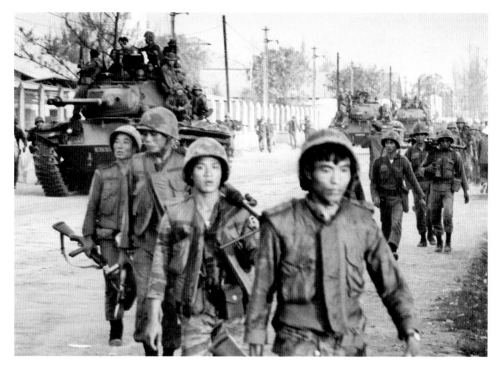

May 16, 1966—Backed by tanks, government troops move into Danang to take control of the city's strategic areas in brisk fighting with Buddhist-organized 'struggle movement' forces.

that time, every time the press wanted to know something about the war,' says Ky, they would ask 'Mr Johnson or General Westmoreland, but never our opinion. As the leaders of South Vietnam we never had any consideration. It's very funny, and also very tragic that it happened. The other side, the Communists, always treated us as a puppet of America. But then the American people themselves also considered us as a puppet of America, not as true leaders of the Vietnamese people.'

'If they indeed had been puppets, then we could have manipulated them', says military analyst Brian Jenkins, 'to do all the things that were considered necessary, toward improving the political situation, improving the quality of military leadership or eliminating the corruption. It was the worst of both worlds in the sense that they were perceived as puppets and yet could not be manipulated,' Quite simply, the huge American presence 'began to create', says Jenkins, 'a very distorted mirror image' so that South Vietnam's administration 'appeared as very much a foreign creation.'

'At that time', says Nguyen Cao Ky, 'they called me a Johnson man,' but he says the fault was with the Americans – their impatience. 'I told Johnson many times, if you go to war, go fast and win it. Over a long suspended war you cannot win because you are a very impatient people.' Ky says he tried to help formulate policy and told Johnson at a second meeting in 1966 'that we should carry the war to the North with South Vietnamese forces . . . with me commanding the troops'. Johnson had always ruled this out as risking confrontation with China, but it was equally unrealistic, says Ky, '. . . when Westmoreland said, and McNamara said at that time to the American people that next Christmas we'll bring our boys home. And the American people waited for one, two, three, four, five Christmases and they didn't see any light at the end of the tunnel. And in the end they became impatient. And in the end we lost our own identity.'

General Westmoreland, who regarded Ky as 'highly intelligent', would develop somewhat less regard for ARVN capability: 'Well, the pace was rather slow. They did take off on weekends. They had extended holidays. They were far from diligent in their pursuance of the war – it was somewhat business as usual.' The South Vietnamese soldier, says Westmoreland, 'performed very well when he had good leadership' but there was a 'shortage' because 'they'd inherited from the French a policy of taking their leaders from the educated group'.

However, at least some American officers felt the US deliberately failed to encourage the ARVN. A Marine, author Jim Webb, says 'Westmoreland and other policy makers had decided that the United States would conduct the major engagements and that the South Vietnamese would be back in their base areas. I always believed that we emasculated the South Vietnamese army. We stripped them. They lost their ability to fight. It's only partially because of any national character. I think it was something that we in many ways forced on them.'

One of the longest serving Vietnam veterans, General Edward Lansdale, blames those in the US military who '. . . didn't have the patience and would jump in and do things themselves' and so 'robbed the Vietnamese of initiative'. Vietnam was the shortest duty tour of any war for American combatants – one year. As another American general put it in 1967. 'Americans haven't been in Vietnam ten years. They've been here one year ten times.'

For Premier Ky the GI duty tour was another example of the 'home by Christmas' approach to the war, which necessitated massive troop deployment but with only a few of the 2.8 million rotating soldiers understanding or caring anything about the country or the cause. 'How can you expect for a short period of just one year', he summarizes, 'that they could understand fully the Vietnamese. They were not even able to speak a few words of Vietnamese. So I can say that the mutual understanding was none. Zero.'

Ky's special assistant, Bui Diem, concedes that there was corruption and 'bad people, like everywhere else, but mainly I think that there were millions of South Vietnamese who were willing to bear their own responsibilities in waging the war. And if they had been asked, and if it had been explained to them what they had to do, I'd say they would have done the job willingly.'

In the Central Intelligence Agency there were those like Frank Snepp who had a much harder, unheroic assessment of both sides. Snepp would become the Agency's Chief Strategy Analyst in Saigon. He saw the cancerous corruption, saw Washington ignore it and saw both the Vietnamese and American soldiers pay the final price. 'It was the policy of the CIA and other elements of the US government', says Snepp, 'not to report extensively on corruption. Why? Because then we would have to question our involvement in Vietnam. Certainly it would be difficult to get Congress to vote additional aid for the South Vietnamese. So there was very little intelligence reporting on corruption among the South Vietnamese generals.

'It meant that we ignored the rot that was destroying the country's will and capacity to fight – because as the generals siphoned off the aid money we were directing to the government, the foot soldier on the ground suffered.' Snepp asserts that the ARVN did not get enough ammunition or hand-grenades because of the corruption and that this was known: 'It was one of the most cynical acts on our part to disregard [such] important intelligence.'

One quarter of a million South Vietnamese soldiers gave their lives in combat. But as the GIS

rotated, the newcomers could see only the consequence, not the cause, of the overall malaise. In 1967 the US military evaluated ARVN performance as 'eighty per cent ineffective'. Its operations were bitterly known as 'Search and Avoid.' US combat deaths increased with ARVN's demise. In 1967, more than 16,000 Americans were killed in Vietnam, triple the 1965 figure which was triple that of all the previous years. The toll would keep rising. Each year there would be new Americans to decide what color the lights of Saigon's fountains should be and each year feelings would darken towards an ally these foreign troops could neither comprehend nor fully command. No solution appeared, except General Westmoreland's 'More'.

Westmoreland's solution was one of attrition; the greater the fire-power, the quicker the end, it was assumed. But the Vietnamese had been fighting for a lifetime: they had adapted to war in all its forms, as soldier-author Tim O'Brien would discover. He had a personal valet, a boy who had latched on to him at the camp: 'I called him Champion. A nice kid who would give me a back rub after a hard day on the march, who would clean my rifle for me. This little kid seven years old knew how to take an M-16 apart. I didn't.' There seemed to be a message in that.

Map shows the location of American, South Korean, Australian and New Zealand troops in South Vietnam in late 1965. Shaded areas indicate the site of most of the fighting during the same period between those troops and the Viet Cong.

Above: April 1, 1965—South Vietnamese troops burn a hut belonging to Viet Cong guerrillas during an operation near Xuan Loc, about 30 miles northeast of Saigon.

Right: April 13, 1965—Two A-1 Skyraiders dive-bomb a Viet Cong barracks along a canal (right), near Thanh Minh.

Bottom: April 4, 1965—A pain-ridden Vietnamese soldier covers part of his face against the hot sun along the Vaico Oriental River. His legs were shattered by Viet Cong fire.

Above: April 1965—A propeller-driven A-1 Skyraider fighter-bomber carries bombs and napalm on a combat mission. Skyraiders, with a design that dated from World War II, saw extensive action in Vietnam.

Right: April 4, 1965—A Vietnamese infantryman jumps from the protection of a rice-paddy dike during a run-and-fire assault on Viet Cong entrenched in rice lands west of Saigon. Fire was set by guerrillas as a distraction.

April 28, 1965—U.S. Marine helicopters drop troops in an area suspected of Viet Cong activity near Da Nang. The Marines were mounting a full-scale helicopter assault.

April 5, 1965—Vietnamese infantry move past smoke from burning fields toward the enemy, a concentration of about 200 Viet Cong along the Vaico Oriental River, 15 miles west of Saigon.

Above: April 4, 1965—A South Vietnamese infantryman with a bullet wound in his shoulder holds a crucifix as he waits evacuation by helicopter after fighting the Viet Cong in a rice paddy 15 miles west of Saigon.

Right: April 15, 1965—Viet Cong terrorist Le Dau, 24, charged with attempting to bomb a Danang hotel filled with American servicemen, is tied to a stake in a soccer field and executed by South Vietnamese troops.

April 5, 1965—A Vietnamese soldier wears the traditional conical hat over his steel helmet while on patrol near the Vaico Oriental River west of Saigon. The hat serves as both as disguise against Viet Cong snipers and protection from the sun.

May 26, 1965—An American soldier looks back at his companions as he advances on a Viet Cong position.

May 1967—U.S. infantrymen take cover behind a tomb as they advance through dried rice paddy near Phu Loi, 12 miles north of Saigon. Tombs like these dot the countryside because of the Vietnamese tradition to bury their dead on their own land.

Above: May, 1965—Nguyen Van Giap and Ho Chi Minh are shown together at a communist party function in North Vietnam.

Right: April 24, 1965—A Marine looks in wonder at the split end of his M-14 rifle barrel. It was hit by a Viet Cong round as he fired at enemy snipers near Danang.

May 16, 1965—U.S. Air Force B-57 bombers burn at the Dak To airbase after bombs exploded in a chain reaction.

Above: May 8, 1965—Minutes after they had been handing out candy and schoolbooks to local children, two U.S. Marines bend over the body of a fellow marine shot through the chest by a sniper in the village of Le My on the outskirts of Da Nang.

Right: May 20, 1965—Helicopters carry members of the U.S. 173rd Airborne Brigade to landing zones marked by smoke bombs, northwest of Bien Hoa. The unit encountered sniper fire on the ground, but made no direct contact with the Viet Cong.

Below: May 28, 1965—His face scratched from the jungle, a U.S. paratrooper of the 1st Battalion, 173rd Airborne Brigade searches for snipers in the ruins of a hilltop pagoda near Hat Lang in northeast South Vietnam.

May 16, 1965—Smoke rises from the Bien Hoa airbase after a chain reaction explosion among the aircraft stationed there. At least 20 U.S. servicemen were reported dead as bombs, fuel, and planes—including 10 B-57 bombers—exploded and burned.

May 31, 1965—U.S. paratroopers of the 173rd Airborne Brigade charge from helicopters during a major operation near Saigon in support of South Vietnamese forces.

May 12, 1965—Civilians and soldiers wounded in battling the Viet Cong at Song Be await attention in the local hospital 74 miles north of Saigon.

Above: May 1965—The flooded Saigon River spreads across the landscape like a many-clawed dragon in this view from an armed helicopter returning from a mission.

Right: June 3, 1965—Crew members and pilots prepare A-1 Skyraiders aboard the carrier U.S.S. *Midway* before bombing runs over North Vietnam.

Below: June 21, 1965—A Huey helicopter fires a cluster of rockets at a Viet Cong position in the jungle at Ban Me Thuot.

Top Left: June 26, 1965—Trying to avoid intense sniper fire, two American medics carry a wounded paratrooper to an evacuation helicopter after their company dropped directly into a Viet Cong staging area in the jungle near Thoung Lang, South Vietnam.

Top Right: June 2, 1965—A paratrooper of the 2nd Battalion, 173rd Airborne Brigade, searches one of three peasants who had been tending water buffalo. At dusk, one of the peasants apparently threw a grenade that wounded a lieutenant in this unit.

Left: June 2, 1965—A U.S. reconnaissance team of the 1st Battalion, 173rd Airborne Brigade, conducts a search-and-destroy operation of guerrilla hideouts in jungle about 40 miles northeast of Saigon.

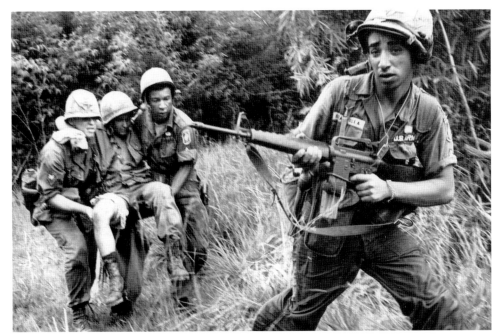

Above Left: June 29, 1965—Troop-carrying UH-1 Huey helicopters fly over the Plain of Reeds, 40 miles southwest of Saigon, as smoke rises from Allied napalm strikes on Viet Cong positions.

Above: June 1965—A U.S. paratrooper with the 173rd Airborne Brigade wears a helmet slogan while defending the Phouc Vinh airstrip north of Saigon.

Left: June 24, 1965—U.S. paratrooper covers for two medics carrying a wounded paratrooper from the jungle about 10 miles northeast of Bien Hoa. The medics crawled through the jungle to treat and evacuate the soldier wounded by sniper fire.

Below Left: June 1965—With their rifles propped nearby, U.S. Marines splash in the water near the coastal airbase at Da Nang.

Below: June 24, 1965—Medic Pfc. Andrew J. Brown of Chicago draws his pistol while protecting a wounded U.S. paratrooper from sniper fire in the jungle near Thuong Lang. Brown and another medic crawled through the jungle to treat the paratrooper while a live grenade lay nearby.

Above: June 1965—A long line of suspects, including three confirmed Viet Cong guerrillas, marches from Le Son village to an interrogation point during a U.S. Marine search-and-destroy operation near Danang.

Left: June 11, 1965—A wounded Vietnamese ranger keeps his weapon ready to answer a Viet Cong attack during the battle at Dong Xoai.

Below Left: May 6, 1965—Viet Cong prisoners await transport to an interrogation center after they were captured overnight in the Mekong Delta area. South Vietnamese troops trapped 42 prisoners, many of whom were hiding in the overgrown reeds of a river as they tried to slip into Cambodia.

Below: June 12, 1965—A seriously wounded Vietnamese militiaman is carried to an evacuation helicopter. He was one of a few government troops to survive heavy fighting when Viet Cong forces overran their post at Dong Xoai before Vietnamese airborne came to their relief.

June 25, 1965—Waiters and others carry an injured man from a Saigon floating restaurant after two terrorist bombs exploded, killing and injuring diners.

June 25, 1965—An injured child is rushed to ambulance after two terrorist bombs ripped through a crowded restaurant on the Saigon River.

June 25, 1965—The dead and injured are sprawled on the sidewalk after a terrorist bomb exploded at a floating restaurant on the Saigon River.

Dong Xoai, site of a major battle.

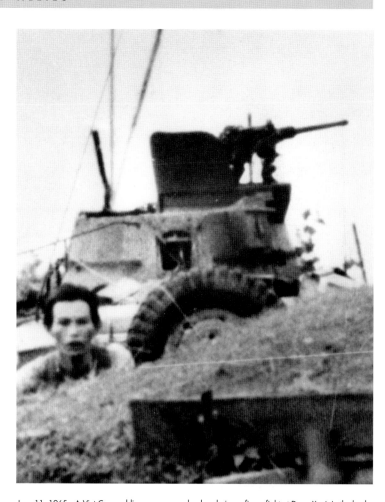

June 11, 1965—A Viet Cong soldier peers over a bunker during a fierce fight at Dong Xoai. In the background is a government tank abandoned moments before.

June 11, 1965—A Vietcong, right, shoots a South Vietnamese who lies wounded on a mud wall at Dong Xoai. The soldier was trying to cross the wall to join government Rangers who had just landed by helicopter 100 yards away.

June 10, 1965—Clutching his jouncing equipment against his body, a Vietnamese Ranger dashes for cover in the battle at Dong Xoai. The Rangers were landed on a soccer field by helicopter.

Above: June 6, 1965—A survivor of the Dong Xoai battle.

Left: June 6, 1965—Government troops reoccupied the post at Dong Xoai after driving off a fierce Viet Cong attack. Though safe now, this woman screams hysterically after emerging from a bunker where she took cover during the two-day conflict. Despite the bunker's protection she suffered burns and cuts.

Below Left: June 6, 1965—A weeping mother holds her child, killed in an air strike that preceded the recapture of Dong Xoai by South Vietnamese Rangers. Hundreds of villagers were caught when the Viet Cong swept into the village. The death toll was high on both sides.

Below: June 6, 1965—A bandaged Vietnamese youngster cries as she limps along in Dong Xoai where her father was killed in the fierce battle with Viet Cong attackers. The girl was injured in a bunker, then taken to a provincial hospital.

Left: June 6, 1965—Wounded and shocked civilian survivors of the Dong Xoai battle crawl out of a bunker where they took cover during murderous ground fire and air bombardments over two days.

Above: June 10, 1965—A girl, her parents slain in a ferocious Viet Cong attack on Dong Xoai, stares into the jungle after the fight subsided.

Below: June 12, 1965—A Vietnamese ranger struggles to retrieve the weapon he dropped when shot in the legs during fighting with the Viet Cong at Dong Xoai.

June 11, 1965—Civilian survivors huddle together after intense fighting between Viet Cong and South Vietnamese forces near the jungle town of Dong Xoai. The bodies of about 150 civilians and 300 South Vietnamese troops were recovered after South Vietnamese Rangers recaptured the town.

June 13, 1965—A Vietnamese militia commander weeps after learning that his entire family was killed in the cross fire at Dong Xoai. The battle, between government forces and Viet Cong units, lasted two days.

June 1965—Villagers, many of whom had hidden in the jungle during the battle of Dong Xoai, begin an exodus after finding their homes destroyed and many of their relatives dead. A massive Viet Cong assault against the U.S. Special Forces compound at Dong Xoai, followed by U.S. air strikes on enemy positions, left the village in ruins.

Left: June 1965—A South Vietnamese soldier helps a U.S. serviceman from a jungle hiding place after a major Viet Cong assault against the U.S. Special Forces base at Dong Xoai.

Below: June 11, 1965—A wounded Vietnamese ranger keeps his weapon ready to answer a Viet Cong attack during the battle at Dong Xoai.

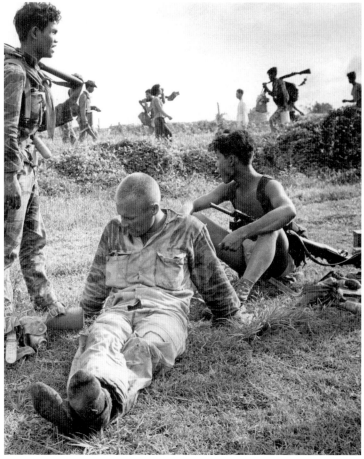

June 14, 1965—A Vietnamese soldier with broken leg gazes at his wife and child when they were reunited at a first-aid station in the Dong Xoai battle area in South Vietnam before a U.S. helicopter moved them to a safe area.

July 2, 1965—A Marine stands on one of the two dominant hills overlooking Qui Nhon, on the watch for enemy movements in the area.

July 14, 1965—U.S. Army nurses Capt. Gladys E. Sepulveda *(left)*, of Ponce, Puerto Rico, and 2nd Lt. Lois Ferrari, of Pittsburgh, Pennsylvania, rest on sandbags at Cam Ranh Bay in South Vietnam. They were waiting for transportation to Nha Trang, where they worked in the 8th field hospital.

July 1965—Vietnamese Rangers climb aboard U.S. Army Huey helicopters at Bien Hoa for airlift into Viet Cong–infiltrated mountains. Valued for their versatility and mobility, the U.S. military was reportedly using about 5,000 helicopters in Vietnam at the time, most of them operated by the army.

Above: July 1965—A party of U.S. Marine night raiders return to their Navy landing craft in the South China Sea near Han Son Cha Island, 12 miles north of Danang. A night of probing the island found no evidence of the Viet Cong.

Left: July 2, 1965—U.S. Marines and a Marine helicopter overlook the harbor at Qui Nhon, where troops of the carrier U.S.S. *Iwo Jima* landed in response to threats of Viet Cong mortar attacks in the area.

July 9, 1965—Villagers evacuate An Hoa as a battle raged between the Viet Cong and U.S. Marines who had made an amphibious landing on the island.

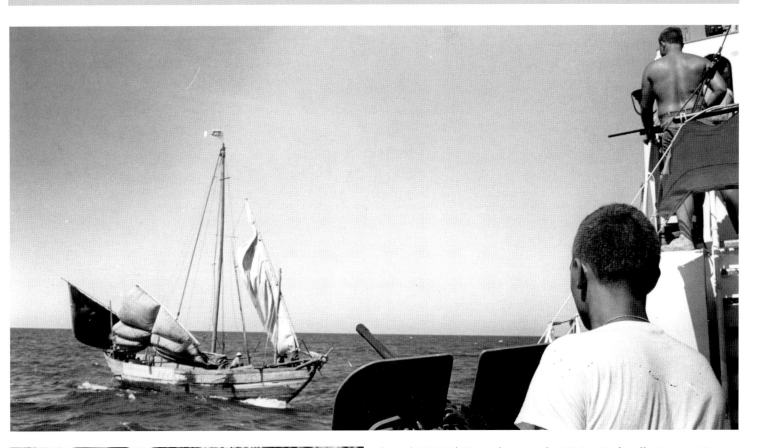

Above: July 1965—With 50mm machine guns ready, a U.S. Coast Guard patrol boat intercepts a Vietnamese junk in the South China Sea. To prevent communist infiltrators or supplies moving at sea, Coast Guard vessels were patrolling the coast near the 17th Parallel dividing North and South Vietnam.

Left: July 25, 1965—Rounding up Viet Cong suspects, a U.S. Marine orders a man and boys to sit during an operation at Tam Loc. U.S. and South Vietnamese troops launched the major assault following a recent Viet Cong attack against the marine defenses around the Chu Lai beachhead.

Bottom: July 1965—A B-52 bomber takes off from Guam for a strike against communist position in Vietnam, more than 2,000 miles away.

Above: July 10, 1965—U.S. Sgt. Marvin C. Runyon *(right)*, wounded by Viet Cong sniper fire, is helped to an evacuation helicopter in War Zone D. Runyon was one of about 50 U.S. casualties in a four-day search-and-destroy mission.

Right: July 23, 1965—A U.S. Marine of the 4th Regiment uncovers a 105mm recoilless rifle overlooking the Dai Giang River Valley. The outpost guards the Phu Bia airfield to the east.

July 29, 1965—U.S. Marines wade through flooded rice paddies during an assault on the village of Duc An.

Above: July 1965—Huey helicopters lift off after depositing U.S. and Vietnamese troops in the ruins of Xo Ba Da, 40 miles north of Saigon.

Below: July 1965—Viet Cong fighters in the central part of South Vietnam cross rivers and jungle in their pursuit of government soldiers.

Right: July 19, 1965—A long line of trucks of South Vietnam army engineers halts on Route 19 between Pleiku and Qui Nhon in the central mountains in an area susceptible to Viet Cong ambushes.

Above: March 1965—An A-1 Skyraider bombs a Viet Cong position concealed in the South Vietnamese jungle.

Right: Undated—U.S. Supersabre fighters in flight after a combat mission in Vietnam.

August 19, 1965—Two Marines assist a third wounded Marine during a land and sea assault against the Viet Cong near Van Tuong.

Above: August 19, 1965—A wounded Marine is taken to an evacuation area after he was rescued after fighting off Viet Cong from inside an embattled amphibious tank near Van Tuong.

Right: August 5, 1965—A Marine helps his buddy find a medic after a clash with Viet Cong near Danang.

Above: August 27, 1965—A Vietnamese soldier drags a woman by her hair through a canal in Ap La Ghi, Mekong Delta. The woman, suspected of being a Viet Cong collaborator, had her hands tied and was submerged repeatedly as soldiers interrogated her for information about the identity and location of local guerrilla forces. She was later imprisoned.

Right: August 28, 1965—Under Viet Cong fire, Vietnamese medics evacuate a seriously wounded soldier on a stretcher through a canal north of Rach Gia.

Above: August 6,1965—A U.S. marine looks over his shoulder at the blazing thatched houses of Duc An, 60 miles south of Da Nang, after a raid on the village. As leather-necks charged Viet Cong positions, 3.5-phosphorous rockets were fired ahead of their advance by U.S. Marine rocket crews.

Right: August 1965—With rifles and cigarettes held above the water, U.S. Marines cross the swollen An Tan River in Chu Lai.

Above: August 19, 1965—Sharpened bamboo sticks rise from a clearing on the Van Tuong Peninsula as U.S. Marines patrol for Viet Cong guerrillas. The Viet Cong planted the stakes to prevent helicopter landings.

Right: August 26, 1965—A B-52 bombs a Viet Cong target 30 miles north northeast of Saigon, the third such strike in the area.

Above: August 1965—A U.S. soldier bandages the arm of the wife of a village chieftain in the Montagnard village of Plei Bon, east of Pleiku. When U.S. troops arrived, the woman was being tortured by Viet Cong who had killed her husband and son. Other villagers were shot in the legs as the guerrillas sought information about government supporters.

Left: August 1965—A U.S. Coast Guard cutter pulls alongside a Vietnamese junk for boarding off the coast of South Vietnam. The cutters were patrolling a 60-mile section of coastline to guard against infiltration of enemy troops or supplies.

Above: August 7, 1965—U.S. 1st Division soldiers wade through a stream near Bien Hoa while searching for Viet Cong guerrillas around their base. The unit had been conducting patrols since arriving in Vietnam one month earlier.

Left: August 19, 1965—Flares dropped by U.S. Air Force planes light the battlefield on the Van Tuong Peninsula for the U.S. 4th Marine Regiment. Paul Dean of the Arizona Republic shot this time exposure from the rim of his foxhole, and camera movement created the pattern.

Above: August 1965—Huey helicopters carrying troops of the 173rd Airborne Brigade settle in for a landing near the Montagnard village of Plei Ho Drong. The unit found friendly mountain tribal people, but no Viet Cong.

Above Right: August 28, 1965—A Vietnamese soldier grimaces as a medic dresses a severe shoulder wound during battle in a rice paddy north of Rach Gia in South Vietnam.

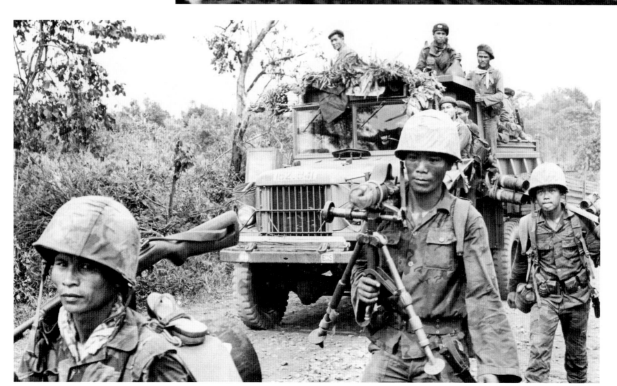

Above: August 1965—Puffs of white smoke mark the positions of six 57mm flak emplacements as North Vietnamese gunners fire at U.S. Air Force jets as they continue the destruction of military targets.

Left: August 12, 1965—Vietnamese troops and trucks proceed down Route 19 near Duc Co as they brought reinforcements and supplies from Pleiku to the besieged government outpost of Duc Co.

Above: August 25, 1965—Smoke from a napalm bomb curls around the rising sun as a U.S. Air Force F-100 jet pulls out of a bombing run near Ap La Ghi.

Above Right: August 26, 1965—A Vietnamese woman, suspected of aiding the Viet Cong, is questioned at bayonet point after her capture near Ap La Ghi in the Mekong Delta. She carried Viet Cong documents.

Above: August 26, 1965—A government soldier threatens a Viet Cong woman, trying to get her to disclose the locations of an arms chache near Ap La Ghi. She refused to talk and was taken to prison.

Left: Mourners gather around the body of the chief of Plei Bon, a remote Montagnard village east of Pleiku. The village leader was executed by the Viet Cong, who also attempted to get the names of government supporters. U.S. troops forced the VC to flee and a television cameraman with the American forces made the film from which this picture was obtained.

Above: September 10, 1965—A Vietnamese paratrooper carries his buddy to a first-aid station during an assault on a Viet Cong encampment in the jungles near Ba Xom, 22 miles north of Saigon.

Above Right: September 25, 1965—Paratroopers of the U.S. 2nd Battalion, 173rd Airborne Brigade, hold their automatic weapons above water as they cross a river in the rain during a search for Viet Cong positions in the jungle area of Ben Cat, South Vietnam.

Above: September 5, 1965—A U.S. Marine carries a baby during the evacuation of Vietnamese farm families from their homes near Vinh Quang. The families were relocated to a safer area as Marine units searched for Viet Cong guerrillas in the hamlets north of Qui Nhon. Two platoons of Viet Cong were reportedly defeated in the operation.

Left: September 19, 1965—U.S. paratroopers of the 1st Battalion, 173rd Airborne Brigade, lead two girls from a captured Viet Cong training camp in the Long Nguyen area. The girls, 17 and 14, said they had been at the camp for two and three months respectively.

September 24, 1965—A sampan carries Vietnamese peasants past South Vietnamese troops on an armored personnel carrier in the Mekong Delta. Government troops were patrolling the area about 20 miles south of Can Tho.

Above: September 1965—Four c-123 aircraft spray a suspected Viet Cong jungle position with a defoliation liquid. The four specially equipped planes cover a 1000-foot swath on each pass over the dense jungle.

Right: September 11, 1965—U.S. soldiers of the 1st Cavalry Division climb down from the U.S.S. *Boxer* as they disembark at the Qui Nhon beachhead, 260 miles northeast of Saigon.

Above: September 11, 1965—A U.S. medical corpsman carries an injured baby to an evacuation helicopter after an assault on Ap Son Thuy, 12 miles from the U.S. base at Da Nang. U.S. forces advancing on the village in Operation Golden Fleece had come under Viet Cong fire. Eleven injured civilians were airlifted to Da Nang.

Right: September 26, 1965—U.S. paratroopers of the 2nd Battalion, 173rd Airborne Brigade search burning huts in a jungle area south of Ben Cat. Viet Cong guerrillas had reportedly burned the huts before fleeing the arrival of U.S. troops.

Above: September 18, 1965—Two wounded U.S. paratroopers help each other to an evacuation helicopter at An Ninh. Units of the 101st Airborne Brigade, surrounded by enemy fire as soon as they landed, were pinned down for 24 hours before reinforcements and evacuation helicopters could reach them.

Left: September 19, 1965—Vietnamese soldier kicks Viet Cong prisoner during an interrogation.

Above: September 18, 1965—Members of the U.S. 101st Airborne Brigade carry a wounded paratrooper to cover after the Viet Cong opened fire on an evacuation helicopter at An Ninh, 17 miles east of An Khe. Viet Cong guerrillas had surrounded the landing zone, pinning down units as soon as they were on the ground.

Right: September 9, 1965—Tape covers the eyes and mouth of a suspected Viet Cong guerrilla captured during a joint U.S.-Vietnamese operation on the Batangan Peninsula, 20 miles south of Chu Lai.

Above: September 15, 1965—A U.S. Marine holds a Viet Cong suspect flushed from a rice paddy south of Danang. The marines were supporting South Vietnamese troops engaged with a communist regiment in the valley dubbed Death Valley.

Right: September 1965—A U.S. Navy A-4E Skyhawk based on the carrier U.S.S. Independence pulls up during a missile raid on railroad cars at Van Hoi, North Vietnam.

Above: September 3, 1965—A makeshift stretcher is used to carry a wounded government soldier on a paddy dike during a clash with the Viet Cong on Tan Dinh Island.

Right: October 6, 1965—U.S. paratroopers of the 173rd Airborne Brigade stay with the poncho-draped bodies of men killed during a Viet Cong ambush in War Zone D. Dense jungle prevented air support and helicopter evacuations.

Above: October 28, 1965—Men of the U.S. 1st Cavalry hit the ground for protection from sniper fire after being delivered by helicopter to a position south of the outpost at Plei Me, South Vietnam.

Left: October 8, 1965—A U.S. Marine guards a suspected Viet Cong sympathizer in a barbed wire enclosure near Danang. The woman was captured during Marine search-and-destroy operations.

Above: October 30, 1965—The bodies of Viet Cong guerrillas, many of them apparently teenagers, are lined up after they launched a human-wave assault against a U.S. Marine position 10 miles southwest of Danang. Fifty-six Viet Cong were reported killed in hand-to-hand fighting; U.S. casualties were described as moderate.

Above Right: October 26, 1965—A U.S. adviser prepares a mortar position in the beleaguered post at Plei Me, 210 miles north of Saigon. The town, defended by Montagnard soldiers and American advisers, was under repeated attack by about 500 Viet Cong.

Right: October 1965—A wounded U.S. Marine in a sling is lifted to an evacuation helicopter after the 3rd Reconnaissance Battalion captured a Viet Cong complex during a weeklong patrol. Eleven marines were wounded, four seriously, and four Viet Cong were reported killed.

Above: October 14, 1965—Navy pilot Lt. Jack Terhune ejects over the Gulf of Tonkin after antiaircraft fire disabled his F-8 fighter. A helicopter from the U.S.S. *Coral Sea* rescued Terhune.

Left: October 14, 1965—A disabled and unmanned f-8 fighter *(bottom)* falls out of the air as Navy pilot Jack Terhune *(top right)* successfully ejects over the Gulf of Tonkin. A helicopter from the U.S.S. *Coral Sea* rescued Terhune.

October 20, 1965—Bodies of Viet Cong guerrillas lie in a muddy moat surrounding the South Vietnamese outpost in Ba Long Valley near Quang Tri in the Central Highlands. The guerrillas used bamboo poles, top, in an unsuccessful assault on the base.

October 6, 1965—Wounded paratroopers of the 1st Battalion, 173rd Airborne Brigade wait for a medical evacuation helicopter in War Zone D, 25 miles northeast of Saigon.

Above: October 28, 1965—A South Vietnamese serviceman pushes a Viet Cong prisoner from a burning hut near Canh Duong during a search-and-destroy operation in a suspected guerrilla tunnel complex.

Right: October 22, 1965—U.S. flares light up the beleaguered Special Forces camp at Plei Me during a steady Viet Cong attack against the base. Despite U.S. air strikes against enemy positions and heavy return fire from the camp itself, the outpost continued to take incoming fire.

Above: October 13, 1965—A Viet Cong guerrilla, despite capture and under threat by a pistol, snarls defiance at a soldier of the 1st U.S. Cavalry Division near Plai Me. The prisoner, one of 20 taken in a raid on a communist hospital, refused to walk to an evacuation helicopter and was finally carried.

Left: October 1965—Montagnard soldiers make a sunset patrol near Plei Me, about 210 miles north of Saigon, after an attack by Viet Cong guerrillas.

Above: October 23, 1965—A Vietnamese Ranger with a head wound waits for evacuation from Plei Me in the central highlands of South Vietnam. He was part of the force that came in to reinforce defenders of the post as Viet Cong hit with a heavy attack.

Right: October 20, 1965—Parachutes billow in the wind after landing supplies at Plei Me during an attack on the Special Forces Montagnard post by the Viet Cong.

**274**

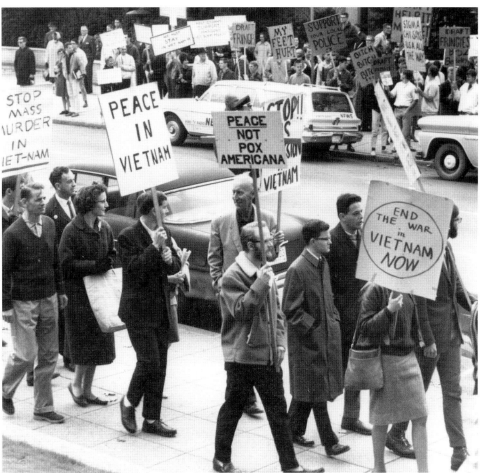

Above: October 1965—Sadness and suffering is mirrored in the face of an elderly woman at a refugee center at Quang Ngai.

Right: October 16, 1965—Demonstrators in foreground protest the war in Vietnam while those in the background protest the antiwar protestors. The two sides marched in Seattle.

October 15, 1965—Antiwar demonstrators in Berkeley, California, protest the U.S. presence in Vietnam.

Above: November 18, 1965—U.S. troops carry bodies of air cavalrymen to an evacuation helicopter as more bodies are strewn on the ground at the site of an ambush by communist forces in South Vietnam's Ia Drang valley. Dozens of soldiers in a battalion of the 1st Cavalry Division were killed the night before.

Left: November 17, 1965—2nd Lt. C. R. Rick Rescorla moves carefully with fixed bayonet through the under-brush in an attack of North Vietnamese sniper pockets outside the American perimeter in South Vietnam's Ia Drang Valley.

Below Left: November 17, 1965—A wounded American soldier, his arm in a sling, crawls toward a medic attending to other wounded as remnants of the ambushed 1st Cavalry Division battalion came under heavy fire by communist troops in Ia Drang valley.

Below: November 15, 1965—North Vietnamese soldiers, wounded in fighting against the 7th Regiment of the U.S. 1st Air Cavalry Division in the Ia Drang Valley, await helicopter transport to an interrogation point.

Above: November 1965—A U.S. Navy F-8 Crusader launches a Zuni rocket at a Viet Cong target in South Vietnam. The fighter was based on the carrier U.S.S. *Midway.*

Left: November 18, 1965—During a beach landing 40 miles south of Danang, U.S. Marines maneuver past bamboo spikes and a cactus ridge erected by the Viet Cong. The tall poles in background made a helicopter landing difficult, and some of the poles were wired to land mines.

Above: November 14, 1965—South Korean Marines of the Blue Dragon Brigade respond to sniper fire while patrolling a Viet Cong–infiltrated area about 10 miles west of Nha Trang.

Left: November 19, 1965—Flares light a jungle clearing covered with U.S. dead and wounded after a battalion of the 1st Cavalry Division was ambushed north of the Ia Drang Valley. Many of the wounded struggled from the ambush site to this field several hundred yards away, some dying overnight before aid could reach them.

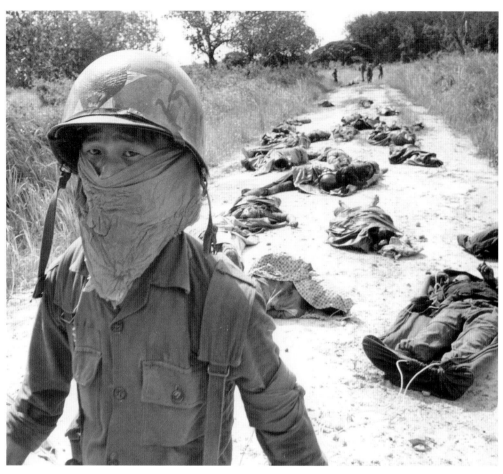

Above: November 25, 1965—U.S. advisor Capt. Glen Blumhardt, of Mondovi, Wisconsin, watches a South Vietnamese battalion reoccupy a battlefield in the Dau Tieng Michelin rubber plantation. Blumhardt had fought for hours beside South Vietnamese troops as Viet Cong forces overran their positions, leaving many of his fellow advisers dead.

Right: November 27, 1965—A Vietnamese litter bearer wears a mask as he passes the bodies of U.S. and South Vietnamese soldiers killed in fighting at the Michelin rubber plantation, 45 miles northeast of Saigon. The Viet Cong overran a Vietnamese battalion and a regimental headquarters, leaving more than 100 dead.

Above: November 14, 1965—As U.S. infantrymen pursue two Viet Cong companies about 18 miles north of Saigon, a Vietnamese woman pours harvested rice onto a straw mat, letting the wind separate the chaff from the grain.

Right: November 1965—Spiked poles placed by the Viet Cong prevent landings at the village of Hoa Ninh, 50 miles northeast of Saigon. The simple but effective devices forced paratroopers to use another landing zone by helicopter.

November 1965—Col. James P. Kelly, commander of the 1st Battalion, 7th Marine Regiment, displays punji sticks found by U.S. Marines during an operation near Chu Lai. The punji's barbed points are designed to penetrate the boots of enemy soldiers.

November 22, 1965—The bodies of Viet Cong dead are loaded on trucks for transport to a mass grave after a reinforced Viet Cong battalion attacked a South Vietnamese regimental command post at Dau Tieng, about 40 miles northwest of Saigon. South Vietnamese troops repelled the assault, leaving more than 100 Viet Cong dead.

November 15, 1965—U.S. helicopters line up on Route 13, near the headquarters of the 1st Infantry Division's 3rd Brigade, before ferrying troops on a search-and-destroy mission in the Michelin rubber plantation, long a Viet Cong stronghold.

November 4, 1965—U.S. 1st Regiment Marines pay their respects at the grave of eight fellow Marines who died securing the port city of Qui Nhon.

**279**

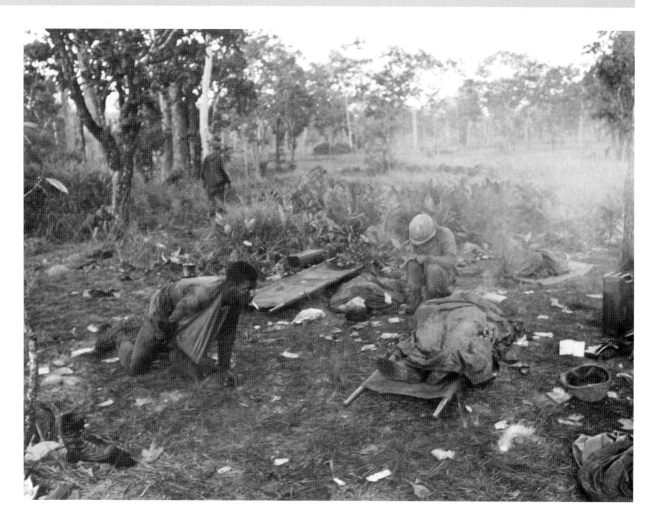

Right: November. 17, 1965 - A wounded American soldier, his arm in a sling, crawls toward a medic attending to other wounded as remnants of the ambushed 1st Cavalry Division battalion came under heavy fire by communist troops in Ia Drang valley.

Left: December, 1965—Boats bring visitors to a Tet celebration in Binh Tan. Each boat carries an armed Viet Cong soldier and helmeted troops march across the bridge. Tet celebrations usually center around family reunions though this one turned out to be a Viet Cong meeting.

Above: U.S. Air Force F-105 Thunderchiefs line up to refuel from a KC-135 jet tanker on their way to targets in North Vietnam.

Above: December 12, 1965—Pfc. Herman D. Kottwitz of Belfast, New York and his sentry dog, "Match," maintain a vigilant watch overlooking the Dalat Valley in South Vietnam.

Right: December 27, 1965—Actress Carroll Baker snaps her fingers at sailors cheering from bridge of aircraft carrier U.S.S. *Ticonderoga* as Bob Hope leads her across stage set up on flight deck. More than 2,500 sailors saw the Hope troupe's show on the carrier off the coast of South Vietnam..

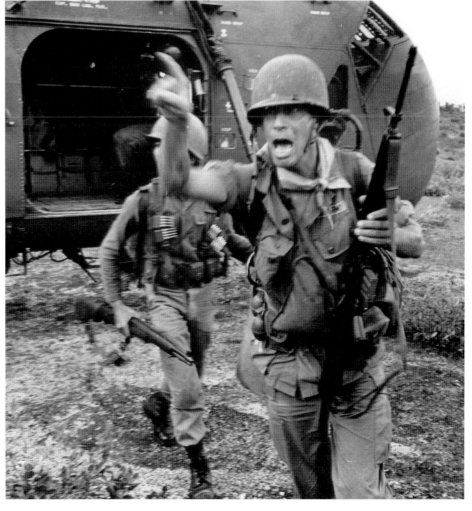

Above: December 1965—Platoon Sgt. Lowell Willhite of Pontiac, Michigan, sports a five-day growth of beard as he takes a cigarette break during a long patrol through the Michelin rubber plantation. Willhite's unit of the 1st Division made no enemy contact during the patrol, about 35 miles northeast of Saigon.

Right: December 8, 1965—A U.S. adviser shouts orders as he leads a group of South Vietnamese soldiers from a helicopter landing at Tam Ky. The troops were reinforcing a Vietnamese Ranger battalion that took heavy losses in a Viet Cong assault earlier in the day.

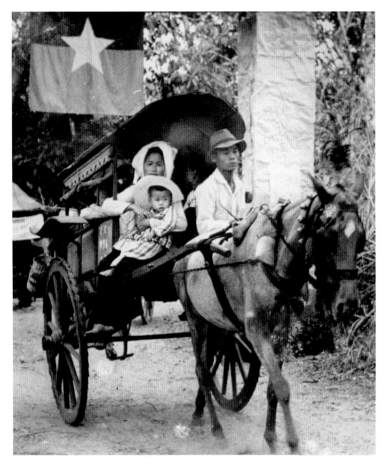

December, 1965 - With a large Viet Cong flag hanging overhead, a Vietnamese family leaves a village in the Chu Chi district by horse cart for a New Year's visit with relatives.

December 12, 1965 - During a helicopter assault 13 miles northwest of Ben Cat, U.S. paratroopers of the 327th Airborne take cover from sniper fire at the edge of a jungle clearing.

November, 1965 - Commander Robert R. King, flying a U.S. Navy A-4 Skyhawk, drops a 2,000 pound bomb on a Viet Cong position in South Vietnam. King was commanding officer of an attack squadron based on the carrier USS Midway.

December 21, 1965 - A helicopter gunner, left, helps a medic carry a wounded Viet Cong soldier to a medical evacuation helicopter. The wounded Viet Cong had been abandoned when the U.S. 1st Cavalry Divison advanced on a communist battalion in the La Thinh Valley, 180 miles northeast of Saigon.

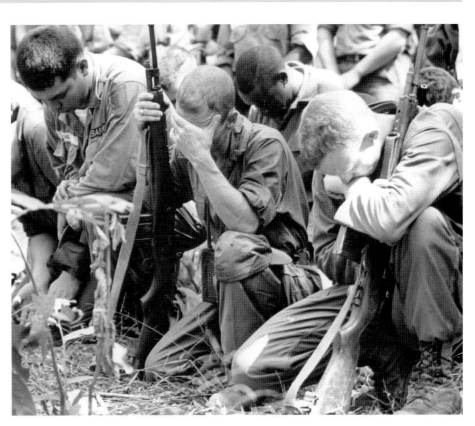

December 6, 1965—Draped with machine-gun ammunition, U.S. soldiers of the 1st Infantry Division carry the body of a fellow soldier afer a battle near Ap Nha Mat, 40 miles northwest of Saigon. A U.S. battalion reported heavy casualties in dense jungle fighting with a Viet Cong regiment.

December 9, 1965—U.S. soldiers of the 2nd Battalion, 2nd Regiment, 1st Infantry Division, pray during services at the Michelin rubber plantation commemorating soldiers who died a few days earlier in a fierce battle with Viet Cong forces near the plantation.

December 1, 1965—With various fighters and bombers on its flight deck, the nuclear-powered carrier U.S.S. *Enterprise* cruises the South China Sea for the first time during the Vietnam War.

December 1965—In an area heavily infiltrated by Viet Cong, a U.S. 1st Division soldier guards Route 7 as Vietnamese women and schoolchildren return home to the village of Xuan Dien from Ben Cat.

Above: December 24, 1965—A U.S. Navy engineer playing Santa Claus delivers gifts on Christmas Eve to Montagnard women and children in Mang Yang, a remote area of the Central Highlands.

Right: December 21, 1965—After a firefight in the La Thinh Valley, the wife of a suspected Viet Cong leans over her husband while begging U.S. soldiers of the 1st Cavalry Division to release him. The man was transported with scores of other suspects to an interrogation center.

December 20, 1965—Radio antennas probing the air, the headquarters unit of the 2nd Battalion, 7th Regiment, 1st Air Cavalry Division, patrols through rice paddies 30 miles northwest of Qui Nhon.

December 23, 1965—A captured Viet Cong guerrilla lies on machine-gun ammunition in a U.S. helicopter under the guard of the helicopter's gunner. A fleet of helicopters delivered troops of the 1st Cavalry Division to rice paddies 30 miles northwest of Qui Nhon on a search-and-destroy operation.

Left: December 22, 1965—A wounded Viet Cong sniper, left behind by his guerrilla unit, is bandaged by a specialist as the U.S. 1st Cavalry Division patrolled the area 30 miles northwest of Qui Nhon.

Above: December 23, 1965—U.S. soldiers carry religious statues from a church in Binh Tan to a waiting helicopter. The 3rd Brigade, 1st Cavalry Division, evacuated the parish priest and most of his church from the Viet Cong–controlled area to a protected area 10 miles away in Phu Phong, about 260 miles northeast of Saigon.

Above: December 1965—A memorial service for seven men of the U.S. 101st Airborne Brigade is held in a clearing near a former French rubber plantation in Lai Khe, South Vietnam. Their boots, helmets, and M16 rifles are set up with a field altar. They were killed during a search-and-destroy mission against the Viet Cong in the jungles and plantation areas about 40 miles north of Saigon.

Left: December 22, 1965—A U.S. soldier of the 2nd Battalion, 7th Regiment, 1st Air Cavalry Division, carries a spare M-79 grenade in the band of his helmet as his unit joined an assault on an area 30 miles northwest of Qui Nhon.

December 20, 1965—Cattle graze as U.S. soldiers of the 2nd Battalion, 7th Regiment, 1st Cavalry Division, wait to move out during a helicopter-borne assault 30 miles northwest of Qui Nhon.

December 23, 1965—A Viet Cong prisoner is interrogated by a Vietnamese militiaman during a search-and-destroy operation by the U.S. 1st Cavalry Division near Binh Khe, 240 miles northeast of Saigon. The prisoner was captured with a grenade.

December 2, 1965—Viet Cong suspects are led to a helicopter for transfer to an interrogation center near Vo Dat. More than 200 suspects were rounded up as the 173rd Airborne Brigade moved into the "Rice Bowl" area to secure the rice harvest in the previously Viet Cong–controlled area.

December 23, 1965—Soldiers of the U.S. 3rd Brigade, 1st Cavalry Division, take up defensive positions during evacuation of the Catholic church at Binh Tan. The unit evacuated the parish priest and most of his church from the Viet Cong–controlled area to a protected area 10 miles away in Phu Phong, about 260 miles northeast of Saigon.

November 1965—Commander Robert R. King, flying a U.S. Navy A-4 Skyhawk, fires a cluster of rockets at a Viet Cong position in South Vietnam. King was commanding officer of an attack squadron based on the carrier U.S.S. *Midway*.

December 1965—Staff Sgt. Vernon Larson of Downing, Wisconsin, shows a beard after nine days in the jungle without a razor. His unit expected to be in the field only two days, and he was traveling light; water had to be dropped in to the patrol.

December 1965—The shadow of a U.S. Air Force RF-101 Voodoo reconnaissance plane sweeps across a North Vietnamese antiaircraft emplacement of 57mm guns.

December 22, 1965—A Vietnamese woman reaches over her slain son to cover the body of her husband, both killed by the Viet Cong in Tan Thuan Dong, just south of Saigon. By custom, it is the duty of the Vietnamese wife to prepare the body for burial. On the table are Buddhist articles of mourning.

December 4, 1965—A Vietnamese mother carrying her injured child escorts a bandaged woman from their apartment opposite the bomb-damaged Metropole Hotel in Saigon.

December 3, 1965—The U.S. enlisted men's billet in Saigon is damaged by Viet Cong attack.

December 4, 1965—A U.S. sailor and a Vietnamese nurse help a wounded woman from a demolished shop near a U.S. enlisted men's billet attacked by Viet Cong.

# WESTY'S WAR

At 10,000 feet aboard his command plane General William Westmoreland was once again conducting an aerial survey of the battlefield. It was his custom to invite one or two reporters 'selected' by his press officer and it was a popular invitation if only because of Westy's self-admitted 'penchant for acronyms and catch phrases' which extended to his oddly named personal aircraft. It was a converted C-123 cargo plane with a big white-painted belly and Westmoreland called it the *White Whale*. For several months before assuming command Westmoreland had taken the *White Whale* over every part of South Vietnam for a first-hand reconnaissance, while educating the press on the terrain and the difficulties. Westmoreland, as he wrote in *A Soldier Reports*, wanted to improve the 'deplorable' relations arising from the military's 'overly optimistic' progress reports, and 'in those early days the newsmen were sometimes closer to the truth than were American officials'. In particular, he wanted to dispel any public illusions about

> '*And throughout the war we never lost a battle.*'
>
> – GENERAL WILLIAM WESTMORELAND

a quick and easy end to the war: American 'impatience', he foresaw, could defeat him. Forty per cent of the interior was uninhabitable jungle, swamp and scrubland – or elephant grass 'ideal for nourishing' guerrilla warfare; the enemy had to be 'found and fought' there: the American tactic must be to 'search and destroy'. The US Commander was frank but confident flying over the narrow, variable land which for twenty centuries had been the graveyard of foreign armies.

Though some reporters thought of the two Vietnams as shaped like an hourglass with the top half filtering remorselessly into the bottom, Westmoreland preferred the image of the Vietnamese peasant's carefully balanced pannier. The two weighted baskets represented the heavily populated deltas of the Red River in the North and the Mekong in the South, and the long bamboo shoulder pole was the politically pliant Laos-Cambodian border. This was where Communist troops and supplies were actually filtering in along

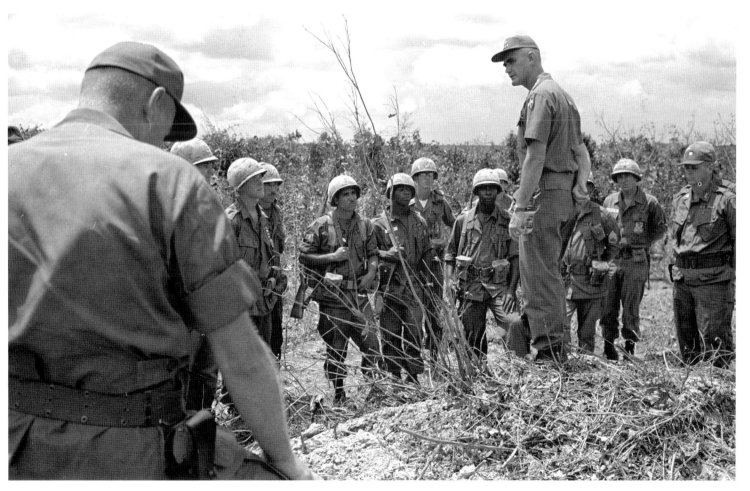

August 1965—Gen. William C. Westmoreland talks with officers and men of the 18th Regiment, 2nd Brigade, of the U.S. 1st Infantry Division, in a field near Bien Hoa, South Vietnam.

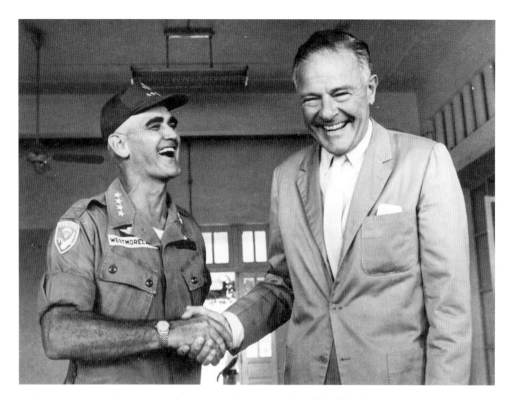

April 30, 1966—Henry Cabot Lodge, U.S. ambassador to South Vietnam, gets a farewell handshake from Gen. William Westmoreland, commander of the U.S. military in Vietnam, as Lodge prepared to board a flight in Saigon to the United States.

six-inch guns, while fighter-bombers pounded and napalmed a complex of guerrilla tunnels and caves. After three days, with Marine 'KIA's' (Killed in Action) put at forty-five, an enemy 'body-count' of 688 was reported, plus 'an undetermined number of persons caught in these caves as indicated by the odor pervading the area'. The impromptu American-only attack, the first regimental-sized US battle since the Korean war, was viewed as an illuminating combination of mobility and fire-power and was thereupon called Operation Starlight. Now, on the coast at Qui Nhon, the 1st Cavalry Division was coming ashore. The 'Cav' came with a fearsome reputation earned in the Pacific war and in Korea, and with a new and potentially deadly punch. The Division and all its support mechanism had been remodeled for total rapid helicopter deployment, though as Westmoreland noted 'the concept was still to be tried under fire'. But within hours of its landing the Division had vaulted on hundreds of Hueys to a new base deep in the Central Highlands protecting Pleiku. To the press it seemed that in just a few days Westmoreland had demonstrated his equation: mobility + fire-power = attrition.

Operation Starlight was quickly followed by Silver Bayonet as the 1st Cavalry Division was pitted against North Vietnamese main force units in the Ia Drang Valley, with '1771 known enemy casualties'. But the month-long battle, though co-

a thousand kilometers of mountain trails. This, effectively, was the Western front – a longer one, Westmoreland would point out, than in World War I, and the solution had to be the same as in that war: attrition. Westmoreland believed that his enemy was also greatly extended and vulnerable – or would be if denied the succor of the populated areas. Having so often pointed out the problems, Westmoreland could now finally demonstrate some answers.

The time was the end of August 1965, just one month after President Johnson's commitment of 125,000 American combat troops. A battalion of Marines had secured the landing beaches at Qui Nhon. An entire division – America's newly devised airmobile division – was approaching at sea. From this midway point of South Vietnam, the coastal flats curved north towards the Marine enclave at Chu Lai, where a week earlier a threatened guerrilla siege had been dramatically broken. To the West lay the Central Highlands, where the February attacks on the plateau cities of Kontum and Pleiku, positioned like eyes overlooking the six largest provinces, had led to the US air and land intervention. Beyond, where the mountainous jungles of the Cambodian border descended to the great Ia Drang valley, three North Vietnamese divisions were reported probing toward Pleiku, but Westmoreland was now confident that he had the manpower and mobility for a counter-offensive.

At Chu Lai, Marine reinforcements had immediately engaged in a major battle which Westmoreland called 'an auspicious beginning for American arms'. Suspecting a sizeable guerrilla attack, Marine commander Lieutenant General Lewis W. Walt had deployed a battalion by helicopter to 'pin the VC' against the shore and had then re-embarked another, newly arrived battalion to attack from the sea. Amphibious tanks were sent in; a navy cruiser delivered devastating fire' from

1966—American troops land in Vietnam.

ordinating the first use of B-52 bombers in Vietnam, saw fighting – in Westmoreland's words – 'as fierce as any ever experienced by American troops'. US combat losses of 300 were almost twice the ratio of the counter-guerrilla Chu Lai action.

In a critique after the Ia Drang battle the senior officer pointedly held up a new, lightweight, fully automatic rifle and said, 'Brave soldiers and the M-16 brought this victory.' The M-16 was still considered unreliable compared to the equivalent Communist AK-47, yet the majority of American troops were then equipped only with the older and heavier semi-automatic M-14–and for fully two years there would not be enough M-16s to go round. At the start, at the most basic level, Communist fire-power was in fact superior, and the other part of Westmoreland's equation, mobility, would throughout prove only of moment to moment advantage in terrain that could be constantly swept but seldom held.

But in the Fall euphoria of 1965, before Communist infiltration escalated in response, there was a dramatic about-turn in the US military evaluation. Instead of the Communist victory once predicted for the end of 1965, or the countrywide 'collapse' envisaged only weeks earlier, the war was now not only winnable but a victory date was anticipated. Westmoreland, however, was still concerned that Washington might miscalculate the cost. He was nervous about an 'incredible' conversation – recorded in his memoirs – in which his predecessor, General Paul Harkins, had been asked by Defense Secretary McNamara, ' "Paul, how long will it take to pacify this country?" General Harkins replied, "Mr Secretary, I believe we can do it in six months. If I am given command of the Vietnamese, we can reverse this thing immediately." '

On taking over the command, Westmoreland was reassured by the Defense Secretary that the resources of the United States were at his disposal. Though the American public knew nothing of this arrangement, Westmoreland says in the interview for this history that 'I was told by Mr McNamara on innumerable occasions that I should ask for the troops I felt needed to bring about the end result. I should not worry about public opinion. I should not worry about the economy. I should not even concern myself as to the availability of the troops. His direction to me was to ask for the resources I needed to carry out a military mission.'

Westmoreland records that he and McNamara had agreed during the summer to seventy-one battalions – or twice the number of troops which President Johnson had just announced as the force to be dispatched. Now, as the year ended with 180,000 troops in place or en route, Westmoreland was preparing personally to confront the President and the Defense Secretary with a request for a 1966 force level of 102 battalions – twenty-three of them to be drawn from five Allied nations, including Australia and New Zealand, which were assumed to be readily supportive. Westmoreland was asking for 429,000 American troops by the end of 1966.

On the assumption that he had 'unrestricted use of American troops' Westmoreland had prepared a tactical timetable for victory. He believed that the first large contingent of US forces would serve to halt both 'the swift disintegration' of the ARVN, and the Communist advance. He would have time to build a logistical base for an enlarged force and this phase would take to the end of 1965.

1966—U.S. soldiers pick their way through the landscape in the mountainous area close to the North Vietnamese border. Snipers are a never-ending danger.

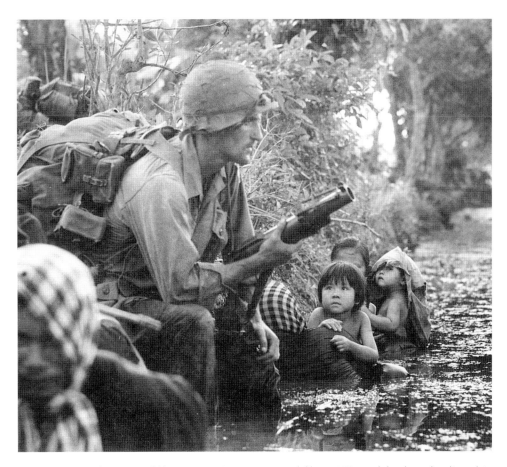

January 1, 1966—South Vietnamese children gaze at an American paratrooper holding an M79 grenade launcher as they cling to their mothers who huddle against a canal bank for protection from Viet Cong sniper fire as the 173rd Airborne brigade made a sweep in Bao Trai area, 20 miles west of Saigon.

January 8, 1966—Followed by tanks of the U.S. 1st Infantry Division, oxen strain to pull a Vietnamese farm family and a load of rice toward Trung Lap, 20 miles northwest of Saigon. The tanks were moving to support infantry units during a massive search for Viet Cong in the area.

In the second phase he would search out his enemy and destroy it in the jungle while the ARVN engaged in counter-insurgency in the villages, pacifying the countryside and winning hearts and minds. This two-fisted offensive – striking out with one hand at the Communist main forces while keeping a grip on the populace with the other – was to be applied with maximum force by mid-1966. The combination of fire-power and pacification would force the North Vietnamese to contemplate open battle or withdraw. If enemy infiltration persisted, then coupled with the bombing of the North a further eighteen months would be required for the destruction of Communist base areas – given the resources to do it. Following this third phase US forces would start withdrawing.

Whereas his predecessor had predicted victory in six months, Westmoreland was conditionally projecting it within two years, or by the end of 1967. He would later insist that he made no specific promises and that planning was predicated on there being no 'restraints', specifically that he would be permitted to attack Communist border 'sanctuaries' inside Laos and Cambodia. Pentagon records show that McNamara informed President Johnson, 'The course of action recommended stands a good chance of achieving an acceptable outcome within a reasonable time.' With this timetable Johnson agreed to the increased combat commitment without setting any ceiling on troop levels. The timetable apparently did not project how many US troops might be needed should Communist troop levels also rise.

Westmoreland says however that he knew the Communists were preparing to escalate the war.

January 29, 1966—A Vietnamese woman sits with her children near An Thi after she was wounded during an intense firefight between the U.S. 1st Air Cavalry Division and combined North Vietnamese and Viet Cong forces.

The US Commander had diligently studied Communist war methodology in Asia. Westmoreland's timetable was a counter to Mao Tse-tung's own classic three-phase strategy: 1. to base in distant inaccessible terrain; 2. to merge with and command the local population; 3. conventional warfare when the time was right. 'Everything indicated – the evidence was totally convincing', says Westmoreland, 'that the North Vietnamese were on the verge of phase three: to move into conventional war, which is subsequently what they did. There were battalion, regimental, even division-sized units coming down from the North.'

But despite this knowledge the US Command felt that it had the situation in hand as 1966 began. In the largest yet 'Search and Destroy' mission, the Marines and the 1st Cavalry linked up after a North-South sweep on the central province of Binh Dinh. The awkward moment came at the start of what was called Operation Masher. President Johnson, seldom cautious with his epithets, 'objected' that Masher was a bit much. Two angelic words were added and when Operation Masher/White Wing was over Westmoreland's MACV command reported a 'body-count' of 2389. His phase two tactic of massive attrition was now well-advanced. The new 'big unit' campaign was beginning to look invincible, and for once the military had few vociferous critics. As America's first combat year ended General Westmoreland was *Time* magazine's Man of the Year.

William Childs Westmoreland – 'Westy' to his friends and to his men – was First Captain of his West Point class of 1936. At graduation he ranked 112 out of 276 in overall academic studies but was eighth in tactics. He was considered 'born to be a general'; certainly he grew up with an acute sense of American military history. His family had served in the Civil War and still tended to fight it. He records in his memoirs that when he told a great-uncle who was a die-hard Confederate that he was attending the same school that 'Grant and Sherman went to' there was a long silence, then: 'All right, son – Robert E. Lee and Stonewall Jackson went there, too.' Westy's campaigns began as an artillery officer in North Africa, then Sicily, then the Utah Beach in Normandy in 1944. With the rank of Colonel he was Chief of Staff of the 9th Infantry Division in Germany until 1945; then Brigadier-General commanding the 187th Airborne Regiment in Korea 1952-53. At the age of fifty-one, his all-round experience led to four-stars and Vietnam in 1964.

For Westmoreland soldiering meant a textbook loyalty and code. One of his first directives in Vietnam was that every soldier should carry at all times written rules of conduct towards civilians, yet his critics would say his tactics brought horrendous civilian suffering. Westmoreland, though in uniform for almost thirty years when he went to Vietnam, was no military crusader. He appeared sceptical of the political rhetoric of policing the world, even doubtful of the specific cause. He wrote that during the political chaos in South Vietnam 'between 1963 and 1965 . . . the United States could have severed its commitment with justification and honor, though not without strong political reaction at home'. Yet given the assignment, only tradition prevailed: 'A soldier', he says, 'must be prepared to cope with the hardships of war and bear its scars.' He had known the most famous American generals of the era –

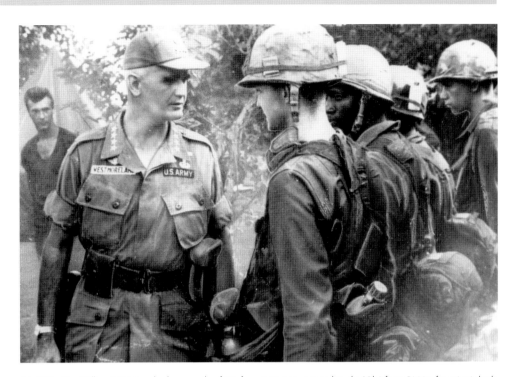

July 1966—Gen. William C. Westmoreland, commander of U.S. forces in Vietnam, congratulates the 25th Infantry Division for action in battle during Operation Paul Revere in which they defeated an overwhelming Viet Cong force.

April 1, 1966—Television covers the war as a crew from the ABC network rides on top of a tank of the U.S. 25th Infantry Division west of Pleiku.

**293**

Pershing, Patton, Eisenhower, Stilwell, MacArthur – and now their sons and grandsons were serving under him in Vietnam. He was the inheritor; he carried the baton, and Lyndon Johnson would describe his mission as 'the most complex war in all American history'.

With his assignment Westmoreland had sought out General Douglas MacArthur and the 'old soldier' had told him: 'Do not overlook the possibility that in order to defeat the guerrilla you may have to resort to a scorched earth policy'. MacArthur urged him always to have 'plenty of artillery, for the Oriental greatly fears artillery'.

Westmoreland recalls getting a quite different reading from the outgoing US Commander in Vietnam, General Harkins, who veering from optimism to pessimism would 'constantly' quote a version of Kipling:

> The end of the fight is a tombstone white,
> With the name of the late deceased.
> And the epitaph drear, a fool lies here
> Who tried to hustle the East.

'I'm very fond of Kipling because he's a soldier's poet,' says Westmoreland, but he confesses, 'I didn't take it quite to heart.' After all, neither Kipling nor even MacArthur – no one in the history of war – had ever known the mobility and fire-power that Westmoreland now had.

'The most spectacular development', he considers, 'was the coming of age of the helicopters. It saved innumerable lives through air evacuation. It gave us a battlefield mobility that we never dreamed of years previously.' With the helicopter – and MacArthur's advice in mind – Westmoreland devised a system of hilltop artillery fortifications called firebases, positioned in remote areas and supplied by air. From these, forward infantry patrols – protected by the artillery – would act as bait, seeking contact with the enemy, then calling in the helicopter 'Search and Destroy' battalions. The firebases, says Westmoreland, were 'designed to channel the enemy into well-defined corridors where we might bring air and artillery to bear and then hit him with mobile ground forces'.

By early 1966 the war had taken strange new forms and a new language which tended to camouflage the grim business of attrition. The 'Daisy-Cutter' – a 15,000 lb monster bomb – would blow a hole on a hilltop 300 feet in diameter or 'the size of the Rosebowl' to create an instant firebase. 'Jolly Green Giants' – Sikorsky helicopters – would ferry in huge 105mm howitzers and this artillery would glint in star formation from the heart of the jungle, thundering in every direction. American forces and imagery rapidly pervaded every area and aspect of the country as Westmoreland built his logistical base. The 'Big Red One' or 1st Infantry Division and 'Tropic Lightning' or the 25th Infantry now formed a 'donut' defense for thirty miles around Saigon. The 'Ivy' or 4th Infantry had joined the 'Cav' in the Central Highlands and the Marines (who preferred to be called just that) were on SOS – 'Strongpoint Obstacle System' or firebases – with South Korean 'Tiger' and 'White Horse' brigades helping seal the coastline.

Westmoreland still felt a general concern about the ARVN, now largely confined to village defense in populated areas, and he expressed particular disbelief when told that one South Vietnamese divisional commander would only contemplate battle if

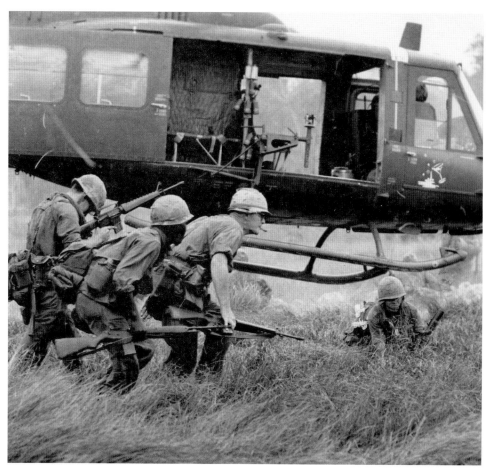

April 1966—U.S. infantrymen hurry across a jungle clearing during a helicopter landing 70 miles northwest of Saigon near the Rach Beng River on the Cambodian border. The 1st Battalion, 2nd Infantry Division was attacking Viet Cong supply points, and captured or destroyed hundreds of tons of equipment and supplies.

so advised by his astrologer, but the US military found comfort in its catalogue of fire-power. Very soon 'Riverine' gunboats were sweeping the Delta; squadrons of giant 'Rome' plows, looking like a centurion's prong, were trying piecemeal to bulldoze the jungle; 'Agent Orange' defoliants were burning off the foliage; 'People Sniffers' or electronic sensors shaped like small trees were strewn over the forests to transmit sounds of men or vehicles, while 'Huey' platoons vaulted from sighting to sighting supported by the new 'Cobras' of the jungle – helicopter gunships with nose-painted fangs. At night there was 'Spooky', a prop-plane carrying enough flares to floodlight a mile radius while firing 6000 rounds a minute and also known as 'Puff, the Magic Dragon'.

But there was the dilemma over much of the rural area of how to direct all this fire-power. Some districts with villages known to be under guerrilla control were declared 'Free Fire Zones' in which anyone could be shot. Villages suspected of aiding the enemy could be ordered destroyed by the search commander. By now the sweep operations, and the difficulty of distinguishing between the guerrilla and the black-clad villager, were producing quite different casualties. In a follow-up to Operation Masher/White Wing in the densely populated coastal region of Binh Dinh, the US military summarized the fire-power deployed. B-52 strikes coupled with a staggering 1126 fighter-bomber sorties unloaded 1.5 million pounds of bombs, and 292,000 pounds of napalm. From off-

shore, navy gunships offered support. The operation left 1884 refugees. An additional 10,779 had been previously evacuated from areas under guerrilla control. By 1967 Communist captives numbered 17,000. But by then civilian refugees had reached 1.2 million. 'Search and Destroy' was earning the acronym SAD.

'It was an unfortunate choice of words,' says one of its architects, General William DePuy. 'What it meant back in 1965, long before it became unpopular, was simply that US units or Vietnamese airborne units and marine units would patrol in the jungle – not in the populated areas – to search for the main force Communist units, fight them and destroy them.' But as the war enlarged and enveloped South Vietnam's 16,000 villages the tactic 'became associated with pictures of troops searching villages and setting them on fire. The word "destroy" became a dirty word. It started out with the best of intentions.'

General Westmoreland would admit to being warned that in the television age he was his 'own worst enemy' in using the discredited phrase. The times dictated that generals, much like politicians, be media-conscious, but Westmoreland no longer considered the press 'closer to the truth'. In an article entitled 'A Military War of Attrition' he charged that 'a few graphic newspaper photographs and TV shots of American troops setting fire to thatched-roof huts were enough to convince many that "search and destroy" operations were laying waste to the land.' He says the opera-

April 12, 1966—A South Vietnamese soldier watches over the wrapped bodies of other Vietnamese government troops slain in a battle with the Viet Cong. The bodies were lined up for helicopter evacuation.

tions were 'directed primarily against military installations – bunkers, tunnels, rice and ammunition caches, and training camps'.

To Westmoreland – believing that he had adhered to General MacArthur's guideline that the military code 'has come down to us from even before the age of knighthood and chivalry' – the criticism was unjust. 'Search and Destroy' was only the tactical element of the 'hearts and minds' strategy. The countryside could not be pacified until it was cleared, and 'the people living in those [burned] villages were humanely relocated'. Speaking with the gravity of a man taking an oath, he says: 'As one who has fought in three wars, I can say categorically that never in the history of warfare, certainly never in the history of American arms, has more attention been given to the avoidance of civilian casualties than we did in Vietnam.'

But between principle and practice lay the different perspective of the High Command and the foot soldier. Hardly any of the veterans interviewed for this history expressed any great concern for civilians in combat situations – if only because they were never certain who among the people were friends or foes. Frustration, fear and moment to moment concern for survival outweighed all else, and an alien land and culture completed what Captain Brian Jenkins remembers as 'the Fort Apache mentality' among American combat troops. In a fairly typical comment he says that for the GI 'going outside of his military base, wherever it was, was going into Indian country, and the safety catch comes off the rifle and there was a great willingness to react with force'.

Modern revolutionary war was not within MacArthur's experience: it did not allow for chivalry or even much compassion. 'It was, in essence, a war of attrition,' wrote Westmoreland, and '. . . there was no alternative to "search and

January 4, 1966—A U.S. paratrooper walks away after setting fire to a house on the banks of the Vaico Orientale River, 20 miles west of Saigon. Civilians were relocated, then houses and crops burned in a scorched earth operation against the Viet Cong.

destroy" operations.' Yet the paradox was more glaring with each operation. By 1968 the effort to secure the people had resulted in no less than one third of the population being uprooted from their ruined or abandoned ancestral villages: this was the number who had been 'relocated' apart from the wandering refugees. There was the question of how 'humane' this could possibly be, and anyhow the cost could only be acceptable if the strategy could also be measured. That became the larger question.

In his subsequent study of attrition, Westmoreland wrote that as a strategy it had been in 'disrepute' since the battles of the Somme and Verdun and it 'appeared particularly unsuited for a war in Asia with Asia's legendary hordes of manpower. Yet if one carefully re-examines the strategy of attrition in World War I. one must admit that, for all the horrendous cost, it eventually worked. Furthermore, the war in Vietnam was not against Asian hordes but instead against an enemy with

March 9, 1966—As helicopters deliver more men, troops of the U.S. 173rd Airborne Brigade use rubber boats to cross the Song Be River at the edge of War Zone D, a Communist stronghold 20 miles northeast of Saigon.

relatively limited manpower.' In fact, year by year. North Vietnam would closely match American troop deployment until the US tired. World War I. of course, had clear-cut cause: Europe was integral to America's identity, the source of its sons and its first line of defense. More specifically, it was a war fought for territory: the horrendous could be measured; the dead could be tallied. Military historians may judge that in Vietnam US mobility and fire-power deployed at random – 'search and destroy' rather than seize and hold – produced only the illusion of progress. If so, then the miscalculations appear to persist.

'Victory', says General William DePuy, 'goes to the side that is able to concentrate its forces at a critical place at a critical time on the battlefield.' He can therefore argue that America was militarily victorious in Vietnam, though from Hanoi's point of view it was the long-term political strategy and not military tactics that would decide the war. DePuy, a senior deputy to Westmoreland, had a large role in the early planning of 'Search and Destroy'. Known as a skilled commander, he would lead some of the largest offensive operations of the war. He gives a concise picture of how the opposing forces maneuvered. The cardinal principle of the guerrillas was never to attack unless able to concentrate superior force, and in choosing when to attack towns and communications the guerrilla 'has all the advantage', but DePuy says that helicopter mobility 'went a long way toward turning that around'.

'We were able', he says, 'to put very small units, platoons and companies, sometimes smaller patrols, out into the jungle to find and fight. And then from the first shot and every minute there-

after the advantage turned in our favor, because the Viet Cong or the NVA were seldom able to reinforce. They started the battle with whatever they had. But every minute we would be able to bring in fighters, attack helicopters, artillery and then additional troops by helicopter. So it reversed what was an exclusive advantage to the guerrilla, and when used well it resulted in frustration for the guerrilla and victory for our own army.

'There were many occasions where we were able to bring in – in the course of a short battle, and most battles were short: maybe an hour or so – two or three battalions. In addition to all the air force fighters and the artillery and the attack helicopters.'

The GI patrols, or 'Grunts', provide a less enthused description. The VC or 'Charlie' knew American tactics well enough never to stay and fight unless trapped. He had no territory to defend, no fixed base; Charlie could float – he was nicknamed 'ghost' – and at night would strike at the firebases where often the Grunts on guard would mutter, 'The ghosts are out there – the ghosts are coming.' On patrol, the GIS were inviting certain ambush beyond the range of the firebase artillery. The guerrillas would recede then advance, biding their time while the patrols searched and searched.

Major Joe Anderson was an exception in Vietnam: he served two years. In 1966, on his first duty tour, he commanded a platoon of the elite 1st Cavalry. 'We very seldom knew', he says, 'exactly where the enemy was and so it was almost always a case of us stumbling on to them and then perhaps following up with a major operation – an immediate reaction force.' That, he agrees. 'was

the great value of the helicopter'. But it was a strict gamble as to which side got mauled, recalls Lieutenant Jim Webb.

The Marine officer – and future author on Vietnam – led numerous patrols, called 'dangling the bait'. 'We had our mission – a sort of military mission – saturation patrolling. We would dive into an area, set up as a company, and platoons would patrol out from the company operation base, hoping to make contact. It was almost like seducing the enemy into making contact with you. Then you could fix the position and bring in other units and supporting arms – and destroy, which is very nice when you start tallying numbers on a tote board but which can be really devastating for the smaller units.'

The guerrillas simply avoided patrols operating within the safety perimeter of the firebase, and deep patrols of company size could never be sure of what they would encounter. Major Anderson remembers when one company 'happened to land in the midst of a North Vietnamese battalion' and 'when the Americans unloaded from the helicopters, they were destroyed: twenty-two out of twenty-seven were killed on the spot'. The survivors radioed their position and Anderson's company '*moved through the rest of the day into the night to reach them* [author's italics]'. A major engagement developed. 'We looked on it as a victory,' says Anderson, 'but it was a very tragic loss for the platoon that we went to rescue.'

As Anderson would say later, 'Looking for all the support we could get, there was never too much fire-power.' But for the forward patrols – essential to 'Search and Destroy' – fire-power could only save them, not shield them. A large

Top Right: February 14, 1966—U.S. troops exchange fire with the enemy in the area known as "Hell's Half Acre," about 30 miles northwest of Saigon.

Center: February 14, 1966—A U.S. infantryman shouts down the line as fellow soldiers return fire against camouflaged snipers north of Cu Chi. The 25th Division was attempting to expand its perimeter in the area known as "Hell's Half Acre," about 30 miles northwest of Saigon.

Below: January 28, 1966—Meeting no resistance, U.S. Marines move up the beach south of Quang Ngai in a major amphibious assault, believed to be the largest since the Korean War.

factor in this in-and-out tactic was the assumption that mobility would minimize American casualties. However, a careful study of the statistics shows that before any decisive fire-power and Medevac helicopters could be called in, US forces paid a higher price in Vietnam. Ambush and face to face combat involving primitive weapons and small arms caused half the American deaths in Vietnam compared to one third in World War II and Korea. (In Vietnam, however, the US survival rate for the seriously wounded was the highest of any modern war due to helicopter evacuation and advanced medical facilities, which, included portable field hospitals. In Vietnam, eighty-two per cent of the seriously wounded were saved, compared to seventy-one per cent in World War II and seventy-four per cent in Korea. On the other hand, the US suffered in Vietnam, largely from ambush, some 10,000 amputees – more than in World War I and Korea combined for American forces.)

Crude but deadly hand-made weapons used as booby-traps often proved the most destructive. After the unreality of his early beach patrols, infantryman Tim O'Brien would find carnage in the jungle, while seldom finding the enemy. Grenades were turned into tiny landmines almost impossible to detect, buried in tin cans with a trip wire: these were 'toepoppers'. but others would shred their victims. 'The most feared mine', O'Brien remembers 'was the "Bouncing Betty". It was conical shaped, three prongs jutting out of the soil. When your foot hit the prong, a charge went off that shot the mine into the air, a yard high, showering shrapnel everywhere. It's a mine that goes after the lower torso: a terrible mine.'

The guerrillas made huge mines from converted mortar and artillery shells. O'Brien saw the results. On one occasion after his company had encamped and sent out patrols there was a large explosion only 200 yards away. Says O'Brien, 'I put out a radio call but no answer – and the captain was kind of joking, saying it was probably just a stray artillery round. Half an hour later one of the survivors hobbled back and said, "They're gone – they're all gone." We raced out there and only two men were living out of a patrol of eight or so. Just a mess. It was like a stew, full of meat and flesh and red tissue and white bone.'

The search missions were therefore very much a two-edged sword, for while the American tactic depended on contact, the guerrilla – particularly in more populated areas – had only to know or anticipate the American patrol routes or pattern. The

May 14, 1966—A U.S. sergeant of the 101st Airborne Brigade displays one of the Chinese-made heavy machine guns that kept his company pinned down for nearly six hours along the Cambodian border 90 miles northeast of Saigon. Five-man teams eventually crawled through the jungle to knock the guns out with grenades.

Undated—Viet Cong guerillas set up a trap of spiked wooden sticks in a rice paddy.

high US death rate *without actual combat* (about eleven per cent killed in ambush) would greatly contribute to the later breakdown of American military discipline and morale, leading to frequent mutiny on patrols and the 'fragging' or murder of unpopular officers, and increasingly a venting of frustration on civilians which – in an uncensored war, and media advances effectively render all contemporary war uncensored – was the most self-defeating aspect of all. By the end of 1967, with the worst fighting to come, US combat deaths again tripled within one year to more than 16,000.

At this juncture the 'enclave' policy of 'waiting and waiting' until there was a negotiated settlement seemed to its advocates the right but irretrievable course. The struggle was still one for military control; until this was achieved the political objective, of village pacification, would be as elusive as the enemy. Short of enlarging the war (which would become the recommendation) some basic questions had now to be posed: 1. were the patrols sufficiently effective to warrant the tactics; 2. was the rank-and-file leadership experienced enough to conduct a counter-guerrilla war; 3. were mobility and fire-power offset by inappropriate fighting techniques; and 4. allowing for corrective measures in these areas, was the basic strategy sound: was the opponent really being attrited?

On the question of patrols Major Joe Anderson, one of the longest serving and most decorated officers, describes his platoon as 'professional . . . quite anxious and willing to come in

contact with the enemy' but the contacts 'were rather infrequent'. 'During the months that I was a platoon leader in the field,' says Anderson, 'there were probably only four or five significant contacts in that whole period. Other times there would be fleeting engagements but no real fights.'

Anderson, a black officer, emphasizes that Americans in Vietnam would always accept and follow experienced leadership. Another black veteran, Marine Corps rifleman Charles Johnson, considers that inexperienced officers were a losing factor. Johnson was eighteen – the average infantry age – when he arrived in Vietnam in 1967. He was part of a 'roving battalion', meaning 'we went where the action was or wherever they needed a unit to plug the gap'. He had the most hazardous job in his platoon – 'walking point' as the advance man. He was wounded twice and decorated twice – receiving his second 'Purple Heart' personally from President Johnson – but the experiences of foot-soldier Johnson would subsequently necessitate psychiatric treatment for ten years.

On an early jungle patrol Johnson found that his company commander was not only 'fresh from the United States, he was fresh from Officer School.' With rations for only one day's patrol 'we stayed in the bush for three days and three nights simply because we were lost. This gentleman wouldn't listen to anyone. I know for a fact that we crossed the same river three times and I made every attempt to indicate that to him, but of course I had no jurisdiction as to which way we should go.'

Against a hostile terrain and an opponent who had lived and fought in it for years, the US with its reliance on mobility and technology gave its men officers who often had no combat experience and who, in the majority of cases, were rotated after six months – or half the duty tour of the men whose lives they commanded. General Westmoreland is highly critical of this: 'It may have been that the career management people in the Pentagon, who wanted to give every career officer enough tour for

a command experience, encouraged that. There was a far greater turnover among commanders than I would like to have seen.'

Military analyst Brian Jenkins feels that 'many people in the American military' regarded Vietnam as 'the exotic interlude between the wars that really count – World War II in the past and World War III in the future'. He contends that even the one-year duty tour for enlisted men made no sense: it improved morale but, he predicted, would only produce 'high-morale losers'. The US Army was 'like a recording tape that is erased every twelve months. It condemns us to learning the same lessons over and over again.' A long-time Special Forces officer, Jenkins had joined Westmoreland's MACV headquarters staff as a member of its Long Range Planning Task Group. He prepared numerous written critiques (which he felt went unread) for MACV, and later for the Rand Corporation. Among the higher echelon, Jenkins says, 'there was a tendency to simply say that Vietnam was not worth it. To put it in the words of one senior military commander, "I'll be damned if I see the US army, its history, its doctrine, its institutions, alter just to win this lousy war". And that attitude, of course, was a tremendous impediment to making the kinds of changes that some thought were necessary; doctrinal changes in the style of fighting.'

On this next related question of fighting techniques, Captain Dave Christian says that for all the rapid deployment the US in Vietnam was 'fighting a defensive war' – airlifting in every support mechanism. Christian's unit was part of the 1st Battalion/26th Infantry command of General Alexander Haig, later NATO Supreme Commander and US Secretary of State from 1981. Christian, who has seven of the highest medals to show for his multiple wounds and who twice received the last rites on the battlefield, says that large infantry units when deployed were like 'a herd of elephants coming'; the guerrillas would go to ground – literally, in huge tunnel complexes – letting the Americans 'walk right through and then when they were through set up camp again'. In Christian's view the new airmobile support system was 'outmoded' in Vietnam.

Even when deployed in force, says analyst Brian Jenkins, US infantry was 'fighting the last war' or worse. 'They carried an enormous amount of equipment; just far more than was necessary. It was burdensome in the environment, in the climate, to move.' The doctrine was of old: '. . . two companies up and one back; almost eighteenth-century style of fighting'. This seemed 'belied' by the helicopters, but 'on the ground it was a very ponderous thing'.

As might be expected, the North Vietnamese view of Westmoreland's tactics is wholly negative: Premier Pham Van Dong at the time likened the American soldier to a blind heavyweight boxer and 'the heavier he is, the easier target he becomes'. Yet the analysis of Colonel Ha Van Lau hardly differs from that of American critics. 'The GI was a fighter that we believed had a certain technical and theoretical molding,' he says. 'He was very well equipped and trained. Nevertheless, in terms of being a fighter in a sophisticated army like the American army he didn't adapt easily. Heavily equipped, the GI didn't get around easily and made himself a vulnerable target for guerrillas. Can you imagine a GI operation in the jungle which had fresh water flown in by helicopter? In these conditions the GI could not support for a long time the deprivations and the difficulties of war.'

On the one hand, searching out the smaller, roving Communist units was exacting a high cost on American forces and objectives; on the other hand, attacking large known enemy bases necessi-

Top Left: June 18, 1966—U.S. Special Forces troops cross a bamboo bridge hanging over a jungle stream near Dak To in the Central Highlands. The unit was trying to win support by bringing medical aid to Montagnard mountain tribesmen in an area infiltrated by North Vietnamese troops and local Viet Cong reinforcements.

Bottom Left: October 14, 1966—A heavily loaded soldier of the U.S. 1st Cavalry Division kneels briefly in the sand while searching for elements of a fleeing enemy battalion along the central coast of South Vietnam during Operation Irving.

October 1966—A U.S. Marine of the 2nd Battalion, 5th Marine Regiment, carries a rocket and launcher across a monsoon-swollen creek south of the demilitarized zone.

tated enormous effort for marginal results. As Westmoreland himself notes, the US had 'the military muscle' to go in and 'disrupt' these bases. It did not have the means to occupy them and disruption, on whatever scale, could therefore only be a temporary setback. One of the largest and longest US offensives was Operation Attleboro (September-November 1966) against the heavily forested war zone C, spreading north and west of Saigon towards the Cambodian border. Westmoreland describes what it took to attack a base area 'developed over a period of decades'.

'The Vietnamese, before we arrived,' he says, 'would never dare go in there because it was totally dominated by the enemy. The enemy had great tunnel complexes in there. They had their headquarters well dug in and camouflaged. They had their supply dumps there. And it was necessary for us to go in and disrupt that – but you couldn't go in with companies or battalions. They would have been chewed up, ambushed and decimated. It took a massive troop effort to go in there with safety and get the job done with minimum losses.'

The operation was launched. Westmoreland deployed 22,000 men. Within hours the helicopters had lifted in the equivalent of two divisions. 'Dust Off' helicopters brought out the wounded from initial scattered resistance. After artillery and air force pounding, the troops searched for bunkers. GIS called 'tunnel rats' sealed the entrances with hand grenades, then pumped acetylene gas into suspected tunnel-complexes, detonating the gas with dynamite. But left-wing journalist Wilfred Burchett, who briefly stayed under fire in this Communist base, says the tunnels were a series of sealed chambers, each elaborately constructed with bamboo, and in just one underground area which he observed 'this particular tunnel extended for about twenty kilometers' with numerous side branches. He was told 'if things get too hot here we can come out under another village' and enter another complex, and 'there was nothing to worry about'. Operation Attleboro lasted seventy-two days. According to US military records there were '1106 known enemy casualties', hardly more than from the original three-day Chu Lai action.

Was the strategy of attrition working? As military analyst Brian Jenkins puts it: 'Ultimately the superiority of weapons would prevail. Hard fought battles were ultimately won. But that was the whole point – if the opponent wanted to give battle it would have been an easy military contest. The other part is that the military success did not translate into political success.' Or there was no territorial gain.

By mid-1967 the US force level in Vietnam had risen to 431,000, and Westmoreland had Defense Secretary McNamara's approval for a troop ceiling of 543,000. But McNamara – now privately doubting the war's cost effectiveness – wanted clearer evidence that additional troops were necessary. Attrition of the enemy, the only measure of any eventual political success, had to be proved. 'I desire and expect', McNamara told Westmoreland, 'a detailed line by line analysis of these requirements to determine that each is truly essential.'

'Mr McNamara', says Westmoreland, 'was very strong on statistics; as a businessman that was his main tool.' In the General's words there were not enough troops to occupy 'the real estate and nail it

Above: Schematic drawing shows the layout of a huge Viet Cong tunnel complex in the Iron Triangle about 25 miles from Saigon. U.S. Army tunnel rats explored the tunnel which may have been headquarters for the Viet Cong local military region. Searchers found 18 graves, rifles and pistols, maps, diagrams, and detailed plans of past attacks.

Left: July 31, 1965—A U.S. paratrooper of the 173rd Airborne Brigade crawls from a Viet Cong tunnel at Long Cat after setting explosive charges to destroy the tunnel.

Top Left: January 1967—Pfc. Jerry L. Lawson of Phoenix, Ariz., a "tunnel rat," emerges from a Viet Cong tunnel in the Hobo Woods, 25 miles northeast of Saigon. The unit of the 25th Infantry Division had earlier uncovered enemy maps, documents, weapons, and 18 graves, leading to the suspicion that the tunnel was part of a Viet Cong headquarters.

Top Right: 1966—A combined operation of American and Vietnamese troops locate a cache of Viet Cong weaponry in an extensive tunnel complex. The cache included 20,000 rounds of ammunitions and 700 weapons. The ammunition was removed and exploded, and the tunnel blasted closed.

Bottom Left: January 21, 1967—American trooper specializing in tunnel searches climbs out of a hole, silencer pistol in hand, after pursuing Viet Cong. GIs who specialize in this work are called tunnel rats. In this instance, nauseating gas was pumped into the tunnel complex to drive out the VC.

Bottom Right: April 18, 1966—A paratrooper of the 173rd Airborne Brigade crawls from an enemy tunnel about 60 miles north of Saigon near the Cambodian border. The Airborne troops uncovered several Viet Cong hideouts, including bunkers, tunnels, and air raid shelters.

down'; therefore 'it was not unreasonable to try to set up some rules of measurement as to progress and we had to do this and we had to report them on a weekly basis'. Westmoreland had been critical of his predecessor's optimistic reporting, and of inflated statistics by ARVN commanders, but now American forces found themselves in the position of being judged in a numbers game. It was easier to tell Washington what it presumably wanted to hear: indeed, careers, promotions, privileges might depend on it. The 'body-court' now became the measure of the war – a highly inflated one, it would later be admitted. MACV's unheard critic Brian Jenkins wrote 'tactics rather than strategy' are the measure; hence 'Good tactics are evidenced by a large number of enemy read on the battlefield.'

But the apparent rapid decimation of the enemy that followed at least had political value in the United States, where the burning of draft cards and an organized anti-war movement was developing. Senior planners like William Bundy were now beginning to worry that Vietnam might become an albatross' around the nation's neck. 'I can remember all too vividly,' says Bundy, 'that when the Korean war dragged on inconclusively a very great counter-tide grew up against this politically.' Bundy was prescient, and he felt a need more fully to 'explain to the country what was being done to keep support strong'. Westmoreland felt the same: he had long since advocated a program 'to get American people more emotionally involved and more appreciative of what was going on. But that suggestion was not accepted. There was a real fear . . . that the hawks would be stirred up.'

Yet the American people had to be told something. As President Johnson put it on television, 'Our American people, when we get in a contest of any kind, whether it's in a war or an election or in a football game, want it decided and decided quickly, and get in or get out, and they like for that curve [raising his arm] to rise like this, and they like for the opposition to go down [dropping his arm] like this.' The 'kill' curve would now rise dramatically if deceptively.

A study by the author of US military operations listing 500 or more 'known enemy casualties' shows that in 1966 only seventeen such operations were recorded; in 1967 there were twenty-eight and in the first half of 1968 (at the point President Johnson de-escalated the war and opened peace negotiations) there were twenty-five. Whereas Operation Attleboro, one of the largest offensives of the war in late 1966, resulted in 1106 enemy casualties, future comparable operations would report casualties ranging from 3000 to 10,000. Over the three-year period the official body-count in these operations rose from around 15,000 in 1966 to 50,000 in 1967 and to more than 50,000 by mid-1968. Though the number of such operations increased only fifty per cent in each period, the kill-claim increased more than 300 per cent. As Brian Jenkins says, 'There were no auditors of the system. The body-counts were enormously inflated.'

Jenkins, joining MACV headquarters with its pressure for a weekly death watch, recalls one operation in which 'nineteen dead could be verified – soldiers that had been killed, soldiers with weapons – and the estimate was that perhaps thirty had been killed'. But the estimate went through different reporting channels which dealt with it in

March 1967—U.S. infantrymen crawl over an insect hill while taking sniper fire in heavy jungle on the northern fringe of War Zone C near the Cambodian border. Viet Cong concealed in bunkers had ambushed the unit.

March 17, 1967—As a CH-47 Chinook helicopter hovers with an artillery piece, U.S. artillerymen of the 196th Light Infantry Brigade fire a 105mm howitzer in War Zone C during Operation Junction City, the biggest U.S. operation of the war to that point.

March 17, 1967—An Air Force B-57 Canberra swoops over a suspected Viet Cong jungle position in South Vietnam and drops its load of bombs.

an 'accumulative' fashion: so many may have been killed but not verified, so many may have died later from wounds, so many may have been killed in air strikes '. . . so that a relatively small engagement, in this particular case perhaps involving thirty casualties, would by the time it had been briefed at headquarters, and entered in the books, begin to approximate the Battle of the Bulge.'

At times the body-count was no more than black comedy. Corporal Matt Martin grew up in a rough area of Philadelphia and volunteered for the Marines – and for a second year in Vietnam. He spent half the time on active duty and says 'The more regular you were, regular Marine, regular army, the higher the body-count was. We had a colonel call in and he was all excited, and he said. "What's the body-count, what's the body-count?" because we had called in a lot of heavy artillery, we were really putting the job on this one village. So he wanted a real heavy body-count. Well this second Louie we had with us – he'd come up through the ranks – and he yelled, "Over 300". So then the radio man said, "You can't give them an even number. They're not going to go for an even number". So he said "Well, okay, 311". Three hundred eleven flat out deaths, sure kills. Well this officer loved it. He started yelling "Great, great, you did a great job".

'Well actually what had happened was one of our jeeps had turned over and killed this old man. And we had one sure kill. And it was an accident.' Adds Martin. 'It was always better if you had a good kill count 'cause everything would come your way. You'd get better supplies; steaks, booze once in a while. Everything would come your way.' It should be noted that such individual accounts are impossible to verify, but Westmoreland himself subsequently agreed that the statistics 'were somewhat overdone.'

Yet in November 1967, Westmoreland on a visit to Washington publicly stated: 'I could quote a number of meaningful statistics such as the roads that are being opened, the increasing number of enemy that are being killed, the number of defectors that are coming in from the Communist side to the government, the numbers of weapons being captured, and other statistical information that we are making progress and we are winning.'

Responds Jenkins, 'In the absence of geographically measurable criteria, we substituted quantitative criteria, counting this and counting that, and according to those criteria we were always succeeding. We may not have won but we were always, in a sense, winning.' The MACV analyst says 'inflated body-counts' were a major factor in 'suggesting to us that we were doing better than we were'. But he points out that even had the figures been true the policy of attrition had 'an inherent flaw' by assuming that it would have a 'deterrent effect on the enemy – and that simply was not the case'. North Vietnam's leaders were 'prepared to fight to the year 2000'.

In Jenkins' analysis, the exaggerated measuring of the war arose from other problems fundamentally far more serious and with contemporary implications. There was the impatience for vic-

tory and the enormous commitment of resources, yet an inability to adapt military doctrine and command structure to the situation. The ultimate responsibility – and blame – lay with the political Cabinet in Washington, a failure of intelligence and authority; the culpability lay with the military which failed to advise change and indeed resisted it. In this Jenkins sees Westmoreland as the victim: '. . . his powers in some cases were quite limited' and there was 'a tremendous amount of interference' even at 'very low levels' from 'various entities in Washington. There were a good many people running that war. There was no American proconsul.'

Westmoreland was subordinate to the US Ambassador, and by extension various levels of the State Department, and to CINCPAC (Pacific) headquarters in Honolulu. The US Air Force, Navy and Marine Corps engaged in Vietnam were under the ultimate authority of CINCPAC – and were not loath to exploit this. The air war against the North was also commanded from CINCPAC with personal direction from President Johnson. General Westmoreland felt that he was not permitted the input and direction vital to the success of his mission.

'The responsibility of the war', he says, 'was a divided one. It was divided between the Ambassador and myself, and the Commander in Chief of the Pacific. I am somewhat critical of this because I feel that it would have been better if it could have been a unified effort – which would have gone contrary to some of the service doctrine."

The extent of division between the two senior US officials in Vietnam is only now revealed. Ambassador Henry Cabot Lodge subsequently expressed what could not be expediently voiced during his second posting to Saigon, 1965–67. 'I liked General Westmoreland and he's a great friend of mine,' says Lodge, 'but I thought we had a lot to learn from the way the British handled the situation in Malaysia. Sir Robert Thompson was an official advisor to us and he was also an official advisor to Sir Gerald Templar who was Chief of the British Mission (in former Malaya) and it took them twelve years to bring about a political and economic set up in Malaysia which would enable them to get order and keep it – but not if you did it in a hurry. It took them twelve years. The idea in our camp was that we haven't got the time; we've got to clean this thing up in not more than two years.

'Well you couldn't for many reasons. If you do it in twelve years and focus on the political and on the economic you reduce your casualties to very, very little – and you get lasting results. Well now, I don't think that that was what General Westmoreland thought, but that's what I thought.'

Ambassador Lodge implies that in the enlarged combat period Westmoreland subscribed to or had resigned himself to supporting this unreality. Westmoreland would tell the press in November 1967: 'The enemy has failed in achieving its objectives. We have succeeded in obtaining our objectives.' At the same time he was requesting 75,000 more troops. But in fairness Westmoreland had consistently warned Washington that it should prepare for – and counsel the public to expect – a protracted war. By 1967 the enlarged, undeclared and therefore uncensored war was by its very scale tilting to defeat. The media or the messenger could be blamed for videoing scenes of death and destruction, but it had little more to show: 'Hearts and Minds' was still an abstraction, and perhaps another apt acronym. Westmoreland felt that the press and domestic political repercussions – rather than his enemy – would defeat him unless there was an immediate all-out effort. America was succeeding but there had to be a big push before the public tired. He sensed that he had perhaps twelve months, certainly not twelve years.

Westmoreland would describe Sir Robert Thompson's advice. It was that 'American preoccupation with the enemy's big units was wrong, that the first priority should be to identify and break the guerrilla infrastructure [also advocated and belatedly tried by the CIA], thus denying the big units their sustenance'. But, says Westmoreland, 'Sir Robert's analysis of where the big units were getting their supplies was incomplete and oversimplified'. In his article on the strategy of attrition, Westmoreland points out two basic differences between the insurrections in Malaya and Vietnam. In Malaya 'the bulk of the insurgents were ethnic Chinese and thus were identifiable within the population' and 'there was no immunity for the insurgents in sanctuaries outside the country. It was not until Tet occurred [February 1968] that Sir Robert truly understood the magnitude and potential of the enemy's main forces.'

Westmoreland would break the Communist Tet Offensive – only to see America recoil from the cost: a vindication of his fears but not of his tactics. Tet would deliver what Westmoreland was now asking for – heightened confrontation, but prior to Tet the war would seem relatively slow paced, relatively acceptable, and the sudden escalation of a distant war would wipe out the years of effort. At Tet it could be argued that the Communists were doing what the British had advised the Americans to do: they were concentrating military force against towns and cities to try and break the government infrastructure and public morale. Until one side or other achieved this what meaning had military victories or setbacks? It was said of North Vietnam's General Vo Nguyen Giap that he lost many battles but never lost a war. In a revealing comment on the conceptual differences, General Westmoreland says: 'Throughout the war we never lost a battle. We had some companies that were badly hurt . . . but we did not lose a battle of consequence.' The point, of course, is that in a struggle of political ideas there is no battle of consequence until the final one.

Some of the criticism of Westmoreland would be extremely harsh – 'the most disastrous American general since Custer' says historian Arthur Schlesinger Jr. A fairer criticism would be that Westmoreland was in a no-win situation. A politically oriented war was not, anyhow, his mandate. He was just the assignee of a man in a hurry, President Johnson, whose directive was the proverbial 'Git thar fustest with mostest'. And the military restrictions placed on Westmoreland – however wise – allowed him no final battle. Yet until the very end of his command (June 1968) he was given whatever he asked for, and given to understand, he says, that he could geographically expand the war – even though Washington, as now clearly emerges, had begun to doubt both the arguments for more troops and fire-power and Westmoreland's direction of these.

The influential Secretary of the Navy, Paul Nitze, a confidant of Defense Secretary McNamara, describes Westmoreland: 'I know him to be an absolutely outstanding man, a man of great character and honor. So that isn't the question. The question at issue is whether he was as subtle a general and as wise in his dispositions and . . . in his actions as one could have hoped for.'

McNamara himself in June 1967 was quietly preparing the historic internal study of decision making and strategy, to be known as the *Pentagon Papers*. From 1966 he had become tormented by doubts. His principal Deputy Assistant at that time, Adam Yarmolinsky, says McNamara already believed that 'this was not a war that could be won, or not at a cost that could be justified either to the American people or to the jury of the civilized world. It was a terrible mistake to have gotten into it: that we had made it an issue when it should not have been an issue.'

The war leaders were telling the public one thing while knowing the actual picture to be very different. Johnson did not want to hear McNamara's doubts, dismissing them as 'a nervous breakdown,' and he did not want Westmoreland's enlarged war: he simply wanted the boys home, somehow, by this Christmas or the next. In Washington in July 1967, while telling the press that America was 'succeeding', Westmoreland discloses what occurred at a White House meeting with Johnson and McNamara.

Westmoreland, though publicly optimistic, had not stated when the war might be over. His earlier three-phase, two-year projection was always predicated, he claims, on the understanding that if needs be 'restraints' would be lifted. His new optimism coincided with a reduction in Communist battle activity (what proved to be one of Hanoi's cyclical moves to re-evaluate and rebuild, preceding the Tet Offensive). Now was the time for the big push and Westmoreland presented plans worked out with the Joint Chiefs of Staff: 'I had two troop lists; I had what I considered a minimum essential and then I had an optimum.' His minimum position was for a new ceiling of 543,400 troops to consolidate; his optimum was whatever were needed to take the ground war beyond South Vietnam.

'I was asked by Mr McNamara', Westmoreland says, 'how long it would take with those two increments to wind the war down. I said, with the minimum essential it will take at least five years, but my estimate is that if we had the optimum we could probably do it in three years. We could cut the Ho Chi Minh Trail; we could clean out the enemy sanctuaries in Cambodia, we could block his lines of supply by sea and by land, and we could also take action against those troops immediately north of the demilitarized zone.'

The US President was hearing a recommendation to invade North Vietnam while being told that even then victory was at least three years away. And, Westmoreland reveals, 'plans were prepared to do all of that'.

President Johnson, however, merely announced that '. . . the troops that General Westmoreland needs and requests – as we feel it necessary – will be supplied'. Johnson then authorized only the minimum increment. Johnson and McNamara would be portrayed as going along with military planning only to control it.

Says Assistant Secretary of State, William Bundy: 'Then, or at any other time when the question of American forces being used against the North itself came up, the arguments against doing so – to all of us in the Johnson administration – seemed overwhelming. It would change the whole nature of the war. It might or might not work militarily. We always thought there was a flash point along the way, as there had been in Korea, where if we moved against North Vietnam itself we would very likely see a massive Chinese counter-intervention with ground forces.'

Westmoreland's conclusion is that the US military would have won if 'it hadn't been for political decisions that prohibited that'. The military, he says, 'did not have the liberty to exercise the mobility we acquired starting in 1966. We didn't have the political authority to extend the battlefield. We had the capability.'

On the differences between the military and political authorities over limitations of the war, analyst Brian Jenkins wrote that the military 'could search for the flaws in its own doctrine' or it could 'try to save face with "stab in the back" theories'. In a 1970 government-commissioned study, Jenkins viewed the US military as being the victim in Vietnam of 'its own doctrinal and organizational rigidity'. He drew an accurate scenario in which US methods would be passed to the South Vietnamese and they would quickly lose. He challenged 'the view that the war in Vietnam is an aberration and does not represent the future demands that the army might have to face.' He caustically noted that if progress in war was to be judged by statistics then the military had ignored the ones that mattered: 'It has been demonstrated statistically that the enemy initiates contact most of the time and avoids it when he desires. He therefore controls his own rate of casualties, negating any strategy based upon attrition.'

Future wars involving direct national survival or territory would not likely be conventional ones; in other politically oriented wars which influence the ideological balance toward direct confrontation, the US – Jenkins was saying – was poorly prepared. 'The case can be made', he wrote, 'that superior fire-power and mobility have been perhaps irrelevant in this war.'

Though perhaps irrelevant to success in Vietnam, there was the paradox that in this war to 'defend the Free World' the expenditure of fire-power in fact endangered Western security. The research for this history shows that the sheer range of fire-power was often wasteful, duplicated and difficult to co-ordinate. For instance, navy guns did what the artillery firebases could do; helicopter mobility was slowed – or troop deployment held back – until the fighter-bombers had finished; each had to have a shot and each waited on the other. On a cost example, the artillery expended on any given day was 10,000 rounds or so. At $100 per shell, this minor fire-power alone cost a million dollars each day. It would certainly have been cheaper to have given each South Vietnamese the lump-sum equivalent of a lifetime earnings with the inducement to fight for this.

Perhaps the greatest question mark is whether the helicopter 'came of age' in Vietnam. In South Vietnam, the US lost 4865 helicopters, each costing about $250,000, destroyed by Communist ground fire only. In a truly conventional war, against an enemy with an air force, the helicopter would seem to offer no greater troop mobility except at horrendous cost. In Vietnam, the United States would spend 110 billion dollars over and above its normal defense costs.

A large part of this was unauthorized, and the cost was hurting Allied world security, says future Defense Secretary Melvin Laird: 'We were borrowing against our spare parts, ammunition, aircraft, ships. When I became Secretary of Defense [1969-73] I found over ten billion dollars worth of supplies and equipment that had not been funded and used in Vietnam. I found tremendous deficits that had been run up by robbing our NATO forces and robbing military equipment all over the world to support that activity of fighting now, paying later. And the effect that had on our domestic economy was very grave.'

Despite this situation, obviously long since evident to the Johnson administration, troop increases continued to be authorized and General Westmoreland would soon ask for another 200,000, arguing that he was having to fight a complex war 'on the cheap' (as he described it in Harper's magazine, November 1970), that the air war against the North and against the Ho Chi Minh Trail was ineffective, that he had to cut the infiltration routes (which a later joint US-South Vietnamese operation would fail to do) and that 'in any war you would try to attrite the enemy's ability to wage war. You try to break down the national will.' The military leaders would not accept the argument that it

could not be done and the political leaders could not afford to say it.

But they knew it. In the autumn of 1966, when US troop levels in Vietnam were 300,000 or about half of what they would rise to, and when accumulative US combat deaths were fewer than 7000 or one-seventh of what they would finally total, it was concluded that Communist infiltration could not be stopped. Former Pentagon planner Adam Yarmolinsky had then joined 'a study group working with a very effective staff'. North Vietnam was 'a giant funnel' with supplies pouring in via the Ho Chi Minh Trail, and Yarmolinsky's group 'tried to figure out' how bombing of the routes might change the results: 'And what we concluded, after trying all the possibilities that we could think of, was "No way".'

1966—North Vietnamese workers move heavy sacks of produce through the countryside. North Vietnam claimed that four such bicycle loads could transport one ton of material about 18 miles a day.

February 5, 1966—A Vietnamese woman sits by a U.S. soldier holding his head after a battle between the 1st Air Cavalry Division and the Viet Cong near Bong Son, 290 miles northeast of Saigon.

1966—A napalm strike erupts in a fireball near U.S. troops on patrol in South Vietnam.

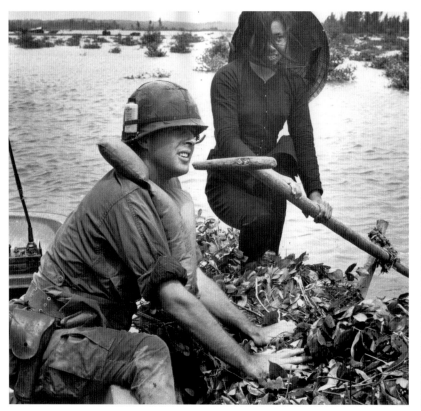

Above: 1966—A GI checks farm produce headed for market in the southern part of South Vietnam. Viet Cong sometimes smuggle military equipment by boat to the cities for use in terrorist attacks.

Right: 1966—Water-filled bomb craters from B-52 strikes against the Viet Cong mark the rice paddies and orchards west of Saigon. Most of the area has been abandoned by the peasants who used to farm on the land.

Above: 1966—American medical technician examines teeth of a young boy as part of the pacification program to win the loyalty of villagers in the fight against the Viet Cong.

Above Right: January 21, 1966—North Vietnamese President Ho Chi Minh, wearing a light military uniform and cap, celebrates the Lunar New Year with a visit in a North Vietnamese village.

Above: January 1966—Paratroopers of the 173rd Airborne Brigade watch for Viet Cong snipers as a village burns along the Vaico Oriental river, 20 miles west of Saigon. Troops evacuated the civilians, then set fire to the houses and fields to prevent use by the enemy.

Left: January 23, 1965—Buddhist monks and a nun stop a policeman from arresting a girl, seated, who attempted to smuggle a knife into the National Buddhist Institute in Saigon.

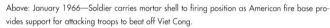

Above: January 1966—Soldier carries mortar shell to firing position as American fire base provides support for attacking troops to beat off Viet Cong.

Above Right: January 1966—GI machine gunner takes up a position behind a concrete gate.

Right: January 9, 1966—An American patrol scatters and ducks for cover as they corner under attack from Viet Cong snipers. The patrol sought to flush out Viet Cong positions in the area.

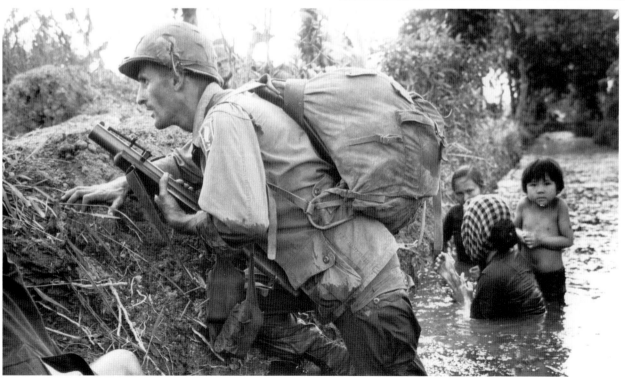

January 1, 1966—A U.S. paratrooper of the 173rd U.S. Airborne Brigade crouches with women and children in a muddy canal as intense Viet Cong sniper fire pinned down his unit near Bao Tri. The first U.S. casualties of 1966 occurred when the paratroopers hit immediate sniper fire during a New Year's Day assault on a densely populated Viet Cong stronghold along the Vaico River.

Above: January 1, 1966—Women and children crouch in a muddy canal as they take cover from intense Viet Cong fire at Bao Trai, about 20 miles west of Saigon. Paratroopers in the background escorted the South Vietnamese civilians through a series of firefights during the U.S. assault on a Viet Cong stronghold.

Right: January 29, 1966—Captured Viet Cong soldiers, tied and blindfolded, are kept in a sandy ditch awaiting evacuation for interrogation.

Above: Thomas Cole from Richmond, Virginia, a medic with the 1st Cavalry Division, wearing a bandage over the left side of his face, tends to an unidentified soldier in a trench during battle. The trench had been the first line of Viet Cong and North Vietnamese defense until it was taken by American forces.

Left: 1st Cavalry Division Medic Thomas Cole from Richmond, Virginia, wearing a bandage over the left side of his face, continues to treat a wounded Staff Sgt. Harrison C. D. Pell from Hazelton, Pennsylvania, in a trench during battle in South Vietnam's Central Highlands.

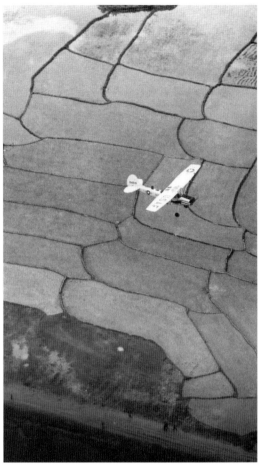

Above: January 17, 1966—A Vietnamese woman and three children take cover in a roadside ditch with soldiers of the U.S. 1st Infantry during a Viet Cong attack near Trung Lap, 20 miles northwest of Saigon. The U.S. convoy suffered light casualties.

Right: January 4, 1966—A U.S. spotter plane flies reconnaissance for South Vietnamese troops, bottom, advancing through flooded rice paddies to a Viet Cong outpost in Quang Ngai province.

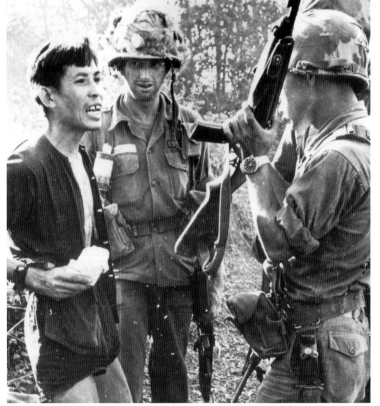

Above: January 31, 1966—A captured Viet Cong guerrilla is questioned by U.S. 1st Division soldiers during a day-long battle at An Thi.

Left: January 1966—Bombs are unloaded at Cam Ranh Bay on South Vietnam's central coast. The base was quickly built to accommodate the heavy shipping demands of the war effort.

January 28, 1966—U.S. Marines wade ashore south of Quang Ngai in what was described as the biggest amphibious assault since the landing at Inchon during the Korean War. About 4,000 craft of the U.S. 7th fleet participated.

January 30, 1966—Three officers of the U.S. 27th Infantry Regiment, 25th Division, take a coffee break as smoke rises from U.S. napalm and bomb strikes outside their encampment near Co Chi, 25 miles northwest of Saigon.

1966—Defense Secretary Robert S. McNamara talks with South Vietnamese Chief of State Nguyen Van Thieu as President Lyndon B. Johnson carries on another conversation with Nguyen Cao Ky.

January 28, 1966—A wounded Viet Cong guerrilla is captured by the U.S. 1st Cavalry Division during a firefight near An Thi.

June 28, 1966—A wounded GI is caught in sniper fire during an action near An Thi along with other American soldiers. They were trapped as they crossed a rice paddy.

June 28, 1966—Caught in heavy sniper fire, this GI hugs the dike of a swampy rice paddy until covering fire can let him escape.

June 28, 1966—A U.S. soldier helps his buddy as they rush to escape withering sniper fire in action near An Thi, along Vietnam's central coast.

Above Left: January 29, 1966—Soldiers of the U.S. 1st Air Cavalry Division advance on entrenched Viet Cong positions near An Thi on South Vietnam's central coast. The battle lasted about 24 hours.

Above Right: January 29, 1966—Troops of the U.S. 1st Air Cavalry Division take cover in the hills near An Thi, along the central coast of South Vietnam, after day-long fighting in Operation Masher.

Left: 1966—A senior American soldier waits out an air strike against enemy troops at An Thi.

Right: 1966—Taking a break while on patrol, these American troops take their relaxation in the relative safety of a ditch.

Below: 1966—U.S. troops take cover in a sandy ditch while under fire from Viet Cong snipers.

Above Left: January 1966—Winging past a bomb explosion from another Crusader jet, a U.S. Marine VMFAW-312 goes after the Viet Cong near Danang who were dropping mortar fire on landing zones used by Marine helicopters.

Above Right: February 14, 1966—Skirmish line of infantrymen of the U.S. 25th Division throw grenades and fire weapons near a Cu Chi rubber plantation. The soldiers sought to drive back Viet Cong forces and expand the division's perimeter.

Above: February 14, 1966—Two Marines help a wounded mate to an evacuation helicopter after he was wounded battling Viet Cong at rubber plantation near Saigon.

Left: February 14, 1966—U.S. troops exchange fire with the enemy in the area known as 'Hell's Half Acre,' about 30 miles northwest of Saigon.

Above: February 27, 1966—A U.S. paratrooper of the 173rd Airborne Brigade sits with his head in his hands after an intense and costly firefight with entrenched Viet Cong guerrillas.

Right: February 1966—A South Vietnamese Special Forces team moves downriver near the Cambodian border, firing at the Viet Cong snipers along the banks during a patrol from the camp at Cai Cai, 90 miles west of Saigon.

Above: February 1966—Soldiers of the South Vietnam Liberation Army (Viet Cong) are "ready to defend against U.S. aggressors," according to the caption of this photo released in Hungary.

Left: February 1966—U.S. Air Force F-105 Thunderchief fighter-bombers drop bombs on North Vietnam.

Above Left: 1966—A U.S. Air Force reconnaissance plane photographed this compound 25 miles northwest of Hanoi. It was described as a surface-to-air missile site containing six launching pads and at least five missiles.

Above Right: February 1966—A woman soldier in the South Vietnam Liberation Army (Viet Cong).

Above: 1966—A typical North Vietnamese antiaircraft post about 50 miles south of Hanoi includes 57mm cannon and a Soviet-built radar unit, lower left.

Right: Members of the Women's Strike for Peace picket the White House in protest against the escalation of the war in Vietnam.

Right: March 24, 1966—Some 10,000 South Vietnamese march across a bridge over the Perfume River in Hue during a demonstration against the policies of the government in Saigon.

Below: September 3, 1966—The night sky is marked by the white light of tracer bullets as defenders fire on Viet Cong troops attacking a fire base in the Vietnamese countryside.

Above: March 1966—A U.S. Marine has a private bunker built of C-ration cases as shelter from the scorching sun at Quang Ngai airfield. There were 12 basic C-ration meals issued to U.S. troops at the time.

Left: March 26, 1966—U.S. Marines run around the nose of their helicopter after landing on the Saigon River delta 35 miles southwest of Saigon. American troops participating in Operation Jack Stay were believed to be the first U.S. combat troops in this delta.

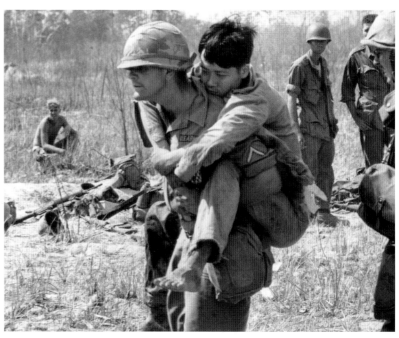

March 1966—A U.S. Marine bounces a South Vietnamese boy on his boot at a village near Danang. The 3rd Antitank Battalion was making an effort to befriend local villagers.

March 5, 1966—A U.S. infantryman of the 2nd Battalion, 28th Infantry Regiment, 1st Infantry Division, carries a wounded Viet Cong guerrilla to a first-aid station near Bau Bang, 30 miles north of Saigon. The infantryman found the wounded guerrilla in a foxhole when the Viet Cong retreated after a morning assault.

March 1966—A South Vietnamese farmer tends a flock of ducks near a U.S. Army helicopter.

1966—North Vietnamese pilots run to their MiG fighters at an unnamed airbase.

March 26, 1966—Clouds of smoke and steam generated by air strikes of Guam-based B-52 bombers rise above mangrove swamps 20 miles from Saigon. The strikes aimed to clear out Viet Cong positions that threatened river traffic. In foreground, a U.S. Navy landing craft cruises the Saigon River.

March 26, 1966—The Fifth Avenue Vietnam Peace Parade proceeds down New York's Fifth Avenue. Police kept marchers and bystanders separated to insure there would be no serious conflict.

March 26, 1966—Hecklers, contained behind police barricades on New York's Fifth Avenue, shout at marchers demonstrating against the war in Vietnam. The demonstration was part of a three-day series.

March 1966—A weeping woman consoles her husband who was wounded in air strikes that preceded an assault on a known Viet Cong village.

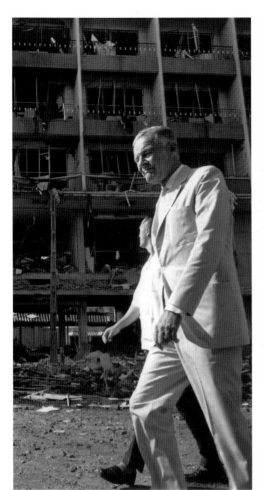

April 1, 1966—U.S. Ambassador to South Vietnam Henry Cabot Lodge tours the wreckage of a U.S. officers' billet in Saigon after a Viet Cong attack with machine guns, grenades, and a truckload of explosives.

April 13, 1966—Oil tanks burn after a Viet Cong mortar attack on Tan Son Nhut airbase in Saigon.

April 20, 1966—Chairman J. William Fulbright (right) of the Senate Foreign Relations Committee engages in an animated discussion with Defense Secretary Robert S. McNamara before a hearing into the conduct of the war in Vietnam.

April 6, 1966—Antigovernment demonstrators in Saigon set fire to bicycles after ransacking the offices of a newspaper.

Top Left: April 29, 1966—A U.S. 1st Air Cavalry Division soldier leaps to the ground from a helicopter prevented from landing by debris of trees shattered by blistering artillery bombardment and air strikes near Pleiku, South Vietnam.

Top Right: April 2, 1966—Young demonstrators in Saigon run from riot police after tear gas was thrown to break up antigovernment and anti-American protests.

Center: April 13, 1966—Oil tanks burn at Saigon's Tan Son Nhut Air Base after a mortar attack by the Viet Cong.

Below: April 25, 1966—Troops scramble from both sides of a helicopter as they are dropped off for an operation. The choppers, easy targets for enemy fire at these moments, hover for only a few seconds over the ground while discharging troops.

April 1966—A U.S. paratrooper of the 173rd Airborne Brigade sits on his duffel bag, waiting for an airlift from Song Be to his base at Bien Hoa.

April 16, 1966—A U.S. landing craft loaded with Korean infantrymen approaches the Vietnamese coast near Qui Nhon. Some 3,600 men of the 26th Korean Regimental combat team landed at Qui Nhon to reinforce the Korean Tiger Division.

April 28, 1966—On the border between South Vietnam and Cambodia, two U.S. soldiers of the 1st Infantry Division sit in a former Viet Cong trench watching for activity in Cambodia, on the opposite side of the Rach Beng River, 75 miles northwest of Saigon. Several infantry battalions were patrolling the area for Viet Cong supply points.

April 27, 1966—As U.S. soldiers of the 173rd Airborne Brigade bathe in the background, a Vietnamese woman washes their fatigues at river's edge near Song Be, in the Central Highlands about 60 miles north of Saigon. The soil in the area had a high clay content, which turned the olive drab uniforms a rusty color.

Above: April 27, 1966—Only their helmets are seen above the high grass after soldiers are dropped off for an attack against Viet Cong opposition. Their mission of getting the troops on the ground completed, helicopters begin to pull away.

Right: April 25, 1966—A Vietnamese woman pours water to relieve a sweaty U.S. Marine patrolling for Viet Cong west of Quang Ngai during Operation Hot Springs.

Above: April 1966—A veteran Viet Cong, who fought over the years against the French, South Vietnamese, and U.S., is held prisoner by the U.S. 25th Infantry northwest of Saigon.

Right: April 1966—A U.S. warplane crashes after being shot down in the Gianh River area of Quang Binh province, in a photo released by North Vietnam.

Above: 1966—North Vietnamese soldiers defending the Ham Zhong bridge fire at U.S. warplanes in a photo released by the Soviet Union. The Soviet caption claimed that the U.S. attack did not interrupt traffic on the bridge.

Right: 1966—A site believed to be a North Vietnamese surface-to-air missile base is shown in the photo by a U.S. reconnaissance plane.

April 1966—An F-100 Super Sabre dive bombs a Viet Cong camp 10 miles west of Saigon, believed to be the base used for the Viet Cong's April 15 attack on Tan Son Nhut airbase.

April 19, 1966—A woman holds her children close as a helicopter lands nearby. Wife of a Viet Cong suspect, she was taken to a military base for questioning.

Above: May 19, 1966—A U.S. paratrooper of the 1st Cavalry is silhouetted at daybreak during Operation Davy Crockett in the Central Highlands near Bong Son, 280 miles northwest of Saigon.

Left: May 9, 1966—U.S. military police advance down Hai Ba Trung Street in Saigon after an apparent terrorist explosion near the Brink Bachelor Officers Quarters, which touched off an hour-long firefight in the streets of the capital.

Above: May 1966—U.S. troops of the 2nd Battalion, 16th Infantry pick their way through jungle foliage blasted by a B-52 bomber near the Cambodian border. Two weeks of patrolling suspected Viet Cong camps had turned up large enemy supply caches.

Right: May 1966—A U.S. Air Force C-130 Hercules drops South Vietnamese paratroopers into a zone marked by an Air Force combat control team that had jumped into the Viet Cong–infiltrated area earlier.

Above: May 1966—Paratroopers of the U.S. 173rd Airborne Brigade pause at a jungle plantation in South Vietnam's Phuoc Tuy province to honor fallen comrades.

Left: May 1966—After landing by helicopter, U.S. paratroopers of the 173rd Airborne Brigade cross the Song Be River into a communist stronghold in War Zone D, 20 miles northeast of Saigon.

Above: May 1966—A North Vietnamese rocket is prepared for launch, in a photo released by the North Vietnamese News Agency.

Left: May 10, 1966—Terrified women and children emerge from a house on Saigon's Hai Ba Trung Street as U.S. military police round up civilians following a mine explosion and gun battle in the heart of the capital that left at least five people dead. The MPs arrested virtually all the men in this area.

Above Left: 1966—A photo caption released by North Vietnam states that, 'The missile battalion 61 of the Vietnam People's Army has fought many outstanding battles and brought down 23 U.S. aircraft.'

Above: May 10, 1966—A U.S. military policeman carrying an M60 machine gun arrests a suspect on Saigon's Hai Ba Trung Street after a terrorist blast near the U.S. Bachelor Officers Quarters.

Left: May 10, 1966—A U.S. military policeman arrests a Viet Cong suspect on Hai Ba Trung Street near Saigon's Brink Hotel after a terrorist mine set off a bloody gun battle. Five people were killed and 32 wounded.

Below: May 31, 1966—Books and chairs fly as students clash inside Saigon University's College of Pharmacy. Progovernment students had attempted to disrupt a rally by antigovernment students.

May 23, 1966—Demonstrators wave a Vietnamese flag in the rain and haze of tear gas used by troops to disperse the antigovernment crowd.

May 1966—A 100-ton coastal freighter at the southern tip of South Vietnam breaks up and goes ashore. Large quantities of weapons and ammunition were seized.

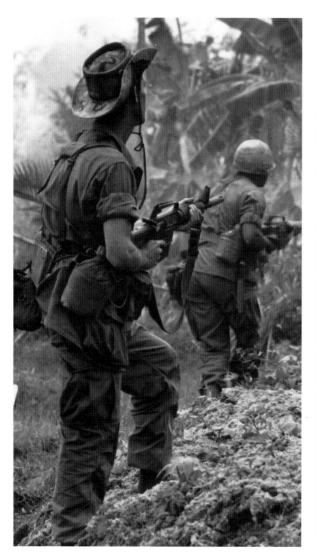

1966—U.S. soldiers pick their way through the landscape in the mountainous area close to the North Vietnamese border. Snipers are a never-ending danger.

1966—A photo, captured by American paratroopers, shows an enlistment ceremony for Viet Cong forces in Cu Chi, near Saigon. Women as well as younger people were signed up to fight with the hardened VC regulars. Note with the pictures reported the gathering was a farewell ceremony.

Above: June 1966—Wounded and weary American soldiers lie in a sandy ditch during an airstrike on enemy positions near An Thi, South Vietnam. Two companies of the 1st Cavalry Division battled Viet Cong-North Vietnamese forces for more than 24 hours across paddies and coastal villages.

Left: June 1966—A demonstrator is carried off by policemen during a protest outside the American embassy in Grosvenor Square in London They protested the United States bombing of Hanoi, North Vietnam.

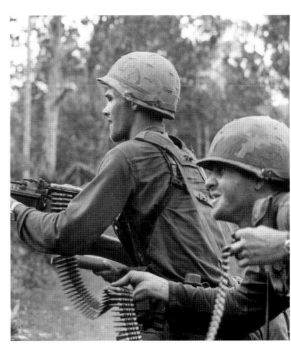

Left: June 1966—A heavily armed fire team of the 3rd Brigade, 25th Division, wades through a flooded jungle clearing along the Cambodian border near Duc Co in the Central Highlands. The 3rd Brigade was patrolling for Communist infiltrators crossing the border.

Above: June 25, 1966—A marksman of the 1st Cavalry Division fires an M-14 machine gun at North Vietnamese sniper position during Operation Nathan Hale in the central highlands. Nathan Hale operated 230 miles northeast of Saigon and was searching for a large force of North Vietnamese soldiers.

June 29, 1966—Hanoi defense forces at Hoan Kiem Lake in the center of the capital support an antiaircraft gun on a railing of Huc Bridge.

June 28, 1966—The crew of a U.S. Air Force C-130 Hercules transport plane makes a low altitude supply drop to the Army's 1st Cavalry Division at An Khe.

June 14, 1966—Soldiers of the 101st Airborne defend the outpost at Toumorong, in Kontum province, against communist assaults. At one point during the siege, the U.S. commander, desperate to stop the enemy attacks, called in air strikes against his own position.

June 1966—A U.S. soldier shoulders a sack of peanuts, part of a huge supply cache captured from the Viet Cong. Tons of peanuts, flour, rice, and dried foods, captured without a shot being fired, were to be distributed to South Vietnamese families in the area.

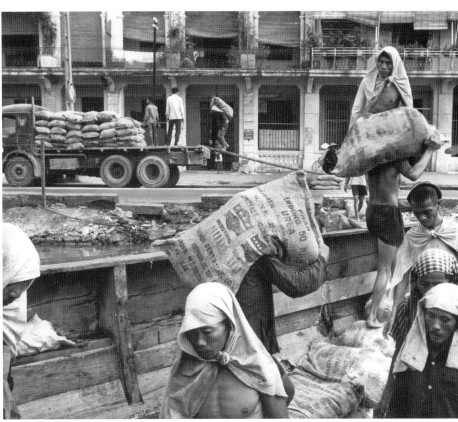

Left: June 29, 1966—Thick smoke rises from an oil depot northeast of Hanoi after U.S. air strikes.

Above: June 1966—Bags of American Aid fertilizer are unloaded from a barge and put aboard trucks in Cholon, the Chinese sector of Saigon. Many supplies find their way to the hands of black marketeers and Viet Cong agents.

June 20, 1966—The U.S. Coast Guard cutter Point Slocum and Point League flank a 125-foot trawler of unidentified nationality that the two ships ran down off South Vietnam. A large shipment of arms and ammunition was seized in the action. The materiel was apparently destined for the Viet Cong.

July 19, 1966—American Marines scramble for their foxholes as North Vietnamese mortar fire hits a battalion command post south of the DMZ during Operation Hastings.

Above: July 15, 1966—U.S. Marines scatter as a CH-46 helicopter burns after being shot down near the Demilitarized Zone.

Right: July 1966—Marines move through high grass single file toward a hill suspected of being the site of a North Vietnamese command post about 2000 yards south of the DMZ. The patrol was part of Operation Hastings.

Above: July 15, 1966—The gunner of a downed CH-46 helicopter staggers to safety after being pinned down by enemy fire near the demilitarized zone. Two other crewmen also survived the crash that killed 12 Marines and one crew member.

Left: July 18, 1966—A U.S. Marine helicopter crashes to the ground, killing Marines on the ground at a landing zone in the Song Ngan Valley, just south of the demilitarized zone. Another helicopter, *top*, also tries to get into the landing zone.

July 1966—U.S. troops of the 173rd Airborne Brigade lead South Vietnamese women and children through dense elephant grass after the civilians were found huddled in a muddy river bank cave. Adult men had fled as the U.S. unit searched the area for a suspected Viet Cong hospital along Route 20, about 120 miles north of Saigon. Helicopters carried the women and children to a safe area.

July 24, 1966—A medic assists a wounded U.S. Marine of India Company during Operation Hastings near the demilitarized zone. India Company reported almost 50 percent casualties. Helicopters evacuated the wounded, then returned for the dead.

Above: July 24, 1966—A U.S. Marine of India Company, wounded during Operation Hastings just south of the demilitarized zone, is hoisted to a medical evacuation helicopter.

Left: July 1966—A wounded U.S. Marine of India Company wears a rough cast as he waits for evacuation near the demilitarized zone during Operation Hastings. The company suffered almost 50 percent casualties.

July 24, 1966—A member of the evacuation crew signals to the helicopter hovering overhead while another member adjusts a sling around a wounded Marine to be airlifted from the area near Dong Ha during Operation Hastings.

July 15, 1966—A CH-46 Sea Knight helicopter is engulfed in smoke and flames seconds before it crashed just south of the demilitarized zone, killing one crewmember and 12 marines during Operation Hastings. Three crewmen escaped with burns.

Above: July 24, 1966—A U.S. Marine on India Company, wounded in Operation Hastings, waits for helicopter evacuation from the area just south of the demilitarized zone between North and South Vietnam.

Right: July 19, 1966—As CH-46 Sea Knight helicopters land at first light, U.S. Marines of the 3rd Battalion, 4th Marine Regiment, 3rd Marine Division, report to the airstrip at Dong Ha, eight miles south of the demilitarized zone, for an assault against North Vietnamese units just south of the DMZ.

Above: July 2, 1966—A U.S. soldier of the 2nd Battalion, 18th Infantry Regiment, 1st Infantry Division, calls for help for a wounded fellow infantryman in a jungle clearing near Quan Loi, about two miles from the Cambodian border. Two infantry companies repelled an overnight Viet Cong assault.

Left: July 24, 1966—After a three-day patrol through mud and monsoon rains during Operation Aurora, U.S. paratroopers of the 173rd Airborne Brigade wash themselves and their laundry in a jungle stream 120 miles north of Saigon.

Above: July 1966—A skull-and-crossbones trooper fires at pigs that ran from a burning house in Vietnam's Mekong Delta. The kerchief he wears is the sign of a leader in the special unit.

Right: July 1966—U.S. Marine helicopters scout an artillery impact area for damage estimates after shelling a suspected Viet Cong emplacement in South Vietnam.

July 7, 1966—The caption of this photo found at a captured Viet Cong camp reads, 'Two youths – one Montagnard and one Vietnamese – offer a bouquet of flowers to the chief of the National Liberation Front, Nguyen Huu Tho.'

July 1966—Two farmers are guarded by a South Vietnamese soldier of the skull-and-crossbones platoon before being taken away for interrogation. The special government outfit operates in known Viet Cong areas with techniques similar to those of the enemy.

Above: July 6, 1966—A soldier of the 1st Vietnamese Infantry Division comforts a woman crying over the wrecking of her home during a day-long battle with the Viet Cong in Phu Lieu, 30 miles north of Hue.

August 22, 1966—North Vietnamese leaders gesture during celebrations in Hanoi for the 21st anniversary of North Vietnam. From far left: Vo Nguyen Giap, commander of the armed forces and vice premier; Truong Chin, chairman of the national assembly standing committee; Le Duan, first secretary of the Communinist Party; Ho Chi Minh, president of North Vietnam and chairman of the Communist Party; and Ton Doc Thang, vice president.

Above: August 14, 1966—A U.S. Army medic wraps the arm of a wounded soldier as another GI cradles the injured man's head behind a rice paddy dike near Phu Loi.

Right: Lance Cpl. Perron Shinneman, who lost a leg to a Viet Cong mine in South Vietnam, is greeted at the airport by his wife, Shirley, as he arrives home in Sioux Falls, South Dakota. Shinneman was on a 30-day convalescent leave from Bethesda, Maryland, Naval hospital.

Above: August 16, 1966—A U.S. radioman of the 1st Infantry Division crouches against a rice paddy dike as sniper fire whistles overhead near Phu Loi, about 15 miles north northwest of Saigon. The unit was leading a helicopter assault in Viet Cong–held territory.

Right: August 16, 1966—U.S. soldier wades through the deep mud of a rice paddy during an assault by the 1st Infantry Division near Phu Loi, 15 miles northwest of Saigon. Advance platoons were pinned down, but U.S. troops eventually seized an enemy battalion headquarters and medical center.

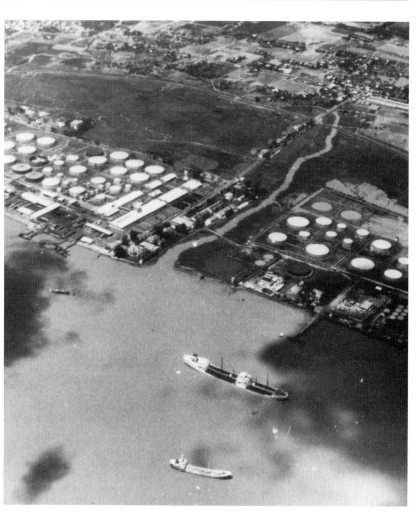

Above: August 23, 1966—A U.S. infantryman hurries civilians from a village near the Michelin rubber plantation, 35 miles northwest of Saigon during an intense firefight with Viet Cong snipers. Civilians were moved to safety outside the village, and some were later flown to an interrogation center.

Right: August 24, 1966—South Vietnam's largest petroleum and fuel storage depot at Nha Be, on the Saigon River about 10 miles south of the capital, is believed to be a prime target of the Viet Cong. In addition to allied ground patrols, the area was declared a free fire zone, and the surrounding area was bombarded every night to disrupt any enemy activity.

Above: August 1966—Huey helicopters lift off after dropping troops of the 1st Battalion, 16th Infantry Regiment, near the Michelin rubber plantation, 35 miles northwest of Saigon.

Right: August 14, 1966—A Vietnamese woman pins a flower on the uniform of a soldier stepping off a landing craft at Vung Tau, southeast of Saigon, as 3,800 men of the 196th Light Infantry Brigade arrived from Fort Devons, Massachusetts.

Above: August, 1966—Paratroopers of the 173rd Airborne Brigade take cover behind a road marker about 25 miles from their Bien Hoa base camp after their convoy came under sniper fire. The troops were en route to landing zone Grenada to take part in Operation Toledo.

Right: August 12, 1966—U.S. Marines of the 1st Battalion, 5th Marine Regiment, carry a captured guerrilla to interrogation following a Viet Cong assault on Marine positions near Tam Ky, 40 miles southwest of Danang.

August 1966—A Viet Cong prisoner is directed toward an interrogation center after his capture.

August 13, 1966—Two Viet Cong guerrillas wade through muddy water in the Mekong Delta, surrendering to South Vietnamese troops in Kien Giang province, 120 miles southwest of Saigon. South Vietnamese helicopters drove the men out hiding in a swamp area.

Above: August 1966—An irrigation dam for farmers near Qui Nhon, South Vietnam, constructed by troops of the Korean Tiger Division who donated their time and labor, is inspected by Vietnamese and Korean officers, led by Vietnamese Chief of State Gen. Nguyen Van Thieu and Gen. Myung Shin Chae, commander of Korean forces in Vietnam.

Right: August 22, 1966—A U.S. soldier of the 1st Battalion, 16th Infantry Regiment, carries a child from the village of Cam Xe after dropping a phosphorous grenade into a bunker cleared of civilians. After taking sniper fire from the village northwest of Saigon, the infantrymen had charged in, firing into houses, clearing bunkers and shelters, and dragging civilians from the village for questioning about Viet Cong activity.

August 1966—Sgt. Elwood Frazier of Fredrickton, Missouri, leans on his rifle after a firefight with Viet Cong guerrillas in the jungle south of Phuoc Vinh, about 35 miles north of Saigon. Frazier was sergeant of an infantry weapons platoon.

August 13, 1966—A U.S. Infantryman of the 1st Battalion, 26th Infantry Regiment, guides a blindfolded Viet Cong suspect through a rice paddy while moving toward cover from sniper fire near Phu Loi, 14 miles north of Saigon.

August 28, 1966—Pfc. Eugene Cabbagestalk of Pittsburgh, Pennsylvania, pushes back his helmet to wipe the sweat from his face. Cabbagestalk was killed in Vietnam the following January.

August 1966—Students of Vietnam's Transportation University undergo compulsory militia training, in addition to their transportation studies.

Above: August 1966—Government election workers in Saigon parade in front of city hall to stir up enthusiasm for the upcoming national elections. The large banner reads: 'Voters of the Gia Dinh province shall put only one vote in the ballot box.'

Right: August 1966—A North Vietnamese soldier, flushed out of tall grass by the scout dog in background, is captured by a machete-wielding U.S. soldier of the 1st Infantry near the Cambodian border.

Top Left: August 13, 1966—Vietnamese soldiers cling to the remains of a bridge to wait for sampans to carry them across a Mekong Delta canal in Kien Giang province southwest of Saigon. The bridge was cut several months earlier by Viet Cong.

Center Left: A peasant and his wife leave their hiding place full of fear after South Vietnamese Rangers raked it with grenades and weapons. The Rangers were flushing out Viet Cong units some 140 miles southwest of Saigon in the An Dien district. The man was taken into custody.

Bottom Left: September 1966—One GI weeps over the body bag that holds his slain buddy. Others run down the trail to seek snipers who fired on their patrol.

August 1966—A mother and her children wade into a river as they move from their hiding place near a delta hamlet 140 miles from Saigon. The area, known as a Viet Cong sanctuary, was assaulted by government troops.

September 1966—North Vietnamese leader Ho Chi Minh joins high-ranking officials at a party in Hanoi to mark the 21st anniversary of North Vietnam's declaration of independence after World War II.

September 17, 1966—U.S. Marines, crouched along a road in a rice paddy, turn for a last look at a comrade being carried by corpsmen to the rear. The unit was attacked by Viet Cong positioned in a tree line just south of the DMZ.

September 1966—The wife of a Viet Cong soldier holds her mortally wounded husband in her arms after he was shot and subsequently captured during a clash with government troops.

September 15, 1966—U.S. Marines are brought ashore in a swarm of landing craft near the demilitarized zone. The Marines were transferred from troop ships to the assault carriers for a surprise attack against enemy controlled settlements near the beaches.

Left: September 1966—U.S. Marines, exhausted after three nights of fighting North Vietnamese troops, emerge from foxholes as sun rises on their hilltop position in the demilitarized zone. The helicopter in background was shot down while bringing supplies to the unit.

Above: September 1966—U.S. paratroopers of the 173rd Airborne Brigade cross the Song Be River during Operation Sioux City in War Zone D. Helicopters couldn't find landing zones in the dense jungle.

September 1966—A U.S. Marine, looking for snipers, orders a Vietnamese peasant out of an air raid shelter in a small village near the demilitarized zone. The Marines found only civilians; the snipers had fled.

September 4, 1966—A young Vietnamese girl joins a U.S. artilleryman in covering her ears as an 8-inch howitzer blasts a shell from the 25th Division base camp at Cu Chi, 20 miles northwest of Saigon. The unit was firing harassment rounds, intended to disrupt Viet Cong operations and transportation routes.

September, 1966  September 1966—A South Vietnamese woman and her child follow U.S. troops carrying the body of her husband, a Viet Cong suspect who died fighting U.S. troops near Linh Hoi on the central coast of Vietnam. The soldiers offered to bury the man, but the widow said she would do so herself.

September 1966—U.S. Marines of the 1st Battalion, 26th Marine Regiment, crouch on a dirt trail with a rocket launcher after coming under sniper fire near the demilitarized zone. The unit made contact with elements of the North Vietnamese 324B Division during Operation Prairie.

Above: September 7, 1966—A landing craft carries troops of the U.S. 11th Armored Cavalry Regiment to a beach at Vung Tau, about 45 miles southeast of Saigon. Some 1,600 men from Ft. Meade, Maryland, arrived aboard three transport ships. Total U.S. troop strength at the time was more than 300,000.

Right: September, 1966—Exposing enemy positions, U.S. Air Force planes spray the chemical defoliant Agent Orange over vegetation in South Vietnam.

September 29, 1966—Captured Viet Cong are tagged and guarded by soldiers of the U.S. 1st Air Cavalry Division at a village near Bong Son, on the central coast of Vietnam, during Operation Thayer. Most of the enemy had fled, but the few prisoners were turned over to South Vietnamese authorities.

September 16, 1966—Following a futile search for Viet Cong, soldiers of the U.S. 1st Air Cavalry Division struggle to carry the body of a dead comrade from the jungle 15 miles northwest of Bong Son on Vietnam's central coast. Soldiers searched for several hours before finding the body, killed by a sniper's bullet.

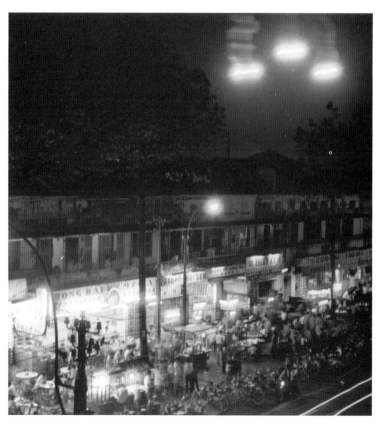

Above: September 24, 1966—U.S. Marines of the 1st Batallion, 4th Regiment, follow tank tracks through elephant grass several miles south of the demilitarized zone during Operation Prairie. The Marines were facing the North Vietnamese 324B Division for control of the area.

Right: September 9, 1969—With Saigon nightlife continuing in the Cholon section, flares burst just two miles away as U.S. planes and helicopters attacked Viet Cong guerrillas infiltrating two southern precincts of the capital.

September 1966—Medics of the U.S. 173rd Airborne Brigade give aid and plasma to a wounded paratrooper as fighting continues around them in the jungles of Phuoc Tuy province, about 30 miles east of Saigon. The wounded man was shot in the arm and chest by snipers.

September 10, 1966—Boats, some with election signs, assemble on the Mekong River at Chau Doc where peasants arrived to listen to campaign speeches of candidates running for the constitutional assembly.

Above: September 27, 1966—Delegates to the Vietnamese National Constituent Assembly attend the opening session in Saigon. In front are, from left: Premier Nguyen Cao Ky, Chief of State Nguyen Van Thieu and Lt. Gen. Pham Van Chieu, secretary-general of the National Leadership Committee.

Left: September 1966—A member of the 173rd Airborne heats C-rations under a Buddha statue in the ruins of a pagoda near Xuan Loc, 35 miles east of Saigon. The battalion had flown in by helicopter hoping to trap Viet Cong guerrillas, but the enemy had fled.

Left: September 8, 1966—Vietnamese infantrymen ands their American advisor crowd in a fiberglass raft as they cross a river in Vinh Long province, about 50 miles south of Saigon. The advisor, with glass, is S.Sgt. Raymond Spivey of Ft. Pierce, Florida.

Bottom Left: An elderly woman listens to speeches in Saigon as politicians seek votes in the coming elections.

Bottom Right: Vietnamese farmer from a village 280 miles northeast of Saigon, near Bong Son.

Above Left: October 1966—Mortar unit fires away at enemy positions during the night hours to fight off assaults on a fire base.

Above: November 1966—A GI offers food to a small child during a visit to a village.

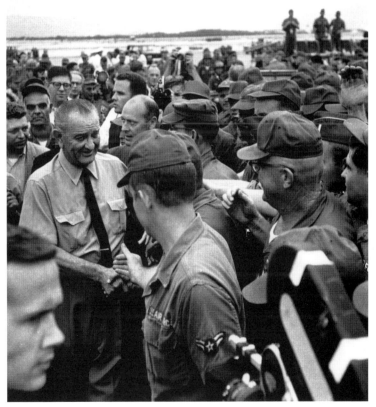

Above: October 26, 1966—A crowd of American soldiers greets U.S. President Lyndon B. Johnson on his arrival at Cam Ranh Bay to visit the troops in South Vietnam. At left is Gen. William Westmoreland, commander of U.S. forces in Vietnam.

Left: October 1966—Spc. Ruediger Richter, of Columbus, Georgia, 4th Battalion, 173rd Airborne Brigade, gazes into the smoke of a directional grenade for the arrival of an evacuation helicopter in a jungle clearing in Long Khanh Province of South Vietnam. Sgt. Daniel E. Spencer of Bend, Oregon, stands by the poncho-wrapped body of a dead comrade.

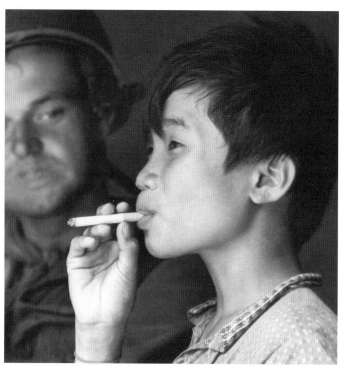

Above: October 1966—A young Vietnamese boy smiles with every puff as he tries an American filter cigarette, his first experience with anything other than hand-rolled cigarettes in his mountain village. The boy asked for the cigarette from a U.S. soldier of the 1st Air Cavalry *(background)* during Operation Irving along the central Vietnamese coast.

Left: October 1966—Villagers in Loc Ninh, 90 miles north of Saigon, gather around a column of U.S. tanks and armored personnel carriers patrolling remote routes near the Cambodian border.

Above: October 1966—North Vietnamese high school boys dig trenches for an underground shelter during a defense training session in Hanoi. Their heavy straw hats are designed to protect them against shell fragments in case of attack.

Left: October 1966—A Viet Cong suspect, flushed out of a muddy bunker by the South Vietnamese 7th Infantry, talks to an interrogator after hearing shouting and a shot fired behind him in Kien Hoa province in the Mekong Delta. The shouting and the shot were a deception to start the prisoner talking.

Top Left: October 1966—Taking part in Operation Irving, U.S. troops of B Company, 1st Battalion, 12 Cavalry Regiment, 1st Air Cavalry Division, land on a mountain in the Phu Cat range, about 30 miles north of Qui Nhon. The unit, searching for any enemy troops remaining in the area after a battle a few days earlier, met with no resistance.

Top Right: October 1966—A wounded North Vietnamese soldier who posed as a farm boy is evacuated by helicopter for interrogation. He had apparently been abandoned by his unit and was captured by the 1st Battalion, 12th Cavalry Regiment, during Operation Irving in the Phu Cat Mountains of Vietnam's Central Coast.

Left: October 10, 1966—Flanked by his wife and child, a Vietnamese peasant, trembling with fear but forcing a weak smile, is interrogated by a Vietnamese army officer in the Mekong Delta near Mo Gay.

Below: October 26, 1966—President Lyndon B. Johnson shakes hands with U.S. troops in Cam Ranh Bay during his tour of South Vietnam. Riding with him is Gen. William Westmoreland, commander of U.S. forces in Vietnam.

Above: November 23, 1966—With artillery firing in the background, U.S. soldiers of the 2nd Battalion, 14th Infantry Regiment, splash through muddy marshland in War Zone C, near the Cambodian border, during the second phase of Operation Attleboro.

Left: November 15, 1966—A U.S. squad leader of the 1st Battalion, 2nd Infantry, 1st Division yells to his unit while taking sniper fire near Dau Tueng, northwest of Saigon.

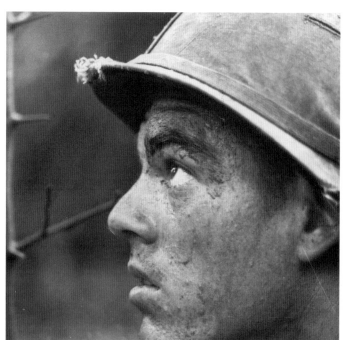

Left: November 14, 1966—With an artillery post in the foreground, the villas and administration buildings of the Michelin rubber plantation in Dau Tieng, 40 miles northwest of Saigon, serve as headquarters for the U.S. 1st Infantry Division. The airstrip is a staging area for scores of helicopters shuttling troops to and from the jungle, and cargo planes land frequently on resupply missions.

Above: November 26, 1966—A soldier of the 25th Infantry Division, coated with sweat and grime, patrols thick jungle near the Cambodian border. B-52 air strikes had driven out snipers that stalled the unit for three days.

Above: November 1, 1966—Saigon's new Independence Palace glows during a National Day reception. The $2 million palace was built at the former site of President Ngo Dinh Diem's presidential palace, bombed in a failed 1962 coup attempt.

Left: November 1966—A canal leads from Saigon harbor to warehouses and depots inland. U.S. aid and supplies arriving by ship were funneled into South Vietnam on these canals, and an estimated 25 percent of the goods were lost before they reached their destination.

Above: November 20, 1966—U.S. troops of the 1st Battalion, 18th Infantry Regiment, 1st Division, deep in War Zone C, crouch in a sandbagged mortar position as smoke rises from B-52 strikes against suspected Viet Cong positions along the Cambodian border during Operation Attleboro.

Right: November 1966—Wearing heavy straw hats to protect against possible shell fragments, North Vietnamese high school girls train by digging individual shelters in a hillside.

Above: November 13, 1966—After flushing out several Viet Cong guerrillas, a U.S. Marine tank fires a flamethrower into the jungle undergrowth south of Danang.

Right: November 1966—A G.I. of the 25th Infantry Division washes his fatigues in floodwater at the Ben Loc base camp, 20 miles southwest of Saigon on the northern edge of the Mekong Delta.

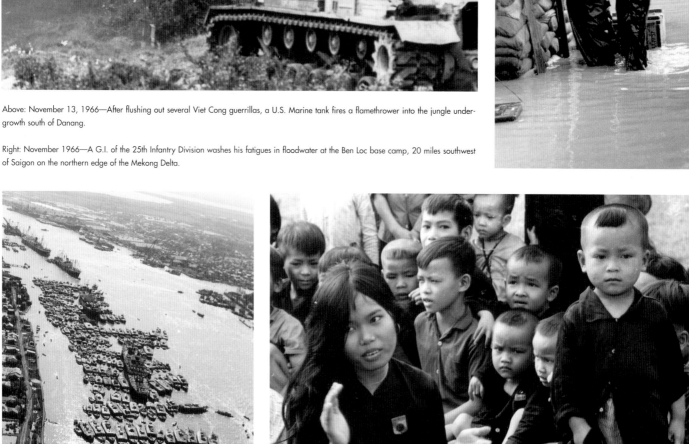

Above: November 15, 1966—A 17-year-old South Vietnamese girl, dressed in black pajamas and surrounded by children, sings sentimental songs about the good life in government-controlled areas whose people are loyal. She is a member of the government's pacification team, whose assignment is to help win over the population.

Left: November 1966—The chaotic collection of barges, sampans, and cargo ships in the Saigon harbor has led to countless instances of pilferage and missing cases of negotiable items going astray.

Above: December 1966—Fighters of antiaircraft Unit X are visited at their post by North Vietnam's President Ho Chi Minh to celebrate the 22nd anniversary of the Vietnam People's Army.

Left: December 1966—A Vietnamese Ranger leaves a village market in the Mekong Delta after buying provisions for the field. Two ducks are strung from his rifle and he carries vegetables, a bag of rice, and fish sauce. Vietnamese troops are not provided with food.

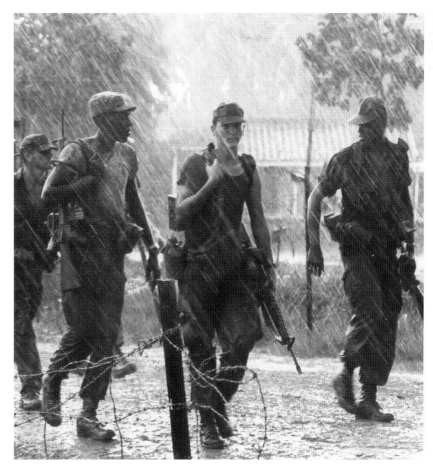

Above: December 10, 1966—U.S. Secretary of State Dean Rusk (left), South Vietnamese Prime Minister Nguyen Cao Ky, and U.S. Ambassador to Vietnam Henry Cabot Lodge meet in Saigon.

Right: December 1966—Monsoon rain does not stop troops just in from a multi-day patrol to make their way through the base camp to their bunker area.

Top Left: December 1966—A reconnaissance company of the U.S. 1st Cavalry searches for a reported Viet Cong squad among rocks and boulders on the central coast of South Vietnam, about 20 miles north of Qui Nhon.

Top Right: December 1966—A U.S. reconnaissance company of the 1st Cavalry searches a coastal area 20 miles north of Qui Nhon.

Left: December 3, 1966—A Korean soldier of the Tiger Division stands hip deep in swamp water as he throws a hand grenade into fortified caves at Bac Ma Mountain. Korean troops were patrolling the Phu Cat Mountains in Operation Fierce Tiger VII to drive out Viet Cong guerrillas and protect the area's rice harvest.

February 27, 1966—Seeking to expand the perimeter of their base, soldiers of the U.S. 25th Infantry "Wolfhound" Division tramp through a dusty area laced with Viet Cong tunnels and trenches near Cu Chi, 25 miles northwest of Saigon.

December 1966—U.S. soldiers of the 1st Battalion, 9th Cavalry Regiment, stand on the skids, prepared to jump as a UH-1D Huey helicopter approaches a landing zone in Binh Dinh province, 300 miles northeast of Saigon. The reconnaissance company jumps as the helicopter hovers at low altitude so that the chopper doesn't spend time on the ground in an unsecure area.

December 1966—A U.S infantryman wounded during Operation Paul Revere IV, northwest of the village of Plei Djereng, is hoisted to an evacuation helicopter near the Cambodian border.

December 1966—Sgt. Jimmy L. Mabry of Birmingham, Alabama, helps fill sandbags at Vo Dat, about 60 miles northeast of Saigon, where the 11th Cavalry Regiment helped secure the area's rice harvest.

Top Left: December 1966—Foot traffic is not stopped by a damaged bridge 60 miles from Saigon on the road to Vo Dat, a district capital in a 'rice bowl' area. The Viet Cong blew up the bridge to stop military convoys and trucks, but bus passengers walk across the bridge to transfer to another bus to continue their journey.

Top Right: December 1966—A U.S. soldier of the 25th Infantry Division stands on a rice paddy dike during a probing mission 20 miles southwest of Saigon, on the northern fringe of the Mekong Delta. The infantry unit was evaluating conditions before more U.S. troops entered the delta region.

Center: December 8, 1966—Stalls across from the Redemptorist Church in Saigon feature black market U.S. cigarettes, canned foods, soaps, and C-rations despite a government crackdown.

Below: December 1966—Armored personnel carriers churn through rice paddies in the Boi Loi Woods, a Viet Cong–controlled area 35 miles northwest of Saigon. The battalion of armored vehicles destroyed much of the rice harvest, and peasants showed little good will toward the government in this Communist stronghold.

# THE TRAIL

The September monsoon had come to the high peaks of the Truong Son – Long Mountains – when journalist Tran Mai Nam of the People's Army began his diary in 1966. He described the grim storms of war and nature nature already raging across the mountains – which the Americans called the Ho Chi Minh Trail. 'We march', he wrote 'in the desolate gray of the forest. Around us, giant trees stripped of their foliage by poison chemicals thrust out their stark branches. Their ghostly silhouettes rise to a low, cloudy sky – heavy like a soaked quilt. Our feet tread on many seasons of fallen leaves. Over them all the rains have hastened the rot.'

Tran Mai Nam's dispatches, published in Hanoi, did not disguise the terrors of the journey: 'The bombers hide above the clouds. The whistle and explosion of bombs thunder in every corner of the forest. There are formations of Phantoms with

'At times the Ho Chi Minh Trail was like the Long Island expressway – during rush hour.'

– US COMMANDO

the howl of death in their jets. The worst is the continuous growl of the reconnaissance planes.'

In one of those planes a little earlier that year an American journalist had scanned the Trail and noted with amazement the nature of the enemy. Sharing the cockpit of a T-28, flying at times below 1000 feet around the peaks, Sol Saunders could see 'traces of red clay and white limestone where the road had been newly cut . . . clearly marked with deep ruts made by wheeled vehicles. In many stretches it was wide enough for two trucks to pass abreast.'

But Saunders, writing for *US News and World Report*, was equally astonished by what he did not see. US military intelligence believed that some 36,000 North Vietnamese had passed down the Trail the previous year; it estimated that 90,000 would do so during 1966. Thousands of supply trucks were known to be using this jungle web of

November 20, 1966—A column of U.S. 3rd Brigade, 25th Division, infantrymen patrol through high jungle in the Central Highlands about 100 yards from the Cambodian border. The unit had been operating along the border west of Pleiku for about six months to prevent communist infiltration from Cambodia and Laos.

man-spun roads, but Saunders could see no men or movement. 'The whole flight had an eerie quality. Although there was no doubt that we were flying over a heavily traveled road, I saw no sign of life during the entire time.'

'We climb and climb endlessly,' Tran Mai Nam wrote, and when the planes had gone he too felt an 'eerie silence'. The bombs and chemicals had driven off the wildlife; there was now only the roar of his own labored breathing. Nam was with a platoon of thirty. They did not use the maze of rough roads – these were for the supply convoys and safe only at night. The platoons, with their guerrilla guides, each worked their own route between the relay camps, marching twelve miles or as many hours a day. 'Our road becomes tougher. Road? It is not even a path,' Nam's diary records, 'just a simple track opened by our guides in the low brush on the sides of the mountains, sometimes only crude steps cut into the bare rock.' They reached the higher tree-line and there after a B-52 attack '. . . a space opens up. Uprooted trees lie fallen at every angle. We see a country of the apocalypse, as if some Fury in an impotent rage had turned her axe without rhyme or reason against these inanimate, harmless forest beings. . . . What do they want? Is it possible they have flown all the way from Guam just to bomb this impenetrable jungle?'

As the army journalist recorded these scenes, the full fury of the battle for the Trail still lay ahead. In 1966 there was indeed a sense of impotence in Washington over how to tame an unseen jungle adversary 9000 miles away. Two years of round-the-clock bombing had failed to slow the infiltration. Almost in Nam's words, an American air force commander likened the use of B-52s against the Trail to 'an unwieldy axe'. Defense Secretary McNamara had presented President Johnson with a simple but devastating summary of the war: quite apart from its main force units, the North needed to deliver only sixty tons of supplies a day to the South – just twenty truck-loads – to sustain the guerrilla offensive. By late 1966 the Pentagon had already concluded that direct bombing of the North was no deterrent. The only solution was to block the Trail – somehow. Strategically, it was the only battle of the Vietnam war that really mattered – and the only one that never ceased. It amounted to whether a score of trucks could outrun the greatest gauntlet ever devised.

US military experts later said that their computers knew 'the entire 3500 miles [5645 kilometers] of the Trail system – every crossroad and gully'. But in his account for this history the Hanoi strategist Ha Van Lau says. 'It was a road system of more than 13,000 kilometers.' It paralleled the thousand kilometers of South Vietnam's border with Laos and Cambodia, looking on the map like the curved pipe of a car fuel pump with North Vietnam as the filling station. But the grid system winding either side of the border was thirteen times as long, according to Ha Van Lau. 'It was begun', he says 'in 1959, and was enlarged and modernized until it became a network of strategic communications provisioning our armed forces in every area of the front.'

For most of the war the Hanoi leadership again and again denied that any North Vietnamese had infiltrated South. In fact in 1959, three years after the deadline for joint elections on

Left: This map, based on information from the South Vietnamese government in the summer of 1966, shows the increased infiltration of North Vietnamese troops between 1960 and 1966. Infiltration routes along the Ho Chi Minh trail, and through South Vietnam directly are also indicated. U.S. intellience sources believed infiltration had not been as great as reported.

reunification, Hanoi made the pivotal decision to help organize guerrilla resistance in the South – at first sending back cadres born in the South who had migrated North with the Partition.

In early 1960 the US doubled its advisory force in South Vietnam from 342 to 685. At the same time the guerrilla movement formed the National Liberation Front (NLF), later pejoratively known as the Viet Cong. That same year an estimated 5000 political cadres infiltrated from the North, and from 1962 the cycle of escalation greatly increased with the political settlement of the once larger war in Laos. The CIA's covert air war was then redirected at the infiltration routes. But because Laos was now neutral, and because the guerrilla war in the South was said to be the NLF's struggle, both Washington and Hanoi denied their activity on the Trail.

Though finally the battle of the Trail would presage the twenty-first century, it was second century BC in its beginnings. The first groups sent south used elephants to help carry supplies over the immediate barrier – the crossing of the 1300-foot Mu Gia Pass into Laos – as Hannibal had in the Alps. Though Laos was known as the 'Kingdom of the Elephants' the herds were soon gunned down in the CIA's secret war. By 1964, when the first North Vietnamese army units were detected on the Trail, it was still a journey to the extremes of human endurance. Along the 7000-foot heights from above the 17th Parallel to the 11th, or the furthest exit west of Saigon, there were footpaths – no more. On this winding trek of several thousand kilometers, nature's hazards were always the greatest. In early 1964 Wilfred Burchett became the first Westerner to make the journey.

'When I first started down,' recalls Burchett, 'it took a good six months to get from the 17th Parallel anywhere close to Saigon. It went through very, very rugged mountainous country, using hair-raising swaying bamboo-bridges.' Years later, the journey would take only six weeks, but with the same perils. In the long rainy season, September to February, catastrophic floods would constantly wash away the man-made trails, turning streams into rapids and the gorges into monstrous rivers. Flimsy, meter-wide bridges, with bamboo foot planks and ropes for handrails, were strung between the high peaks, then hastily dismantled to avoid detection. In the dense forests the knapsacks of the marchers were so weighted by the rains that the men could not walk upright. Then under the palest sun they would steam and suffocate. Malaria and amoebic dysentery were the main scourges. In the early days it was believed that ten per cent of those who set out died from disease.

'The medical problems were bad – especially malaria,' says Burchett. But even in 1964 there were 'pretty good little jungle clinics producing pharmaceuticals'. Like the soldiers, Burchett trained for the journey with several weeks of rigorous climbing and exercise. Starting out, each man's eighty-pound pack held (according to 'conversations' with captive soldiers issued by the Rand Corporation) two pairs of sandals, an extra olive-green uniform, one set of traditional black pajamas, a raincoat, a nylon tent, a hammock, a mosquito net, ten meters of rope and enough medicine and vitamin pills for one month until the first major base camp was reached.

'One thing that was absolutely obligatory for

Below: November 1966—A gravestone provides protection for a 1st Infantry Division GI providing cover for others crossing an open field. The operation was designed to cut infiltration routes from War Zone D.

everybody to carry – which I also carried,' says Burchett, 'were dice-shaped cubes of anti-snake venom. If you got bitten, you had to break this cube very quickly, apply half of it to the actual bite and swallow the rest. You had to do it within three minutes otherwise you'd be stiffened up by the death adders.'

The Australian-born journalist had reported the Viet Minh campaigns during the war against colonial France. As correspondent for some of Europe's most enterprising newspapers he had met Ho Chi Minh in the jungles of Dien Bien Phu. But Burchett would pay a high personal price for his extraordinary eye-witness exploits. After Australia entered the war it was alleged that he was support-ing his country's enemy and his passport was re-voked. In 1965, as the Allied war began, Burchett published *Vietnam: Inside Story of the Guerrilla War*, detailing the Trail and guerrilla methods, and it was essentially a retelling – and a warning – of the fortitude of a decade earlier.

In the early 1960s supplies for the South again depended on thousands of human porters – ponies and bicycles could only occasionally be used. Discipline and camouflage again hid this great march; the last man in a group would swish back leaves and twigs to disguise any movement. Burchett could never forget 'the little green leeches that dropped from the branches as you brushed past, softly and coldly, like drops of water. You only knew the difference when your blood started trick-ling.' The only respite was occasional beauty: 'ser-ried folds of mist-covered forest stretching away into purple infinity'.

Near the end of the Trail there were suddenly four 'dark shapes, flying quite low' and as Burchett and his guides ran for cover he thought the roar of the helicopters left 'no space in the ears for any-thing more, but still above the motors was the dev-astating clatter of their machine-guns and the piti-fully unequal reply of the guerrillas' two light machine-guns'. The helicopters 'circled and hov-ered, as if trying to make up their minds where to land' but then left because, says Burchett, unless they could 'dive straight down on their prey' they were too vulnerable to ground fire. The coming of the bombers, with B-52s flying unheard and unseen seven miles high, was still a few months away.

Above: A truck convoy rolls along a road into Laos and the Ho Chi Minh trail as it transports supplies to North Vietnamese troops fighting in South Vietnam.

Left: 1971—North Viet-namese drivers and guards line up in front of camou-flaged trucks at a staging point along the Ho Chi Minh Trail in North Vietnam. During the course of the war, thousands of young recruits drove the trail, providing a critical supply line for Com-munist forces.

US fighter jets began interdiction and strafing missions over the Trail in late 1964, when it was estimated that the infiltration rate was tripling each year. These flights were in support of the CIA-funded Royal Lao Air Force, using T-28 propeller aircraft. Though officially neutral, with a coalition government, Laos remained physically divided between the Royal Lao forces which held the few towns and cities, and the North Vietnamese-supported Pathet Lao, which held much of the countryside, including the border supply routes. With Vietnam now center-stage, a major proxy war developed in Laos, which was largely unre-ported and totally denied. Even after the Rolling Thunder bombing of North Vietnam was announced in early 1965, the air war conducted within Laos against the Trail – code-named Steel Tiger – was kept secret, though for a long time it was of far greater intensity. By then as many as 300 sorties a day were being flown.

Whereas the US had all along been openly sup-porting the defense of South Vietnam, the American Ambassador to Laos, William Sullivan, was in the extraordinary position of commanding a large, unacknowledged war from within his Embassy at Vientiane. He would do so throughout

his posting from 1964 to 1968, or throughout the most bitter combat years of the Vietnam war. After 1965 Ambassador Sullivan's war was no longer much of a secret – but it was no longer just a CIA-financed affair, or the dual, shadowed side of diplo-macy. The Ambassador was helping to co-ordinate the might of the US Strategic Air Force against tar-gets inside neutral Laos (through which 3000 North Vietnamese troops were believed to be infil-trating South each month).

'Laos wasn't the center of activity,' Sullivan explains, 'and since we didn't wish to get the United States forces directly involved in a con-frontation there while the confrontation was being pursued in South Vietnam, it was decided not to take an overt cognizance of this breakdown [of neutrality], and to continue to operate in a covert way.'

This meant that while breaching neutrality Sullivan had to prevent it from getting out of hand. He had to have final approval of targets. Sullivan had been a US delegate at the 1961 Geneva Conference held to guarantee the neutral-ity of Laos, and before becoming Ambassador he had chaired a working group of Pentagon and CIA experts on how to co-ordinate Vietnam war policy.

He argued unsuccessfully that the scenario for bombing the North should be restricted to targets further removed from population centers, but as Ambassador in Laos he exercised total control, opposing Pentagon plans to use US ground forces against the Trail. Part of the infiltration routes came within his jurisdiction. Though these fed the war in South Vietnam Sullivan's orders at times had precedence over General Westmoreland's in order to disguise a war which didn't officially exist.

'I was restrictive not only on B-52 strikes', says Sullivan, 'but also on strikes of tactical aircraft. These were fast moving aircraft and their navigational controls were not all that precise in those jungle areas, and we wanted to be absolutely certain that they were not indiscriminately striking into inhabited areas. This meant that we insisted on photography beforehand and several times I'm sure that Westy was impatient with the delay.' In fact, some critics in the military now called the Trail the Sullivan Freeway.

General Westmoreland was equally impatient with Washington. He argued that bombing of the Trail was no more effective than bombing of the North. He wanted to invade far enough into Laos to cut the Trail and in 1966 he 'prepared detailed plans for such an operation'. He estimated it would take 'at least a corps-size force of three divisions' to keep the Trail blocked. Washington viewed the likely casualty rate, and risk of escalation, as far too great. But in mid-1967 Westmoreland found a strong supporter in the new American Ambassador to Saigon, Ellsworth Bunker. 'Shortly after I arrived,' says Bunker, 'I sent a message to the President urging that we go into Laos. If we cut the Trail, the Viet Cong – I thought – would wither on the vine. The only thing that kept them going were supplies, weapons and ammunition from Hanoi.'

A one-time sugar magnate, Bunker had learned his business the hard way as a New Jersey dockhand. It had earned him the reputation of an accomplished trouble-shooter: 'an inspired contriver of compromises'. He had been a US delegate to the United Nations, Chairman of the Organization of American States and Chairman of the American Red Cross, but now exchanging the business of the wounded for the Vietnam war – where he would serve six years – Bunker was against compromise over the Trail. He 'recognized' that invading Laos would violate its neutrality, 'but my point was that the other side had violated the agreement ever since they had signed it'. As to fears of escalation, specifically Chinese intervention, Bunker simply felt: 'We had friends in Peking. The British and the French were there. They could explain to the Peking government that we had no designs on China, or on North Vietnam – that North Vietnam could have any kind of government it wanted but that they were not going to take over the South.'

However President Johnson ordered that there be no further discussion of invading Laos; he was then, anyhow, putting his faith in a quite opposite, remote-control scheme for blocking the Trail, known as the McNamara Line. This was an electronic 'fence' intended to straddle the northern borders for 100 kilometers. At a projected cost of a billion dollars, this barrier would comprise conventional barbed-wire and minefields several kilometers deep, strewn with thousands of seismic and accoustic sensors.

Westmoreland was sceptical. He felt Washington was still looking for simplistic or easy way out solutions. His deputy, General DePuy, describes the sensors as 'shaped like little bushes, trees and bamboo shoots'. Dropped from planes, each sensor had its own code locating its area and the various sensors could transmit the sounds and presence of men and vehicles. With this information, artillery and fighter-bombers could be brought to bear. But Westmoreland argued that the McNamara Line, or the minefields necessary to protect the electronic devices, could not be built

without initially deploying a lot more supporting troops which he could not spare. He was proved right. When actual construction began in early 1967, concentrated North Vietnamese attacks forced a halt.

At this time Westmoreland's command estimated that troop reinforcements from the North were at least 90,000 a year. While refining its plans for electronic warfare Washington ordered that air strikes against the Trail, already 300 a day, be gradually tripled. On the Trail itself, journalist Tran Mai Nam recorded the 'tight surveillance by reconnaissance planes, to say nothing of unpredictable brushes with patrols of the enemy's Special Forces. We are issued passwords, special signals, recognition signs, both for the day and night, in case contact is broken.'

By now, Tran Mai Nam had spent several months on the Trail. From a base camp in the mountains overlooking the border province of Quang Tri, battalions would descend into the lowlands, divide into platoons, attack, then regroup back in the hills. The days were no less arduous: on the climb 'the veins on your forehead swell with your rapid pulse', and frequently caught by storms or commando raids the units would have to camp for days in the forest 'eating only rice soup, wild roofs and leaves'. Without any time limit on their assignment the men on the Trail wondered when they might again see their homes, but the political officer told them: 'These forests and mountains are our homeland; our weapon.' Political cadres were attached to each platoon to maintain morale. One likened the Trail to 'a giant python feeding on pigs'.

The python had swelled. With the intensified bombing the North had placed its elite divisions, a 25,000-man force coded Duan 559, on permanent guard. This force staffed the base camps, which constantly relocated with the B-52 bombing, and manned the checkpoints and artillery positions. Somehow, an estimated 10,000 artillery pieces had been hauled into the mountains for thousands of kilometers. An equal number of trucks were spaced out, racing the bombers, and youth volunteers recruited from the North repaired and re-repaired the routes. Recalling it, Hanoi's future Ambassador to the United Nations. Ha Van Lau, says the routes were 'permanently maintained by groups of young pioneers, men and women, who were ready every moment to repair the roads immediately after every bombing in such a way that despite the very strict surveillance by American planes this road network was never cut. Every night the roads were immediately repaired.'

One US Special Forces soldier, Ivan Delbyk, who went on commando raids, says that 'at times the Ho Chi Minh Trail was so busy it was like the Long Island expressway – during rush hour'. Another Special Forces officer, Captain Dave Christian, says from experience. 'Well, it wasn't one trail. There were thousands of trails, thousands of rest spots along the way where the enemy troops could seek refuge and build up – and I have to commend them: the NVA were some super soldiers.' But back in the US people would keep asking him. 'Why don't we just plug up the Ho Chi Minh Trail?'

In Washington the question of how to do it was taxing the nation's coffers and, evidently, its intelligence. At CIA headquarters Frank Snepp, who would become the Agency's chief analyst in

Above: Map locates the disposition of North Vietnamese and Viet Cong units in South Vietnam in the summer of 1966. It was estimated that communist combined forces numbered 250,000 soldiers.

Right: The South Vietnamese called the infiltration of nine North Vietnamese regiments in December, 1965, an invasion. Map indicates the location of the North Vietnamese forces, some identified, others not.

Saigon, was hearing the brain-strain. He recalls that among the ideas discussed was a plan to kidnap the entire North Vietnamese leadership, but – he told the author – 'We never knew where to find them all'; (three years out of four the author saw Hanoi's leadership convene at Ba Dinh Square Hall in the capital). The CIA, says Snepp, believed that Hanoi's Chief of Secret Police was partial to Vietnamese apricot brandy and so tried to figure how to get a poisoned bottle to his table.

'Some of the contingency plans were ludicrous,' says Snepp. 'There was consideration at one particular point of dropping Budweiser beer along the infiltration areas in Southern Laos because we discovered that the North Vietnamese forces loved Budweiser beer and we thought it might slow them down. That particular plan died on the drawing-board. We couldn't come up with enough intact cartons to drop on the infiltration system.'

A new super-secret intelligence group known as the Jasons now took over. In early 1967 it had presented very hard information. It concluded that in dollar terms the cost of the bombing was at least ten times as great for the United States as for North Vietnam. The air war over Vietnam was conservatively estimated to be costing a billion dollars a year. The economic damage to the North up to that time was assessed at less than 100 million dollars – with East-Bloc replacement aid valued at several times this loss. No matter how many

factories or facilities lay in ruins, the North had only to keep this aid moving South to maintain the war. Once more President Johnson sought verification from his trusted former Secretary of the Navy, Paul Nitze: was Rolling Thunder really just a storm in an Oriental teacup? Was no knock-out blow possible other than the saturation bombing of civilian areas (which the Johnson administration, at least, consistently avoided)? Nitze had been asked to help revitalize the US Strategic Bombing Survey group which had proved so accurate in its World War II findings. He soon confirmed the negative assessment: there was no means of stopping the source of supplies to the Ho Chi Minh Trail.

'Most of the material,' says Nitze, 'came from either China or Russia. You couldn't destroy the factories that produced the material. You could cause North Vietnam a great deal of difficulty but it didn't look feasible to bring decisive pressure through air attack.' Despite these separate assessments the bombing continued for another five years with an overall loss of some 1000 planes and 800 US airmen killed over the North. Nitze was equally doubtful whether any amount of bombing could block the infiltration routes: 'We had the experience in Korea of trying to interdict the movement of material and we found it very difficult.' And the Trail was vastly more intricate.

Another independent study indicated that the B-52, while potentially the most destructive and

feared weapon, was generally an expensive gamble against a target like the Trail. Bombing by co-ordinates, a B-52 could unleash more than a hundred 750-pound bombs within thirty seconds, cutting a scythe through the forest a mile long and a quarter-mile wide. But the estimated kill ratio was one infiltrator for every 300 bombs – or 100 tons – at a cost of $140,000. US military records show that in the peak year when an estimated 150,000 North Vietnamese were sent South, 171,000 tons of bombs were dropped over the Trail, or about one ton for every suspected infiltrator. If the kill ratio was correct, then the B-52s were accounting for fewer than one in every hundred infiltrators – perhaps 1500 men that year at a cost of more than two billion dollars. Certainly against a jungle enemy America's mightiest conventional weapon was of very questionable value: the B-52 had to rely on something more instant than normal photo-reconnaissance information. With all these negative findings, President Johnson now asked 'Jason' to search for the solution to the mythic Trail.

The self-named Jason Group had existed for several years as a semi-official Think Tank comprising top university scientists, Nobel Laureates, technocrats, computer experts and military strategists. But by 1967 it had been very much enlarged and secretly ensconced in Washington under the new, innocuous title Defense Communications Planning Group (DCPG). It had been given fiscal

July 1967—Heavy artillery at American fire base blasts away at Viet Cong and North Vietnamese positions.

Above: This map, from information provided by several non-official sources, showed effective control of South Vietnam at the beginning of 1966. Black areas indicate government control; white areas indicate Viet Cong or no control.

carte-blanche and a priority rating which had its alumni talking in 'reverential and enthusiastic terms', comparing 'their pace, daring, level of excitement and freedom from bureaucracy' to those who worked on the Manhattan project which produced the atomic bomb, says observer Paul Dickson, author of *The Electronic Battlefield*. As an example he quotes a DCPG member as saying that if the group 'needed 10,000 chocolate cream pies from the army by noon the next day, it would get them and without any questions'.

The Jasons – as they still called themselves – would continue until the end of US involvement in Vietnam five years later to develop and perfect electronic warfare. They had conceived the McNamara Line, and the sensors devised for this were now being dropped over the Trail together with minimines camouflaged to look like leaves, twigs and things of nature (these would later be used by international terrorists). Some of Jason's early brainwaves were painfully felt – by their own side.

There were the 'Button Bomblets' – pill-size explosives which, while inflicting minor injuries, were designed to make enough noise to activate

any nearby sensors – and thus the bombers. In effect, the fighter in the distant jungle stepping on one of these was to press the button for his own destruction. It was envisaged ordering 300 million of these, but then in a test trial a batch of 5000 got scattered on the beaches of Florida's Choctawhatchie Bay and one fine Sunday 10,000 sunbathers had to be evacuated. During this, reports author Paul Dickson, 'an air force demolition expert was blinded while moving a box of several hundred bomblets that exploded' – and that was the end of that.

There was the 'Lava' plan – an unsuccessful search for a chemical formula that could turn the moist forest soil of the Trail into slippery grease. There was 'Project Pigeon', a Strangelovian plan foreseeing limitless flocks of bombers. Strapped with bomblets the pigeons would home in on North Vietnamese vehicles, one and all being blown to bits as the metal triggered the explosives. This too was abandoned when the pigeons, tested against American and North Vietnamese trucks, failed to identify their ideology.

Author Dickson quotes one Jasonite as saying, 'Did you hear about the sensor we came up with in the shape of a dog turd?' It was a Seismic Intrusion

Detector (SID) and '. . . we called it TURDSID'. Jason appropriately discovered the Dragonteeth – bombs weighing only about half an ounce, to be strewn over the Trail from a mother bomb – and, helped by the Air Force, it built a bigger Daisy-Cutter, calling it the 'Cheeseburger' because its explosive mixture had everything.

But by late 1967 Jason had found a combination ultra-weapon, which it was boasted had changed the balance of conventional war (with the danger in the nuclear age of rendering conventional war obsolete). This was code-named Igloo White, a system of remote-control warfare. Elements of it included the ground sensors, and relay aircraft kept in 'orbit' over the battle area to transmit the sensor signals to distant computers, whose instant printout would activate aircraft bombing by co-ordinates. For extra round-the-clock vigilance of moving targets the system gave birth to INFANT (Iroquois Night Fighter And Night Tracker), a helicopter gunship with infra-red scopes able to magnify star or moonlight up to 50,000 times, then follow the target on television monitors. Said an official study of Igloo White: 'The Trail has in effect been a field laboratory for testing and perfecting the apparatus for an electronic battlefield.'

Even in terms of conventional fire-power deployed, there was nothing comparable in all of history. The bomb ordnance expended along this single battle front exceeded that used in all theaters of war during all the years of World War II. (In World War II two million tons of air ordnance were dropped. From 1965 to 1971 2,235,918 tons of bombs were dropped over Laos infiltration routes.) Air strikes against the Trail soon exceeded 500 each day.

However, at the start of 1968 – when the drama would shift to South Vietnam's cities – the 'electronic battlefield' system was not sufficiently enlarged to become operational across the vast infiltration routes. But the first element of it – the sensors developed for the McNamara Line – were in place, some 20,000 of them. Accoustic sensors, dropped by 'invisible' parachutes to suspend from the high foliage, recorded the sounds of human and vehicle activity. Seismic sensors, disguised like tiny trees and plants and spiked to dig into the earth where they fell, registered the pressure wave on the earth's surface of groups of men or machines.

There were also the 'People Sniffers' – a kind of radar with a long snout that hung from the helicopters and registered body heat or smell. Officially called Personnel Detectors, they were appraised at the time by *Ordnance* magazine as having 'proved invaluable in detecting the unseen enemy'. Instead of more troops, General Westmoreland was getting gadgets and finding it frustrating. 'The "People Sniffers" ', he says 'could pick up concentrations of individuals in the jungle by the odor they generated, and the excretion therefrom, without physically seeing these people.' But his deputy, General DePuy, says: 'They were never very successful. The fact that we don't have them today may be sufficient evidence that they weren't. Those sniffers sniffed ammonia from body functions and the problem was that animals and other distracting influences made them ineffective.' The distracting influences included a crudely effective North Vietnamese counter-measure. They were known to hang bags of buffalo urine along unused

areas of the Trail – and the urine reportedly fetched the B-52s like flies.

'They were tough soldiers, very persevering,' admits Westmoreland, 'and this was typical all the way from the Politburo in Hanoi down to the lower ranks. Their commanders were well disciplined, well trained; but they were ruthless in demanding strict obedience.'

With 150,000 North Vietnamese estimated to be moving down the Trail at the start of 1968 Westmoreland clearly did not think that electronic warfare was going to change the balance in time. 'On the battlefield of the future', he would pointedly say a little later, 'enemy forces will be located, tracked and targeted almost instantaneously' – and then 'the need for large forces will be less important.' But in the pivotal year of 1968 the organization and discipline of the Trail was vividly recorded by another North Vietnamese journalist, Khanh Van, who later wrote of it in a Hanoi military newspaper *Quan Doi Nhan Dan*. Setting out from the main staging area at Dong Hoi, north-east of the Demilitarized Zone, the troops could now reach almost any part of the Trail within six weeks – a journey that three years earlier had taken up to six months. But still, in Van's words, 'aircraft roared continuously overhead'. The Trail routes closest to the North were now naked from the bombing and defoliants.

'I gradually realized', he wrote, 'that almost no part of this road section was well concealed. Along the roadside, trees had been stripped of leaves and

branches. There remained only bare trunks with pointed tops. I was told that on certain days aggressor aircraft, in formations of three, sprayed toxic chemicals over this road. At night dozens of fires flicker on the crests of hills where the broken remnants of the forest go on burning from one raid to the next.'

Whether traveling or in action the platoons were divided into three-man cells. They were to assist each other in times of illness, or combat, or in maintaining morale against war-weariness and home-sickness. The soldiers were younger now, often under seventeen, and the cell-system evidently combined paternalism and Big Brother. They now began marching before sunrise, taking only one break before dusk for a rice-ball lunch prepared the previous night. The ration per man was two pounds of rice per day, some vegetables and occasional fish – often caught by tossing a grenade in a stream. On the march they had one day's rest a week at base camps which now had field hospitals, news-printing facilities, and telephone lines from one camp to the next. At each camp the troops received exhaustive briefings on the way ahead.

'The on-duty cadre', wrote Khanh Van, 'was always conversant with everything – from weather conditions to the level of the water along the overall route. He knew how many bombs were dropped at key points, how many bombs had hit the surface of the road, how many cubic meters of earth and stone were required to do the repair job, and at what time the repair would be finished.'

*Right: March 13, 1967—Under fire, a U.S. soldier of the 1st Air Cavalry races for cover carrying the rifle of a dead fellow soldier. The unit hit heavy fire as it moved down a rocky slope, trying to relieve a company pinned down in flatland near the village of My Phu, about 290 miles northeast of Saigon. They were forced to pull back, leaving behind some of their dead.*

Above: July 6, 1967—A U.S. Marine runs for cover as U.S. jets blast North Vietnamese positions between Con Thien and the demilitarized zone. The marines had met heavy enemy fire as they tried to move into the area to recover the bodies of marines killed earlier in the week.

The functioning of the Trail, he reported, was due to 'skillful signal operations'. At one camp during one day '600 messages were received or dispatched'. After a typical bombing raid '286 cuts in telephone wires were repaired by telephone combatants' on the immediate route. There were specialist teams for every function. The road repair gangs – 'Youth Shock Brigades Against the Americans for National Salvation' – numbered 50,000, according to the Communist press, and they were as young as fifteen, volunteering for three years service on the Trail. With males drafted into the army at eighteen, the majority of the Shock Brigades were young women.

The casualty rate among this civilian defense force on the Trail must have been considerable, judging from Khanh Van's report: 'There's an enemy trick to use bombs of many different types.

If we want to fill in the bomb craters we must first of all destroy enemy time bombs. If we want to destroy the time bombs we must destroy the [small, disguised] magnetic bombs. To destroy the magnetic and time bombs, it is necessary to sweep away the barrier formed by the trigger mines that the enemy drops on both ends of the [road] control point in order to keep us from moving up to repair the damaged road sections.'

Control points, each with a company of fifty or sixty troops, guarded the truck parks spaced out under jungle cover every three miles or so, with other fuel, food and ammunition depots similarly spread out to minimize losses. The trucks worked in relays, driving back and forth along one section of the Trail. No truck traveled the whole route South – again to reduce losses. Most routes, some now paved, had a lay-over system. If a sector was

bombed the trucks could safely pull off under covered bays until the route was repaired. Says Hanoi strategist Ha Van Lau, 'Along each section of the road we'd constructed barracks so that our drivers could rest. And around these barracks there were always vegetable gardens, chickens and pigs. It was almost a normal life. Very active because there was combat – it was exposed all the time. But very normal.'

But from his earlier first-hand observations and later information, journalist Wilfred Burchett says bomb damage to the Trail transportation system was 'very considerable. At one point they calculated that to get 600 trucks to their destination they would have to start out with a thousand.' The US Air Force claimed that in the late, peak bombing period it damaged some 25,000 trucks on the Trail and 'actually destroyed' half of them. If so, then toward the war's end North Vietnam had to replace its entire truck armada in one year – and faced doing so annually. But with Sino-Soviet military and economic aid exceeding one billion dollars a year this replacement would have been a relatively minor cost compared to the 500 planes which the US officially lost over the Trail (one seventh of the total lost in South Vietnam) during the air war.

By the early 1970s, as American troops started to withdraw, the US 'electronic battlefield' was fully ready. New, deadly 'Hobos' – Homing Bombs – and 'Smart' bombs, guided by a laser beam to their target, would be used in the last days of American involvement. But Soviet Sam-2 missiles would then also be pointing from the jungles of the Ho Chi Minh Trail, and the outcome of an electronic war in this improbable arena would never be known. The decisive factor remained the same: how many trucks could run the gauntlet.

In 1967 the Pentagon had estimated that the North's war against the South could be sustained with only sixty tons of supplies a day (though some specialists argued that it could be done with far less). During 1970, with the US ground war winding down, the Secretary of the Air Force cited figures that '68,000 tons of material started down the Trail and 21,000 tons managed to reach their final destination' – almost exactly sixty tons a day.

Human endurance had prevailed on the Trail – but only just. Perhaps for the last time in a major conventional war man had outlasted or outwitted the machines. The Trail veterans, as General Westmoreland said, were a tough persevering bunch, and perhaps the terrors of Jason were nothing compared to those of nature on the Trail itself. In his science-future account, author Paul Dickson recounts how various sensor recordings of North Vietnamese voices on the Trail were rushed back to Washington for urgent analysis. He quotes Jason's deputy-director as saying 'We were very eager to find out how the enemy would react. They shot some, burned others and in what was perhaps the ultimate act of contempt we actually heard them pissing on one of our accoustic sensors.'

By early 1968 the thousands of sensors were recording something more extraordinary: the entire Trail seemed to be hissing, uncoiling, like a giant python about to strike.

Left: March 27, 1967—U.S. troops of the 2nd Battalion, 173rd Airborne Brigade, advance on suspected Viet Cong positions during the second phase of Operation Junction City in War Zone C.

Below: January 12, 1967—Black smoke rises from B-52 air strikes in the Iron Triangle, about 35 miles northwest of Saigon, during Operation Cedar Falls, the prelude to Operation Junction City. The bombing revealed bunkers and trenches of five enemy base camps as ground troops of the U.S. 1st Infantry Division moved into the area.

Above: 1967—Bob Hope and Raquel Welch share the stage as they entertain the troops in South Vietnam.

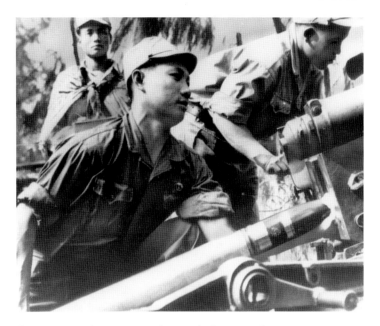

Above: 1967—A North Vietnamese coastal gun crew loads its weapon during operations against U.S. warships shelling targets in North Vietnam.

Above: 1967—Ho Chi Minh, president of North Vietnam, speaks to the 4th Congress of Heroes and Elite Fighters in Hanoi.

Left: 1967—Viet Cong guerrillas pose together for a photo found on the body of a dead guerrilla by U.S. 1st Infantry troops during Operation Cedar Falls in the Iron Triangle area north of Saigon.

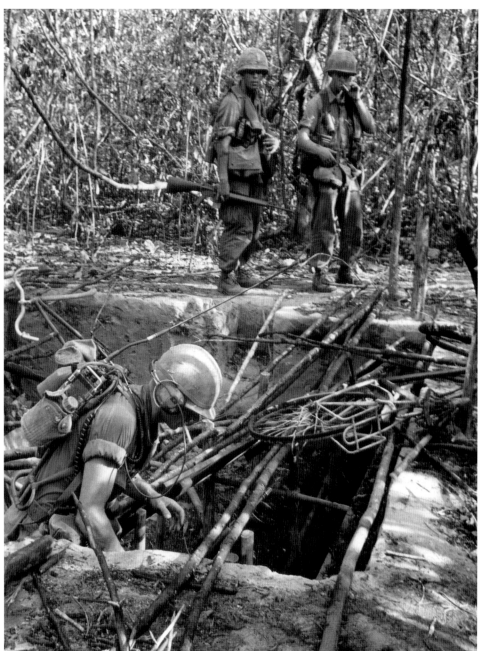

Above: January 1967—The bodies of former President Ngo Dinh Dien and his brother, Ngo Dinh Nhu, are buried in their third resting place, in unmarked graves in Saigon's main public cemetery, four years after they died in a coup. Superstitious South Vietnamese reburied them twice to keep their souls from stirring up further trouble. Lack of headstones is supposed to make it less likely that the spirits will wander.

Above left: 1967—North Vietnamese soldiers with bayonets on their rifles march a captured U.S. airman to a press conference with foreign journalists in Hanoi.

Above: 1967—President Lyndon B. Johnson addresses troops at Cam Ranh Bay.

Left: January 1967—A U.S. soldier of the 1st Battalion, 26th Regiment, 1st Infantry Division, inspects a Viet Cong base camp in the jungle 30 miles northwest of Saigon. The unoccupied camp in the Iron Triangle area had been struck by B-52 bombers before the infantry moved in.

Above: January 1967—The U.S. Department of Defense released this photo, described as a South Vietnamese man tortured by the Viet Cong. Vietnamese officials said more than 2,000 civilians had been executed by the Viet Cong in the previous three years.

Above: January 1967—A U.S. military convoy moves into the Mekong Delta town of Rach Kien, which had fallen to the Viet Cong in 1965. A battalion of U.S. troops was now occupying the area, securing the road for U.S. military traffic.

Above: January 1967—A Vietnamese man who lived his life in the Mekong Delta area south of Saigon.

Above: January 1967—A refugee child confused by the chaos in her village in the Iron Triangle. The villagers were being removed to a resettlement area.

Right: January 1967—A South Vietnamese mother carries her children in one of two baskets attached to a stick she holds over her shoulder in Ben Suc. Villagers leave their homes to be resettled at a refugee camp in another area. They are part of some 10,000 peasants evacuated from the Iron Triangle, a Viet Cong stronghold, as U.S. troops push through.

Left: Febuary 1967—A field is littered with bodies of dead North Vietnamese soldiers dragged with ropes to a central area for mass burial after a battle. Korean Marines claimed they killed 243 of the enemy.

Below: January 29, 1967—An infantryman of the U.S. 25th Division moves through jungle underbrush in South Vietnam to help his unit seal off a cave entrance for a tear gas and grenade attack.

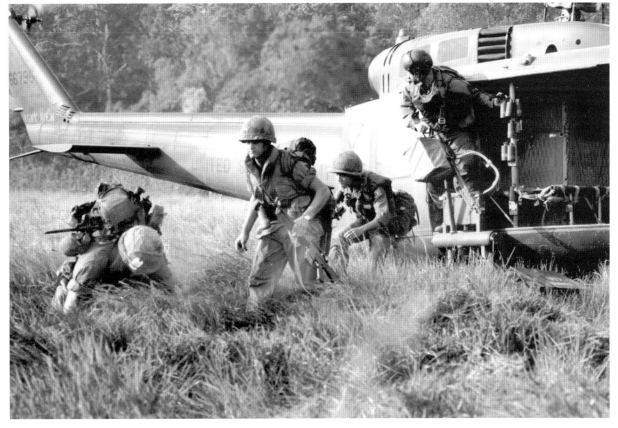

Above: February 1967—Korean troops of the White Horse Division sit in the jungle of the Hon La Mountains during an operation 230 miles northeast of Saigon.

Left: February 23, 1967—Troops of the U.S. 196th Light Infantry Brigade leap from a helicopter into a landing zone close to South Vietnam's Cambodian border during Operation Junction City.

Above: February 23, 1967—U.S. soldiers take up positions along the rim of a bomb crater during Operation Junction City, about 60 miles northwest of Saigon. The operation to clear Viet Cong strongholds in War Zone C was one of the largest of the war, eventually involving some 25,000 allied troops.

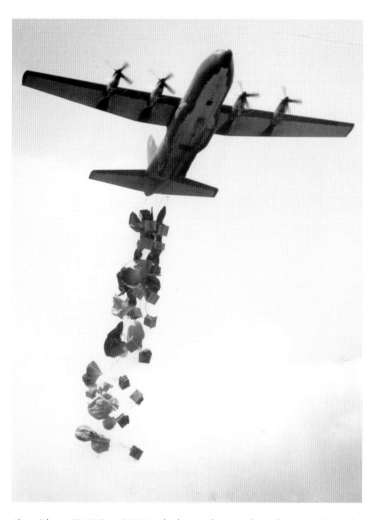

Above: February 22, 1967—A C-130 Hercules drops supply crates with parachutes in War Zone C during Operation Junction City, one of the largest operations of the war.

Above: February 22, 1967—Paratroopers of the 2nd Battalion, 503rd Infantry, 173rd Airborne Brigade jump over a landing zone in War Zone C, about four miles from the Cambodian border during Operation Junction City. More than 700 paratroopers were dropped in the first major U.S. Airborne assault since the Korean War.

Above: February 16, 1967—Viet Cong dead are piled outside a Korean base near Quang Ngai, about 340 miles northeast of Saigon, after Korean Marines of the Blue Dragon Brigade repelled repeated attacks by two Viet Cong battalions. The Koreans reported 243 enemy killed.

Right: February 19, 1967—U.S. infantrymen of the 25th Division pass the skull of a water buffalo in a jungle clearing during Operation Junction City in western Tay Ninh province, 65 miles northwest of Saigon.

Below: February 20, 1967—Ammunition and other supplies for troops of the U.S. 173rd Airborne Brigade drift toward a landing in War Zone C during Operation Junction City, a massive assault on Viet Cong strongholds northwest of Saigon.

Above: February 1967—The command group of the 1st Battalion, 5th Marine Regiment, huddles together under sniper fire during Operation Rio Grande south of Quang Ngai, 330 miles northeast of Saigon.

Above: February 2, 1967—A young woman peasant of Vietnam's Mekong Delta.

Left: February 25, 1967—Members of Vietnam's Roman Catholic organization participate in a sanctioned demonstration in Saigon to protest 'false peace moves.' They hold effigies of French President Charles de Gaulle, North Vietnamese President Ho Chi Minh, and U.S. Sen. J. W. Fulbright.

Above: February 14, 1967—Enemy sniper bullets crackle overhead as a wounded GI lies in a ditch and others return the fire. This soldier was hit in the eye as the 1st Cavalry unit was attacked crossing a rice paddy near Bong Son, some 300 miles northeast of Saigon.

Right: February 1967—An elderly Vietnamese woman reaches into a large jar for water to fight the flames consuming her home in a village 20 miles southwest of Danang, where U.S. Marines fought a Viet Cong force.

Above: February 1967—Antiwar demonstrators jam the corridor in the administrative offices of the University of Wisconsin. The students threatened to keep the chancellor in his office unless 17 persons arrested in an earlier protest are freed. The siege was lifted three hours later.

Left: February 1967—A battery of 105mm Howitzers are spread over an open area, set in place to support ground troops in Operation Junction City.

Right: Capt. James D. Bruton of Salina, Kansas, a military chaplain, conducts dawn services for troops of the U.S. 9th Marine Division at Dong Tam, 45 miles southwest of Saigon, in South Vietnam's Mekong Delta.

Above: March 8, 1967—Spent shell casings pile up at Soui Da, 60 miles northwest of Saigon on the southern edge of War Zone C. This was just one of the bases firing artillery support during Operation Junction City, one of the largest operations of the war.

Above: March 10, 1967—After emerging from a tunnel in the jungle of Vietnam's Iron Triangle, Viet Cong members head for a central surrender point under the Chieu Hoi (Open Arms) policy.

Above: March 1967—A soldier of the U.S. 11th Armored Cavalry Regiment writes a letter as another hangs wash from a radio antenna during a break after Operation Junction City.

Right: March 27, 1967—During the second phase of Operation Junction City in War Zone C, U.S. troops of the 2nd Battalion, 173rd Airborne Brigade, advance toward suspected Viet Cong positions, passing through the smoke and dust of an earlier artillery barrage.

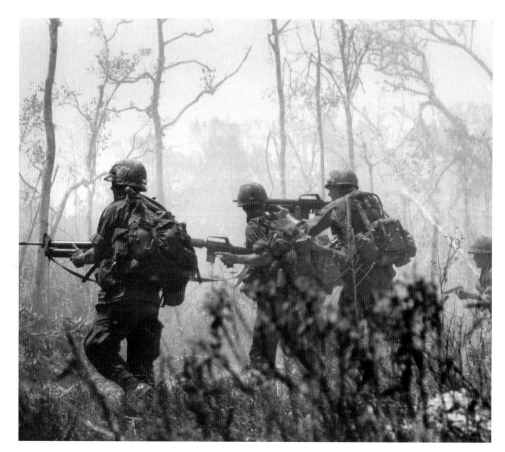

Right: March 3, 1967—U.S. Marines of the 1st Battalion, 9th Regiment, man a mortar on Hill 162 near the demilitarized zone while taking mortar fire from North Vietnamese positions. The North Vietnamese had lobbed more than 1,000 mortars at Marine positions south of the DMZ in the previous three days.

Above: March 1967—With M60 machine gun ammunition over his shoulders Pfc. Filomeno E. Castaneda of Denver, Colorado, uses a mirror while applying camouflage grease paint.

Above: March 1967—Camouflaged troops of the Korean Tiger Division's armored cavalry cross the Ky Lo River in an assault on a suspected Viet Cong stronghold about 230 miles northeast of Saigon. Operation Oh Jak Kyo was intended to open and secure some 50 miles of Route 1.

Above: March 23, 1967—Burning trucks and other debris block the road near Gio Linh after the Viet Cong attacked an ammunition convoy with mortars and artillery. A least seven trucks en route to the Marine camp at Gio Linh were destroyed.

Right: March 8, 1967—Troops of the U.S. 1st Air Cavalry Division's elite reconnaissance unit return fire, right, as a wounded member is carried to a more secure area in a tree line near Bong Son on the central coast of Vietnam. The unit encountered a stronger-than-expected enemy presence in the area.

Left: March 16, 1967—An infantryman shouts a sniper warning as troops of the 4th Infantry Division were setting up a mortar position in Plei Djereng, 20 miles northwest of Pleiku near the Cambodian border. The infantrymen exchanged fire with an estimated platoon of North Vietnamese soldiers.

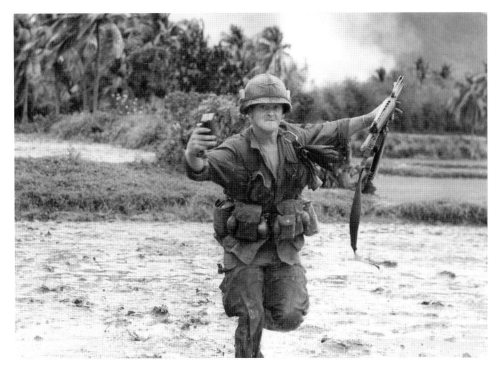

Above: March 8, 1967—A Blue Team member of the 1st Battalion, 9th Infantry Regiment – the 1st Air Cavalry Division's elite reconnaissance unit – runs through North Vietnamese fire while carrying his dismantled rifle and a magazine of bullets. He was cleaning the rifle near Bong Son when the enemy zeroed in on his position, forcing him to dash for cover.

Right: March 1967—A guard mans an isolated post at Huong My in the Mekong Delta. He is one of South Vietnam's 140,000 popular forces, part-time warriors poorly armed and poorly paid.

Below: March 1967—A .50-caliber machinegun in a Marine helicopter covers the 'Rock Pile' and 'Razor-back' mountains near the DMZ of Vietnam, focal points of Marine battles in the area.

Left: March 1967—A surface-to-air missile (SAM) site is highlighted in an Air Force photo of a residential area in North Vietnam. Two other SAM sites were located within five miles, also in heavily populated areas.

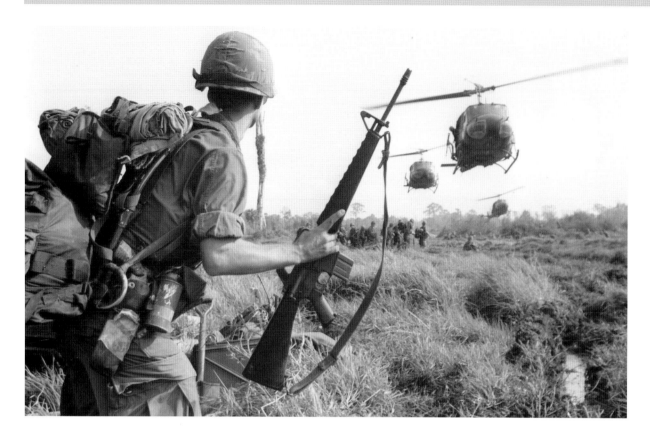

Left: March 1967—U.S. troops disembark during a helicopter assault on suspected Viet Cong positions.

Above: March 1967—Youths of the village of Phu Huu wear black pajama outfits and use bamboo staves as they are taught to drill by an armed member of Vietnam's pacification cadre. Rifles will replace the staves and the youths will defend the area against the Viet Cong when the pacification cadre moves on to a new village.

Above: March 9, 1967—U.S. troops leap from helicopter at the beginning of a mission to search out Viet Cong positions. Frequently helicopters, in a vulnerable position at this point in an attack, only hover momentarily over the drop zone and troops leap from the craft.

Left: March 1967—A small mountain, dubbed by U.S. Marines as the 'Rock Pile' is scene of constant battles with the North Vietnamese along the DMZ. In a strategic valley overlooking a main highway, the Communists had stored tons of ammunition and food supplies in hundreds of small natural caves.

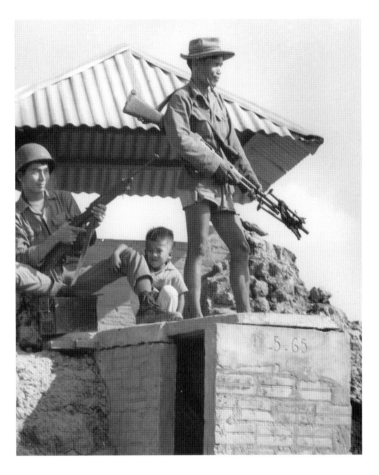

Above: March 3, 1967—American troops move cautiously through the high elephant grass as they seek out Viet Cong positions during one of many patrols.

Right: March 1967—A youngster joins two militiamen on guard against Viet Cong at Huong My in the Mekong Delta. When not on duty, the men tend their farms.

Right: March 1967—Despite his wounds, an American soldier keeps a lookout for enemy troops during an ambush by Viet Cong. In background medics tend to the wounds of others hit by Viet Cong fire.

Above: March 10, 1967—U.S. Secretary of Defense Melvin R. Laird steps from a helicopter after arriving at Danang following a four-day tour of South Vietnam bases.

Right: Anti–Vietnam War demonstrators fill Fulton Street in San Francisco. The five-mile march through the city ended with a peace rally at Kezar Stadium. Domed building is San Francisco City Hall.

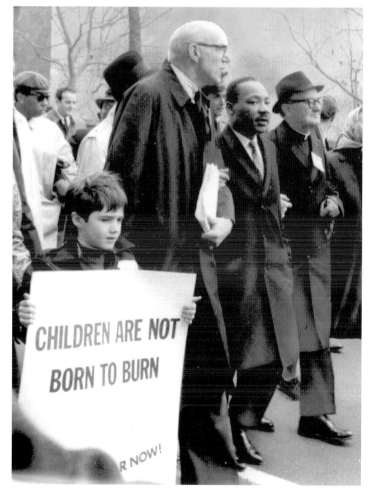

Medics give first aid to a wounded American soldier seconds after he was shot. The 1st U.S. Division troops fought the Viet Cong 271st Regiment in the South Vietnamese jungles of Zone C close to the Cambodian border.

Dr. Benjamin Spock, Dr. Martin Luther King Jr., and Monsignor Charles O. Rice link arms as they march in an anti–Vietnam War rally in New York's Central Park.

Left: April 1967—U.S. Marines take shelter in a Buddhist pagoda during a monsoon shower near Gio Linh, just south of the demilitarized zone. The Marines were providing security for engineers and bulldozer crews clearing a no-man's-land to stop infiltration across the DMZ from the north.

Below: April 17, 1967—Richard M. Nixon, running for president, chats with Lt. Gen. Lewis W. Walt, commander of U.S. Marines in Vietnam, during a visit to Da Nang.

Right: April, 1967 The U.S. Marines rest on ammunition boxes at Gio Linh, just south of the demilitarized zone. The Marines were taking regular mortar and artillery fire from Communist forces.

Left: April 1967—A phosphorous grenade leaves a spidery trail as it ignites napalm falling into the jungle of the An Lao Valley. A plane of the 1st Cavalry Division dropped the firebomb during Operation Thayer II.

Above: April 24, 1967—U.S. Navy Ensign James W. Laing ejects from his F-4 Phantom over the Gulf of Tonkin off the coast of North Vietnam. Laing and his pilot shot down a Communist MiG on a raid near Hanoi, but ran low on fuel as they returned. Both ejected and were rescued.

Left: April 1967—A 175mm gun at Camp Carroll near the demilitarized zone blasts enemy positions in support of Marines operating in Quang Tri province. The gun was manned by the 2nd Battalion, 94th Infantry Regiment.

Above: April 1967—An RF-101 reconnaissance plane on a photographic mission crosses the enemy airfield at Kep, North Vietnam, 39 miles northeast of Hanoi.

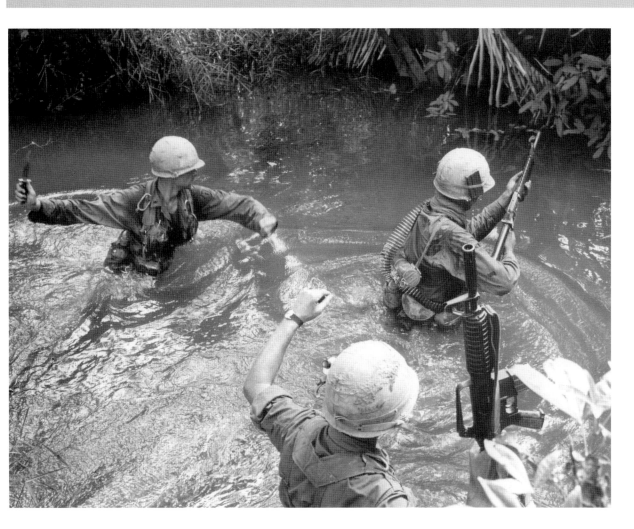

Left: April 1967—U.S. soldiers of the 25th Infantry Division wade through a canal in pursuit of a sniper who opened fired on them during a mission west of Cu Chi near the Cambodian border. The sniper escaped.

Below: April 5, 1967—The sun setting behind him, a U.S. Marine uses high-powered binoculars to monitor the demilitarized zone from a 90-foot watchtower at Camp Carroll, an artillery base just south of the DMZ.

Right: April 18, 1967—Watched by a Vietnamese peasant, a U.S. soldier of the 3rd Battalion, 39th Regiment, 9th Infantry Division, searches a village in the Mekong Delta during Operation Enterprise in Long An province.

Above: April 9, 1967—A U.S. helicopter gunner overlooks a fleet of fishing sampans in Danang Bay. The sampans, loaded with their day's catch, often have to maneuver among U.S. Navy warships.

Left: April 19, 1967—With a cold rain falling, Vietnamese children watch as U.S. Amtracs pull a mine-damaged bulldozer from an area just below the demilitarized zone. The children and their families are being relocated from the no-man's-land cleared near the DMZ.

Below: April 1967—Three F-105 Thunderchiefs release their bombs over North Vietnam.

Right: April 1967—As the sun sets behind them, gunners of the U.S. 1st Cavalry Division finish their daylight firing mission near Bong Son on the central coast of South Vietnam.

Above: April 9, 1967—A soldier of the U.S. 1st Cavalry Division aims a flamethrower at the mouth of a cave after Viet Cong guerrillas believed hiding inside had been warned to surrender. Viet Cong units in the An Lao Valley had dispersed in small groups as U.S. troops entered the region, about 300 miles northeast of Saigon.

Below: April 2, 1967—U.S. Army engineers build trenches and bunkers for a Special Forces camp near the Saigon River in War Zone C. The camp would be home to about 400 Vietnamese militiamen and U.S. Special Forces when thousands of U.S. troops pulled out of the area following Operation Junction City.

Above: April 1967—The French-built fort at Long Huu, 25 miles from Saigon, lies on a channel to the capital from the South China Sea. The fort, originally built in 1910 to protect French colonial interests, had since been occupied by Japanese, Vietminh, South Vietnamese government troops, the Viet Cong, and U.S. troops.

Left: April 1967—U.S. infantrymen hitch a ride back to base on the beach near Duc Pho during Operation Oregon in southern Quang Ngai province, about 325 miles northeast of Saigon.

Above: April 27, 1967—A U.S. Marine quickly dons his helmet as a Chinook helicopter drops supplies on a hill west of Danang. Because of jungle terrain, they were unable to land.

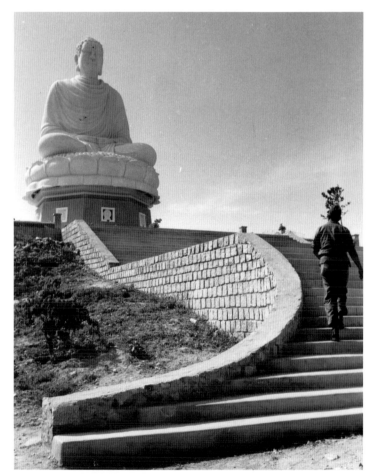

Above: April 30, 1967—A huge concrete Buddha image built to commemorate the Buddhist struggle to overthrow the late President Ngo Dinh Diem dominates the skyline at the coastal town of Nhatrang, a center of Buddhist opposition to Diem.

Above: April 1967—With his machine gun shouldered, and with a splendid view of sprawling flatlands and a curling river, a Marine treks down a hill 20 miles from Danang in search of a North Vietnamese headquarters installation said to be in the area.

Above: April 1967—The French-built fort at Long Huu, 25 miles from Saigon, lies on a channel to the capital from the South China Sea. The fort, originally built in 1910 to protect French colonial interests, had since been occupied by Japanese, Viet Minh, South Vietnamese government troops, the Viet Cong and U.S. troops.

Above: April 1967—A Marine watchtower just south of the DMZ looks over North Vietnamese positions in and north of the demarcation lines. A self-propelled 155mm artillery piece can hit targets spotted from the tower.

Left: Bodies of three young Vietnamese girls, hands tied behind them, lie in a road at Suoi Chon, 40 miles from Saigon. The girls, members of a government pacification team, were executed on the spot by Viet Cong who also killed a score of others and burned the village.

Above: May 5, 1967—Gen. William C. Westmoreland, commander of U.S. forces in Vietnam, introduces his new deputy and eventual successor, Gen. Creighton D. Abrams (right) to Prime Minister Nguyen Cao Ky at Independence Palace in Saigon.

Below: April 2, 1967—An aged Vietnamese farmer studies a billboard in Binh Phong Thanh to select his candidate before casting his ballot in South Vietnam's village and hamlet council elections.

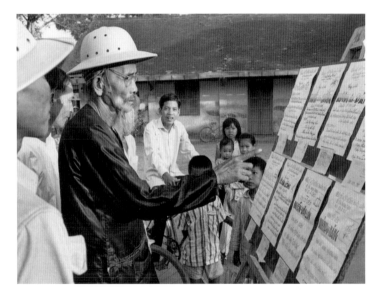

Above: April 16, 1967—Former Vice President Richard Nixon bends for a better look at a Montagnard woman's headdress as he shake hands during his visit to the village of Boun Kram, about 70 miles north of Saigon. Nixon observed voting for local council members in the village.

Above: May 5, 1967—A U.S. Marine of the 2nd Battalion, 3rd Marine Regiment, pistol in one hand and an active grenade in the other, inches his way forward to Hilltop 881 North in South Vietnam.

Left: May 1967—A U.S. Marine of the 3rd Battalion, 4th Regiment, crouches in a pagoda entrance during a patrol along the Ben Hai River in the southern sector of the demilitarized zone.

Right: May 2, 1967—A U.S. Navy corpsman dives for safety after the injured Marine he was aiding died. The U.S. Marines stormed Hill 881 near Khe Sanh in South Vietnam's Laotian border, where they fought a bloody, often hand-to-hand battle for two days.

Below: May 3, 1967—U.S. Marines stand on Hill 881 North after a fierce nine-day battle near Khe Sanh, South Vietnam.

Right: May 1967—Taking fire from enemy snipers, U.S. troops of the 2nd Brigade, 1st Infantry, charge toward the cover of bomb craters and rice paddy dikes at a landing zone near Phu Loi, 12 miles north of Saigon. Troops moved toward the center of Binh Duong province, once a Viet Cong stronghold.

Below: May 16, 1967—U.S. Marines rest on the altar of an abandoned Roman Catholic Church south of Con Thien. The church was later hit by mortar fire when helicopters landed to evacuate wounded troops.

Right: May 1967—Photos from Hanoi television are identified as captured U.S. airmen. Top left: James Shively; bottom left: James L. Hughes; and Gordon A. Larson in both photos at right.

Above: May 6, 1967—Col. Gordon Albert Larson is escorted to the International Club in Hanoi to meet with journalists one day after his F-105 Thunderchief fighter-bomber was shot down over North Vietnam.

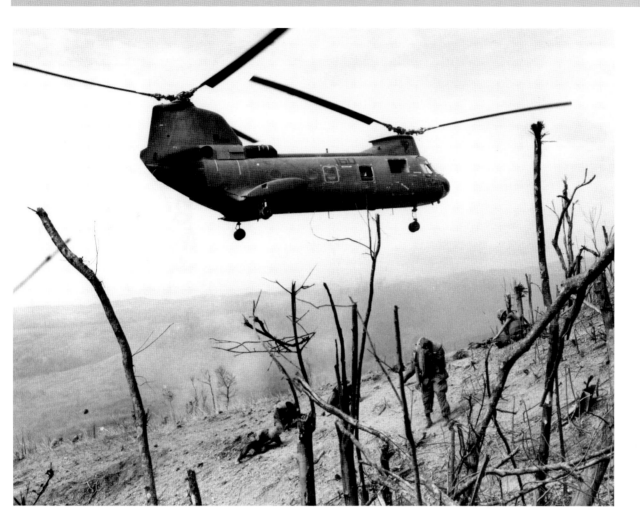

Left: May 1967—A CH-46 Sea Knight helicopter lands on the blasted slopes of embattled Hill 174, on the southern edge of the demilitarized zone, during a resupply flight. A U.S. Marine unit was trying to take the hill against resistance from North Vietnamese troops dug into bunkers.

Above: May 6, 1967—Captured U.S. pilot James R. Shively is taken before journalists in Hanoi after his F-105D Thunderchief fighter was shot down the previous day over North Vietnam.

Left: May 1967—A Viet Cong woman prisoner huddles behind barbed wire after U.S. Marines captured her during a battle 22 miles southwest of Da Nang. Two women were captured, and several others were killed.

Left: May 2, 1967—A fully automatic machine gun sprays covering fire as U.S. Marines, taking heavy casualties, advance on Hill 881 near the Marine combat base at Khe Sanh.

Below: May 1967—A grimy and wounded U.S. Marine drinks from a canteen after heavy fighting near Con Thien, just south of the demilitarized zone in the northwestern corner of Leatherneck Square.

Above: May 1967—Viet Cong guerrilla suspects wear blindfolds after South Vietnamese Rangers captured them in swampland about 50 miles southwest of Saigon.

Below: May 1967—U.S. Marines sit atop Hill 881 South, recently established after bitter fighting as a patrol base in the northwestern corner of South Vietnam near the Laotian border.

Above: May 1967—A U.S. radioman dashes through enemy fire just south of the demilitarized zone. Marines of the 2nd Battalion, 3rd Regiment, were pulling out of the area when they ran into North Vietnamese troops dug into bunkers and foxholes. Hours of close fighting and a night-long artillery barrage drove the enemy out.

Right: May 1967—North Vietnamese men and women undergo militia training in Hanoi.

Above: May 4, 1967—Gen. Creighton Abrams *(left)* is welcomed at Saigon airport by Gen. William C. Westmoreland, commander of U.S. Armed Forces in Vietnam. Abrams, who arrived to be deputy, would later succeed Westmoreland.

Left: May 19, 1967—An American infantryman is comforted by a buddy after surviving a battle with the North Vietnamese in the central highlands near the Cambodian border. The GI was upset because, watching a North Vietnamese unit set up a trap, his patrol unit was unable to sound a warning because of a jammed radio. There were serious casualties for the trapped unit.

Above: May 4, 1967—A Vietnamese woman goes about her work amidst the ruins of a special forces camp at Long Vei near South Vietnam's Laotian border after a Viet Cong rocket and mortar attack.

Right: May 1967—A 1st Infantry Division soldier is ready for battle, armed with his M60 machine gun and a case of ammunition. His unit searched for Viet Cong that harassed the unit's home base with mortar fire.

Right: June 15, 1967—American infantrymen crowd into a mud-filled bomb crater and look up at tall jungle trees seeking out Viet Cong snipers firing at them during a battle in Phuoc Vinh, northeast of Saigon in South Vietnam's War Zone D.

Above: May 4, 1967—A Marine cradles the head of his buddy after he was wounded in fighting near Khe Sanh on Hill 881. Twenty-two Marines were killed and 69 injured in the fighting.

Above: June 1967—A Vietnamese woman carries her two children and household goods in two baskets attached to a stick she holds over her shoulder as she travels barefoot during evacuation from Ben Suc, Vietnam. A third child walks in front carrying pots and pans.

Right: June 15, 1967—An American soldier is positioned over his rifle as he protects his wounded buddy crouched in front of a log in the thick mud during battle against the North Vietnamese in War Zone D near Phuoc Vinh, South Vietnam.

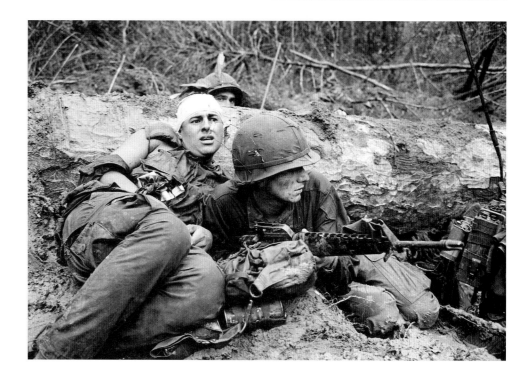

Below: June 16, 1967—Wounded American GIs wait in ankle-deep mud from the monsoon rain as they receive first aid and evacuation after a half-hour fight with Viet Cong snipers in War Zone D, 50 miles northeast of Saigon.

Above: June 18, 1967—American troops run for cover when their unit comes under sniper fire during an operation.

Left: U.S. Marine Corpsmen lead a wounded Marine and carry bodies toward a helicopter in Con Thien, South Vietnam.

Right: June 1967—A U.S. soldier of the 1st Infantry Division presses himself to the jungle floor while taking sniper fire during Operation Billings in War Zone D, about 50 miles north northeast of Saigon.

Above: June 14, 1967—U.S. troops of the 3rd Brigade, 1st Infantry Division, wait at Lai Khe airfield for helicopters flying them into War Zone D.

Right: June 12, 1967—Released North Vietnamese prisoners cross a bridge over the Ben Hai River in the demilitarized zone between North and South Vietnam after South Vietnamese President Nguyen Cao Ky granted amnesty to about 40 prisoners in observance of his second year in power. Many of the prisoners showed their defiance by tossing clothes and gifts received from South Vietnam into the river.

Above: June 1967—A U.S. bomb explodes near Hoi An, 20 miles south of Danang as a Marine walks by the blast. U.S. Marines of the 2nd Battalion, 3rd Regiment, called in air strikes to clear out a cluster of snipers they encountered while patrolling the coast in Operation Beacon Torch.

Left: June 24, 1967—Australian infantrymen, on their first mission in Vietnam, wade through a pond of water lilies during Operation Geraldton, about 30 miles east of Saigon. They reported one Viet Cong killed.

Above: June 1967—Camped in War Zone D during Operation Billings, a U.S. soldier of the 1st Infantry Division carries a case of mortar shells across a flooded jungle clearing after a night of monsoon rains.

Left: June 22, 1967—A U.S. infantryman in a flak jacket wades through muddy swamp during an assault against Viet Cong positions near Can Duc on the fringe of the Mekong Delta, 19 miles south of Saigon. The U.S. 9th Infantry Division had lost more than 30 men in a day-long firefight the previous day.

June 17, 1967—With sniper fire overhead, medic James E. Callahan treats a head wound to a soldier of the U.S. 1st Infantry Division. A Viet Cong bullet reportedly pierced the infantryman's helmet during a three-hour battle in War Zone D.

Above: June 17, 1967—U.S. medic James E. Callahan gives mouth-to-mouth resuscitation to a dying soldier after a guerrilla ambush in War Zone D, about 50 miles northeast of Saigon. Thirty-one men of the 1st Infantry Division were killed in the operation.

Below: June 17, 1967—Medics James E. Callahan (left) and Mike Stout wrap the bodies of dead soldiers in ponchos for evacuation from a battlefield after a three-hour battle with Viet Cong guerrillas in War Zone D. Thirty-one soldiers of the U.S. 1st Infantry Division were killed, and 115 wounded.

Above: June 21, 1967—Pfc. John T. Hogle of Syracuse, New York, is covered with mud after the 9th Infantry Division engaged the Viet Cong in a 19-hour firefight near Can Duc, 19 miles south of Saigon on the fringe of the Mekong Delta. The 9th Division reported 32 men killed, 126 wounded, and 4 missing.

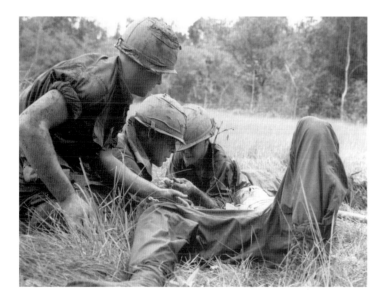

Above: June 18, 1967—As a medical evacuation helicopter was repeatedly driven away by Viet Cong ground fire, three U.S. infantrymen talk to one of their buddies five minutes before he died of an abdominal wound in War Zone D, about 50 miles north northeast of Saigon. The 1st Battalion, 16th Infantry Regiment, reported 31 dead and 113 wounded.

Above: June 18, 1967—Chaplain Capt. Duane Redding of Waco, Texas, tries to cheer a seriously wounded infantryman who could not be evacuated for several hours because of heavy Viet Cong ground fire in War Zone D, about 50 miles north northeast of Saigon.

Below: June 19, 1967—A wounded U.S. infantryman runs for a bomb crater sheltering the wounded during a firefight in War Zone D. Surrounded by Viet Cong, the 1st Battalion, 16th Infantry Regiment, lost more than 30 men, with more than 100 wounded.

Above: June 3, 1967—A North Vietnamese MiG-17 is targeted in the gun sights of a U.S. F-105 Thunderchief piloted by Maj. Ralph L. Kuster. Kuster shot the enemy fighter down with a 20mm gun.

Above: June 1967—An armored vehicle tows an antiaircraft gun down a Hanoi street as an air-raid warning sounds in the North Vietnamese capital.

Left: July 9, 1967—American soldiers stay close to the protection of sandbags as they weather a barrage of fire from North Vietnamese and Viet Cong mortars at their firebase.

Right: June 1967—An amphibious vehicle carries a detachment of marines into Operation Arizona in Quang Nam province about 25 miles southwest of Danang. Marines say they feel safer atop the vehicle than inside. If they hit a mine, they are thrown off, not trapped.

Left: June 23, 1967—Blood streams down the face of a demonstrator as police put him into handcuffs outside the Century Plaza Hotel in Los Angeles. President Johnson was inside speaking to a fund-raising dinner.

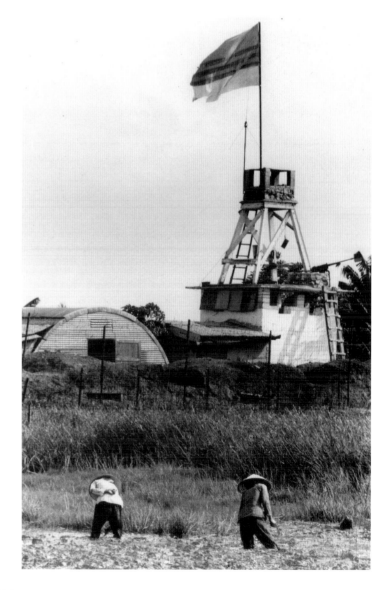

Above: June 19, 1967—A wounded GI waits patiently for evacuation from a jungle clearing in War Zone D some 50 miles north of Saigon. Snipers keep the rescue choppers from making a safe pickup.

Right: June 1967—In war as in peace, a Vietnamese farmer prepares his field at the start of the rainy season. A watchtower is a reminder that danger is not far away.

Right: May 13, 1967—A wounded Marine, trapped in an open field under fire from North Vietnamese infantry, looks up to comrade who approaches to help him. Marines fought for six hours in the area just south of the DMZ.

Above: July 1967—Under fire from enemy snipers, a wounded Korean infantryman clutches the runner of an American medical evacuation helicopter. The Korean soldier stepped on a poisoned punji stick during a sweep of a communist training camp along the South Vietnamese coast near Phan Rang, 75 miles northeast of Saigon.

Above May 13, 1967—A U.S. Marine lifts a wounded buddy as they make their way to cover while under fire in the Leatherneck Square area south of the demilitarized zone.

Left: May 13, 1967—A U.S. Marine lifts a wounded buddy as they struggle to cover while under fire in the Leatherneck Square area.

Above: September 30, 1967—Plainclothes police use sticks against students after they ripped down part of a large election tally board in downtown Saigon.

Left: June 1967—A wicker basket is a boat for this young pair in a quiet water corner of Danang harbor.

Above: July 1967—Machine gunners ride lookout as a U.S. Marine tank rumbles through shallow water during an amphibious landing on the South Vietnamese coast near the demilitarized zone.

Right: July 1967—Suspected Viet Cong are blindfolded and tagged as they await interrogation by intelligence officers of the South Vietnamese army.

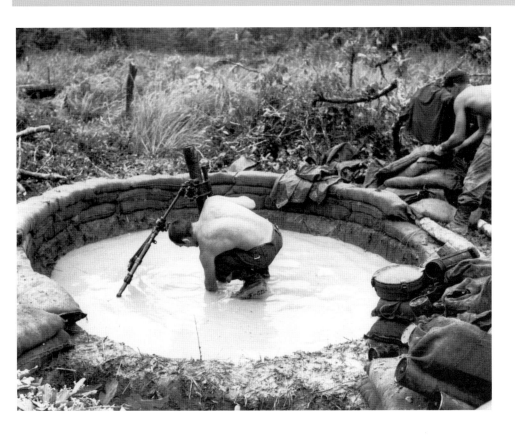

Left: July 15, 1967—An Australian soldier tries to position an 81mm mortar in a flooded gun emplacement at a base jointly operated by U.S., Vietnamese, and Australian troops about 25 miles east of Saigon. Monsoon rains were flooding the base daily.

Above: July 6, 1967—A U.S. Marine M-48 tank advances between Con Thien and the demilitarized zone to recover the bodies of Marines from B Company, 1st Battalion, 9th Regiment, who had been killed in a fierce firefight with North Vietnamese troops four days earlier. A bomb exploded as U.S. jets provided air support.

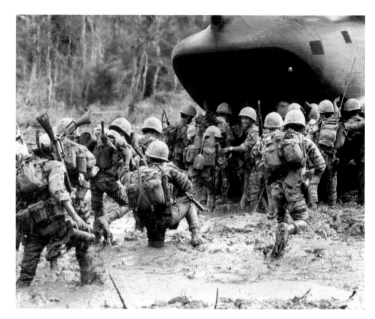

Above: July 1967—After heavy monsoon rains turned their staging area into a quagmire, Vietnamese Marines in full battle gear board a Chinook helicopter for transport to a joint operation on the edge of the Mekong Delta in Phuoc Tuy province.

Above: July 1967—A U.S. Marine guzzles water from a jerry can after returning from a dry and dusty operation near Con Thien, south of the demilitarized zone.

Below: July 1967—Mired in hip-deep mud of the Mekong Delta, a U.S. 9th Infantry Division soldier is pulled by his M-16 rifle during a search-and-destroy mission about 20 miles southeast of Saigon. The area was hit by monsoon rains at least twice a week.

Above: July 4, 1967—A U.S. helicopter, one of three shot down by Viet Cong gunners near Phan Rang, burns on the South Vietnamese coast about 75 miles northeast of Saigon. Two U.S. crewmen and two Korean soldiers on board were killed en route to an attack on a Communist training camp.

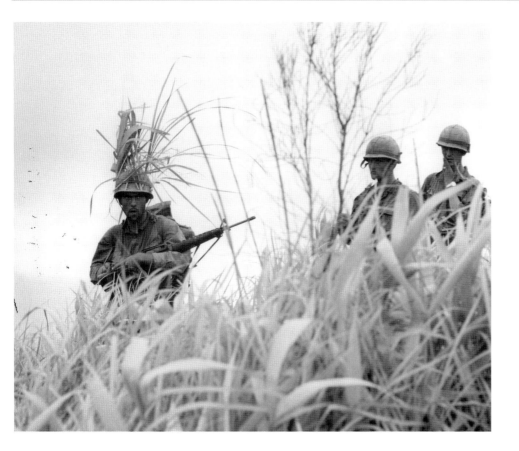

Above: July 1967—A U.S. soldier of the 9th Infantry Division holds his M-16 rifle over the water as he crosses a monsoon-swollen stream in the Mekong Delta during a search-and-destroy mission about 20 miles southeast of Saigon.

Left: July 1967—A point man, carrying camouflage in his helmet, leads a U.S. Marine patrol in the mountains of northwestern South Vietnam, near the Laotian border. Two companies of the 3rd Battalion, 26th Regiment, found abandoned bunkers but made no significant enemy contact.

Right: July 1967—A U.S. armored personnel carrier cuts a wide path through sandy mud in the Mekong Delta about 30 miles southeast of Saigon. Monsoon rains turned already soggy terrain into a quagmire reducing the effectiveness of the armored vehicles.

Below: August 1967—South Vietnamese troops gather in groups along side a creek as helicopters arrive to take them back to base after a patrol seeking Viet Cong regulars.

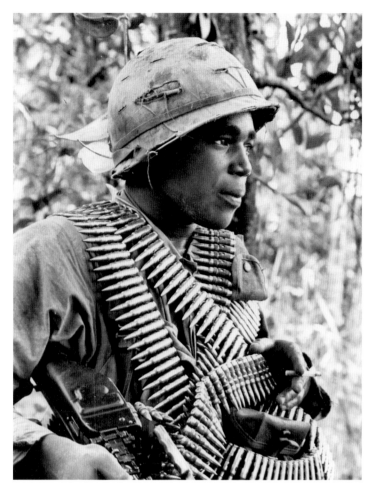

Above: August 1967—A U.S. paratrooper of the 101st Airborne Division wears bands of M60 machine gun ammunition during a sweep of the South Vietnamese coastal area about 25 miles south of Chu Lai. The unit met stiff resistance, including mortar attacks, during the patrol.

Below: August 1967—The constant arrival of troops on U.S. Marine helicopters raises a dust storm during Operation Cochise near Danang.

Above: August 1967—A column of U.S. Marines set out along rice paddies during a joint operation with South Vietnamese troops in the coastal plains 25 miles south of Saigon.

Above: August 1967—A Vietnamese Ranger shoulders his machine gun prior to a mission in South Vietnam's swampy Mekong Delta area.

Left: August 1967—U.S. servicemen and Vietnamese women enjoy the beach at Vung Tau, the last beach resort unaffected by the war. 'In Vung Tau, there simply is no war,' said a U.S. official.

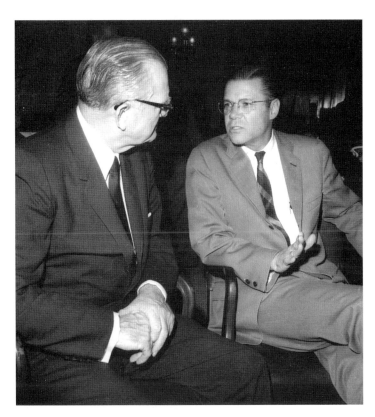

Above: August 25, 1967—U.S. Defense Secretary Robert McNamara (right) chats with Chairman John Stennis of the Senate Preparedness Investigation subcommittee before testifying on administration bombing policies in Vietnam. McNamara told senators that no U.S. bombing campaign, short of attacks on North Vietnamese cities, would alone force Ho Chi Mihn regime into submission.

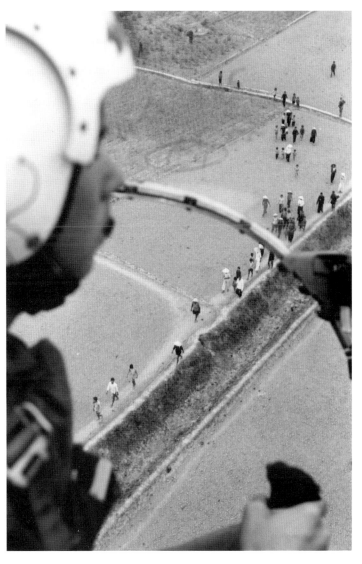

Above: August 21, 1967—As troops of the U.S. 1st Air Cavalry help South Vietnamese authorities round up Viet Cong suspects on the ground near Bong Son, a scout helicopter keeps watch for a possible ambush by guerrillas or North Vietnamese soldiers.

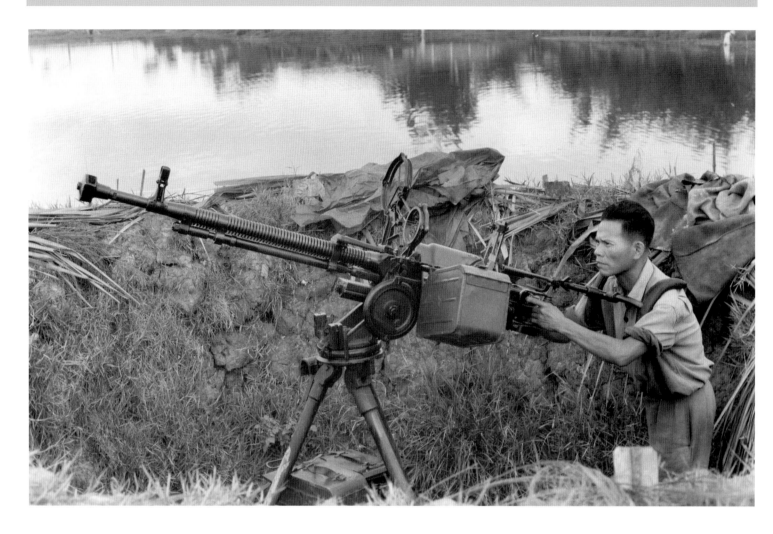

Above: August 10, 1967—A North Vietnamese solider mans an anti-aircraft weapon at his post on the outskirts of Hanoi, according to the caption with this picture released by the North Vietnamese news agency.

Left: August 10, 1967—Carrying food, water, and ammunition, a U.S. Marine convoy makes its daily high-speed supply run from Con Thien to the embattled outpost at Dongha, just south of the demilitarized zone. Dong Ha had been under almost constant North Vietnamese artillery fire for weeks.

Right: August 1967—North Vietnamese personnel operate an anti-aircraft gun in Hanoi.

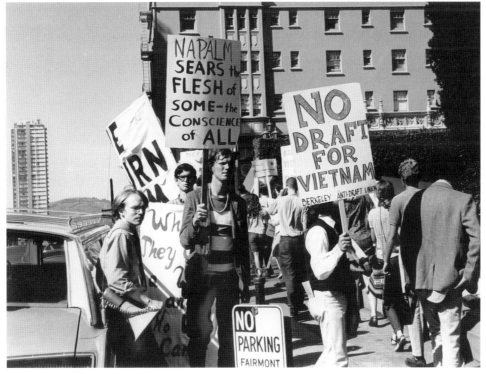

Above: August 28, 1967—
A luncheon vendor sets up
shop beneath a propaganda
poster in a Mekong Delta
town. The poster shows Ho
Chi Minh on his knees making an offering to Mao Tse-
tung. The caption reads:
'Friendship and Brother-
hood between Communist
Countries.'

Above: August 24, 1967—
A U.S. medic patches up the
shattered arm of a Viet
Cong prisoner after he and
several others were discov-
ered in a bamboo thicket at
Duc Pho during Operation
Oregon.

Left: September 19, 1967—
Demonstrators protesting U.S.
involvement in the Vietnam
War parade in front of the
Fairmont Hotel, where
Defense Secretary Robert S.
McNamara was holding a
conference in San Francisco,
California.

Above: September 1967—A Korean Marine of the Blue Dragon Brigade dashes through smoke during an assault landing on the Batangan Peninsula, about 350 miles northeast of Saigon. The peninsula was long considered a Viet Cong stronghold for arms smuggling into South Vietnam.

Below: September 13, 1967—A bandaged U.S. Marine gets a helping hand from a fellow Marine after fighting near Cham Son in northern South Vietnam. Twenty marines were wounded as they repelled North Vietnamese and Viet Cong forces trying to overrun the command post of the 3rd Battalion, 5th Marine Regiment.

Above: September 13, 1967—A U.S. Marine helps a blinded Marine through flooded fields near Cham Son, South Vietnam, to a medical evacuation area after a bitter battle with Communist troops. Another Marine holds his wounded arm and has a bandaged shoulder and chest wounds. The leathernecks repelled the North Vietnamese in the battle, killing 14 men.

Below: September 5, 1967—A squad of the 1st Cavalry Division moves down a mountainside into the Bong Son Valley, about 290 miles northeast of Saigon in Binh Dinh province.

Right: September 1967—South Vietnamese soldiers grapple with a Viet Cong suspect captured after a brief exchange of gunfire in Vinh Long province in the Mekong Delta.

Below: September 8, 1967—A Viet Cong suspect rushes from a 'spider hole' as a soldier of the 1st Cavalry Division continues to fire into the hole. The U.S. platoon swept through the village near Bong Son, about 300 miles northeast of Saigon, during Operation Pershing, reporting five enemy captured and one killed.

Above: September 1967—Near the mouth of the Dong Ha River, U.S. Marine tanks and armored vehicles make their way over sand dunes, packed hard by monsoon rains during Operation Fortress Sentry.

Left: October 21, 1967—Protesters meet a wall of police in front of the Clay Street Induction Center in Oakland, California. Protesters were trying to stop the draft and the Vietnam war. The protest turned violent, as police used mace for the first time.

Above: October 1967—An soldier tosses a straw basket used for rice harvesting into the flames of a burning structure during a search and destroy mission in South Vietnam. In most cases the residents of the villages, known Viet Cong areas, were evacuated to other camps.

Right: October 29, 1967—Demonstrations such as this one were held in the U.S. in support of the U.S. goverrnmet policy in Vietnam.

Left: October. 19, 1967—Anti-war demonstrations and clashes with police were held in a number of foreign cities, as well as in the U.S.

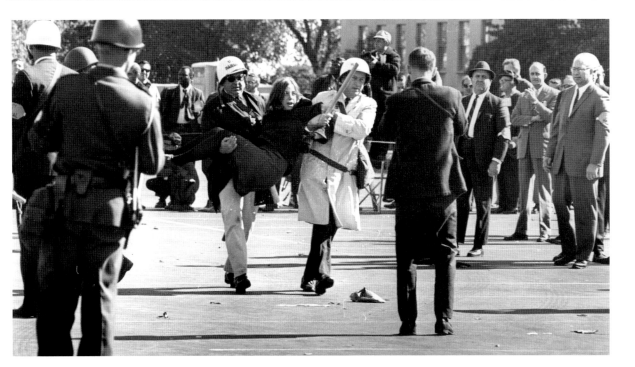

Left: October 22, 1967—U.S. Marshals carry an anti–Vietnam War demonstrator away from the mall entrance of the Pentagon. She was one of a group that staged an all-night vigil in the area declared out-of-bounds by authorities.

Below: October 21, 1967—Anti–Vietnam War demonstrators use the steps of the Lincoln Memorial in Washington for a resting place before their march to the Pentagon.

Above: October 10, 1967—Military police face screaming anti–Vietnam War demonstrators at the Pentagon.

Right: October 21, 1967—U.S. Marshals use force to try to control anti–Vietnam War demonstrators near the Pentagon.

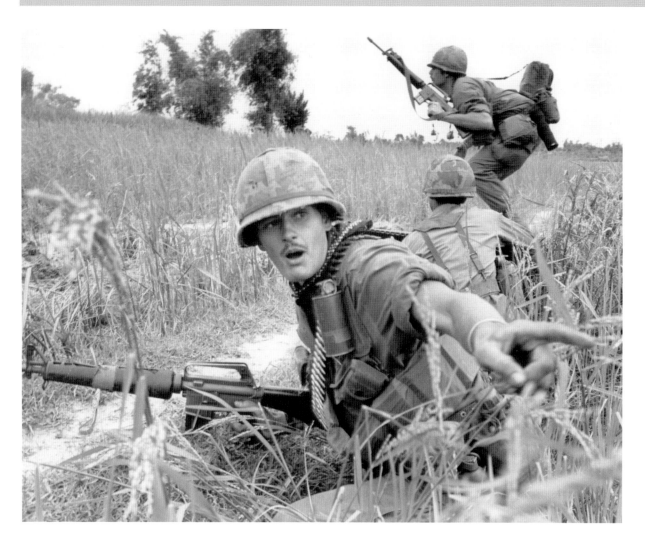

Left: October 1967—A U.S. 1st Air Cavalry Division soldier throws a rice basket into flames after a peasant woman retrieved it from the burning house in background. American troops destroyed everything of value to the enemy after overrunning the village near Tam Ky, 350 miles northeast of Saigon.

Below: October 1967—A U.S. Marine reads *Stars and Stripes* as he rests against an artillery piece at Con Thien. The crew was prepared for a renewed exchange of shelling with North Vietnamese artillery across the demilitarized zone.

Above: October 18, 1967—A North Vietnamese MiG-17 trails smoke as it plunges to Earth after a hit from a U.S. Air Force F-105 Thunderchief, 19 miles northwest of Hanoi.

Left: October 29, 1967—With gunfire crackling around him, a U.S. soldier of the 1st Cavalry Division lobs a grenade at an enemy machine-gun bunker in the opening minutes of a fire-fight near Binh Yen, 23 miles south of Danang.

Above: October, 1967—A North Vietnamese solider and his woman companion man an anti-aircraft weapon in North Vietnam. Women fighting side by side with men was common practice in both North Vietnamese and Viet Cong military organizations.

Left: October 8, 1967—A U.S. Marine CH-53 Sea Stallion helicopter hovers over a smoke marker as it prepares to drop a sling load of ammunition and C-rations to the embattled outpost at Con Thien, just south of the demilitarized zone. The supply mission was made on a rare break in the monsoon rains.

Above: October 30, 1967—Lt. Gen. Nguyen Van Thieu takes the oath as the elected president of South Vietnam in Saigon. At right is Premier Nguyen Cao Ky, who stepped down to second spot as vice president after the ceremony. Thieu immediately offered to hold peace talks with Hanoi.

Below: October 1967—GI crouches down in his bunker safe from North Vietnamese incoming artillery and mortar fire. Only a direct hit could do personal damage.

Above: October 2, 1967—A machine-gunner of the 101st Airborne hangs up his ammunition to dry after a heavy thunderstorm in Chu Lai.

Above: October 1967—U.S. helicopter crew members scramble for a rescue helicopter after they were shot down in wetlands while flying support for a Vietnamese military operation near Vam Co Dong River in Long An province.

Right: October 29, 1967—A rally of some 25,000 gathered in Wakefield, Massachusetts, in support of the U.S. policy in Vietnam.

Left: October 20, 1967—A street urchin in Saigon puffs on a cigarette. Thousands of children lived in the streets of the capital during the war.

Right: October 29, 1967—Demonstrators pose with the effigy of Ho Chi Minh they hung in Wakefield, Massachusetts, during a pro-Vietnam rally attended by some 25,000.

Left: October 24, 1967—A woman pleads with U.S. soldiers to spare her home during an operation in a small village about 350 miles north of Saigon. The troops had spotted Viet Cong in the village from helicopters.

Below: November 11, 1967—A spectator witnessing the Veterans Day Parade gives the thumbs-down sign to anti–Vietnam War demonstrators in Denver, Colorado. The demonstrators became the target for boos, rock throwing, and later punches in the nose from veterans and uniformed high school ROTC students.

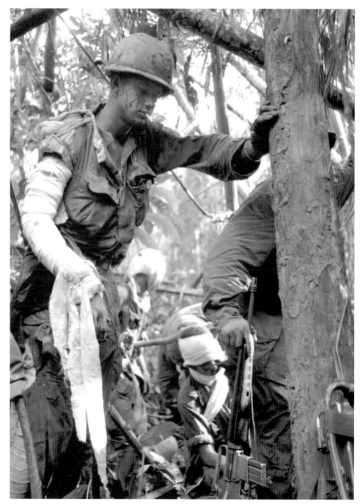

Right: November 15, 1967—A U.S. trooper of the 173rd Airborne Brigade, bleeding from a slight head wound and with other wounds swathed in bandages, limps along with other walking wounded through the jungle to an evacuation point near Dak To, South Vietnam.

Right: November 18, 1967—Soldiers of the U.S. 173rd Airborne Brigade crouch in a jungle clearing after a rocket landed close by in a battlefield 11 miles south of Dak To, South Vietnam.

Below: November 1967—U.S. troops move toward the crest of Hill 875 at Dak To after 21 days of fighting. The hill in the central highlands of South Vietnam, of little apparent strategic value to the North Vietnamese, was nevertheless the focus of intense fighting and heavy losses to both sides.

Above: November 18, 1967—An American medic pauses to look for the sniper fire as he works over a severely wounded comrade in the jungle near the crest of Hill 882, 11 miles southwest of Dak To, South Vietnam.

Right: November 1967—A soldier of the U.S. 1st Air Cavalry Division rests his gear, including mortar shells, near Loc Ninh and the Cambodian border.

Below: November 1967—A soldier of the U.S. 1st Cavalry Division looks over a field of North Vietnamese punji sticks near Tam Ky, about 350 miles northeast of Saigon. U.S. troops were advancing against a North Vietnamese unit when they encountered the punji sticks.

Above: November 1967—Smoke and dust swirl around heavy guns of the 1st Infantry Division as they lob shells at enemy positions around Loc Ninh, near the Cambodian border. Communist forces were attacking almost nightly, and had nearly overrun the tiny outpost on several occasions.

Below: November 15, 1967—Smoke and flames engulf two U.S. C-130 transport planes on the Dak To airstrip after an enemy mortar attack. A second attack destroyed the camp's ammunition dump.

Above: November 24, 1967—A U.S. paratrooper of the 173rd Airborne passes the poncho-covered body of a fellow soldier on Hill 875 in South Vietnam.

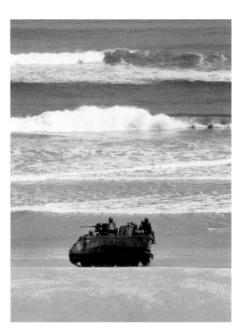

Below: November 4, 1967—A U.S. armored personnel carrier makes its way beside the surf of the South China Sea between Tam Ky and Hoi An, about 370 miles northeast of Saigon. North Vietnamese troops had been sighted in a village nearby.

Above: November 30, 1967—The landing light of a medical evacuation helicopter silhouettes U.S. soldiers moving wounded to the landing zone during the battle for Bu Dop.

Below: November 29, 1967—Bombs explode outside the Bu Dop camp as U.S. troops defended the tiny outpost during a Communist assault. Defenders in a bunker, *foreground*, fire at attackers outside the camp perimeter.

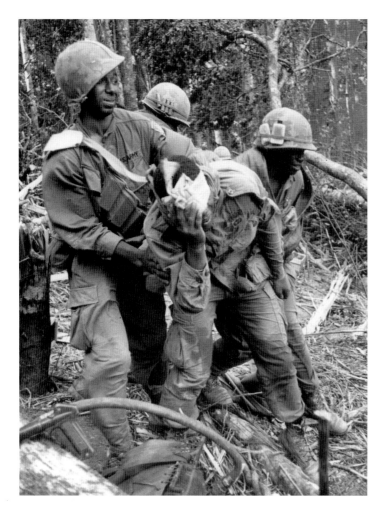

Above: November 21, 1967—A seriously wounded paratrooper of the 173rd Airborne Brigade holds his bandaged head as he is helped to the rear during a hill side battle with North Vietnamese army troops.

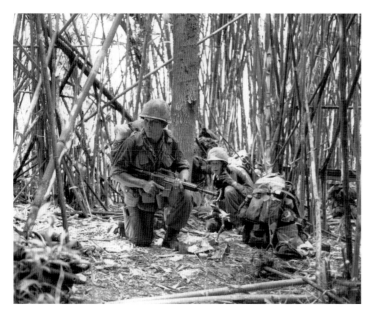

November 13, 1967—A platoon sergeant and radio-telephone operator of the 173rd Airborne Brigade peer into thick bamboo jungle atop a hill during a clash near Dak To in the Central Highlands.

Right: December 4, 1967—U.S. troops cross a graveyard littered with spent shell casings during a mortar and artillery exchange that had lasted for several days at Bu Dop, 80 miles north of Saigon and 3 miles from the Cambodian border. A Viet Cong regiment continued to harass infantry and artillery units of the U.S. 1st Division, which were sent to reinforce positions at the rubber plantation town.

Above: November 5, 1967—An M-1 pressed against her head is used to convince this woman to provide information about Viet Cong activities near Tam Ky, some 350 miles northeast of Saigon.

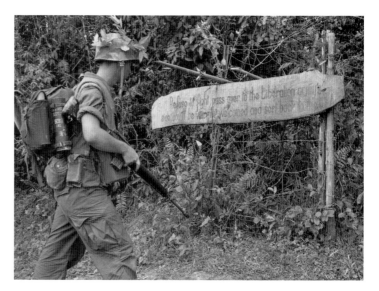

Above: November 13, 1967—A U.S. Marine reads a sign posted by the Viet Cong that says: 'Refuse to fight, pass over to the Liberation Army side. You'll be warmly welcomed and sent back to the U.S.A.' The Marine was on Operation Foster, six miles northwest of An Hoa near Danang.

Right: December 5, 1967—Machine-gunner James R. Pointer of Cedartown, Georgia, takes cover in the undergrowth of a rubber plantation near the Bu Dop Special Forces camp during a half-hour firefight. The patrol narrowly avoided an ambush, opening fire when the unit's patrol dog sniffed out the enemy.

Left: December 9, 1967—A puppy is delighted from a petting by an infantryman of the U.S. 25th Division in My Le.

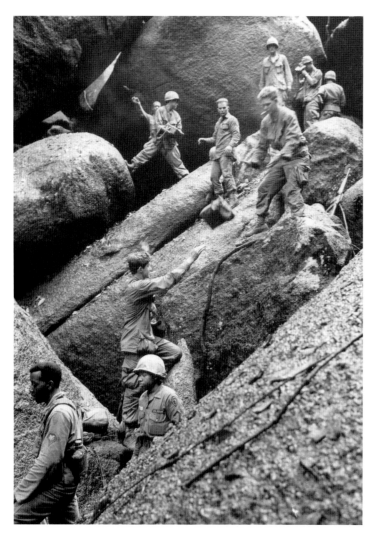

Above: December 1967—U.S. troops of the 3rd Brigade, 25th Division, prepare explosives to blast the entrance of a mountain cave near Phu Cat, 275 miles northeast of Saigon. Viet Cong units were believed to be using the cave as a hideout.

Above: December 5, 1967—Men of a company-sized patrol move through the rubber plantation bordering the Bu Dop airstrip after repelling an enemy ambush attempt. The patrol withdrew to the Bu Dop Special Forces camp after a half-hour firefight.

Above: December 1967—Huddled against the chill, a U.S. Marine radios headquarters during Operation Kentucky, near the demilitarized zone. Monsoon rains and temperatures dipping into the 40s at night made conditions unpleasant in the northern provinces.

Left: December 1967—Blood from shrapnel wounds streaks the face of Lt. Robert D. White of Livonia, Michigan, after a North Vietnamese recoilless rifle hit his armored personnel carrier. White's company of the 1st Air Cavalry Division was attacking dug-in enemy positions near Bong Son, about 350 miles northeast of Saigon.

Right: December 6, 1967—A chaplain gives Communion to U.S. 1st Infantry Division soldiers standing in a trench at Bu Dop during an evening service. Because the base was under constant threat of mortar and rocket attack, the men were prepared to take cover in the trench.

Below: December 1967—An HH-3E Jolly Green Giant helicopter refuels from a C-130 Hercules over the Gulf of Tonkin. The helicopter was on duty near the carrier U.S.S. *Ranger* to pick up downed pilots returning from raids over North Vietnam.

Above: December 1967—After taking fire from the enemy, U.S. soldiers of the 1st Infantry Division patrol through a smoke screen near the air strip of the Special Forces camp at Bu Dop. After a brief firefight, the patrol withdrew to allow air strikes.

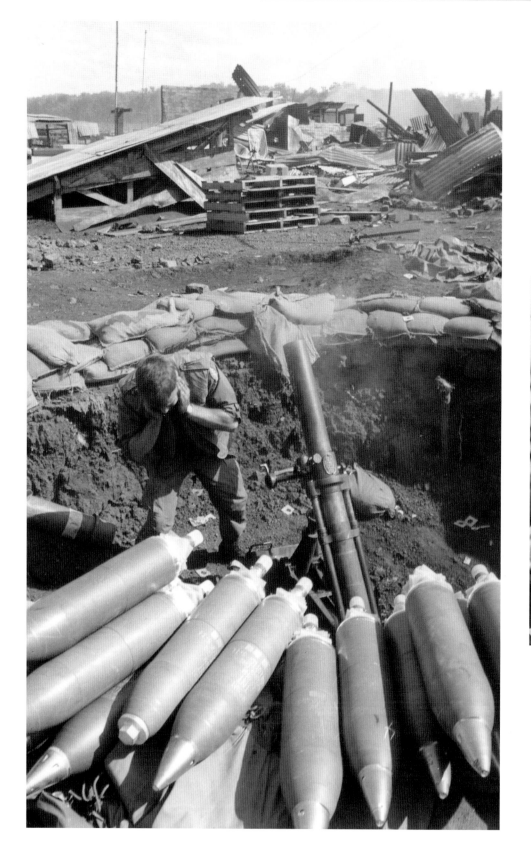

Left: December 3, 1967—Working alone while incoming mortar fire destroys the base around him, a determined U.S. officer at the Bu Dop Special Forces Camp fires a 4.2-inch mortar at enemy positions near the Cambodian border.

Above: December 1967—President Lyndon B. Johnson addresses American troops at Cam Ranh Bay in South Vietnam.

# SIEGE

Even when the wind stirred, thinning the fog, the reconnaissance planes scanning the north-west border area of Vietnam could detect no movement except the slight sway of the high elephant grass, its ripples like those of a green lake filling the lowland. Even months earlier the planes would have turned back, radioing negative. Now, from below, strange new signals kept them searching. Though the peace of the valley seemed complete what was hidden there would soon raise thoughts of nuclear deterrent.

There were certain obvious dangers in the very geography of this north-west corner, a place where major battle could anytime erupt. It could be avoided or invited. It had one tempting feature – an old French airstrip positioned between the border infiltration routes. Just like the one-time French base at Dien Bien Phu in the more distant north-west it had been ignored for years, its name forgotten. But a year earlier a battalion of US Marines had seized and activated it for forward patrols, just as the French had done thirteen years before at Dien Bien

'A shell came right in this man's trench and what they had to send home would probably fit inside a handkerchief.'

—US MARINE AT KHE SANH

Phu. The setting was almost a duplicate: the furthest Communist hills were at the Partition line fourteen miles north, the nearest formed the border with Laos only six miles to the west, and in the pattern of history these hills were studded with undetectable artillery. There were, however, some major differences. The Marine base was 1477feet above sea level on a single plateau, half a mile long and a quarter of a mile wide. Though it presented a flat, confined target, dependent on air supply, it could quickly call in superior fire-power and it could no longer be surprised by a ground assault.

Now, in January 1968, the Americans immediately knew what the French only belatedly discovered. Hundreds of the new acoustic sensors reported what the reconnaissance planes could not see: the Marine base was being rapidly surrounded. James Hebron remembers the beginning all too well. He had just turned eighteen when the patrols 'started to catch sniper fire. Tempers started picking up, and you knew there was something coming down – something major.'

Right: January 29, 1968—
A big U.S. gun goes into
action at Khe Sanh.

**431**

Left: January 1968—A Marine gunner carries a 155mm shell to an artillery piece in Khe Sanh. The fighting at Khe Sanh, close to the DMZ, largely took place with daily exchanges of cannon and rocket fire. Air Force strikes also were used against the North Vietnamese installations.

Below: The various distances, bases, outposts, hills and towns in and near Khe Sanh are located on this map. The Marine base was under siege for many weeks.

Above: February 7, 1968—U.S. Marines on the besieged base at Khe Sanh dig in as the North Vietnamese, using Soviet tanks, captured the nearby Lang Vei Special Forces Camp.

Below: January 1968—As thousands of North Vietnamese troops were assembling in the hills, a U.S. Marine cleans his M-16 in a sandbagged position on the perimeter of the Khe Sanh combat base. The North Vietnamese launched the expected attack just after midnight on the morning of January 21.

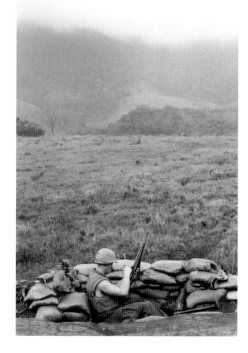

Two elite North Vietnamese divisions, the 325th and the 304th, were identified coming down from the Trail, a force of between 15,000 and 20,000 men. The 304th was the same division that had led the assault on Dien Bien Phu. The Marines braced – and the base was quickly reinforced to six battalions totalling 5600 men. Hebron's unit 'heard rumors that there were anywhere up to 80,000 enemy out there – and that's not very welcome odds'. Traditionally trained as an attack force, the Marines felt like target-range ducks in this 'dusty backwater' and Hebron believed that even the officers while 'getting geared . . . didn't know exactly for what'.

For Hebron's commanding officer, Colonel David E. Lownds, tradition did not allow for questions: 'Marines have one funny habit – they do what the hell they're told.' A veteran of twenty years he now had orders new 'in my career as a Marine'. Lownds was told to dig in – and hold. There was to be no retreat. Suddenly one morning, says Hebron, there were sappers running

barbed wire all around his position: 'That was really freaky. Either they didn't trust us to dig the trenches, or else they expected us to get overrun.

'My Colonel came around and asked if anybody needed any water, or any food. That was it.' Hebron presumed that 'people back home knew a lot more about what was happening than we did'. His platoon then 'swore oaths up and down' that they would not be taken alive: 'We all pulled out our grenades and started waiting.'

At dawn, 21 January 1968, North Vietnamese long-range artillery began the siege with devastating accuracy. On the first day eighteen US Marines were killed, another forty wounded. 'They just shelled the hell out of us up there,' Hebron recalls. 'On the first day alone they dropped 300 rounds.' Seventy-seven days of siege became 'just death and destruction'.

It was as if the shells had landed directly on Washington. From the first moments of the siege the press, public and President Johnson himself feared a bloody blunder. Johnson would proclaim:

'The eyes of the nation, the eyes of the entire world, are on that little brave band of defenders who hold the pass at Khe Sanh.'

But the nation had never before heard of Khe Sanh; what purpose or meaning had it suddenly acquired? The criticism built with the siege: what use was a forward interdiction base that could be so easily surrounded? Why had it not been evacuated at first warning? If it was to bait and draw out the enemy, had the US military calculated the cost of attrition in American lives? And if this were the policy why, anyhow, choose an old French outpost whose every position had long ago been mapped by North Vietnamese artillery?

From the start Khe Sanh became the most controversial battle of the war, bringing the first serious debate on US military strategy in Vietnam. It was an election year and the public was already beginning to tire of the war. In the Oval Office, President Johnson constantly sat with a switch-console facing three outsize television screens, one tuned to each major US network. He had a terrain model of Khe Sanh set up in the White House basement. The Joint Chiefs of Staff pointed out to him the factors which they said made a repetition of Dien Bien Phu impossible. Johnson rounded on them, demanding a formal paper – 'signed in blood' as he put it – that Khe Sanh would not fall. The presidential finger pointed directly at General William Westmoreland. 'The Chairman of the Joint Chiefs called me,' says Westmoreland, 'and I told him to tell the President not to worry about Khe Sanh, that I had no concern about it, and if there was any mishap – which I did not expect – it was my full responsibility.'

As seen in America the broad picture was the grim one of 3500 Marines and 2100 ARVN rangers pinned inside their own barbed wire. But Westmoreland's confidence was unshaken. The Khe Sanh defenders, he says, were only 'the minimum force which I thought could be supplied by air if necessary'. It was necessary. Although Khe Sanh, unlike Dien Bien Phu, was accessible by road – or Route 9 – the danger of a major ambush precluded any ground relief operation while the siege continued. A generation earlier General Henri Navarre had decided that once the siege had begun he could not abandon Dien Bien Phu without losing vital terrain – and perhaps the war.

'I made the decision to hold Khe Sanh', says Westmoreland, because 'if the enemy could roll up Khe Sanh he would outflank the forces we had south of the Demilitarized Zone. He could move immediately into the [east coast] city of Quang Tri and those troops could connect with others along the coastline into the city of Hue.' Westmoreland does not make clear why Khe Sanh, if it was such an important blocking position, had been ignored for years, or why a North Vietnamese thrust at the cities could not be dealt with if or when it

occurred, as indeed it was about to – helped rather than hindered by the attention on Khe Sanh. Essentially, Westmoreland, like Navarre, had sought a set-piece battle believing that superior fire-power could decisively undermine his enemy's immediate war capability and confidence. 'I was influenced' he says, 'by a desire to fight the enemy away from the populated areas.'

Westmoreland was influenced in his choice of Khe Sanh because his troops held the high ground. A company of Green Berets had used the plateau base as early as 1962, but had then shifted camp to the Montagnard hill village of Lang Vei closer to the Laos border. A contingent of twenty-four US Special Forces had remained at Lang Vei, training more than 900 of the mountain tribesmen, and for six years nothing much had happened to them. When North Vietnamese artillery units made known their presence in 1966 by shelling US patrols, the area seemed the long-sought stage for a showdown. In October 1966 a battalion of the 3rd Marines occupied Khe Sanh and its three adjacent hills – and waited. Though the first assault came without warning in heavy fog six months later, the Marines were able to fight off a regimental-size attack because the hills were their 'eyes' directing US air-power. Even so, the fight for the

hills was 'extremely bitter' and lasted eleven days. At the end of it the 'body count' was 940 North Vietnamese dead. American fire-power had left the valley 'cratered like the moon' – but it then became as silent.

After another three uneventful months a battalion of the 26th Marines, fresh from Okinawa, took over. But their commander, Colonel David Lownds, was a veteran of jungle war. He had fought at Iwo Jima, and now as he first surveyed the plateau, looking down into the fog, the only comforting sight was the protective crests of Khe Sanh's satellite hills. These formed a triangle north and north-west, or between Khe Sanh and any assault from the borders. These 'eyes', only 5000 meters apart, kept watch over each other and the airstrip, mutually supportive with a total of forty-six star-formed 105mm artillery – twice as many heavy guns as the French had at Dien Bien Phu. The hills, like so many which men again and again died for in Vietnam, had no names. They were simply designated as Hills 861, 881 and 881S. The plateau base was as bleak as anything men had ever fought for: an old French bunker served as the command post, and, Lownds recalls, 'that was basically it'.

The patrols began descending into the fog like live bait in muddied waters, but for months

Left: February 23, 1968—A wounded Vietnamese Ranger, hit during an enemy rocket attack at Khe Sanh, is carried through a sandbagged trench to an underground aid station. The remote outpost, under siege, was shelled daily by North Vietnamese artillery and rockets.

Below: February 24, 1968—Parachutes carry food and ammunition into the embattled U.S. Marine base at Khe Sanh as the North Vietnamese siege of the base entered its second month. With enemy gunners zeroed in on the base's runway, aircraft landings had become extremely dangerous.

Left: February 1968—Marine cleans his weapon at Khe Sanh alongside sign whose grim humor reflects the attitude at the base, long under siege by North Vietnamese.

nothing happened. 'We were patrolling with one battalion – just a modest operation,' says the ever-casual Lownds. But now the sensors could warn of impending danger, and by the start of 1968 their constant signals alerted Westmoreland. 'We picked up very good intelligence', he says, 'that the enemy was massing over two divisions to take Khe Sanh.'

Westmoreland sent in another five battalions and prepared for a siege. Enlisted Marine Anthony Astuccio then had two months of his Vietnam duty tour remaining – and he would spend it at Khe Sanh. He found that the high ground was only relatively safe – the Marines had dug in so deep that 'the highest thing you could see were just people walking around'. The bunkers just capped the ground and except for the barbed wire it was 'like a compound without a building'. Says Colonel Lownds, 'We'd tell each other, dig another foot and we're into China.' Lownds had now readied the airstrip to take heavy C-130 transports. Helicopters would ferry supplies to the battalions on the nameless hills. Both tanks and anti-tank vehicles were positioned to repel any breach of the giant coils of barbed wire. Only the occasional 'Search and Destroy' mission was to leave the base. Three long weeks of boredom and tension ensued for the 5600 men who would trap, or be trapped by, a force several times larger. The lives of a great many of them were probably saved by nothing more than sheer luck.

On 20 January 1968 a Marine patrol bumped into a North Vietnamese one and after a fire-fight captured its officer. Says Lownds, 'They took him in and somebody interrogated him.' The prisoner told his interrogators what the acoustic sensors could not: the attack on Khe Sanh would begin during the coming night. Lownds: 'I said to my intelligence people, "Do you believe this guy?" They said, "We don't know." I said, "Okay, let's react like it's going to happen. See if it does." '

Even forewarned, with all artillery co-ordinated and all units on 'Red Alert', eighteen Marines died and Khe Sanh lost its main arsenal in the opening round at dawn, 21 January. From six miles away North Vietnamese artillery saturated the familiar base, ceasing fire before their distant guns could be located. Khe Sanh's main ammunition dump was hit almost immediately. In a searing fireball, 1500 tons of explosives blew up. In a ground assault against the outlying hills, North Vietnamese sappers advanced high enough to fire rockets at the plateau airstrip, ripping open its aluminum planks. But the hills had held, and for Lownds, on balance, it was 'a good fight . . . if the enemy got that high terrain then the effectiveness of his rockets and mortars becomes 100 per cent'.

Lownds knew that the North Vietnamese had first to take the hills: 'If I were on the other side, and my commander said "I want that airstrip – take it", then my first step would be to get you off the hills, to take away your eyes.' Lownds was convinced it could not be done. He could rely on unlimited air strikes. In addition to his forty-six heavy guns he could call in as many more from firebases within range to the south and east. And though Khe Sanh was now accessible only by air, supplies had no great distance to come. But with the relief planes came the press – and the emotive question.

'Every new reporter who came up', says Lownds, 'tried to equate it with Dien Bien Phu,

Right: February 23, 1968— Deep trenches are the pathway around Khe Sanh.

Below: April 1968—North Vietnamese troops advance on a hill near Khe Sanh in a photo displayed at the North Vietnamese Embassy in Laos.

Below: March 18, 1968— An area of the besieged U.S. Marine base at Khe Sanh is fortified with sandbags and bunkers. The base was taking fire from enemy artillery, rockets and snipers, and was preparing for a possible ground attack.

and I kept trying to tell them, and I'll tell you today, that the comparison is not a good one because we did hold the high terrain which the French at Dien Bien Phu did not. Secondly, we had enough artillery and support, and this of course is where the French ran into a lot of problems.'

Lownds also had his problems. In the first days of the siege the hundred guns at his disposal were responding with as many as twenty shells for every incoming one. Up to 2000 rounds a day rained on the North Vietnamese hills, but like the siege fourteen years earlier the 'steel elephants' were secreted in mountain caves: they could be rolled out and back again immediately after firing. Despite the now intense bombing, an average 150 rounds a day kept the Marines pinned in their trenches. And for all the lessons of the French experience, the Marine bunkers had not been fortified enough. Extra timber had to be flown in to shore up 8 × 8 ft dug-outs, roofed with aluminum runway matting and three layers of sandbags.

The strengthened runway was also found not strong enough for the heavy C-130s. One of the first to skid in ripped its wing, spewing gasoline, and Khe Sanh had now to rely on the smaller, lighter C-123s. It increased the logistical problems – and the dangers of the airlift. To provision Khe Sanh planes were also having to land at night with only limited flares permissible. Day and night the planes found the shelling so intense that they dared not stop: ingeniously, rollers were built into the floor of the cargo hold so that supplies could

be jettisoned from the rear door, with the planes merely slowing down before taking off again. The spectacle had an undiminishing drama, like a constant hazardous landing on a damaged carrier far at sea. The press speculation of a Dien Bien Phu disaster persisted – and irked General Westmoreland. 'There were certain similarities but many differences,' he says. 'Dien Bien Phu was far more remote from supply bases than was Khe Sanh.'

But the trauma of siege was the same. Says Peter Braestrup, one of the scores of reporters who flew in on brief visits to Khe Sanh, 'It had all the ingredients, especially for television, of melodrama and impending doom. Here we were, 5000 Marines on a plateau surrounded, it seemed, by the North Vietnamese under the direction of General Giap – who was the victor over the French in a similar situation at Dien Bien Phu. It had a certain irresistible appeal.' (Press rumors that General Vo Nguyen Giap was personally leading the siege somewhere in the hills were later laughingly dismissed by his aides in Hanoi, who told the author, 'We fully trust our commanders in the field.')

Braestrup describes the press 'coming in by air and scrambling from an airplane under fire, or under the threat of fire, always feeling that you were under enemy observation; confined to trenches and dug-outs with the Marines – melodrama at its purest. And no such prolonged confrontation between the Americans and the North Vietnamese had taken place up until then. So you had visions of Dien Bien Phu in your head.'

Left: March 1968—A U.S. Marine at the besieged base in Khe Sanh wears graffiti on his flak jacket.

Right: March 1968—A U.S. Marine fires on suspected North Vietnamese positions outside the perimeter of the besieged base at Khe Sanh.

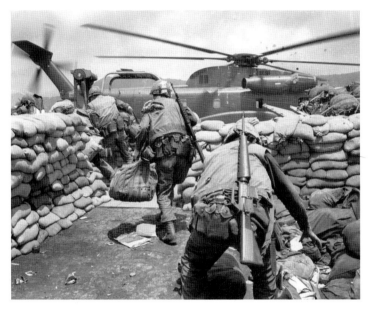

Left: March 1968—Marines dash for waiting helicopters that will take them out of Khe Sanh. The chopper loading is a high speed affair; helicopters are prime targets for enemy rocket fire.

The media visions seemed not unreasonable, and their questions perhaps warranted, since the specter of Dien Bien Phu tormented the President himself. Says Braestrup, who considers the press coverage overly influential, 'Khe Sanh was probably the most terrifying part of the Vietnam war for Johnson, despite the assurances that he got from the military, and which he insisted on getting.' Johnson had instructed the Joint Chiefs that Westmoreland must report directly to him on every aspect of the battle. The US Commander now slept on a cot at the Combat Operations Center in Saigon. He would do so for two months. Daily he cabled Johnson in minute detail – on the condition of the runway at Khe Sanh, on the supply situation, on casualties and morale on the nameless hills where helicopter missions had to get in food, and get out the wounded, under heavy fire and torrential monsoon weather.

Johnson was spared much of the chaotic, gung-ho atmosphere of what was known as Operation Super Gaggle. It was described years later in the official Marine history: 'These missions looked much more orderly on paper than they did in the air, and the operation fully lived up to its name. Only those who have experienced the hazards of monsoon flying can fully appreciate the veritable madhouse that often exists when large numbers of aircraft are confined to restricted space beneath a low-hanging overcast. The aircrew involved in the Gaggle were mindful of the standard warning issued to fledgling aviators: "Keep your eyes out of the cockpit – a mid-air collision would ruin your whole day." '

For all the hazards, the spirit of Khe Sanh was as strong as at Dien Bien Phu, and for young James Hebron out on Hill 881 the visiting reporters were a positive factor: 'We saw the newsmen walking around and we thought, hell, we've got to be safe now. Helicopters brought in new supplies. The NVA blew all six guns one morning, and the next day they brought in six new guns and we thought, wow, fantastic, and our morale was up. And now we were just waiting for them to come on. Come on baby and try to get us.'

But the immediate North Vietnamese objective was quite different. For a time the attention of the newsmen, and of the world, turned to an even more jolting, parallel event. On the night of 31 January 1968, the Communists launched a nationwide offensive timed to the Vietnamese New Year holiday, Tet. Simultaneously, every major South Vietnamese town and city came under attack. A force of perhaps 80,000 guerrillas and North Vietnamese regulars had materialized within the urban defenses. With the exception of Hue, the assault on the cities was quickly repelled with heavy Communist losses, but, combined with Khe Sanh, the Tet Offensive exacted its own attrition – psychological. In the CBS television studio America's father-figure, the venerable newscaster Walter Cronkite, was heard to exclaim: 'What the hell is going on? I thought we were winning this war.'

Cronkite spoke for the nation, and American hopes that Khe Sanh was but a brief diversionary feint for the surprise Tet Offensive were brutally dispelled as the siege continued with its harrowing television scenes. One fifth of the Khe Sanh force were defending the hills outside the main strongpoint and on Hill 861, closest to Khe Sanh, the cameras were there as North Vietnamese units overran the

perimeter on 5 February before being turned back in costly hand-to-hand fighting. Two days later, using (Soviet PT-76) tanks for the first time in the Vietnam war, the North Vietnamese broke through the minefields and defensive wire at the Special Forces base at Lang Vei, midway between Khe Sanh and the Lao border. Lang Vei's 1000-man force called on Khe Sanh for urgent ground reinforcements, but none could be sent along the ambushed route and no supporting air strikes were possible with the close-in fighting. Lang Vei was doomed. Only fourteen of the twenty-four Americans and sixty of the Montagnard militia broke out and were rescued by helicopter. In one brief action more than 900 men had been wiped out.

General Westmoreland remembers 'great consternation in Washington'. The President, he says, was 'very much influenced' by press and television reports and very often 'would receive that information before the official reports. Official reports would be evaluated and verified, but reports of the battle by the media were instantly transmitted events of the moment. Mr Johnson and his advisors were concerned to the point where, I think, they over-evaluated the importance of the battle and the prospect of defeat.'

The President was 'extremely nervous', says journalist Peter Braestrup, because 'he thought of Dien Bien Phu and he thought of the political repercussions'. Braestrup later wrote *Big Story*, a critical study of the press coverage of Khe Sanh and Tet – and its political impact. He claims that during the two peak months of the seventy-seven day siege, Khe Sanh accounted for twenty-five per cent of all Vietnam film reports on US evening network news programs (and at times, he says, fifty per cent on CBS which had the highest ratings) and thirty-eight per cent of all Vietnam reports filed by Associated Press.

However, interviewed for this history because of his research, Braestrup says that 'even prior to the bulk of the reporting' President Johnson was 'sufficiently nervous' to ask Westmoreland for assurances 'that he – the President – would not be called upon to use the atomic bomb to save Khe Sanh'. 'Westmoreland', says Braestrup, 'hadn't thought about the atomic bomb until that moment, but never one to throw away a good idea said he didn't think it would have to be used, but if worst came to the worst he would like to be allowed to consider using it.'

Westmoreland does not use the term 'atomic bomb', but states in his own personal account,

'There was another possibility at Khe Sanh: tactical nuclear weapons.' The US Commander felt it would be 'imprudent' not to consider 'the possibilities in detail' because 'the region around Khe Sanh was virtually uninhabited; civilian casualties would be minimal.' (The area until that time had a considerable civilian population. After the fall of Lang Vei, Montagnards from surrounding villages which had often supported the Special Forces fled toward Khe Sanh. An estimated 6000 refugees were refused protection in case some were Communist saboteurs. Only after strong protests from Ambassador Sullivan in Laos were the Montagnards safely evacuated. Considering these numbers there may well have been other civilians, or tribal groups, in the general area.)

Westmoreland admits that he 'established a small secret group to study the subject' but Washington 'so feared that some word of it might reach the press that I was told to desist. I felt at the time, and even more so now, that to fail to consider this alternative was a mistake.'

Thus, with the first direct set-piece confrontation, the 'unthinkable' became a 'possibility'; not least, the policy of conventional attrition – the main US military strategy – was now evidently regarded, even by Westmoreland, as perhaps not good enough. This would seem sufficient evidence that a policy based on inflicting 'unacceptable losses' could only be theoretical. It presumed that any given nation would surrender its territory or ideals rather than die for these, and in Vietnam that policy totally collapsed with the sacrificial Tet Offensive.

In the ancient north-east capital of Hue, the last action of the Tet Offensive was proving as bitter as Khe Sanh – but this time with 12,000 North Vietnamese besieged. At Hue, fighting fanatically block to block, Westmoreland's enemy was providing the set-piece confrontation he wanted, but on the battleground of their choice. Though the Marines would clearly win at Hue, the people at home could not understand this sudden bitter street fighting when they had been told that the war was but a mopping up of the countryside. The battle of Hue made it seem that the fight was everywhere, and made Khe Sanh seem more like a beleaguered action rather than a measured demonstration of US might.

At Khe Sanh, too, the human drama overshadowed US military superiority. Literally and figuratively, press and public could not see much beyond the barbed wire, but there the battle had to rank as history's best co-ordinated use of firepower up to that time. An average of 300 air strikes were being flown in support of Khe Sanh each day, or a ratio of one bombing mission every five minutes. Guided by the new array of electronic detectors, the jets struck swiftly at the computered targets even in zero visibility. The rapid strikes almost immobilized Vietnamese AA guns; only two fighter-bombers were lost. Though the ground artillery of the Trail had been secreted too long and too well for detection, new showers of sensors precisely registered any large movement of men and vehicles, saving the hill positions from being overwhelmed.

As the base commander, Colonel Lownds, summarizes it, 'Sensors had come into being and they went wild where I figured the enemy would come from. We took out our maps and figured out where the enemy would assemble. We'd wait until he had closed the assembly area because we wanted to get them all.' Then, in Lownds' words, the B-52 strikes would be 'a god-send, miraculous thing. It's almost scary when you think of it. You don't even see them but, boy, the bombs sure come down right on target.'

Above Left: Four North Vietnamese soldiers barely visible on the horizon flee bombs dropped just 50 yards from a South Vietnamese position at Khe Sanh. The North Vietnamese, equipped with rockets and mortars, attacked the Khe Sanh air strip.

Left: April 1968—A wounded U.S. Marine is helped to helicopter evacuation at the top of Hill 689 by two fellow Marines – one with his own arm in a sling. The Marines fought their way to the top of the hill, about two miles west of Khe Sanh, to retrieve the bodies of Marines killed there a week earlier.

Left: April 1968—U.S. cavalrymen move through a once-fertile area four miles south of the Khe Sanh Marine base. The U.S. dropped hundreds of tons of explosives on the area as the Marines held the base during a 77-day siege.

Westmoreland personally chose the name Operation Niagara for the B-52 strikes to 'evoke an image of cascading bombs'. The explosive equivalent of five Hiroshima-size atomic bombs was dropped in the Khe Sanh area. The daily average was 5000 bombs – 'the most concentrated bombing in the history of warfare'. For two miles around Khe Sanh the valley was a leveled wasteland.

'All you saw,' recalls Marine James Hebron, 'was the air being ripped apart and the ground tremoring underneath you – and you bouncing in the air. You weren't aware of where the planes had been, yet it was happening yards from our front lines. Some were really massive bombs; the trenches would shake, the sandbags would come loose; there was a really tremendous vibration.'

Yet still the North Vietnamese infantry came, and, as at Dien Bien Phu, the defenders could hear them digging in the night, their trenches zigzagging to within 300 meters of the hills. Each dawn, as the cameras rolled, Skyhawks and Skyraiders dived on the trenches, 'cleansing' them with napalm. Halfway through the siege thousands of tons of napalm had been dropped on North Vietnamese lines. MacArthur's suggested 'scorched earth' was a fact.

After a month of siege, with no lessening of the shelling, only the seriously wounded were getting out on the helicopters – which brought in the press. And the press had 5600 harrowing stories. 'We had a man who caught an artillery round,' remembers Anthony Astuccio. 'A shell came right into this man's trench, and what they had to send home would probably fit into a handkerchief.'

'The rats – huge,' would always remain with James Hebron. In the bunkers 'you could hear them scurrying all about. Even if you were exhausted you just couldn't fall asleep: you'd wake up and they would be crawling on you. Guys would grab a pistol and start shooting at them.' 'I'd seen rats, being from New York,' says Johnny Bryant, a black in Company Foxtrot, 'but never that big. You took a blanket and you tucked in like a cocoon. If you didn't, well the first night there a guy showed us what would happen. He refused to sleep with his face covered and a rat bit a hunk out of his face. The rats', says Bryant, 'owned Khe Sanh. We were just roomers.'

Some of the Marines like Hebron had now been at Khe Sanh six months, and there was no way 'to keep clean'. Astuccio longed for something as simple as a proper haircut: 'We cut each others', but none of us were barbers – and it showed.' Hebron's stomach was mutinying over C-rations. 'You ate them', he says, 'because it was the law.'

'You'd eat them in your hole,' recounts Astuccio, 'so that you didn't make a light. Above ground, heating them, would be almost like a spotlight.' Astuccio thought at the time that he was lucky. His duty tour was up: he could leave – if he could get out. He tried jumping the open rear cargo door of a C-123 as it slowed between its landing and take-off: 'I didn't make it, and the plane didn't make it out. It was just lifting off and it got blown away.' Astuccio went back to his trench: 'The NV got into the trenches of the company next to us. It was hand to hand combat.'

'When people are hit,' he reflects, 'it comes home very rapidly. You feel it very deeply, over and over again. It doesn't matter how many times it happens. It doesn't lessen it any.'

This first prolonged face-to-face battle for some forgotten cause was coming home to

Above: Map locates the Dimilitarized Zone separating North and South Vietnam and the area just south of the DMZ which was the scene of contant fighting during the course of the Vietnam war.

Right: An unidentified American GI, wounded in the head during his unit's assault on Hill 549, waits for medical evacuation southeast of Khe Sanh, South Vietnam. His unit, the 1st Battalion, 5th Cavalry of the U.S. 1st Cavalry Division, was three miles southeast of the besieged Marine base when North Vietnamese attacked.

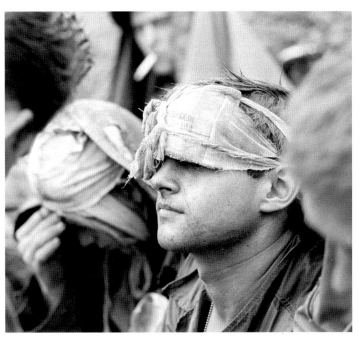

America, and thirty days, fifty days, seventy-seven days, would not lessen it any. An entire nation was an almost instant eye-witness. The six o'clock news had become the living-room war. The faces on the 'box' did not just haunt from 9000 miles away: they were the boys from next door, and sometimes one's own son. The faces, so youthful, trustful, scarred, scared or brave, peered from every newspaper and every magazine – under the heavy black ink of news agency flashes:

MARINE OUTPOST OVERRUN JUST 500 METERS WEST OF KHE SANH. THREE HOUR BATTLE.

MARINE C-130 HIT BY ENEMY FIRE DURING LANDING APPROACH, CRASHES IN FLAMES. SIX-MAN CREW DEAD.

HEAVIEST DAY FOR 'INCOMING' – A RECORD 1,307 ROUNDS LAND ON KHE SANH.

C-123 SHOT DOWN EAST OF RUNWAY, 48 KILLED.

In the fine print it was clear that the battle would be won, but it was agonizingly endless, and when Khe Sanh was won and held, what was to prevent it recurring anytime? And if it was not held then what was all the pain and sacrifice for? There was, on the one hand, an intense pride in traditional Marine fortitude (after one news agency story about an embunkered group who kept raising the Stars and Stripes each morning until it was shot to pieces, hundreds of flags were mailed to Khe Sanh); on the other hand, the ceaseless air-lift of 'beans, bullets and bandages' was largely impressing only the military. There was the sense that the military had forgotten to mention the body-bags. There was the sense of something vitally profound – like a reproach more deeply felt for being unsaid – in the television pictures of shell-tilted signs above the Marine bunkers, saying 'Home Sweet Home' and 'Room For Rent'.

Such images, satellite-born from jungle to the family den, now produced a collective image: Khe Sanh suddenly was not freedom's plateau but the peak folly of an older generation. In mid-February, as the President personally saw off Marine reinforcements for Khe Sanh declaring, 'This is a decisive time in Vietnam', the American people were for the first time rejecting Johnson – and, by extension, the war. A Gallup poll showed that since the siege the President's public standing had reversed, with fifty per cent disapproving of his war policy and thirty-five per cent approving.

Critics and supporters alike were now distraught by Khe Sanh's eternity. An American Dien Bien Phu was no longer the fear: there was the larger specter of three years of combat which seemed only a struggle of questionable honor at a very high price. In successive days, cost and cause were questioned as never before: on 14 February the administration budgeted $32 billion for the war in the fiscal year of 1969; on the 15th the Air Force reported the loss of the eight-hundredth aircraft over North Vietnam; on the 20th the Senate Foreign Relations Committee began public hearings challenging the necessity of the war; on the 22nd Westmoreland's command announced the highest weekly total of American combat deaths – 543; on the 24th fighting ceased at Hue but at Khe Sanh on the 25th a Marine patrol was ambushed with twenty-three killed – and on the same day Westmoreland requested an additional 206,000 troops. As Secretary of State Rusk would later say, the 'daily hammering' was too great – and on the 27th newscaster Walter Cronkite ('the most trusted man in America') delivered perhaps the

Above: April 5, 1968—U.S. cavalrymen run to helicopters during Operation Pegasus to relieve the Marine base at Khè Sanh, under siege for more than two months. The cavalry officially relieved the base on April 8.

Left: March 19, 1968—Two Vietnamese Rangers stationed at Khe Sanh pose with captured Bangalore torpedoes after a short patrol outside the base perimeter. The torpedoes are crude enemy devices made by sandwiching bamboo with sticks of dynamite. The North Vietnamese use the Bangalores to blow gaping holes in the barbed wire perimeter.

final blow to any further escalation. In a rare personal report he called the war a stalemate and said negotiation was the only way out. In the Oval Office listening to Cronkite, the President reputedly turned to his press secretary, saying, 'If I've lost Walter I've lost Mr Average Citizen.'

But Khe Sanh raged on – and Westmoreland's inclination was to shoot the messenger. 'The operation', he says, 'was given such visibility in the United States that it did play into the hands of the enemy psychologically. They were smart enough to realize that they couldn't defeat us on the battlefield. But they realized that we were vulnerable to political defeat because they had defeated the French that way, and they were sufficiently self-confident to believe that they could defeat us by the same strategy, and indeed they did.' Westmoreland, in effect, was saying that his enemy had accepted attrition, used it against him, and that Khe Sanh was, after all, an American Dien Bien Phu – politically.

The role of the press would have some self-critics, foremost Peter Braestrup. He had served in the Korean war, won a Nieman Fellowship at Harvard, and began covering Vietnam from 1960. His first base posting in Saigon for the *Washington Post* began in January 1968, when the Khe Sanh and Tet campaigns started. After Tet, says the author of *Big Story*, the 'only melodrama left for television in particular, and for wire photos and for the newspapers, was Khe Sanh. This was the continuing drama. That is why Khe Sanh came to have such enormous visibility in journalistic terms, quite aside from what was really happening there. There were a lot of incentives journalistically to make it a bigger story than it turned out to be.'

These criticisms miss or obscure the crucial point that, given the war's high visibility at any time, the deliberate setting of a siege was itself contrived drama – technically well-staged but lacking plot or climax, a psychological blunder – and this, in fact, was the war's big story. A great many newsmen had lived years in Vietnam; at least fifty gave their lives covering stories big or little in the region; collectively, in the experience of Colonel Lownds, they acted responsibly. The Khe Sanh commander was getting his water supply from outside the base and he feared that if this was ever known the supply would be cut or poisoned. He asked the press not to report this – and they never did, and, he says, that was 'the only thing that really astounds me, and I respect them for it'.

Says Braestrup, 'Newsmen never had a very clear grasp of the relative strengths of the opposing forces, or of significant changes occurring at Khe Sanh. All that seemed to happen was that it got bombarded and people were killed and wounded.'

Another Vietnam observer, Bernard C. Nalty, suggested that it was the US military which had no clear grasp of the Communist perception of the battle. Nalty, author of *Airpower and the Fight for Khe Sanh* and contributor to an exhaustive study *The Vietnam War*, had served with the centers of military history of both the US Air Force and US Marine Corps. Nalty writes that it was General Westmoreland who 'believed that the Communists intended to make Khe Sanh "an American Dien Bien Phu" – confident the attempt would end in disaster for the enemy'. But, states Nalty, '. . . it is unlikely that the North Vietnamese ever envisaged the base as a second Dien Bien Phu'. The military historian cites the 'enemy's failure to

storm Khe Sanh' and the final 'feeble resistance' when the North Vietnamese 'seemed to melt away and the body count [officially 1602 confirmed dead] and number of weapons captured was disappointingly small'.

At the time the US military version was that the air strikes broke the North Vietnamese will, that this was expected and Khe Sanh was intended to be the staging ground to invade and cut the Ho Chi Minh Trail. It was to that end, says Westmoreland, that he requested 206,000 additional troops midway in the siege. Historian Nalty suggests the North Vietnamese politically and militarily blocked Westmoreland by sustaining a

controlled siege at Khe Sanh 'to pin down troops and aircraft needed elsewhere in the aftermath of the Tet Offensive'. Westmoreland dismissed Tet as a serious Communist defeat, but, says Nalty, Tet 'constituted the main Communist effort', or strategy.

On 28 February, which would prove exactly the halfway point of the seventy-seven day siege but then with no end in sight, President Johnson acted on Westmoreland's huge new troop request by ordering a watershed analysis of the origins of Tet and of American options and prospects in Vietnam – and at the end of it what Westmoreland got was his ticket home.

Above Left: Shaded area locates the central highlands of South Vietnam where, in 1965, some 22,000 North Vietnamese and Viet Cong regulars roamed at will.

Above Right: Map locates the four military corps areas in South Vietnam.

Below Left and Right: Map shows were U.S. troops were assigned in the spring of 1966.

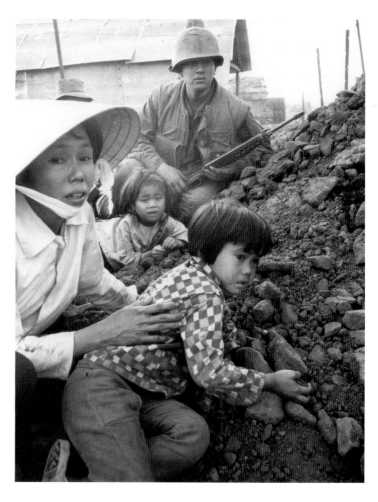

December 4, 1968—U.S. Marines at Khe Sanh man positions in trenches in front of their bunker and keep lookout for enemy movement.

Right: January 23, 1968—Vietnamese refugees and a U.S. Marine crouch behind an earth embankment as enemy mortars explode near the air strip during the first days of the siege of Khe Sanh. Refugees were evacuated from the base by emergency airlift.

Left: February 23, 1968—It looks like World War I but these trenches are dug into the Marine base at Khe Sanh where constant improvement in sandbagging and digging protects the troops from the constant shelling by North Vietnamese artillery.

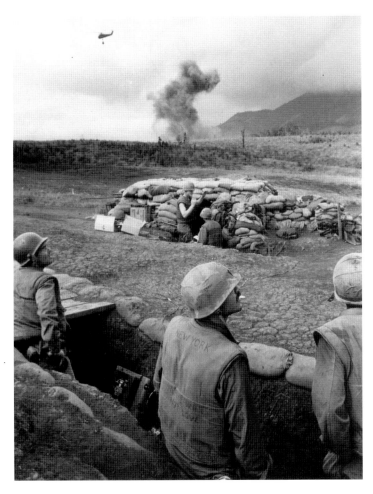

Above: February 1968—U.S. Marines play basketball during an uneasy calm early in the siege of the Khe Sanh Marine base. Earth banks, sandbags and timbers protect the men from enemy gunners and snipers surrounding the base.

Above: January 1968—Smoke from napalm strike rises in background as GIs at Khe Sanh relax in their bunkers.

Above: January 24, 1968—A U.S. medical corpsman tries to calm a wounded Marine after a Communist rocket and artillery attack in the first days of the siege of Khe Sanh.

Left: February 1968—Dr. Joseph Wolfe, center, wearing a flak jacket along with other physicians in attendance, treats a wounded soldier at Charlie Med, the makeshift underground hospital at the besieged Khe Sanh Marine base. Working under combat conditions, doctors of C Company, 3rd Marine Medical Battalion were making daily treatment decisions with life and death consequences.

Right: February 11, 1968—U.S. Air Force medics under sniper fire carry seriously wounded Marines to an evacuation plane on the besieged Khe Sanh combat base. The rescue aircraft stayed on the ground just long enough to board the wounded.

Below: February 1968—An artilleryman tosses a shell casing onto the nearby heap after firing a Howitzer into enemy positions in the hills around Khe Sanh.

Above: February 23, 1968—A U.S. Marine stands atop his post, a sandbagged bunker, and watches clouds of black smoke rise at the Khe Sanh Marine Base during a North Vietnamese artillery barrage.

Left:: February 1968—Marine at Khe Sanh prepares his rocket launcher in its bunker near the base perimeter.

Above: February 10, 1968—An unexpected shelling by North Vietnamese troops sent these Marines to cover at the nearest point, in this case stacked boards to be used in construction.

Right: February 1968—Marines hunker down in a trench during shelling of the Khe Sanh camp by North Vietnamese artillery and mortars.

Left: February 1968—Marines hug the nearest the cover they can find when unexpected shelling from North Vietnamese hits the Khe Sanh camp.

Above: February 17, 1968—A deep trench connecting machine gun bunkers and fighting holes defends the perimeter of the besieged U.S. Marine base at Khe Sanh. The base was receiving frequent rocket and artillery fire from the surrounding hills.

Left: February 1968—Barbed wire, trenches and sandbag bunkers topped with empty shell casings reinforce the besieged Marine combat base.

Right: March 1968—U.S. Marines watch supplies drift into the drop zone at the combat base in Khe Sanh, under siege for more than two months.

Below: February 1968—A U.S. Marine stands in a trench while doing his laundry at the besieged Marine combat base in Khe Sanh. Under constant threat of shelling from North Vietnamese units ringing the base, the Marines worked from trenches and bunkers whenever practical.

Above: March 3, 1968—A U.S. Marine at right waves his jungle knife to bring forward others of his squad into no-man's land outside of Khe Sanh base, South Vietnam, to try and rescue an ambushed and trapped Marine platoon. Several men in the rescue squad were killed or wounded.

Above: March 25, 1968—Marines walk through a man-high trench connecting two bunkers on the besieged U.S. Marine combat base at Khe Sanh. In the event of a direct hit by the enemy, the zig zag pattern is designed to limit shrapnel injuries to one section of the trench.

Above: March 1968—As U.S. Marine gunners clean their 105mm gun, the American flag flies briefly over the besieged Marine base at Khe Sanh. The flag was hoisted daily, but not long enough to become a target for North Vietnamese observers in the hills surrounding the base.

Left: March 4, 1968—A U.S. Marine targets North Vietnamese positions about 100 yards outside the perimeter of the embattled Khe Sanh Marine base. The base was in its second month under siege.

Above: March 1968—U.S. Marines at Khe Sanh use telescopic sights attached to their M-16 rifles to target the North Vietnamese troops surrounding the base.

Above: March 10, 1968—A white phosphorous bomb leaves smoke trails to create a smoke screen for supply planes landing at the beleaguered Khe Sanh Marine base. Enemy mortars, snipers and artillery ringing the base had already hit a number of supply planes.

Left: March 1968—During a North Vietnamese artillery barrage, a helmetless U.S. Marine struggles through barbed wire to reach the protection of a bunker during the siege of Khe Sanh.

Right: March 2, 1968—U.S. Marines take cover in a trench during an enemy artillery attack during the siege of the Khe Sanh Marine base.

Above: March 1968—An aircraft destroyed by enemy fire on the airstrip at the Khe Sanh Marine base in early March forces supplies to be air dropped from a C-130 transport. Only helicopters were able to land at the base, already under siege for nearly two months.

Above: March 1, 1968—A U.S. cargo plane burns after being hit by enemy mortars while taxiing at Khe Sahn, South Vietnam. The crew escaped.

Left: March 24, 1968—Holding his helmet in place a Marine dives into his bunker as North Vietnamese artillery attack on Khe Sanh begins.

Right: March 8, 1968—U.S. Air Force bombs create a curtain of flying shrapnel and debris barely 200 feet beyond the perimeter of South Vietnamese ranger positions defending Khe Sanh.

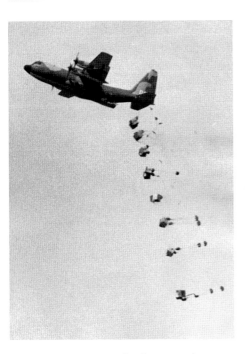

Above: March 1968—A camouflaged C-130 Hercules transport plane drops supplies to the besieged Marine base at Khe Sanh. Communist shelling prevented landing at the base.

Left: March 5, 1968—A 1,000-pound bomb explodes outside the perimeter of the U.S. Marine Khe Sanh combat base, sending shrapnel and dirt 300 feet in the air.

Left: March 14, 1968—A fuel dump burns at the U.S. Marine base at Khe Sanh after a mortar attack, while a Texas state flag flies from a radio mast on a communications and command hut labeled 'The Vatican.'

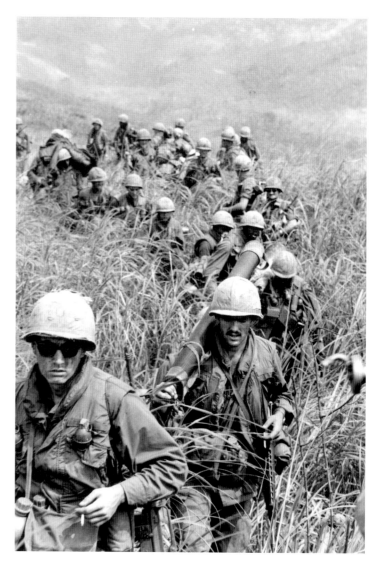

April 1968—A Marine patrol walks along a ridge line near Khe Sanh. Regular patrols keep tabs on North Vietnamese and Viet Cong movements in the area of the besieged outpost.

Right: A platoon of U.S. Cavalrymen struggle on foot through the high elephant grass on their way to the Khe Sanh Marine combat base. They are taking part in Operation Pegasus, a joint Marine and cavalry drive to relieve the base, which had been under North Vietnamese artillery fire.

Left: The bodies of U.S. Marines lie half buried on Hill 689, about 2½ miles west of Khe Sanh, South Vietnam. Fellow Marines stand guard in the background after battling entrenched North Vietnamese troops for the hill.

Left: April 7, 1968—As a relief force of Operation Pegasus neared the long-besieged U.S. base at Khe Sanh, Marines captured two North Vietnamese soldiers near the perimeter of the base. The two prisoners were evacuated for interrogation.

Above: April 1968—With ponchos covering dead soldiers in the foreground, U.S. soldiers of the 1st Battalion, 5th Cavalry Regiment, carry wounded to evacuation from Hill 549, three miles southeast of the besieged Marine base at Khe Sanh. The unit was fighting its way to forge a ground link with the base, which was officially relieved April 8, after 77 days under siege.

Right: March 1968—Supply containers drop by parachute to the besieged Marine outpost at Khe Sanh.

Above: April 19, 1968—Storming Hill 689, just west of Khe Sanh, to retrieve the bodies of Marines killed a week earlier, a U.S. Marine fires his grenade launcher at North Vietnamese positions.

Above: April 6, 1968—A helicopter patrols the area surrounding the base camp at Ca Lu, the headquarters for Operation Pegasus to relieve the beleaguered U.S. Marine base at Khe Sanh, 11 miles to the west. The camp, foreground, was established only one week earlier, but was already fortified with bunkers, *foreground*.

Above: April 19, 1968—Marines fight their way up Hill 689 about two miles from the main base at Khe Sanh. They were on a mission to recover the bodies of Marines slain in an earlier action.

Left: April 7,1968—South Vietnamese troops advance cautiously on enemy trenches within 25 yards of the Khe Sanh base perimeter. The trenches were a source of constant harassment to the base defenders.

Right: April 1968—Marines carry a recoiless rifle to a position where they can hit North Vietnamese infantry on Hill 689, about two miles from the main Khe Sanh base. They will support an assault on the hill by other Marines who will recover bodies of their fellows slain in an earlier action.

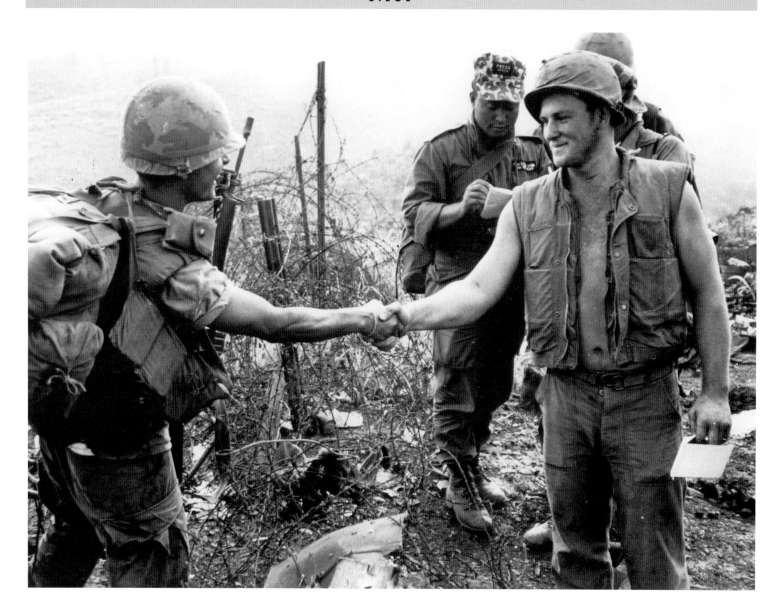

Above: April 7, 1968—A soldier of the 1st Cavalry Division, *left*, shakes hands with a U.S. Marine at the barbed wire perimeter of the Marine base at Khe Sanh. It was the first time ground troops of the 1st Cavalry had reached the besieged Marine garrison.

Left: April 6, 1968—A U.S. 1st Cavalry soldier, slightly wounded on Hill 549 waits for the morning mist to lift for a helicopter to evacuate the wounded. The unit was hit by North Vietnamese artillery just three miles southeast of the beleaguered Marine base at Khe Sanh.

# THE TET INQUIRY

In the early morning hours as Saigon's New Year crowds receded, the thousands of men emptying from as many bars and cafes went unnoticed. The street vendors seemed naturally busy, handing out last bundles of flowers and boxes of rice-cake from sidewalk stalls. Outside their barracks and government buildings ARVN soldiers alcoholically slumbered as the last fire-crackers brought in the Year of the Monkey. In a shadowed alley some of the late-night strollers piled into a small truck and an empty taxi, unwrapping their bundles as the vehicles set off toward an imposing white building nearby. As the taxi pulled up outside the iron gates of the Embassy of the United States of America, a 'Death-Defying Volunteer' leaped out and opened fire. It was around 2.30 am on 31 January 1968, and the Tet Offensive was under way.

The impact of that moment was the beginning of the end of American involvement in Vietnam, but like the slow rise and retreat of an Asian typhoon the extrication from the ruins would last longer than the storm, the casualties still mount-

> '**It was startling to me to find out that we had no military plan to win the war. . . . It was a real loser.**'
>
> — US SECRETARY OF DEFENSE
> CLARK CLIFFORD, 1968

ing as the fury lingered. And those who had believed the storm could be weathered would soon be gone: Defense Secretary McNamara, General Westmoreland and President Johnson himself. The paradox was that they were right. Militarily, Tet was a clear-cut American victory; psychologically, it was the decisive reversal. The storm defenses were sound, but no alert had been given: rather, an all-clear. In a war that had produced too many surprises, none stunned harder than Tet, especially the symbolic assault on the Embassy which had so often declared that the worst was over.

Ambassador Ellsworth Bunker remembers suddenly being 'wakened when it started by Marine guards', who took him to a 'safe house' in the compound. As Bunker puts it, 'My bunker then was the wine cellar, which was fortified with sandbags. After Tet they built a proper bunker for me.' Marines at the main gate had cut down the first attackers and alerted the duty guards inside the Embassy. But during the suicidal distraction at the

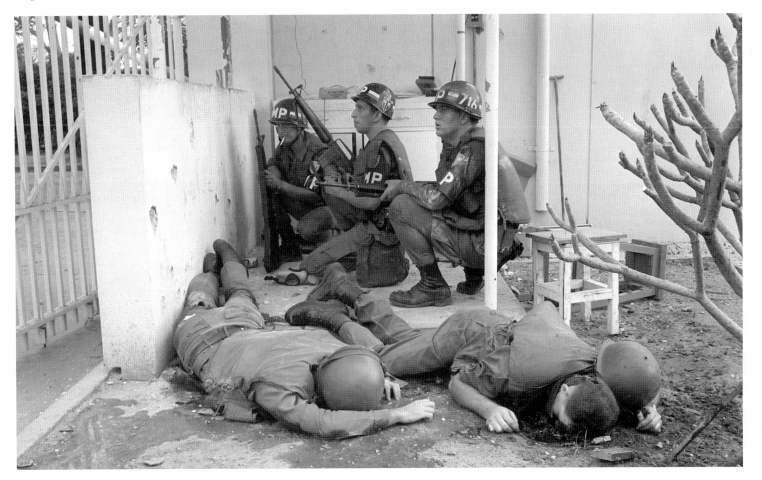

Above: January 1, 1968— With dead U.S. soldiers in the foreground, military police take cover behind a wall at the entrance to the U.S. consulate in Saigon on the first day of the Tet Offensive. Viet Cong guerrillas had invaded the grounds of the U.S. Embassy compound in the earliest hours of the coordinated Communist offensive.

January 31, 1968—Vietnamese soldiers search for Viet Cong guerrillas in an uncompleted hotel one block from the presidential palace in Saigon during the Tet offensive.

Right: January 31, 1968—Two U.S. military police help a wounded fellow officer through the U.S. Embassy compound in Saigon as the embassy came under attack in the Tet Offensive. A Viet Cong suicide squad held part of the compound for about six hours before they were killed or captured by the Marines.

gate other guerrillas had blown a hole in the Embassy wall and entered the grounds. For six hours the press were spectators to an extraordinary no-quarters gunfight, with US Marine reinforcements rushing their own Embassy and with some diplomats shooting it out from the windows. The first news-flash – and headlines across America – mistakenly reported that the Embassy had been seized.

Westmoreland was furious. 'I inspected the Embassy', he says, 'as the battle was being concluded, and visited every floor and got on the phone and called Washington – and came out and had a press conference. At which time I said, "No enemy got in the Embassy building" and that I felt this was a relatively small incident . . . we shouldn't be deceived by this incident.'

Saigon was only one of a hundred towns, cities and US bases in the throes of a simultaneous attack. In Saigon a guerrilla force estimated at 4000 was barricaded in the central populated areas, having infiltrated disguised as farmers and vendors in the traditional holiday influx from the countryside. Other commando groups were still attacking Saigon's main Tan Son Nhut airport, ARVN military headquarters and the presidential palace as the Embassy shoot-out ended. At the Embassy, nineteen guerrillas and seven Americans had been killed. The bodies still lay around the compound early the next morning as Ambassador Bunker inspected the scene, with news cameras tracking from him to the corpses. Even the Ambassador was 'surprised that there was as much infiltration into the city as there had been. Surprised', he says, 'that they had got into the Embassy grounds itself, but they had been repulsed. The reports that I had from General Westmoreland was that militarily the situation was under control.'

'The enemy', says Westmoreland, 'had attacked in force and he was going to be defeated. But the press was unbelieving. The character of the press reports was doom and gloom.' Some 80,000 troops had been committed to the first wave of attacks, the great majority of them being Southern guerrillas who knew every urban street.

But at Hue, the symbolic cultural and religious center, an advance force of 5000 men had shed disguises to reveal North Vietnamese uniforms at the moment of its synchronized attack. Within twenty-four hours the attackers had seized most of the historic city and had been reinforced by another 7000 regular troops.

Across South Vietnam scores of towns had fallen. In Saigon, with half the ARVN force on holiday and many others deserting, five American battalions were in action by the end of the first day, fighting block to block in some areas of the capital. In the ensuing days, as the guerrillas fought to the death, US fighter-planes assigned to the defense of the capital were having to fire on it, strafing and rocketing pockets of resistance in densely populated areas. To defend the capital against further assault, nearby guerrilla-occupied towns like Can Tho and My Tho were devastated by air strikes, with tens of thousands of civilians left wounded or homeless. After the total leveling of one town, Ben Tre, an American officer stated, 'We had to destroy it to save it.' Like the symbolic embassy attack, Ben Tre came to epitomize for many Americans the overall questionable sacrifice.

With the exception of Hue, the Tet Offensive was largely smashed within the first ten days and by the end of it, late February, Westmoreland claimed '37,000 enemy dead'. But the Offensive had cost some 2500 American lives and left half a million refugees. Even with a million-man Allied army the cities had proved vulnerable. As *Time* magazine of 9 February stated, 'It was undoubtedly a *tour de force*: the spectacle of an enemy force dispersed and unseen, everywhere hunted unremittingly, suddenly materializing to strike simultaneously in a hundred places throughout the country.' It was the nature of the Offensive, rather than the defeat of it, which impressed the American public. The questions were larger than the victory: how had such a massive country-wide attack been possible; who was responsible; what was the plan now?

On the very eve of Tet, Johnson had appointed a new Secretary of Defense, Clark Clifford, to take over from 1 March. Clifford, who would be called on to provide the answers, recalls his own initial shock to the Tet Offensive: 'It was rolled back, but in the early days it looked like the bottom was dropping out. . . . What led up to it explains it better,' says Clifford. 'The expression being used was that we could see "the light at the end of the tunnel". And returning visitors would comment on when we might be able to get our men back from Vietnam. There was quite a lot of euphoria by the end of 1967. It looked like we were ultimately prevailing. That's why the Tet Offensive was such a shocking event to the public and to the administration. It was so unexpected.'

The administration, however, had been warned by Westmoreland. In December 1967 he informed Washington that the North Vietnamese seemed to be preparing for 'a major effort' and perhaps 'a radical switch in strategy' to begin in the New Year. This warning was then publicly voiced by General Earle G. Wheeler, Chairman of the Joint Chiefs of Staff, in a speech in Detroit devoted largely to an attack on the US anti-war movement.

Journalist Peter Braestrup is critical of the press for not giving equal prominence to Wheeler's warning – 'showing that the press can only think about one thing at a time' – but, he says, 'an equally heavy burden rested on the President. . . . Troubled by growing anti-war sentiment, particularly in Congress in 1967, President Johnson launched what in retrospect seems a fairly deliberate campaign to put the Vietnam war in its most favorable light. In his January 1968 State of the Union message, which came before Tet, he did not tell the American people or the press what he had been told by his own military, namely that the enemy was preparing to launch a major effort; that hard times lay ahead.' Says Braestrup the 'general state of mind in the country' was one of progress in the war.

On 15 January, as shown in the records of his Saigon MACV, Westmoreland in a military briefing foresaw 'a sixty/forty chance' that the Communists would launch a major strike of some kind before or around Tet. But the beginning of the siege of Khe

Sanh ten days before Tet fully preoccupied the President, and perhaps the military command. At that time, Marine Lieutenant-Colonel Myron Herrington was commanding an infantry company twelve miles south of Hue and he says that military intelligence 'indicated a great deal of enemy movement throughout the countryside; they were massing for some sort of attack, but exactly where we weren't sure.' Yet the largest Tet attack was at Hue.

'I can remember', says Lieutenant-Colonel Ronald Christmas, commenting on the eve of Tet atmosphere, 'having a very ill feeling about it.' He was commanding a Marine company guarding Route 1 into Hue and like Herrington his men would have to fight street to street for a month to recapture the city. Christmas had noted 'a very tense feeling' in the villages quite contrary to 'other ceasefires'. But he only received orders to call off the holiday truce a few hours earlier on 'the night that we were hit'.

'To be quite frank,' he says, 'I think we were just totally let down. I think no one realized the North Vietnamese forces would go after such a large objective. We were moving the entire 3rd Marine Division south of Hue and didn't expect an offensive to occur at that time. And obviously the ARVN forces did not expect it either . . . at least fifty per cent of them were on holiday leave.'

Therefore, although Westmoreland's command knew of large movement 'throughout the countryside', indicating an unusual offensive, the nature of it could not be analyzed because the Communist urban infrastructure (the neglected factor in the view of the British and the CIA) was too extensive and efficient. As Colonel Herrington says, the North Vietnamese must have been infiltrating Hue 'for several days, perhaps even weeks'. A *New York Times* post-mortem commented that Communist security was 'so effective that despite the North's using tens of thousands of men neither the United States or the South Vietnamese army had any real advance inkling of the plan'.

The evidence is that the US command, with its emphasis on military tactics and its mind on Khe Sanh, judged North Vietnamese objectives as the same. An attack on the cities could not succeed; therefore it was not expected – and when it occurred, and failed, it was rightly judged as a costly military failure. The people had not risen up: Hanoi had suffered an overall setback. But Hanoi's view, expressed by Ha Van Lau, was that the Tet Offensive also demonstrated that the US could not win militarily. 'The American command', he says, 'had always been under the illusion that victory was in the palm of their hands. Tet destroyed that illusion. As to the actual losses in human life on our part, I don't recall the exact number, but . . . that was the price that had to be paid to win this strategic victory.'

An American expert on North Vietnamese strategy, William Turley, agrees that Hanoi's objective was to demonstrate military 'stalemate'. Turley, a professor of political science and research associate at the Ford Foundation, prepared numerous studies on Vietnamese Communism. (He was also a contributing editor to *Vietnamese Communism in Comparative Perspective*, 1980). He states that 'the immediate objectives were the occupation of a few cities, not necessarily permanently, in order to reveal the revolution's strength

Left: January 30, 1968—U.S. military policemen and an embassy employee dash past the body of a Vietnamese on the lawn inside the embassy compound during the height of a battle with Viet Cong sappers.

Left: January 31,1968— U.S. soldier lies wounded on a bridge in Siagon after being shot by Viet Cong infiltrators during The Tet Offensive.

Left: February 7, 1968— South Vietnamese rangers and police fire automatic weapons at trucks and people in the streets of Cholon, the Chinese sector of Saigon. The street barricades had been set up by Viet Cong guerrillas.

in urban as well as rural areas'; to weaken faith in the structure of government and to gain an edge 'for negotiations that were thought to be inevitable'.

International pressure for peace negotiations had been building for a year. It is an important part of the record that peace efforts began fully six years before a settlement was reached; three-quarters of the war years – accounting for one million dead –

were spent 'negotiating' while both sides sought a military edge, only to finally adopt the cease-fire in-place formula proposed all along. The prolonged negotiations grew from early mutual distrust.

American historian Gareth Porter, who closely studied the course of negotiations throughout, says a 'promising' development in early 1967 was abruptly terminated by the White House. After mediating with Hanoi, British Prime Minister Harold Wilson was discussing with a Johnson envoy a formula by which the US would cease the bombing of the North 'if the North Vietnamese would agree in advance to slow down infiltration considerably'. Wilson was then to exert pressure on Soviet Premier Aleksei Kosygin to support the plan as a first step toward formal talks (British and Soviet premiers were permanent co-chairmen of the Geneva Accords). But, says Porter, 'in the midst of these London talks' Johnson's National Security Affairs advisor Walt Rostow, 'suddenly stepped in and prevented the American position from being put forward'.

Rostow's action reflected Johnson's own hardening position, influenced by the confident field reports he was then beginning to get. Among Johnson's inner circle only Defense Secretary McNamara was having serious doubts, while keeping them silent. Rostow and McNamara had once been co-architects of the 'surgical' bombing strategy, supposed to prevail within a matter of months. The war's duration now worried McNamara, who feared it must increasingly escalate. If the President had trust in the military reports, then the time had come for statesmanship, McNamara argued. He proposed a new formula for initiating

peace talks – one with a major concession. The US would halt the bombing without setting preconditions other than a negotiating timetable. In September 1967, after privately conveying the package to Hanoi, Johnson publicly outlined it in a speech at San Antonio. Hanoi, in turn, now rejected the peace opportunity. It waited a full month before dismissing the plan as 'nothing new', stating that a bombing halt had to be totally unconditional. By then, Hanoi was obviously preparing for the Tet Offensive, and the reports of increased North Vietnamese infiltration further alarmed McNamara.

His peace plan had failed, and his 'limited' war concept was widening out of control. His Vietnam policy, he confided to aide Adam Yarmolinsky, arose from 'a more fundamental concern about the danger of nuclear war. He wanted to be remembered', says Yarmolinsky, 'as a great teacher; the first high government official who really addressed the proposition that nuclear wars are unwinnable.' Technological war was to be the alternative; the world could 'get away from Armageddon', but now McNamara's new electronic war was haunting him as much.

As this program developed in early 1967, former Navy Secretary Paul Nitze had joined

McNamara's personal staff. He helped McNamara draft the unsuccessful San Antonio formula, and now saw him 'agonizing' over the difficulty of trying to wage war 'more intelligently and less brutally'. Ironically, Nitze reveals that it was the press reportage, which the military consistently discounted, that finally convinced the Defense Secretary to step down – thus setting in motion the process of military withdrawal. McNamara had obtained confirmation of a *New Yorker* report that there had been 'tremendous destruction' of villages from random artillery fire. 'The results had been horrible,' and, says Nitze, McNamara felt 'this was not the way to fight a war'.

McNamara now considered that the military effort he had orchestrated for seven years was futile and immoral. In November 1967 he persuaded Johnson to accept his resignation. The fact that the man who more than any had formulated military policy was now renouncing it did not cause Johnson to pause at all. 'At that point', says biographer Doris Kearns, 'Johnson was having even less doubts; he was growing more sure of his actions.' The way the President 'liked to think about it was that McNamara was being wracked by doubts; he wasn't just doubting the policies, he was becoming emotionally disturbed; near the point of

Left: February 1968—U.S. Marines hold a tower position overlooking a street in the stone fortress of Hue, Vietnam's ancient imperial capital, during the Tet Offensive.

Right: February 1, 1968—A South Vietnamese soldier takes a wounded Viet Cong soldier, left behind by his comrades, from a battered building in the northern sector of Saigon.

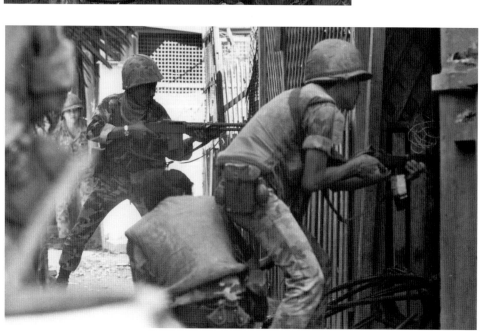

Left: February 12, 1968—South Vietnamese army rangers fire into a building in Cholon, the Chinese section of Saigon, in house-to-house fighting against Viet Cong forces.

Above: February 17, 1968—U.S. Marines, under fire from snipers, carry their seriously injured wounded atop an army tank to a helicopter evacuation point.

Above: February 6, 1968—A soldier calls for a medic in Cholon, the Chinese sector of Saigon, as he helps the commander of a South Vietnamese ranger force and district police chief who was wounded in street fighting with the Viet Cong.

cracking up. So then Johnson liked to tell that magnanimously he'd allowed McNamara to go [to head] the World Bank as a way of preserving his sanity.' Johnson, says Kearns, 'just didn't want a dissenter around, and he didn't want McNamara out there saying that he had dissented.' It was agreed that McNamara would 'just sort of slip away into the night' – but only after a politically healthy interval, effective on, appropriately, Leap Day – 29 February 1968.

In letting his most senior war policy maker go, Johnson proclaimed that at the World Bank McNamara would 'try to build the kind of world that alone can justify' military strength. The man so long regarded as the war's dispassionate generalissimo now publicly revealed his inner torment as he tried to respond. His voice breaking, McNamara said 'Mr President, I cannot find the words to express what lies in my heart today. And I think I'd better respond on another occasion.' (As of 1981, still President of the World Bank, McNamara has kept totally silent on the Vietnam war for thirteen years.)

Johnson himself now concentrated on military strength. In an election year he wanted more Allied help. Once again Johnson turned to a trusted, politically like-minded friend, his legal advisor Clark Clifford, asking him to visit all of America's Vietnam allies. He was to 'persuade them to make a greater contribution to the war'. Clifford spent several weeks trying. 'I kept finding', he says, 'that the important officials of these nations, who were much closer to the trouble, did not share the degree of concern that was apparent in our country. Many of them were right on the border and yet they did not see the same danger in it as we did. And it troubled me deeply.'

Clifford had been peripherally involved in Asian politics for years. He had worked for the Kennedy administration on the Foreign Intelligence Advisory Board, then in 1965 as Chairman of the Board he had toured South-east Asia at Johnson's request. He had been a Johnson advisor at the 1966 Manila conference, and 'I accepted the philosophy and reasoning that was widespread at that particular time – that this was Communist aggression in Southeast Asia and that it was in our own enlightened self-interest to help the South Vietnamese stem the tide of Soviet and Chinese expansionism.'

But on returning from his 1967 tour Clifford 'passed onto the President my concerns'. Johnson told Clifford that the Allies were only being tight-fisted with arms and money: they were still behind the war. Despite Clifford's worries, the President then asked him to be the new Secretary of Defense. 'At that time', says Clifford, 'I supported President Johnson fully. I supported the war. I thought it the right course of action. I had been a confidant of Johnson's for twenty-five years and I think he felt that it would be a strengthening factor if I was to replace Secretary McNamara. The result of that shift proved to be quite paradoxical.'

Clifford's appointment was announced on the eve of Tet – and in the month before he took office the Offensive was over. But related events would cause Clifford to emerge as the most decisive voice of the war. The intervening month would be the hardest yet for Johnson. He was rapidly losing his health and his public. He was being hard-tugged in opposite directions. The Allies were pressuring for a negotiated settlement, and conversely Westmoreland was lobbying for an all-out military effort. One way or another, the turning point in the war had come for Johnson.

In the second week of the Tet Offensive, Johnson was faced with the biggest decision of the war. Westmoreland wanted more troops – some immediately, with consideration for the optimum force he had proposed in 1967 – another 200,000 men. Though the date coincided with the worst setback at Khe Sanh, or more precisely the annihilation of 900 men at Lang Vei, Westmoreland contends that his submission was 'a contingency plan' for a counter-offensive. Except at Hue, the most serious Tet assaults had been repelled. Now was the time, he felt, for hot pursuit of Communist forces into Laos and Cambodia.

Westmoreland's various troop needs were not yet public knowledge. It would still be another three weeks before Clark Clifford took up his post – and in the vacuum, with McNamara as a lame-duck Defense Secretary, the Joint Chiefs of Staff now rallied behind Westmoreland. And Johnson himself initially considered – and appeared to support – both an extension of troop levels and of the battle front, judging from new evidence which Westmoreland cites here. Certainly Westmoreland's proposal was only totally ruled out after adverse publicity. The exact chronology of events at this time are critical to any final assessment of President Johnson and of his senior advisor for a realization of how slowly and narrowly the decision swung against Westmoreland.

At a White House meeting on 12 February 1968, Johnson and the Joint Chiefs are recorded as discussing a possible change of political restrictions – meaning pursuit of the enemy across the borders. The meeting decided 'against deploying the additional forces requested by the field commander, in the absence of other steps to reconstitute the strategic reserve' – that is, a call-up of reserves. This was ambiguously phrased: the recommendation could be in the first part or the last part. The Pentagon Papers summarized: 'A fork in the road had been reached – the alternatives stood out in stark reality . . . at long last, the resources were beginning to be drawn too thin.' Certainly approval of Westmoreland's request would mean in effect an extension of the draft age and vastly increased costs, while a denial would mean that the US had declared a limit to its Vietnam commitment – knowledge which Hanoi could exploit. The administration had indeed come to a fork in the road, but had it really paused on the issue of resources?

A day later, 13 February, despite Johnson's Gallup poll reversal that day, the Pentagon formally announced that 10,500 troops were being sent immediately to Vietnam. This increment was relatively so small as to be meaningless in the context of the immediate battle situation. Though immediate second-wave Communist assaults on the cities were anticipated, neither the US troop increment nor Saigon's call-up of 65,000 reserves

Right: February 1968—A unit of the 1st Battalion, 5th Regiment, U.S. Marines rests alongside a battered wall of Hue's imperial palace after a battle for the Citadel of the ancient capital city. The Marines reported heavy casualties in street fighting in Hue.

Left: May 9, 1968—Saigon residents remaining in the embattled southern quarter of the city crouch on the bank of a canal to avoid crossfire between government troops and Viet Cong sapper squads setting off explosions.

seem retreat. Whichever fork in the road he took, he needed the strongest support. The day after hearing from Wheeler (and Cronkite) the President summoned the man who was about to take charge of the Pentagon. He ordered Clark Clifford immediately to form a 'Task Force' to be operative on 1 March when Clifford took over as Secretary of Defense. It was to render an urgent 'A to Z' assessment of US options. At that point the outcome in Washington was as unpredictable as the continuing siege of Khe Sanh.

Clifford's Task Force was in no sense a tribunal on past policy, or it would have been largely sitting in judgement on itself. The eleven-man committee was drawn from all major departments and its members were to provide a frank analysis of future prospects. They included General Maxwell Taylor from Defense, William Bundy from State, Richard Helms from the CIA and Walt Rostow from the White House – and though they differed somewhat on Strategy they were all considered fully behind the war. Task Force member Paul Nitze, now Clifford's deputy, regarded his new boss as the 'great hawk'.

Clifford makes clear that his Tet inquiry resulted from Westmoreland's huge troop request because the US had already sent 'more than we ever intended'. The Task Force was to report within days on the need and effectiveness of additional troops, and then continue its study of strategic options. The new Defense Secretary was aware of his predecessor's feelings, saying McNamara had 'concluded that the bombing was valueless, it risked the lives of our men [air crew], it killed civilians and it was not preventing the North Vietnamese from moving to the battle area'. Coincidentally Clifford was getting field analysis in the aftermath of Hue, corroborating McNamara. The US military victory at Tet was not, it emerged, altogether comforting. It was a victory more of fire-power than tactics.

Hue, embodying centuries of Vietnamese history and cultural values, had become a shattered monument after a month of 'house to house, room to room' fighting. Lieutenant-Colonel Herrington's Delta Company had helped lead the assault and he felt the paradox expressed by so many field officers, saying, 'There was a reluctance initially, of course, to use our heavy armament to destroy the city in order to save it.' He had found the North Vietnamese soldier to be 'an extremely tenacious fighter. He did not flee and run when the Marines came in – he held his ground. He was well indoctrinated; he knew what his mission was.' Towards the end, several thousand North Vietnamese troops had fallen back and entrenched in the Citadel, a fortress once the Imperial Palace, and 'they had this perhaps emotional attachment to the fact that they had liberated this ancient capital, and they saw this as a great crusade'. Facing prohibitive casualties, the US military had finally decided to bomb the Citadel.

Hue was 'devastated', says Herrington. The Vietnamese 'small wooden' homes had been 'completely blown away'; the business district was 'rubble all over' and generally, 'I can't really describe how devastated it was but it'd really been destroyed.' In Hue alone, the civilian dead exceeded 5800 – ten times the combined American-ARVN troop losses. The US military would later say that half the civilian deaths were Communist executions. Another Hue veteran, Lieutenant-

could be ready in time. Anyhow the US Command placed even less reliance on ARVN as a consequence of Tet and this ARVN addition was again numerically insignificant for any major counter-offensive. The 10,500 deployment therefore signalled that the US was not about to retrench after the psychological shock of Tet, and was perhaps taking a small step towards larger moves. This deployment went almost unnoticed.

The Joint Chiefs were meantime endorsing the estimate of 30,000 to 40,000 Communists killed or captured in the Tet Offensive – or upwards of half the force involved: a strong argument for Westmoreland's hot pursuit. On 23 February, after eleven days of intense Washington debate, the Chairman of the JCS, General Wheeler, flew to Saigon. Westmoreland claims he was then told that his extended war policy was being considered, with Wheeler himself supportive.

Westmoreland provides this new account: 'Joe Wheeler came over to see me and he said that consideration was being given to mobilization of reserves, and there was a possibility that the polit-

ical strategy could change: we might be allowed to take the fight to the enemy, permitting us to move into Cambodia and Laos.' Westmoreland then told Wheeler what this change would require – 206,000 additional American troops.

It was the Field Commander's largest troop request of the war – a huge forty per cent increase. And Wheeler implicitly endorsed it. On the 27th President Johnson received a much altered recommendation. He was told by the Joint Chiefs that 'we must be prepared to accept some [call-up of] reserves. . . . The forces currently assigned to MACV, plus the forces yet to be delivered, are inadequate.' It was on this day that the venerable Walter Cronkite of CBS was calling for a negotiated settlement. The last Tet fighting had just ended at Hue; UN Secretary-General U Thant had returned from a tour of world capitals, including Moscow, saying that peace talks 'could begin within days'. At the same time the French Government stated it had 'specific information' that with a bombing halt peace talks could begin.

Johnson faced the double election year dilemma of choosing between escalation or what might

Colonel Christmas, says that early on 'a number of Vietcong formed goon squads' and took away anyone who 'may have worked for the government' and 'I think this is where many of the mass graves [report] come from.' But he says 'the North Vietnamese commander did put a stop to this eventually when he found out about it. And I think that's something that should be said – the differences. The North Vietnamese soldier was a good, crack soldier.' (MACV says a captured guerrilla document listed '1892 administrative personnel, 38 policemen, 790 tyrants' as executed. Radio Hanoi referred to 'lackeys who owed blood debts'.)

Christmas, the son-in-law of Colonel Lownds in charge at Khe Sanh, was commanding Marine Company H fighting alongside Herrington's and he says tactical errors 'prolonged the battle' because 'our side failed to ever really isolate the city of Hue'. In fact, he says, throughout the month-long battle the North Vietnamese had 'a corridor that ran along the Perfume River' from the city to the countryside and in terms of rough combat 'we didn't recognize what we really had on our hands'.

One of the significant contradictions that the Tet inquiry would reveal was that the Marines, traditionally accustomed to close-in fighting in previous wars, had experienced combat in Vietnam only in the rice-paddies and the jungles. Herrington notes that the Marines had not participated in combat in a built-up area since Korea fifteen years earlier '. . . so that our training was not completely efficient in that area, because we do train in that area, but our experience at that time [Hue] was absolutely zero. Initially as we went in we did not have any real concept of how we were supposed to fight.'

Under these circumstances, both officers felt, the Marines had acquitted themselves remarkably well at Hue. Now in Washington the Clifford Task Force had to consider such field reports. Although elsewhere the Tet Offensive had been smashed relatively easily, the great majority of the defeated Communist force had been guerrilla irregulars. On the one hand, the Task Force had evidence that guerrilla strength had been so weakened it might never recover – an argument for an intensified US effort; on the other hand, infiltration from the North was unabated and there would be a tougher adversary replacing the guerrilla network who would still choose the time and method of attack. There was the evidence of Hue that North Vietnamese fighting ability had been underestimated, and that after two decades of conflict they were certainly more experienced than the Marines in ambush and urban warfare, which might at any time resume. What would it take in Vietnam either for a US counter-force or for a counter-offensive?

Clifford was not a career politician, he was a tough corporation lawyer who had given up a $500,000 practice for a $35,000 job. He began it with a personal no-nonsense cross-examination of the Pentagon chiefs. 'I swear to you it was a revelation to me,' says Clifford. 'I spent four days down in the "Tank" – that's the situation room of the Pentagon where you're in touch with every US location in the world. And I tried to get answers to questions like "How long in your opinion – and you are the military experts – do you think the war will last?" I could get no satisfactory answer. "Now if we send 200,000 more men will that be the end,

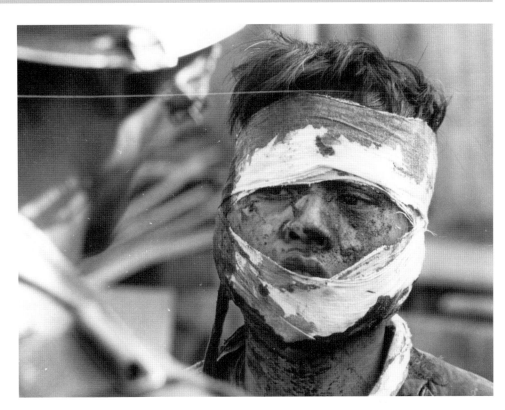

Above: February 3, 1968—A wounded North Vietnamese prisoner undergoes interrogation by U.S. Marines during street fighting for the old imperial capital of Hue.

or must we send more?" "Well, we really don't know." "Well, are we actually prevailing?" "It all depends on how you look at it." I could not get sound and solid answers.'

Clifford recalls questioning one US general who had 'moved a hundred thousand men' in a sweep of one zone. 'I said, "How did it go?" and he said, "Badly". I said "What was the trouble?" and he said "Damn it, they won't come out and fight." It reminded me', says Clifford 'of the complaint by the British general in the revolutionary war that the American troops wouldn't come out and fight. We hung behind brick fences, rocks and trees and knocked off those Red Coats. And this was the same kind of problem.' Clifford was now doubting that even if the US 'doubled or trebled' its forces it would end the war 'because the other side was not fighting that kind of war'.

In the Pentagon 'War Room' Clifford 'finally asked the ultimate question and that is, "What is the plan for the United States to win the war?". . . . It was startling to me to find out that we had no military plan to win the war. The answer was that the enemy will ultimately be worn down so severely by attrition that the enemy will eventually capitulate. And that was our policy in the war.'

Only the CIA continued to dismiss this strategy, concluding in its Task Force study that Hanoi could withstand a war of attrition regardless of large US troop increases. But perhaps the most devastating submission came from the ISA, or the Office of International Security Affairs of the Department of Defense. In a commissioned paper entitled 'Alternative Strategies', it had this bleak summary: 'We lost our offensive stance because we never achieved the momentum essential for military victory. "Search and Destroy" operations can't build this kind of momentum and the South Vietnamese forces were not pushed hard enough. We became

mesmerized by statistics of known doubtful validity, choosing to place our faith in the ones that showed progress. . . . In short, our setbacks were due to wishful thinking compounded by a massive intelligence collection and/or evaluation failure.'

On 4 March, four days after Clifford's immersion in the Pentagon 'Tank', the Task Force submitted an interim memorandum to President Johnson. Despite Clifford's doubts and the damning ISA report, the memorandum compromised on Westmoreland's request – neither approving nor rejecting it. The President was simply told, 'There can be no assurance that this very substantial additional deployment would leave us a year from today in any more favorable military position. All that can be said is that additional troops would enable us to kill more of the enemy and provide more security if the enemy does not offset them.' Johnson was hardly any wiser.

On 10 March the *New York Times* disclosed Westmoreland's massive troop request, shocking the nation. As Westmoreland puts it: 'Unhappily this top secret plan was leaked to the press, and the headlines were that I was asking for 206,000 troops in the context that I was desperate. One report said that Westmoreland had panicked and asked for these reinforcements to save the day.' Clifford continued his inquiry but now seemed isolated. When Clifford was named Defense Secretary one press review noted that Johnson had 'picked a man he knows and trusts, one who could hardly repudiate any basic policy decision, particularly in an election year'. On 11 March, at a concurrent Senate inquiry, Secretary of State Rusk reiterated the basic policy, saying that if South Vietnam was put at risk it would be 'catastrophic not just for South-east Asia but for the United States'. On the same day a *Newsweek* cover bannered 'The Agony of Khe Sanh'.

On the 12th, Democratic presidential 'peace candidate' Senator Eugene McCarthy, though considered a long shot, almost tied Johnson in the traditional barometer primary in New Hampshire. Yet on 13 March, despite the adverse press and the new public mood. Johnson secretly approved the phased deployment to Vietnam of a further 30,000 troops. On the 17th the *New York Times* again disclosed this latest troop plan, and now the headlines and editorials were thunderous. Westmoreland felt that the press leaks 'put pressure on Mr Johnson that pretty well closed the door to any other course of action except withdrawal'.

Johnson by now, says biographer Doris Kearns, was going through 'the most difficult period in his entire life: the way he described it is that he felt stampeded on all sides'. And leading the stampede was Johnson's most feared political rival, Senator Robert Kennedy, who had just announced that he, too, would oppose his party leader for the Presidency. 'Worst of all and symbolizing all these problems', says Kearns, 'was that Robert Kennedy, the very person that he feared his entire presidency, would somehow come back and haunt him about John Kennedy. And he had come in March to finally announce that he was going to try and – as he [Johnson] put it – reclaim the throne for the lost brother.'

Johnson began to feel that 'there was no way he could fight that stampede' – and the stampede was gathering force. On the 19th, the day after Kennedy's decision, 139 members of the House of Representatives – including forty-one Democrats – passed a resolution calling for an immediate review by Congress of US war policy. In fact, Defense Secretary Clifford had just finished his confidential inquiry and he now decided to confront the President directly. Biographer Kearns says at this period Johnson feared 'becoming paralyzed – not just that he might lose, but worse than that – that in the middle of all those forces – he would literally become paralyzed'.

In this mental and physical condition the advice of his politically trusted Defense Secretary was in every sense a body blow. Since his compromise memorandum Clifford – in his conclusions – had become a one-man task force. His deputy, Paul Nitze, had watched as 'the great hawk became the great dove'. Clifford did not just 'change his mind – he reversed it 180 degrees'. The Defense Secretary wanted to get out of Vietnam and 'to get out right away'. Even Nitze, an advocate of negotiations, found himself 'in as much disagreement with Clifford after his change of mind as I was before'.

Says Clifford, 'I then reported my *personal view* [author's italics] to President Johnson, and said that it was very clear to me that the one course of action that the United States should take was to get out of Vietnam. It was a real loser.' (At that time, US combat deaths in Vietnam were fewer than 19,000 with 115,000 wounded – overall forty per cent of the eventual toll. ARVN deaths were 57,000 – one-fifth of what they would become. A point of interest is that the US Defense Department did not issue casualty figures for the other five Allies whose forces then fighting in Vietnam totaled 61,000. The Allied losses from 1965 to 1973 exceeded 5200 – 4407 South Koreans, 469 Australian and New Zealand dead and 350 Thai – but these tended to get overlooked.)

Left: February 3, 1968—A large section of rubble is all that remains in this one block square area of Saigon after fierce Tet Offensive fighting. Rockets and grenades combined with fires laid waste to the area. An Quang Pagoda, location of Viet Cong headquarters during the fighting, is at the top of the photo.

Right: Map shows the Citadel, an ancient stone fortress, where fierce fighting took place during the Tet Offensive of 1968. Map shows location of the opposing forces.

CITY Limits

**THE CITADEL**

Airborne Strikes North and West Walls

SOUTH VIETNAMESE

U.S. MARINES

U.S. SUPPLY ROUTE

Canal

Dong Ba Canal

City Limits

IMPERIAL CITY

Ngo Mon Gate

Controlled by Enemy

River of Perfumes

Bridge DESTROYED

Bridge DESTROYED

Marines Storm South Wall

**SOUTH VIETNAM**

Hue University

Provincial HQ

U.S. MILITARY COMPOUND

**HUE**

An-Dinh Palace

City Limits

0   1/2   Mile

It would seem that one man's strength of conviction largely contributed to America's change of course in Vietnam. As Clifford himself puts it, 'I think the major impact on the President was the fact that I had supported the war, supported it strongly; he knew me very well after twenty-five years. And the fact that I had gone into the position, went through this exhaustive inquiry, had then changed: I think that had more impact on President Johnson than perhaps any one development.'

At the time, however, Clifford 'didn't know what impact it was having on him'. Clifford continued to 'persuade anybody who would listen to me that we ought to get out of the war'. But Johnson still needed consensus of whatever kind, not least from the private sector. In the ensuing

days, between 18 and 20 March, he convened what amounted to a nine-man jury of retired presidential advisors. They were to get 'candid' briefings from department experts; they would then face and question Johnson's department heads, and after that the President would hear their verdict. These meetings were to be informal lunch and dinner gatherings, perhaps in the spirit of *in vino veritas*.

The ex-advisors included respected generals like Matthew B. Ridgway of Korean war fame and national icon Omar Bradley; distinguished State Department elders like Dean Acheson and George Ball, as well as Cyrus Vance, formerly Deputy Defense Secretary, and McGeorge Bundy, previously National Security advisor to both Johnson and Kennedy. This second post-Tet inquiry began

NORTH VIETNAMESE AND VIET CONG
UNITS IN SAIGON AREA

Above: The sites of Viet Cong and North Vietnamese battalions in provinces surrounding Saigon in the spring of 1968 after the Tet Offensive are located on this map. Their mission was to harass the central government and influence peace talks in Paris.

Left: March 30, 1968— President Lyndon B. Johnson works on his speech in the White House Cabinet Room. The following day he announced that he would not seek or accept the nomination for re-election.

with a briefing from three experts: George Carver, a senior Vietnam political analyst at the CIA; Phillip Habib, a deputy to William Bundy at the State Department, and – representing the Pentagon – General William DePuy, now Special Assistant to the Joint Chiefs on counter-insurgency. State Department evidence was that the Saigon government had emerged even weaker after Tet; corruption and refugees were serious problems. The CIA and the Pentagon once more gave differing assessments of Communist strength and durability, and the contradictory testimony continued as the former policy-makers confronted their successors – including Rusk and Bundy from the State Department, Walt Rostow from the White House, Helms from the CIA, General Wheeler from the Pentagon and Defense Secretary Clark Clifford.

When the jury delivered its verdict to Johnson, Clifford had not wholly won his case. The past and present advisors had hammered out a consensus: they recommended against further troop increases and advocated negotiations.

Johnson was said to be 'surprised' at this advice. Still undecided, he summoned the three men who had briefed the arbitrators, telling them to be as candid with him. They were, and the circle around Johnson was now complete – though completely reversed. Among all those who had embarked with him on the war he now found no whole-hearted confidence that the war could be won.

Though the fork in the road had been faced, and chosen, Secretary of State Dean Rusk nevertheless found the reverse course hard to understand. 'The result of the Tet Offensive', he says, 'was a very severe military setback for the North Vietnamese and Viet Cong forces. It is a great mystery to me as to how it was translated into such a brilliant political success for the North Vietnamese – here at home in the United States.'

But Rusk's deputy, William Bundy, who had helped draw up the bombing scenario that was to end it all within six months, now exactly three years later could foresee no end. 'It would be a tremendously long, costly and bloody struggle,' he says, explaining the March turn-about. 'Essentially it represented a conclusion that there was not a military solution that was possible within the political capacity of the United States and the American public to carry it through. That's what it amounted to.'

On 22 March, Johnson formally announced that General William Westmoreland was to leave Vietnam by June. Westmoreland was promoted to Army Chief of Staff. With this move, the US abandoned the big unit 'Search and Destroy' strategy of attrition. (The Pentagon list of Americana-coded operations abruptly switches style as of June 1968 with Operation 'Toan Thang' – 'Complete Victory' – signaling the process of 'Vietnamization'.) However, Westmoreland contends that 'after the enemy was defeated at the Tet Offensive and withdrew across the border to lick his wounds', the new US Commander General Creighton William Abrams, was able 'to break his forces into smaller groups without jeopardizing the safety of those forces'. Westmoreland further says that he was informed in December 1967 that 'they planned to move me in the summer of 1968' and that 'the Tet Offensive really had nothing to do with the relief'. 'It was the turning point of the war,' he says, however. 'It could have been the turning point for success, but it was the turning point of failure.'

Above: Map locates the infiltration routes and the sites and size of North Vietnamese forces in South Vietnam in the spring of 1968.

Right: The tempo of fighting stepped up in May, 1967. Map locates some of the hot spots..

Above: July 1968—A U.S. Marine adds fuel to the fire destroying the Khe Sanh 'Hilton,' considered the most comfortable and secure bunker on the base. The Marines were destroying anything useful to the enemy as they abandoned the base, which they had successfully defended during a grueling 77-day siege just three months earlier.

Right: June 2, 1968—A Vietnamese Ranger pauses from the heavy street fighting of Cholon to place burning sticks of incense on a temple altar.

Left: April 4, 1968—People at a Hanoi newsstand buy Nhan Dan newspaper to read the government's statement regarding U.S. President Lyndon Johnson's announcement of de-escalation in the Vietnam War.

Fourteen years earlier General Navarre admitted failure but not any guilt. Westmoreland denies failure and says 'I have nothing to apologize for'. He was 'center-stage, the war had become considerably unpopular, and needless to say a lot of that rubbed off on me. I was not elated with some of the venom that was cast my way. But as a soldier prays for peace, he must also be prepared to cope with the hardships of war, and bear its scars. I have borne those scars.'

Of 1968, he says, 'We had as fine a military force as America has ever assembled – a force that could have brought the war to an end if it hadn't been for political decisions that prohibited that.' As Westmoreland sees it, 'doom and gloom' reporting 'gave the American people the impression that the Americans were being defeated on the battlefield, swayed public opinion to the point that political authority made the decision to take all the pressure off the enemy at a time when he was virtually on the ropes'.

His worst enemy, Westmoreland would go out feeling, was the press: 'At one time in Vietnam we had 700 accredited reporters – all practicing, seeking and reporting news as they were accustomed to in the United States, all looking for the sensational stories. If we get involved again and we hope we won't, but we have to assume that we will, and if the enemy controls the information on his side and we continue the practice of reporting only the off-beat, the unusual or the bizarre in any future war, well then the American public are going to be influenced as they were during Vietnam. I think the bottom line in this subject [Vietnam] is how an open society, and how our political democracy are vulnerable to manipulation by an autocratic flow of society. This is a lesson to be learned.'

In Saigon, Ambassador Bunker shared Westmoreland's feelings: Tet 'militarily was a massive defeat for the other side, but a psychological victory – there's no question about it'. Though the free press had openly reported an undeclared war, Bunker also paradoxically argues that 'it is questionable whether a democracy can fight war successfully without censorship'. He adds that 'a democracy can't fight a war successfully unless there is a consensus in support of the war'. This raises the question of how there can be meaningful consensus without free debate.

'If, God forbid,' says Dean Rusk, 'we ever got into this sort of situation again, then when the Congress passes a resolution of involvement it must address itself to the censorship problem at the same time.' It would certainly be a problem. With modern communications censorship in the field can be quickly circumvented. For instance, film reports on Vietnam could have been flown from Saigon to Bangkok and sent by satellite with only an hour or so delay. The alternative, domestic censorship, would mean actual autocratic government as distinct from Westmoreland's view of the press. The dilemma of Tet and Khe Sanh which altered America's perception of Vietnam had also altered the nature of any great future war.

As Dean Rusk says, 'This was the first struggle fought on television in everybody's living-room every day. What would have happened in World War II if Guadalcanal and the Anzio beach-head and the Battle of the Bulge or the Dieppe raid were on television and the other side was not doing the same thing? War is an obscene blot on the face of the human race. But whether ordinary people,

Above: Map of Paris highlights important sites in the French capital during peace talks between U.S. and North Vietnam.

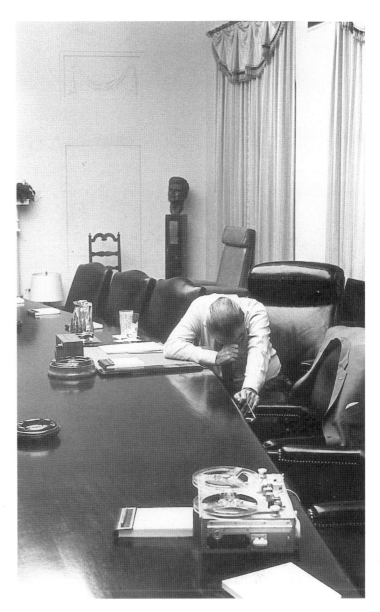

Right: July 31, 1968—U.S. President Lyndon B. Johnson listens to a tape recording from his son-in-law, Capt. Charles Robb, at the White House. Robb was a U.S. Marine Corps company commander in Vietnam.

Left: March 11, 1968—Secretary of State Dean Rusk testifies before the Senate Foreign Relations Committee with an offer to stop bombing North Vietnam to get war settlement talks going.

Right: May 13, 1968—French protocal chief Bernard Durand gestures as he invites negotiators to take their seats at the opening of Vietnam Peace Talks in Paris. North Vietnam's Xuan Thuy (behind outstretched hand) and U.S. representative Averell Harriman (second from right) opened the talks.

Left: October 8, 1968—South Vietnamese President Nguyen Van Thieu, *left*, meets in Saigon with Gen. Duong Van Minh, known as 'Big Minh,' who returned from exile in Thailand. The general, leader of the 1963 coup that overthrew Ngo Dinh Diem, was invited to return as an advisor to broaden popular support for the government.

Right: October 30, 1968—President Nguyen Van Thieu leads the way in ceremonies to open the high-level Inspection Directorate in Saigon. Following are Vice President Nguyen Cao Ky and Prime Minister Tran Van Huong.

who prefer peace to war in any country, whether ordinary people can sustain a war effort under that kind of daily hammering is a very large question.'

The only answer might be that in World War II there was clear-cut cause, and even grave defeats like Dunkirk were perceived as victories of the spirit. In contrast there was nothing inspiring about the military's victory claim at Tet. The Tet debate seemed sure to bring a repeat of the agonizing at some future place and time, but on 25 March 1968, a Harris poll showed that a majority of Americans – sixty per cent – regarded the Tet Offensive as a defeat for US objectives in Vietnam.

On 31 March, as the siege of Khe Sanh was lifted, a gaunt President Johnson faced the television cameras in his Oval Office and addressed the nation. 'Tonight', he said, 'I want to speak to you of peace in Vietnam, and South-east Asia. No other question so preoccupies our people.'

Clark Clifford recalls that he had worked with Johnson on this speech for several days and that an early draft began, 'I want to talk to you about the war in South Vietnam.' Says Clifford, 'Some of us were strongly in favor of saying, "Good evening, fellow Americans. I want to talk to you about

*peace* in Vietnam." Ultimately, that was pretty much the way it started. Still, we were not sure that he was going to go through with it. He finally came through all the way.' The President announced that he had decided to freeze troop levels, limit the air war against North Vietnam and seek a negotiated peace. (Peace talks began in Paris on 12 May. American historian Gareth Porter, who studied the talks throughout, claims that 'most people advising the President felt that the North Vietnamese would probably reject it [negotiations] and that we would gain public points for having made the offer'.)

The President then delivered the last shock of the Johnson years. Clifford and his wife had been invited to join Lyndon and Mrs [Ladybird] Johnson for dinner at the White House before the speech: 'He and I had been through a very difficult time together. I'd been urging a change in policy, and he had been resisting it, and our relationship had become quite fragile. So I was glad that we were there. And as we got near the time for the speech, he stood up and said "Clark, will you step in my bedroom with me." And we went in and he handed me a little extra piece of paper and said,

"This is a part of the speech that you've never seen." It was the paragraph that announced that he would not run again for the presidency.'

'With America's sons in the fields far away,' Johnson told the people, 'and with America's future under challenge here at home; with our hopes and the world's hopes for peace in the balance every day, I do not believe that I should devote an hour or a day of my time to any personal partisan causes, or to any duties other than the awesome duties of this office – the presidency of your country. Accordingly, I shall not seek, and I will not accept, the nomination of my party for another term as your President.' Then in words almost paraphrasing those of John F. Kennedy long before the war began, Johnson concluded: 'But let men everywhere know, however, that a strong and confident and a vigilant America stands ready tonight to seek an honorable peace, and stands ready tonight to defend an honored cause, whatever the price, whatever the burden, whatever the sacrifice that duty may require.'

Clifford remembers that Johnson's 'close staff were terribly despondent' and his two daughters 'both cried – they didn't want him to do it'. But Johnson himself just felt 'a sense of relief' and Ladybird 'was radiant, she was glowing; she wanted very much for him to get out. She had a serious doubt that he would live through another term.'

Although Lyndon Johnson would live the equivalent of another term, or for almost another five years, his close friend Dean Rusk maintains that Johnson's decision on the presidency was based on his physical condition, not on Vietnam. Says Rusk, 'The way in which he made the announcement not to run again would leave it open to people to make a close connection between that decision and the Vietnam problem. Actually he discussed this matter with me a year earlier, and he talked about Woodrow Wilson lying there paralyzed while Mrs Wilson was trying to run the Cabinet. He talked about men in other high positions who had health problems – Winston Churchill, Anthony Eden, John Foster Dulles and Eisenhower – and he said "I'm not going to inflict that problem on the United States government, nor on my family." Health was ninety-eight per cent of the problem in his mind when he decided not to run again.'

Johnson would tell biographer Doris Kearns that during the 'stampede' period he would have a recurring dream that 'he was awake in the Red Room of the White House where Woodrow Wilson's portrait hung, and somehow he had the body of the thin gaunt Woodrow Wilson after the stroke. And he heard all of his advisors out in the corridor trying to take his power away from him. And he said the dream symbolized for him why he couldn't stay in the presidency anymore. Far better to be out of the thick of the action, back home on the ranch, at least controlling your own small destiny, than to be in the middle of the stampede and look like a coward, unable to control your own destiny.'

Johnson, it seemed, in getting out of Vietnam still had the same concern that led him into it – a fear of appearing cowardly. And later, after being carried by the stampede one way then another (as compared to Clifford who faced it), Kearns remembers Johnson 'on the ranch all alone, with absolutely nobody to really command other than four Mexican field hands; with no reports to receive at night except how many postcards had been sold at the LBJ ranch . . . you literally watched him withering in those last years. There was no purpose left to his life anymore.'

Rusk had said that no one agonized more than Johnson over the soldiers in Vietnam, and Kearns says that history will counter the idea that Johnson was 'a warmonger'. In Kearns' summary, 'Reigning ideology had a hell of a lot to do with what got us into Vietnam. And he didn't make those assumptions – they came with him. They were part of the whole baggage of ideas that he had inherited from another generation. History is going to have to say that here was a man who had been a leader all of his life, an effective leader, who always tested everything by "Will it work?" – he was the most pragmatic of sorts – and yet on this particular case of Vietnam he lost that whole instinctive sense for what is practical. . . . He never understood it at the beginning. As time went on it assumed a proportion for him that left him unable to extricate himself.'

The last act of the Tet period, the relief of Khe Sanh, seemed symbolic of what happened in Vietnam and what would follow. With the siege lifted, the Khe Sanh base was then abandoned. Its defender, Colonel Lownds, says of it, 'I was told to go there and I was told to stay there. I went there, I stayed there. When they told me to come out, I came out. The same thing with the troops that went there. I am not a politician.'

In May, peace talks began in Paris, but the 'stalemate' on the battlefield was now reflected in the negotiations as – based on past climate – both sides continued to seek military or psychological advantage. The fighting became even more bitter. That month, as Johnson awarded Colonel Lownds and his men the Presidential Unit Citation, he kept to the old rhetorical question and answer. 'Some have asked', he said, 'what the gallantry of these Marines and airmen accomplished: why did we choose to pay the price to defend those dreary hills?' But America, he said, had 'vividly demon-strated to the enemy the utter futility of his attempts to win a military victory in the South.'

But privately Johnson would concede that at Tet the real battle fought and lost was for the hearts and minds of his own people. Unlike Westmoreland and Rusk and so many others who led the war, Johnson's bitterness would be directed not at the press but at the public. He had loved them. Soon he would see his Great Society crumble like the glory of Hue. He would grieve for it and for himself. Somehow he had destroyed it in trying to save it – and no one understood. Finally, says biographer Kearns, 'he had begun to question not so much Vietnam but whether a life that is lived, as his was, always for public approval, is really going to produce that sense of satisfaction in the end' – and Johnson would think only of '. . . the fickleness of this public that has turned against me'. In the last few months of Johnson's presidency, and for the two-thirds of the war still to be fought, the decisive front line would remain America.

Above: November 1968—Fog drifts up from the valleys below the demilitarized zone as U.S. Marines of the 4th Regiment, 3rd Division, untangle air dropped supplies. The Marines had made minor enemy contact during a week-long sweep for infiltration south of the DMZ.

Right: February 27, 1968—Displaced persons in Hue crowd a bridge partly wrecked by the Viet Cong after the government permitted the refugees to return to their ravaged homes in the Citadel and old city. They use a walkway to reach a temporary pontoon bridge or wait for boats to ferry them between spans.

Above: February 22, 1968—People of Hue stream back through the ruins of the narrow gate of the Citadel, where more than half of the homes shown at the top of the photo were destroyed in the Tet fighting.

Right: February 24, 1968—South Vietnamese soldiers carefully enter a gate of the old imperial palace in the Citadel of Hue, as scattered fighting continues after they captured the palace grounds.

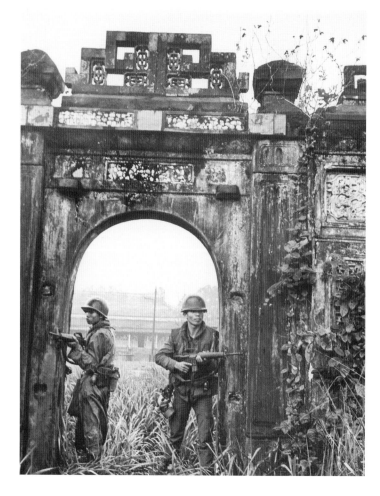

Below: February 12, 1968—A building burns during a gun battles in Hue, killing several Viet Cong prisoners held inside.

Above: February 1968—A U.S. Marine carries an American flag as he charges across a rubble-strewn courtyard in the old citadel in Hue,
South Vietnam. The Marines secured the flag atop a wall of the ancient fortress as fighting continued.

Above: February 26, 1968—Vietnamese soldiers pose in victory in the ornate throne room of the Imperial
Palace in the Hue Citadel.

Left: February 1968—U.S. Marines hold a tower position overlooking a street in the stone fortress of Hue,
Vietnam's ancient imperial capital, during the Tet Offensive.

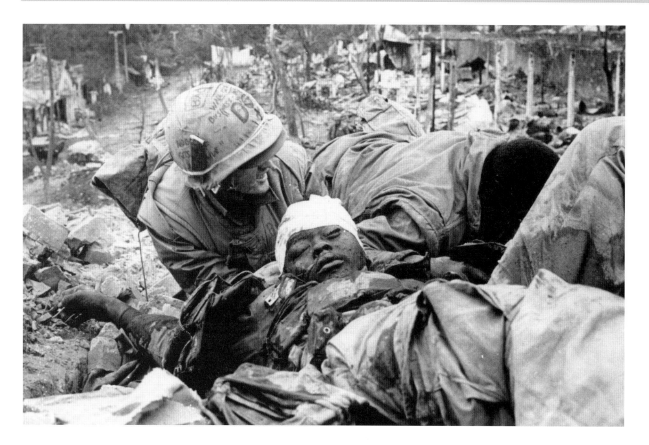

Left: February 1968—A wounded Marine is protected by his buddies during the fierce fighting in the stony, rocky crevices of the Citadel in Hue. It was difficult to evacuate troops hit during the fighting and often wounded had to wait until the action subsided.

Below: February 16, 1968— Dug in behind columns of the old Imperial Palace, South Vietnamese Marines survey the palace courtyard during fighting in Hue's walled Citadel.

Left: February 4, 1968—U.S. Marines, supplemented by a tank, take cover behind a tree near the southern bridgehead on the Perfume River, in Hue, South Vietnam, as they fight well-armed North Vietnamese troops for the fifth straight day. The Communists continued to hold on to the major portion of the city.

Right: February 1968—A U.S. Marine tank guards the residential section of Hue as fighting in the city finally wound down. More than half the ancient capital's buildings were damaged or destroyed during the month-long fight for control of the city.

Below: February 1968—A U.S. Marine takes a red scarf from the uniform of a dead North Vietnamese soldier in the rubble of Hue's Citadel. Hundreds of North Vietnamese and Viet Cong troops were believed to be holding positions in the walled Citadel of the ancient capital.

Above: February 13, 1968—South Vietnamese troops and U.S. Marines hold a gate to the Citadel, Hue's ancient walled fortress. With North Vietnamese soldiers still holding a corner of the Citadel, fighting in Hue entered a third week.

Above: February 16, 1968—
U.S. Marines prepare to carry
a wounded Marine through
the eastern wall during an
assault on the Citadel in Hue.
Air strikes left much of the
walled Citadel in ruins.

Left: February 7, 1968—
Wounded U.S. Marines
wait for ambulances on a
Hue street corner after a
week of fighting for the
ancient imperial city during
the Tet Offensive.

Above: February 27, 1968—Two Communist prisoners await transport to an interrogation center after South Vietnamese Rangers overran enemy positions in Hue's Citadel.

Left: February 9, 1968—U.S. Marines set up a skeleton next to their 81mm mortar position in the garden of the Vietnamese provincial government headquarters at Hue. The skeleton was taken from the medical school in the city.

Right: February 26, 1968—A U.S. soldier of the Military Assistance Command, Vietnam (MACV), uses his rifle to guide wounded Viet Cong troops down a street during the battle of Hue.

Above: February 26, 1968—Image of an old Vietnamese warrior from a past century contrasts sharply with a U.S. Marine on a patrol and mopup operation in the Citadel of Hue.

Above: February 23, 1968—A South Vietnamese soldier fires at a sniper from rubble that was once the tower at the southwest gate of the Citadel in Hue. A torn South Vietnamese flag flies above, while below is the shredded remains of a Viet Cong flag.

Above: February 1968—Gunners atop a Citadel wall keep a lookout for enemy movement as they attempt to drive the Viet Cong from their hiding places.

Left: February 16, 1968—A South Vietnamese soldier fires from the window of a Buddhist pagoda as allied forces fight to dislodge Communist elements holed up in Hue's walled Citadel.

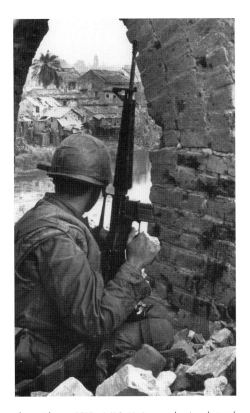

Above: February 1968—A U.S. Marine crouches in a battered stone arch atop a tower of the Citadel, the ancient stone fortress in the heart of Hue. The battle for Hue was three weeks old; it took three days of bitter fighting to take the tower.

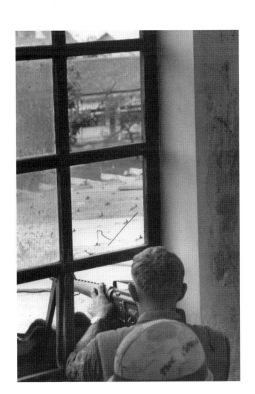

Above: February 1968—Marines crouch low in the rubble of one of the towers of Hue's Citadel. They await an artillery strike before advancing against North Vietnamese positions in the ancient stone fortress that provided protection against Marine attacks for several weeks.

Left: February 3, 1968—A U.S. Marine fires from a window during house-to-house fighting for Hue during the Tet Offensive.

Above: February 2, 1968—A family carrying personal belongings returns to their partially wrecked home in Hue after Viet Cong units were driven from the city. Some 140,000 residents of the ancient capital were refugees from the battle.

Below: April 1968—Shafts of light filter through the jungle cover as American troops look skyward to helicopter moving downward to pick up wounded.

Above: April 29, 1968—A medic looks up at a medical evacuation helicopter while treating a wounded man of the U.S. 101st. Airborne Division west of Hue. The unit was on a five-day patrol through the Communist-controlled area, making regular contact with the enemy.

Left: February 22, 1968—Wounded Marine sits in a sandbagged emplacement awaiting evacuation from Hue's Citadel.

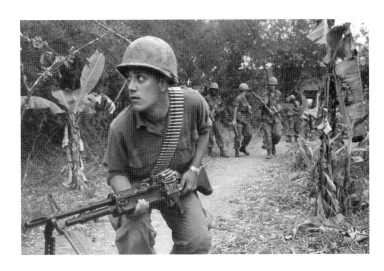

Above: April 1, 1968—Alert, cautious movement forward is the key to survival for these soldiers as they seek out Viet Cong on a rubber plantation not far from Saigon.

Above: April 18, 1968—A South Vietnamese soldier stands guard outside a damaged wing of the ancient Imperial Palace in the Citadel of Hue.

Left: April 1968—A U.S. paratrooper of the 101st Airborne Division sits under the damaged archway of a small temple west of Hue. The unit was patrolling for remnants of the Communist units that attacked Hue during the Tet Offensive.

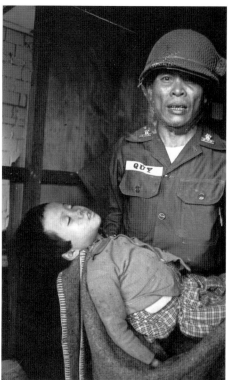

Above: February 1, 1968—
South Vietnamese Marines
carry a seriously wounded
buddy to an ambulance
during battle with the Viet
Cong for the northern suburbs of Saigon.

Above: February 1, 1968—South Vietnamese military officer carries his dead child from his home. The officer's family was executed by Viet Cong the previous night when they overran his home
in a Saigon military compound.

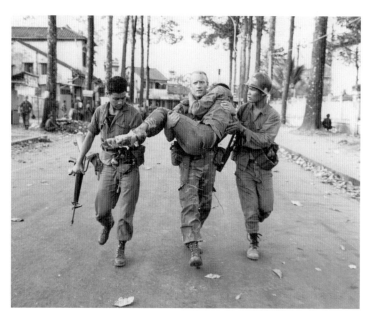

Right: February 6, 1968—
1st Lt. Gary D. Jackson of
Dayton, Ohio, carries a
wounded South Vietnamese
Ranger to an ambulance
after a brief but intense
battle with the Viet Cong
near the National Sports
Stadium in the Cholon section of Saigon.

Right: February 6, 1968—
Mourners line the grave site
of South Vietnamese Col.
Nguyen Tuan, his wife and
five children in Saigon. Tuan
was beheaded by the Viet
Cong when he refused to
support them in their attack
on Saigon. His wife and
children where killed in a
bomb shelter that was fired
and grenaded.

Above: February 9, 1968—A Vietnamese doctor treats wounded
Viet Cong prisoners who were wounded during house-to-house
fighting in Cholon, the Chinese section of Saigon, during the Tet
Offensive.

Above: February 19, 1968—A South Vietnamese soldier fires a machine gun into burning buidings in northeastern Saigon where Viet Cong forces occupied several city blocks.

Above: February 9, 1968—The bodies of some of the seven blindfolded people executed by the Viet Cong lie near gas pumps in the Cholon section of Saigon during the Tet Offensive. The area had not yet been secured to recover the bodies.

Left: February 2, 1968—A South Vietnamese infantryman fires a bazooka into a house in the southeastern section of Saigon, where Viet Cong snipers were in hiding.

Right: February 7, 1968—With an enemy machine gun firing down the street, paratroopers advance through the deserted Xom Moi suburb in northern Saigon, engaging a Viet Cong battalion believed to number 400 men.

# SAIGON EXECUTION

EDITOR'S NOTE: A lasting icon of the Vietnam war was the picture of a Vietcong summarily executed on Saigon street, a photo made by Eddie Adams of Associated Press. Here is the story of that photo.

February 2, 1968—It was the second day of the Tet Offensive and Vietnam was under massive attack at multiple fronts by the Vietcong and by the North Vietnamese army. The enemy struck with surprising strength in many cities and into the courtyard of the U.S. Embassy in Saigon.

Photographer Eddie Adams, working his third stint for AP in Vietnam, and National Broadcasting Co. cameraman Vo Su, prowled the streets of Saigon looking for war. The two photographers, office neighbors who frequently shared transportation and news tips, teamed up to investigate reports of fighting in Cholon, Saigon's Chinese section.

The two photographers looked around Cholon but it appeared that fighting had eased up. The debris of aftermath littered the street, but not much more. They were about to depart when they heard shots a block or so away. The two moved toward the action.

Eddie saw two Vietnamese soldiers pull a prisoner out of a doorway at the end of a street. The soldiers pushed and pulled what appeared to be a Vietcong infiltrator in a plaid shirt, his arms tied behind his back. He had been captured at a nearby pagoda in civilian dress and carrying a pistol.

Eddie recalls:

> It looked like a 'perp walk' (covering crime suspects) in New York. And I covered it that way. I just followed the three of them as they walked toward us, making an occasional picture. When they were up close – maybe five feet away – the soldiers stopped and backed away. I saw a man walk into my camera viewfinder from the left. He took a pistol out of his holster and raised it.
>
> 'I had no idea he would shoot,' Adams says. It was common to hold a pistol to the head of prisoners during questioning. So I prepared to make that picture – the threat, the interrogation. But the man just pulled a pistol out of his holster, raised it to the VC's head and shot him in the temple. I made a picture at the same time.'

Left: South Vietnamese troops capture a Vietcong fighter in Cholon, the Chinese section of Saigon. Hands tied behind his back, he is pushed and pulled through the street.

Left: The soldiers keep the Vietcong moving forward.

Below: The Vietcong was known under two names – Van Ken and also Bay Lap.

The Vietcong fell to the pavement, blood gushing from his head. Eddie made a shot or two of the man falling but then couldn't take any more and left. But not before the shooter, later identified as Lt. Col. Nguyen Loan, police chief of South Vietnam, walked up to Adams and said, 'They killed many of my people, and yours, too.' And he walked away.

Back in the office Adams turned in his film and went to his hotel room, exhausted emotionally and upset by the incident. The pictures, the full sequence of the incident, were sent by radio-photo to the world.

The picture was a sensation. It became a political statement, printed and reprinted, appearing on placards at anti-war demonstrations and used by anti-war advocates as an example of the kind of allies the U.S. had in Vietnam. One writer described it: The shot not heard 'round the world, but seen 'round the world.

What never caught up with the impact of the picture was the fact that in the first hours of the Tet Offensive before Loan shot the man, Vietcong had beheaded a Vietnamese colonel and killed his wife and six children.

Above: Colonel Nguyen Ngoc Loan pulls out his pistol and executed the Vietcong on the spot with a single shot to the head.

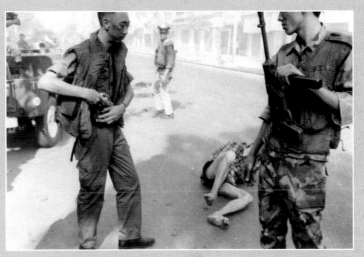

Left: Loan holsters his pistol and walks away.

Left: Offical photographer looks over the scene after Loan has gone.

Above: February 6, 1968—South Vietnamese rangers struggle to carry a wounded comrade across a street in Saigon under machine gun fire from the Viet Cong.

Above Right: February 2, 1968—A South Vietnamese soldier fires his bazooka at Viet Cong guerrillas while advancing along a Saigon street.

Right: February 13, 1968—South Vietnamese rangers, weapons ready, move cautiously into a burning block of houses in the Cholon sector of Saigon. The houses were the last stronghold of a band of Viet Cong guerrillas.

Left: February 1968—South Vietnamese army tanks and ranger troops fight at the Saigon end of the Saigon-Bien Hoa highway. Smoke rises from villages shelled by the tanks.

Right: February 10, 1968—Destruction to the residential area along Minh Mang street in the Cholon district of Saigon is evident after fires raged through this Chinese quarter following a battle between government troops and the Viet Cong.

Below: February 19, 1968—South Vietnamese combat police assault a burning building in northeastern Saigon as they battle Viet Cong forces who occupied several city blocks.

Above: February 1968—South Vietnamese soldiers stand near the bodies of a commander of a training camp and his family, slain in an enemy attack, after the camp was retaken from the Viet Cong in a northern suburb of Saigon.

Above: U.S. soldiers of the 9th Infantry Division run past burning homes on the southern edge of Saigon during intense fighting near the 'Y' bridge. Heavy air and artillery strikes were called in on suspected Communist positions.

Above: May 5, 1968—Slightly wounded and covered with dirt and blood, this mother and child were caught in a crossfire they sought to flee the fighting in the southern section of Saigon.

Above: April 27, 1968—The body of a victim is removed from the scene of a Viet Cong bomb explosion at a bus stop in Saigon which was crowded with Korean and other workers. Eleven died and 23 were wounded.

Left: May 7, 1968—Residents of Saigon flee a section of city that is under attack by Viet Cong and North Vietnamese.

Right: May 25, 1968—Vietnamese soldiers help evacuate civilians wounded by a Viet Cong rocket during a street battle northeast of Saigon.

Above: May 7, 1968—A U.S. Army helicopter pulls up after dropping two rockets on suspected Viet Cong positions in the southwestern part of Saigon.

Below: May 19, 1968—Civilians search debris of homes destroyed by Viet Cong rockets in downtown Saigon that marked the 78th birthday anniversary of North Vietnamese President Ho Chi Minh.

Left: May 9, 1968—An American serviceman hurries two Vietnamese girls to safety in an area of Saigon under Viet Cong attack.

Below: May 5, 1968—U.S. military police run through sniper fire in an alley in the northeastern corner of Saigon. Following an early morning mortar barrage, Viet Cong squads continued to harass allied forces.

Below: May 31, 1968—A young South Vietnamese soldier carries a fatally wounded fellow soldier after street fighting in the central market of the Cholon Chinese section of Saigon. Viet Cong infiltrators on the western edge of the capital penetrated more than a mile into the city, triggering a battle that sent thousands of civilians fleeing in panic.

Left: May 9, 1968—A U.S. soldier of the 9th Infantry Division throws a grenade into a suspected Viet Cong position in the southern sector of Saigon. The American troops were called in to assist the South Vietnamese in the capital's latest battles, which were now going into a fifth day.

Left: May 30, 1968—South Vietnamese troops use a tank to blast Viet Cong snipers from their hiding places in office buildings and apartment houses in southeast Saigon during a heavy monsoon rain storm.

Below: May 30, 1968—A South Vietnamese Marine, loaded with bandoliers and an M-79 grenade launcher, scurries for cover as a tank maneuvers for firing position in western Saigon. Enemy elements had moved in the previous night and were firing on government troops.

Left: May 12, 1968—Flares glow over western Saigon, a suspected area of Viet Cong infiltration. During the previous week, flares were dropped closer and closer to the center of the capital.

Right: May 6, 1968—A group of South Vietnamese rangers, ready to dive into available cover should the Viet Cong open fire, edges past burning homes during heavy fighting in southern Saigon.

Below: May 9, 1968—Two South Vietnamese soldiers crouch behind the concrete base of an electronic pole during heavy fighting in southern Saigon.

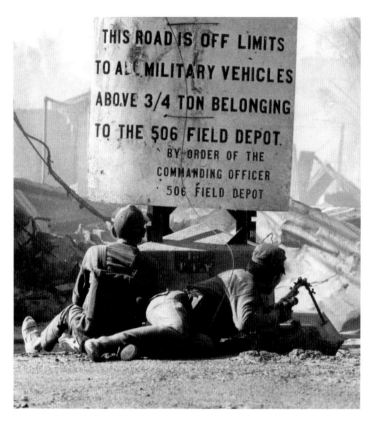

Right: May 9, 1968—A South Vietnamese soldier looks over a street in Cholon from his vantage point on the roof of building.

Above: May 28, 1968—A South Vietnamese Marine tries to crawl forward after being hit in the leg by a Viet Cong sniper in western Saigon. Another Marine moves quickly from the area.

Right: May 8, 1968—South Vietnamese rangers aim their rifles at Viet Cong positions in the western part of Saigon as smoke rises from burning tin and thatch homes.

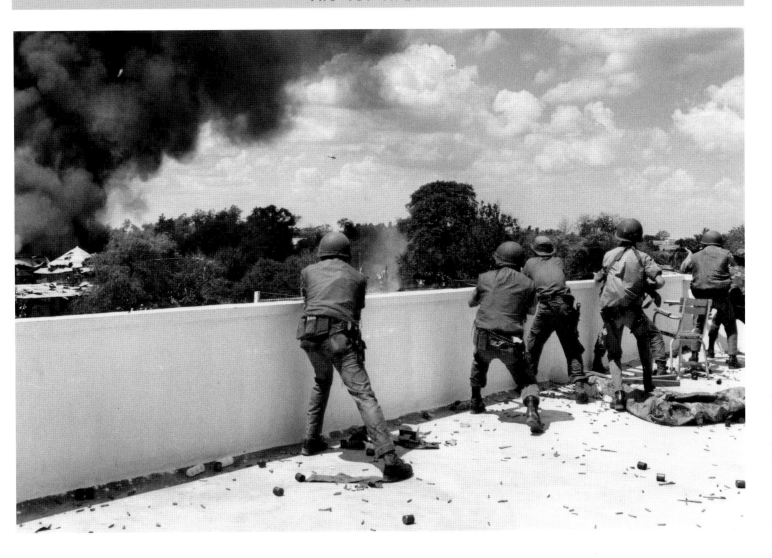

Above: May 26, 1968—
South Vietnamese Marines
fire from the roof of an
apartment building in the
northeast section of Saigon.

Right: May 9, 1968—A
South Vietnamese soldier
carefully steps out of a doorway in Saigon to locate Viet
Cong snipers.

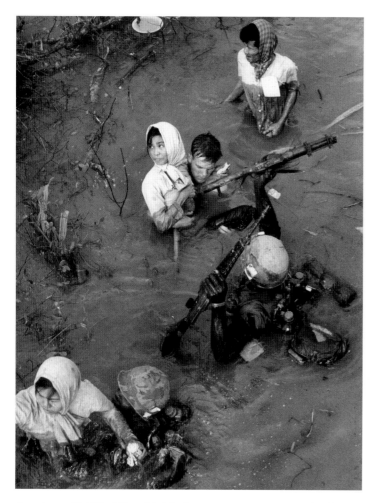

Above: January 22, 1968—Soldiers of the U.S. 9th Division move Viet Cong suspects through swamp water near the Ham Luong River, 25 miles east southeast of Saigon. The suspects were rounded up in an area known for Viet Cong activity. After questioning they were released or transferred to Vietnamese authorities.

Above: January 30, 1968—With a dead guerrilla in the background, a South Vietnamese soldier fires on a street in Danang, South Vietnam's second largest city, which was infiltrated by the Viet Cong.

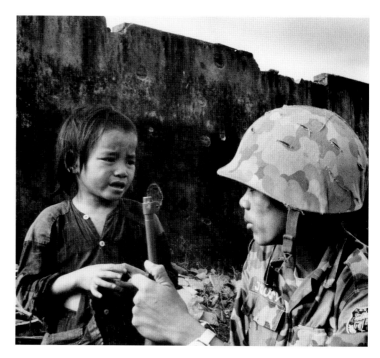

Above: January 1968—A young girl is questioned by a member of the National Police Field Force attached to the U.S. 1st Air Cavalry operating in the Que Son valley about 35 miles south of Danang. The child later led U.S. troops to a Viet Cong rice cache.

Below: January 1968—Cpl. W.L Files of Charleston, W.Va., distributes his candy supply amongst these South Vietnamese children who were being evacuated from their village near An Hoa.

**490**

Left: January 31, 1968—A South Vietnamese army captain and his family lie dead on a pile of rocks in Saigon after they were shot by Viet Cong early in the Tet Offensive.

Right: January 1968—U.S. soldiers of the 1st Cavalry Division man a mortar position in landing zone Leslie, 30 miles southwest of Danang in the Que Son Valley.

Left: January 1968—A soldier drops a mortar round into the tube as he and his companion launch attack on Viet Cong forces nearby.

Above: February 24, 1968—The Rev. Daniel Berrigan speaks to anti-war demonstrators gathered in front of the U.S. Mission to the United Nations in New York City. Berrigan, who had been in Hanoi trying to arrange for the release of three captured U.S. pilots, told the crowd he brought 'greetings from the premier of North Vietnam.'

Left: February 13, 1968—South Vietnamese President Nguyen Van Thieu inspects an old U.S. water-cooled 30-caliber machine gun during his visit to My Tho in the Mekong Delta. The weapon was captured from Viet Cong forces that overran the town.

Left: February 8, 1968—Wounded U.S. Marines wait for evacuation from a rice paddy six miles south of Danang after fighting elements of the North Vietnamese 2nd Division. The Marines reported 15 dead and 63 wounded.

Above: March 1968—A Viet Cong prisoner looks from behind a bandage after a South Korean Division captured him near the coastal city of Qui Nhon.

Above: April 3, 1968—U.S. troops of the 1st Cavalry Division carry cases of artillery shells from a Chinook helicopter east of Khe Sanh during Operation Pegasus. The operation to link up with the beleaguered Marine base at Khe Sanh finally succeeded on April 8 when the cavalrymen officially relieved the base, under siege for 77 days.

Left: April 19, 1968—Saving a few trips, a soldier of the U.S. 4th Infantry Division balances spent artillery casings on his shoulders, seven at a time, at Kontum's 'Mile High' fire support base in the Central Highlands.

Below: March 1968—Soldiers of the Americal Division wait to move into a village south of Danang as U.S. air strikes hit suspected Communist positions.

Above: April 8, 1968—Three tons of TNT send dirt flying as South Vietnamese demolition experts blow up a tunnel which had been used by Viet Cong as a supply dump about 10 miles north of Saigon.

Above: April 2, 1968—U.S. Marines, part of Operation Pegasus to relieve the besieged combat base at Khe Sanh, take a break in a stream-fed pond off Route 9. This unit was providing security for an engineering company repairing a bridge 12 miles east of Khe Sanh.

Right: April 1968—Two Navy swimmers help Maj. Carl R. Webster, a U.S. Air Force pilot, board a landing craft after ejecting from his F-4 Phantom off the coast of South Vietnam.

Above: May 31, 1968—Passengers and crew escape from a Caribou transport plane as a section of the plane burns on the runway at the Dak Pek Special Forces camp in South Vietnam. The plane was apparently hit by enemy ground fire as it was landing.

Above: May 1968—U.S. troops of the 101st Airborne Division withdraw to a dry rice paddy after calling in artillery strikes against suspected enemy positions outside the village of Cao Xa, near Hue and the demilitarized zone.

Below: May 5, 1968—Specialist 4 Robert Scott of the U.S. 716th Military Police Battalion carries two children to safety during fighting in Saigon.

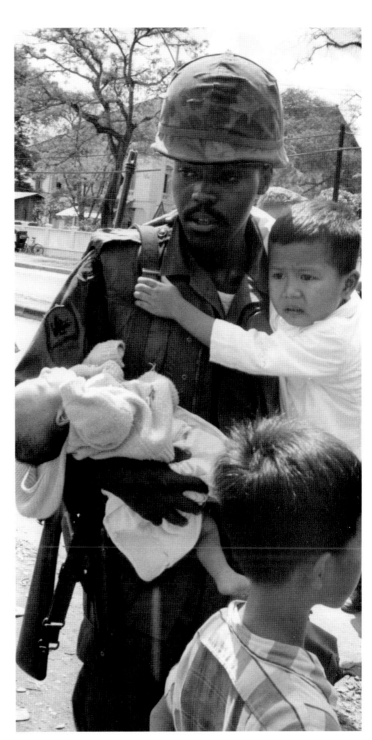

Left: May 1968—Thatched huts of the Dak Pek Special Forces camp stand on a hilltop at the end of Dak To Valley, near the Laotian border. Montagnard tribesmen built the huts and lived with about a dozen Green Berets monitoring North Vietnamese activity along the border.

Right: May 18, 1968—A fireball erupts at Bein Hoa during Viet Cong rocket attack on the key military airfield on the outskirts of Saigon.

Above: May 30, 1968—A CH-47 Chinook supply helicopter lands at Fire Support Base 29 in the Central Highlands west of Dak To. The base, manned by the U.S. 4th Infantry Division, was the scene of intense fighting the previous fall.

Right: July 1968—A line of South Vietnamese soldiers carrying M-16 rifles crosses a river in their way back from patrol in the Soc Thang area, 100 miles southeast of Saigon.

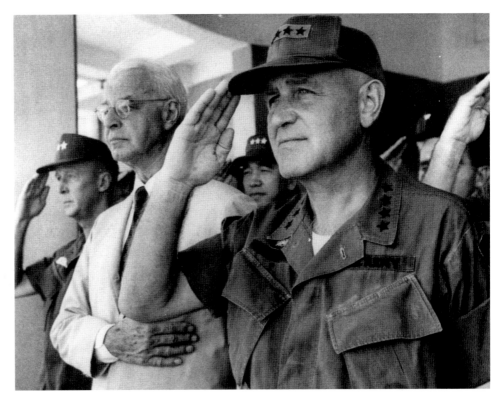

Above: June 1968—Gen. Creighton W. Abrams salutes in ceremony as Gen. William C. Westmoreland leaves Saigon's Tan Son Nhut airport. Abrams, moved up from deputy to replace Westmoreland as commander of U.S. forces in Vietnam. With him is U.S. Ambassador Ellsworth Bunker in white suit.

Above Left: June 1, 1968—A South Vietnamese combat policeman carries a crying child out of the area in Saigon where government troops were battling the Viet Cong. Her parents followed with their belongings.

Above: June 1, 1968—Children run past rubble and damaged cars in the Cholon sector of Saigon to escape street fighting between Viet Cong and government troops.

Above: June 20, 1968—A U.S. C-130 cargo plane drops artillery ammunition to the Special Forces camp at Dak Seang, 320 miles north of Saigon. Supplies are dropped by parachute because the camp's airstrip is too small for the C-130s.

Above: June 26, 1968—U.S. soldiers of the 199th Light Infantry Brigade rest in hammocks over muddy swamp and rice paddies after a night patrol west of Saigon. Allied patrols, trying to prevent another Tet-style attack on the capital, were continuously sweeping the area surrounding Saigon.

Left: June 2, 1968—A U.S. Army helicopter lands in front of the post office in the Cholon Chinese section of Saigon in support of an isolated Vietnamese Marine unit. The Viet Cong had pushed about 11 city blocks into the capital despite the efforts of government troops.

Right: June 29, 1968—The Khe Sanh combat base, where U.S. Marines weathered a 77-day siege earlier in the year, is dismantled as the Marines prepare to deactivate the base. Virtually everything at the base, including the airstrip, was being removed, bulldozed or burned.

Left: June 1968—A helicopter full of U.S. Marines lifts off from the Khe Sanh combat base on a patrol near the demilitarized zone. The base, which endured a 77-day siege just months earlier, was soon to be deactivated.

Below: June 6, 1965—U.S. Marines patrolling the western edge of the demilitarized zone near Khe Sanh carry their dead and wounded to a waiting evacuation helicopter after North Vietnamese troops attacked the unit's night perimeter.

Right: June 29, 1968—A heavily-armed convoy pulls out of the U.S. Marine combat base at Khe Sanh, carrying equipment down Route 9 to landing zone Stud. Khe Sanh, where the Marines survived a 77-day siege earlier in the year, was being dismantled and abandoned.

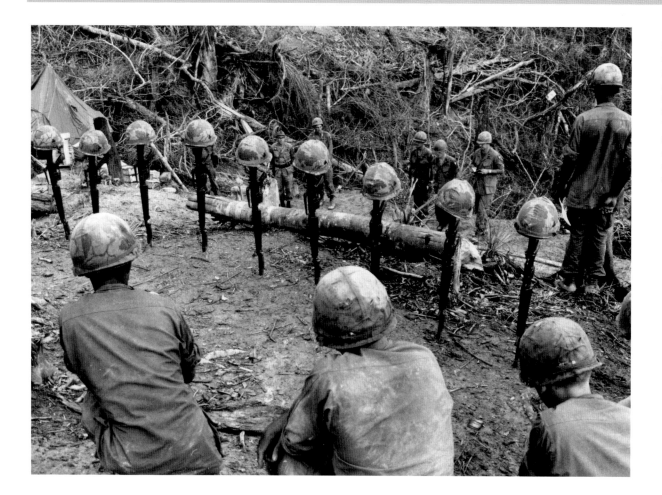

Left: June 1, 1968—With the helmets of dead paratroopers resting on their M-16 rifles, members of the 101st Airborne Division mourn their men who died in fighting near Hue one day earlier. The unit uncovered a huge enemy weapons cache, including 49 Russian trucks, anti-aircraft guns, artillery and mortars.

Below: June 16, 1968—Vietnamese Black Panthers fire from the second floor window of an abandoned house into Viet Cong positions in northeast Saigon.

Left: June 10, 1968—A Vietnamese Special Forces soldier sits behind the protection of a statue of Buddha during fighting in the northeast section of Saigon.

Right: June 7, 1968—A Vietnamese army tank slowly advances through the rubble-strewn streets of Cholon, firing its recoilless rifle and machine gun into Viet Cong positions.

Below: June 14, 1968—With his pistol in one hand and a spare ammo clip in the other, a South Vietnamese combat policeman, accompanied by an MP, kicks in a door looking for Viet Cong infiltrators in the Cholon section of Saigon.

Right: June 1, 1968—A South Vietnamese tank moves into position to fire into Viet Cong strongholds during fighting in the northeast section of Saigon, a densely populated area near the Binh Loi bridge. Smoke rises from homes caught in house-to-house fighting and air strikes.

Above: June 1968—South Vietnamese combat police crouch behind a taxi hit by Viet Cong snipers in Cholon, the Chinese sector of Saigon.

Left: June 3, 1968—South Vietnamese troops cluster in a square where, supported by tanks, they have been attempting to push out Viet Cong infiltrators in Saigon's Cholon area.

Below: June 7, 1968—A Vietnamese army tank advances through the rubble-strewn streets of Cholon, firing its recoilless rifle and machine gun into Viet Cong positions. The area was slowly destroyed in heavy fighting in an attempt to weed out Viet Cong infiltrators.

Left: June 20, 1968—U.S. Green Berets watch ammunition cases drift to a drop zone at the Dak Seang Special Forces camp 320 miles north of Saigon. The camp's landing strip cannot accommodate C-130 Hercules transport planes.

Right: June 18, 1968—A patrol with American advisors moves through the South Vietnamese jungle using elephants, their centuries-old method of transport.

Left: June 2, 1968 A U.S. soldier fires a grenade launcher into an alley during street fighting in the Cholon Chinese section of Saigon.

Below: June 17, 1968 The body of a U.S. Marine is carried to an evacuation point on a hilltop south of Khe Sanh, nine days after 18 Marines were killed in a firefight with North Vietnamese troops building a road from Laos into north-western South Vietnam. A flag found with one of the bodies was posted at half staff on the hilltop.

503

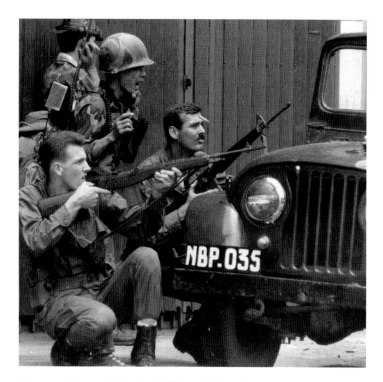

Above: June 1968—Spent shell, in front of soldier at right, flies out of an M-14 rifle fired at Viet Cong in street fighting in Cholon, Chinese section of Saigon.

Below: April 1968—U.S. Cavalry troopers move into the A Shau valley from a landing zone on the fringe of the valley during Operation Delaware. Allied forces were trying to regain control of the valley, 25 miles west of Hue, for the first time since abandoning it to the communists more than two years earlier.

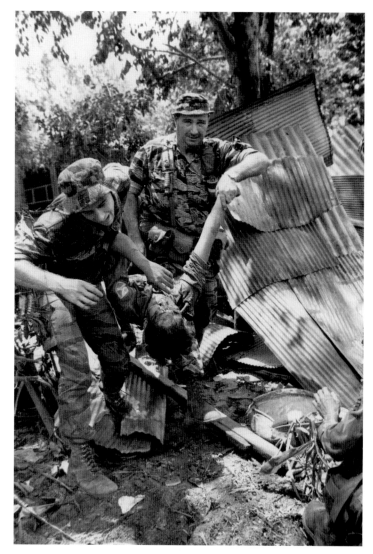

Above: June 16, 1968—American special forces carry a Vietnamese soldier wounded in face-to-face fighting which wiped out a Viet Cong stronghold at Gia Dinh near Saigon.

Below: Civilians ride past damaged buildings in a street cluttered with debris in Saigon's Cholon section. Civilian traffic resumed after tanks blasted the last Viet Cong snipers from the ruins of the buildings.

Above: July 7, 1968—Dependents of South Vietnamese infantrymen look through barbed wire that surrounds their compound. Families of soldiers usually accompany them to the battle areas, in this case the Mekong Delta.

Below: July 7, 1968—Portrait of an American fighter in South Vietnam.

Above: August 26, 1968—Searching for a suspected Viet Cong unit in nearby structures, U.S. troops of the 1st Brigade, 9th Infantry Division, charge from assault helicopters across flooded rice paddies near Tan An, about 25 miles south of Saigon.

Above: August 1968—Providing fire support for men operating in the central A Shau Valley, 105mm howitzers overlook the valley from a sandbagged firebase set up by the 101st Cavalry Division.

Right: August 16, 1968—Marine loadmaster directs a helicopter pilot bringing in a sling of supplies to a Marine base in the mountains west of Danang. Setting sun and monsoon clouds silhouette the operation.

Above: August 23, 1968—After fighting all day to drive the North Vietnamese from a village two miles south of Danang airbase, U.S. Marines read graffiti pockmarked by machine gun fire.

Right: August 25, 1968—A Viet Cong prisoner is questioned by South Vietnamese troopers near Danang. The prisoner was captured when he and others attacked a Danang radio station.

Left: August 11, 1968—Marine loadmaster directs a helicopter pilot bringing in a sling of supplies to a Marine base in the mountains of west Danang. Setting sun and monsoon clouds silhouette the operation.

Above: Gen. Creighton Abrams, commander of U.S. forces in Vietnam, chews on a cigar during a visit to Chan Luu, a village near Saigon that was newly retaken from the Viet Cong.

Below: September 5, 1968—A Vietnamese boy peers out from behind the barbed wire fence which surrounds the outpost in which he and his parents live northwest of Saigon.

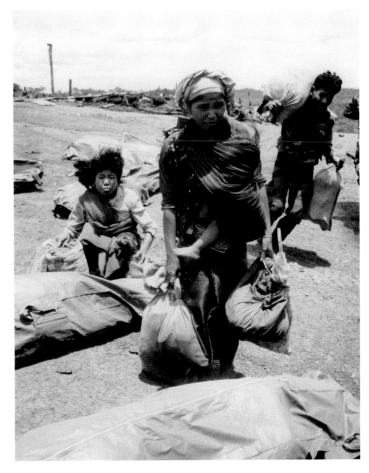

Above: August 24, 1968—Relatives of Montagnard soldiers stand by their shrouded dead at the U.S. special forces camp at Duc Lap in South Vietnam. More than 60 Montagnards died as a North Vietnamese assault was beaten back.

Above: September 1968—Members of the Montagnard tribe are transported by U.S. Army helicopters to a nearby refugee camp from the village of Bu Lach, 60 miles northeast of Saigon. The tribe of some 700 asked the South Vietnamese government for help in moving to a more secure area during fighting in the Vietnam War.

Above: September 3, 1968—A terrorist hand grenade thrown at the U.S. aid office in Saigon claims two lives, with several wounded. The policeman shown here was killed; the woman injured.

Right: September 1968—Saigon's many rivers and canals are densely populated and always teeming with life. Junks and sampans provide housing and transport.

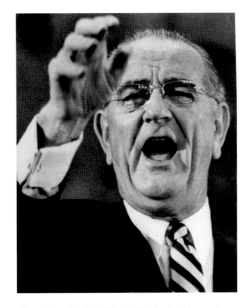

Left: September 16, 1968—U.S. commanders inspect a captured 12-barrel 107mm rocket launcher, one of the newest weapons in the enemy arsenal, as they tour the tons of equipment and supplies recovered from Viet Cong hiding places near Saigon. From left are Adm. John S. McCain, commander of U.S. Forces in the Pacific; Gen. Creighton W. Abrams Jr., commander of U.S. Forces in Vietnam, and Col. Ira A. Hunt, commander of the 1st Brigade of the 9th Infantry Division.

Above: September 10, 1968—President Lyndon Johnson rejects a complete bombing halt in Vietnam in a speech to the 50th National Convention of the American Legion in New Orleans, La.

Left: Members of the Montagnard tribe are transported by U.S. Army helicopters to a nearby refugee camp from the village of Bu Lach, 60 miles northeast of Saigon. The tribe of some 700 asked the South Vietnamese government for help in moving to a more secure area during fighting in the Vietnam War.

Right: September, 14, 1968—A South Vietnamese paratrooper disarms and North Vietnamese soldier who emerged from a bunker underneath the smoldering ruins of a farmhouse on the Thai Dong rubber plantation, southwest of Tay Ninh. The paratroopers fought a battalion of North Vietnamese and Viet Cong who had infiltrated Tay Ninh earlier in the week.

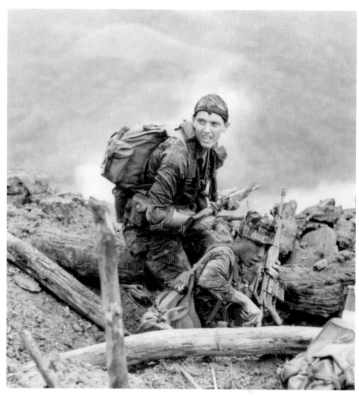

Above: September, 1968—A U.S. Special Forces officer yells orders to Montagnard mercenaries as they try to retake a hilltop outpost near Ha Thanh. The post, 325 miles northeast of Saigon, had been over-run by the North Vietnamese three days earlier, and two previous attempts to retake it had failed.

Left: September 27, 1968—Soldiers of the Americal Division order villagers from their homes during a sweep through a hamlet near Tam Ky, about 30 miles south of Danang. Soldiers cleared civilians from bunkers and homes while searching for North Vietnamese 2nd Division troops.

Right: September 11, 1968—South Vietnamese militiamen, supported by armored personnel carriers, move through Tay Ninh during a heavy monsoon rain toward the last remnant of enemy soldiers who had earlier invaded parts of the provincial capital about 45 miles northwest of Saigon.

Right: September 29, 1968—A South Vietnamese soldier attached to a mobile strike force and carrying an M-79 grenade launcher, uses a stone wall for protection while advancing on a enemy position near the Vu Gia River in South Vietnam. His unit was on its way to reinforce the Thuong Duc Special Forces Camp, 30 miles southwest of Danang, when the North Vietnamese were encountered.

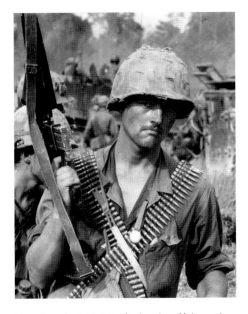

Above: September 27, 1968—After three days of fighting with no sleep, Pfc. Bob Whitworth of Albany, Ore., continues on patrol as the 11th Light Infantry Brigade pursues remaining elements of the North Vietnamese 2nd Division 30 miles south of Danang. The infantry unit had inflicted heavy casualties on Communist forces in fighting through rice paddies, underbrush and villages.

Left: September 11, 1968— South Vietnamese militiamen take cover around their armored vehickle as smoke rises from air strikes on enemy positions inside Tay Ninh, a key provincial capital 45 miles northwest of Saigon.

Above: September 10, 1968—The body of Ky Hung Lam lies under a table at Chinese High School in Saigon. The 49-year-old teacher was one of four shot by terrorists who escaped.

Left: September 1968—After fighting on the outskirts of Tay Ninh, some 45 miles northwest of Saigon, one wounded Vietnamese soldier helps a more seriously wounded trooper onto a waiting truck to be evacuated.

Below: September 29, 1968—Vietnamese Special Forces troopers take cover behind a low wall as white phosphorous grenades make arcs through the sky. They were engaging North Vietnamese troops who overran outposts near the Thuong Duc Special Forces camp 30 miles west of Danang.

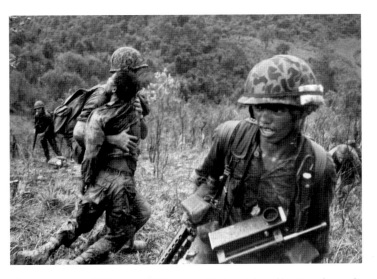

Above: September, 2, 1968—A wounded Vietnamese soldier is carried out of harm's way by a medic during action near the Ha Thanh Special Forces Base. Efforts were underway to dislodge North Vietnamese units that had overrun the base.

Above: September 1968—Members of the Special Forces camp at Ha Thanh, about 300 miles from Saigon, watch supplies drop by parachute from an American plane. The frequent sky drops are the only means of supply to the remote post.

Above: September 2, 1968—A medic attends to an American Special Forces soldier wounded during an uphill battle near Ha Thanh, some 300 miles northeast of Saigon. The strike force sought to retake an outpost which had been overrun by Viet Cong. They drove the enemy out the next day.

Right: September 2, 1968—Experienced Montgnard fighter, once allied with the French, and now connected with Special Forces Mobile Strike Force. He was involved in an action in Quang Ngai province, more than 300 miles northeast of Saigon.

Above: September 7, 1968—A Saigon policeman carries a child injured in a school yard after a terrorist bomb exploded in a nearby unoccupied office in the Cholon section of Saigon.

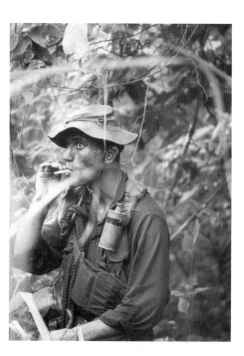

Below: October 1968—A U.S. Marine 'lurp,' a member of a long range reconnaissance patrol, rests after a sweep along the western edge of the demilitarized zone near the former Marine combat base at Khe Sanh. Members of these elite patrols would stay in the field for days at a time with minimal supplies, scouting enemy positions.

Above: September 6, 1968—Rescuers carry victims away from the site of a Viet Cong terrorist attack in Saigon. Eight died when a bomb exploded in a government office causing the building to collapse.

Above: October 1968—A bomb handler pushes 500-pound bombs to a plane on the flight deck of the carrier USS Constellation. With a bombing halt in effect above the demilitarized zone, U.S. pilots were targeting enemy positions in South Vietnam.

Left: September 2, 1969—Armed landing craft and troops of the Riverine Force patrol a meandering tributary of the Mekong River in the southern part of South Vietnam. The highly mobile force includes armed assault convoy ships. When the enemy is contacted the troops are put ashore and the ships provide covering fire.

Left: October 1, 1968—A U.S. Green Beret lobs a grenade at a North Vietnamese position near the embattled Special Forces camp at Thuong Duc, southwest of Danang. Troops had defended the camp against an earlier assault.

Below: October 1968—A badly-injured South Vietnamese paratrooper is pulled from the wreckage of a U.S. helicopter which lost power and crashed after an all-day operation near Tay Ninh. Two South Vietnamese and two Americans were seriously injured in the crash.

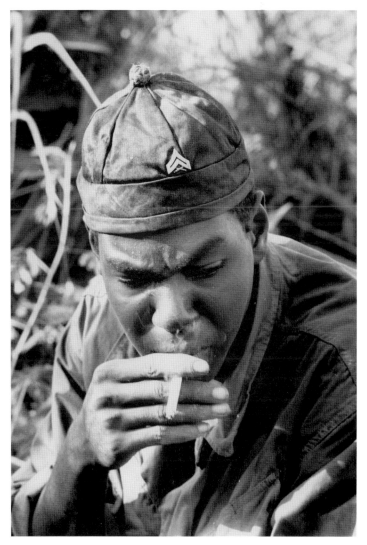

Above: October 12, 1968—A U.S. Marine lance corporal wears a Chinese cap with his stripe pinned to it during a search operation through blistering heat and rugged terrain around the now-abandoned Khe Sanh Marine base.

Left: November 1968—On a firebase of the U.S. 3rd Marine Division, just below the demilitarized zone, artillery is pointed in the direction of North Vietnam. Earth mounds and sandbags ring the gun positions.

Left: October 10, 1968—U.S. Marine Sgt. Herbert Day blows taps at Khe Sanh for the hundreds of Marine casualties during the 77-day siege of the combat base there earlier in the year. Despite surviving the Communist siege, the U.S. had abandoned the base in July.

Above: November 1968—A GI and a CH-46 Sea Knight helicopter are reflected in a puddle near the Cambodian border north of Saigon.

Left: A Skyhawk, loaded with six 500-pound bombs, takes off for a bombing mission from the flight deck of the USS Intrepid.

Above: December 31, 1968—Villagers take cover with rangers behind a rice paddy dike about 20 miles southwest of Danang while under fire from North Vietnamese machine guns.

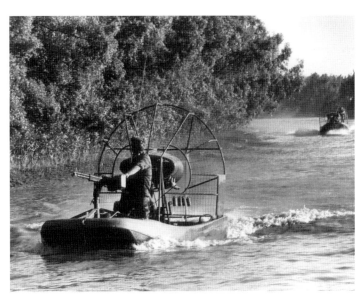

Above: November 1968—A rivercraft patrols the shoreline in Vietnam

Left: November 17, 1968—South Vietnamese rangers make their way through high elephant grass as paratroopers float to the ground in an operation to take over the old Viet Cong stronghold of Mount Coto, 100 miles west of Saigon.

Left: December 1968—A concrete bunker rests atop one of the old gates leading to the Citadel of Hue, the ancient capital of Vietnam.

Below: December 14, 1968—A sergeant with the South Vietnamese popular forces, described as a brutal and tough fighter, receives his new equipment, an American M-16 rifle. He commands a platoon charged with the security of a government pacification team in the Delta area.

Above: December 1968—U.S. Marines wallow in mud during a two-week patrol south of Danang in the Dien Ban area, long an area under communist influence.

Left: December 12, 1968—A U.S. Marine aims at a North Vietnamese bunker amid the ruins of a South Vietnamese village in the Bien Dan district.

Right: December 17, 1968—A U.S. Marine CH-46 Sea Knight helicopter lifts off after dropping a unit at a landing zone south-west of Danang. U.S. troops were searching for elements of a North Vietnamese division reported in the area.

Below: December 1968—Americans in Vietnam unroll a huge, long Christmas card sent to them by students in the U.S. to assure them of their support.

Left: December, 17, 1968—Aerial view of a well bunk-ered outpost, protected by sandbags and with canon aimed at the location of enemy troops in the country-side.

Right: A South Vietnamese Ranger, shot several times in the arm and chest, is evacuated after field treatment near Dai Loc, 20 miles southeast of Danang.

Left: December 6, 1968—Pistol in hand, a Marine pulls a wounded North Vietnamese soldier from a half collapsed bunker during an operation just south of Danang. The enemy soldier hid in the bunker for two days with a 16-year-old girl before surrendering.

# FRONT LINE AMERICA

'We set up a hospital just to bring these people in and sew them up,' recalls Eugene McCarthy. The action involved 26,000 men in uniform. Army intelligence viewed the situation as 'dangerous' and McCarthy considered that it was really weird'. It was indeed. This was not Vietnam but Chicago in August 1968, and the Senator was describing what had happened to anti-war supporters of his presidential candidacy at the Democratic Party national convention.

Five months had passed since Lyndon Johnson had thrown in the presidential towel to 'seek peace' but the bodies of the young soldiers were returning at a greater rate than ever before – at least 1000 a month. They came back in canvas bags piled inside reusable aluminum containers. Sorted into burnished oak coffins, draped with the flag, one was being delivered on average every half hour of the day – and something was happening in the country. The war's front line was extending to a thousand more places across America every month – a front line as diffuse and hard to gauge as Vietnam's, but which in August erupted in anger and frustration at Chicago.

By this time in 1968 Vietnam had aroused three quite distinct anti-war sentiments – and groups. David Dellinger sensed a new concern when 'the GIS started coming home in canvas bags and there was a realization that in addition to napalming a peasant civilization "our sons were being killed".' Dellinger was a life-long pacifist – and Vietnam was 'moral horror'. Jerry Rubin saw the war as the 'vital edge of all that we were feeling inside our gut about this country's limitations'. Rubin was for militant social revolution – and Vietnam was 'a mirror for America to look at

> '**I said the opposition to the war would begin when the bodies started coming back to the small towns. Something would happen in the country.**'
>
> — PRESIDENTIAL CANDIDATE SENATOR EUGENE MCCARTHY

itself'. Eugene McCarthy represented a middle-ground, or 'my children and others who felt really kind of desperate that the American political system would not even allow them an instrument by which they could register even minimal opposition'. McCarthy was a Democratic Party liberal – and Vietnam obliged him 'to challenge Johnson'.

McCarthy, Rubin and Dellinger, reflecting the diverse views and character of the optimistically named 'Anti-War Movement', had arrived at Chicago by politically very different routes. Rubin and two associates, Abbie Hoffman and Paul Krassner, had just founded the militant Yippies or Youth International Party. It had been conceived more as a joke to scare the 'squares' but when the authorities took it seriously, so did Rubin. He planned to hold in Chicago 'the kind of demonstration that would end the war; a trumpet call for young people to rise up. So we called for 500,000 people to come.' It was to be 'our own convention on the other side of town – our music, our politics, our expression'.

Dellinger wanted a passive protest outside the convention as 'non-violent witness that we would not accept the war'. He was uncertain even about this because 'McCarthy wanted to solve the war by changing the President' and the Senator feared that any demonstration 'would antagonize the country'. McCarthy was regarded as a passionate libertarian but also as a self-conscious, unemotional man whose campaign had oratorically faltered. His low-key approach was to 'take a chance' on de-escalation of the war – and the vote would decide the extent of it. His own Party called this 'surrender'. Vice-President Humphrey's platform was insistent on mutual troop withdrawal. With

Left: August 26, 1968— Chicago police lead a demonstrator from Grant Park during demonstrations that disrupted the Democratic National Convention. The convention became the focal point of bitter confrontations between police and anti-war demonstrators.

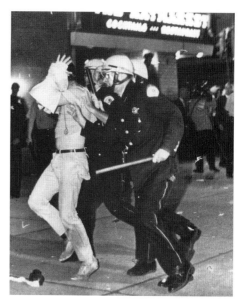

Above: August 28, 1968—Chicago police push a demonstrator off the street during a clash near the headquarters of the Democratic National Convention.

the Party rancorously divided, the Anti-War Movement had become increasingly militant – and this worried Dellinger, who saw the movement getting 'a bad image, as if it didn't care about the rest of the American people'.

'We said crazy things,' admits Rubin, 'like putting LSD in the water. That was a joke. We didn't even spend one minute trying to find out how to put LSD in the water.' But as a result Chicago's Mayor Richard Daley 'put a policeman in front of every water-main that week and when he did that he was organizing our demonstration for us'. Rubin wanted confrontation; he was excitable, impatient. Dellinger was fourteen years older, a quiet seeker of consensus, gray-haired and suited like a professor among the hippies. When the anti-war coalition was denied a permit to demonstrate, Dellinger as its chairman was swayed by 'our constitutional right to march anyway, come what may'.

'Mayor Daley and the people running the convention', says McCarthy, 'anticipated 100,000 demonstrators so they had enough police and military to deal with 100,000'. Daley, more monarch than mayor, called out 26,000 police and National Guardsmen. Says Rubin, 'Finally only five or six thousand people showed up for the demonstration.' It was a sign of the movement's decline because of its militancy. 'We were very scared that so few showed up,' says Rubin. 'There had to be some dramatic, moral conflict.' Daley provided it, in McCarthy's opinion: 'There was no proportion between the numbers, and between what the police and the military did and what the threat to them was.' The demonstrators were outnumbered perhaps five to one. They were confronted by more men in uniform than were then engaged in any battle in Vietnam.

'What happened', says Dellinger, 'was that the government decided it could not afford to have demonstrators in Chicago at that time. And they

Above: August 28, 1968—Chicago policemen with nightsticks in hand confront a demonstrator on the ground in Grant Park, Chicago. The police force converged when protesters opposing the Vietnam War climbed on the statue of Civil War Gen. John Logan.

Right: August 28, 1968—Police squirt mace into a tightly packed crowd at an anti-war demonstrators outside the Conrad Hilton hotel in Chicago. Hundreds were injured in a bloody clash.

began with threats. We were told ahead of time that the police were going to be armed, and that they would shoot to kill.' As the anti-war group gathered it was 'met with clubs and tear-gas'. Dellinger persuaded the demonstrators to get off the streets and rally in Chicago's Grant Park: 'And early in the rally a bloodied, beaten-up demonstrator shinnied up the flag-pole and replaced the American flag with his bloodied shirt, saying "Let the world see what's happening in Chicago". That became a signal for the police to charge the crowd, and I shall never forget them. They marched across the field swinging their clubs and chanting "Kill, kill, kill".'

Says McCarthy, the ratio was 'usually five or six policemen beating up one or two protestors. They were waiting to charge, and when there was no provocation they charged anyway. I saw some

of the fighting in the park.' The candidate for the presidency of the United States then ordered his convention offices at the Hilton Hotel to be turned into 'a sort of field hospital' for his bloodied voters. One had his 'scalp split open four inches' and 'there was lots of blood, broken hands and things'.

In the park, Dellinger tried to rally his bruised followers for 'a non-violent march' but was turned back by 'tanks and tear-gas'. They sat around and waited. They 'smoked' and played guitars and sang 'We Shall Overcome' – but there were doubts now. Dellinger was 'discouraged and dejected' hearing them say that 'non-violence is no longer working. So many of the people I had been working with had come to that conclusion – and we did look helpless.'

'They're a pitiful handful,' one of the mayor's

aides was telling the press at City Hall. 'They're referred to as kids, they're referred to as Yippies. Gentlemen, the hard core leadership of this group are Communists.' Rubin saw his Yippies as 'cultural style becoming politics, content and form merging'. He knew he was hurting Eugene McCarthy's chances. McCarthy, he says, 'told people to go clean for Gene, but we felt that the image of beards and long hair and even not taking baths, and getting stoned and being crazy was the nightmare of the American family come back to haunt them. Very, very important. And it wouldn't have worked if we all got short hair and told people to vote for Gene and be reasonable, because the issue was deeper than that.' But neither did Rubin's way work in rich, righteous Chicago – a city encapsuled in the mid-West in a time plane a generation behind New York or San Francisco. Yippies-Hippies: the new culture as much as the new politics had the old gangster city shuddering. Men just did not wear their hair that long, and love-beads were not macho. Women might just don blue jeans but preferably with matching Saint Laurent bras, which were unnervingly absent in any color. To Chicago it all spelled Red.

On the next night the marchers were surprised to get as far as the convention hotel and Rubin felt 'pride that we were center-history; we were on history's main street'. They halted, facing the hotel from across the street. Inside, Vice-President Humphrey was giving his acceptance speech when police buses suddenly unloaded and 'the police charged the crowd, flailing with their clubs,' says Dellinger. 'They were just unmerciful,' says Rubin. 'It was unjustified, unnecessary violence,' says McCarthy.

After the 'frustration and then excitement', says Rubin, 'came the absolute terror when the police showed they had no restraint, and the police went through the crowd clubbing and beating up people. And it was just total anarchy. Then the fact that this anarchy was being televised world-wide showed the total paradox and irony of this country that arrests you and beats you up and then televises it. Because we knew we were morally right. And we knew when truth speaks up to power, truth eventually wins.'

Earlier that month the Republicans had quietly chosen Richard Nixon on a 'peace with honor' platform, which sounded doubly reassuring. But now the television cameras showed the front line as America. The concern over the Democratic mêlée transcended Vietnam; there was the sense of civil war, and of so much paradox: the rampaging police were like the frustrated 'Search and Destroy' missions, a spectacle of attrition, brought home. The power in Chicago that night of 29 August was unleashed against even the presidential candidate who had opposed his party machine. The police charged the hotel entrance, clubbing to the ground newsmen and ordinary spectators gathered there, then stormed to the fifteenth-floor offices of the already defeated Eugene McCarthy.

The Senator only later discovered 'forty to fifty of our workers sitting on the floor, surrounded by about twenty-five policemen. They were like prisoners-of-war. And I said "Who's in charge?" to these police – and nobody was in charge. The real Nazi stuff.' One staffer described how in 'trying to fend off some of the blows I came back up and they said "Get out of here" – and I tried; I said "I'm trying to" and they hit me again and hit me again.'

McCarthy decided to pull out with his staff before the convention closed the next day: 'I was prepared to leave and the secret service said, "We suggest you don't leave because the minute you're out of town they're going to arrest everybody in town who has a McCarthy button." '

McCarthy learned that in a few terrifying minutes 800 of the anti-war protesters had been injured, some seriously, in what a federal investigation later described as 'a police riot'. McCarthy could not sleep and from his hotel window he could see some fires in Grant Park where the scattered youth now huddled. He decided to join them and phoned his secret service guard to advise what he was doing. He discovered later that 'army intelligence' had listed him as 'communicating with a dangerous subversive group'. His phone had been wire-tapped.

It had been twenty-six years since McCarthy had decided as a novice in a Benedictine monastery that he should actively campaign for a better world. Ironically, he first entered politics as a supporter of Hubert Humphrey. When he had announced his candidacy, McCarthy had com-

Above: February 1970—Anti-war activist Jerry Rubin, along with other defendants in the Chicago Seven conspiracy trial, speaks at a news conference. Front row, from left: Rennie Davis, Rubin, Abbie Hoffman. Back row, from left: Lee Weiner, Bob Lamb and Thomas Hayden. (Lamb was not one of the Chicago Seven.)

Left: April 27, 1968—A Viet Cong flag is waved during an anti-war rally in New York City's Central Park. Violence erupted when groups favoring the government position on Vietnam demonstrated at the fringes of the rally.

mented: 'I don't think it will be a case of political suicide. It might be an execution.' Now the Anti-War Movement, and the Democratic Party, had emerged crippled from within. 'In my case,' says McCarthy, 'I concluded that the Democratic Party which I'd worked in and trusted and defended for years was really not to be trusted, and that some of the persons whom I'd believed in as decent and responsible were alright unless it came to a matter of the presidency.'

In the park, the anti-war factions had gathered, fittingly, around their separate fires, and as Dellinger tried to rally them he heard talk that 'stronger methods, which I actually do not believe are stronger, had to be involved'. Rubin felt that the point had been made: 'By forcing the government to over-react at home we were spotlighting the over-reaction of America in Vietnam. Chicago was an education – about Vietnam, about oppression in the ghettos, about the whole use of physical force to solve social problems.' But Dellinger sensed that the public, while wanting peace, wanted it foremost at home: it was 'unfortunately a time when on the one hand the entire country was turning against the war and realizing it had to end, and when the movement was not as clear and precise in its imagery as it should have been'.

The movement had become too diffuse; it sought too many solutions all at once, though Rubin argued for this: 'You can't treat others, poor people, blacks, Vietnamese, without any humanity, and have a safe and secure home yourself; you have to address these social problems.' But if the war was the 'vital edge' then Dellinger felt 'the protest was somewhat muddied'. There was general agreement that the outcome in Chicago had been to elect Richard Nixon, and they agreed that there should be one last march, a torchlight parade – a requiem.

Chicago had been the one opportunity for effective organized protest within the system. The movement had failed to influence policy and thus shorten the war, and now its critics could say it had merely encouraged Hanoi and therefore prolonged the war. National honor was Nixon's approach; the movement would be increasingly dismissed as unpatriotic, though patriotic conscience was its only common motivation. Says Rubin, 'I felt throughout the war that I was a patriot, a nationalist, fighting for America. In the year 2000 without a doubt we're going to look back at the Sixties and say that the people who represented George Washington, the real patriotism of America, were the people who were opposing the war because the war was against America's interests. It hurt America.'

Indeed, after Chicago, it was already time to look back at the movement: to those who shaped it and why, the voices and issues that would persist long after Vietnam. The movement would have lasting significance for the very reasons it then failed: it had shown Americans that McCarthy's fears remained – the public's right of protest was far too arbitrary, and in seeking a government 'instrument' to express opposition, McCarthy had encountered only a blunt one. The movement had bared extraordinary xenophobia – not inspired by the public but inculcated by ideological elitists or what McCarthy saw as 'a sort of religious strain running in our State Department'; it had bared social divisions then harder to face than Vietnam but which meant that some day, as Rubin puts it,

America 'had to really face its own soul' and choose between its global aspirations and those of its ghettos; and finally it brought home, as Dellinger says, that 'the opposition did not begin in a vacuum' but was 'a long slow process of *building*'.

Though they saw themselves as fighting for America, Jerry Rubin was labeled a Communist and David Dellinger, in the mood of the times, was something worse – a pacifist. At the time Johnson defaulted the presidency in March 1968, both Rubin and Dellinger had been anti-war activists for three years, or from the beginning when the Marines went into Vietnam in March 1965. Rubin was then twenty-six, held a BA from the University of Cincinnati in Ohio where he had started out conventionally as a sports reporter for the *Cincinnati Post,* becoming its youth editor. He then drifted through Europe, India and Israel before discovering the counter-culture of Berkeley in 1964. In the fashion that went with the anti-establishment clothes, music and drugs at Berkeley, Rubin quickly 'dropped out' from the University of California, drawn instead to the rebel curricula of the campus. He was Jewish, the son of a poor truck driver, his political activism limited to 'shop-ins' at stores which did not hire blacks, when America went to war in Vietnam. Rubin then saw the chance 'to wake up the slumbering morality' and 'build a mass movement that would reach into every level of American society'. Rubin's militancy or his taste for what he called 'guerrilla theater' would make him nationally prominent.

Rubin's appearance in Berkeley coincided with a ferment among America's young people, many of whom were in the process of becoming radicalized through their involvement with the burgeoning Civil Rights Movement in the South. Not long before a group of students in Michigan had drafted the charter of the Students for a Democratic Society (SDS), which in coming years would evolve into the far more violent Weathermen. The Free Speech Movement in Berkeley was born out of confrontations between students and the school administration, and became the inspiration for countless demonstrations and seizures of school buildings in the coming years. At the same time groups like the Black Panthers were propagating the concept of Black Power in answer to ever more

violent resistance to desegregation. A new spirit of social resistance was being kindled, and Vietnam would turn it into a conflagration.

Some opponents of the war traced their resistance back much further. David Dellinger was already forty when America's war in Vietnam began. He had opposed violence all his life, and through this he became allied with what was called the 'New Left' – though he never joined any political party, and his background and personality were moderate-conservative. His family traced back to pre-Revolutionary New England. He was the son of a Boston lawyer and himself graduated from Yale *magna cum laude* in economics. He went on to study theology, and in World War II he twice refused the draft and was jailed for a year, then for two years. In the postwar years, coinciding with the cold war, he devoted his entire efforts to pacifism, founding a pacifist newspaper and co-operative to take up such causes as Martin Luther King's passive struggle for racial equality.

It was these separate protest groups, known collectively as The Movement, that organized opposition to US combat intervention in Vietnam from its start in March 1965. An immediate demonstration in Washington drew 25,000 people, and Dellinger recalls the 'heady sense people had, after the lonely vigils, that the country was beginning to wake up to what was happening'.

But as the US widened the offensive, committing 125,000 troops that July, a 'depression set in', says Dellinger. 'People said the Anti-War Movement is doomed because the American public will react to support the GIS over there.' At that time 'a lot of the early inspiration for the Anti-War Movement came from blacks, who had already tangled with the system and had learned not to trust the explanations that came out of Washington'. Initially, dissent arose not over the war but over who had to fight it. The blacks and poorer groups saw the draft as additional discrimination, favoring those who could afford college and get a deferment. This dissent swelled with the troop demands.

In mid-1965 there was strong anti-war sentiment but no strong structure among the campuses whose critical fraternity did not, anyhow, have to go. At Berkeley, Jerry Rubin began the 'teach-in'

Left: April 26, 1968—Black power militant H. Rap Brown speaks to the media as he and Stokely Carmichael leave Hamilton Hall where black students take part in a anti-war sit-in protest at Columbia University in New York City.

Right: April 27, 1968—Anti-Vietnam war protesters march down 5th Avenue near 81st Street in New York City.

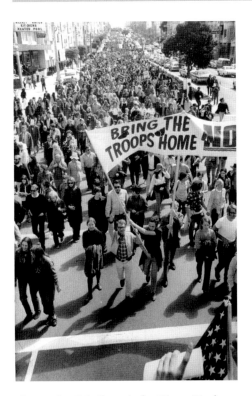

Above: April 6, 1969—Thousands of anti-Vietnam War demonstrators march for peace on Van Ness Avenue in San Francisco, Calif.

Left: May 22, 1969—People's Park demonstrators of Berkeley, Calif., wait to be arrested after bayonet-wielding troops maneuvered them into a downtown parking lot. At least 200 people were arrested a week after a bloody riot in Berkeley.

and saw the potential for 'moral crusade' as 12,000 students sat through a continuous two-day series of anti-war speeches by such luminaries as Norman Mailer, Isaac Deutcher and Dr Benjamin Spock. Recalls Rubin, 'Dr Spock the baby doctor against the war – what could have been more American than that? He tells you how to raise your kids, and then he tells you don't send them to Vietnam. Without Benjamin Spock it wouldn't have worked. He was crucial.'

But for the most part it was the youth who saw themselves as the conscience of their elders. The general public were fully behind their President on Vietnam, confident that the new US offensive would at long last resolve the mess. Jerry Rubin 'as an ex-reporter' understood 'how to make news, and I knew we had to make dramatic news in the streets to counter the news from Vietnam'. David Dellinger recalls these dramatics as 'things like trying to stop the troop trains going to the ports of embarkation, or the shipment of munitions, or trying to organize communities to have vast demonstrations, and I had mixed feelings about it'.

Dellinger, however, felt that the passive teach-ins were not sufficiently educational: those Americans delving into Vietnamese history were concluding that the war was a civil one; Ho Chi Minh's nationalism, rather than his Communist backers, was the issue they tried to convey. But it was not enough for Americans just to hear this – they had to see the nature of the war and of their adversary, Dellinger believed. And he also had to see for himself.

The television images were then still softened by the early successes, and television could not go behind the lines. In 1966 David Dellinger became the first American to take all the risks of going to the wartime capital of his country's enemy. Says Rubin, 'Dave was the spiritual soul of the movement. His integrity was an inspiration to people all over the country.' Dellinger met Ho Chi Minh – 'He amazed me by speaking of the sincere idealism of some Americans, including many GIS who went to Vietnam actually believing they were going to help the Vietnamese people' – and he toured the bombed areas.

The President had pledged that the US was bombing 'only steel and concrete' but, says Dellinger, 'when I got there I found that churches, schools, hospitals, houses, entire villages were being wiped out'. The US bombing, in Dellinger's view, was 'a violation of all the international laws of war. I brought back, for example, an anti-personnel bomb. They dropped what they called "mother bombs" and each of these released 120 of these smaller bombs and each of them released little pellets which were absolutely useless against steel and concrete and were good only against people.'

Dellinger's findings received attention internationally, presented as evidence at a so-called War Crimes Tribunal organized in Stockholm by philosophers Bertrand Russell and Jean-Paul Sartre, but this only left the US public distrustful and resentful. At the same time, categorizing Washington's view of the Anti-War Movement Jerry Rubin was subpoenaed by the House Un-American Activities Committee. To convey Vietnam, he turned up wearing a Revolutionary War costume accompanied by Abbie Hoffman wearing a shirt made from the American flag. There was an angry uproar and the Committee dismissed them in disgust.

The heart of the movement was still the campuses – and it beat faster now. Rubin had provided passion, Dellinger had provided reason – the war was 'unclean', it was 'David and Goliath' – but it was General Westmoreland who gave the movement impetus. His 500,000-man requirement was a rotating figure, and whether they fought it or avoided it the war was marking the lives of millions of young Americans. The majority accepted the draft as their fate. Others married young, entitling them to deferment, or hastily enrolled in college or graduate programs. Others chose exile, some going to known havens in Mexico and Sweden, the great majority going to Canada. (Canadian Immigration records show that 30,000 legally settled there, but Amex – an exile organization – estimates that another 50,000 lived on the run in Canada.)

There was one other choice apart from fighting, deferment and exile. And David Harris chose it – jail. Harris was student Vice-President at Stanford University in 1966. His decision, he says, was not emotional: 'The more I investigated it the more it became clear to me that far from fighting for freedom and democracy we were fighting something, at best, much more confused than that. It was hard to tell which side was freedom and democracy and which side wasn't.'

Harris was married to folk singer Joan Baez at the time, and a folklore quickly built around his resistance. He could not, he says 'play the game of student deferment: you know, let the poor people who weren't going to college go fight the war. It was grossly unfair, and if Americans were going to fight wars, white college kids ought to fight them every bit as much as blacks and Chicanos.' His options were to go to war, or 'go to the physical and fake it – pretend that I was a homosexual or a drug addict', or leave the country.

'I felt that if anybody ought to leave that Lyndon Johnson ought to be the one leaving, not me. My family had been in the country since the Revolution in 1776. I felt a very strong love for the United States, and for what it was supposed to stand for. I saw myself as one of those who were defending those values.' Harris decided to mail back his draft card and having done so 'felt I was walking ten feet off the ground'.

The movement now entered a new phase. It set up counsel centers on how to avoid the draft, and staged much publicized burnings of draft cards. For his refusal, Harris served twenty months of a three-year sentence (the sentences were harsher than in World War II). Of those who openly resisted the draft on conscientious grounds, 3250 went to prison. An estimated 250,000 avoided draft registration and one million committed draft offenses, with only 25,000 indicted – according to a special study, *Chance and Circumstance* by Lawrence M. Baskir and Wm A. Strauss. The study found that the number of eligible Americans who managed through student and occupational deferments and other factors to avoid military call-up totaled fifteen million. 'It meant', says historian Arthur Schlesinger Jr, 'that the war in Vietnam was being fought in the main by the sons of poor whites and blacks whose parents did not have much influence in the community. The sons of the influential people were all protected because they were in college.'

The crucial swing of middle-America against the war coincided with the period from 1969 when it was announced that deferments would be abolished.

Left: April 5, 1969—Thousands of anti-Vietnam war protesters march along the Avenue of the America's in New York City. Many of the protesters wore black arm bands bearing the number '33,000,' referring to the American deaths in Vietnam.

Below: November 15, 1969—A sea of faces fills the hillside near the base of the Washington Memorial as demonstrators protest the war in Vietnam at a Moratorium Day peace rally in the nation's capital.

Below: January 22, 1966—Chairman William Fulbright questions Secretary of State Dean Rusk as the Senate Foreign Relations Committee met to discuss additional funds for the war in Vietnam.

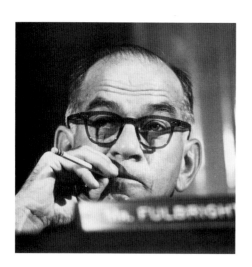

Full enactment of this only began in late 1971 when US troops had started withdrawing from Vietnam. Johnson's opponent for the presidency, Eugene McCarthy, charges that the deferment system was a deliberate policy to reduce opposition to the war.

'The Johnson administration expected the war to end quickly,' says McCarthy. 'The whole thrust of it was to allow people whom they thought would be critics of the war, the better educated, to stay out of the fighting. And progressively the military was made up more and more of people drawn from minorities. It became a completely unrepresentative military.'

Civil rights leader Martin Luther King urged that all black and white Americans should declare themselves conscientious objectors. 'Negroes', he said, "are dying in disproportionate numbers in Vietnam. Twice as many negroes as whites are in combat.' Research for this history shows that Martin Luther King was correct. Black Americans comprised thirteen per cent of the troop force in Vietnam – about equal to America's black population. But a disproportionate number of blacks, twenty-eight per cent, had combat assignments. Only two per cent of the officers were black.

Blacks, poverty and civil rights were the causes Lyndon Johnson had held most dear. During his presidency he introduced a national health care program, wider voting rights, a department of housing and urban development, greater federal aid for schools, and numerous anti-poverty measures. But as defense spending cut into the domestic budget, Congress refused to pass some civil rights measures. The Great Society was being literally vetoed by the war, even as civil rights leaders pressed harder for the slums of America to take precedence over the jungles of Asia. The dissent was greatest among those Johnson had desired to help. As the ghettos smoldered, then burned through successive long hot summers, elected Democrats openly joined the anti-war cause – notably Senators Fulbright, Kennedy, McCarthy, McGovern, Mansfield, and, the earliest Senate dissenter, Wayne Morse – bringing it a public credibility it had lacked. In retrospect, their numbers were dismally few, but their position was strong.

From 1966 the Senate Foreign Relations Committee began Congressional hearings which the policy-makers, when summoned, dutifully attended. Senator Morse – one of the only two Senators to vote against the Gulf of Tonkin reso-

lution – had an exchange with General Maxwell Taylor typifying the Committee's anger, and typical for the inattention it received. The public was growing disenchanted with the war, said Morse. 'That', responded General Taylor, 'is good news for Hanoi.' Replied Morse, 'That's the smear you militarists give to those of us who have honest differences of opinion with you, but I don't intend to get down in the gutter with you and engage in that kind of debate.' Essentially, the elected leaders blocked public debate, says Committee Chairman William Fulbright: 'We made efforts in Congress to restrict or stop the war but we didn't get anywhere. The clear majority of both Houses wouldn't support it. They didn't know anything about it [Vietnam], but they always support the President.'

Senator Fulbright had remained the product of his beginnings – lecturer in law at George Washington University. He began to speak and write prodigiously against the war from 1966, stating that the real risk in Vietnam was that America would adopt the oppression it was ostensibly fighting. 'My assistant', says Fulbright, 'said you shouldn't make such speeches. You'll be ruined politically. The President and the administration will punish you in every way they can. The other side was, well, you're Chairman of this Committee: if you don't do it, who will?'

Attending an official ceremony with President Johnson, Fulbright's once close friend tried to shame him publicly: 'He used the phrase of the "Nervous Nellies" and the "Sunshine Patriots" and no one stands up to support the President, and everyone hoots and hollers. You were made to look like a traitor.' (Johnson was using a quotation from Thomas Paine, who wrote in 1776: 'The summer soldier and the sunshine patriot will, in this crisis, shrink from the service of his country.' One anti-war group composed of Vietnam veterans would see a reverse truth in Paine's words, calling themselves the 'Winter Soldiers'.)

But through 1966 to 1967 the opinion polls showed that a clear majority of Americans supported the President's policies. Numerically, there were probably as many small demonstrations all across the country in support of the war as there were against it, often with big labor union backing; 'hard hats' and 'flower children' and at times fathers and sons were confronting in a totally un-American, unconversable way.

The anti-war demonstrations grew in 1967 as the wounded veterans came home in sizeable, highly visible numbers, often leading the demonstrations. In one protest, by coincidence, six Vietnam veterans found themselves marching side by side. They formed the Vietnam Veterans Against the War – and within a short time they numbered 600. But, duty done, the veterans increasingly found themselves alienated, arousing guilt among their elders and anger among their own generation who often shunned them, and damned them, as killers. There was never – for any of them, any year – any 'homecoming', no official welcome back as in other wars, no special thankfulness beyond family and friends, no great understanding that a war unwon exacted the same blood as a victory. There was no sense, no dignity in their sacrifice, so many came to feel.

Most, though emotionally pent-up, made their lonely, individual way back into society, to wait years for some debate and sympathy. Others, distraught that America seemed neither to question nor care, publicly burned their uniforms and Purple Hearts and became anti-war activists. They sought out the GIS yet to go; encouraged desertion and the draft-dodge, and raised through their fury a large doubt among the troops who went in the later years.

This was probably the largest single factor in the final public misgiving: the lowered morale of the military and the interaction, unique to Vietnam, as the troops so quickly rotated between battle front and home front, until suddenly – in terms of hearts and minds – the fronts were indistinguishable. The television coverage of the war only really began to register in this context. In other wars the boys went and came back together, if at all. But by 1967 Americans did not even have to see the television images. The casualties of body and mind were everywhere they turned, perhaps even an amputee son bitterly watching the 'box' like a daily dark journey back and forth through a looking-glass.

Anti-war leaders David Dellinger and Jerry Rubin sensed that only now was the public beginning to understand physically Vietnam, as the scenes of the big unit war coincided with the large numbers of returning veterans, some scarred by what they had gone through, others by what they had done. The war policy – attrition and random fire – seemed finally in question, Dellinger thought, when there were 'pictures of [US] napalm falling on American troops. This roused an emotional reaction and moral revulsion that I don't think anybody had anticipated.' Rubin felt that the Anti-War Movement now 'had to be bold, confrontational, had to really grab the imagination of the country. So we would close down the Pentagon.'

The movement had grown, with a committee representing its many factions. Dellinger was persuaded that the demonstration would peaceably seal off the Pentagon through sheer numbers. No one would get in or out. The protesters would include all sectors of society in what Rubin saw as 'a massive outpouring of public reaction against the war'. Rubin had new supporters – psychologist and left-wing radical Abbie Hoffman ('an absurdist genius' who thought it would hurt more if 'we burn dollar bills, not draft cards') and drug-indulgent Professor of Psychology Timothy Leary, who purportedly called Rubin 'Merry Jerry, the Lysergic Lenin, the Grass Guevara, the Mescaline Marx'. But the committee members also represented student and teacher associations, women's groups, war veterans, movie stars, major authors and intellectuals, civil rights pacifists and black militants, family doctors and anarchists. Except for the war, the movement was a contradiction of opposites, and, says Rubin, 'If the Vietnam war did not exist, we would have had to create it.'

On 21 October 1967, probably the strangest group of people ever to keep company rallied at the Lincoln Memorial in Washington, camping on the lawns in what at first seemed a grand outing with household names as the after-picnic speakers. Baby expert Dr Benjamin Spock told them: 'The enemy, we believe, is Lyndon Johnson, whom we elected as a peace candidate and who betrayed us within three months.'

The crowd exceeded 50,000. With white professors marching alongside black Muslims, chanting together 'Hell No, We Won't Go', the vast procession made an orderly advance on the Pentagon.

Below: October 15, 1969—The flag of the Viet Cong flies from one of the masts surrounding the Washington Monument during a Moratorium Day demonstration in Washington, DC.

Left: October 15, 1968—New Orleans college students shout stop the war as they march on the federal building on Moratorium Day. About 2000 participated in the peaceful demonstration.

Above: November 15, 1969—The scene from the top of the Washington Monument looking toward the Potomac River. More than 250,000 gathered at the base of the Monument for a Moratorium Day rally.

There, for some time, a vigil was held. A force of 10,000 US army troops, state marshals and National Guardsmen surrounded the Department of Defense. Their rifles were unloaded, but they had orders to use tear-gas and truncheons if necessary. A new chant swelled from the crowd, 'Peace Now, Peace Now.' There was a moment when young girls placed flowers in the rifle barrels held at half-guard by the soldiers, and between them, fleetingly, there were the same shy smiles as on the beaches at Danang.

No one ever resolved how it started. There had been no serious disorders at any previous demonstrations held by the movement. There was sudden scuffling at the main Pentagon entrance and Dellinger's voice was heard pleading, 'It has been peaceful so far – let's keep it that way.' But the scuffling became a running battle that lasted an entire weekend. It was called the most violent dissent in America since the Civil War, with 1000 arrested. In the only light-relief statistic the government solemnly disclosed that the cost of defending the Defense Department had been exactly $1,078,500.

Rubin saw the Pentagon demonstration as 'the turning point in the antiwar effort – the most important demonstration in the entire decade, including Chicago. It captured the imagination of young people.' He recalls feeling that 'the only way this war is going to end is if we have war in the streets'.

Left: May 6, 1970—Ohio National Guardsmen patrol the empty Kent State University campus after a three-day riot with students. Four persons were killed and 10 were injured during the anti-Vietnam War protests.

Secretary of State Rusk viewed the protest as prolonging the war: 'If we had seen 50,000 people demonstrating around the headquarters in Hanoi, calling for peace, we would have felt that the war was over, and we would have been right. But they could see 50,000 people demonstrating around the Pentagon.' Rusk believes this 'persuaded them [the North Vietnamese] not to try to find a peaceful solution but to persist and win politically what they could not win militarily'.

However, the opinion polls were no comfort for Hanoi. Shocked by the violence, a majority of the public expressed confidence in the President. It was for the last time. Johnson's rating slipped as Democratic opponents provided the public with an alternative to the movement, perhaps also in response to unusually violent anti-American riots in London and Paris protesting against intensified bombing of North Vietnam. Taking a public stand, Robert F. Kennedy denounced as a 'fraud' the South Vietnamese elections confirming President Thieu's regime. In November 1967 Senator McCarthy announced that he would oppose Johnson in several primaries in 1968. Belatedly, Johnson ordered an administration campaign to explain the war. General Westmoreland and Ambassador Bunker were summoned from Saigon for cross-country television appearances, but Bunker thought the effort came too late. 'The President', he says 'could have emphasized more than he did publicly what our objectives were. I don't think the President took a strong enough lead.'

It was safer not to, says Dean Rusk. 'We did not take steps to whip up war feeling among the American people. For example, we didn't parade military units through our cities; we didn't send pretty movie stars out to factories to sell bonds, all those things that were done during World War II. We thought that in a nuclear world it was too dangerous for an entire people to become too angry. . . . This creates a problem – because we were trying to do in cold blood what we were asking our men on the battlefield to do in hot blood. And this imposes a very severe morale problem at home and abroad.'

Johnson personally encountered this in visiting Australia in December 1967. Though Australia then had 8000 combat troops in Vietnam, the US

President was confronted by constant demonstrations and was considered safe only on military bases. By now, more than 16,000 Americans had died in the combat, and the draft was reaching wider and wider.

Recalls McCarthy, 'I said the opposition to the war would begin to develop when they were sending bodies back not to Louisville, Kentucky, or Memphis and New York – where nobody in the next block – or next house – knows that somebody's dead – but when they begin to come back into towns of 5 or 10,000 or smaller communities; that these are historic events in a town of that size: so-and-so's son has been brought back dead; that this would make the country papers and eventually something would happen in the country. There was I think a very gradual growth of opposition. I think the real impact came with the Tet Offensive.'

Prior to Tet, one public opinion poll showed that Johnson was preferred over McCarthy by sixty-three to eighteen per cent. After Tet, just two months later, another poll showed them about evenly rated. With his strong forty-two per cent of the New Hampshire primary vote on 12 March, the fifty-two-year-old McCarthy had given the mass of young Americans new political faith. An army of 10,000 young volunteers, largely unassociated with the Anti-War Movement, had canvassed for him. This innovative 'New Politics' seemed nationally regenerative. McCarthy had served in Congress exactly twenty years, had a strong pro-labor voting record, had long lobbied for a curb on presidential powers, and had now revealed the mood for consensus all too well.

His unpredicted showing against Johnson – with new polls favoring McCarthy two to one – brought Robert F. Kennedy into the race on 16 March. Kennedy was also influenced by Tet, says historian Arthur Schlesinger Jr. Seeing the destruction, Kennedy told him, 'A lot of decent people are becoming accomplices in evil happenings.' Kennedy now campaigned against violence and the Vietnam war in words which became for America a rediscovery of its traditional compassion. In his first 18 March campaign speech, Kennedy described America in Vietnam: 'As Tacitus said of Rome:

"They made a desert, and called it peace." Can we ordain to ourselves the awful majesty of God: to decide what cities and villages are to be destroyed, who will live and who will die, and who will join the refugees of our creation?'

And yet any prospects of an anti-war President died with those words. By the time Johnson bowed out on 31 March, Kennedy was favored over McCarthy. There was the greed of the bandwagon, and for the young there was now a whiter knight who charged head-on, and a great many switched to his banner. It brought bitter rivalry, weakening the anti-war cause. Like Johnson, McCarthy would never really recover from this sudden withdrawal of faith. The entrance of Kennedy, he says, 'set up a division among the anti-war people. Up until that time you could really be quite impersonal about it: they were just against the war. But once he came in they began to fight over what would appear to be the possible victory, and that ran all the way through the organization in both his campaign and mine.'

Kennedy's fear of 'evil happenings' now proved eminently prophetic. On 4 April civil rights leader Martin Luther King was shot dead in Memphis. King's words 'I have a dream . . .' had reached the heart of black and poor America; now rage replaced hope, and from Washington to Los Angeles – in ghettos whose names had been as unknown as Can Tho and My Tho – the cities burned. Kennedy attended King's funeral, then the New York Senator continued on his campaign, winning the California primary. There on 6 June, five years after the assassination of his brother whose 'throne' he sought, Robert F. Kennedy was shot down in the Hotel Ambassador in Los Angeles.

In a scathing comment on the politics of power, McCarthy relates what Kennedy's death meant in American history, five years before the war would end: 'Once he was killed I was pretty well certain we couldn't even carry on the issue for several reasons. There were really three kinds of people supporting Kennedy. There were those who were against the war; there was another group that would have been for Kennedy if he'd been for bombing Peking. And they were among his delegates. And there was a third group of his delegates who were simply there because they had been left out either of the regular party or mine, and they were in it for power. When Kennedy was killed we figured that two-thirds of his people would leave us on the [anti-war] issue, and that's just about what happened.'

Had Kennedy lived to win the presidency, historian Schlesinger Jr says 'he would have pulled out American troops. In his private conversation there is no doubt that this was his determination. He just felt that our foreign policy should have some rational relationship to our national interest. If Robert Kennedy had been elected,' concludes Schlesinger, 'he would have ended American participation in the war in 1969.'

A few weeks after Kennedy's death, in the continuing violence at Chicago, Vice-President Humphrey beat McCarthy for the Democratic nomination 1760 to 601. On 5 November, Richard Nixon won the presidency for the Republicans by an extremely narrow margin on a platform of 'progressive de-Americanization of the war'. The war, in fact, would continue as long again, building in ferocity, and McCarthy believes that despite the public revulsion as the bodies came home it had no great influence on Nixon, nor would it have influenced Humphrey. 'I'm inclined to believe,' says McCarthy, 'that the war would have ended just about when it did, even if there had been no protest, if I had not campaigned, because they didn't end it on policy finally: they just ended it because they were losing it, and – you know – the soldiers wouldn't fight.'

Secretary of State Rusk maintains that a new Democratic administration would have pursued an early peace. 'The real decision to bring this to an end', he says, 'was not made on college campuses or in the streets but when the people at grass roots – maybe the first half of 1968 – came to the conclusion that if we could not tell them when this struggle was going to be over, we might as well chuck it.' As Nixon took over, Rusk – who had headed the State Department for eight years – felt that his party and his country had been sabotaged by dissent. A 'tolerable' settlement would have been 'much closer', he says, 'if a good many of my own fellow countrymen, including some Senators, could have just been silent for a while. I think we helped to persuade the North Vietnamese to persist and to me that is a tragedy.'

Those who led the Anti-War Movement judge it as having had only peripheral impact. As they see it the movement's motivations are of lasting importance: the effort to register political

opposition and the insistent social grievances that spawned the movement, but these objectives, they say, were only highlighted, not won. Says David Dellinger, 'The protest movement could not have ended the war without the successes of the Vietnamese people.' Long-time militant Jerry Rubin says, 'Looking back, the movement fell apart: it moved much too quickly into aggression, violence, secrecy and military tactics.' Rubin confesses: 'We looked at the Viet Cong as our models, many of us – and I think that was a mistake. We made it too much good guys versus bad guys. It was a moral struggle, but the Vietnamese were not our model and we, in a sense, romanticized guerrilla war and by 1970 we were fighting guerrilla war. And that was too much.'

And finally the man who failed to become President, Eugene McCarthy, would just like to believe that politicians and public were influenced: 'I'd hope that they would not let themselves be maneuvered into a position again where you can be forced into a war on what's said to be an ideological issue – something which is quite outside of history; and also that we would recognize the limits of our military power under all circumstances.'

Whether the protest was encouraged by the press coverage, and whether either delayed the peace, can only be conjectural. In the view of Eric Sevareid, perhaps the most respected television commentator of the period, the television coverage

Above: May 4, 1970—Mary Ann Vecchio screams as she kneels next to the body of a student, one of four people killed by National Guardsmen during an antiwar demonstration on the Kent State University campus in Kent, Ohio.

was only marginally influential: 'You must remember that in spite of the freedom to report it all, in spite of a lot of horror pictures in your living-room every night, most people according to all the polls for years believed the war was probably justified. They were not persuaded until late in the game.'

Sevareid provided a nightly editorial on the CBS Cronkite newscast, and over the years reported from Vietnam. 'I'm sure that Hanoi', he says, 'kept a very close watch on press coverage, public reaction to it, the demonstrations and so on, and no doubt they were encouraged by that. But the activity they had to respond to was in front of them – a constant reinforcement of the American air force, infantry, artillery, navy, everything else. There may have been a lot of anti-war feeling here but what was coming at them was more and more pro-war American power. So I never quite believed that the reason they fought so hard and tenaciously was because of things going on here.

'You weren't really fighting just a military force. You were fighting a society, a society equipped with a total faith.' It was the point which took so many people 10,000 days to grasp.

Left: November 14, 1969—The New York City skyline forms the backdrop for an anti-war demonstration in Central Park. Activists released balloons as a sign for peace and in protest of U.S. government policy in Vietnam.

Above: November 11, 1969—Flags, signs and people are massed on the grounds of the Washington Monument during a Veteran's Day rally by supporters of President Nixon's Vietnam policies.

Right: November 13, 1969—Participants in the 'March Against Death' place name cards of U.S. military killed in Vietnam in coffins at the foot of the capital in Washington.

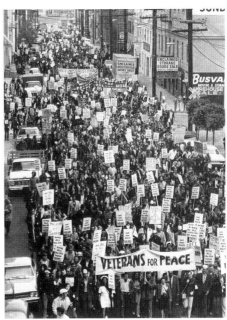

Above: November 15, 1969—Marchers walk out of the waterfront area in San Francisco and head for Golden Gate park in a seven mile demonstration to protest the war in Vietnam.

Above: November 13, 1969—The U.S. capitol in Washington, DC, is alight over a scene in which anti-war demonstrators have lined up coffins to represent those killed in the Vietnam war.

Right: May 1970—Demonstrators showing sign of protest as ROTC cadets parade at Ohio State University during a ceremony in Columbus, Ohio.

Above: May 20, 1970—Construction workers, longshoremen and office employees rally in downtown Manhattan to support President Richard M. Nixon's Vietnam War policy.

Below: May 4, 1970—An overturned ROTC panel truck burns on the campus of the University of California in Berkeley. The truck driver escaped as anti-war marchers turned over his vehicle and set it on fire following a rally.

Above: May 15, 1970—New York workers, angered by the mayor's apparent Anti-Vietnam War sympathies, wave American flags as they march in a demonstration near City Hall.

Left: May 11,1970—Some of the more than 2,000 blue collar workers march around New York's City Hall shouting 'USA All the Way!' and 'Lindsay Must Go!' Violence resulted from the workers' anger at Mayor John Lindsay's orders to have the American flag flown at half-staff for the four students killed at Kent State University.

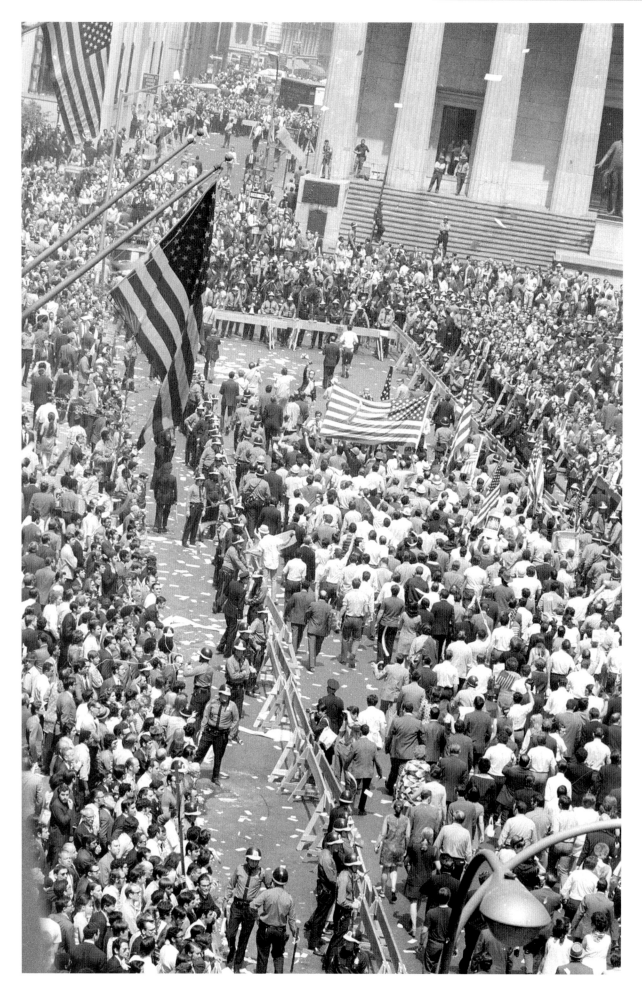

Left: May 12, 1970—A mass rally in support of U.S. policy in Vietnam makes its way through Wall Street in New York City.

# THE GUERRILLA SOCIETY

On 1 November 1968, the war across North Vietnam became strangely problematic. In the capital of Hanoi, the sirens had not sounded and the city's three million sidewalk 'man-holes' were empty all through the day. At Vinh Linh near the Partition Line, 70,000 people emerged from their underground city for their first full day in the sun in three and a half years. After a thousand days and two million bombs the seventeen million population faced a new test. The North had now to cope with the US government's dilemma: the problem of sustaining the war effort at home.

As his last important decision of the war, President Johnson had announced on 1 November an immediate cessation of all air and naval bombardment of the North except for contingency 'protective strikes' in support of reconnaissance flights. Except for these, the North now owned its skies. But there was only relative comfort.

'They had been in the same prisons, had fought together shoulder to shoulder.'

– HA VAN LAU ON HANOI'S LEADERSHIP

The bombers had totally destroyed urban life, or anything of brick and mortar, in the provinces below Hanoi. Life here had been reduced to the simplest village level. The bombing had made it so, and now policy kept it so: 'The bombers would return,' said Hanoi. Only the straw world of the villages, essentially indestructible, could safely be rebuilt. The war's privation and tension – sustained by the over-flights – continued unaltered through the Johnson-Nixon transition; with the embittered years of bombing conditioning as many years of peace talks.

With the cessation of bombing and the change of US administration there was the opportunity for a serious re-evaluation. There was now significant evidence that the North was fundamentally untouched by the air war, or by its absence. Though Hanoi's long-term objectives remained unchanged, 1969 brought political con-

Right: June 1, 1969—North Vietnamese President Ho Chi Minh is surrounded by children he invited to his official residence in Hanoi.

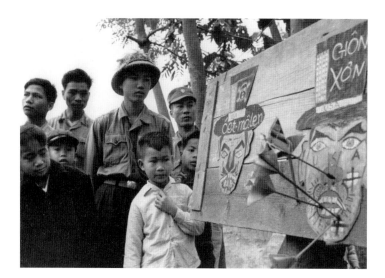

cessions from both sides – and the only major difference in the final settlement was that it came four years later. Many observers would feel that the latter half of the war was especially tragic, that both sides misinterpreted the de-escalation as weakness, and that the new US administration continued to ignore the old maxim, 'Know your enemy'.

Then, as now, an understanding of what lay ahead was provided by the nature of North Vietnamese society. The best measure of this was a comparison of North Vietnam during the bombing and after.

The unprecedented bombing which was supposed to resolve the war within six months had lasted seven times as long, and had produced only awesome statistics – 350,000 missions flown, 655,000 tons of bombs dropped over the North, 918 US aircraft lost, 818 American airmen killed – when Johnson 'ended' it. His decision was presented as a humanitarian one, heeding the pleas of the Allies and of the United Nations, yet since mid-1967 or for fifteen months Johnson had disregarded a McNamara memo, published in the *Pentagon Papers* which stated: 'There may be a limit beyond which many Americans and much of the world will not permit the United States to go. The picture of the world's greatest super-power killing or seriously injuring one thousand non-combatants a week, while trying to pound a tiny backward nation into submission on an issue whose merits are hotly disputed, is not a pretty one.'

Ignoring his Defense Secretary, Johnson had continued personally to approve the bombing targets at a regular Tuesday White House lunch reserved for the purpose. CBS correspondent Dan Rather described the atmosphere in a WTOP Radio report of 17 October 1967 (reproduced in the *Pentagon Papers*): 'After a bit of chatter over drinks in the sitting room, the President signals the move to the dining room. It is semi-oval, with a huge chandelier, a mural around the wall: brightly colored scenes of Cornwallis surrendering his sword at Yorktown. The President sits at the head, of course – sits in a high-back stiletto chair. Rusk is at his right, McNamara on his left, Rostow is at the other end, and the extras, if any, in between. Lunch begins, so does the serious conversation. There's an occasional pause, punctuated by the whirl of Mr Johnson's battery-powered pepper grinder. He likes pepper and he likes the gadget.'

'At those Tuesday luncheon sessions,' says Rusk, 'there were times when we'd require our fliers to go in to the more heavily defended areas to deliver their bombs on military targets rather than easier areas because of the possible threat to civilian neighborhoods.' Yet McNamara was saying that a thousand *civilians* were being killed each week. On this evidence 182,000 civilians had been killed so far during the air war in the North alone.

Perhaps to discourage 'attrition' or perhaps for internal reasons the North never revealed its casualties. Interviewed for this history, Prime Minister Pham Van Dong says, 'We did not keep statistics. That is the truth. We fought year after year in extremely hard conditions which went beyond all imagination.' But, the premier says, 'Our human losses were not so great as in other wars' considering that 'the quantity of bombs and shells used

were several times larger than that of World War II. We Vietnamese continued to live, to work and fight.' But how? 'Our collective leadership', he points out, 'had remained the same throughout the last few decades and this symbolizes the unity of the entire population.'

Contrary to Dean Rusk's contention that the US suffered because there were no film or press reports from the other side, the very lack of these prevented the American people from knowing the full extent of the death and destruction, or the capability and morale of the North. The US public had no means of judging either the main strategy – the air war – or the resistance of the North and what it implied in terms of US casualties. Although in the early years a succession of British, French, Scandinavian and East European journalists and academics provided first-hand accounts of the bombing and its ineffectiveness, Washington was able to dismiss these as partisan left-wing reports. The US press, while considered irresponsible by the administration, in fact gave Washington the benefit of the doubt by largely ignoring these reports. When the distinguished journalist and Communist affairs expert Harrison Salisbury visited the Hanoi-Haiphong area in late 1966 the administration sought to discredit his reports on the basis (ironically) of statistics rather than observations.

The overall result amounted to a news blackout from behind the lines throughout the bombing, and this prevented any serious public evaluation – and perhaps prolonged the war. While much of the early reporting was highly emotional, and of no interest to the bombing planners, some provided factual – and fascinating – detail on North Vietnamese counter-measures and morale. The always descriptive reports of Wilfred Burchett were perhaps the most overlooked intelligence. He recalls examples of what he saw during 1966.

Above: July 17, 1966—Soldiers of a Hanoi rocket unit hold a rally dedicating themselves to the defeat of the United States in Vietnam, according to the caption of this photo released by North Vietnam.

Above: 1966—North Vietnamese antiaircraft troops defend the bridge in Thanh Hoa province, according to the caption of this photo released by Hanoi. The unit claimed more than 100 encounters with U.S. aircraft.

Right: 1968—The Soviet agency Novosti released this photo, described as an antiaircraft missile 'guarding the skies of Hanoi.'

'The use of camouflage was something quite fantastic,' says Burchett. 'It was compulsory for the kids to wear green camouflage when they attended school – and normally the schools in the countryside might be a mile from where the peasants were living. I remember once driving through an area and to my great astonishment the whole field of maize suddenly got to its feet and charged across the road.'

Burchett described how the bombed bridges were replaced by wooden ones camouflaged under water. 'Bamboo bridges', he says, 'would be lowered by inches at dawn and would be winched up at night for the truck convoys. And there were pontoons: half of a bridge would be on one bank of the river, the other half on the opposite bank, and they'd be floated out around dusk and put together. They reckoned that no bridge could be put out of action for more than four hours.'

No fewer than two million civilians formed 'shock brigades' traveling where needed to man the bridges, or repair road and rail-lines, ensuring the flow and pocket-storage of food, fuel and ammunition. In industry and agriculture, some seventy per cent of the work-force were women. 'They did jobs', says Burchett, 'which previously women never handled at all. It was much different talking to a woman than a man. They were very proud they could do more or less the same and they'd remark, "Things will never be the same afterwards." ' He found that women made up 'half or more of the local village self-defense units. They knew how to handle rifles, grenades, AA guns.'

In the cities a simple but effective defense kept casualties relatively low. Concrete cylinders, just large enough for one person, were embedded every few feet on every street. In Hanoi there were three for each of the estimated one million population, says Burchett: 'The system worked on the principle of one shelter close to home, one close to the place of work and one along the commuter roads in case they were caught between home and work. Each shelter had a thick concrete cover which you just pulled over the top.' The population would just dissolve into these individual shelters whenever the sirens sounded: 'I never saw any panic. People would run when they were told to.'

The majority – the peasantry – were rallied by means exactly opposite to those in the countryside of South Vietnam: they were given more autonomy. Unlike the South, the villages – though organized as State co-operatives – still elected their own chiefs, keeping ancient tradition nominally intact. With the bombing, Hanoi simply relaxed controls, permitting farmers to contract land and sell any produce above their co-operative quota. Food production rapidly improved, and this took care of the higher-paid city workers evacuated to the countryside. Early rationing was severe to enable stockpiling. The average rice allotment was a pound a day, but this was doubled in the later war years. During the bombing, the cloth ration was five yards per person – enough for an annual change of shirt and trousers: the standard dress for both men and women.

All industrial and government workers – including the Politburo members – received the same pay: the equivalent of ten dollars a month. Some major factories were divided into as many as fifty different locations, so that no industry could be seriously crippled. Ninety per cent of industrial workers were relocated in this way, with their children evacuated to rural communes and the youth assigned to local defense and the road repair gangs. In contrast to the South, the policy was a decentralized, self-sufficient, hold-your-ground approach. In heavily bombed strategic areas which had to be held at all costs this meant going underground.

The most extraordinary example was the 'city' of Vinh Linh, a complex of villages which had burrowed thirty feet beneath its former location along the 'Demilitarized' border. Linked by tunnels, this community was officially said to number 70,000 people and to extend for several hundred kilometers. For successive years these people tended the crop-land and repaired the border supply routes at night, and abandoned the earth's surface by day to the ceaseless air strikes and offshore bombardment of the US 7th Fleet. Children born below the earth were cradled in cots in the wells of deep shafts where the light hardly filtered; they were carefully exposed to the sun for a few minutes each day. Families lived in small catacombs of their making, with canvas-covered floors and – if fortunate – tin or bamboo-shored walls, faintly warmed and lit by oil lamps from China. Each sector or 'village' had its clinic, school, nursery and recreational center, and, as in the age before the bombers, tended to its own fields and communal affairs.

This demonstration of the North's morale – known through diplomats in Hanoi – had Washington thankful, despite its protestations, that there were no cameras on the other side: Vinh Linh was more intensely bombed for a longer period than any other area in Vietnam and though it had a military function its population was predominately civilian. (Hanoi officials say 'half a million tons of bombs and shells' were dropped in the area, or 'treble the amount dropped in Japan in the whole course of the Second World War'. The North Vietnamese extensively filmed Vinh Linh under bombardment during the mid 1960s and say twenty cameramen died in the bombing while making the film.)

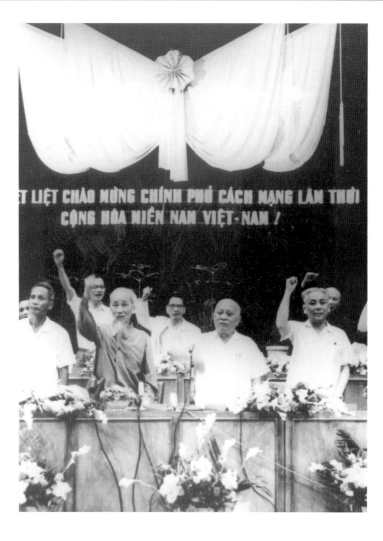

Left: June 14, 1969—North Vietnamese President Ho Chi Minh, second from left, celebrates establishment of the Provisional Revolutionary Government in South Vietnam at a rally in Hanoi. From left are North Vietnamese Premier Pham Van Dong, Ho Chi Minh, Vice President Ton Duc Thant, and Nguyen Van Thien, ambassador from the provisional government.

Below: May 6, 1967—Captured U.S. pilot James Lindberg Hughes, whose F-105 fighter was shot down the previous day, is escorted to the International Club in Hanoi, where captured airmen were presented to journalists. Hughes was imprisoned in the 'Hanoi Hilton' compound.

At the time Wilfred Burchett reported the mood in this devastated countryside. 'Maybe for morale purposes', he recalls, 'they established what they called "plane cemeteries" in various provinces. And I just happened to come across a convoy of ox-carts bearing bits of an F-105 – one had a bit of a wing, another a bit of fuselage, a bit of tail and so forth; a strange procession of ox-carts and people. There was one old chap with a long white beard and a spear, which his ancestors probably used against the Mongols, and they were quite solemnly taking this stuff to the "cemetery".' The prize catch was a large chunk of a B-52 kept in a cage at Hanoi's municipal zoo.

Burchett talked to Prime Minister Pham Van Dong and asked, ' "What's in you: what makes you tick?" And he laughed and said, "Well you know, what is our history? There's nothing else in our history except struggle. Struggle against foreign invaders, always more powerful than ourselves; struggle against nature – and we've had nowhere else to go, we've had to fight things out where we were. And the result of this after two thousand odd years is that it has created a very stable nervous system in our people. We never panic. And whatever new situation arises, our people say, Ah well, there it goes again." He repeated this three times, "There's nothing else in our history except struggle." '

In few countries had history repeated itself so constantly and exactly as in Vietnam. Even the physical division of North and South was not a new pattern. The war with America had lasted a

Above: 1968—In a captured photograph, Viet Cong chant slogans to boost morale and maintain a 'high degree of ideological awareness.'

Left: December 1972—Snapshots of young North Vietnamese men were found on the body of a North Vietnamese soldier after air strikes against the village of Tam Binh, seven miles north of Saigon. An enemy rocket attack against the Tan Son Nhut airbase had been launched from the area the previous day.

mere four years at this point. Resistance to the Chinese had taken a thousand years, from 111 BC to AD 959. For an entire millenium the people known as the Viets had withstood not only Chinese domination but Chinese culture and philosophy because the villages had always retained their indigenous roots. The centuries had been a succession of armed uprisings and prolonged rebellions led from rural hideouts historically as familiar as birthmarks. Nor was a super-power adversary anything new. Alone in mainland Asia the Vietnamese Tran Dynasty had fought off the armies of Kublai Khan in the thirteenth century. The war between South and North had been waged before. In the sixteenth century the Nguyens of the Mekong and the Trinhs of the Red River had exhaustively fought each other and for a time divided the country very close to the 17th Parallel. This latest halving of the country came after a century of French rule – and in the history books of the North the Americans had merely replaced the French. As military analyst Brian Jenkins says, in Vietnam the United States was fighting not just Communism but a long history of uncompromising nationalism.

'Hanoi's leaders', says Jenkins, 'attached themselves to these powerful traditions. They made history work for them, psychologically and politically.' They had preserved the village structure with its inherent nationalism 'passed down orally' and they could claim 'they were the legitimate inheritors of Vietnam. If one looks at things traditionally they had a certain validity to that claim, going back to 1945 when the last emperor of Viet-

nam, Bao Dai, ceremonially passed on his power to their leadership.' Trust and tradition minimized dissent; Marxism was part of a national crusade among 'a society that historically was well disciplined'. It meant, says Jenkins, 'a society where everything, the production, the economy, every newspaper, virtually every poem, artistic activity, was all geared toward the war effort'.

As Ha Van Lau puts it, 'Against the American air force we led a popular war.' The future UN Ambassador was then helping organize civilian counter-measures. 'When the enemy planes arrived,' he says, 'everyone participated in the anti-aircraft defense – whether it was active defense such as manning the guns or passive defense such as organized use of shelters. And after the planes left everyone would recommence work and repairs – whether in the fields or the factories. We had a slogan "Combat and Construct".' Everyone was regarded as being in uniform, and civilians were kept closely identified with the military in a competitive spirit. 'This was the business of the cultural section of the army.' says Ha Van Lau. 'There was a cultural team that offered dances, singing, music. They organized basketball, volleyball. Teams of athletes would compete against one another.' This interchange not least aided military morale and 'We attached a great deal of importance to it for our fighters.'

'Naturally,' says Ha Van Lau of the bombing, 'it was terrifying. We had to adapt ourselves to a life of war, or we would have been beaten. We would have lost the war.' When the air strikes halted in November 1968 the North for a long

time remained on full alert and remained suspicious. In the summer of 1969, at the time when the formal Paris peace talks seemed to the Americans frustratingly unproductive, the author met Ha Van Lau in Hanoi and was then told that US reconnaissance flights over the North had increased from 600 in November 1968 to 800 in April 1969, 1300 in May and 1450 in August. In claiming this, Hanoi took the position that President Nixon was not intending to implement Johnson's peace program. Hanoi then wanted to document the extent of the bombing and North Vietnamese resistance to it. The author, as correspondent for the Canadian Broadcasting Corporation, was invited to produce the first film documentary on the devastated areas in the 'hope' that it might have 'an impact on your American neighbors'. What followed was a journey through a wasteland extending down Highway 1 toward the Partition Line.

On the map the distance was 250 miles, once a journey of only four or five hours. But travel time was logged at four days. The awesome bomb craters along the 'highway' interlocked almost end to end, negotiable only by jeep. There was just a very rough route stitched from broken-down rock, thousands of loose planks and nerve-wracking bamboo platforms bridging the craters and canals. Wrecked vehicles and twisted rail lines littered the entire route, with rusted metal rising in grotesque shapes from the adjacent rice-lands. With side visits, three weeks was spent covering 1000 miles of five of the worst hit provinces – residing in 'guest centers' which were straw-roof huts near former towns. Often it was a case of searching for places which on the old maps had once existed.

Simply stated, urban civilization had been erased in a region containing one-third or about six million of the North's population. Statistics from the French era showed that five per cent or 300,000 of these people had been town and city dwellers (most of the US estimate of 182,000 civilian dead had been killed in this region). Whatever the French had built in eighty years of occupation, and whatever the North had achieved in fifteen years of independence, had been wiped out.

The journey showed that five cities had been leveled. These, traveling south, were the cities of

Phu Ly, Ninh Binh, Thanh Hoa, Vinh and Ha Tinh, each formerly with populations between 10,000 and 30,000. The North's third largest city, Nam Dinh – population 90,000 – was largely destroyed but at least recognizable. Another eighteen destroyed centers were classified as towns – but though the place names checked on the map, it was now impossible to know what these collections of overgrown debris had once been like. Traffic still passed through, peasants still marketed their produce along the highway, but there remained only ghost towns from the nightmare of Rolling Thunder. Across the whole landscape, journeying far from the highway, not a single habitable brick edifice could be seen: the schools, hospitals, and administrative buildings that had certainly once existed were now, like the factories, just so many heaps of rubble.

At Phu Ly, only thirty-five miles south of Hanoi, local officials said the city had been leveled in eight successive days between 1 and 9 October 1966. It had been a cross-roads food marketing town of 10,000. Ninh Binh, a provincial capital sixty miles south, was described in an old guide book as a cotton and coffee trading center of 25,000 people – and the main center of Roman Catholicism in the North. The cathedral spire, but little else, had somehow survived.

Thanh Hoa, capital of the most populous southern province eighty miles from Hanoi, had been a major food distribution center, also trading in cotton, jute and timber. It was a total ruin; to find a place to sleep one traveled ten miles to a bamboo cluster of 'provincial offices' hidden in the hills. Vinh, 160 miles from Hanoi in Nghe-an province where Ho Chi Minh was born, once served a fertile and densely populated plain of 1.5 million people. Formerly a city of 30,000, Vinh had the only immediately obvious military installations: a central rail terminal and airport. It had been built in 1954 – the year of the Geneva 'Accords'; now it was at waist-level. Year after year, said district officials, the bombers had kept bombing the rubble. At Ha Tinh, provincial capital on the 18th Parallel 250 miles from Hanoi, the local mayor-without-a-city produced files citing that between 1965 and 1968 this province of 800,000 people had been bombed 25,529 times. This would equal one air strike every ninety minutes for some 1500 days. In the first raid, March 1965, it was claimed that Ha Tinh's municipal hospital containing 170 people and its secondary school filled with 750 students had been simultaneously destroyed. This was called 'a conscious massacre'. The hospital's Red Cross markings were still discernible amid the ruins.

After the account of this journey had appeared in a score of major world newspapers, from the *New York Times* to the London *Sunday Times*, and after the American NBC network had televised the film, the US Defense Department insisted that only military targets had been bombed – though it knew otherwise from Defense Secretary McNamara's own findings.

Perhaps there is a certain detachment about this long ago death-list of places which few people outside the North had ever heard of. But the systematic silencing of these places needs to be recorded. There were some outside witnesses at the time – but not much questioning. An equally important part of the record was the degree of human resilience and defiance. Somehow, the

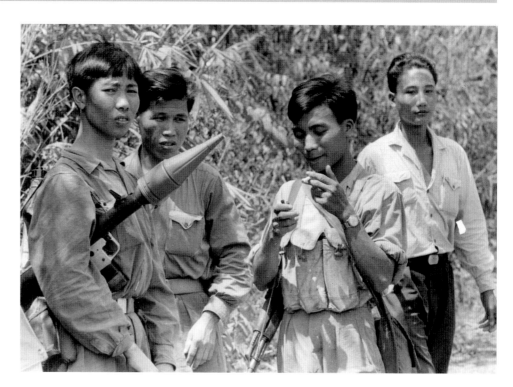

Above: May 1971—Viet Cong soldiers armed with automatic rifles and a B-40 antitank rocket launcher hold an outpost in Communist-controlled Binh Long province north of Saigon.

Above: May 6, 1967—Col. Gordon Albert Larson is escorted to the International Club in Hanoi to meet with journalists one day after his F-105 Thunderchief fighter/bomber was shot down over North Vietnam.

Above: October 1969— Rifles stand nearby as North Vietnamese farmers harvest their rice crop.

Left: President of North Vietnam Ho Chi Minh is surrounded by North Vietnamese children at his official residence in Hanoi to celebrate International Children's Day.

urban people had adjusted to life in the hills and caves: there was the strange yet moving sight of the old city people still treading their textile looms in bamboo groves, or welding bayonets in dim caverns where their ancestors had plotted against the armies of Kublai Khan. The hardest part was continuing this existence in the months after the bombing halt. At first only the village structure was renewed.

Beyond the 18th Parallel, where the people had gone underground, the 'new' village of Cam Binh seemed typical. It was a cluster of thirty hamlets straddling Highway 1. Cam Binh – 'Precious Peace' – had reputedly taken 6756 direct hits during the bombing years, with some 200 villagers killed. But it was said that within a week of the bombing halt Cam Binh was 'its old self' – 570 neat households of latticed-bamboo and woven straw. There were still the earthen mounds – like

blisters on the earth's skin – which led to deep shelters and tunnels, and when the daily practice alert sounded thirty little communities suddenly melted into the ground.

In the fields, anti-aircraft guns still poked skyward from clumps of bushes, and in the rice-paddies young women still wore pigtails to keep their tresses free of their rifles. In one hamlet four stretcher-bearers were carrying a maternity case to the village clinic, gouged under the ground. At the afternoon gong, adults replaced the children in mud-walled classrooms for lessons in midwifery or animal husbandry – or for political lectures. Outside, the older children were taking PT and rifle lessons from locally based army instructors. The largest hut was at the edge of a bomb crater filled with water lilies: this was Cam Binh's 'museum' – and in it were bits and pieces of US planes along with tools said to date from 2000 BC. The

forty-three months of Rolling Thunder were only a heartbeat in as many centuries.

This was the uncompromising nature of North Vietnam before and after the bombing. The foreign press and diplomats, including the British and French who maintained consuls in Hanoi, had provided clear evidence that the bombing was a strategic failure. It had not broken the war capability, nor the morale, of the North. And, among many others in US intelligence, Brian Jenkins continued to present analyses suggesting that whatever the pressures, Hanoi's goals and unity would not change. After two years on the Long Range Planning Task Group at military headquarters in Saigon, Jenkins became a consultant for the Rand Corporation. From 1969 he was commissioned by the State Department to prepare numerous war scenarios.

Though both the Johnson and Nixon administrations came to accept that the bombing would not end the war, there remained the belief that Hanoi's ageing leadership must eventually tire and seek a political settlement. US Presidents were conditioned by their four-year terms whereas, says Jenkins, Hanoi's leaders thought in half centuries: 'That leadership by virtue of its tenure, and the rigid authoritarian structure, was a very, very stable leadership. I hadn't seen anything to indicate at any time, even at the height of the bombing, that there was any threat to the stability of that leadership. There may have been discussion and debate as to tactics, methods, timing, but as to the pursuit of the contest: that was a given which those members shared.'

The contest began to seem like a re-run. On 22 February 1969, a month after President Nixon's inauguration, a hundred towns and cities in the South came under prolonged assault in an echo of Tet a year earlier. In this latest offensive 1140 Americans died. Nixon then took the first step in the old scenario for extended war. He approved B-52 strikes against North Vietnamese 'sanctuaries' inside Cambodia – and like Johnson's B-52 bombing in Laos this was to be kept top secret. As with the bombing of the North, the method was to be 'surgical' – and with the code-name Operation Menu it sounded like a variant of the White House target luncheons. A suspected North Vietnamese base area designated 'Breakfast' was struck first. Washington then paused for Hanoi's reaction before directing the bombers at 'Lunch', 'Snack', 'Dinner', 'Dessert' and 'Supper'. There was never any response.

At the Paris 'negotiations' it had taken seven months just to resolve the seating arrangements (so that the Saigon and NLF delegations could avoid face-to-face recognition and discussion), and the formal weekly talks had become a marathon in name-calling. Henry Cabot Lodge had re-emerged once more as chief US negotiator – and while the B-52s secretly attacked the menu, Lodge secretly took tea with his Hanoi counterpart eleven times. The answer was always the same: the US had first to withdraw militarily, and the two Vietnams would then negotiate a political settlement. Nixon's celebrated trouble-shooter, National Security Advisor Henry Kissinger, now privately appealed to Moscow (then providing North Vietnam with one billion dollars a year in aid) only to be told that the Soviet Union could not 'deliver' an independent Socialist republic. Asked to define Moscow's influence in Hanoi, a Soviet diplomat said 'There is absolutely none.'

In mid-May, Kissinger took the first positive step towards a political settlement, proposing mutual troop withdrawal phased over twelve months, an early release of prisoners, an internationally supervised cease-fire and new elections with 'all parties agreeing to observe the Geneva Accords' disregarded fifteen years earlier. Kissinger's formula allowed for Communist forces to withdraw to base camps, a concession which foreshadowed the eventual cease-fire in-place settlement. Hanoi did not react.

As American historian Gareth Porter analyses it, Kissinger's package amounted to 'a proposal to freeze the situation in the countryside' at a time when the North Vietnamese had anyhow decided 'to pull back from the battlefield in terms of major offensive operations. So it was a period when the North Vietnamese were essentially playing for time; they would wait for the moment when they would throw their main forces into the battle again.'

North Vietnam's political re-evaluation became apparent in June, when an ailing President Ho Chi Minh summoned Southern guerrilla leaders to Hanoi. Ho now recognized them as a separate government – and the NLF became the PRG or Provisional Revolutionary Government. It signalled a period of military retrenchment in which the North was to rebuild from the debris of the bombing. But though perhaps playing for time, Ho Chi Minh – like Kissinger – had provided the essential structure of the settlement that would come four years later.

One of America's most respected analysts on North Vietnamese affairs, David Elliot of the Rand Corporation, wrote in *North Vietnam since Ho* that the formation of the PRG 'marked a major shift in the diplomatic strategy of the Vietnamese Communists. This move ultimately led to the promulgation of a concept of "two administrations, two armed forces, and two zones of control" that provided the political basis of the peace agreements in Paris, 1973.' Elliot noted that 'along with the formulation of the PRG, there were efforts to stabilize and ultimately scale down the relatively high level of warfare in the south'.

Only one month later, President Ho Chi Minh responded positively to a private letter from President Nixon. In yet another twist of the war, the exchange of letters had been arranged through the man whose mission it had once been to keep the Americans out of Vietnam, former Major Jean Sainteny. In his letter, Nixon proposed secret peace talks between Henry Kissinger and Hanoi's senior negotiator, Politburo member Le Duc Tho. Ho agreed, and on 4 August 1969, the first meeting took place in Sainteny's Paris apartment. Then on 3 September, aged seventy-nine, Ho Chi Minh died of a heart attack.

He had founded the Democratic Republic of Vietnam and led it for twenty-four years. Now, while the Western press speculated on the rivalry and disunity that might result, the North Vietnamese in fact drew closer in their grief. As Ho's body lay in state at Hanoi's Ba Dinh Hall, millions queued to pay homage. The men wore white smocks or jackets, and the traditional *ao dais* of the women were all white – the Vietnamese color for mourning. This line of white stretched to the city limits until it was finally turned away.

As the mourners left the bier none, it seemed, could lift their eyes from the ground. Hundreds fainted, suddenly collapsing in the exiting queue; others fell in a paroxysm so violent that it took the strength of several people to restrain or remove them. The author – the only visiting Western journalist in Hanoi at that time – reported: 'It is both very moving and very disturbing to see this. People act as if entranced. It is more than just a people's sorrow: almost a people possessed. There can be no doubt that if called upon every single one of Ho Chi Minh's people will fight all the fiercer.' (As some measure of America's need to know the CBS Cronkite newscast ran the report as a seven-minute lead item actually uninterrupted by commercials.)

The funeral oration took place on 9 September at 7.00 am under a 107 degree sun. In the square the sobbing of 100,000 people was mercifully drowned out by military bands, whose finale was a march called 'Liberate South Vietnam'. On a make-shift dais, the site where Ho Chi Minh would eventually lie embalmed in a Leninesque mausoleum, Prime Minister Pham Van Dong stood at the center of foreign dignitaries but was at times doubled over, weeping uncontrollably. Premier Kosygin represented the Soviet Union. China had sent only a vice-premier, Li Tien-Nien – evidence of Peking's displeasure with the nation that the US perceived as an instrument of Sino-Soviet expansionism. Kosygin and Li did not once exchange greetings or even a glance.

After the eulogy, the First Secretary of the [Lao Dong Workers] Party, Le Duan, read from a document – also printed in English – titled 'Will of Ho Chi Minh'. It reproduced his written words, dated four months earlier, 10 May 1969. In the English translation of the author's copy, it says: 'First I will speak about the Party. *Unity* is an extremely precious tradition of our Party and people. All comrades, from the Central Committee down to the cell, must preserve unity of mind as the apple of their eyes.' The final words were Ho's last poem:

> Our rivers, our mountains, our men
> will always remain;
> The Yanks defeated,
> we will build our country
> ten times more beautiful.

As a measure of what Ho meant to the Vietnamese, one of the Saigon leaders, former Vice-President Nguyen Cao Ky, who fought

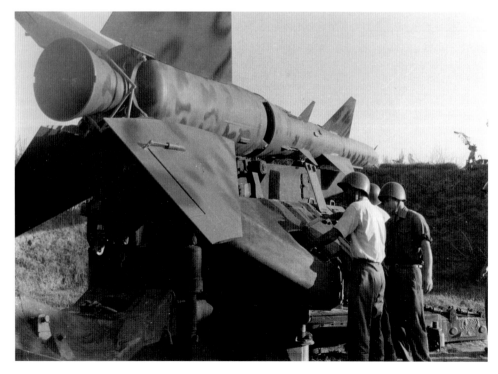

Above: July 1967—A camouflaged two-stage antiaircraft missile is readied at a site in North Vietnam.

against him had this unqualified tribute years after the defeat: 'He led the fight against the French and foreign domination. When I was young – and I don't think only myself but the majority of Vietnamese – at that time we considered Ho Chi Minh a great patriot. I myself had a great admiration for him.'

But in the month Ho died the Ky-Thieu Saigon government publicly rejected Kissinger's peace formula. 'We will not agree to a cease-fire', Thieu said, 'without first arranging that which will follow it' – meaning prior agreement on the political future. From this point on, Saigon's intransigence as much as Hanoi's kept America at war. The White House, noting 'substantial decline in infiltration', had already announced current withdrawal of 60,000 American troops. President Nixon was committed to 'Vietnamization' or the principle that the South would have to stand or fall on its own merits after a cease-fire. Unlike Saigon, Washington needed only a military pact to validate US withdrawal. But to get that pact in time Nixon was now prepared to escalate the war.

Operation Menu continued; the old plans for invading Cambodia and Laos were redrawn and readied, and in a veiled warning of a bombing resumption Nixon that same month declared that if peace came it would be because 'Americans, when it really counted, did not buckle and run away, but stood fast so that the enemy knew that it had no choice but to negotiate'. In fact the US still hardly knew the enemy it had opposed or fought for almost twenty-five years. In Hanoi, Chairman of the National Assembly Truong Chinh was saying: 'Our enemies fancy that after President Ho Chi Minh's death we will be bewildered and divided. But they are grossly mistaken.'

'Looking back at the war,' says former intelligence chief General Edward Lansdale, 'it strikes me as very odd that we really didn't know any of the leaders on the other side: we meaning not only the American people but probably our leadership in Washington. I have often wondered if any of our Presidents knew the names of more than two or three members of the Politburo that directed the war council. They might have known [General Vo Nguyen] Giap, but I don't know that any of them knew Le Duan, who laid out the strategy and organized the South's resistance originally.'

And yet Le Duan, born in Quang Tri in the South, was now the guiding voice or 'first among equals'. If Washington had no knowledge of him – or the others – it could have asked the French. Le Duan had spent seven years in French jails, then another decade organizing the Southern guerrilla structure before joining Ho in China in 1940. Prime Minister Pham Van Dong had spent six years in the notorious Con Son island prison – as had Paris negotiator Le Duc Tho. Deputy-Premier Pham Hung and the Party's chief theoretician Truong Chinh had been jailed for almost ten years, and the new father-figure President, Ton Duc Thang, had been imprisoned there for seventeen years. Though General Giap was known at least as a legend, his Defense Deputy, General Van Tien Dung, who would direct the final offensive, was virtually unknown – yet he was prominent at Dien Bien Phu, was Chief of Staff and the only other military member of the Politburo. (After Ho's death the eleven-man Politburo comprised First Secretary of the Party Le Duan, Chairman of the National Assembly Truong Chinh, Prime

Above: August 14, 1969—Ambassador Henry Cabot Lodge, Chief of the U.S. delegation at the Vietnam Peace talks in Paris, arrives at the International conference Center for the 50th session of the discussions.

Minister Pham Van Dong, Senior Deputy-Premier Pham Hung, Defense Minister General Vo Nguyen Giap, Military Affairs Liaison Le Duc Tho, Foreign Affairs Minister Nguyen Duy Trinh, Chairman of the State Planning Commission Le Thanh Nghi, Senior Vice-Chairman of the National Assembly Hoang Van Hoan, Public Security Minister Tran Quoc Hoan and Army Chief of Staff General Van Tien Dung.)

Ho Chi Minh had once calculated that the thirty-one members of the Central Committee, comprising the various ministries, had spent a cumulative 222 years in prison. As Vietnam's Ambassador to the UN reflects, 'They fought under the same conditions. They were in the same prisons. They'd been together shoulder to shoulder.'

By September 1969 the principal leaders had held their various offices without major change for fifteen years since Partition, had been part of the government for exactly twenty-four years since Independence, and in some instances had worked alongside each other for forty years or more – without any of the dramatic power struggle common to the Communist world. Yet in a fairly typical comment after Ho Chi Minh's death an American South-east Asia correspondent referred to 'rival groups' in Hanoi 'who seek to seize power'.

North Vietnamese expert Brian Jenkins felt that the US press and administration failed to understand the 'dedication' of Hanoi's leaders. 'The pursuit of their goals', he says, 'had taken up their entire adult lives. And the notion that one could change the mind of a number of people sixty and seventy years old in the politburo in Hanoi was a bit far-fetched. There was no changing of mind.' Jenkins thought that North Vietnam's 'Marxism, while legitimate and true to those leaders, was very, very much something put on top of Vietnamese nationalism.

'Ho Chi Minh's boast that they were willing to

fight ten years, twenty years, thirty years or longer if necessary was not an idle boast, but really reflected the Vietnamese perception of history. It made probably little difference to them whether ultimately they would achieve their ends in the year 1969, 1970, 1975 or the year 2000.'

Ho Chi Minh's dying words had been of 'the precious tradition' of unity, and his last orders had been a retrenchment from the battlefield in order to rebuild the North. Now his political heir, Le Duan, began stumping the countryside in support of his own decree that 'leading cadres should visit every locality and every co-operative to assess the situation, recommend bold measures, build a rational economic structure and carry out a redivision of labor'. This even extended to formation of new 'Ho Chi Minh brigades' diverted from military service to reconstruction in the countryside. To achieve this reconstruction Le Duan directed that 'material incentives must be brought into play' as it was now possible to 'put an end to all unnecessary shortages and complications in the daily life of the people'.

As to the war, he said: 'The strategic guideline is to fight a protracted war, gaining strength as one fights.' And he declared that to 'engage in military struggle under unfavorable circumstances is a serious mistake'. The Party Chief was clearly signaling that the North, while conceding nothing further at the negotiations, was pulling back from the war, and, to some extent, from Socialist ideology. In effect he had declared an indefinite truce in which the US could consider total withdrawal, leaving the Saigon government and the new Provisional Revolutionary Government to deal with each other – for however long.

By October 1969, US Secretary of State William Rogers was telling the press that 'combat activity is down' and North Vietnamese infiltration 'is way down – by two thirds this year'. It was possible, Rogers said, that the war might 'just de-escalate until it sort of fades out'. But the State Department was by now a facade. The President and Henry Kissinger alone decided foreign policy – and quite simply, they did not consider an unsigned withdrawal as 'peace with honor'. In 1969, US combat losses in Vietnam totaled 9414, down from 14,592 in 1968. Another 10,000 Americans would die before the paper peace of 1973, and in that period of 'Vietnamization' the South Vietnamese military losses would rise fifty per cent to more than 250,000; civilian casualties – including deaths – would also rise fifty per cent to 1,435,000.

Through 1970 the North Vietnamese continued to turn away from the war as dramatically as the American public. Le Duan had first demonstrated organizational flair and flexibility when he turned around the disastrous land reforms of the 1950s. He was considered highly pragmatic. He had favored the Tet Offensive; militarily it had failed; conditions in the South were 'unfavorable'; now he would wait – the new front line would be the North. The transformation in a few short months was astonishing. In the previous year the total lack of rebuilding was as much a surprise as the totality of the destruction. Now, revisiting some of the same provinces, one saw a uniformity of change.

Everywhere the landscape gleamed with the bright red of brick and tile – new homes, schools, factories standing out like beacons in towns which had seemed permanently extinguished. Evacuees had returned to rebuild their own homes, and a common sight was thousands of galvanized citizens moving acres of stacked bricks. Hundreds of small machine tool and repair plants had once more been dismantled and brought back from the countryside to their original sites. Visibly, the bamboo and straw metropolis left by the bombers was taking new concrete roots. On the co-operatives farmers were being paid cash for excess produce – and the money could be used to buy bricks, or a new life-style, from the State. Consumerism seemed the new danger.

It all seemed to imply intent and belief in a workable peace and a new workers' society, though perhaps it was all just an exercise in keeping busy. Red banners strung everywhere proclaimed one word, 'Vigilance'. And everywhere people fatalistically repeated that 'the bombers would return' – if only because of the reconstruction. In Hanoi, two adjoining posters said it all. One announced that the circus had come to town. The other proclaimed that the bombers would return.

In the North the countryside was rapidly recovering, largely through its own muscle, morale and village traditions. In the ebbing war in the South the US was making an extraordinary $1.7 billion effort at rural renewal, giving everything from food to a nuclear reactor. It was the largest single handout in the history of US aid, but it was no equalizer. And very soon the bombers returned.

'In those times, our people showed unimaginable strength,' Premier Pham Van Dong recalls. 'We were one-minded and united. And we will forever remain such a nation.'

Left: This is the layout for an 'L' ambush in 1967 Vietnam. As troops enter the open end of the 'L' the Viet Cong opens fire. Escape to the right makes soldiers easy targets in the open race paddies; those in the 'L' likewise are trapped.

Above: Diagram shows how a 'U' ambush is sprung. Enemy takes elevated positions on both legs of the U and open fire when opposition troops move in. The Viet Cong prefers this ambush because they are able to fire down on the trapped unit and avoid the possibility of hitting their comrades.

Above: Diagram shows how a Viet Cong 'Open U' ambush is sprung on U.S. and South Vietnamese forces during the 1967 period of the war. Patrols enter between the two legs of the 'U' and the well dug in enemy opens fire with automatic weapons. Special Forces respond by hitting the head of column to break out.

# THE VILLAGE WAR

The shattering of guerrilla strength in the 1968 Tet Offensive coincided with a huge new American aid program which combined the diffuse military and civilian effort under a new agency called CORDS – Civil Operations and Rural Development Support. It was the brainchild of Robert Komer who had taken over the American aid effort in mid-1967.

Pacification had become a catch-all description for the self-interests of a dozen different US agencies, all with their Saigon government counterparts. The results were little more than a shared cliché – 'winning hearts and minds', and with the military in overall control the priority was reflected in a slogan bandied by the Marines: 'Get 'em by the balls and their hearts and minds will follow.' The military attitude was conditioned by South Vietnam's apathetic record, and Komer persuaded Washington to back a single agency that was part of the US MACV command but operationally separate.

Komer realized that pacification had a prolonged and poor history: the French had tried and failed with the 'agrovilles'; the early South Vietnamese 'Strategic Hamlets' – involving forced relocation of villagers from their ancestral lands – had been a disaster, but Komer was convinced that

'The hit teams were going out, arresting a great many people. And the prisons came to overflowing. Well, the hit teams became impatient. They began killing them. Piecemeal.'

– FRANK SNEPP, CIA, SAIGON

the war could only be won politically in the villages and 'there was no way to go but up'.

Pacification was in fact a French colonial term which Saigon and Washington had unwittingly adopted. Komer, having read the French history, was worried that the US might be learning from it too late. 'The French', he says, 'discovered at the end rather than the beginning that pacification should have been a far more important component of their effort that it was. We went through a very similar process, I'm sorry to say.' Komer considered that intensive pacification could have preceded – and perhaps prevented – US combat: 'Military operations tend to alienate people', says Komer, 'as fast as the pacification operations are trying to help them.'

Robert Komer was a former CIA man who had served both the Kennedy and Johnson administrations as an aid expert. He was known as a nonconformist – at times outrageously outspoken, a mixture of ebullience and abrasiveness. When first given the job of monitoring the US aid effort from Washington his swingeing cables to Saigon were called 'Komergrams'. In Vietnam his nickname was 'Blowtorch' – and he was scorchingly critical of how the Saigon government ran the countryside.

Above: April 1969—A young woman stares into a mass grave being uncovered that contained victims of a Viet Cong massacre in a village east of Hue.

Left: September 1969—A young member of a self-defense unit sits in a guard tower on the perimeter of his village near Hue. The South Vietnamese government created the million-member self-defense units after the 1968 Tet offensive.

'Only a shadow structure existed out there,' recalls Komer. 'The Vietnamese local military forces – so-called Regional and Popular forces – were extremely weak. The Vietnamese police were a farce – they were called the "White Mice". The economy was in a shambles. The enemy was very shrewdly pursuing a policy of terrorism and assassination against village chiefs and the few public works engineers and schoolteachers that we could get to go out into the countryside. It was very difficult to restore security.'

Komer had faith in those individual South Vietnamese who did not hide the difficulties. One was Colonel Nguyen Be, the deputy province chief in charge of pacification in the central Binh Dinh region. Though the guerrillas initially used terror to gain control of a village, Colonel Be kept arguing that counter-terror was by itself no answer. 'The Viet Cong', he says, 'were often from the same hamlet. Most of the time they lived among the people; they shared the misery of the people, they shared all the concern of the people in their area so they were really protected by the people and by their information. They were not separate from the people.'

As Colonel Be summarized the problem for Komer, 'Our police appointed to the villages are afraid to go near them'; the ARVN would patrol only during the daytime, and the old solution of relocating or amalgamating the villages had just increased sympathy for the guerrillas. For a thousand years the village units and their elected councils had kept intact; their philosophy of Buddhist and Confucian thought held that loyalty was to the family and immediate community – and it was the guerrillas who lived among them who therefore had the people's loyalty, said Colonel Be. He wanted civilian teams skilled in defense and social work who would be assigned to live in the villages. 'They were to be dressed in black pajamas just like the guerrillas,' recalls Komer. 'They were a very innovative effort.'

The CIA took on the financing and training of fifty-nine-man teams, thirty of them self-defense experts and the other twenty-nine specialists in every kind of village need. 'My plan', says Colonel Be, 'was to demonstrate to the people that we were not trying to rule them, but trying to aid the basic social and political institutions of the village.'

But this South Vietnamese effort began badly. 'The difficulty', says Komer, 'was recruiting in the countryside where the Viet Cong either drew off or shanghaied most of the young people. This meant we had to recruit very largely in the cities, so a bunch of city boys were put in black pajamas and sent out to protect the hamlets against the Viet Cong. It wasn't all that successful.'

Komer had a 1.7 billion dollar economic aid fund he could draw on. If only he could reach the villages, his hoard of goodwill might effectively disarm the guerrillas. He had ready thousands of tons of multi-crop miracle rice, thousands of tons of soya-bean seeds, thousands of tons of fertilizer, thousands of gallons of cooking oil, tons of pharmaceuticals, acres and acres piled high with cement mixture and corrugated tin, and great warehouses full of wonders from tooth-brushes to dentist drills, sewing kits to the latest in plumbing – and, like a promise of a peaceful future, South Vietnam would even get an atomic reactor.

And there it all sat – the ammunition for 'the other war' that was to captivate eighteen million

Above: January 1969— U.S. soldiers of the 2nd Brigade, 9th Infantry Division, move through coconut groves in the Mekong Delta on a patrol to assess B-52 bomb damage to the enemy-held groves of Kien Hoa province.

Left: June 9, 1969—A boy holds his younger brother and studies the remains of what was their village, Thanh Son, about 45 miles northwest of Saigon. It was destroyed after civilians were driven out by the Viet Cong.

hearts and minds. But the reality in the countryside by late 1967 was two rampaging military forces which had already left some 800,000 refugees. Komer, like so many who had joined the CIA or Defense, was from the Harvard School of Business. And though he seemed to have the same dispassionate statistical approach, he differed in two respects – he believed that so many tons of bulgar wheat rather than bombs would do it, and he also believed there would be no early harvest. Komer thought it was 'foolish' to expect 'yet another pacification to achieve things in two or three years, and we started from the beginning with the idea that this had to be a painstaking, long-term effort'.

But Komer also sensed American impatience – and it began to influence his thinking: 'How can you have a schools program when the VC come in and blow down your schools as soon as you build them and assassinate your teachers? How can you provide miracle rice when the VC come and steal the crop? How can you provide the civil economy and improve the standard of living when the VC are blowing up the roads and bridges?' Komer found himself obliged to concur with the opposition approach: 'You see, the security dimension had to come first.'

But Komer had still tried an alternate to military measures. He had launched *Chieu Hoi* – an open-arms amnesty program pledging that defectors would be integrated without reprisal into the South Vietnamese economy. Presaging the methods that Saigon preferred and would adopt, Komer recalls that the amnesty program was 'very strongly opposed by ARVN who said, "These fellows are rebels – and they ought to be put in jail, if not shot." ' Komer went ahead and 'we distributed millions of leaflets by airplane and artillery shells, saying: "We will be happy to welcome you, feed you well, not put you in prison." The program was very successful.' It was claimed that 27,178 guerrillas had 'rallied' to the Saigon side by early 1968. But the Tet Offensive then shattered not just the cities but Komer's long-term plans for the villages.

'It was apparent to me', says Komer, 'that Washington, indeed the American people, were turning off the Vietnam war; therefore I switched my emphasis to try for enough short-term results to convince the people back home that we were really accomplishing something – and that turned out to be very difficult.' In the wake of Tet, Komer saw in the guerrilla rout his first chance literally to gain ground. He revised his plans to concentrate all his resources on the security dimension. He intended it to last three months and he called it APC – Accelerated Pacification Campaign: 'The campaign was launched and it proved like nothing else up to that point. The enemy had exhausted his rural cadres to a great extent.'

Prior to Tet, Komer had dismissed Saigon's claims of rural progress as 'wildly exaggerated'. His own evaluation system showed that the guerrillas then still held sixty per cent of the 16,000 hamlets and villages in the South. Now 'we reoccupied much of the countryside very quickly and then moved on to expand our daytime control to most of the country'. But after the initial use of US and ARVN combat units the village control rested (and there is no better word) with the Regional and Popular Forces – which Komer had called 'weak' – and the police which were a 'farce'. Under the 'corrupt' district chiefs, these forces would now

Above: February 28, 1969—Information officer Maj. Robin Luketina of Fayetteville, N.C., carries a Vietnamese baby after pulling her from the ruins of a house destroyed between lines of North Vietnamese troops and South Vietnamese Rangers on the edge of Bien Hoa.

Right: January 1969—Portrait of a woman who has lived the hard years of a long war.

have a large role in the exaggerated information which – for three years instead of three months – fed the security drag-net called Phoenix.

Komer had conceived the plan which came to be known as Phoenix as an integral part of pacification – but it was only activated after Tet when Komer left Vietnam. By then he saw that the fundamental dilemma remained: even if the villages were secured, 'You can't tell a Viet Cong from a Vietnamese nationalist when you see him walking down the village street.' How to ensure that all those soya-bean seedlings and sewing machines got to the right people? Identification cards were Komer's answer – and soon, he says, 'We had a whole set of computer banks, where you could check ID cards against a central file in Saigon.' When Komer left, this program which eventually contained some eight million names was itself nameless.

Komer's successor was William Colby, the former Saigon CIA chief, who returned in 1968 after several years absence. He explained that the pur-

January 1969—A bullet-scarred wall is the backdrop for this picture of a young child in Cholon playing with his toy rifle. The shattered wall is a reminder of the fighting that gripped Saigon and Vietnam the previous year during the Tet Offensive.

the countryside in the night without any concern for my safety'. By the end of 1971 only three per cent of the South's population was officially considered to be living in 'contested' areas.

Colby persuaded President Thieu on a measure which the paranoid Diem had opposed; arming the villagers. Both the local militia and the regular army now belatedly received modern M-16 rifles. Through 1969 to 1971 the US pacification effort emphasized the security aspect, while President Thieu actively promoted the return of village elections and land reform. Thieu was spurred by the need for a popular base as US troops withdrew, and the American pacification effort was now shaped by the same reasoning: they had not much time and a new Communist offensive was considered inevitable. The parallel retrenchment and reconstruction in the North was ignored or considered insignificant, and the priority of eliminating the Communist infrastructure in the South proceeded without close examination.

Another priority, as Colby saw it, was to strengthen the forces directly commanded by the province chiefs. Previously 'the province center was like a beleaguered castle in the middle of a great sea of guerrilla warfare'. Now, before such warfare renewed, Colby felt it opportune to enlarge the PRU – the Provincial Reconnaissance Units – better known to the US Special Forces who worked with them as 'the hit teams'.

On the one hand the pacification effort was supposedly racing the Communist clock, on the other hand its organizers were amazed – even puzzled – by its rapid, almost unopposed progress. By mid-1970, the Saigon government was claiming that ninety-one per cent of the hamlets were 'secure' and had elected local councils and chiefs. President Thieu then began a gradual but major program of land grants to tenant farmers called 'Land to the Tiller'. However, some of the statistics had the press referring to the pacification people as the 'New Optimists'. Saigon was saying that the continuing *Chieu Hoi* amnesty program had brought in 79,000 guerrilla defectors from 1969 to 1970 (Colby later estimated 17,000), while cynics were suggesting that perhaps this was the figure incarcerated under Phoenix.

Once again, the progress reports did not tally: Tet had 'decimated' the guerrilla ranks, but now the number said to have given up was greater than the number which took part in the Tet Offensive, and still the Phoenix squads were packing the jails with suspects – that is if they bothered with arrests at all. Something was wrong, and President Thieu would eventually wash his hands of it, saying that he did not have overall control of pacification and all it required was American money 'to do it ourselves'.

Critics would say that the CIA-financed Vietnamese special forces, while using Phoenix to rule by fear, simply provided their paymaster with what they presumed it wanted – 'suspects'. Having itself long criticized the US military for rough-shod tactics and reliance on body counts, the CIA was now – in the kindest interpretation – duped into repeating the error. William Colby responds that the very reason for the new centralized, computerized intelligence operation was to correct the previous 'sloppy basis of information'. It began as a logical effort to 'refine our knowledge' of the guerrilla infrastructure: 'not just the military units, but what kinds of tax collecting, what kind of prosely-

pose of the program was 'to centralize the central intelligence concept', for, as with earlier aid effort, there were numerous American and South Vietnamese intelligence agencies 'running around after each other'. In essence, the CIA wanted direct control but did not want direct association. 'We couldn't think of another name,' says Colby, 'so we called it Phoenix.' South Vietnam's Phoenix, many critics would feel, was the reverse of the mythical bird that rose from the ashes.

Colby had been a strong advocate of pacification all along, beginning it at the start of the decade with the co-operation of President Diem – whose assassination Colby regarded as the greatest mistake of the war, leading to US military intervention. When the accelerated pacification program became fully operational in November 1968,

coinciding with the bombing halt in the North, Colby was doubly pleased: 'I never thought the bombing had much to do with the real issue'; the US wasted 'time, effort and resources in the North better used organizing the villages in their own protection.' The United States, felt Colby, had belatedly learned from its mistakes: Vietnam was 'not an affair for soldiers'; 'Americans finally understood the nature of the war as existing primarily at the village level. And we began to work on it.'

The social transformation in the South now seemed as rapid as in the North, suggesting that the two Vietnams could negotiate from political as well as military strength. In 1968 Colby recalls going to provincial towns 'ringed with barbed wire and tanks'. By early 1971 'I could drive through tizing, what their terrorist programs were and all the rest. To put agents into it, to get defectors out of it, and to interrogate prisoners from it.'

Simply put, the infrastructure meant the upper echelon of the political cadres and party members. These were estimated to number two per cent of the population, or some 360,000 Communist organizers and supporters who were well cloaked as members of teacher or farmer associations.

'Two per cent of the population is a lot of folks – and when you grab that many bodies, you grab a lot of the wrong bodies,' says Barton Osborne who helped direct counter-terror operations at Danang, the second largest city. Osborne was attached to a US army intelligence unit in 1967 to 1968 before the operations were amalgamated, so he saw only the start of Phoenix. But he states that 'by late 1968 the Phoenix program was not serving any legitimate function that I know of, but rather had gone so wrong that it was the vehicle by which we were getting into a bad genocide program'.

Above: February 26, 1969—An American advisor and a Signal Corps photographer drag a wounded North Vietnamese soldier with them as they withdraw from a Bien Hoa suburb.

Left: February 27, 1969—North Vietnamese prisoners are led away while South Vietnamese rangers assault enemy positions in the ruins of Gia Kien, a suburb of Bien Hoa. A Communist attack on the Bien Hoa airbase was routed by air strikes.

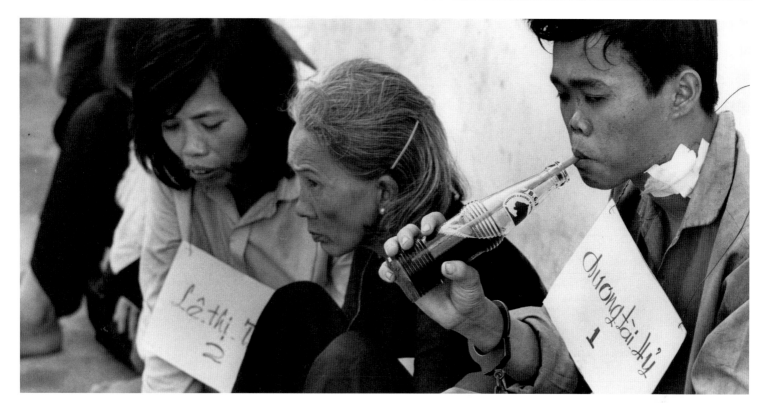

Above: September 12, 1968—A three-member Viet Cong propaganda team sit on the sidewalk after their arrest by police in Saigon. They operated in Cholon, Chinese section of the capital.

Right: September 17, 1968—North Vietnamese prisoners, including three women, are detained after a sweep of an island southeast of Hue. Two of the women were reported to be medics; the third was a tax collector.

Colby rejects this accusation, saying Osborne was not present during the 'more intelligent approach' of Phoenix. Colby says he set up a system of 'three different reports' to distinguish whether a suspect was 'a leader, a cadre, or a simple follower. And if he was the third – forget it, we're not interested in him.' But Jeff Stein who succeeded Barton Osborne at Danang states, 'I certainly would have heard about some of those correctional measures and none was taken.' He too says it was mostly the ordinary Vietnamese who suffered under Phoenix.

Phoenix offices were set up at the provincial and district levels, largely staffed from the participating Vietnamese agencies. But Osborne and Stein say an American advisor was assigned to each Phoenix sector, and that extreme torture was routine. Stein says he learned of 'the insertion of a six-inch dowel into the circular canal of one of my detainee's ears and the tapping through to the brain until the person died; the starving to death of a Vietnamese woman suspected of being part of the local political education cabinet'.

Colby says he told the Phoenix operatives, 'If you want to get good information, you'd better get good methods. Torture and so forth – and I saw the Nazis do this in World War II – gives you bad information because the people will either give you something to make you go away and stop and satisfy you with what you want to hear, rather than really what is true, or they will very courageously die.' The American pacification chief says he

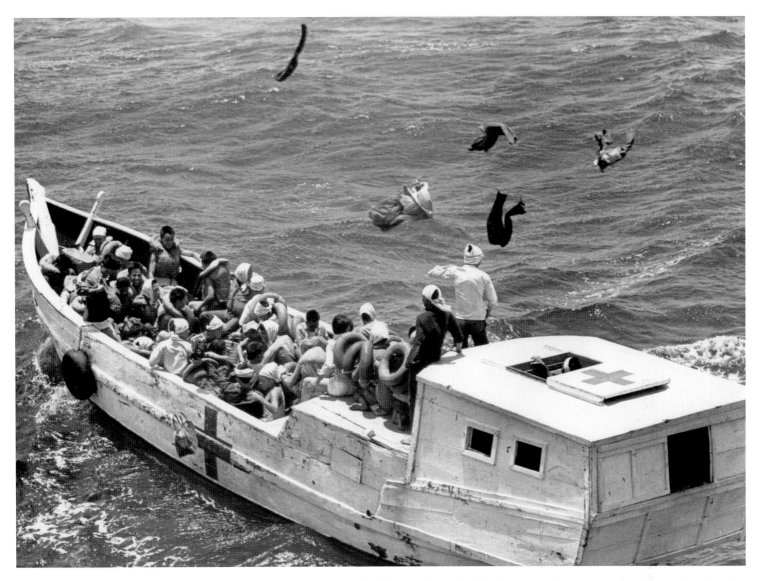

July 12, 1970—Defiantly tossing their prison clothes and belongings overboard, members of a group of 24 fishermen and 62 war-disabled North Vietnamese soldiers return to North Vietnam in a Red Cross boat. They had just been released by South Vietnam in the largest repatriation of the war to date.

stressed that 'as a practical, as well as a moral reason' it was wrong to 'kill someone who should not have been killed – who was not properly identified; you'd make the community furious.'

A senior CIA agent, Frank Snepp, insists that there was 'never a firm definition' of a Communist operative, and that mostly the innocent died. Snepp was an undercover agent at the US Embassy and was its principal analyst of North Vietnamese affairs from 1969 to 1971 – the entire Phoenix period. His duties took him regularly to the National Interrogation Center in Saigon. Snepp, who would later resign from the CIA and become one of its severest critics, describes Phoenix as 'jerry-built' and says 'the CIA was the principal mover. We funded most of the Phoenix operations; we put together some of the hit teams, which were called the PRU teams, and we also commanded in effect a detached [US] special force of officers who were running these various hit teams.'

Snepp charges that 'because of the lax definition, the PRU – the hit teams – were going out arresting and pulling back to our interrogation centers a great many people. And the prisons came to overflowing. Well the hit teams became impa-

tient, and they decided to take the law as such into their own hands. And instead of bringing the sources in they began killing them. Piecemeal.'

Colby concedes that Pheonix became an instrument of reprisal: 'a lot of very bad things were done on both sides', so that terrorist acts of the mid-1960s led 'the [Saigon] government side to go out and get at the people who were doing this'. But Colby says he set 'an early regulation that Phoenix will not be a program of assassination. And I said further that if any American sees anyone being assassinated under this program he is not to turn away and say "Well that's none of my business – that's just the Vietnamese"; he's to object and he is to report it to me. And I received a few of those reports.'

Snepp says it took a year before he realized what was happening: 'When I first got to Saigon in 1969 I was charged with identifying who the opposition was that we were trying to eliminate through capture or killing. I would put together a list and I would turn it over to Mr Colby's people. He would feed this list out to the strike teams, and they would go to work.'

In late 1970, reviewing statistics on the size of the Communist network, Snepp found that the

figures hardly differed for the past three years: 'Then I looked at the list of the Phoenix program's latest casualty count – and I discovered it ran about 20,000 killed. Quite obviously somebody was being killed, but it wasn't the Viet Cong. And I wrote a memo to Mr Colby and never got an answer. That is the way it was in Saigon at the time. And that is how you became a collaborator in the worst of the terrorist programs, in the most atrocious excesses of the US government.'

As Colby sees it, 'Most of those killed had been killed in the course of military combat. If there was a fight outside the village at night, you went out in the morning and found that people had been killed on both sides. Some on your side, some on the enemy side – one of them the head of the guerrilla force who had been on your list. Now he hadn't been assassinated – he had been killed.' Explains Colby, 'Names on your list were killed in the course of attack. Obviously you'd prefer to capture them, but they were killed.'

Snepp says it did not and could not work like that: generally 'it was impossible to bring out a particular cadre'. Snepp gives this example of the method used: 'Let's say a Mafia chieftain was out to nail one of his opponents, and he knew his

February 1969—North Vietnamese prisoners under the guard of South Vietnamese rangers run past the ruins of a church in Gia Kien, near the Bien Hoa airbase 15 miles north of Saigon. The rangers were counter-attacking after North Vietnamese troops infiltrated the village overnight.

opponent was having dinner in a particular restaurant in New York, so he sent his hit-men in. Now the hit-men go in and they open up with a shotgun. They get the bartender, they get the bartender's son, a waiter, and they also get the opposition figure – the target himself. Well that is basically how the Phoenix program operated, except of course it wasn't a bar or a restaurant – it was a village, and a great many innocent people were killed.

'Now one should add in this context that the hit teams took their leaf from the Communists' own book, and the Communists were perhaps no less brutal or lethal in their particular way.' But, says Snepp, this didn't justify 'the American involvement in Phoenix'. He says that 'enough high ranking cadres were killed as well to make it very difficult for the Communists to continue to operate'. But this meant that 'the Communists finally had to opt for a main force offensive' – which quickly overran South Vietnam.

When the US army intelligence officers Jeff Stein and Barton Osborne returned home they spent two years trying to expose Phoenix. Says

Stein, 'But nobody gave a damn.' Osborne finally got his Congressman to conduct a Senate hearing in late 1971. This was Osborne's sworn testimony in answering Congressman Reid: ' "I never knew in the course of all those operations any detainee to live through interrogation. They all died." Reid: "They all died?" Osborne: "They all died. There was never any reasonable fact that any one of those individuals was in fact co-operating with the Viet Cong. But they all died." '

There were never any figures for the number of suspects imprisoned. Colby, who had then returned to Washington duty, was summoned to testify. He cited figures only for what he called 'members of the enemy apparatus', stating that up to mid-1971 "some 28,000 had been captured, some 20,000 had been killed, and some 17,000 had actually rallied by that time.' The inquiry was brief – and it was the first and last. In Colby's summary, 'I was not able to say that no one had been wrongly killed' but – he concludes – 'the purpose and the effect of the Phoenix program were to bring decency and intelligence to our side of that

battle.' Two years later Colby became Director of the CIA.

Snepp, who stayed on in Saigon, estimates that in the course of Phoenix 'probably thirty thousand people gave their lives'. But only suspected (not confirmed) Communists were counted and 'going into a village to hit a particular cadre, to get that cadre you killed several others'. In Snepp's opinion the real toll was 'impossible to say and Colby should know it'.

The man who reorganized the US aid and intelligence effort comments that in the final offensive 'pacification just absolutely fell apart' along with the South Vietnamese army: 'It just got swept up in the resulting debauch.' The single cause of failure, says CORDS innovator Robert Komer, 'was really the weakness of the South Vietnamese, their inability to pull themselves together, their incompetence, their corruption, their factionalism'. The majority of the villages had been secured, village elections had been restored, generous land reforms implemented, yet it all 'fell apart'. There would be no national spirit of resistance at grass roots, nor among the ARVN troops who were the sons of the 'secured' villagers.

President Nguyen Van Thieu blames the Americans for beginning to withdraw without having really severed Communist roots in the villages. He says Saigon should have had overall control of pacification in the period when it had a chance. 'Pacification could only be conducted by the Vietnamese. The foreigner could never control the people. It is impossible.'

In a concise summary in *The Counter-Insurgency: US Doctrine and Performance*, a CIA analyst and former National Security staffer Douglas S. Blaufarb wrote: 'In the end, the peasant was left to his own resources, with no organization to speak for him above the village level. The government thus failed – despite the economic and development benefits of its programs, despite the increased security in the countryside – to create among the peasantry a strong, positive motivation to engage in the struggle on the official side. It was still, in peasant eyes, a government of "them", remote, arbitrary, and often abusive.'

In the village tug-of-war an unknown number of unknown people had been cut down in the crossfire of Phoenix; an estimated 37,000 had been executed earlier for opposing the guerrillas, and the selective terror was only a relatively minor horror in a decade of random fire-power which had left almost 1.5 million of the villagers dead or injured and another one million homeless by late 1971. The villager had been threatened and cajoled by both sides, had paid taxes and lip allegiance to both sides, had been offered a 'better life' by both sides, but in the end – in the words of America's first intelligence chief in South Vietnam, Edward Lansdale – 'Ninety-nine per cent of the people hoped that the war would go away and leave them alone. That was their deepest sentiment.'

The story of the village war had been first one of missed opportunity in the early 1960s and then one of lost opportunity in the early 1970s. There was a grass-roots potential in pacification for a different or long delayed political outcome and while the two allies would each regard the other as culpable, the final political failure, Phoenix, was a shared one in which each had put its faith in force. With President Nixon's haste for a military solution, pacification became a rushed and rough effort like the unproved 'Vietnamization' which was to quieten an irate American public. In the end Saigon's political authority – to paraphrase Mark Twain – was country-wide but an inch deep.

Perhaps the GIS who fought in the villages can best chronicle those years. Infantry platoon leader Robert Santos, 1967: 'All you represented to them was a force that was in place fighting, killing, saving – it didn't matter: someone was going to die, and you were going to leave.' Special Forces member Ivan Delbyk, 1968: 'One thing stands out in my mind more than anything else. I saw a woman who had just done breast-feeding her child, looking at me with an expression of hate. Pure unadulterated hate. And at that point I knew I was in Vietnam.' Marine Captain Jim Webb, 1969: 'The civilians had this thing washed over them for twenty years by then. You know, we would go through some hamlets and find French coins, which really gave this thing a feeling of *déjà vu*.'

There was also the question, hardly ever addressed, of what the village war did to the GIS. Phoenix operative Jeff Stein, seconded from army intelligence, was concerned that in the general tension and hostility 'atrocities become normal; atrocities are taught to us as being normal'. And Phoenix corrupted the military, he says: 'Example: I would send in a report which would say, one person who was suspected of being Viet Cong, unconfirmed, uncorroborated, should be at this point, co-ordinate, at this time, on this day, and I would find out later that a B-52 strike had hit that spot at that time and wiped out the whole village. That I think is an extreme example of how involved the military machine got in the cutting edge of Phoenix.' Stein sensed that the GIS were becoming 'traumatized one way or another'; so many who had been sent to win hearts and minds were losing their own.

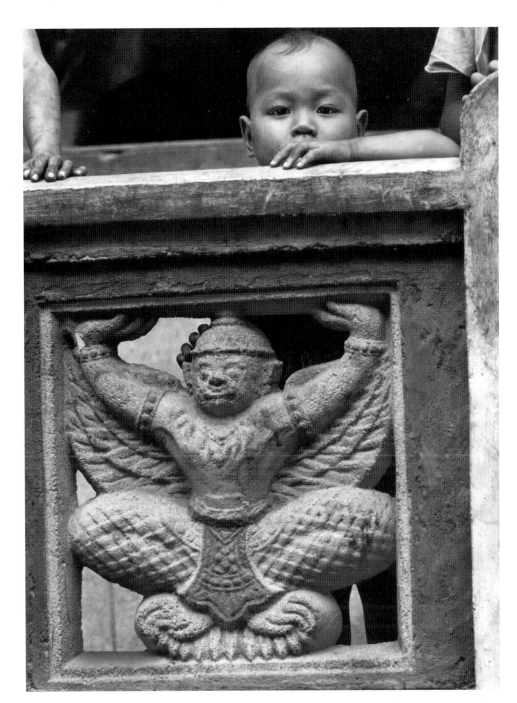

February 1969—A Vietnamese child is just tall enough to be able to peer over the top of a Buddhist pagoda balcony to view troops in a village near the Cambodian border.

At left are dancing girls as recorded by an ancient artist on the wall of Ankor Wat. At right, dancing girls in a nightclub in Saigon.

At left is the face of an elderly man carved centuries ago into the face of a wall at Ankor Wat. At right, a modern day man in South Vietnam.

August 1969—In the 13th century, a thirsty soldier drinks from a dried squash container as depicted in a temple carving at Angkor Wat, Cambodia. In the Vietnam War, a wounded GI with the same thirst drinks from a plastic bottle.

The dead of war, etched on the ancient wall of Angkor Wat in Cambodia, and in the village battlefields of Vietnam.

Top Left: January 1969—The ornate gate to the inner imperial city of Hue still bears the marks of bitter fighting from the Tet offensive. While most of the damage remains, the rubble has been removed.

Top Right: February 7, 1969—Motorized and human-powered vehicles clog one of Saigon's main thoroughfares. At the time, no license was needed for drivers of small motorcycles, but the South Vietnamese government has considered a compulsory license.

Left: February 5, 1969—President Nguyen Van Thieu is greeted by a line of pacification workers during his visit to an outlying village in Quang Tin province. They are part of the South Vietnamese government's pacification plan to win back areas long under Viet Cong control.

Right: 1969—During an ambush by Viet Cong guerrillas, an officer shouts orders as a wounded American soldier awaits evacuation near Saigon. The soldier is attended by a medic as they seek cover beside an armored troop carrier.

Below Left: 1969—GIs of the 9th Infantry Division relax on the long boat trip back to their base camp after a long day trudging through the coconut groves of Kien Hoa province in the Mekong Delta.

Below Right: 1969—Gen. Creighton Williams Abrams was commander of U.S. forces in Vietnam from 1968–1972. He died in 1974.

Above: A U.S. soldier glancing backwards as he crawls toward enemy emplacements in the South Vietnamese jungle. His unit, B Company, 31 Infantry of the American Division, was engaged in ferreting out enemy bunkers and field fortifications in the Hiep Duc Valley, 30 miles south of Danang.

Left: February 26, 1969—With the bodies of enemy soldiers in the foreground, South Vietnamese troops assemble on the steps of a bombed-out church after a furious battle for the village of Gia Kien, near the Bien Hoa airbase.

Below: A woman wails over the plastic-wrapped remains of the body of her husband, one of 47 bodies discovered in a mass grave at Dien Bai. She covered the skull with her conical hat after identifying him through his teeth.

Above: A Cobra helicopter gunship pulls out of a rocket and strafing attack on a Viet Cong position near Cao Lanh in the Mekong Delta of South Vietnam. Large craters from air and artillery strikes cover the area which is largely uninhabited and scattered with abandoned rice paddies and small coconut groves.

Right: A helicopter lifts a 155mm howitzer cannon to the top of a hill during a U.S. Marines–South Vietnam thrust around Khe Sanh, South Vietnam.

Above: January 3, 1969—U.S. Marine artillerymen prepare 105mm howitzers airlifted to a hilltop firebase near the Laotian border earlier in the day. Some 5,000 U.S. and South Vietnamese troops were sweeping the area near the abandoned U.S. combat base at Khe Sanh.

Left: January 12, 1969—An air cavalry trooper moves through a muddy rice paddy during a patrol in Tay Ninh province near the Cambodian border.

Above: January 1969—Gunners protect their ears as Howitzer 105mm fires its shell at Viet Cong and North Vietnamese positions outside a fire base.

Above: February 1, 1969—Troops relax at a U.S. Special Forces bunker, with their target, Superstition Mountain, nearly a mile away in the Mekong Delta. The barren outcrop was a Viet Cong stronghold.

Above: January 1969—Barefooted guerillas rush across a road past a burning Vietnamese army truck in a village. Picture from captured film.

Right: February 25, 1969—Part of Operation Dewey Canyon, U.S. Marines of the 9th Regiment stand around a captured 122mm artillery piece on a jungle hill near the Laotian border in the northwestern corner of South Vietnam. The assault on the artillery position left 15 Marines dead, and about 60 wounded.

Above Left: February 1969—A U.S. soldier of the U.S. 1st Cavalry Division peers through dense-jungle foliage while patrolling War Zone D north of Saigon for Viet Cong base camps and arms caches.

Above Right: February 1969—A U.S. Navy seaman fires twin machine guns into the free fire zone on the shoreline along the Mekong Delta southwest of Saigon. Navy boats would often fire into the area in the event that Viet Cong troops were concealed in the canals of the Delta.

Right: February 27, 1969—South Vietnamese troops use an armored personnel carrier to drag North Vietnamese dead to a mass grave following a North Vietnamese assault on the city of Tam Ky, about 380 miles northeast of Saigon. Allied forces repelled the attack, leaving 168 enemy dead.

Bottom: February 1969—U.S. Army Huey helicopters fly in formation over Vietnam. In 1968 allied helicopters reportedly flew more than six million missions, carrying more than one million men in and out of battle zones and transporting more than one million tons of supplies.

Above: March 1969—A U.S. Marine splashes some water over his head as his patrol crosses a jungle stream south of Khe Sahn. The unit was on a search-and-destroy mission for enemy arms south of the demilitarized zone.

Left: February 1969—A mud-soaked soldier crosses a Mekong Delta waterway.

Above: March 1969—Two U.S. 7th Regiment Marines move carefully across a bombed-out hillside southwest of Danang following an hour-long air strike on enemy positions. The unit counted 11 enemy bodies.

Left: March 1969—Carrying an 81mm mortar, a U.S. Marine leads a patrol about five miles south of the Danang airbase. A combination of Marines and South Vietnamese infantrymen were searching for Viet Cong positions used for rocket attacks on Danang.

March 1969—Staff Sgt. George T. Adkins of Lorain, Ohio, a tank commander, watches as tanks and armored personnel carriers of the 11th Armored Cavalry Regiment advance through jungle about 37 miles north of Saigon.

March 19, 1969—Six 122mm rockets, assembled and ready to fire from bamboo bipods were found five miles due east of Saigon. Maxim range of the rockets would be the middle of the city. The pending attack was detected by a patrol working with night glasses.

Above: March 30, 1969—Montagnard mercenaries probe for caves hiding enemy soldiers on the slopes of Superstition Mountain in the Mekong Delta near the Cambodian border. The mountain stronghold was captured after a three-month battle.

Right: April 4, 1969—A dead north Vietnamese soldier hangs from a gate along Route 1 between Quang Tri and Dong Ha, about six miles south of the demilitarized zone. U.S. troops killed the man during a night ambush, and South Vietnamese soldiers displayed the body with a sign reading, 'Surrender quickly to avoid such a tragic death.'

Above: April 1969—U.S. Marines charge from landing craft on Barrier Island, 20 miles southeast of Danang. The assault, supported by South Vietnamese and Korean troops, was made to restore government control of the 40-square-mile island, long a Viet Cong stronghold.

Left: April 1969—A mortar gunner pulls a round from its casing at a newly-established base west of Saigon, near the Cambodian border. U.S. troops of the 25th Division were digging in and preparing for a possible overnight attack.

Above: April 26, 1969—'Frontier City,' a new patrol base near the Cambodian border, rises out of a rice paddy as men of the 25th Infantry Division work through the day to finish the base in about 14 hours. The base was built to slow Communist infiltration across the border.

Right: April 27, 1969—A soldier watches a huge smoke ring in the blackened sky over the U.S. Air Base at Danang. The blast at a nearby ammunitions dump destroyed several hundreds of tons of ammunition.

Right: April 14, 1969—Like a modern version of the old wagon trains, American armored unit forms a circle for its night perimeter during a patrol northeast of Saigon. Command vehicles are in the center, tanks and armored personnel carriers on the rim.

Below: May 3, 1969—An allied firebase sits in a dried-out rice paddy near the Cambodian border, one of a string of such bases along the border west and northwest of Saigon.

Above: May 1969—A paratrooper of the U.S. 173rd Airborn Brigade uses high-powered binoculars from an observation post on a mountain in the Central Highlands.

Below: May 15, 1969—A line of armored personnel carriers of the U.S. 25th Infantry Division makes its way back to base at dusk after three days of fighting the North Vietnamese near Dau Tieng.

Above: May 18, 1969—A resupply helicopter settles into heavily-fortified Firebase Berchtesgaden overlooking the A Shau Valley. Two weeks earlier the hill was covered with trees, until the 3rd Brigade of the 101st Airborne Division built the firebase in support of Apache Snow, the operation to take Ap Bia Mountain, also known as Hamburger Hill.

Above Right: May 18, 1969—Firebase Berchtesgaden on the eastern edge of the A Shau valley provides fire support for troops sweeping the communist-held valley in Operation Apache Snow, which became known as the battle for Hamburger Hill.

Above: May 19, 1969—A medic of the 101st Airborne Division attempts to save the life of a fellow medic seriously wounded during an assault against the North Vietnamese at Ap Bia Mountain, also known as Hamburger Hill, on the western edge of the A Shau Valley. The wounded medic later died.

Left: May 1969—A U.S. infantryman holds his M-16 out of the water while crossing a waterway in the Mekong Delta.

Above: May 1969—Surrounded by protective sandbags these artillerymen fire their heavy guns to support patrols that encountered Viet Cong outside the perimeter of their firebase.

Right: May 8, 1969—A bomb explosion inside the Saigon central post office claimed four lives with many others injured. An injured man is assisted by police.

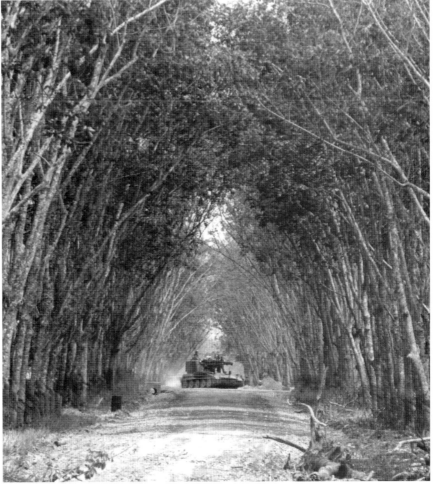

Above: June 1969—A U.S. 9th Infantry Division soldier of the 2nd Battalion, 60th Infantry, takes advantage of a stream in the Mekong Delta of South Vietnam to cool off while cleaning his weapon.

Right: May 5, 1969—An armored vehicle maneuvers among rubber trees on a plantation that serves as the base camp for the 1st Infantry Division about 30 miles from Saigon.

Above: June 27, 1969—An American soldier at Ben Het runs for a bunker as North Vietnamese artillery and mortar hits the camp.

Top Right: June 11, 1969—A U.S. soldier of the 1st Air Cavalry Division carries a captured North Vietnamese rocket launcher and shells after an enemy demolition team tried unsuccessfully to penetrate the brigade base camp at Quan Loi, 60 miles north of Saigon.

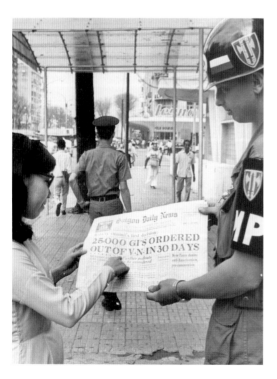

Above: June 1969—U.S. 11th Regiment Marines hold onto a tank as it climbs the dike of a rice paddy 15 miles southwest of Danang. The Marines were searching for enemy bunkers or fortifications among several deserted hamlets.

Left: June 9, 1969—A South Vietnamese woman and a U.S. military policeman pose with a Saigon newspaper announcing President Nixon's decision to withdraw 25,000 troops in 30 days. Servicemen in Saigon expressed little surprise at Nixon's announcement.

Top Left: June 27, 1969—A smoke screen rises from the besieged outpost at Ben Het as U.S. planes prepare to drop supplies by parachute. The smoke blocks enemy observers from directing fire during the supply drop.

Top Right: June 1969—South Vietnamese fill the beach at Vung Tau, a favorite weekend excursion with the route from Saigon safe during daylight hours.

Above: June 2, 1969—U.S. 1st Division Marines gather atop a tank during a patrol near Danang. The tanks often carried coolers of cold soda and better food than the standard-issue C-rations.

Right: June 1969—A U.S. supply convoy slowly makes its way along a crude road near Hue. Ground convoys remained the primary means of transporting large quantities of heavy materials over long distances, while cargo planes and helicopters handled most day-to-day resupply of units in the field.

Top Left: June 24, 1969—A U.S. Special Forces soldier carries a Vietnamese trooper with a shrapnel wound to safety during a North Vietnamese rocket and mortar attack on Ben Het Special Forces camp in South Vietnam.

Top Right: American artillery men take cover behind a truck at the besieged Special Forces camp at Ben Het during a North Vietnamese artillery attack. Their exposed position atop a hill made them a prime target for enemy barrages.

Above: June 28, 1969—Smoke rises after enemy artillery impacts in the Ben Het Special Forces camp in South Vietnam.

Left: June 6, 1969—A helicopter hovers overhead to provide protective fire for ground troops in action near the Special Forces camp of Ben Het.

Top Left: July 6, 1969—Members of the 9th Infantry Division, the first American combat troops ordered home by President Richard M. Nixon, carry their belongings at Dong Tam as they prepare to leave Vietnam.

Top Right: July 30, 1969—President Richard Nixon is surrounded by combat infantrymen of the U.S. 1st Infantry Division at their headquarters at Di An, 12 miles north of Saigon.

Right: July 10, 1969—Tilled land near Danang, with dikes around rice paddies, presents a unique mosaic dotted with the mounds of ancestral graves, but none of the scars of war found in most of South Vietnam.

Above: August 19, 1969—With the help of a spotter, members of a recon platoon of the American Division zero in on snipers hiding in a nearby gully who had been harassing incoming helicopters west of Chu Lai.

Left: July 27, 1969—A Thai soldier fires an M-79 grenade launcher while pursuing a Viet Cong suspect in the jungle east of Saigon. The Thai Panther Division found Viet Cong bunkers and supplies, but made little contact with the enemy.

Above: August 19, 1969—A soldier of the 198th light infantry brigade of the Americal Division crouches atop his bunkered position west of Chu Lai in South Vietnam.

Right: August 26, 1969—U.S. Marines take fire as they charge toward entrenched troops of the North Vietnamese 2nd Division on Hill 441 near Hiep Duc Valley.

Above: August 27, 1969—A U.S. infantryman of the 196th Infantry Brigade, American Division, yells a warning to his unit that he has spotted a sniper ahead during a patrol in the Hiep Duc Valley, 30 miles south of Danang.

Right: September 1969—Members of South Vietnam's self-defense unit use a bamboo structure to guard their village. Gongs are used to sound the alarm.

September 19, 1969—Twelve M-16 rifles capped with helmets represent the 12 American soldiers killed when two helicopters collided, during a memorial service at Tan An, 25 miles west of Saigon, attended by Gen. Creighton Abrams, commander of U.S. Forces in Vietnam, *right.*

September 1969—U.S. Marine helicopter gun ships fire tracer rounds at enemy positions around the Marine headquarters complex near Danang. The complex provided supplies and support for all Marine operations in Vietnam's five northern provinces.

Above: September 7, 1969—A Chinook helicopter delivers a sling of ammunition crates to an artillery position to landing zone Ike, an active patrol and firebase for the 1st Cavalry Division in War Zone C.

Right: September 1969—U.S. soldiers at the 1st Cavalry Division's Phuc Vinh artillery base, 50 miles north of Saigon, read of the recent death of North Vietnamese President Ho Chi Minh. Allied commanders said that operations would be scaled back to match the enemy's activity during the Communists' three-day period of mourning.

**574**

Top Left: September 10, 1969—U.S. 25th Division soldiers at Cu Chi read *Stars and Stripes*, headlining a possible cease-fire during the funeral for North Vietnamese President Ho Chi Minh. U.S. commanders said they would match the level of enemy activity during the period of mourning.

Top Right: September 7, 1969—The U.S. combat base at landing zone Ike sits in the center of War Zone C. The 2nd Battalion, 8th Regiment, 1st Cavalry Division, supported companies operating within range of the base's 105mm howitzers.

Above: October 14, 1969—President Nguyen Van Thieu talks to newsmen outside a pagoda on Ninh Loc island near Hue. He invited U.S. anti-war students to South Vietnam to dissipate misunderstanding about the war.

Left: September 5, 1969—GIs read a Saigon newspaper's story of the death of North Vietnamese President Ho Chi Minh.

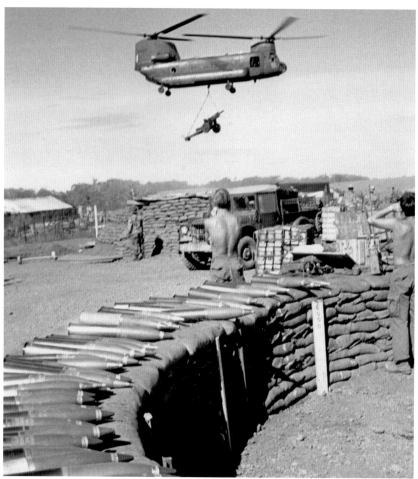

Above: October 14, 1969—South Vietnamese President Nguyen van Thieu throws a handful of dirt onto some of the 400 coffins during a mass funeral service for victims of the Hue 'Tet' massacre.

Right: October 1969—As a Chinook helicopter lifts a 105mm artillery piece out of Firebase Annie for repair, shells are laid out at the Bu Prang Special Forces camp near the Cambodian border, in an area that had recently come under heavy North Vietnamese fire.

October 24, 1969—During ceremonies at Black Horse Camp, 40 miles east of Saigon, the base is turned over to the 18th Vietnamese Army Division. Black Horse was the second largest base that had so far been turned over to the ARVN as part of the Vietnamization program.

November 15, 1969—An estimated 200,000 demonstrators gather at the Washington Monument for the Moratorium Day peace rally to protest the Vietnam War.

Above: November 8, 1969—A Montagnard mother and son peer out of a window in the sand-bagged home at Duc Lap Special Forces camp, where dependents live along side soldiers on the Cambodian border about 135 miles north of Saigon.

Right: November 23, 1969—A U.S. Green Beret covers his ears while firing a 62mm mortar at enemy positions near the Special Forces camp at Bu Prang, 110 miles northeast of Saigon.

Above: November 1969—Staff Sgt. Rodney Namauu of Hilo, Hawaii, dashes for cover after setting the fuse of a Claymore mine aimed at a hedgerow concealing enemy troops.

Left: November 23, 1969—A South Vietnamese infantryman waits for a safe time to leave his sandbagged bunker, looking for a lull in the mortar bombardment of Bu Prang camp, about 110 miles northeast of Saigon.

Above: November 21, 1969—A Viet Cong guerrilla captured by the South Vietnamese in the U Minh Forest, at the southern tip of South Vietnam, is bruised and bandaged. Prisoners were sometimes beaten during interrogation.

Left: November 1969—U.S. troops stand at attention as South Vietnamese soldiers march forward to take command of six 105mm howitzers during a turnover ceremony in Danang. The guns had been manned by the U.S. 108th Artillery Group.

Above: November 3, 1969—Still wearing torn, dirty uniforms after 60 days in the field, U.S. artillerymen who escaped Firebase Annie prepare to be flown from the Bu Prang Special Forces camp to a base at the rear. The gunners abandoned Firebase Annie, fighting their way out while under an intense North Vietnamese ground assault.

Left: November 26, 1969—U.S. artillery observers stand atop a fortified post at the Bu Prang Special Forces camp as they call in fire on suspected enemy mortar positions near the Cambodian border, north of Saigon.

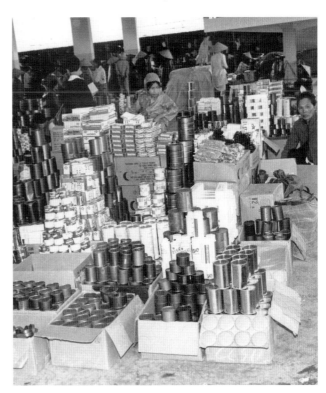

Above: November 28, 1969—Black market vendors in the Hue market display stacks of PX and military food items, stolen from warehouses or bought from people having access to the PX.

Left: November 21, 1969—Black market vendors scatter as police stage a routine clamp-down on the sidewalk stalls of Saigon. Such raids are staged off and on during the day, and the sharp-eyed dealers quickly gather their goods to lay low until the police leave.

Above: November 14, 1969—Vietnamese soldiers rush to board Huey helicopters in a rice paddy near their forward command post. The men were transported to the interior of the U-minh forest, a large marsh, swamp, and forest area that is a Viet Cong stronghold at the southern tip of Vietnam.

Left: November, 21 1969—A super bunker rises high above ground level. Made of sandbags and fortified with heavy timber, not even a direct hit would penetrate the interior of this fortification.

November 23, 1969—Wearing traditional turbans and robes, these elderly North Vietnamese Catholic refugees attend a rally in Gia Kiem, 50 miles northeast of Saigon. Some 1,000,000 Vietnamese fled Hanoi when the French were defeated. They arrived in Saigon and eventually took up residence northeast of the city.

Top Left: November 19, 1969—A Montagnard mother, baby in a sling, runs for her bunker as incoming artillery hits Pu Brang Special Forces camp 110 miles from Saigon on the Cambodian border. Families live in the camps with the Montgnard fighters.

Top Right: December 1969—A Popular Force soldier is on guard at Vinh Xuan hamlet beside an old gravestone, his M-16 rifle hangs ready to fire on a wire attached to the thatched roof. The government regained control of the area 70 miles southwest of Saigon after 10 years under the Viet Cong.

Right: December 1969—Wearing the conical straw hat, a peasant leaves the farm to take up guard duty as a member of South Vietnam's self-defense force in the Mekong Delta.

Below: December 1969—Government troops wade through a deep canal during patrol in U-Minh forest of South Vietnam, part of a 4,000-man operation to gain control of the forest. Sampans carry their equipment.

Top Left: December 16, 1969—Vietnamese army outpost along the DMZ guards the border against North Vietnamese infiltration.

Top Right: December 22, 1969—South Vietnamese soldiers take blindfolded Viet Cong prisoners to a helicopter following a firefight south of Danang near An Hoa. The prisoners were flown to a provincial capital for interrogation.

Above: December 17, 1969—A bunker at Con Thien is reinforced against North Vietnamese artillery attacks across the demilitarized zone. The 1st Brigade, 5th Infantry Division, was stationed there to prevent infiltration across the eastern section of the DMZ.

Right: December 1969—Late in a Saigon evening, people stroll around illuminated fountains and sidewalk cafes. With the war not as evident in the capital, Saigonese were staying out later.

Above: December 3, 1969—Under the watch of military police, disabled North Vietnamese prisoners enter the courtyard of the Bien Hoa prison camp. The South Vietnamese government said it had offered to send the men home, but Hanoi had declined the offer.

Right: December 17, 1969—A U.S. Army Huey helicopter returns to base at Con Thien after a patrol inside the southern sector of the demilitarized zone. The 1st Brigade of the 5th Mechanized Infantry Division is assigned to the base to stop Communist infiltration through the DMZ.

Above: December 17, 1969—A Vietnamese woman with the wrinkles of years of hard labor in the rice paddies watches soldiers searching for Viet Cong in Phong Dien, Thua Thien province, in northern South Vietnam.

Left: A cavalryman balances himself on a support frame as he and other troopers of the U.S. 11th Armored Regiment check out a shelter that was used by North Vietnamese who had passed through the area hours before them.

Top Left: Judith Hillenbrand, New York State's representative on the Youth Advisory Committee of the Selective Service System, picks a capsule in Washington for the birth-date drawing of the 1970 draft lottery. Opening the capsules at right is Helen F. King. Man in background is unidentified.

Top Right: December 1969— Aerial view of a typical special forces camp in Vietnam.

Left: December 1969—A guard watches the peaceful farm scene at My Lai hamlet, soon after a fight with the Viet Cong which razed the huts, killed two villagers and brought in a U.S. artillery barrage.

# SOLDIERING ON

From the air base at Bien Hoa to the giant naval yards at Cam Ranh Bay, and north to the Marine stronghold at Da Nang and beyond to the distant, lonely hilltop firebases, the scene and sound were much the same. An army was watching the clock. At base it was steak and waiting. In the 'boonies' it was C-rations and waiting. Everywhere it was bitching and waiting, dealing the cards and waiting, passing a joint and waiting, giving the peace sign and waiting.

It was June 1969 and President Nixon had announced immediate but gradual withdrawal of US troops – now at a peak of 543,000. After 40,000 dead and 260,000 wounded so far, an unvictorious army had withdrawal symptoms. For the most part duty and the enemy would still be faced – but reluctantly. The objective was clear now in a common slogan: 'Don't be the last GI to die in 'Nam.'

'In Vietnam,' wrote Colonel Robert D. Heinl Jr

> ## 'The final effect was of a moron wandering through a foreign land.'
> — COMBATANT TIM O'BRIEN

in 'The Collapse of the Armed Forces', 'the best army the United States ever put into the field is numbly extricating itself from a nightmare war which the armed forces feel they had foisted on them by bright civilians who are now back on campus writing books about the folly of it all.'

But if it was folly, then fighting on was harder. It was now a different war – unpopular, all over except for a date, but for the soldiers the dangers were the same. Courage was no less, but motivation and morale had gone like the victory. Combat, if not avoided, was no longer sought. 'I think the major aim of anybody over there at the time', says Marine Bobby Murdoch, 'was just to take care of himself. The main objective was just to live through it, to get out of there.' But Murdoch had to soldier on – and when he got out it was as a paraplegic.

Dave Christian was with the Special Forces in

August 20, 1970—American and South Vietnamese soldiers help a wounded GI to an evacuation helicopter despite intense enemy fire.

August 10, 1970—South Vietnamese soldiers tote artillery rounds to firing pits at Firebase O'Reilly in jungled hill country west of Hue. The base was under heavy pressure from the North Vietnamese.

1969: 'They'd drop us in and say "Go get 'em".' By the time he left Vietnam Christian had been 'shot in both legs; stabbed in the left arm through hand-to-hand combat; paralyzed in my right hand; shrapnel in my back, my feet, my head, and I had forty per cent of my body – my last wound – burned with napalm [dropped by his own side].' He was only nineteen.

It was a different war, or it was no longer America's war, or it was a mistake: 'the Vietnam experience' as the policy-makers so often called it, or the 'Vietnam Conflict' as they inscribed on the cenotaphs. 'It still boils down to suffering,' says infantry sergeant Tim O'Brien, 'and the thing about Vietnam that most bothers me is that it is treated as a political experience, a sociological experience, and the human element of what a soldier goes through – and what the Vietnamese went through – is not only neglected: it is almost cast aside as superfluous.'

In Vietnam there was the trauma of having to fight on while questioning the rationale, and then after – in the homecoming – the devaluing of the soldier's sacrifice along with the cause. It was a different war only in that, without national valor, the soldiers were left without any feeling of individual honor – all too often left without any feelings at all, brutalized by the terrible sameness of war which in this case they could never redeem.

'Vietnam in essence for the foot soldier was really identical to every other war,' considers infantryman O'Brien. 'I'm talking about things that a foot soldier sees: maiming, death, orphans, widows, pain, loneliness, boredom.' O'Brien was part of the tough-reputation Americal Division and his year's tour was spent largely on combat patrol in the central coastal region. His war was a waiting one but no less grim as it began to wind down in mid-1969: 'Looking at your watch, counting the days, marking off the days you have left in Vietnam on a little calendar drawn on your helmet. It is monotony punctuated by moments of sheer terror, just horrible stuff. And after the war is over you don't remember the monotony and the boredom and the mosquitoes and the heat. You remember those few moments of real terror.'

'I had the last rites twice on the battlefield,' says Dave Christian, who won a dozen medals. 'I remember the priest giving me the last rites: I woke up in a semi-state of shock and I started screaming: you know, there can't be any justice, there is no god, why me; you know, I'm only nine-teen years old. Father, please . . .' In combat it was like any other war; as one soldier put it, 'When I was wounded in Vietnam my blood ran just as heavily and my pain was just as heavy as my father's and other fathers' in other wars.'

It was different when they first went off to the war, as if each generation is fated to learn for itself. They believed they were brighter, stronger, morally better: 'And that's why we take young people into war,' says Christian. 'You're looking for peer recognition, you're looking for recognition from the people back home, and you think everything you're doing is right.' They looked to their fathers; believed in the elders who sent them. It was the major influence on those who went to Vietnam, a values reference outweighing the controversy. After two world wars, then Korea, America's patriotism could not be questioned and had to be upheld by service, as most of them saw it.

Dave Christian enlisted at seventeen, leaving college and his wife of a few months: 'I told her, "Look, don't worry about it, men fight wars and women have babies, and that is our role in society. I'm going off to fight my war and you'll have our children." I didn't think of Vietnam as a political war at the time. My father had served, everyone in our community had served. My two brothers served over in Vietnam. I hailed from a steel community and we handed out 29,000 boys from my county alone.'

Tim O'Brien was twenty, already above the average age of the 1,759,000 Americans who served in Vietnam. He was a student at McAlister University in St Paul, Minnesota, when he got his military papers. He accepted the draft: 'I was a mixed up kid. I was against the war in a kind of abstract way, in an ideological way. And simply hadn't been prepared for the realities of army life, the reality of perhaps going to Vietnam. And almost immediately I began to think, "This isn't for me – the war is wrong." It was like a sleep-walking kind of thought where I just let gravity pull me into the war. I was young, I was scared of exile, of [the alternative] of leaving my country: that was a heavy price to pay as a kid. A month later I got on a plane and went to Vietnam.'

Like O'Brien, Lieutenant Jim Webb arrived in Vietnam in early 1969. But Webb began as a career officer whose family had 'a very strong military tradition – all the way back to the American Revolution'. He says he 'never related to Vietnam politically' – it was just 'my responsibility to go. When I first got there, because of Marine training, I was ready to jump off the boat like at Iwo Jima. Then you come very quickly to realize that the most important thing is to husband your own people, to get as many people back as you can.' Webb had a naval academy education but his unit 'were largely working-class Americans of various ethnic backgrounds'. They had in common 'a sense of pride' but, he says, the GI in Vietnam was 'basically an immature human being. The average age of an American soldier in World War II was twenty-six years. The average guy in a grunt [infantry] unit in Vietnam was nineteen years old. And you had a collection of young, immature, very emotional people. And these guys tried like hell.'

The one-year duty 'tour' in Vietnam – which limited domestic dissent – meant rotating younger men. The avoidance of a call-up of reserves meant that the country generally did not actively share in the commitment, duty, sacrifice, nor in the soldiers' understanding of the war. And once the soldiers had arrived in Vietnam, whether in the first or the last years, their values reference was gone: they were in alien country and alienated from the mass of their people who talked of cause without feeling its cost.

Says Marine medic Jack McCloskey, then nineteen: 'I bought an American dream,' but in Vietnam after a few weeks 'I saw my buddies blown away. I never saw a Viet Cong; never saw my enemy. And listening to some of the guys that had been over there for a time – me being enthusiastic and saying, "Hey, let's go, let's go out there" – and they're saying, "Let's not – if we can avoid it. We're only here for a year." ' Louis Packer, a First Cavalry medic, says: 'I knew little except what I read in the newspapers. I was young, full of excitement; I wanted to see what it was all about. After a while I thought about it and said, "Why? Here I am 10,000 miles away from home – for what? Here we are trying to wage war in another country. It has never done anything to me. People I have never seen before. And what am I doing here, for what reason, what purpose?" '

They were young and green, but not insensitive – or not at first, though often the numbing

March 9, 1971—Helicopter kick up a dust storm at Khe Sanh base in South Vietnam as they prepare to airlift waiting South Vietnamese troops to Laos.

March 1971—An ammunition dump explodes after being hit by Viet Cong rocket-propelled grenades. The firebase on the Mekong River supported an operation through the Chup rubber plantation.

was rapid. McCloskey could not shake a dream about 'having my medic bag by me and reaching down, reaching for a battle dressing, and that battle dressing turns into a body bag'. Medic Louis Packer, when first called in to a fire-fight, 'couldn't believe what I saw. I'd seen the kids at base camp, but when I got out there it was an entirely different story. Just bodies laying there. Kids' arms and legs. People screaming – the awful 'sight of blood all over the place. It was unreal. Unreal.'

Since the abandonment of large-scale 'Search and Destroy' operations, life for the small percentage of combat troops had become more and more a guerrilla existence: ambush and counter-ambush, living out of a pack, patrolling endlessly. If anything, the winding-down war made it tougher for Marine Captain Webb's platoon: 'I don't think that anything or anyone could have prepared me for what I was going to see in the bush: the Marine living conditions, and the people – the way they lived.' He was patrolling the 'badlands' south-west of Danang.

'My real frustration', says Webb, 'is trying to explain what the infantry went through. I was not prepared for the continual primitiveness; I had three hot meals in nine months. I carried my pack – it had a poncho, a tooth-brush, letter-writing gear and that was it. That was all I carried for nine months. We moved every two days; didn't take a bath for months literally: maybe wash off in a stream, or find a well. We ate C-rations continually. And virtually every single person in my unit

got either ring worm, hook worm, dysentery or malaria. And some of us had them all.'

Webb watched as one by one his platoon of twenty-five fell to the attrition of the bush, only to be replaced in the war that was over except for a date: 'During one period – not quite seven weeks – I took fifty-one casualties, and when number fifty-one got his arm blown off I sat down next to him and cried like a baby. I had had it.'

They kept going because 'when you're up to your neck in alligators you don't sit there and keep talking about why you came to drain the swamp'. The objective was to get through the day: strategy, cause, the politics of it were inexplicable subjects, almost taboo, bad for morale. 'You didn't talk about what the patrols were about,' says Webb, 'you talked about whether you were getting mail; how many days you have left on your tour.' This countdown was 'really emphasized' because of the awareness that the great majority had beaten the calendar altogether. Webb points out that "only eleven per cent of the draft eligible males in America ever made it to Vietnam" and he says his platoon 'averaged tenth or eleventh grade education'. They were 'very courageous people, but they were not political people'. There was awareness, too, that at most 'ten per cent of the Americans in Vietnam were actually in a combat unit'.

Webb himself was an exception – most officers served only six months. He stayed on as a company commander with the rank of captain for another three months: still less than his men. Major Joe

Anderson, one of the few black officers, was assigned to a second tour. He had led a platoon in 1966, returning as a company commander in 1970, and 'the tactics had changed, the attitudes had changed'. Ironically, now that the US was withdrawing, it had become 'much more of a guerrilla war and we were hiding and searching as the North Vietnamese and Viet Cong were hiding. So it was more of a jungle war and jungle warfare concepts being applied.' But now the attitude of his Company was 'not to aggressively search out and destroy the enemy but "Let's do whatever is necessary to do the job so that we can get back home safely".' American combat involvement had now lasted five years but in Anderson's company of 200 men 'only myself, one platoon sergeant and one squad leader had more than two years of service. So it was a fairly inexperienced army.'

Although the Americans were belatedly applying jungle warfare concepts, the soldiers knew it was a holding operation until the South Vietnamese took it over – if they could; they knew that territory gained was even less likely to be held; they knew they were not pursuing military victory – they were just to fight and die while 'bright civilians' talked on in Paris. And while tactically green they were motivationally blank. There was virtually no political training, nor even much basic education on the country for which they were being asked to die.

Tim O'Brien was a college graduate, and a perceptive author – much later. 'My time in Vietnam', he says, 'is the memory of ignorance. I didn't know the language. I knew nothing about the culture, nothing about the religion, nothing about the village community. I knew nothing about the aims of the people – whether they were for the war or against the war. And I knew nothing about the tactics we were pursuing.

'It was hit and miss. Like hunting a humming-bird. You would get to one village: nothing there. Another village – and nothing there. The enemy, the humming-bird that we were after, was just buzzing around. You secure a village, you search it, and you leave, and the village reverts to the enemy. It seemed a senseless strategy – and yet I thought perhaps there was some rhyme or reason behind it. I never found out. I knew nothing about the regime in Saigon, and what they were after. I knew nothing about the war.

'The final effect was of a moron wandering through a foreign land, or a blind man wandering through a foreign land. Vietnam was like walking a maze: you didn't know where the maze was leading. You would leave a point and you would walk blindly through some hedgerow, take a right and then a left and then a right, and you would end up sometimes back where you started. No sense of progression. And all along the way mines were going off – feet going, legs going, balls going.'

The continuing high casualty rate – on average, 800 American dead and 6000 wounded each month during the phase-out of 1969 – increasingly strained military discipline and the code of conduct, finally bringing a considerable degree of mutiny and the murder of over-zealous officers. The last wave of GIS to arrive came not with the traditional gung-ho of Fort Bragg but in step with the public revulsion of 1968: they in fact brought the anti-war movement with them. In the US and in Vietnam, both on and off base, illicit GI anti-war publications flourished, (there were 245 at dif-

October 25, 1970—The door gunner on a South Vietnamese helicopter uses a minigun instead of the usual 60 caliber machinegun. The minigun is electrically operated and can fire up to 6,000 bullets per minute.

ferent times), along with organizations to aid desertion.

With general morale near zero and with at least 500,000 or nine-tenths of the US force as rear-echelon and preferring it that way, the US military command ordered what Congressmen called 'an absolutely senseless' offensive of the A-Shau Valley close to the Laotian border. Some 2800 infantry of the American 101st Airborne Division and of the 1st ARVN division were deployed in what only seemed a training exercise in 'Vietnamization' with the objective of sweeping the Ap-Bia mountain range. To the GIS this remote region had always been the worst of 'Indian country'. The US command, further revealing how out of touch it was with the times – or how desirous for times past – called this war-path to the mountains 'Operation Apache Snow'. At a 3000-foot nameless hill designated No. 937 the Allied force found the North Vietnamese firmly entrenched.

So began the battle for 'Hamburger Hill'. For ten days in early May, 1969, in assault after assault, more and more troops were pressed into the attack. One million pounds of bombs were dropped; 152,000 pounds of napalm scorched the hill. It was captured on the eleventh attempt – and abandoned the following day. American casualties – killed or wounded – totaled 476; with 'an enemy body count of 505'.

The public fury in the United States was such that Defense Secretary Melvin Laird had to rebuke openly the military command, stating: 'It's our goal to keep the maximum pressure on the enemy consistent with the lowest possible casualties.' President Nixon personally went to Saigon on 30 July to direct field commander General Creighton Abrams to allocate full responsibility for the security of South Vietnam to ARVN forces. In 1970 the US casualty rate was halved. But in Vietnam after 'Hamburger Hill', according to Colonel Robert Heinl Jr in his 'The Collapse of the Armed Forces', a GI protest newspaper, 'GI Says', offered 'a $10,000 bounty on Lieutenant-Colonel Weldon Honeycutt, the officer who ordered and led the attack. Despite several attempts, however, Honeycutt managed to live out his tour and return Stateside.'

Top: May 1969—A wounded U.S. paratrooper of the 101st Airborne Division is helped through a blinding rainstorm by two medics after being evacuated from Dong Ap Bia during the 10-day battle for Hamburger Hill. U.S. and South Vietnamese forces eventually dislodged Communist forces from Dong Ap Bia, but the action touched off further political controversy in the United States.

Center: May 21, 1969—U.S. paratroopers of the 101st Airborne Division rest atop the damaged crest of the 3000-foot Ap Bia Mountain on the western edge of the A Shau Valley in South Vietnam, one mile east of the Laos border. The battle involving heavy ground fighting against North Vietnamese troops holding Hill 937, known as the battle for Hamburger Hill, resulted in 46 American casualties with 400 wounded. More than 500 enemy soldiers died.

Right: May 19, 1969—U.S. paratroopers come to the aid of a fallen buddy after being evacuated from Hamburger Hill on the western edge of the A Shau Valley. Troops of the 101st Airborne suffered heavy casualties in 10 days of close quarters fighting before finally taking Ap Bia Mountain.

The bounty for the life of the Lieutenant-Colonel was not unique except for the amount. There were bounties (pooled sums) ranging from $50 to $1000 offered for the killing of unpopular officers. By now, military indiscipline was such that victory in the ground war, although not sought, was anyhow considered unobtainable. A subsequent study called *Crisis in Command* by two career officers, Major Richard A. Gabriel of the US Army Reserve, a graduate of the Army Advanced Intelligence School, and Lieutenant-Colonel Paul L. Savage, a general staff veteran of campaigns in Europe and Asia, blamed not the ranks but the officer corps. The book had its beginnings in a series of articles at the time, when the two officers say that they were 'strongly warned' against speaking out. They state: 'It is difficult to escape the charge that the troops failed to follow most often because their officers abandoned their responsibility to lead.' This was the very charge which, over the years, the American command had leveled at the South Vietnamese.

There were too many officers, yet too seldom seen. In the last years, American officers in Vietnam comprised fifteen per cent of the total personnel, compared to seven per cent in World War II and nine per cent in Korea. The Grunt slogan of CYA – Cover Your Ass – was also the higher sentiment. The officers were generally despised for directing combat operations from helicopters and distant command posts (CPS). There was a derogatory epithet for each officer class, and collectively they became known (as acknowledged in *Crisis in Command*) as REMFs. 'That', says multi-medal winner Dave Christian, 'stands for Rear Echelon Mother Fuckers. And that is what we thought of them. They were collecting their combat pay at our expense, and telling their war stories at our expense.' Christian's own extraordinary combat exploits later earned him the rank of captain.

In an army no longer 'driven by success', as one major put it, even those officers who did lead their men in combat were by now, like as not, regarded as anxious 'to get their ticket punched', hungry for ribbons and promotion. And these six-month commanders, often fresh from cadet class, were more jungle-green than the eleventh-graders they led. Combat refusals by individuals and platoons reached an unprecedented level. Though the Department of Defense kept no statistics, Senator John Stennis of the Armed Services Committee disclosed in 1971 that in the traditionally fearless First Air Cavalry Division alone there had been thirty-five individual combat refusals the previous year. According to Congressional data. US army convictions for 'mutiny and other acts involving willful refusal' in Vietnam rose from 82 in 1968 to 117 in 1969 and 131 in 1970.

Mike Beaman, a Grunt who was a company scout in Vietnam and later a veterans counsellor, recalls numerous intra-army conflicts: 'I spoke out a lot in Vietnam about missions. We used to refuse certain missions because we thought they were brutal. If I didn't want to go in a certain direction, if I felt that we were going to have a confrontation and shoot people for no reason at all, other than to get a body count, I'd say "No – I'm scout, I'm going this way. You, officer, can go that way, but the other people will follow me."'

From 1969 Vietnam brought a grim new word in the military lexicon – 'fragging': in plain English,

September 1970—A GI mortar platoon fires away at enemy positions near the DMZ.

murder. The term fragging derived from the use of a fragmentation weapon, usually a hand-grenade, as the surest way of dispatching an unpopular officer. Between 1969 and 1971, according to Congressional data, the total number of 'fragging incidents' – including actual attempts at murder and intimidation – was 730, and eighty-three officers were killed this way. But these figures do not include assaults on officers with other weapons – rifles or knives – and by one official estimate there was sufficient evidence in only ten per cent of suspected 'fraggings' to warrant investigation. The ratio of violence against officers in Vietnam was believed to be almost fifteen times as great as in the grim trench-warfare of World War I.

'We were aware that officers were being fragged,' states Mike Beaman. 'In our particular unit our officer was aware that I felt pretty strongly about some things and so did some of the other men. And although we got to some pretty severe confrontations where there were some threats of shooting him in the field, that never had to be done. And that was like a behaviour modification: when you're out in the field there's no court of law, you just have to reconcile these problems out in the field.'

A black Marine corps rifleman, Charles Johnson, relates circumstances which 'did not occur in my particular company but it occurred in another company. There were some associates of mine who were experiencing some problems from a gunnery sergeant: he was an older guy, a career man, gungho. He liked the war; he was very petty in terms of how Marines should be dressed, even in a war zone, and he made sure that everything was spit and polish and he just generally made a nui-

sance of himself. At one point the company was out – they'd gotten pinned down by the enemy. When they found the gunnery sergeant there were more holes in his back than in his front, so that would lead one to believe that some of his own men made every attempt to kill him too.'

A black officer, Major Joe Anderson, felt that indiscipline did not 'stem from the soldiers but from the people leading them or failing to lead them in a responsible way'. The High Command approach to Vietnam as an opportunity for officer field experience meant not only rapid rotation but rapid commissions with the criteria irresponsibly lowered. And this, says the study *Crisis in Command*, created situations like My Lai.

The My Lai massacre of civilians was only disclosed by journalists in late 1969 after the known facts had been suppressed by the military for more than a year. On 16 March 1968, Lieutenant W.L. Calley led a platoon of thirty men into a village complex in the central Quang Ngai province, and subsequent accounts estimate that between 200 and 500 unarmed villagers were slaughtered. Says the study by career officers: 'Even the staunchest defenders of the army agree that in normal times a man of Lieutenant Calley's low intelligence and predispositions would never have been allowed to become an officer if the army had maintained its normal standards for officer selection, and that because the army did in fact lower its standards it must share in the guilt and culpability for the My Lai affair. The lowering of standards was a wound that the officer corps inflicted upon itself.'

Seymour Hersh, the journalist whose investigation brought the first full national exposure of

March 1968—Bodies of women and children lie on the road leading from the village of My Lai following the massacre of South Vietnamese civilians by American troops.

April 23, 1971—Lt. William L. Calley Jr. arrives for his court-martial at Fort Benning, Ga., in connection with the massacre of civilians at the village of My Lai in South Vietnam.

the massacre, wrote in *My Lai 4: A Report on the Massacre and its Aftermath:* 'If there was any concurrence among former members of Calley's platoon in Vietnam, it is the amazement that the army considered Calley officer material.' Author George Walton, a retired Lieutenant-Colonel, gives this description of William Laws Calley, nickname 'Rusty' in his book *The Tarnished Shield: A Report on Today's Army:* 'The lieutenant was a below-average, dull, and inconspicuous boy, his father, a World War II naval veteran, had made a modest success as a salesman of heavy construction machinery, and being moderately affluent the Calleys maintained a residence in Miami and a home in the mountains near Waynesville, North Carolina, where Rusty and his three sisters spent happy summer months. He first attended the Edison High School in Miami and thereafter the Georgia Military Academy but his grades in both schools were such that he was unable to attend a college and ended by going to Palm Beach Junior College in Lake Worth, Florida. There his grades were even worse than they had been in high school. At the end of the first year he flunked out with two Cs, one D, and four Fs.' Calley enlisted in 1966, was named for Officer Candidate School and 'although Calley graduated in the middle of his class, he had not even learned to read a map properly'.

Calley was a platoon leader in Charlie Company, 1st Battalion, 20th Infantry of the newly formed American Division. Charlie Company arrived in Vietnam in December 1967. It was the height of 'Search and Destroy', and just weeks before the ultimate attrition of the Tet Offensive

with its random killings of civilians by both sides. The towns of Can Tho and My Tho had been destroyed in order to 'save' them. Ancient Hue, Vietnam's Mecca, was a ruin and its victims reportedly included hundreds of civilians executed by the guerrillas. Walton quotes Calley as having spoken of the My Lai massacre as '. . . no big deal, Sir'.

My Lai-4 was one of several hamlets in a village known to the Vietnamese as Son My. Among the GIS the area was known as 'Pinkville' – the guerrillas were entrenched there, though in which hamlet no one was certain. On 25 February, a patrol from Charlie Company stumbled onto a minefield and six men were killed and another twelve severely wounded. On 14 March there were more casualties, and early the next day battalion commander Lieutenant-Colonel Frank A. Barker Jr, a veteran of twenty years, summoned the commanding officer of Charlie Company, Captain Ernest L. Medina, who had advanced through enlisted ranks and after eight years graduated fourth in his officer class of 1966. The Colonel told the Captain, according to published accounts, that a guerrilla force of perhaps 250 men was believed operating from My Lai-4. The intelligence reports were that on Tuesdays the women and children went to the market by 7 am. Medina's company was to attack the village after that hour and destroy it. They had twenty-four hours to prepare; some are quoted as regarding it as their 'first real live battle'; others as having 'a score to even up'.

Tim O'Brien, who would search the same area a year later before the disclosure of the massacre, describes the atmosphere: 'I knew it was a bad place. We were afraid to go to Pinkville. It was a sullen, hostile, unpeopled place. We'd go among the My Lai villages and there were never any people: deserted, and yet there were smoldering fires – people obviously lived there. It was a place where men died. It was a heavily mined area. There was no tangible object to attack except the land itself. And in a sense the area of My Lai itself became the enemy, not the people of My Lai, not even the Viet Cong, but the physical place – the sullen villages, the criss-cross paddies, the bomb craters and the poverty of the place became the enemy. We took revenge, burning down huts, blowing up tunnels.'

At sunrise on Tuesday 16 March 1968, the Hueys airlifted the entire Charlie Company west of the hamlets to a clearing designated Landing Zone Dotti. The company commander, Captain Medina, set up his CP in an old graveyard. As the gunships put down, other senior officers were described as observing the operation from aircraft stacked at 1000 and 2000 feet. Calley's thirty men advanced on My Lai-4, just a cluster of thatched roof huts. The accounts note that with platoons spread out through 'Pinkville' no one observed the entire events. The accounts, however, state that at My Lai-4 there was no opposing fire and that Calley ordered his platoon to go in shooting and to throw grenades into the dwellings. As women and children ran out they were mowed down by automatic fire, and soon 'the contagion of slaughter was spreading throughout the platoon'. Other civilians – all women, children or old men – were described as being led with hands above their heads to a large ditch and there systematically shot. Two other platoons beyond the hamlet cut down the few who had managed to run from My Lai-4.

The author of *The Tarnished Shield*, retired Lieutenant-Colonel George Walton, is a former attorney and a professor of political science. He wrote this account: 'Within My Lai-4 the killings had become more sadistic. Several old men were stabbed with bayonets and one was thrown down a well to be followed by a hand grenade. Some women and children praying outside of the local temple were killed by shooting them in the back of the head with rifles. Occasionally a soldier would drag a girl, often a mere child, to a ditch where he would rape her. One GI is said to have thrown a grenade into a hootch where a girl of five or six lay that he had just raped. The young were slaughtered with the same impartiality as the old. Children barely able to walk were picked off at point blank range.'

In an observation helicopter Hugh C. Thompson, a warrant officer on second duty tour, saw what was happening and put down in My Lai-4. After threatening a shoot out with Calley's platoon, Thompson is credited with saving the lives of sixteen children and was awarded the Distinguished Flying Cross. It was at 9 am – two hours after it all began – when battalion commander Colonel Barker was described as arriving over the area in his helicopter and only then realizing what had occurred. He radioed Captain Medina at the graveyard CP to cease all action.

The army chain of command in Vietnam kept silent on the reports it received of My Lai-4. The usual practice of submitting such findings to Washington was not followed. My Lai-4 might never have been known – or at least never proved – except for the fact that a *Stars and Stripes* reporter on the operation took photographs of the Belsen-style bodies piled in the ditch. One soldier, GI journalist Ronald Ridenhour, investigated the rumors and for months persisted in trying to get US political and religious leaders to recommend an inquiry. He sent written evidence to thirty prominent people, including President Nixon and sixteen Congressmen. Only two of these thirty people – House Member Morris K. Udall and Chairman of the House Armed Services Committee L. Mendel Rivers – took vigorous action, demanding a Pentagon investigation. The chief of Army Reserve, Lieutenant-General William R. Peers, was assigned to conduct the inquiry.

Officially, it was estimated that about 200 civilians were murdered in My Lai-4. Among others who investigated was the American international law expert Richard A. Falk who estimated there were 500 civilian victims, and in his survey US army author George Walton estimates 700 were massacred.

General Peers, himself a former divisional commander in Vietnam, concluded: 'The principal failure was in leadership. Failures occurred at every level within the chain of command, from individual squad leaders to the command group of the Division. It was an illegal operation, in violation of military regulations and of human rights, starting with the planning, continuing through the brutal, destructive acts of many of the men involved, and culminating in abortive efforts to investigate and, finally, the suppression of the truth.'

Despite this uncompromising indictment, only thirteen officers and enlisted men were charged with war crimes and an additional twelve were charged with cover-up. Of the twenty-five men charged, only William Laws Calley was court-

martialed, found guilty and sentenced to life imprisonment. Calley spent just three days in military jail, then on White House orders he was transferred to house arrest where he spent three and a half years pending appeals to various military courts. All these appeals were denied, but after its final review the White House concurred in suggestions for parole. In effect, President Nixon pardoned Calley.

Wrote General Peers, 'I think it unfortunate that of the twenty-five men charged with war crimes or related acts, he was the only one tried by court-martial and found guilty. . . . Above and beyond that, he personally participated in the killing of non-combatants. So I don't consider him a scapegoat.' George Walton in his study of 'today's' army states: 'When an army is required to fight a war without the support of society it is forced to commission its Calleys.'

Wrote law authority and military consultant Richard Falk: 'The Vietnam war has amply demonstrated how easily modern man and the modern state – with all its claims of civility – can relapse into barbarism in the course of pursuing belligerent objectives in a distant land where neither national territory nor national security is tangibly at stake.' And he added: 'It would be misleading to isolate the awful happening at Son My from the overall conduct of the war [or from] the general line of official policy that established a moral climate in which the welfare of Vietnamese civilians is totally disregarded.'

In the most searing verdict on My Lai-4, the mother of platoon member David Paul Meadlo was reported in the *New York Times* of 30 November 1969 saying: 'I sent them a good boy, and they made him a murderer.'

Few would question that the boys America sent to Vietnam were, as they set out, a cross-section of humanity as good as any – but they were just boys, and years later, unable to comprehend, few Americans would care to ask how the boys came back so different. My Lai was a collective consequence of the individual emotional overload which almost every American ground combatant in Vietnam came to endure in a war without any recognizable front, enemy or cause, waged without national participation or unity.

Sergeant Tim O'Brien had just patrolled the My Lai area when he heard of its infamy: 'On the one hand I was shocked and I thought that this is terrible: you don't kill the people. And then I wasn't shocked. After all the frustrations we had been through, I understood the frustrations that were felt by Calley's company. This is not to excuse his behaviour. I hated what he did. I thought it was wrong and terrible and I still do. I think that he should have been sent to jail for life. But at the same time, as a man who was there, and who saw men die in the My Lais, I understand what happened.'

But some GIS would feel that their training as much as Vietnam's environment conditioned them – and the events. Marine medic Jack McCloskey remembers the mock Vietnamese village at training camp: 'It was taught to us, go into this Ville, and you have to blow everything away in this Ville. Your basic mistrust of the Vietnamese people is already ingrained in you: anything with slant eyes was a "gook" – they were not human beings.' McCloskey, with his body full of shrapnel, would later devote a decade to counseling emo-

tionally disturbed veterans through his self-help organization 'Twice Born Men'.

Special Forces member Lou Carello recalls: 'We were always told, "As long as you don't make human contact with them, you will always see them as the enemy." ' He was 'part of a team that killed civilians, civilians who were in key spots. I was like a hired gun, you know. I still can't sleep without a light on. All the people that I either put away or helped put away are going to get me.' Carello lost both legs in Vietnam. Back home, he returned to school to study sociology. Condemned for life to a wheelchair, he says, 'I don't want people to know my whole story. But understand me when you see me.'

All wars brutalize, but in Vietnam the war's nature and strategy produced a schizophrenic norm. Ivan Delbyk, Special Forces, remembers: 'You could be walking and it was quiet and peaceful, and you are listening to the birds singing, and the air smells good, and the trees and the greenery look beautiful. And then all of a sudden all hell breaks loose. From a rocket or a mortar. And a few seconds later it is quiet again. And if nobody is wounded you continue on your way. And if they are, you wait until you have Medevac. One second you were up, the next you were down. And you just never knew when those times were coming.

'I really didn't think about the war – about winning or losing. I just tried to stay alive. And in the process I'd say I became very animalistic in my outlook towards life. A very blasé attitude towards life and death and indifference to the suffering and misery that was around us. All I really cared about was seeing the light of the next day, having a meal. I just wanted to stay alive.' After one action Delbyk had 'a piece of shrapnel sticking out of my head'. He was urgently flown to Japan for advanced surgery: 'When the neurologist came to look at me – he was Japanese – I had developed a large distaste for Orientals, and plus he had a nervous twitch, so as soon as he left the room I pulled it out myself.'

In combat in Vietnam each soldier had to struggle to find the inner safety net between man and animal; each had to question himself, says Tim O'Brien: 'What does fear do to a man? How do we react to ignorance? My general feeling about Vietnam was that I was dumb. I didn't know anything. I compensated for that ignorance in a whole bunch of ways – some evil ways: blowing things up, burning huts. That's the frustration of being ignorant and not knowing where the enemy was.'

Even their marching songs were negative. O'Brien titled a book on this one, 'If I die in a combat zone, box me up and ship me home.' They would chant it, louder and louder; another was 'Every night while you are sleeping, Charlie Cong comes a creeping all around' – and, says O'Brien, 'these seeped into your dreams at night, those songs used to just reverberate in your dreams. And going from village to village those songs resonated in the imagination.'

Says another soldier-author, Jim Webb: 'The military mission became to inflict casualties and the primary reason for existence became to minimize your own casualties. And you were sort of walking that tightrope the whole time. Ethical confusion is the only word that I can use. It just sort of mounts. People would flash. You have really good people, and one individual who was a terrific Marine saw his best friend killed. His friend only

August 11, 1970—Five 105mm Howitzers respond to North Vietnamese mortar and recoilless rifle attacks from Firebase O'Reilly, a flattened mountaintop in South Vietnam, 27 miles west of Hue.

had something less than a month left on his tour. His friend was killed and we made a sweep two days later through a village and this guy killed someone, killed a civilian as payback, and in his own mind he was sort of justified. This is the sort of thing that would happen again and again in Vietnam.'

Special Forces Captain Brian Jenkins says: 'The minute they got beyond their very, very tightly circumscribed circle of familiarity it was a foreign, alien – in the sense of "other" – world. They were frightened. Anything might set them off: a pig running across the road, a chicken running out of a door, in fear operating against an enemy they seldom saw. And in some cases it led to outlets of violence against the population in general.'

A Marine volunteer, Laird Busse, remembers a dawn patrol on his third day in Vietnam: 'We were walking along and I was impressed with how beautiful the countryside was; little pagodas, and the people were just waking up, dogs coming out, chickens scratching and this blue mist coming off the rice-fields. It was the first time that I actually saw Vietnamese people – saw them in front of their houses, as they rolled up their bamboo curtains; the curtains would raise and I would see them coming out and it was a very beautiful thing to see.

'And we were walking along and the scout yells, "Gooks in the tree-line on the left" – and everybody just starts turning and fucking cranking fire. And there are some people over there and they are shooting at us. And I remember one bullet went right over my shoulder, and one hit the dirt. I stood there: I didn't have any instinct to take my rifle off and participate, and I did not run for cover. I just actually stood there, and I watched it, like I had watched so many movies as a child.

'And then it was over, and we walked about seventy yards, and there were four people lying on the ground. Three were dead, the other one was about fifteen years old, and all of his guts were hanging out – spilled out. And this person who was fifteen years old looked exactly like I did except that he was Oriental. The person that was in charge of the squad started stamping on his intestines, kicking him, jeering; and the man's ears were carved off while he was alive.

'From that day forth,' says Busse, 'I was at least a hundred years old.' Busse's veterans' counsel describes him as 'one hundred per cent psychologically disabled'.

Some in their century-felt tour would find a moment that restored their values. A soldier called Christian found it on the body of his dead enemy, a North Vietnamese: 'As I was searching the guy's fatigues I saw a cross around his throat. And he believed in God, and I believed in God, in the same God. And I thought, "What are we doing here – we are brothers in this same world here, and here we are killing each other because the politicians can't resolve this war and their differences."

Says Marine Captain Webb, 'You see people around you stripped down to their basics as human beings. We always seem to realize the one element of the paradox – that it is debilitating. But because the war lost its political meaning we have tended to deny people the basic dignity of the experience.'

Says Dave Christian, 'I came back with hundreds and hundreds of crippled men whose bodies were wrecked in Vietnam and we aren't perceived with dignity.' It was an individual struggle to come out of it not just physically but mentally intact, and it remained an individual struggle in putting the war behind them. Christian, with multiple wounds, spent the first two years of his homecoming as a hospital in-patient and another six years as an out-patient, only to find through those years that his service was unsaluted: 'Society said, "You didn't win your war. We won our wars. You guys are losers." And they're not losers. And when I go around I tell them they're somebody.'

For a period of eight years – and for far longer back home – those who saw combat endured exceptional stress because, as Christian points out, only a tenth of the US force had to face the fighting: 'When we were at full strength, about 550,000, you may have had 50,000 men in combat

593

August 1970—Firebase Kathryn, a hilltop west of Hue once covered by jungle, is one of several U.S. and South Vietnamese bases intended to stem enemy infiltration into the coastal lowlands to the east. It is manned by 101st Airborne Division troops.

roles, and out of those you may have had 5000 a day in combat – and that would be a lot; that's really extending the situation.'

But the situation was one of overall demoralization in the phase-out period, 1969 to 1972. The knowledge that US forces were steadily disengaging increased the trauma and thinned the rationale for the 100,000 Americans wounded in those years. And for the vast army of 500,000 that was on base or facing the prospect of combat, watching the clock was watching a self-rot that would account for most of the 1.7 million who – almost a decade later – would still be considered emotionally scarred. In his 1971 report Colonel Robert Heinl summarized the state of US forces: 'By every conceivable indicator, our army that now remains in Vietnam is in a state approaching collapse with individual units avoiding or having refused combat, murdering their officers and non-commissioned officers, drug-ridden and dispirited where not near-mutinous.'

There was a simple enough explanation. In a confused war, there was still the need to find military honor. And the 'kids who left their hearts and souls there, and who died there' so desperately needed some vestige of that, says Christian. 'I had a kid die in my arms: he was shot severely, and I was holding him and I was saying, "Scotty hold on, hold on, we're going to beat the bastards, hold on." And Scotty started shaking, and his eyes started rolling, and he started talking about his mother. I think in death everyone thinks about their mother because that's who brings you into this world. And Scotty, he died, his eyes rolled back. And before he died he asked me to give this medal that he got two weeks earlier to his mother. A little bronze star. A little medal.'

Quite tangibly, the US army in Vietnam lost heart from the time Lyndon Johnson did. He had led them into the war, and no matter what the reasoning or lack of it they were pursuing a military outcome: there was valor if only in duty. Dave Christian's story summarizes 2.8 million others: 'I was only seventeen when I went in. I couldn't explain the magnitude of Vietnam at that time. And at twenty years of age, I knew how to fight a war but I didn't know the reason why or why not.' When Johnson, himself unable to explain the magnitude, de-escalated and sought peace in November 1968, the army was still physically intact, if somewhat morally tarnished. The soldiers were now being told that the reasoning had changed. There was to be a political, not a military settlement. But there was still military honor in laying down arms to avoid the shedding of blood.

The rot began when the army was required by President Nixon to continue an open-ended fight for political 'honor', or for a signed agreement that South Vietnam would remain as it then existed – if it could; and for this, without US military guar-

antees, the American soldiers found themselves soldiering on indefinitely.

The new policy was to obtain a negotiated peace through pressure, but that pressure was also heavily felt by the troops and by a divided nation. Official intolerance of dissent was sharper; the results more tragic. It had come to the point where the troops were being asked to fight on in Vietnam in the name of democracy while at home their brethren were shot down for asking, Why? Nixon's Vietnam policy would be rationalized both by him and Henry Kissinger as having, through a show of strength, achieved wider geopolitical security. It was a persuasive argument for the general public who could not assess – as the administration could or should have – the huge damage occurring in the military because of the prolonged Vietnam 'sideshow'. The statistics are damning. Far from improving US security, America's military capability was seriously endangered at the time – and considering that the war's domestic repercussions continue, there is the question of whether the wounds inflicted on the military have yet healed, whether institutionally it will have the strength and credibility it once had in time of genuine national need.

At the end of 1968, or before Richard Nixon took office, the US troops in Vietnam, whatever their view of the war, were a cohesive force. Until then the desertion rate in the US armed forces was below that of World War II and Korea. But between 1969 and 1971, compared with the three previous years, the number of desertions doubled, then doubled again – and yet this was the period when US troops were withdrawing. These desertions were both in Vietnam and at US bases worldwide indicating the wider military demoralization.

As the GIs saw it the phase-out from Vietnam was – until the very end – uncertain. Year by year the combat kept escalating: bombing of Cambodia, 1969; invasion of Cambodia, 1970; invasion of Laos, 1971; a new offensive by the North and unprecedented retaliatory bombing, 1972. In the latter twelve-month period, when half of America's troops had withdrawn, the official figures show that the desertion rate was the highest for the US forces of any year of any war: 73.5 per 1000 men. The absentee rate was 176 per 1000 men, double the 1968 figure, so that the combined desertion and AWOL numbers meant that about one in four of the US world forces had mutinied or were defying military orders (desertion is administratively defined as being absent more than thirty days, AWOL as less than thirty days).

Prior to 1969 'fragging' was apparently so rare that official statistics do not record any incidents. Between 1969 and 1971 assaults on officers in Vietnam averaged 240 a year, eleven per cent fatal. The unsubstantiated number of 'war crimes allegations' against US army personnel in Vietnam (and such charges must have been rare and proof even rarer) increased seven-fold to 144. Another forty-seven cases were substantiated in whole or part.

Drugs became the main expression of discontent – in effect, an innoculation against 'Nam. Although marijuana was always readily available, its usage among American troops in Vietnam in the phase-out period doubled from twenty-nine to fifty-eight per cent of the entire enlisted force, according to various surveys. Between 1969 and 1971 those using hallucinogenics rose from about five per cent to fourteen per cent of the force, and heroin users increased from two per cent to twenty-two per cent. In 1971 a Congressional review described heroin addiction among the Vietnam troops as 'epidemic'. This was something of an understatement. The great majority of the troops were using various drugs which, obtained at source, were more powerful and addictive. The heroin – which then cost $2 a capsule on the Saigon streets compared with $50 in New York – was ninety-eight per cent pure as against three to twelve per cent pure in the US. In 1971 fewer than 5000 American soldiers required hospital treatment for combat wounds. Four times that number, 20,529, were treated for serious drug abuse.

The hard drug addiction of this period would significantly contribute to violence in America for far longer than the US combat years. In 1981, a US government survey found that almost twenty-five per cent of those who saw combat in Vietnam had been arrested on criminal charges since their return home – and most of their crimes were drug-related.

Although the boredom and drugs went together, and were largely an on-base problem, there was also the general sentiment among the troops that life, as well as lives, was being wasted to obtain a paper settlement which virtually none of them who knew the ARVN (with its even lower morale) believed was worth the ink let alone the blood. A measure of the demoralization is that for one reason or another more than 500,000 Vietnam era soldiers received what was called 'other than honorable discharge' from the military, one third of these being Vietnam veterans.

It is hard to escape the conclusion that Commander in Chief Richard Nixon, through his doubling of the war years without military objective, left a once proud army morally shattered. The American public would finally judge Nixon for his administration's political degeneracy; the demoralization of the military was probably no less dangerous.

January 10, 1970—A U.S. tank stands in the foreground as air strike bomb blasts hit the slopes of Black Virgin mountains 50 miles north of Saigon. The fighting pitted U.S. troops against an entrenched enemy.

Above: Map shows the location of many of the U.S. bases turned over the South Vietnamese military one year after the U.S.withdrawal from Vietnam began. Also shown are bases still in U.S. hands in the autumn of 1970.

August 15, 1970—South Vietnamese regional force troops, backed by a U.S. army tank, advance on North Vietnamese army positions in scattered village 25 miles southeast of DMZ.

January 8, 1970—President Nguyen Van Thieu whispers to Vice President Nguyen Cao Ky at a news conference at the presidential palace in Saigon.

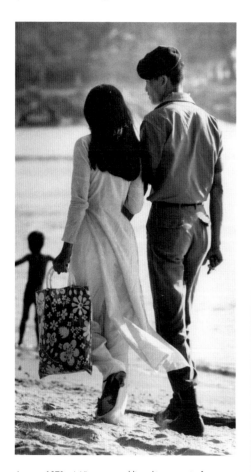

January 1970—A Vietnamese soldier taking a respite from war, strolls along the beach at Vung Tau with a young girl dressed in a flowing Ao Dai dress. The placid village was seldom touched by the war.

1970—A South Vietnamese pilot in an A-37 Dragonfly assigned to the 1st Air Division closely follows a lead plane back to base after air strike.

Above: February 1970—A South Vietnamese Air Force A-37 fires rockets into an enemy bunker at Binh Thuy Ab, providing air support for ground units in the Mekong Delta.

Left: February 12, 1970—U.S. Defense Secretary Clark Clifford speaks at a news conference in St. Louis, Mo., about how he thinks President Richard Nixon should end American involvement in Vietnam.

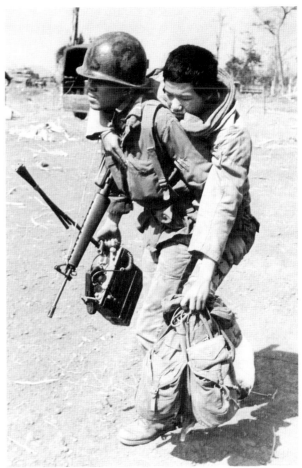

Above: February 12, 1970—U.S. Defense Secretary Melvin R. Laird, *right,* on a three-day inspection tour in Vietnam, meets South Vietnam's Premier Tran Thien Khiem in Saigon.

Right: February 19, 1970—A South Vietnamese trooper carries a buddy, wounded in a mortar attack in Laos, on his back at the Khe Sanh base in South Vietnam.

Above: February 1970—South Vietnamese President Nguyen Van Thieu talks with artillerymen at Firebase Vicki, 20 miles northeast of Tay Ninh, which supports Vietnamese Airborne and U.S. Air Cavalry troops trying to stop North Vietnamese from infiltrating from nearly Cambodia.

Right: March 1970—U.S. Marine Lance Cpl. Charles C. Sead of Portsmouth, Ohio, carries a Vietnamese woman to a waiting helicopter for evacuation to the An Hoa combat base and a refugee processing center.

Above: March 18, 1970—Meo refugees crowd around an Air America helicopter, piloted by U.S. civillian personnel, during the evacuation of Sam Thong base southwest of the Plain of Jars in Loas.

Left: March 18, 1970—A member of the Tactical Operation Center (TOC) at the U.S. base in Long Binh plots an enemy position on a map after receiving the coordinates from the field.

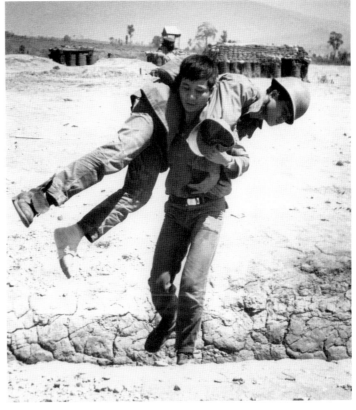

Top Left: March 25, 1970—South Vietnamese Marines, both hospital corpsmen, wade through deep water during an operation in Kien Hoa province, 40 miles southwest of Saigon in the Mekong Delta.

Top Right: April 14, 1970—A South Vietnamese soldier, wounded in the face, carries his injured son at Tan Canh. They had been evacuated from Dak Pek, the site of a special forces outpost on the Laotian border, which was now in its fourth day under communist attack.

Right: April 12, 1970—A South Vietnamese infantryman carries a wounded buddy to an ambulance at Tan Canh base camp. The wounded trooper had been evacuated by helicopter after an enemy attack against the Dak Pek special forces camp.

Below: April 9, 1970—A column of armored personnel carriers of the U.S. 25th Division rumbles toward 'Straightedge Woods,' about one mile from the Cambodian border.

Above: June 1960—South Vietnamese Marines rush to point where descending U.S. Army helicopter will pick them up after a sweep east of the Cambodian town of Prey-Veng. The troops had been searching for a Viet Cong unit reported to be in the area.

Left: April 25, 1970—As the wives and children of Montagnard soldiers watch, a U.S. Air Force C-123 cargo plane drops supplies over Dak Pek Special Forces Camp, in the Central Highlands near the Laotian border. Helicopter flights were kept to a minimum due to the threat of rocket and mortar fire.

Above: June 15, 1970—A Saigon University student throws a molotov cocktail at riot police during an anti-government demonstration to protest repression of the student movement. Tear gas billows from a barrage fired the riot police at the students.

Right: June 22, 1970—Troops of the 7th Royal Australian Regiment cross a stream in Phuoc Tuy province, southeast of Saigon. The regiment specialized in long patrols and night operations.

Above: July 6, 1970—Soldiers of the U.S. 11th Armored Cavalry Regiment are silhouetted atop their tank by the glare of tracer bullets in Cambodia. In an exercise known as Mad Minute, they sprayed the area around them, possibly infiltrated by enemy patrols, before they move on.

Right: July 25, 1970—Black market brokers move through a herd of cattle in an open air market outside Chau Doc in the western portion of South Vietnam's Mekong Delta. The cattle were smuggled across the border from Cambodia. In the background, in front of a Buddhist Temple, a convoy of trucks moves into Cambodia for a military operation.

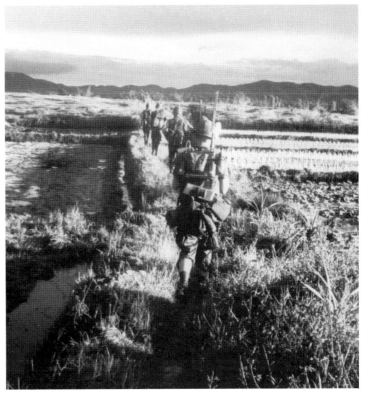

Above: July 8, 1970 Bravo Company of the 1st Battalion, 7th Regiment, 1st Marine Division, sets out on a dawn patrol through flooded rice paddies near the hamlet of Ba Ren.

Left: August 5, 1970— U.S. soldiers of the 101st Airborne Division watch as barrels of Foo gas burn away the underbrush on the perimeter of Firebase Maureen west of Hue. Foo gas was a mixture of oil, gasoline and explosives, dropped by helicopter.

Above: July 11, 1970—Student demonstrators try to evade a barrage of tear gas thrown by Saigon police by climbing over the fence at the University of Saigon.

Left: July 18, 1970—A U.S. Army CH-54A Skycrane helicopter delivers supplies to the former Special Forces camp at Kham Duc as the Americal Division reactivated the base for the first time since May, 1968. The base, still littered with the wreckage of a C-130 Hercules shot down in 1968, was being reopened to support operations along the Laotian border.

Above: August 10, 1970—A column of South Vietnamese artillerymen carry casings with powder charges to a battery of Howitzers, up a staircase protected by concertina wire at Firebase O'Reilly, west of Hue.

Left: August 28, 1970—South Vietnamese troopers, under fire from North Vietnamese positions, take cover behind a tree trunk during an operation to eliminate an enemy mortar which was harassing Firebase O'Reilly, 20 miles west of Hue.

September 1970—A company of the 1st Brigade, 5th Infantry Division, forms a human chain near the demilitarized zone while clearing their overnight position of empty shell casings.

September 17, 1970—South Vietnamese soldiers take a midday siesta atop 17th century cannons in the Citadel in Hue, the former imperial capital of Vietnam.

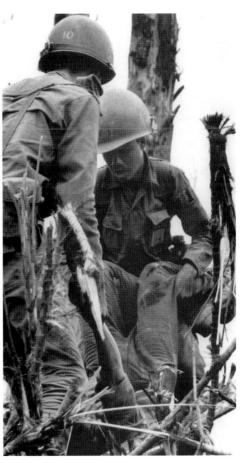

September 1970—South Vietnamese soldiers carry the body of their squad leader who was hit by North Vietnamese fire near Firebase O'Reilly, 25 miles west of Hue.

November 14, 1970—A South Vietnamese soldier screams at a Viet Cong hiding in a bunker in the middle of a burning house to come out and surrender. They were in an area known as the Arizona Territory, 25 miles southwest of Danang.

Left: November 2, 1970—A Vietnamese elder participates in a memorial service in Saigon, marking the seventh anniversary of the death of former South Vietnamese President Ngo Dinh Diem who was slain in a coup.

**604**

# FOUR MORE YEARS

'The greatest honor history can bestow is the title of peacemaker,' declared President Richard Nixon in his inaugural speech on 20 January 1969, and he stated 'This honor now beckons America – the chance to help lead the world at last out of the valley of turmoil and on to that high ground of peace that man has dreamed of since the dawn of civilization.'

On the pledge of obtaining peace in Vietnam, Nixon had been narrowly elected. He had campaigned on nothing more specific than 'de-Americanization' and 'peace with honor', but his inaugural words were taken as intent to pull back quickly from Vietnam. In fact, Nixon's first words as President had re-cast a Vietnam settlement in the context of a new global policy – and it would be a great many years before Americans learned that from the start Nixon was prepared to escalate the war.

'I call it the Madman Theory,' Nixon is quoted as telling his future White House Chief of Staff, H.R. Haldeman. They were walking along a 'foggy beach' *during* the presidential campaign and Nixon explained what he intended: 'I want the North Vietnamese to believe I've reached the point where I might do *anything* to stop the war. We'll just slip the word to them that "For God's sake, you know, Nixon is obsessed about Communism. We can't restrain him when he's angry – and he has his hand on the nuclear but-

> '**Kissinger would go to the negotiations and say to the North Vietnamese, "Look, I represent this crazy fellow Nixon and there's no telling what he might do."**'
>
> – NIXON AIDE JOHN EHRLICHMAN

ton." They'll believe any threat of force that Nixon makes because it's Nixon,' said the future President in a self-characterization. 'The threat was the key,' noted Haldeman in his book, *The Ends of Power*. But the threat would only be credible if first backed by force, and then emphasized by more force. Unknowingly, the American public had just voted for an enlarged war.

Haldeman emphasizes that Nixon 'spoke of his desire to be a peacemaker'. But Nixon, says his Domestic Affairs advisor John Ehrlichman, also saw Vietnam as expedient – as 'a kind of stage where America's bona fides, our intentions, our motives, were being acted out'. As with Presidents Kennedy and Johnson, the motive was perceived as of the highest order: to defuse the forces of world Communism. Nixon believed that by exploiting the rivalry between China and the Soviet Union he could improve US relations with both powers and thus achieve detente and limitation of arms. But the US had to negotiate for these from strength, and demonstrate its alternative readiness to fight. Specifically, in Nixon's perception, the US had to demonstrate dramatically that it had not been weakened in Vietnam. If necessary, the 'high ground of peace' was to be gained through intensified war. Between Nixon and his foreign policy collaborator Henry Kissinger, the Vietnam war 'was always discussed in the larger global context,' says Ehrlichman, 'rather than in

Right: October 4, 1970—President Richard Nixon walks with his aides during a discussion of the Vietnam war. From left: Ellsworth Bunker, U.S. ambassador to South Vietnam, Nixon, Secretary of State William Rogers and National Security Advisor Henry Kissinger

Above: February 10, 1970—Secretary of Defense Melvin R. Laird talks with Gen. Earle G. Wheeler, chairman of the Joint Chiefs of Staff, on their arrival in Saigon to look 'for ways to improve the Vietnamization program and push it forward.' With them are U.S. Ambassador to South Vietnam Ellsworth Bunker, left, and Gen. Creighton B. Abrams, right, U.S. commander in Vietnam.

Below: February 7, 1971—A U.S. Army Sheridan tank takes an overnight defensive position along Route 9 at Lang Vei, just yards from the Laotian border.

Above: April 24, 1971—Anti-war demonstrators gather on the Ellipse south of the White House in Washington to protest the Vietnam War.

the narrow context in which the debate raged in this country'.

As Nixon arrived in the White House the anti-war demonstrations raged outside, and from the Oval Office he could hear the persistent chant, 'What do we want? Peace. When do we want it? Now.' Nixon had inherited both serious domestic dissent and a framework for peace negotiations at the Paris talks. He decided neither was viable. 'His position', says Ehrlichman, 'was that he'd been elected as the individual under the constitutional system responsible for the conduct of foreign policy and the waging of war, if you please, and that foreign policy just couldn't be made in the streets.' As Nixon saw it the correct policy was to get – not make – concessions, and the Johnson people had erred.

Looking back, ex-Secretary of State Dean Rusk felt that 'the American people, at the grass roots, had come to the decision that we should abandon this effort'. Rusk was 'somewhat surprised that President Nixon tried for so long to bring about a particular result, rather than to simply extract our forces'. With the greatly reduced conflict, Rusk then saw no suggestion of military defeat in a US withdrawal: 'We had left behind for the Nixon administration a military position

which the North Vietnamese could not have overrun.'

The ex-Secretary of Defense who had persuaded Lyndon Johnson to abandon the effort now tried again. Clark Clifford met with Henry Kissinger in the transition period 'and I told him that I thought Mr Nixon had one of the most unique opportunities that an American President ever had. I suggested that within ninety days of taking office Mr Nixon could announce that he was starting the withdrawal of American troops and would continue to withdraw them until they were all gone.' Clifford 'explained all the reasons why we had been through all these years of frustrating experience'. Kissinger responded that the President should hear Clifford's presentation directly.

'The call never came,' says Clifford. 'Mr Kissinger never at any time reflected the views that I had passed on to him at that stage. We could

have got out of the war in a year, if we really set our minds to it. We were in it another seven years. We lost another 20,000 men. We spent another sixty or seventy billion dollars. They misapplied a number of the theories that we had found out were fallacious.'

As the war began its rerun, the new Secretary of Defense, in yet another parallel, was again the restraining voice trying to 'get Americans out of Vietnam'. On taking office, Melvin Laird was shocked at the cost of the 'fight now, pay later' policy of the Johnson era: 'We were borrowing against our spare parts, ammunition, aircraft, ships,' says Laird. 'I found over ten billion dollars worth of supplies and equipment that had not been funded and used in Vietnam; tremendous deficits that had been run up by robbing our NATO forces and robbing from military equipment all over the world to support that activity of fighting now, paying later, and the effect that had on our domestic economy

Above: February 8, 1971—South Vietnamese soldiers ride an armored vehicle along Route 9 into Laos.

Right: Map locates movement of South Vietnamese troops into Cambodia in early 1971 at the same time as other troops remained poised to move into Laos.

was very grave.' Yet with this knowledge the war would be continued for as long again.

Laird says he entered the Pentagon stating he would be there 'four years and no more' with the objective of withdrawing American forces from Vietnam 'in an honorable fashion because I did not support the large ground involvement in South-east Asia'. He would in fact resign at the end of Nixon's first term, though by then he was described as 'deeply distressed' that military policy had been taken over by Kissinger. Laird had come highly qualified for the Defense Secretary's post. He had been the Republican Party's chief military spokesman in Congress since the mid-1960s, consistently arguing that the cost of the Vietnam war was jeopardizing the development of strategic weapons and thus Western security.

Though he opposed a political settlement that would give the North any role in the government of South Vietnam, Laird took the view that America's obligation was to provide only arms, not troops. 'You could give them the equipment, but you cannot ensure the will of any nation,' he says. Laird's primary concern was the division in America: for years he had felt that government had to be 'more forthcoming with the American people about the war'. Not least, says Laird, 'I could well understand the concerns of many young people'. As a first act, Laird corrected 'the unfairness of the draft', ending the deferment system, but he felt that the demonstrations and protest were also due to 'the lack of understanding as to what US policy was in that area of the world'. Laird soon discovered that the American people were to be kept uninformed.

Within a month of assuming the Presidency, Nixon had decided on his first move in the 'Madman' scenario. This was Operation Menu – the secret bombing of Cambodia. It originated with a recommendation by the US Field Commander in Vietnam, General Creighton Abrams, for B-52 bombing of the so-called Fish Hook – a small curve of Cambodia north-west of Saigon. Abrams had 'reliable' information that the much-sought North

Vietnamese regional headquarters, known as COSVN (Central Office for South Vietnam), had been located in the Fish Hook area. Abrams proposed concentrated but 'short duration' air strikes as being sufficient for the small target zone. His recommendation went to Laird, who endorsed it and passed it to the White House. Planning immediately began to enlarge the air strikes to include every known North Vietnamese 'sanctuary' – even though these were adjacent to civilian areas. The bombing was planned as a replica of the clandestine air war in Laos at the beginning of the decade: the enemy could not complain without admitting his presence.

Nixon ordered total secrecy; later it was discovered that even the Strategic Air Command records had been falsified. Abrams had initially intended sixty B-52 sorties against one area. But beginning on 18 March 1969 with Operation Breakfast, followed by Lunch and so on, there were 3650 B-52 raids extending over fourteen months, involving quadruple the tonnage dropped on Japan in World War II. The US public only learned the full story four years later as part of the Watergate revelations. At the start of 'Menu' a press report that the President had been requested to authorize B-52 strikes against Cambodia drew little attention except at the White House, where the first wire-tapping of staffers and newsmen became the first ripples of Watergate.

Defense Secretary Laird was persuaded that the bombing would help speed the withdrawal of US troops and 'my disagreement with Kissinger and the President was over the fact that they insisted on keeping the strikes secret'. Laird was sure that the Congress and the public would support measures presented as shortening the war. And, anyway, 'the American people don't understand that kind of secrecy in government'. The administration 'was not being fair or open-handed and frank with the American people' but says Laird 'the State Department and Kissinger took the other position and the President came down in their favor instead of mine'.

Kissinger's military advisor, Alexander Haig, who participated in the discussions, provides the rationale that the North Vietnamese 'sanctuaries' were 'not a source of comfort to the Cambodian regime itself'. Haig asserts that both the neutralist government of Prince Norodom Sihanouk and its pro-US successor 'generally supported' the bombing. 'Their lack of complaint in the midst of it is certainly confirmation of that,' says Haig.

But Sihanouk says the US acted against his country without permission on the basis of an earlier, casual policy discussion on the remote Communist base camps just inside his border. A decade later Sihanouk told the British author William Shawcross, 'I did not know about the B-52 bombing in 1969. In 1968, I had told [US envoy] Chester Bowles, en passant, that the United States could bomb Vietnamese sanctuaries, but the question of a big B-52 campaign was never raised.'

The bombing was only the beginning of a cycle of escalating violence that would leave Cambodia as perhaps the most tragic nation in the history of warfare. The early result would be the overthrow of Sihanouk. The later outcome would be a Chinese-supported regime called the Khmer Rouge, which by various estimates exterminated between 500,000 and two million of the eight million population. After border friction the Vietnamese drove out the Khmer Rouge but continued to occupy Cambodia. In his thoroughly researched account, *Sideshow – Kissinger, Nixon and the Destruction of Cambodia*, Shawcross quotes Sihanouk as saying, 'In the sixties Cambodia survived because Lyndon Johnson rejected all the requests of his military that the United States invade Cambodia.'

The view of Nixon's White House is put by Alexander Haig, who would later become President Reagan's Secretary of State. 'It was enemy territory – it was not Cambodian territory,' says Haig, 'and we had every right, legally and morally to take what action was necessary to protect our forces.'

In the early period of the secret bombing, Defense Secretary Laird says his office 'had a timetable worked out' for the additional training of ARVN and 'the withdrawal of US air, sea and ground combat forces'. Nixon now worried that this might encourage Hanoi to hold back from serious negotiations. The bombing had brought no response and Nixon 'was plagued with the fact', says Laird, 'that once our country had made a commitment you must withdraw from that commitment only in an honorable fashion, and not cut and run'.

But in Saigon President Thieu was angrily though privately accusing the US of preparing to do just that. 'The so-called "Vietnamization" program was a pretext to withdraw American troops – to scuttle and run,' Thieu then recalls feeling. He thought that Vietnamization was 'the wrong terminology', an admission that the Americans had been 'interventionists', and their mistake 'from the beginning was to take over the war themselves'. Now Thieu foresaw 'Kissinger negotiating over our heads' to resolve relations with the Communists; the South Vietnamese would be 'abandoned to be overrun later by the North Vietnamese after a so-called "decent interval".' Nixon privately reassured Thieu that American military support remained steadfast. The President did not commit himself to a timetable for withdrawal, instead he announced that 25,000 American troops would begin leaving Vietnam the next month, July 1969, with further withdrawals contingent on Hanoi's response. 'I was not optimistic,' says Thieu, 'but we had to trust the leader of the free world.'

With the first troop withdrawal, Nixon and Ho Chi Minh exchanged letters agreeing to commence secret negotiations between Henry Kissinger and Le Duc Tho. Defense Secretary Laird remembers that Nixon and Kissinger 'entered into these negotiations with a great deal of confidence that they could have some sort of success'. The early confidence was rooted in Nixon's theory that 'they'll believe any threat of force that Nixon makes'. As the Cambodian bombing chewed up the areas designated 'Dessert', 'Snack' and 'Supper', Nixon coupled the secret talks with an ultimatum: unless the talks produced a breakthrough by 1 November he would 'regretfully' have recourse to 'measures of great consequence and force'. After Ho Chi Minh's death early in September 1969 the ultimatum was repeated.

Nixon was concerned about an unusual anti-war demonstration, a 'National Moratorium' being organized for 15 October. It promised to be the largest protest so far and Nixon raged to his staffers about the 'mindless rioters and professional malcontents' who were undercutting his credibility. Nixon decided to spell out indirectly to Hanoi the kind of force he might use. He admits that he leaked to the press unattributable reports that he was considering a blockade of the port of Haiphong and even invasion of North Vietnam. And Kissinger, who had an informal relationship with Soviet Ambassador Dobrynin, phoned him to say, 'The train has just left the station and is heading down the track.'

Dobrynin, though worried about Kissinger's hints of US rapprochement with China, kept

insisting that Moscow could not influence Hanoi, nor – because of its image in respect to China – could it reduce aid. In Hanoi itself Premier Pham Van Dong scorned 'Nixon's dark maneuvers' as 'desperate efforts doomed to total defeat'. In a maneuver of his own, Pham Van Dong extended greetings to the organizers of the moratorium, stating, 'May your offensive succeed splendidly.'

The 15 October protest brought out hundreds of thousands of demonstrators in cities across the country. When John Ehrlichman told Nixon the extent of it 'his response, in house, was to say, "Look that's a tiny fraction of the American people out there; it's on all the television, the media are killing us with it, but we know that the vast majority of Americans are with us." ' Nixon, however, knew that America was polarized: another huge moratorium was planned for 15 November, this time in Washington, and Nixon decided that he must demonstrate consensus if his word was to have weight in Hanoi. 'He had only been elected by a fraction of a percentage point,' says Ehrlichman, but Nixon believed he could 'build a base of support' among those he called 'the forgotten Americans.'

'He wasn't passive about it – he didn't just sit there and wait for those folks to suddenly appear. He had people like Charles Colson organizing "hard-hats" and labor unions and American Legion groups to come and say, "Mr President, we support you".' (Colson was the White House special counsel and like John Ehrlichman, H.R. Haldeman and other White House aides he was later convicted and jailed for Watergate felonies.)

As in the Johnson years, the anti-war groups were falsely optimistic. A former highly placed Pentagon official, Daniel Ellsberg, was persuaded by the first moratorium on a course of action. He began xeroxing a top-secret critique of the war which he had helped compile. The multi-volume study documented a long history of White House deceit over Vietnam and though it did not extend to the Nixon years, Ellsberg, from his Pentagon soundings, was convinced that the US faced four more years of enlarged war. 'Nixon', he says, 'had planned to do everything that he later did: Cambodia, Laos, dikes, B-52s, the mining of Haiphong; he had meant to do that as early as the

Left: February 9, 1971—South Vietnamese troops prepare to board a U.S. helicopter in South Vietnam after their patrol on the Ho Chi Minh Trail in Laos.

Above: February 8, 1971—South Vietnamese armored vehicles prepare to cross the Laotian border west of Lang Vei in an operation to sever the Ho Chi Minh Trail in Laos. Photographer Henri Huet was killed two days after taking this picture.

Above: March 1971—U.S. Navy armorers aboard the USS *Kitty Hawk* wheel 500-pound bombs to jets flying support for South Vietnamese ground troops in Laos.

Left: March 15, 1971— South Vietnamese troops board helicopters at the Khe Sanh base in South Vietnam to fly to Laos.

Above: Feb. 18, 1971 - Early morning mist shrouds the hills around a South Vietnamese firebase near the Laotian border. The base supports patrols by South Vietnamese troops in nearby Laos.

fall of 1969.' Ellsberg then thought that the moratorium had forced Nixon to 'back down on his threats' and that 'the people who marched in the streets will never do anything more effective than that in their lives'.

Ehrlichman could see that with Nixon the demonstrations were 'very counter-productive – he recoiled, he resisted'. In an emotional speech on 3 November, Nixon appealed to 'the silent majority' – and the response, whether impromptu or *à la* Colson, came in thousands of letters and cables to the White House. As 250,000 people gathered for a weekend protest at the Washington Monument on 15 November, Nixon sat glued to his television set. Asked his reaction to a quarter of a million protestors in his backyard, the President said he had not noticed: he had been watching a football game. Nixon's senior domestic advisor wanted 'some reconciliation'. Says Ehrlichman, 'I was hopeful that he would take this opportunity to try and soften the very sharp division that existed between the anti-war militants and the Nixon administration. I think he could have done some things; I urged him to receive some of the people, talk to them, hear them out. I think those in government owe it to people to listen to them whether you agree with them or not.'

But when Ehrlichman finally got four young demonstrators into the Oval Office 'the thing didn't come off. He was asking them "ho ho ho" kind of things to try and put them at their ease and making it worse, and the whole thing was just awful'. None of those who closely served Nixon would ever claim to know the inner man. In the anomalous way of so many professional politicians, he was strangely withdrawn, with the adulation of the crowd (the right crowd) seeming like a blood transfusion for a shy, awkward, dried-out persona that between the cheers receded in brooding need. Nixon's one detectable passion was pride of country: rightly, for he had, after all, risen from a penurious live-in general store to the presidency.

He had been born fifty-six years before this summit in 'the house my father built' on the wrong side of the California tracks in a farming town of 200 people called Yorba Linda. But for the son of Irish-descended Quakers it still seemed 'a place and time of almost unlimited opportunity'. It would be so for Richard Milhouse Nixon, but two brothers died, one in infancy, the other as a young man from tuberculosis. Perhaps this saddening, impoverished youth taught Nixon to rise to challenges – and more: to set them. He won entrance to Harvard, but the family could not afford to send him. Instead he paid his way through law school and by the age of twenty-seven was married and, so to speak, legally settled – partner in a prestigious company – when the war intervened. He joined the Navy, served in the Pacific, then endlessly fought the cold war with an anti-Communist political crusade. After being a Congressman for only five years he won the Vice-Presidency for another seven, and in 1960 almost won against John F. Kennedy: losing by 113,000 votes, the slimmest margin in any US presidential election.

In defeat, Nixon tended also to lose grace – seeming somewhat like the 'flaky, comic character in George M. Cohan's *The Tavern*', which he recalls in *The Memoirs of Richard Nixon* playing in college. But his strength was that he would not accept defeat, and this quality brought him back and brought him the votes. In his memoirs there is perhaps another detectable passion – for acting, but in the college plays 'I was usually given the character parts'. And Nixon wanted the lead.

As President, did he lead, or was he led? Was Henry Kissinger his man, or the reverse? Certainly Nixon remained impressed, though unenamored throughout, by the German-Jewish immigrant who had made it to Harvard. Kissinger was Nixon's flamboyant opposite but his ideological twin, and with Nixon predominantly interested in foreign policy there was a constant transfusion in that. Together they could brood at geopolitical chess, both playing White against Red, relishing the public cheers of each checkmate. But they seemed to hate their need of each other, according to the two men who formed the so-called 'Berlin Wall' around them.

White House Chief of Staff Haldeman wrote that a magazine cover story on Kissinger left Nixon 'white lipped in anger', and Domestic advisor Ehrlichman says 'Kissinger was very assiduous in his cultivation of the press. He would talk about the President in less than complimentary terms if it established some credibility for him with somebody that he was trying to convince. Henry's a very innovative and facile negotiator, but also an individual who on a personal level has a lot of problems. He cares very much whether people like him or not.' They were the Odd Couple, but with their secretive policy ideas and methods, no one could discern which was the prime mover, nor their ultimate motives on Vietnam. In this period of late 1969, journalist Tad Szulc, the author of a major study of the negotiations and of Kissinger's record entitled *The Illusion of Peace*, felt that 'Nixon, to a larger extent than Kissinger, probably still believed for a short period that a military victory was possible'. But, says Szulc, regardless of the outcome 'essentially Nixon and Kissinger perceived Vietnam, as Kissinger said himself at one point, as a sideshow'.

As to motivations, Defense Secretary Laird thought that both men wanted 'a peaceful accord' but he did not regard Nixon as the policy innovator; 'I would say that in the conceptual view of the world President Nixon was influenced to a great degree by Kissinger, although he had not been a friend of his and did not know him before December of 1968.' Kissinger's conceptual view, in the opinion of former Assistant Defense Secretary, Adam Yarmolinsky, grew from 'a paranoid fear of the consequences of withdrawal [from Vietnam] in terms of right-wing reaction. I take it this was a consequence of Henry's growing up in post-World War I Germany, pre-Hitler Germany, and he saw the same thing happening in the United States and he was not prepared to take what he saw as a serious risk to Americans. And he was prepared to sacrifice large numbers of Americans, and even larger numbers of Vietnamese lives, to avoid what he saw was at risk.'

In Ehrlichman's view, 'It would be very hard to say where the Nixon decisions stopped and the Kissinger decisions started. It was an amalgam; it was almost a blending of the two. Henry's conduct of affairs was almost always in response to a presidential decision, but the presidential decision very often was strongly influenced by Henry's argument.' Did Nixon express the same concern as Johnson over the casualties in Vietnam? 'I think they bothered him,' says Ehrlichman. 'I didn't see very much of that in the early years in terms of his

Left: March 24, 1971—U.S. Cavalrymen fire at enemy positions as they travel along Route 9 to the Laotian border to cover the withdrawal of South Vietnamese troops from Laos.

Right: May 23, 1972—Le Duc Tho, member of the North Vietnamese politburo, reaches out to U.S. presidential advisor Henry A. Kissinger at the end of their week-long series of talks in the Paris suburb of St. Nom La Breteche.

response to that.' But whatever his concerns Nixon 'had a political problem to marshall – to retain consensus'.

By 1970 Nixon concluded that the firmness of his domestic support could be demonstrated to Hanoi. Kissinger was frustrated with the secret peace talks begun six months earlier: there had been only four meetings, all unproductive; perhaps more secret force would oil the peace machinery. In February, Defense Secretary Laird was sent to Saigon to discuss methods. A program of clandestine ARVN attacks against North Vietnamese base camps inside Cambodia was approved. Open invasion, it was decided, would be denounced by Cambodia's Prince Sihanouk. Laird agreed with this tactic. He thought of Kissinger as 'a strong thoughtful foreign policy leader' – but Laird, though the only other relatively strong voice in a tamed administration, felt uneasy. His main objective was US disengagement and he regarded the 60,000 American troops withdrawn in Nixon's first year as insufficient: 'I was always pushing for a higher rate.'

Nixon had a consistent response. 'It would be the easiest thing in the world for me simply to

Above: May 8, 1972—President Richard M. Nixon announces from the White House that he has ordered entrances to North Vietnamese ports mined to keep weapons and supplies from those he termed 'the international outlaws.'

order our toops out of there,' he told Ehrlichman, 'but if I did none of our allies could ever count on the United States' word again.' As the President put it, 'this thing' must not 'destroy the US relationship' with either its 'allies or our adversaries'. Though in fact the major allies, Britain and France, had long been pressing for international negotiations on Vietnam, Nixon essentially considered that the allies did not know what was best for them. Says Ehrlichman, 'He saw Vietnam in a very large geopolitical context.'

In this context, Cambodia now became the sacrificial pawn. On 18 March, Prince Sihanouk was deposed while traveling abroad. His long-time aide, General Lon Nol, set up a military government and immediately began attacks on the Communist border camps. Sihanouk set up a government in exile, protesting that he was the victim of a carefully prepared CIA coup. Washington vigorously denied this, and for the next few days the National Security Council was in urgent session. One of the Council members, Kissinger's Special Assistant, Winston Lord, says, 'There was considerable surprise that Sihanouk had been overthrown – he was generally seen as a force for stability.' Lord insists that 'we had nothing to do with it' He recalls 'disagreement among various advisors on whether you try to bring Sihanouk back or whether you throw your support to Lon No!. The move was to support Lon Nol.' Within two weeks $500 million worth of US military aid was rushed to the rebel general.

Nixon in his memoirs says that a month later, 22 April, he sent Kissinger a memo stating that 'a bold move in Cambodia' was needed to support Lon Nol. Two days later Kissinger summoned Winston Lord and others of his staff to discuss American 'options'. Lord, who had graduated in law in 1960 before starting a Washington career, says 'Kissinger wanted to share and debate with his closest aides major policy decisions, so that the popular image of Kissinger as a man who doesn't like to hear dissent is not true.'

The major policy decision that Kissinger now contemplated was for an entirely new war in South-east Asia – an invasion of Cambodia by ARVN and American ground forces. Says Lord, 'The North Vietnamese were already going further into the interior of Cambodia – they were doing it before any American invasion, which is sometimes forgotten. (Sihanouk would later point out that the North Vietnamese were driven deeper into Cambodia by the previous fourteen months of US secret bombing. In February 1973, after the US had withdrawn from Vietnam, Hanoi backed Sihanouk in an armed bid to overthrow the internationally condemned Khmer Rouge regime, US bombing was then renewed against Sihanouk's front, and, as author William Shawcross notes, 'Within a few months an enormous new aerial campaign had destroyed the old Cambodia forever.')

Lord states that Kissinger 'called five of us into his office' and 'there was a rather vigorous, even stormy discussion where everyone was candid with each other. All five of us with differing rationales and differing degrees of vehemence thought that an American-South Vietnamese incursion in Cambodia would have more problems with it than positive elements. As a result of the Cambodia decision a few of the people in that meeting left the staff.' In fact, the other four – Anthony Lake,

Above: October 14, 1972—Presidential advisor Henry A. Kissinger stands in the window of his White House office. He reported earlier to President Richard M. Nixon on four days of talks with the North Vietnamese in Paris.

Left: November 13, 1972—Dr. Henry Kissinger, *right*, chief foreign policy advisor, and Gen. Alexander Haig, who had returned from talks with South Vietnamese President Nguyen Van Theiu, leave a helicopter for a meeting with President Richard M. Nixon at Camp David near Thurmont, Md.

Laurence Lynn, Roger Morris and William Watts – all resigned.

Nixon says in his memoirs that he made the decision on 27 April (within five days of his memo to Kissinger) 'to go for broke' after weighing the domestic repercussions. 'Now that we have made the decision.' he told Kissinger on the eve of the invasion, 'there must be no recrimination among us – not even if the whole thing goes wrong; in fact, *especially* if the whole thing goes wrong.'

The President then summoned John Ehrlichman to the Oval Office. Their association had been among the closest in the Nixon White House, dating from 1968 when Ehrlichman gave up a law career to join the Nixon campaign. Only with Ehrlichman and Haldeman, certainly not with Kissinger, could Nixon totally relax, talking in an ungrammatical shorthand which they had learned to decipher, translating the presidential language into memos of government with expletives deleted. 'He called me in', says Ehrlichman, 'and said, "Look, for the next ten days or so I'm going to be totally unable to deal with any domestic problems." He said, "Now, for your private information, we're going to do an invasion of Cambodia. I want you to understand what's going on." And they whistled up some Brigadier-General to come in and brief me.'

Ehrlichman then sat down with Nixon and 'we went over everything that I could anticipate might be a problem for him on the domestic side for a couple of weeks in advance.' The President asked what the domestic reaction might be: would ' "there be all this in the streets? If there were," he said, "you're going to have to handle it. I cannot be distracted by that during this period of time." ' And, Ehrlichman says, 'I didn't see him again for a long time because he was involved very much in the day to day command of the Cambodian operation.'

With forty-eight hours remaining, Nixon began preparing his public explanation. Secretary of State William Rogers had softened the ground with an opportune address to the American Society of International Law two days earlier, stating that 40,000 North Vietnamese 'now occupy Cambodia'. Though Rogers unequivocally opposed a US invasion, he did not resign.

Above: Map shows key events of the North Vietnamese offensive in the first five months of 1972.

1—North Vietnamese launch artillery attacks on bases south of the DMZ.

2—South Vietnamese abandon bases near the DMZ in April.

3—Siege of An Loc begins in April.

4—U.S. doubles Naval force off the Vietnamese coast.

5—B52s strike Hanoi and Haiphong April 15.

6—South Vietnamese lose Kontum, key central highlands fire base.

7—South Vietnamese abandon Quang Tri, flee to Hue.

8—Enemy controls part of Binh Dinh province.

9—President Nixon orders mining of North Vietnamese ports in May.

Left: Map locates the 45,000 of the 60,000 American troops in Vietnam in the spring of 1972. The 15,000 not shown were scattered around the country in small units.

However, his law society speech perhaps contained an oblique criticism of Nixon for historians. While referring to the North Vietnamese he said a 'more explicit and unprovoked violation' of the United Nations charter 'could hardly be imagined'. Defense Secretary Laird still thought there might be time to dissuade the President from deploying US troops. But Nixon was adamant: the Cambodian move would show Hanoi that America was not a crippled giant. Laird now attempted to stop the President from saying in his public explanation that the primary objective was to attack COSVN, the North Vietnamese regional headquarters, which in fact had no fixed location.

Says Laird, 'Right up to the time he gave that speech I was pleading to have that taken out because COSVN was never a single unit of a single headquarters. In that type of guerrilla warfare it moves all the time, so again the American people were misled by not having a real understanding of what it was about. But the speech was made and COSVN was listed as a major military target.'

The invasion began on 29 April with 15,000 US troops and another 5000 ARVN soldiers in a separate two-prong strike. The first announcement, issued jointly from the Pentagon and the US command in Saigon stated that the action against Cambodia was 'in response to the request of the government of the Republic of Vietnam'. The US was providing 'advisors, air, logistics, medical and artillery support, as required'. There was no mention that in fact US troops were directly involved, nor that they comprised three-quarters of the invading force. Without specifying the extent of the US action, President Nixon publicly announced on the following day, 30 April, that American soldiers had entered Cambodia 'in co-operation with the armed forces of South Vietnam'. This, said Nixon, was not an invasion of Cambodia but an extension of the Vietnam war 'to protect our men who are in Vietnam and to guarantee the continued success of our withdrawal and the Vietnamization program'.

The New Cambodian government, while receiving US military aid, had apparently not been consulted. On 1 May, Premier Lon Nol denounced the US action as a 'violation' of Cambodian territory and stated he would have preferred additional aid to do the job himself. In the US the Vietnam Moratorium Committee called for 'immediate massive protests' – and these brought confrontational tragedy unknown since the Civil War.

Nixon had anticipated violent protest, telling Ehrlichman: 'I want you to think through what you might have to do in terms of police and national guard and all that sort of thing.' 'Well,' says Ehrlichman, 'we'd been through it so many times by then that it was not an awesome responsibility. We discussed the possibility of various kinds of demonstrations that might occur. We didn't anticipate Kent State, obviously.'

At Kent State University in Ohio the protests had grown in strength day by day, with students occupying the faculty buildings – as they had all across the country. Five days earlier Nixon had

Above: Map shows the progress of the North Vietnamese offensive that moved forward in the spring of 1972. Shaded portion indicates area under enemy control. Square with star indicates enemy regional headquarters. Black squares are district towns fallen to North Vietnamese in 1972. Circle with white star indicates key cities vital to the defense of South Vietnam.

referred to students who had set fires at Berkeley, Yale and Stanford universities as 'bums'. On 4 May the Ohio National Guard, with loaded rifles, surrounded the campus at Kent State. As the guardsmen lined up on a slope overlooking the massed group of young demonstrators, a witness recalls a sudden volley of fire: 'Some kid yelled, "These are live bullets", and this guy says "My God, this girl is hurt" and he picks her up and she has this bloody spot on her jacket and there was blood coming out of her mouth.'

Four students had been shot dead, two of them girls. Eleven others lay bleeding; a scene of carnage on green lawns. In a sorrow that reached across America, the father of one dead girl said, 'My child was not a bum.' Within a few days 450 colleges closed in protest.

Nixon's reaction: 'Look,' Ehrlichman quotes him, 'I can't let this affect how I conduct this thing, and the reasons we're in Cambodia are that this was a sanctuary and the North Vietnamese are beating up our people and we had to get in there and root them out.' Publicly Nixon stated, 'When dissent turns to violence it invites tragedy.'

Kissinger's military advisor, Alexander Haig, thought the President had displayed leadership: Cambodia was 'essential' and 'after all we gave the whole length of South Vietnam free run to the enemy, to enter and debauch in any manner they wanted, and the consequences were grave for American lives'. Haig says that Nixon recognized that Cambodia was 'an extremely controversial decision', but 'that is one of the aspects of presidential leadership. He was prepared to address that controversy, and did so.' '

But Nixon did not know how to address or rally his divided nation, says Ehrlichman, reflecting on 'those times when hundreds of thousands of people came to Washington', with the students camping in continual vigil outside the Lincoln Memorial. 'We had delegations in droves', he remembers, 'and a lot of us in the White House were seeing those people. Henry Kissinger and all kinds of people were seeing them. I had parades of them coming in the office. And they were saying, "We don't like what's happening in Cambodia, and we don't like what happened at Kent State, and we're very upset and why can't we just get out?" '

Then at 2.00 am on 8 May Ehrlichman heard from a White House staffer that the President was about to set off somewhere in his car and Ehrlichman said, 'Go with him, and take a radio and the Signal Corps will patch your radio into my telephone. Keep me posted – the secret service were with him, of course. Next thing I heard he's at the Lincoln Memorial talking to the college students.'

Later, Ehrlichman got a full briefing on what Nixon talked about: 'He generally jollied them up. They wanted to talk about the war, about Cambodia, about college campuses and their concerns, and he missed the point, I'm sad to say. He was talking to them about football teams and

about their hobbies and all that kind of thing – typical Nixon problem of how to relate to the people that he met.' Then the President 'called in his Press Secretary and some others and indicated to them that this was a great rapprochement, this was Nixon and the students burying the hatchet and finding a meeting ground. And he wanted that put out to the press as his version of what had taken place.' But the students were also talking to the press 'and saying, "Gee, this guy is just not on our wavelength." I think it was a net minus, actually,' concludes Ehrlichman.

Defense Secretary Laird felt much the same about the Cambodian operation. American troops were withdrawn on 30 June after a two-month, twenty-mile probe into the 'Fish Hook' region having, it was said, seized large stockpiles of North Vietnamese ammunition, including 143,000 rockets, mortar and rifle rounds and some 200,000 anti-aircraft rounds. Casualties were put at '4776 Communist dead' with US losses placed at 338 killed, 1525 wounded. But the enemy headquarters had not been found. Laird had been right – the headquarters 'floated' and were easily relocated – and he was privately critical of the President: 'By misleading the American people on this fact, and then not finding any headquarters, he took away from the credibility of the whole operation.'

As an enlarged 40,000-man ARVN force continued to press deeper into Cambodia creating 200,000 refugees, the US Senate adopted an amendment intended to prohibit further use of US troops or air support in Cambodia (this was later circumvented). The Senate had meantime repealed the Gulf of Tonkin Resolution, thus legally forbidding further escalation in South-east Asia without Congressional approval.

Like General Westmoreland in his day, the military would now say it was hindered by political restrictions. Military aide Alexander Haig would have preferred an extended operation in Cambodia. Haig had by then been in uniform for

twenty-three years, graduating 214th in a class of 310 at West Point. He had displayed administrational ability, serving General MacArthur in occupied Japan, and later saw action in both Korea and Vietnam. He held the rank of colonel when discovered by Kissinger. From that point Haig was an exceptionally influential force for a military man in US affairs, running the besieged White House in the final Watergate days, then promoted to general, raised above many senior candidates when appointed NATO supreme commander, and finally becoming Secretary of State. On the Cambodian invasion, Haig says; 'If I were to be critical of it, I would say that there were too many definite limitations applied to the conduct of the announcement of the decision to go in there, both in terms of duration and scope of American activity on the ground in Cambodia.'

Early in the Cambodian invasion President Nixon had announced that he would withdraw 150,000 US troops from South Vietnam over the next twelve months. A CBS opinion poll then showed that the public supported the Cambodian action by two to one. A subsequent Gallup poll showed that while forty-eight per cent of the public wanted withdrawal of Vietnam forces immediately or no later than mid-1971, thirty-one per cent supported withdrawal over as long a period as necessary, and another thirteen per cent favored an increase in troop levels to finish off the war. America was almost evenly divided, but Nixon could still claim a very large remnant of his 'silent majority'. He still felt he had a mandate to act firmly with Hanoi, but his problem was that the North Vietnamese showed no signs of being intimidated. With Cambodia, Hanoi had broken off the secret talks, resuming them in September with a tougher stance: demanding President Thieu's removal from office as a condition of any settlement.

At this stage of the 'negotiations', says analyst Tad Szulc, 'the realization had dawned on Nixon

Above: The expanded, aggressive attacks by North Vietnamese and Viet Cong units expanded to three fronts in the spring of 1972. Near the DMZ fighting was heavy around Quang Tri. Enemy tanks were on the attack in the central highlands. A third front was opened as enemy tanks moved out of Cambodia to with 60 miles of Saigon. Shaded area shows location of Viet Cong control. American air bases are indicated plane icons, including those in Thailand.

Right: Black area in map at left shows area of South Vietnam controlled by the Vietminh in 1954 before the defeat of the French. Map at right shows area controlled North Vietnamese and Viet Cong in December, 1972.

Above: October 13, 1972—President Richard M. Nixon hears reports on Vietnam peace talks in the family dining room at the White House. From left are Secretary of State William P. Rogers who met with foreign ministers at the United Nations, Nixon, and presidential advisor Henry A. Kissinger and chief assistant Gen. Alexander L. Haig who met with Hanoi's negotiators in Paris.

Above: November 27, 1972—An A-7 Corsair comes in for a landing on the USS Saratoga after completing an air strike against North Vietnamese targets south of the 20th parallel.

Right: January 23, 1973—Le Duc Tho, right, North Vietnam delegate, shakes hands with presidential advisor Henry A. Kissinger after their meeting on Vietnam peace talks at the International Conference Center in Paris.

Left: January 23, 1973—Hanoi delegate Le Duc Tho waves as he and presidential advisor Henry A. Kissinger leave the International Conference Center in Paris.

and Kissinger that military victory was not possible'. It was now a question of slowly, in some fashion, arriving at a settlement which would at least preserve the Saigon government from total collapse. Yet Nixon had now set the clock against himself: he faced, as a result of Cambodia, clear Congressional checks, and he faced a public commitment to withdraw almost one third of his Vietnamese force in the coming months. But as 1970 ended, North Vietnamese forces were again pouring down the Ho Chi Minh Trail in reaction to Cambodia. The opportunity of withdrawing from a battlefield quietened for two years was now lost; the tentative cease-fire in-place formula of 1969 would, if implemented, confront President Thieu with a far larger North Vietnamese force on his borders. Thieu had all along wanted to take over the war: he was now invited to put Vietnamization to the acid test.

On 18 January 1971, with the concurrence of the National Security Council, President Nixon authorized an invasion of Laos. No American ground troops were to participate, but a US artillery, air and helicopter force of 10,000 men would support an ARVN assault of 17,000 men.

Operation Lam Son – named after a fifteenth century victory – was set for 8 February. 'We agreed', says President Nguyen Van Thieu, 'that in the limited time we have, to do our best to cut the Ho Chi Minh Trail, to destroy as much as possible of the North Vietnamese supplies to delay their offensive.'

Kissinger says in his memoirs *The White House Years*, that he regarded the invasion, supported by the US military in Saigon, as 'conceived in doubt and confusion'. The doubt was whether 17,000 South Vietnamese troops could achieve this objective considering that the US military in earlier plans to attack the Trail had calculated on 60,000 American troops.

The main objective was the North Vietnamese base town of Tchepone, twenty-five miles inside Laos. Airlifted by American helicopters, the ARVN force slowly advanced after building a chain of hilltop firebases. It took them a month of relatively light fighting to reach Tchepone – and then the North Vietnamese responded. In a month-long retreat some South Vietnamese units were annihilated. On 9 April, at the end of this second two-month-long invasion, ARVN losses

were officially put at 1146 dead, 4235 wounded, but were believed to be several times higher. US air-crew losses were 176 dead, 1042 wounded. Only the deployment of every available US helicopter to evacuate the ARVN prevented a greater tragedy—and the overloaded helicopters were coming back with soldiers desperately clinging to the landing skids.

The US military criticized ARVN for not holding, but President Thieu accuses the Americans of being the first to back off. 'Now what went wrong', says Thieu, 'is that after the first week the Americans had so many casualties among the helicopter pilots that they reduced the number of helicopters used for medical evacuation. That's the reason why the Vietnamese troops couldn't advance faster. It slowed down the advance and that gave the advantage to the North Vietnamese to react. The Americans would not accept to pay the high price both in helicopters and pilot losses.'

Thieu's Vice-President, Nguyen Cao Ky, says he was at field headquarters at the start and was then criticized for predicting failure. 'It was a failure', he says, 'because the operation itself was unnecessary. If you sent your troops to make an enclave to draw the Communist troops and then destroy them – Yes. But just to go there in that jungle for a promenade – what for? What for?'

Military analyst Brian Jenkins calls the invasion 'a first rate disaster' which wiped out the best young ARVN officers and, 'It would seem that no one had learned a single lesson from the previous years of warfare in Vietnam, either at the tactical level or higher up.'

Nixon and Kissinger had dispatched Alexander Haig to observe the invasion. He felt there should have been more American input: 'The inability of the South Vietnamese forces alone to conduct that kind of an operation resulted in the less than satisfactory outcome. When I got there,' Haig recollects, 'it was clear that the operation was not receiving the kind of leadership and management from the American force structure that it should have.' The problem, as Haig saw it, was 'our preoccupation with the Vietnamization concept; and the American leadership on the ground, I am sure directed by the Secretary of Defense, was to be one of benign overwatch when it should have been very active management, and had that been applied it would have been a successful operation.'

Haig would seem to imply that somehow Defense Secretary Laird did not fully support White House orders. Apart from this, taking Haig's analysis, Vietnamization was never going to succeed without a large American presence, so that if Haig's views at all reflected those of his White House seniors then the administration's Vietnamization policy was indeed one of expedient escape, not conviction.

Vietnamization, says President Thieu, 'depended on the US heart and mind. I repeated many times to the Americans, it must be honest Vietnamization. You must honestly like to help us fight. If it's fully done, continuous, it could be a way to prevent the collapse of South Vietnam.' At the time, Thieu held a somewhat less than honest 'Lam Son victory' parade in Saigon. It was solemnly announced that 13,000 North Vietnamese had been killed – and 7000 weapons and 1250 tons of rice captured.

In the United States the sense of defeat spurred more than criticism. Violence begat tragedy, quoth Nixon – and now terrorist bombs exploded in American cities. One severely damaged the Senate wing on Capitol Hill. In Congress, the House Democratic caucus, after a stormy debate, voted to cease US involvement in Vietnam by the end of 1972: once more, Nixon had adversely advanced the clock – at least for the South Vietnamese. Senator Edward Kennedy called the Laos decision a 'nightmare'; McGovern said it cast doubt on the credibility of Vietnamization; Fulbright called it a 'massive deception or a massive misjudgement, or both'.

Senator Fulbright then knew the entire history of deception and misjudgement involving successive Presidents – and he had known it for eighteen months. As Chairman of the Foreign Relations Committee he had been the first outside the administration to receive a copy of the Defense Department's secret internal study on US decision-making in Vietnam from 1945 to 1968, to become known as the *Pentagon Papers*. Disillusioned by the very study in which he had participated, Daniel Ellsberg had given Fulbright a copy of the massive, 7100-page study in late 1969.

Left: January 27, 1973— The four delegations sit around the table during the first signing ceremony of the agreement to end the Vietnam war at the Hotel Majestic in Paris. Delegates clockwise, from front: United States, Provisional Revolutionary Government of South Vietnam, North Vietnam and South Vietnam.

Fulbright considered Senate hearings on the study, but had yet to conduct any.

'It really took two more invasions, Cambodia and Laos, to convince me that I couldn't wait for Congress,' says Ellsberg, who had become a senior research associate at MIT. 'I had the feeling that America was eating its young, was destroying some of its most dedicated, most patriotic, most concerned citizens – young Americans subject to the draft, and it was up to older people like me who had been participants to not let that burden fall entirely on their children.

'When I finished reading the *Pentagon Papers* I understood at last that the war was one war; there wasn't a French war followed by a Vietnamese war and an American war – there was one war that we had participated in from the beginning, and it was a war that we had never had any right to be in at all, any more than the French did.'

Ellsberg had consulted his wife about xeroxing the secret papers, if only because the cost of making several thousand copies took 'all our savings of three or four thousand dollars. So I handed her some of the material on the plans to bomb North Vietnam, going back to 1964; the plans to give "another turn of the screw", to use the water-drip technique of occasional raids, followed by a moratorium and then another raid that hit them with "greater pain", "squeezing them", using a variety of such language. She came back to me after she read it with tears in her eyes and she characterized it as the language of torturers, and that hit me very hard.'

After the invasion of Laos, Ellsberg turned the papers over to Neil Sheehan of *The New York Times*, which after several weeks careful deliberation and verification began publishing excerpts on 13 June 1971. The paper's front page of that date showed a picture of Nixon and daughter Tricia at her marriage in the White House rose-garden, and next to the photo was the headline: 'Pentagon Study Traces three Decades of Growing US Involvement.'

Nixon, though not implicated in the damning study, saw it as a slight on the presidency and on him personally, says John Ehrlichman: 'Nixon's feeling about the press was cumulative. There wasn't any one event I'd say that colored it. This was just more of the same as far as he was concerned: the press had no concern for the country's secrets; no concern for the country's well-being; it

was anything to get a story, anything for the sensational headline, and anything to undercut the President.' Nixon obtained an injunction to stop further excerpts in the *Times*. The press then rallied. *The Washington Post* began publishing excerpts; again Nixon obtained an injunction, only to see more and more newspapers across the country defy him with the justification that the issue was not the endangering of national security but the suppression of the truth. *The New York Times* had pleaded to the Supreme Court on the right to publish, and on 30 June the Court ruled in favor of the *Times*.

As a direct consequence of the *Pentagon Papers*, arising from the Vietnam war, the White House began to develop the climate and methods of Watergate. Nixon's senior domestic advisor, John Ehrlichman, says at this time Nixon 'just pushed all the buttons'. Ehrlichman relates afresh how it began: 'It happened that Daniel Ellsberg had been a student and protégé of Henry Kissinger [at Harvard]. They had had a fundamental falling out of one kind or another, and so Kissinger was very much involved in conversations with Nixon about Daniel Ellsberg, telling him what he knew about Ellsberg. One of the problems was that Ellsberg had some Defense Department secrets in his mind, if not in his possession: what might he do with these other secrets? So there was an effort made to try and define Ellsberg's intentions.

'The FBI was given this task. [FBI Director] J. Edgar Hoover, it turned out, was a friend of Ellsberg's father-in-law; Hoover dragged his feet. The upshot was that Krogh on my staff, who'd been given responsibility for trying to anticipate what Ellsberg might do, came to me and said, "Look, we're not getting results out of the FBI. I have an ex-FBI and an ex-CIA man working for me – I'd like to turn them loose on this." These are people from the White House staff. I said, "I think I'd like to check that one." *So I asked Nixon about it. And Nixon said, "If Krogh recommends it, that's what we'll do." '* (Egil Krogh Jr, deputy-assistant to the President for Domestic Affairs, formed the so-called plumbers unit which included former FBI agent G. Gordon Liddy and former CIA agent E. Howard Hunt: all, like Ehrlichman, once lawyers. Ehrlichman approved 'a covert operation' – burglary of the offices of Ellsberg's psychiatrist, Dr Lewis Fielding.)

Left: January 27, 1973—
Agreement to end the
Vietnam war is signed in
Paris by U.S. Secretary of
State William Rogers, rear.

'Among other techniques which the FBI and the CIA were given to pursue in the past were break-ins and black-bag jobs investigating through people's medical files and that sort of thing, and these two fellows reverted to type, in effect, and went into Ellsberg's psychiatrist's office and went through his files in the hope of finding something there.' The precedent for the Watergate break-in had thus been set. With the violation of his rights, Ellsberg – indicted on fifteen counts rendering him liable to 115 years imprisonment for theft and mishandling of classified documents – would have all charges dismissed.

The revelations of the *Pentagon Papers* came at a time which Nixon describes as 'particularly sensitive'. The SALT or Strategic Arms Limitation Talks with Moscow were underway, and in July, after two years of patient negotiating, Henry Kissinger had met secretly with Premier Chou En-lai in Peking. Though 1971 had started badly for Nixon he was now able to announce that he would make an historic visit to China in February, to be followed by a Moscow summit meeting in May 1972. American foreign policy had progressed impressively on all fronts except Vietnam. At the secret talks in Paris, Kissinger had just made the most significant concession of the negotiations. Unknown to Saigon, he had dropped the demand for the withdrawal of North Vietnamese troops from the South. Hanoi had still not responded.

But by now, for the US, says negotiations analyst Tad Szulc, the war 'in a curious sort of way' was unimportant: it 'had to be overcome, had to be solved' but only when 'all the strands came together'. And Hanoi, he considers, was holding back having 'assessed correctly the American domestic pressures' which obliged Nixon, if possible, to end the war in his first term. This gave Hanoi 'a chance to show whether *they* could achieve the military victory which had eluded the Americans'. Historian Gareth Porter, Director of Washington's Indo-China Resource Center and Research Associate of Cornell University, felt that

through 1971 'both sides wanted to see how far they could get with military action'. And events would sustain this.

Whether or not Nixon had decided on his ultimate move he was clearly confident as he began the new year – election year. In January he announced a further 70,000 US troops would leave Vietnam in the next four months, reducing the total US force there to only 69,000 men. And also in January, responding to criticism of the unproductive formal peace talks. President Nixon revealed to the world that Henry Kissinger had been engaged in secret peace negotiations since 1969.

During two and a half years Kissinger had made fifteen transatlantic trips to France, with his aides elaborately plotting to keep the visits secret. 'These trips were almost always on a weekend or on a holiday,' says Winston Lord who traveled with Kissinger. As Lord describes the intrigue, Alexander Haig would cover for Kissinger's whereabouts and 'we had the presidential plane at our disposal and the close co-operation of the French.

'We'd usually go on a Saturday morning, drive out to Andrews air force base to a special hangar, just three or four of us along with Kissinger; get on the plane, fly across the Atlantic all day Saturday, and land in central France, get out and transfer to a small French jet arranged by President Pompidou's office and fly from there to the outskirts of Paris where we'd be met by our military attaché at the Embassy who had rented a car under an anonymous name; drive to a safe haven apartment to get a night's sleep, negotiate with the Vietnamese on Sunday and with the time change we could fly back late Sunday and still go in the office the next morning as if nothing had happened. . . . It had its James Bond aspects.'

Plus a touch of Kafka. Nixon would tell Ehrlichman about the progress of his 'Madman' theory: 'Henry and Nixon played good guy, bad guy in these negotiations, just like a couple of cops. Henry would say – and I have this from Nixon – he would say to the North Vietnamese, "Look, I represent this crazy fellow Nixon, and

there's no telling what he might do. I am a very reasonable man. I am a man of peace. I oppose these bombings and so on. But there's no telling what Nixon might do. So you'd better make your deal with me because I'm going to be much easier to get along with than he is." And then if he got to a sticky point, he would report back and they would unleash the bombs or some kind of an offensive, and Henry could go back and say, "See what happens when you don't make your deal with me – he back there in the White House does something crazy."'

But it was a case of two could play. During the period of the secret talks, North Vietnam rebuilt. Kissinger's opposite, Politburo member Le Duc Tho who had been a founding member of the Party forty years earlier, was in no hurry. He would smile at Kissinger, never saying yes, never quite saying no, but afterwards citing political poems to his aides: 'Rage grips me – so many years their heels have crushed our country – a thousand thousand oppressions.'

As the series of secret talks concluded in early 1972 with Nixon's disclosure of them, the President publicly announced his peace terms: all US forces would be withdrawn within six months of a signed agreement; internationally supervised elections would be held within the same period, and President Thieu, if seeking re-election, would step down beforehand to compete equally with other candidates. Except for this last provision, the terms hardly differed in essentials from those possibly attainable in 1969. The intervening time had benefited East-West relations but not those of South and North Vietnam. In this sideshow, the United States would not write the final acts, nor even guess at the next.

To the total surprise of the other side, 120,000 North Vietnamese troops swept across the Partition line on 30 March in a so-called Spring Offensive, spearing deep into three provinces with Soviet tanks and armored units. It was the North's largest conventional offensive so far, and experts on the peace negotiations differed as to the impact of the offensive. In the view of Gareth Porter, Hanoi sought not military victory but 'to move the balance of forces back to the position before the 1968 Tet Offensive' – in other words, to have more troops in place prior to a cease-fire. But in the analysis of Tad Szulc, the North Vietnamese no longer considered American troops a viable threat; they 'clearly believed they could do it' but they under-estimated 'the resolve or the unpredictability of President Nixon and his very powerful military response'.

With 95,000 American troops then remaining in Vietnam, Nixon ordered massive air strikes in support of ARVN ground forces – and also started heavy B-52 bombing of the North around Hanoi and Haiphong. On 8 May, two weeks before he was due to visit Moscow, the President in a special broadcast declared that 'Hanoi must be denied the weapons and supplies it needs'. He announced that the US was even then mining North Vietnamese ports – used mostly by Soviet ships.

It was a huge gamble, fiercely debated because of the Moscow summit which Kissinger aide Winston Lord describes as 'painstakingly prepared for a couple of years. Several agreements, including a major strategic arms agreement, were in the offing.' Many Nixon advisors, he says, felt that though his action was retaliatory it was not 'worth doing if it meant losing the Moscow summit. Nixon felt it would be impossible for him to go to Moscow, sign all those agreements and link champagne glasses with Russian leaders at the very time the North Vietnamese were overrunning parts of South Vietnam with the help of Russian arms. He felt this would put him in an impossible situation.

So to his credit he was willing to risk major achievements with the Russians, which incidentally could help in his re-election.'

With the North Vietnamese offensive still continuing after two months and with US mines sealing Soviet ships in the Northern ports, Nixon went to Moscow on 22 May. Says Tad Szulc: 'It is one of those terribly curious stories of relationships of super-powers. It was one of the great poker games of history.' The North, he says, risked everything on that one offensive; the Chinese and Russians risked their global image by keeping silent on the bombing and mining of their Vietnam ally; the Nixon government risked the summit – and detente. 'There was this sideshow', says Szulc, 'still going on; people bombing each other; Nixon goes to Peking, Nixon goes to Moscow, and history on the super-power level goes on to its own logical or illogical conclusion.'

By mid-July it was clear that North Vietnam's conventional assault could not succeed against US air-power. Cities had fallen and been recaptured, but there had been no decisive change; and the North Vietnamese ceased the offensive. Both sides had now failed to achieve outright military victory. Hanoi, says historian Gareth Porter, 'had to step back from its maximum hopes – which were a coalition government, and retreat to a position of Thieu's continuing in power. So this represented a true compromise between the two – the United States wanting to maintain Thieu in power without any intermediary structure and the North Vietnamese wanting to change that structure totally to a coalition government.'

The United States, at this stage, also accepted

that it could not gain a military edge, says John Ehrlichman. 'It was increasingly obvious that to continue the war on the same scale was not going to accomplish anything by election time. Probably the best that could be done, Kissinger has told me, was to get the North Vietnamese back to where they'd been a year or two before.' In other words, the bombing and invasions of Cambodia and Laos, with their hundreds of thousands of casualties, had gained nothing.

Similarly the North in its invasion had captured territory it then found it could not hold, resulting only in almost a million new refugees. US troops would soon be all gone – but US air-might remained, and was striking ever closer to Hanoi itself. Hanoi's chief negotiator Le Duc Tho now asked to meet Kissinger and in Paris on 8 October proposed a military settlement: a cease-fire in-place in return for the complete withdrawal of US forces and exchange of prisoners. A 'National Council of Reconciliation' would deal with elections or the political settlement at some future time.

Says Winston Lord, who accompanied Kissinger, 'It was clear to us immediately that it was a breakthrough because it effectively said, "Let's do what the Americans had proposed" – they didn't put it that way, of course – "back in May 1971"; namely a military settlement only, consisting of US withdrawal, cease-fire; return of prisoners, international supervision.' Lord considered that Hanoi was influenced by the impending US election 'because by then, in October, it was clear that Nixon was going to be re-elected over [Senator George] McGovern. It was clear that they were going to have to deal with Nixon for several more years.' Lord acknowledges the historic nature of the 8 October meeting: 'It was on that date, through their plan, that they for the first time after agonizing years of negotiations, separated a political settlement from a military settlement and made a peace that we considered honorable, possible.' This 'honorable' peace would leave an estimated 150,000 North Vietnamese troops in-place in the South or on its borders.

Unlike Lord, other American observers of different political shades would see no US accomplishment in the October formula. Says historian Arthur Schlesinger Jr, 'Nixon could have got American troops out of Vietnam in 1969 on the same terms.' Says Tad Szulc, 'What the North Vietnamese were really giving the United States was the great face-saving device of letting Thieu remain in power, and inevitably their own calculation was, Okay, let's get the Americans out, let's sign the bloody peace treaty, let Thieu stay and let nature take its course; in the next year or two he will disappear – as he, indeed, did.'

Again contrary to Lord, one of Kissinger's own negotiators in Paris, John Negroponte, felt that if anything the US domestic situation – 'fear about political unrest within this country' – influenced the American side, and that the North's spring invasion also 'had a major disruptive effect on our plans because we did not know what the impact would be on the Vietnamization program'. And, says Negroponte, 'One of the most significant flaws of the agreement was that it did not address in any significant way the prospect of a cease-fire in either Laos or Cambodia.'

Finally, South Vietnam's President Thieu still knew nothing of the 'honorable' interim settlement.

Right: January 27, 1973— A huge peace sign is lighted in New York's Times Square as the cease fire goes into effect in Vietnam. The sign was 10 stories tall.

In ten hectic days after the 8 October meeting, Washington and Hanoi settled any remaining differences and details. In an exchange of cables, President Nixon and Prime Minister Pham Van Dong agreed to a limit on arms replacements after a cease-fire, and the North agreed to a schedule for releasing the 566 American pilots held captive in Hanoi. As Kissinger flew to Saigon on 18 October, Nixon cabled Hanoi that the agreement 'could now be considered complete'. The signing date was set for 31 October. There was the matter of informing Thieu – and his reaction.

Winston Lord went with Kissinger to Saigon: 'I'd have to say that this, for me, and I think probably for Kissinger, was one of the most painful episodes throughout those eight years [of the war]. We really thought that we had achieved an honorable peace, with just a few language details to be worked out. We thought that Thieu and the South Vietnamese would be so happy that after years the North Vietnamese had finally dropped their insistence on a coalition government, had agreed that we could continue supplying military equipment to South Vietnam after the cease-fire.

'We presented it to him; he listened impassively and we took encouragement because he didn't immediately denounce it; thought about it overnight, asked some questions which we thought were encouraging, and then came back and blasted the agreement and for a couple of days we had a very painful time.' Thieu recalls that he told them, 'I am not a yes-man. I am not a puppet. I will not agree with everything that the Americans would like to impose on our people.'

Nguyen Van Thieu – whose name means 'One Who Ascends' – had then been President for five years. After the return of the French in 1945, Thieu joined the Viet Minh but within a year abandoned Ho Chi Minh's side, declaring it was Communist. He then entered a French-run military academy which was training an opposition Vietnamese army, fought in several campaigns against the Viet Minh and as a colonel emerged as a key plotter in the 1963 overthrow of Diem. Says Thieu of his confrontation with Kissinger, 'They said I am an unreasonable man. I acted as a patriot, as a Vietnamese, and as a President who is responsible for the fate of our country.'

'We miscalculated', Winston Lord admits, 'on two grounds. We were getting out but we had dropped the mutual withdrawal – which we had dropped a couple of years before – but now he was faced with the actual prospect of these [North Vietnamese] troops remaining in his country. Secondly, he felt that he didn't have enough time to consider this agreement, to prepare his people and his army for the concessions he would have to make.'

Thieu became visibly angry remembering his exchange with Kissinger: 'I said that the life or death of South Vietnam relied on those two points. One, the North Vietnamese troops had been allowed to stay forever; secondly, there's a coalition government camouflaged under the form of a National Council. Mr Kissinger had negotiated over our heads with the Communists. At that point the Americans wanted to end the war as fast as possible to wash their hands, to quit Vietnam because of the domestic problem in the United States. It was not an error in politics. It was a deliberate wrong political choice.'

Both Ambassador Ellsworth Bunker and

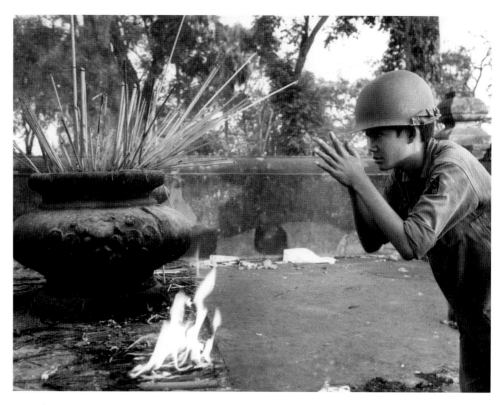

Above: January 24, 1973—A soldier offers prayer of thanksgiving at a temple in Saigon following the announcement of a ceasefire.

Kissinger's military advisor, Alexander Haig, were present at the confrontation and were sympathetic to Thieu. Says Bunker, 'I was not surprised that Thieu was reluctant to yield on the question of North Vietnamese troops remaining in South Vietnam; their presence would make it difficult to hold a fair and free election.'

'With justification, President Thieu was sceptical of a number of things,' says Haig. 'Would these Accords be enforced once they were arrived at? We were asking Thieu to accept some rather severe risks.' But with Congress 'in 180 degree opposition to the further conduct of that conflict, some risks had to be taken'.

Thieu stormed and delayed for four days, then rejected the terms outright on 22 October. On the 25th, Nixon cabled Hanoi and asked for a delay in the treaty, explaining Saigon's dissent. The response came the next day over Radio Hanoi – a full announcement of the terms and the pre-agreed 31 October signing date. Hanoi's reaction was understandable in the view of John Negroponte, who after a long period with the US delegation in Paris was now a member of the National Security Council.

'When we deviated from the timetable because we could not bring Saigon along,' says Negroponte, 'my analysis was then – and remains today – that Hanoi was fearful that it had become the victim of the biggest con job in history and that the US had promised to go through with a peace treaty just for domestic political purposes and that once the election was over there was a danger that the United States might renege on its promise.'

Kissinger reacted to the Radio Hanoi disclosure on the same day. He asserted that 'peace is at hand'. A week later, 7 November, Nixon won the presidential election with 60.7 per cent of the popular vote. At the Republican celebration that night, Nixon raised his arms in a large V-sign and

the crowd chanted over and over, 'Four More Years'.

'Right after the election,' says John Ehrlichman, 'Nixon went to the mountain, he went to Camp David and he locked us in.' Preparing the inaugural address and a new budget was 'very much front-burner' but Nixon was 'very much involved in contacting Henry right along' and wanted 'as early a wrap up of the Vietnam situation as possible'. Kissinger was back in Paris secretly meeting with Le Duc Tho on 20 November and now the US side presented a list of sixty changes and clarifications to conform with President Thieu's demands.

Says Winston Lord who was there, 'We tried to be reasonable; we tried to keep the demands for change within reasonable limits; we tried to accommodate some of Hanoi's changes, but they began to pile up.' Most of Hanoi's counter-demands were seen as stalling technicalities. Most of the US requests were minor – except for the major reversal requiring North Vietnamese troops to withdraw. There was another fundamental change in the peace conditions. To placate Thieu, says US negotiator John Negroponte, 'we promised a significant increase to Saigon in terms of military and economic aid. So my assessment would be that in November and December of 1972 the Politburo in Hanoi was starting to have second thoughts about the advantageousness of going through with the treaty.'

'Specifically in December,' states Winston Lord, 'it was clear that the North Vietnamese were sliding away from an agreement. Every time we would get close, they would slide in new conditions. It was clear that they were playing on public opinion, undercutting us at home and stonewalling us in Paris, and there was no choice but to break off the negotiations.' The talks collapsed on 13 December.

Kissinger, on Nixon's orders, had earlier warned Le Duc Tho that a complete breakdown of negotiations would result in recourse to massive force. At the same time, President Thieu was informed that there would be a total cessation of all American aid if he did not comply with a settlement. Journalist Tad Szulc, after investigating the chain of events, points to the moment *almost two months earlier* when Kissinger first 'listened to Thieu for endless hours in Saigon, complaining, opposing, threatening. Kissinger on the plane flying back to Washington said to one of his associates something to the effect – You know, this war simply cannot go for another four years. We have to end it even if it takes a very brutal – this is a verbatim word – a very brutal way of doing away with this war.

'Brutality becomes important in the reconstruction of events because', says Szulc, 'I believe it tends to explain to an important extent that which was to happen in December – the violent and sudden Christmas bombing of Hanoi and Haiphong as the final paroxysm, final spasm of American military involvement in Indo-China: brutal ending of the war, damaging the North Vietnamese as much as possible.'

On 18 December the 'Christmas' bombs began to fall. There would be eleven days and nights of horrific destruction. On the first day wave after wave of B-52s – in all 121 of the giant bombers – struck at the twin cities; three were brought down by Soviet SAM-2 missiles. Hanoi's future Ambassador to the United Nations describes the bombing. 'Our military', says Ha Van Lau, 'were ready twenty-four hours a day on the loading platform of the anti-aircraft guns or on the ramps of the rockets. Twenty-four hours out of twenty-four hours. And the American strategic air attack was of a breadth never before known in the history of war.'

On the third day, anticipating the B-52 flight pattern, Hanoi's defenders shot down another six of the bombers. Each cost $7,946,780. By the fourth day, with forty-three American pilots killed or captured, there was intense criticism of the planning among the air-crews and Washington briefly considered abandoning the raids entirely. Instead, it decided on a more varied pattern of attacks.

Several of the captured pilots, after being shown the destruction, went before foreign news cameras. 'I was extremely surprised', stated one pilot, 'at the area we had actually hit: the fact that I could observe no military targets anywhere in the area.' The United Nations condemned the bombing. The Pope, unheeded, called for its end. Among major international newspapers there were these comments and headlines: from Japan 'Nothing is more grotesque'; from Buenos Aires 'Genocide'; from West Germany 'A crime against humanity'. Stated *The Times* of London, 'Nixon ordered saturation bombing; this is not the conduct of a man who wants peace very badly.' Said *The New York Times*, 'Civilized man will be horrified.' *The Los Angeles Times* – 'Beyond all reason'.

There was a pause on Christmas Day, then the bombing was intensified. The US military calculated that Hanoi had expended 1000 SAM missiles and had very few left, so that it agreed to return to the peace table. Perhaps it was too much for any people to endure. In the eleven days ending 29 December, 100,000 bombs were dropped on two not very large cities. 'That', says Ha Van Lau, 'is the equivalent of five atomic bombs dropped on Hiroshima.' The US air force reported losing twenty-six aircraft with thirty-three pilots killed and another thirty-three captured. Civilian deaths remain unknown.

'Unpleasant as it is,' reflects Winston Lord, 'one has to, in the agony of those years and in the agony of diplomacy in conflict, weigh the unpleasantness of having to resort to force against the fact that it did achieve the breakthrough. And there's no other explanation for Hanoi changing its attitude.' Lord also explains the precise motives for the bombing: 'The President felt that he had to demonstrate that we couldn't be trifled with – and, frankly, *to demonstrate our toughness to Thieu* – this was the rationale for the bombing [author's italics].'

Thieu now accepted that he would indeed face a total aid cut-off if he did not comply. 'How could I not accept the peace agreement?' he says. 'How could I continue to fight – with what?' In Alexander Haig's words, Thieu 'took the lesser of two evils'.

Hanoi did not consider that it had been bombed to the peace table, rather that Nixon had run out of time and was prepared to settle on the earlier terms. Defiant to the end, Ha Van Lau says: 'It was this decisive victory – an aerial equivalent to Dien Bien Phu – which obliged Nixon to sign the Accords.'

The final settlement, initialled in Paris by Kissinger and Le Due Tho at noon on 23 January 1973, was the same agreed upon in October. (The cease-fire took effect at 2400 Greenwich Mean Time 27 January. The two chief negotiators were later jointly awarded the Nobel Peace Prize. Le Duc Tho declined, stating there was still no peace in Vietnam.) Thieu remained in power, and 150,000 North Vietnamese troops remained in the Southern region.

Says US negotiator John Negroponte, 'The peace treaty did nothing for Saigon. We got our prisoners back; we were able to end our direct military involvement. But there were no ostensible benefits for Saigon to justify all of the enormous effort and bloodshed of the previous years.'

The White House military advisor, Haig, intimates that on the final terms Nixon was, indeed, beaten by the clock: 'Keep in mind that the President and Dr Kissinger were faced with a legislative, mandated cessation of this bombing as the Congress came back from its Christmas recess.' Adds the future Secretary of State: 'I felt as a military man that could we have applied that pressure somewhat more extensively for a greater period of time that the conditions which we could have imposed on Hanoi would have been somewhat more binding. I would have hoped we could have gone on a little longer.'

As it was apparent that Congress would order an end to any wider military action – and, indeed, in earlier amendments had already done so – was the December bombing justifiable legally or morally? Says Ambassador Bunker, 'I thought that it was something we shouldn't have done.' Says administration critic Gareth Porter. 'It was simply to show the American public that we were going out in style. It was a public relations gimmick, essentially.' Says White House insider John Negroponte, 'The Christmas bombing was excessive in view of what it was designed to accomplish.' Says Defense Secretary Laird, 'I did not think it was necessary . . . but I have no objections in the manner in which that decision was made by the Commander in Chief, the President.'

Who conceived the bombing – Nixon or Kissinger? The National Security Council did not participate in the decision – or at least not in full session, reveals NSC member Negroponte. 'I first learned of the Christmas bombing after it had been decided,' he states. Ehrlichman was closer than most to the two men who played out the 'Madman' theory. Asked specifically how Kissinger felt about the December bombing, Ehrlichman says: 'Well, Henry says he opposed it, I guess. The fact is he supported it.'

As to accomplishment of peace, such as it was – peace for America – Ehrlichman stresses that Nixon 'won a great prize in opening China and in forging some kind of alliance with China vs. Russia – and if the price of that was a cynical peace in Vietnam, then historians are going to have to weigh the morality and the pragmatism and all these other things that historians like to weigh.'

Weighing it all, independent observer Tad Szulc says: 'Clearly, intelligent men such as Kissinger had to know that this [peace] was a bandaid, knowing perfectly well it was a question of time, a relatively short time, before that structure we were leaving behind would collapse.' As to what seemed the 'prize' of the time, the elusive detente, Szulc asks; 'Has it really changed the world? No, it has not. I think that as time goes by the extraordinary claims that Nixon and Kissinger made for themselves are being reduced to their proper proportions.'

Alexander Haig thinks otherwise: 'That aspect of Nixon's incumbency looks rather well today in nostalgic terms, and I think history will further enhance his performance in the international sphere over time.' And an historian who served the former Democratic administration, Kenneth Galbraith, states: 'credit belongs to Mr Nixon for bringing our involvement there to an end.'

But President Thieu says Nixon (who rushed one billion dollars worth of military equipment to South Vietnam before the peace signing) vowed to resume US involvement, if necessary: 'He pledged solemnly that if the North Vietnamese violated the peace agreement the United States would react vigorously.' At the time there was surprise and even scepticism that Nixon had committed the US to intervene directly if the North invaded. But Ambassador to Saigon Ellsworth Bunker confirms that Nixon's signed commitment was handed to Thieu when the formal peace treaty was signed.

Bunker states: 'He received assurances – which I gave him personally – written assurances from the President that in case of a violation of the Paris agreement by the other side we would come to their [South Vietnam's] assistance. As a result of those commitments, the South Vietnamese signed the Paris agreement. We, however, never made good on those commitments.'

Says Thieu: 'It's much better to let the Americans speak for themselves – and I have heard many very important men, who had a great responsibility in Vietnam, say that we have no other word than "betrayal". "Betrayal." '

America's longest war, eight years of combat and a military involvement of some twenty years, came to a close on 29 March, 1973. In Hanoi on that date the last American prisoners-of-war were released and in Saigon the last token handful of GIS boarded a flight for home, 9000 miles away. At the headquarters of the Military Assistance Command, Vietnam, there was a ceremonial furling of the flag. Up to that moment 56,962 American soldiers had died, most of them in combat, in this one small country – as many as in World War I. Officially, the only US military personnel who remained were fifty advisors – as permitted under the Geneva Accords, which the United States had refused to sign two decades before.

For those who seek symbols, there were many.

There was the soul-destroyed end of the man who had led America to war. 'When my Great Society dies, when she dies, I too will die,' Lyndon Baines Johnson had told biographer Doris Kearns. On 20 January Johnson died 'alone in his bed' – three days after 'having to listen' to Nixon's four-more-years inaugural address with its statement, says Kearns, 'that he was going to cut the Great Society down to the bone. And there was also a statement that he was bringing peace to Vietnam. These two things happened within the space of two days, and on the third day Johnson had the fatal heart attack.'

There was the death in South Vietnam on 7 April of nine men in a helicopter. It had been shot down by guerrillas – who used a heat-seeking missile. The nine men were Canadian, Hungarian and Polish members of the new, hoped-for International Commission of Control and Supervision. The peace-keepers had been the next to die in Vietnam.

There was the sign that remained at the former US infantry base at Tay Ninh, near Saigon – and it was about all that remained there. Hours after the last Americans had handed over the base to ARVN soldiers it was dismembered surgically. First the furnishings went, then the prefabricated walls, floors and roofs. On a skeletal support a tilted sign had been overlooked, and its English words just hung there. It said, 'Good-bye and Good Luck.'

Above: January 7, 1971—A South Vietnamese village woman stands silently by as her home goes up in flames in the coastal lowlands about 25 miles south of Danang. South Vietnamese troops burned her house after finding ammunition buried in her yard.

Below: March 18, 1971—South Vietnamese soldiers straggle away from a U.S. helicopter which evacuated them from firebases in Laos to Nguyen Hue base in South Vietnam.

Above: January 15, 1971—A South Vietnamese soldier, holding a pistol, questions a woman suspected of being a Viet Cong in the U Monh forest area, 150 miles southwest of Saigon.

Above: January 20, 1971—An elderly Chinese artisan paints good luck signs on a Saigon street prior to the state of Tet, the Lunar New Year. A 24-hour cease fire ban was planned by both sides in the war to mark the holiday

Left: February 16, 1971—A U.S. Marine helicopter delivers fuel to the base at Khe Sanh, which was recently reactivated as a staging point for operations against the Ho Chi Minh Trail in Laos. The base was abandoned in 1968, a few months after it survived a 77-day siege.

Above: March 3, 1971—South Vietnamese paratroopers, reinforcing units inside Laos, pass the wreckage of a previous enemy ambush on Highway 9, about four miles inside the Laotian border.

Above: March 19, 1971—Spent shell casings surround South Vietnamese Marines during a lull in fighting at Firebase Hotel One, just inside the Laotian border. The 155mm howitzers in background are fired in support of allied operations in the area.

Above: March 18, 1971—An American flag flies above a bunker at the Khe Sanh supply base, the frequent target of North Vietnamese artillery.

Above: March 10, 1971—A South Vietnamese solider hitches a ride on the landing skid of a helicopter carrying wounded from a firebase in Laos to its landing at Khe Sanh, South Vietnam.

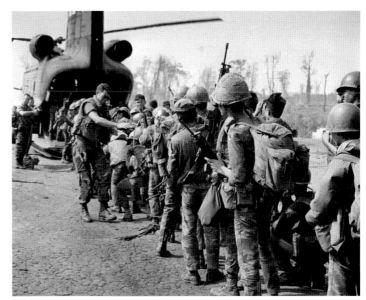

Above: March 22, 1971—An American advisor helps line up South Vietnamese airborne troops at Khe Sanh to prevent overcrowding on helicopters carrying them to coastal bases after heavy fighting in Laos.

Left: March 27, 1971—A U.S. soldier holds an M-79 grenade launcher in his left hand and a radio in his right while taking enemy mortar fire at an outpost near Lang Vei.

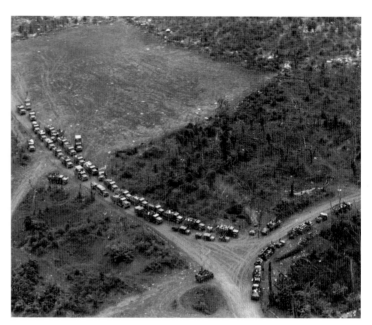

Above: April 2, 1971—A convoy leaves Khe Sanh as U.S. troops withdraw to coastal bases. The base, where U.S. Marines were besieged for 77 days in 1968, was reactivated during operations in Laos.

Left: April 1971—A CH-47 Chinook helicopter, top, and two Cobra gun ships lift off from Mai Loc on a mission providing fire support for a South Vietnamese commando raid into Laos.

Above: April 1971—Seen through a destroyed control tower, U.S. troops ride an armored vehicle as they pull out of the base at Khe Sanh which had been reactivated for operations in Laos.

Right: April 1971—Fresh South Vietnamese troops thread their way through a line of trenches at Firebase 6 in South Vietnam's central highlands. Artillery fire from Communist forces was fired into the base's landing zone as the reinforcements arrived.

Above: April 1, 1971—A small boy stands in what remains of his home in Duc Duc, 25 miles southwest of Danang. An attack by North Vietnamese killed about 100 civilians and destroyed more than 2,000 homes.

Right: April 15, 1971— South Vietnamese airborne troops swarm across a landing zone to help besieged Firebase 6 in South Vietnam's central highlands.

**625**

Below: June 18, 1971—A South Vietnamese soldier dashes for cover as he arrives at Firebase 5 in Vietnam's Central Highlands. The base and supply helicopters had been under heavy enemy ground fire.

Above: April 23, 1971— South Vietnamese troops, members of the 1st ARVN division, carry equipment to reopen an old firebase between the A Shau valley and Quang Tri.

Above: April 27, 1971—A Saigon bar girl greets a passing U.S. soldier on Tu Do street in downtown Saigon.

Left: July 1970—A U.S. helicopter attempts to lift a downed chopper from a river where it had crashed after being hit by enemy gunfire. The attempt failed and the downed chopper was blown up.

Above: June 17, 1971—A South Vietnamese soldier takes aim outside Firebase 5. The hilltop base in the Central Highlands was under siege by North Vietnamese mortars.

Above: July 10, 1971—U.S. tanks of the 5th Mechanized Division pass Vietnamese peasants after withdrawing from Firebase Charlie 2, just south of the demilitarized zone. South Vietnamese units were replacing the U.S. armor.

Above: July 16, 1971—South Vietnamese troops move out on patrol from Firebase Fuller, a hilltop position four miles south of the DMZ.

Above: September 16, 1971—An American soldier checks the pulse of a Vietnamese girl who was wounded when an explosion ripped a downtown Saigon nightclub.

Left: July 10, 1971—South Vietnamese troops move into Firebase Charlie 2 where they are taking over control from units of the U.S. 5th Mechanized Division.

Above: July 26, 1971—Former Gen. Duong van Minh, a popular 56-year-old leader of the 1963 coup which overthrew President Ngo Dinh Diem, announces his candidacy for the presidential elections of October 1971.

Right: July 10, 1971—Buddhist monks and villagers of Ba Thu are searched before they return to their homes in the Parrot's Beak section of Cambodia. They fled in the wake of the South Vietnamese army advance.

Above: August 25, 1971—A South Vietnamese soldier writes a letter while sitting atop sandbags at Firebase 6 about 50 miles northwest of Pleiki in the central highlands.

Right: October 1971—A U.S. cavalryman uses an outdoor shower at Firebase Pace near the Cambodian border, about 85 miles northwest of Saigon.

Left: October 20, 1971—Flares light up Firebase Pace, on the Cambodian border 85 miles northwest of Saigon, as the base sustained almost a month of North Vietnamese shelling. Two days after this photo was shot, U.S. troops were withdrawn from the base.

Above: October 20, 1971—A U.S. cavalryman watches plumes of smoke rise from an air strike near the perimeter of Firebase Pace, 60 miles northwest of Saigon near the Cambodian border.

Left: November 25, 1971—A South Vietnamese soldier radios from one of two helicopters flying near Chrum, Cambodia.

Above: March 11, 1972—A South Vietnamese machinegunner advances in the Mekong Delta near the Cambodian border.

Left: February 24, 1972—Montagnard tribesmen with a South Vietnamese ranger unit carry their wounded to a waiting helicopter near Chu Pa mountain in South Vietnam's central highlands.

Above: October 20, 1971—A South Vietnamese artilleryman sets charges on 105mm howitzer shells at Firebase Pace near the Cambodian border, 60 miles northwest of Saigon. South Vietnamese troops were taking over operations at the base from U.S. forces.

Above: 1972—A South Vietnamese medic and refugees run for cover on the outskirts of Quang Tri, the provincial capital just south of the demilitarized zone (DMZ).

Right: April 5, 1972—South Vietnamese militiamen drag the body of a North Vietnamese soldier killed when his unit tried to cut Route 1, six miles south of Quang Tri, South Vietnam.

Above: April 30, 1972—A South Vietnamese Marine carries the dead body of a comrade killed on Route 1, about seven miles south of Quang Tri. Marines were fighting to reopen the road in order to break the North Vietnamese siege of the provincial capital.

Left: May 1971—A South Vietnamese soldier is captured by two enemy troops in southern Laos, according to the caption on this photo released by Hanoi.

Below: April 12, 1972—A mushroom cloud rises from an air strike against North Vietnamese positions just off Route 13, about 15 miles from the besieged provincial capital of An Loc. An armored personnel carrier was part of the 20,000-man relief force which came under attack as it moved toward An Loc.

Left: October 1971—Viet Cong prisoners clean fish at the Can Tho prison camp. Some or all of these POWs may have been slated for the October 31 prisoner release, a gesture of good faith on the inauguration date of South Vietnamese President Nguyen Van Thieu.

Above: April 16, 1972—A government soldier evacuates the area as an ammunition dump is hit at Lai Khe, 30 miles north of Saigon on Route 13. The ammunition was intended to use by airborne troops at An Loc, 30 miles further up the road.

Above: April 12, 1972—South Vietnamese troops eight miles west of Don Ha watch smoke from B-52 hits on a North Vietnamese tank column.

Left: April 12, 1972—South Vietnamese troops stand atop an armored personnel carrier watching air strikes against North Vietnamese troops who attacked a government relief column 45 miles north of Saigon on Route 13.

Left: April 8, 1972—South Vietnamese paratroopers move along Route 13 as reinforcements for the fighting north of Saigon near the Cambodian border.

Above: April 28, 1972—A civilian bus is loaded with refugees and soldiers leaving the fighting in Quang Tri, South Vietnam.

Left: April 12, 1972—A wounded South Vietnamese soldier is carried to an evacuation point after his tank was destroyed by a rocket grenade on Route 13 north of Saigon.

Right: April 29, 1972—Hundreds of refugees wait for transportation out of Quang Tri as North Vietnamese troops approach the key, provincial capital.

Above: April 3, 1972—A South Vietnamese family carry their belongings on a bicycle as they flee their homes in Quang Tri in the face of a North Vietnamese advance.

Above: April, 28, 1974—A supply convoy is stopped on the highway due to an earlier ambush that resulted in equipment blocking the road. Such actions were typical of the Viet Cong in their attempt to halt or slow supply and reinforcement tactics by the South Vietnamese.

Right: April 5, 1972—South Vietnamese troops aboard a tank watch smoke rise from air strikes on North Vietnamese positions across the river at Dong Ha, 10 miles south of the DMZ.

Above: April 1972—A woman refugee rests at roadside as she and countless other refugees fled Quang Tri city when it fell to North Vietnamese forces.

Above: May 22, 1972—A U.S. advisor carries a seriously wounded South Vietnamese soldier through sand dunes beside Route 1A, 20 miles northeast of Hue. Soldiers clearing the road to the northern front were ambushed by North Vietnamese troops.

Above: May 13, 1972—South Vietnamese Marines relax in a pavilion of Hue's Imperial Palace, where government forces concentrated their defense against a North Vietnamese attack on the city.

Left: May 5, 1972—School children and villagers pass the bodies of 15 Viet Cong soldiers and their North Vietnamese battalion commander after an overnight ambush by local militia in the village of An Ninh in Hau Nghia province.

Above: 1972—North Vietnamese soldiers rush through the rubble of Quang Tri city, key provincial capital south of the DMZ. The city changed hands several times as attacks and counter attacks took place during this period.

Above: 1972—North Vietnamese infantry during an offensive in which they moved south across the DMZ.

Left: 1972—North Vietnamese soldiers fire bazookas and rifles as they advance south though brush in the DMZ.

Above: 1972—North Vietnamese troops stand guard at a captured bunker in Quang Tri City.

Below: 1972—North Vietnamese soldiers carry away ammunition from a U.S. and South Vietnamese dump at a government post south of the DMZ.

Top Right: 1972—A North Vietnamese radio operator takes shelter during an artillery attack from South Vietnam. His unit was south of the DMZ.

Right: 1972—North Vietnamese soldiers carry away ammunition from a U.S. and South Vietnamese dump at a government post south of the DMZ.

Left: May 1972—North Vietnamese soldiers climb over an enemy bunker during the spring offensive across the DMZ. Here they have captured an ammunition dump at a government outpost.

Below: 1972—North Vietnamese infantry advance through barbed wire during their offensive south across the DMZ.

Above: October 11, 1972—Smoke and rubble are thrown in the air during an allied air strike on the hamlet of Xom Suoi along Route 13, about 20 miles north of Saigon. The area was the scene of heavy fighting after enemy forces occupied several villages.

Right: May 19, 1972—South Vietnamese soldiers watch clouds of smoke and dust rise from bombs dropped by U.S. B-52s two miles from their lines along Route 13 near An Loc, north of Saigon.

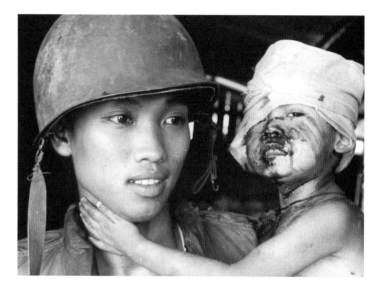

Above: May 1972—A Marine gunner fires his weapon from a helicopter at enemy positions near Quang Tri City. The chopper carried South Vietnamese troops behind enemy lines on a two day raid near the key provincial capital.

Right: May 31, 1972—This bandaged boy was the only survivor when North Vietnamese opened up on fleeing refugees outside An Loc. The boy was found next to the body of his mother and taken to an aid station.

Below: May 25, 1972—Two refugees who slipped through enemy lines around An Loc where the town was under attack by North Vietnamese army regulars.

Above: May 8, 1972—South Vietnamese soldiers and their children, part of the 750,000 refugees from nearby fighting, move a cart of belongings through the streets of Danang, looking for a place to settle after fleeing battle areas.

Left: May 27, 1972—Refugees sit in the shade of a straw cover along Vietnam's Route 13. Masses fled fighting in the north as troops from both sides battled in key cities.

Right: May 25, 1972—Billowing smoke from a North Vietnamese artillery attack is the backdrop for a single woman on Highway 1 north of Hue. The artillery explosions set the village on fire.

Above: May 4, 1972—South Vietnamese Marines and an American advisor help a wounded soldier off a sampan at My Chanh north of Hue.

Right: May 26, 1972—Woman and boy run down Route 13 after escaping through enemy held lines near the besieged city of An Loc. Some 4,000 fled city which was under artillery attack for more than 50 days.

Above: May 2, 1972—Remnants of the defenders of Quang Tri ride on armored vehicles as they reach friendly lines north of Hue. Their arrival marked the end of an all night escape from the abandoned city.

Left: May 2, 1972—South Vietnamese soldiers, many barefoot and without weapons, along with civilian refugees, reach friendly lines north of Hue after an all-night escape from Quang Tri and heavy Viet Cong fighting.

Above: May 1972—The sun sets behind mountains behind the war-torn city of Hue as sampan traffic moves along the Perfume river.

Above: May 26, 1972—Refugees who passed through North Vietnamese lines in their flight from An Loc rest in roadside ditch. Smoke on the horizon is from air strikes.

Right: May 1972—A U.S. advisor helps a wounded South Vietnamese soldier near the My Chanh river north of Hue. The soldier had escaped the North Vietnamese capture of Quang Tri. A Route 1 bridge is burned to prevent it from being used by the North Vietnamese.

Left: May 20, 1972—A wounded South Vietnamese soldier is led from a helicopter at Lai Khe, north of Saigon, after being evacuated from heavy fighting near An Loc.

Right: May 3, 1972—A U.S. advisor helps a straggler, wounded at Quang Tri, who reached My Chanh. Behind them is a bridge set on fire to prevent use by the North Vietnamese.

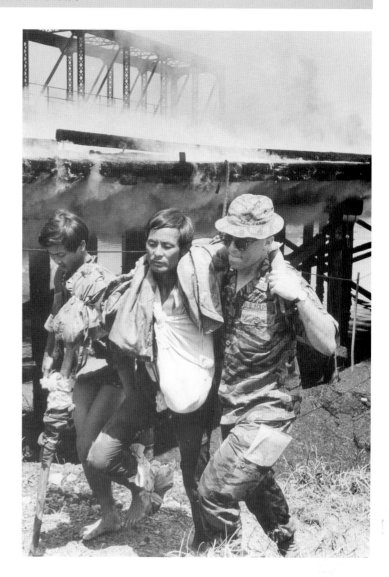

Above: June 10, 1972—Nine-year-old Phan Tai Kim Phuc is comforted by her mother in a Saigon hospital, two days after she was severely burned during a misplaced napalm attack on her village, Trang Bang, South Vietnam.

Right: June 22, 1972—A refugee family from Quang Tri takes a midday rest in a former American camp in Danang, South Vietnam. The camp now serves as a home for more than 50,000 civilians from the fallen province.

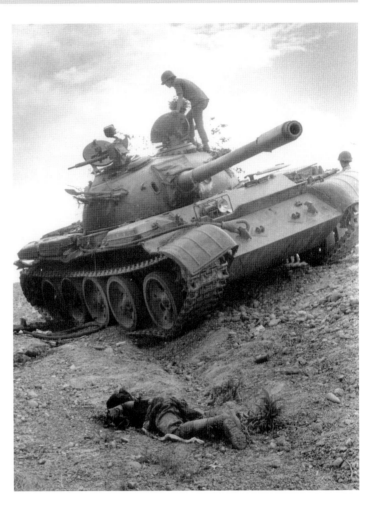

Above: June 24, 1972—Specially trained riot troops spend hours on standby duty at the base of a statue in downtown Saigon. The soldiers routinely carry weapons of war, as well as tear gas and riot shields.

Right: June 29, 1972—The body of a North Vietnamese tanker man lies beside a Chinese-made T-59 tank as a South Vietnamese soldier inspects the tank. South Vietnamese Airborne troops found the tank, disabled by air strikes beside Route 1 between My Chanh and Hai Lang.

Below: May 12, 1972—A South Vietnamese boy rides past a newly built execution post with five stakes, erected in Hue as a warning to looters and army deserters.

Above: June 26, 1972—A South Vietnamese youngster wounded in fighting around the town of An Loc awaits evacuation helicopters.

Left: June 24, 1972—Battle-weary defenders of An Loc cheer atop a knocked out North Vietnamese tank as airlifted reinforcements arrive at the besieged provincial capital. They ignited a flare on the battered vehicle to celebrate.

Right: June 18, 1972—Smoke rises from five fuel tanks at the U.S. Army base at Long Bihn, South Vietnam. They were set afire during a Viet Cong sabotage attack. There were no casualties.

Above: All that remains of a home in An Loc is the bullet-marked statue of Buddha. The town, a provincial capital north of Saigon, was the scene of fighting for more than two months.

Below: June 7, 1972—A South Vietnamese soldier takes a midday siesta under a huge stone elephant at the Ming Mang tombs near Hue. Troops defending the city occupied old tombs dating from the 19th century.

Above: June 25, 1972—Lightly wounded civilians and troops attempt to push their way aboard a South Vietnamese helicopter hovering over a stretch of highway near An Loc. Helicopters were forced to leave more seriously injured behind as they were mobbed by walking wounded.

Above: June 15, 1972—Vietnamese parents and their five children speed down Hjighway 13 on a motorbike. They head south, away from An Loc and toward Saigon.

Left: June 1, 1972—Under a North Vietnamese mortar attack South Vietnamese troops scramble for cover carrying wounded civilians to safety in a village near An Loc.

# THE NAPALM GIRL

EDITOR'S NOTE: One of the most famous pictures to emerge from the Vietnam war showed a naked young girl running down a highway after she and others were hit by a napalm attack. This is the story of that picture, which was made by Nick Ut of Associated Press.

June 8, 1972—It is early morning as Nick Ut swings his AP van out of its Saigon parking lot and begins the 25 mile drive to Trang Bang where North Vietnamese troops have been holed up for several days.

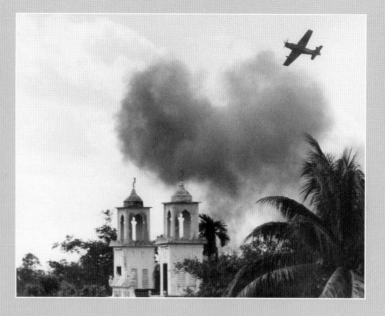

Left: A Vietnamese Air Force Skyraider makes a swing over the Cao Dai temple at Trang Bang where a stubborn enemy force is holed up.

Above: The plane dives and the deadly napalm is released.

Below: A woman runs down the highway carrying her dead child, a victim of the misplaced attack.

Left and Below: In a two picture sequence the napalm explodes in front of the towers of the temple, then mushrooms into a fiery ball. But the explosion misses the enemy and hits friendly troops and civilians who took refuge near the temple. In the foreground are reporters and photographers assembled to cover the conflict.

Above: The tell tale black smoke of burning napalm drifts across the horizon and over the towers of the Cao Dai temple.

Below: Kim Phuc, who had ripped off her burning clothes, runs down the highway. At left is her younger brother who lost an eye in the attack and, at *right*, other members of her family.

The town, site of a major Cao Dai temple, sits astride Highway 1, which is the major artery that connects Saigon and the Cambodian border. South Vietnamese troops for several days fought to eliminate a stubborn enemy from the village but without success. Nick parks his van some distance from the village and walks toward the town. Other cameramen are already on the scene.

Suddenly a South Vietnamese plane appears and, after a swing over the target, dives toward the enemy positions. Nick sees and photographs them as they drop deadly napalm. But there is a miscalculation and the fiery mass falls on friendly troops and civilians.

The explosion seems close enough to touch. Nick recalls: It was hot . . . I could feel the heat on my body. . . . it was too close.

Immediately people from the village run screaming down the highway. One woman carries a badly burned child who dies in her arms before she reaches Nick.

Running children appear, one a young naked girl who had torn off her clothes to escape the fire. Her back is seared by the napalm jelly. Nick photographs her as she runs toward him.

Hot . . . Hot . . . she cries in Vietnamese. Nick pours water from his canteen on the burned child. Her father comes to Nick and asks him to help and the photographer drives the child and her father to a Saigon hospital.

Nick then returns to the AP bureau where the film is developed, a print made and the picture transmitted to New York. It is immediately relayed to the world and becomes a defining photo icon, a symbol for the ages of the horror of war in general and the war in Vietnam in particular. Ut's picture is awarded the Pulitzer Prize.

But the story does not end there. Nick visits the girl the next day—and he sees her on subsequent days also. Nick and Kim Phuc become friends. Ironically, Nick is wounded at a spot very near Trang Bang where the picture of Kim was made. The two—photographer and girl—lose contact in the final chaotic days of the conflict. At war's end, Nick leaves Vietnam and is assigned to AP's Los Angeles bureau. After the war the North Vietnamese send Kim to Cuba to study pharmacy and she is used in propaganda releases. But eventually she and her husband defect at the airport in Toronto and they take up residence in Canada.

Kim and Nick are eventually reunited. She is now married with children of her own; the photographer who took one of the war's most telling photographs covers baseball and OJ Simpson. They meet several times. Kim calls him Uncle Nick.

A quarter century later Kim's back remains severely scarred and painful. Memories of the fiery jelly dropping from the sky that sweltering day in June still haunt her. Nick and Kim stay in touch, united forever by a photograph made near Trang Bang on the highway between Saigon and Cambodia.

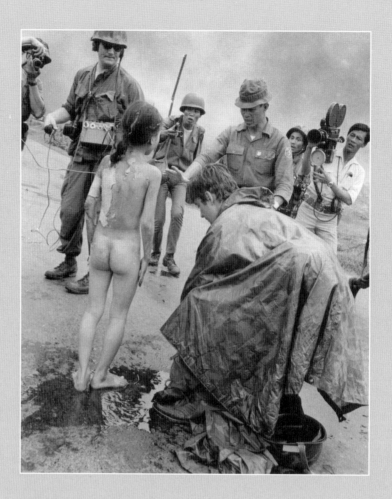

Left: Soldiers and newspeople attempt to help Kim but it is obvious that she is severely burned. Nick Ut minutes later drives her and her father to a hospital in Saigon.

Below: A South Vietnamese soldier, also injured by napalm, receives assistance from a comrade along Highway 1.

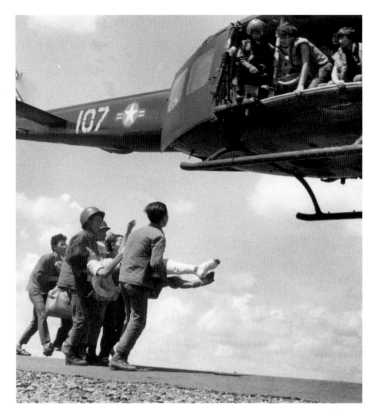

Above: June 11, 1972—A stream of exhausted refugees, in all about 10,000, move down the highway to escape the fighting in An Loc.

Right: June 22, 1972—A wounded woman is carried to a hovering helicopter along Route 13. She was wounded in a North Vietnamese mortar barrage at An Loc.

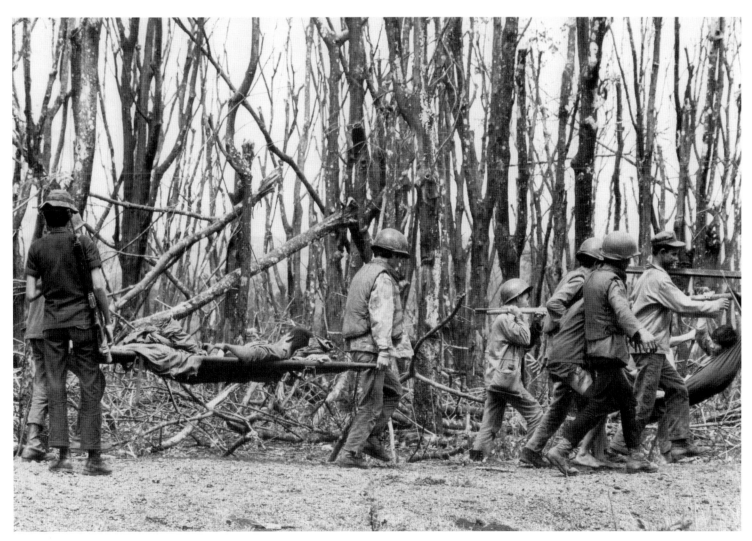

Above: June 18, 1972—Wounded soldiers from the battle of An Loc are carried to a landing pad in the city, past the battered remains of a rubber plantation hit by heavy North Vietnamese fire.

Right: June 15, 1972—South Vietnamese rangers patrol past destroyed buildings in besieged An Loc, 60 miles north of Saigon, which was destroyed in North Vietnamese artillery barrages and allied air strikes.

Above: June 21, 1972—A wounded Vietnamese soldier is helped as he clambers aboard a helicopter taking off from a landing zone south of An Loc as incoming rockets started to hit.

Right: June 16, 1972—Wounded South Vietnamese troops attempt to board a hovering rescue helicopter to leave An Loc.

Below: June 1972—Survivors of the battle for An Loc wander around the battered city's market place.

Above: June 19, 1972—A medic looks for an ambulance to help a South Vietnamese ranger wounded by rocket shrapnel along Route 13 south of An Loc.

Above: July 1972—American actress Jane Fonda visits a North Vietnamese anti-aircraft installation near Hanoi during her controversial visit to North Vietnam.

Right: July 25, 1972— Actress Jane Fonda points to pictures of unidentified American war prisoners during a news conference in Paris. The men were seen in a silent film made during her visit to North Vietnam.

Left: July 1972—South Vietnamese troops run from enemy rocket fire as they were finishing construction of a pontoon bridge.

Below: July 6, 1972—A South Vietnamese paratrooper rests amid the rubble of a Catholic church after it was destroyed by bombs and artillery fire during fighting south of the Quang Tri Citadel.

Above: July 20, 1972—The fender of a blasted truck in Quang Tri City serves as a seat for a South Vietnamese trooper following fierce fighting for control of the provincial capital.

Right: July 21, 1972—A South Vietnamese paratrooper holds his M-16 at the ready as he moves through ruins of homes during house-to-house fighting in Quang Tri city.

Left: July 22, 1972—A tank covers government troops pulling back to the bunker line during fighting along Route 1 south of Quang Triu.

Above: July 2, 1972—A South Vietnamese family weeps for their dead relatives in the rubble of their home in Hue after it was detroyed by enemy rocket fire.

Above: July 1972—A lone South Vietnamese soldier walks the empty, wide road that passes through a large now abandoned U.S. Army logistics command camp at Cam Rahn Bay. Americans pulled out after manning the base for six years.

Left: July 25, 1972—Government troops race through the streets of Quang Tri City as they recapture the provincial capital from enemy forces.

Above: July 1972—A line of South Vietnamese troops move along a devastated street in Quang Tri city as the battle continues for the provincial capital.

Left: July 17, 1972—A South Vietnamese airborne soldier crouches behind the shattered threshold of a house as his unit moves into Quang Tri city.

Above: July 20, 1972—South Vietnamese paratrooper pulls the body of a North Vietnamese off the road during an attack on government positions near Quang Tri City.

Right: July 24, 1972—A Vietnamese family emerges from an underground shelter during a government sweep in Binh Dinh province.

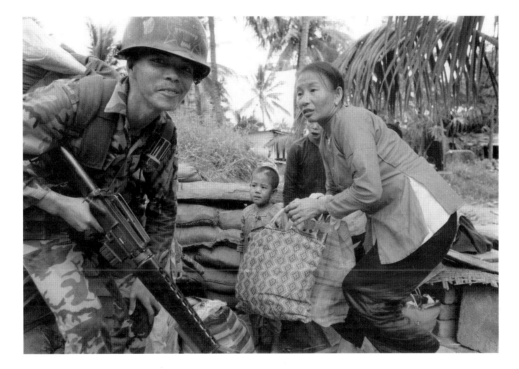

Above: July 31, 1972—Smoke rises from air strikes on North Vietnamese positions hidden inside Quang Tri city.

Left: July 4, 1972—The six-inch guns of the light cruiser USS *Oklahoma City* fire away in support of South Vietnamese forces in operation Lam Son.

Right: July 17, 1972—A South Vietnamese soldier wounded in the hand to hand fighting in Quang Tri city heads for an aid station. He carries the weapons and equipment of a wounded comrade.

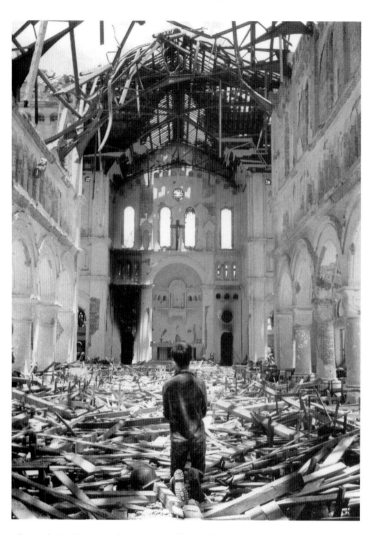

Above: July 8, 1972—A South Vietnamese soldier kneels in prayer amid the ruins of the La Vang Cathedral near Quang Tri. The church for the once prosperous Catholic community was damaged in fierce fighting in May.

Above: July 24, 1972—South Vietnamese troops make their way through the rubble as they move forward against enemy troops in Quang Tri City.

Right: July 7, 1972—A soldier positions a South Vietnamese flag on the wall of destroyed cathedral in La Vang as forces were moving into Quang Tri to dislodge North Vietnamese units.

Above: July 21, 1972—Government troops, laden with weapons, cross a stream near Quang Tri city.

Above: July 1972—North Vietnamese troops launch a combat assault in Quang Tri in South Vietnam.

Right: July 19, 1972—A wounded North Vietnamese prisoner, *left*, is brought to an evacuation truck to ride along with South Vietnamese troops at Quang Tri.

Left: July 18, 1972—A wounded South Vietnamese paratrooper returns to his unit's command post after he was injured in house-to-house fighting in Quang Tri city.

Above: July 24, 1972—South Vietnamese soldiers run for cover behind gravestones in a cemetery hit by Viet Cong sniper and mortar fire outside Tam Quan on South Vietnam's central coast.

Left: July 24, 1972—A Vietnamese soldier helps his buddy through barbed wire during an operation to retake the district town of Tam Quan along South Vietnam's central coast.

Above: July 27, 1972—South Vietnamese soldiers explore a heavily damaged section of Quang Tri city which was taken from Communist troops in heavy fighting.

Above: July 16, 1972—A Vietnamese paratrooper takes a last look at a buddy killed in bitter house-to-house fighting in Quang Tri city.

Right: August 11, 1972—South Vietnamese troops celebrate with a North Vietnamese heavy machine gun they captured from a blasted roadside bunker on Route 13 near the Lai Khe base, north of Saigon.

Above: August, 1, 1972—A U.S. Marine surveys an aircraft storage shed destroyed when more than 70 enemy rockets hit the Bien Hoa airbase 15 miles northeast of Saigon.

Above Left: August 13, 1972—A South Vietnamese Marine, his weapon ready, naps in an abandoned house in Quang Tri city.

Below: August 11, 1972—Crew of an armored personnel carrier waits for the order to advance on enemy positions along Route 13 north of Saigon. Three of the vehicles were lost in the fighting.

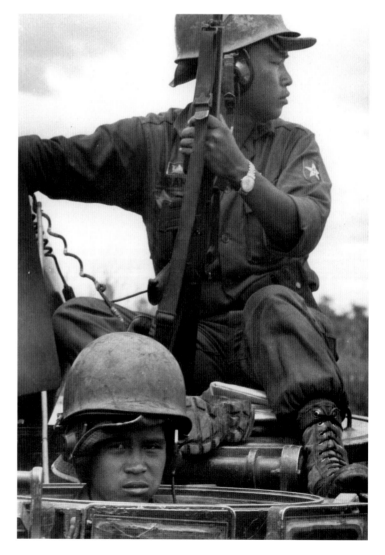

Above: August 25, 1972—A South Vietnamese soldier shows off a captured Viet Cong flag near Cai Bay after Communist troops attacked a government outpost and bridge on the road linking Saigon to the Mekong Delta.

Right: August 7, 1972—Villagers in the Mekong Delta town of Nhi Qui watch government forces passing through the rain-soaked main street.

Below: August 1972—Litter bearers walk through the ruins of Quang Tri city where heavy fighting continued for weeks.

Above: August 3, 1972—A bomb explodes in the ruins of Quang Tri city as North Vietnamese artillery harasses government positions. Much of the city was in ruins from fighting over many weeks.

Left: August 1972—Smoke from air strikes rises over North Vietnamese positions in Quang Tri as government troops attempt to drive the enemy from the key northern provincial capital.

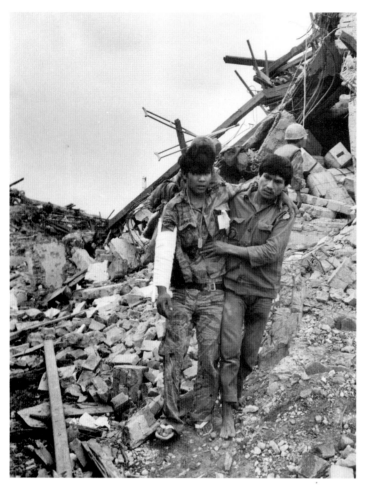

Above: August 16, 1972—A South Vietnamese Marine wounded in house-to-house fighting in Quang Tri city is helped from a destroyed school serving as a hospital.

Right: August 1972—A South Vietnamese Marine fires mortar rounds as government troops engaged in house-to-house combat in Quang Tri city.

Above: August 1, 1972—A peasant woman carries vegetables to market in Phu My along the central coast of South Vietnam. She passes the rubble of houses destroyed in battle.

Left: August 7, 1972—South Vietnamese armored personnel carriers move down a canal in the northern Mekong Delta to retake villages under enemy control.

Right: September 1972—A South Vietnamese officer orders his men to advance as they fight their way into a village near Mo Duc, southwest of Danang.

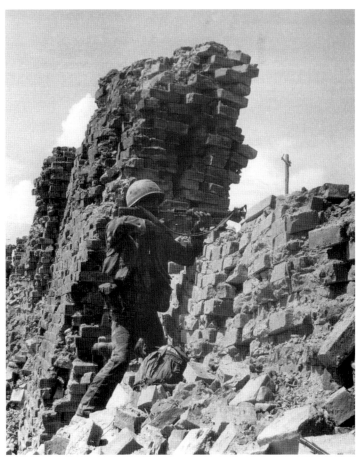

Above: September 1972—South Vietnamese troops aboard an armored personnel carrier watch smoke rise after an air strike on Quang Tri.

Right: September 16, 1972—A South Vietnamese Marine sprays bullets across the bomb-shattered wall of the 19th century fortress into the Citadel at Quang Tri city. Government forces ended more than four months of North Vietnamese occupation.

Above: October 13, 1972—South Vietnamese troops watch as an A-1 Skyraider returns from a bombing run on suspected Communist positions in a hamlet on Route 13 north of Saigon. Troops were trying to reopen the road to the base at Lai Khe, eight miles farther north.

Above: September 1972—The blast of a South Vietnamese 175mm gun, aimed at enemy position in Quang Tri city, shatters the otherwise placid setting of a rural pool.

Right: A South Vietnamese peasant woman carries her two children as they flee fighting along Highway 13, north of Saigon where North Vietnamese outflanked South Vietnamese and cut the road.

Below: September 20, 1072—A South Vietnamese soldier lofts a hand grenade over a wall during fighting in a village near Song Vei, south of Danang, which had been a hotbed of Viet Cong activity.

Above: September 1972—B-52 high altitude bombers leave vapor trails miles long while flying over the Mekong Delta after a bombing mission. Flying at altitude, the planes' trails are often the only evidence visible from the ground.

Above: September 2, 1972—Loaded with grenades, a government ranger walks down the streets of Que Jon southwest of Danang which lies in ruins after bitter fighting to recover the town from the North Vietnamese.

Right: October 11, 1972—A South Vietnamese soldier fires a recoiless rifle at North Vietnamese positions along Highway 13 during attempts to recapture an enemy-held hamlet some 20 miles north of Saigon.

Above: October 15, 1972—A South Vietnamese soldier watches as air strikes hit North Vietnamese bunkers along Route 13 north of Saigon. Communist troops had temporarily cut the road, preventing government reinforcements from reaching forward positions as they advanced toward the base at Lai Khe, 30 miles north of Saigon.

Above: October 17, 1972—A young South Vietnamese soldier crouches behind a knoll during fighting along Highway 13 north of Saigon where North Vietnamese troops captured hamlets, most of which returned to government control.

Above: October 15, 1972—South Vietnamese soldiers watch the explosion from their recoiless rifle, sending sheets of corrugated tin from village hut into the air. The hut, in Bing Duong province northeast of Saigon, was believed to conceal North Vietnamese snipers.

Above: October 26, 1972—Police in Danang cover the eyes of a woman who they said was part of a Viet Cong terrorist unit. She was caught with 15 hand grenades after a running gun battle.

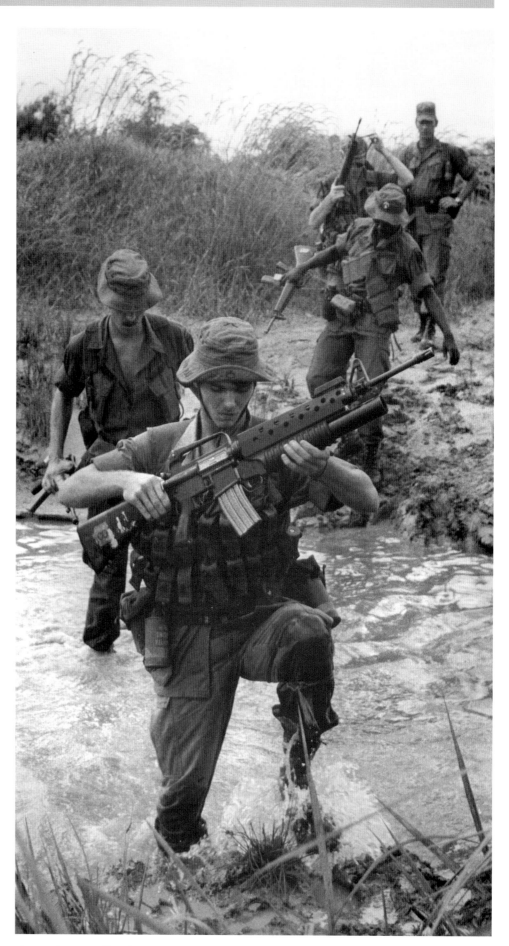

Above: October 1972—Soldiers of the Long Binh supply base cross a stream while patrolling the base's huge perimeter against possible attack. Although the last official U.S. combat patrol had taken place three months earlier, the makeshift unit at Long Binh, the 87th Infantry (provisional), was continuing its patrols.

Above: October 21, 1972—A South Vietnamese soldier throws a grenade at North Vietnamese sniper positions during fighting to retake the hamlet of Bung Cau, 16 miles north of Saigon.

Left: A national flag flies above The Citadel in Quang Tri after government troops completed conquest of the structure, a 19th-century fortress.

Above: October 14, 1972—A wounded soldier is carried during fighting for a hamlet along Highway 13 north of Saigon where government troops tried to reopen the road to the Lai Khe base.

Left: October 14, 1972—In pain, a wounded government soldier is carried along Highway 13 north of Saigon.

Below: October 26, 1972—A man searches among the dead and wounded for his child who was outside the U.S. Embassy when a bomb was detonated.

Above: November 5, 1972—Pfc. Clifford Erickson of Cameron, Wisc., makes his way through thick brush outside the U.S. base at Long Binh, 15 miles northeast of Saigon, on the last day of Charlie Company's patrol.

Above: October 30, 1972—Villagers salvage roof tiles from their war-damaged house at An My, north of Saigon. They are careful not to disturb the national flag which must be displayed on all dwellings.

Above: October 26, 1972—South Vietnamese lookouts take up a position on one of the towers of a Cao Dai temple 25 miles from Saigon.

Right: November 25, 1972—Peasant women squat alongside Highway 4, 45 miles southwest of Saigon, holding South Vietnamese flags in a demonstration in the Mekong Delta. Thousands of villagers demonstrated against Communist support of Thieu government and to prove that government controls the land along the main highway into the Mekong Delta.

671

Above: November 17, 1972—A U.S. Cobra gunship patrols bomb-cratered landscape near the Bien Hoa airbase. Observation teams typically inspect the Viet Cong-infiltrated area after overnight high altitude B-52 bombing runs.

Left: November 1, 1972—An enemy shell explodes before a South Vietnamese soldier, dug in at Hai Van south of Hue, has time to react.

Left: December 15, 1972—A South Vietnamese woman picks through the rubble of her home left devastated by battles between government troops and the Viet Cong.

Left: November 1972—The crew chief signals the pilot of an A-1 Skyraider preparing for takeoff at Bien Hoa air-base near Saigon. U.S. and South Vietnamese pilots used propeller-driven Skyraiders extensively in Vietnam.

Above: November 25, 1972—As armored personnel carriers of South Vietnam's 7th Infantry Division line up for an operation in Dinh Tuong province about 45 miles west of Saigon, a peasant calmly waters his vegetable field.

Above: December 28, 1972—Ice cream comes to the front line as an enterprising vendor does business with the crew of a South Vietnamese tank north of Saigon.

Left: November 1972—Peasants stop along the road to watch air strikes at Cu Chi, northwest of Saigon.

Right: January 20, 1973—South Vietnamese tanks returning to base pass peasants during a patrol off Route 1 northwest of Saigon. South Vietnamese troops were trying to seize control of Communist-held areas before a cease-fire went into effect.

Below: The headline reads 'Cease Fire' in this Saigon newspaper reporting the announcement of a cease fire agreement at the Paris peace talks.

Right: January 24, 1973—North Vietnam's chief negotiator, Le Duc Tho, addresses a news conference in Paris, calling the latest Vietnam peace agreement 'a great victory for the Vietnamese people.'

Left: February 1973—U.S. delegates, headed by presidential advisor Henry A. Kissinger, *left*, dark glasses frames, faces North Vietnamese delegation headed by Prime Minister Pham Van Dong, *fourth from right*, during meetings held in Hanoi.

Above: 1973—An American POW talks though a barred door to fellow POWs at a detention camp in Hanoi.

Right: December 14, 1972— Broken glass is cleaned up from windows of a Saigon airline office shattered by explosions at an ammunition dump several miles away.

Above: January 13, 1973— North Vietnam's Lo Duc Tho and U.S. negotiator Henry Kissinger meet in secret at Saint-Nom-La-Broteche near Paris to seek agreement on a ceasefire in Vietnam.

Above: January 31, 1973—A South Vietnamese woman looks at smoke from air strikes on Communist positions just off Route 15, 18 miles east of Saigon. The strikes temporarily closed the road linking Saigon to the coastal resort of Vung Tau.

Above: January 24, 1973—GIs at their Ton Son Nhut airbase billet listen to President Nixon announcing Paris peace agreement.

Above: January 18, 1973—South Vietnamese armored personnel carriers pass a farmer with his rice harvest in Trang Bang, northwest of Saigon, as three South Vietnamese divisions moved out to occupy the area in the event of an anticipated cease-fire. About six months earlier Trang Bang had been the site of a misdirected South Vietnamese air strike which left civilians dead or horribly burned.

Left: January 28, 1973—South Vietnamese soldiers run for cover as North Vietnamese and Viet Cong open up on their positions with mortar fire at Trang Bang, 30 miles north of Saigon.

Right: January 1973—While South Vietnamese artillerymen prepare to fire in the Mekong Delta, a peasant woman returns from a rice harvest with two bundles of rice straw.

Above: January 30, 1973—South Vietnamese soldiers head into the fighting along Route 1 northwest of Saigon.

Left: January 22, 1973—Pains of war are etched in the face of a South Vietnamese soldier who was wounded, captured, and later escaped during fighting in the U Minh forest southwest of Saigon.

Above: February 1973—Peoples Republic of China Chairman Mao Tse Tung welcomes North Vietnam leader Le Duc Tho to Peking.

Above: February 2, 1973—A South Vietnamese soldier displays a Viet Cong flag captured during fighting for a hamlet along Route 4 in the northern Mekong Delta.

Above: A Vietnamese woman displays her ample jewelry in Cholon, the Chinese section of Saigon.

Right: February 7, 1973—Villagers, mostly women and children, travel in boats to a Viet Cong propaganda meeting at Binh Pong, 45 miles from Saigon. Western newsmen were also invited to the session.

Right: March 1973—Hanoi school children return from school dressed in the white shirts and red scarves of the Communist youth movement.

Above: March 24, 1973—The town of Loc Ninh is under the watchful gaze of a portrait of Ho Chi Minh. The district capital north of Saigon fell to the Communists and served as the Viet Cong capital in South Vietnam.

Left: March 1973—North Vietnamese children wander through rubble in the Kham Thien district of Hanoi several months after a B-52 bomb strike.

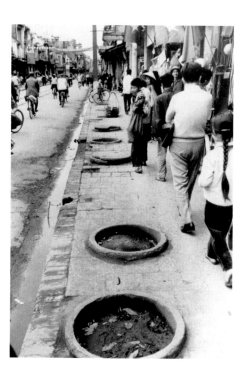

Below: March 1973—Individual air raid shelters line a Hanoi street. Hanoi's mayor said sand and debris could be quickly removed from the shelters, if necessary.

Above: March 29, 1973—The American flag is furled at ceremonies marking official deactivation of the Military Assistance Command-Vietnam (MACV) in Saigon after more than 11 years in South Vietnam.

Below: March 11, 1973—South Vietnamese POWs leave a Viet Cong camp in Binh Dinh province on the Vietnamese central coast. They were released as part of prisoner exchange agreed to under the Paris cease fire plan.

Below: March 1973—Three North Vietnamese men sit on a bench in Hanoi as a foreign delegation passes.

Above: March 1973—North Vietnamese children play on a Hanoi street. Some played around the capital's closed air raid shelters.

Below: March 1973—A Vietnamese man cradles his grandchild in Hanoi. After more than 20 years of hardship and war, many citizens in the North Vietnam were looking forward with hope for a better future.

Above: March 1973—A North Vietnamese man reads a newspaper on the curb of a Hanoi street. The people of Hanoi were reserved around foreigners at the time, presumably because government minders usually accompanied foreign visitors.

Above: March 28, 1973—Viet Cong observer counts US troops as they prepare to board jet aircraft at Saigon's Tan Son Nhut airport. Thousands of Americans departed Vietnam as the American military role decreased.

Right: April 1973—North Vietnamese workers ride a Hanoi streetcar.

Above: March 1973—North Vietnamese children cross a street as a cyclist passes by. Many citizens in the north were hoping that the Paris agreements would secure a peaceful future.

Below: March 19, 1973—The family of Lt. Col. Robert Stirm rushes toward the released POW as he arrived at Travis Air Force Base in California. Stirm's daughter Lori is followed by his son Robert, daughter Cynthia, wife Loretta, and son Roger.

Right: March 17, 1973—Several hundred soldiers and civilians crowd the bank of the Thach Han river to greet a boatload of POWs newly freed by the North Vietnamese across the river.

Below: March 28, 1973—President Thieu's Democracy Party makes its formal debut at a Saigon movie theater under huge banners carrying the party's symbol.

Right: April 1973—Prince Sihanouk, Cambodian chief of state, is embraced by Vietnamese Premier Pham Vahn Dong, upon Sihanouk's arrival in North Vietnam for a state visit.

Above: March 1973—A South Vietnamese soldier peacefully naps in a Danang museum, guarded by ancient Cham statues.

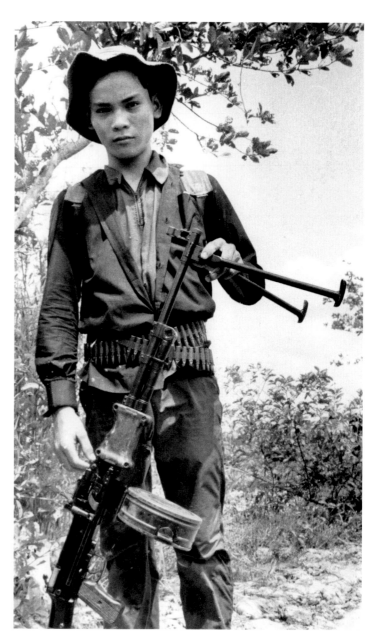

Left: April 1973—A Viet Cong trooper checks out his Chinese-made AK-47 rifle during a militia exercise near Cam Son village in the Mekong Delta. The guerrilla fighter also wears an American web belt and U.S.-made hand grenades and a flashlight.

Above: April 19, 1973—A young Viet Cong machine gunner shows off his Chinese-made weapon near Cam Song village in the Mekong Delta. The Communist guerrillas welcomed visiting journalists.

Left: April 27, 1973—A disabled political prisoner held by South Vietnam waits at the Bien Hoa air-base as a planned prisoner exchange at Loc Ninh was canceled or postponed without explanation by the South Vietnamese.

Right: June 1973—The daughter of South Vietnamese army sergeant Nguyen Bao Toan pauses to look back at her father's grave in a military cemetery at Bien Hoa.

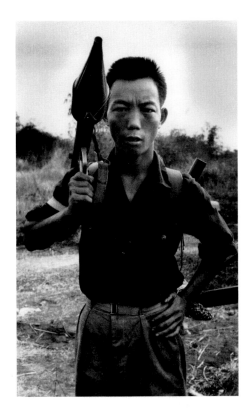

Above: April 11, 1973—A teenage member of the Viet Cong shows his B40 armor-piercing rocket in Binh Long province north of Saigon where Communist forces control most of the area.

Left: May 14, 1973—A Viet Cong guerrilla carries an anti-tank rocket in Binh Long province, a Communist stronghold on the Cambodian border north of Saigon.

k730915

Above: September 15, 1973—South Vietnamese President Nguyen Van Thieu accepts shafts of rice from peasants during his visit to Hai Lang to mark the first anniversary of the recapture of Quang Tri.

Right: January 1973—Presidential advisory Henry A. Kissinger talks with members of the North Vietnam delegation after initialing the Vietnam peace accord in Paris.

Left: August 2, 1973—U.S. Ambassador to South Vietnam Graham Martin shakes hands with Vietnamese officials after signing a $50 million loan agreement in Saigon. The loan allows the purchase of industrial and agricultural machinery.

Above: August 12, 1973—A Montagnard family and its prized possession, a work elephant, move down a winding, hilly road in the southern central highlands to escape fighting in their home district.

Right: October 24, 1973—South Vietnamese commandos, dressed like their Viet Cong counterparts, train at Quang Trung for infiltration of Viet Cong controlled areas. The man in foreground clears a route through sharpened punji sticks in the exercise.

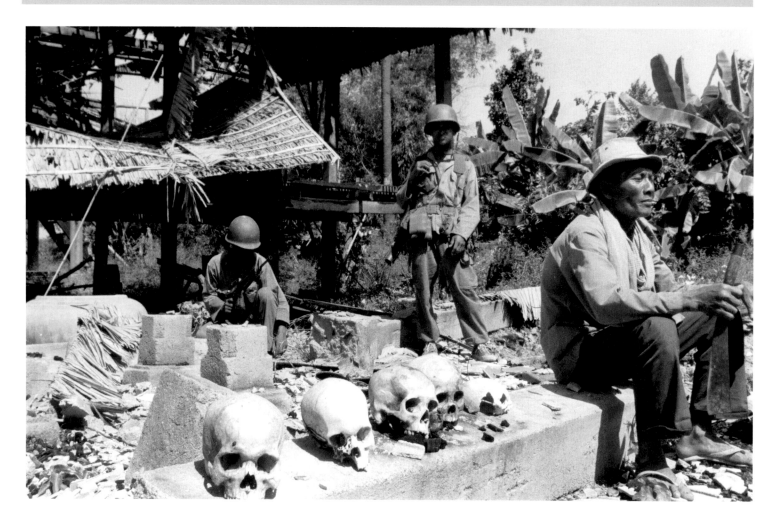

Above: December 1973—A Cambodian villager sits near human skulls recovered from debris in Kampong Tueol, Cambodia, after government troops retook the village on Route 3, southwest of Phnom Penh. The skeletal remains were those of civilians and troopers killed by Khmer Rouge insurgents who captured the town during heavy fighting.

Right: December 8, 1973—Bandaged and bloody, a South Vietnamese casualty of fighting near the Kien Duc district, 90 miles northeast of Saigon, is helped at an aid station.

# FINAL OFFENSIVE

In mid-December 1974 a score of men gathered at 33 Pham Ngu Lao Street – named after a Vietnamese general who had won repeated victories against foreign invaders. They had first convened here twenty years before in what until then had been the French military headquarters in Hanoi. Now they were meeting to plan the greatest victory in all of Vietnam's history. None of the conferees had changed, except for their gray hair and their expressions. They talked and gestured excitedly, which was unusual; their lined, stern faces at times were wreathed in smiles; but this was the conference for which they had long waited.

The senior military and political cadres had been summoned from their bases in the South and together with the eleven members of the Politburo they sat around a long plain-wood table that had once served the French kitchen staff. It was bare except for the inevitable teacups and their favorite cigarettes called 'Dien Bien Phu'. Wearing a worker's cloth cap, First Secretary Le Duan began the meeting by telling them that the end was in sight – and they were all in agreement. Le Due Tho reported on the political situation. Since signing the Paris Accords he had secretly spent several months in the South where, he said, control at the village level was being regained, with Saigon's army demoralized by the uncertainty of US support. The two senior generals who were present were outspokenly confident. Defense Minister Vo Nguyen Giap foresaw no resistance among the population in the South: they knew that Thieu would last only as long as his ammunition; they

> ## 'Some soldiers advanced on foot and ran and made fifty kilometers a day. They didn't eat because their goal, their first preoccupation, was the taking of Saigon.'
>
> – HANOI DIPLOMAT HA VAN LAU

knew in their hearts, he said, that Vietnam must be reunited. But Giap still thought in terms of years: the final offensive might take years, perhaps three, he cautioned. Everything depended, of course, on the response of the United States.

General Van Tien Dung, Commander of the People's Army, reported on the new military situation. Even as they talked his forces were launching a massive thrust from Cambodia into South Vietnam's province of Phuoc Long, a trial invasion to test American reaction. If the climate in Congress was as stringent as they assumed, no B-52s would re-emerge to thwart the new advance. 'Don't worry about the B-52s,' Le Duan told them. He was certain the United States would not re-enter the war: Watergate and the fall of Richard Nixon had turned Americans inward. Regardless, said General Giap, the North was now strong enough to carry out successfully the final offensive. They agreed that it should start in three months time.

Giap expresses Hanoi's attitude after the signing of the peace treaty almost two years earlier. In the days before the treaty the US, he argues, had already broken the spirit of it. They had sent South Vietnam an extra billion dollars worth of military aid. 'The Americans', says Giap, 'thought that even when they withdrew their troops they would still continue to transform Vietnam into a new colony of theirs.' But America had lost the will to defend the South, and Giap felt that short of a new American ground war the final offensive must succeed: 'Even if they deployed their air force

Above: February 7, 1975—Villagers of Binh Phong hamlet pose with Viet Cong flags during a rally in the Viet Cong controlled area 45 miles southwest of Saigon.

Above: March 29, 1975—North Vietnamese Army soldiers enter Danang, South Vietnam's second largest city.

and navy they would again fail.' But they would not do it: by now it was 'obvious' to the Americans that 'the Vietnamese did not fear such things'.

Giap's protégé, General Van Tien Dung, who was tasked with leading the final offensive, felt simply that the United States – even if it had the will – no longer knew how to fight this kind of war. 'They applied a lot of new strategies,' says General Dung, 'such as "Special War", "Local War", "Vietnamization" – and the result of it all was the biggest failure in the history of the United States.' The US might be a super-power but, as General Dung put it, 'A small nation, with a small land mass and a small population which knows how to consolidate and knows its leadership could defeat a greater power.' Dung felt that the North's great offensive at Tet 1968 had been the turning point because it had 'destroyed America's will'.

Recalling his mood before the final offensive, the veteran of Dien Bien Phu thought the outcome had been determined twenty years before. 'Every victory, direct or indirect, contains reasons for the following victory,' he says, and America's main mistake was not in recent years – it was 'in taking the place of the defeated French'.

Thus, Hanoi's leadership embarked on the last phase of its long struggle, supremely confident that it knew its old enemy as well as it knew itself. They had briefly met – and briefly debated. Yet only now, after thirty years of almost continuous war, and – for some of them – fifty years of armed resistance, had they 'reached the historic decision', says diplomat Ha Van Lau, 'that the balance of strength had changed fundamentally in our favor'. They had stoically waited, virtually for a lifetime, for the right moment.

But then, says Ha Van Lau, they moved with exceptional speed. In Hanoi the Foreign Ministry had to create the element of surprise, arranging the diplomatic schedule of the leadership to give an appearance of routine. And though 'we knew the moment had come to undertake the last battle to liberate the South' the North could not totally assume that the bombers would remain grounded. It meant that there were just three months 'to mobilize all the people and all our armed forces'.

In the South the battle had not ceased with the peace treaty. Since then, ARVN deaths had averaged 1000 a month in the renewed struggle for the villages. Although there had been Operation Enhance, the billion dollars of extra aid rushed to South Vietnam in the weeks immediately before the peace treaty, President Thieu now began to worry that US guarantees had gone with Nixon. Under the terms of the Paris treaty, weapons and ammunition could be replaced as expended, and with this safety provision Thieu had fully deployed his forces in the battle for the countryside. His army had fought well: it had proved itself deserving of continued US support, Thieu considered. The Americans remaining in Saigon, he says, 'had been very astonished'.

'Everyone, and above all Kissinger,' says Thieu, 'believed that six months after the peace signing we would have collapsed.' Instead, by the time of Hanoi's final offensive, the South had 'endured two years with a completely reduced military potential and reduced economic aid'. In 1974 Congress had set a one billion dollar ceiling on military aid for South Vietnam in the coming year – as compared to the thirty billion dollar annual military aid bill during the American com-

Above: March 23, 1975— Vehicles of all kinds clog the highway along the northern central coast of Vietnam as a massive evacuation sent tens of thousands of people heading southward ahead of the advancing North Vietnamese.

Left: December 9, 1974— Smoke rises from incoming Viet Cong rockets on a South Vietnamese firebase near Tay Ninh, 55 miles north of Saigon near the Cambodian border.

Right: December 9, 1974— A South Vietnamese woman cries over the body of her soldier-husband killed in Viet Cong shelling on a government fire base near Tay Ninh, 55 miles northwest of Saigon.

bat years. By late 1974, says Thieu, he was without helicopter and artillery replacements and US air support was 'nil'. For years the United States military had believed that the war was winnable because of its helicopter mobility and superior firepower. 'When the North Vietnamese launched the great offensive,' says Thieu, 'we had no mobility and not enough fire-power.'

Thieu in fact had been unable to hold even one province close to his capital. The North Vietnamese test offensive against Phuoc Long succeeded in just three weeks with the capture of the provincial capital. Phuoc Binh, on 7 January 1975. The US State Department now charged Hanoi with serious violation of the Paris Accords. It was a perfunctory statement, and Hanoi's assessment had so far been accurate. The US continued to protest, but did not act.

At the US Embassy in Saigon the principal analyst of North Vietnamese strategy, Frank Snepp, says that he – and therefore Washington – knew that the Phuoc Long offensive was a rehearsal for the final one: that much then depended on how the US reacted. Snepp, operating a CIA network from the Embassy, claims he had a 'deep mole' or agent well entrenched in the North Vietnamese command in the South. Snepp says this agent knew of the decisions and even the discussions of the Hanoi Politburo. And if Phuoc Long 'failed to bring in the B-52s, as Le Duan suggested it wouldn't, then they would move a little bit further,' Snepp was informed. He quotes his Red Mole as saying that beginning in 1975 Hanoi's strategy was 'a two year program of victory. They would escalate their attacks in 1975, testing the US response, and then go for total victory in 1976. Thus they hit the province of Phuoc Long and the United States didn't react.

'It was the first time since 1972 that the South Vietnamese had lost an entire province. The Politburo reconvened and the Party's First Secretary Le Duan said, "That means the Americans won't come in – we can advance our schedule." The Politburo agreed: "Okay", they said, "we'll push for victory next year, but if we see opportunities for victory in 1975 we will go for broke then." '

'By 1975,' says President Nguyen Van Thieu, 'our war potential had been reduced by sixty per cent. Meanwhile, the war potential of the North had been increased by the overwhelming help of Russia. I can tell you, during those two years since the signing of the Paris agreement, the war is more cruel than before the signing.' Thieu recalls that 'every week of every month I sent delegates to Washington – military men, political men, Vietnamese senators, to explain. I wrote to the American President and I explained the danger to the Ambassador in Saigon – and nothing happened.'

Thieu had now to deal with a new US Ambassador, Graham Martin, who says his instructions were to ensure that 'the American military understood that the involvement was ended and that the South Vietnamese also understood that they were on their own in fighting what was obviously going to be a continuing North Vietnamese pressure'. The US 'military' to whom Martin refers were, in addition to the legally permitted quota of fifty advisors, the sizeable aid task force of 7000 Americans, many of them ex-servicemen, who had been contracted by the

Left: December 9, 1974—A woman collects what was left of her house after the North Vietnamese and Viet Cong attacked Doan Ket village, 65 miles northeast of Saigon.

Department of Defense to stay on in South Vietnam after the peace treaty. Ambassador Martin regarded this small army of technicians whom he commanded, and the huge emergency aid program prior to the peace treaty, as evidence that his country would fulfil at least the aid terms of the settlement. As he understood it, South Vietnam, 'was basically on its own, but on its own with promises of economic and military support in the way of logistics and supplies, not fighting men, that we had promised and which was a condition of the South Vietnamese agreement to the 1973 Accords'.

Graham Martin had spent much of the 1960s in South-east Asia, first as US representative to SEATO, then as Ambassador to Thailand, where he had proved a dexterous and sympathetic diplomat, on the one hand getting Thai co-operation for US B-52 bases, on the other hand persuading Washington against pressuring for more than the token 11,500-man force Thailand had committed to the Vietnam war. Martin personally felt the war's tragedy. His adopted son was among the first GIS to die in combat in 1965, and Martin had 'utterly no desire to go back to South-east Asia in any capacity'. He was Ambassador to Rome, and at sixty-one already counting on retirement to a farm in Tuscany, when Henry Kissinger – now Secretary of State – called him to offer this 'final post' in Vietnam.

Martin was a logical choice: indeed, perhaps the best qualified for the Saigon role of any of the long line of Ambassadors. He was the only one to have actively studied jungle warfare techniques in years of liaising between the State Department and the Pentagon – and had concluded that America did not understand this kind of war. He would have been the perfect chief advisor in Vietnam – ten years earlier. Now it was all too late, and Martin declined the job. But then President Nixon – in his own last days – passed word that 'you can't back out when the going gets tough'. And Graham Martin, a loyal career diplomat for thirty years, felt there was 'really no answer to that for a professional'.

By the same code Martin felt that the US had an obligation to the South extending back as many years as his own service, and like a defense lawyer who might be dubious about his client, he nevertheless staunchly fought his case – perhaps sensing that he would be the last American voice,

the last hope and the last measure of the American character for the people whose well-being had once been fundamental to the Free World but whose destiny had been re-cast by his boss as players in a sideshow. In cable after cable to Secretary of State Kissinger, Martin reminded him of South Vietnam's trust and America's honor. 'I imagine that my cables were perhaps a bit tar,' he recalls, 'but they were intended to make certain that there could be no misunderstanding of the gravity of the situation.'

Reviewing the events since the peace treaty, Martin says the first 'great difficulty was that we had suddenly dumped enormous quantities of supplies' in the South in late 1972 and the US before its withdrawal had not had time to set up the logistics for these, nor adequately to train the South Vietnamese in all the technology – from the latest fighter-bombers to the most modern air-traffic control equipment – which they belatedly received. By mid-1973 'other things obviously preoccupied Washington – remember the Middle East shuttle diplomacy'. Kissinger was constantly somewhere between Cairo and Tel Aviv trying to avert a new war – and failing.

'The Yom Kippur war was a disaster for South Vietnam,' says Martin 'because US military aid diverted to Israel from American bases in Europe had to be replaced.' Vietnam 'suddenly became a competitor for the replenishment of the supplies in Europe' and 'received a much lower priority'. On top of this the Arab oil embargo, followed by escalating prices, meant that overnight the military budget for Vietnam was worth only a quarter of its face value. If the US was to continue its commitment to replace supplies and arms on the peace treaty 'basis of one for one' then the US had to accept, says Martin, that 'the cost had quadrupled. Yet there was no recognition of this, and no additional funding and no requests to the Congress for these amounts.' In effect, says President Thieu, 'The economic aid was cut, the military aid was cut – and we had no means to fight.'

Ambassador Martin went to Washington personally to plead Thieu's case following the North Vietnamese capture of Phuoc Long province in January 1975. Washington now had the CIA's reports that Hanoi would briefly pause for US reaction. Thieu was pressing Washington to stand behind Richard Nixon's written assurance that such open invasion would bring US retaliation –

Left: March 1975—Viet Cong and militia women celebrate from a jeep and tank captured undamaged from government forces in Hue, South Vietnam.

Right: March 27, 1975—A girl cradles her young brother aboard an Air America C-46 carrying refugees from the threatened city of Danang. The flight was the first evacuation fight sponsored by the U.S. to move people from Danang where they gathered after fleeing cities in the north that were being overrun by North Vietnamese and Viet Cong forces.

Right: March 25, 1975—A full load of troopers and their families come down in a cargo sling to an already jammed deck as the boat takes aboard during an evacuation. They fled south from Hue, then boarded the boat to escape North Vietnamese.

but Nixon had resigned six months earlier and President Gerald Ford's response, a resumption of reconnaissance flights over the North, was – in Thieu's view – like using doves instead of B-52s. Ford had asked Congress for a mere $300 million supplemental aid for South Vietnam, but it was not yet authorized for 1975. Ambassador Martin had no comfort to offer Thieu – and no trust in past promises.

'If you try to "stiffen somebody's back" by giving them assurances which you yourself do not believe, you are getting nowhere,' the Ambassador concluded. He then felt the situation demanded 'the utmost realism on both sides' and, he says, 'I was very frank with President Thieu on what was happening; very frank on the deterioration of the climate in the United States.' By now, Thieu's trust in Martin had replaced his long belief that the Americans, if needs be, would return. And the Ambassador's gloomy report struck like a prognosis of death for want of treatment. Thieu still could not quite believe it.

'The United States', he says, 'had kept 300,000 troops in Europe for thirty years after the war; had kept 50,000 troops in Korea for twenty years since that war. And now we had let all American troops withdraw; we just asked for help to fight the war. Instead of maintaining half a mil-

lion troops in Vietnam it would be twenty times less expensive for the American people. What more could they ask of a small nation?'

Thieu still had an army of 660,000 and enough small ammunition for two years. His force outnumbered the North Vietnamese left in place after the 'cease fire' by four to one. Now in January 1975 Hanoi set about halving the odds. After two years reprieve from the bombers the Ho Chi Minh Trail had become a paved highway in parts, and a fuel pipe-line had been constructed along most of the Trail. The foliage had regrown; and the jungle canopy camouflaged what now occurred.

Within a few weeks another 150,000 Vietnamese troops secretly and easily completed what had once been one of the world's most perilous journeys. After the capture of Phuoc Long, General Van Tien Dung had halted the advance, but in Phuoc Long he held a key piece in South Vietnam's jigsaw of forty-four provinces. It was one of the largest and it interlocked with half a dozen of the populous southernmost provinces around Saigon and with as many more north of it in the strategic Central Highlands which, if captured, would cut the country in two. With the control of Phuoc Long the North Vietnamese command could co-ordinate its 300,000-man adjacent Trail force from deep within South Vietnam.

General Van Tien Dung now secretly proceeded to do this, setting out from Hanoi with chief political cadre Le Duc Tho on 15 February. The nature of their journey maintained the strange legends of the Ho Chi Minh Trail.

'They went to considerable lengths to keep secrecy,' recounts journalist Wilfred Burchett who later discussed the events with the North Vietnamese commander. 'They kept secret the fact that Van Tien Dung had even gone to the South. They kept putting out messages from Hanoi in his name. His car went to the staff headquarters at the same time every morning.' Van Tien Dung confirmed this story to the author. He had a look-alike, an enlistee who temporarily became a four-star general. Foreign observers in Hanoi would report that Dung was still in the capital.

For Dung the greater danger was not the hazards of the long jungle journey but of being recognized by Saigon agents as he entered the occupied area of the South, so the Commander in Chief of the People's Army simply did what thousands of his cadres had done before. Leaving the Trail he and Politburo member Le Duc Tho put on peasant clothes and went to war riding bicycles. He had done the same during the French years, 'I wore a woven peasant shirt and a conical palm leaf hat,' says Dung.

General Van Tien Dung (the 'D' is pronounced 'Z') had long since taken over active command of the armed forces from his mentor, Defense Minister Vo Nguyen Giap. At fifty-seven, he was the junior member of the Politburo both in years and rank, but since his youth his military reputation had been second only to Giap's in the North. He was a native of Hanoi, starting life as a weaver in a French textile plant, where the conditions drove him to join the Indo-Chinese Communist Party. He was arrested by the French and jailed for several years, escaping in 1943 only to be re-arrested in the following year and sentenced to death. He again escaped and by 1946, when full-scale war with the French began, Dung aged twenty-nine was head of the political department of the Viet Minh. He led some of the most hard-fought campaigns against the French – the battles of the Red River delta – and by the time of Dien Bien Phu he was Giap's Chief of Staff. He was known as a flexible tactician who applied guerrilla thinking and exceptional discipline in shaping a huge conventional army, which he would now lash into action with a mixture of biting criticism and messianic generalship.

The presence of Van Tien Dung in the South, had it been known, would have signaled Saigon that it was facing the ultimate battle. But Dung had achieved his first objective – surprise. Extraordinarily, he had moved a vast army into position largely undetected. 'Orchids were blooming on ancient jungle trees,' Dung remembers, and his men were hidden in the rubber forests on the slopes of the Trail: 'Trucks, tanks and cars pulling artillery could hide securely under the umbrella of their leaves.' Thousands of hammocks were slung between the rubber trees in 'orderly rows' and entering South Vietnam there were 'whole forests of signs at every crossroad' in the form of color codes of different 'sizes and shapes pointing the way for all the units'.

'We did not know in the CIA', admits Frank Snepp, 'that Van Tien Dung or Le Duc Tho were actually in the South. Our intelligence was deficient to that extent.' But the CIA had not even learned of the extent of Dung's forces or anything of his plan of attack from its 'agent' in the North Vietnamese command, suggesting that perhaps the CIA was fed only such information as Hanoi wanted known. Snepp had now been with the Agency for seven years, and had been re-posted to Saigon as the last American ground forces withdrew. In the year America's war had begun, 1965, Snepp had just majored in Elizabethan literature and with this grasp of court intrigue and subsequent master's degree in international affairs from New York's Columbia University, he was snatched from the campus by CIA recruiters. In Vietnam, Snepp did rare double-duty, working both sides of the espionage operation by serving as operative as well as analyst.

He recounts the start of the North's final offen-sive, or what the United States then knew of it. 'The Communists moved into the South a great many more forces than we knew were there,' he says, 'and they concentrated these forces in the Western Highlands which had always been a critical battlefield. They concentrated them around a place called Ban Me Thout. Now Ban Me Thuot historically had always been the anchor for government defense in the Highlands. If Ban Me Thuot went then these defenses could be outflanked. They were very clever. They moved in radio silence. They moved three divisions into the Ban Me Thuot area and we never knew they were there.'

The South Vietnamese had anticipated a repeat of the 1972 offensive with the North invading across the Partition line, and ARVN forces were concentrated at the northern coastal city of Da Nang. After General Dung had positioned his army in central South Vietnam so as to outflank the main ARVN force, he finally broke radio silence to transmit false messages. These indicated he would strike not at Ban Me Thuot in Darlac province but immediately north at Pleiku. 'So we began looking at Pleiku as the danger zone,' says Snepp.

Though Ban Me Thuot was a strategic center, the unprepared ARVN had only 4000 troops deployed there. And they had no knowledge that 30,000 North Vietnamese were hidden only a few miles away. General Van Tien Dung had called together his officers: 'I told them, there are two lines from a poem which burn in my heart – "For thirty years our land has taken up the gun, yet still the disc of our Moon is split in two." ' Dung's narrative is drawn from his own written account, *Our Great Spring Victory*, and from conversations with the author and with journalist Wilfred Burchett. 'They had hidden their tanks the night before in villages only twenty miles from Ban Me Thuot,' relates Burchett, 'and they hid them among the palm groves. They sawed the palms three-quarters of the way through so that at a minute's notice their tanks could leap forward along the road to Ban Me Thuot. The ARVN commander was taken completely by surprise.'

Dung describes how he almost lost months of surprise planning in a bizzare last moment mishap. A 'trumpeting herd of elephants' was suddenly charging his hidden headquarters in the remote Highlands. Some soldiers were about to shoot at the herd, giving away their presence, but Dung instead ordered his men to run, saying afterwards, 'There's nothing wrong with running from elephants.' Then the final offensive began: 'At exactly 2.00 am on March 10, raising the curtain for the attack on Ban Me Thuot, artillery and rockets poured a tempest of fire into the enemy's 23rd Division headquarters and kept up the barrage until 6.30 am, putting the enemy nerve center in an uproar and paralyzing them.'

In General Dung's words, a sapper force took the town airfield 'in just one hour: in the wink of an eye destroying seven enemy aircraft'. The South Vietnamese had no time to reinforce but General Dung concedes that they resisted the opening offensive as best they could. At Ban Me Thuot, he says, 'The enemy had been hit unexpectedly and had responded haphazardly – their armor and artillery were completely paralyzed right from the start. Nevertheless they remained extremely stubborn and sent eight bomber sorties to halt us and sought every opportunity for desperate counter-attacks. But nearly all the enemy counter-attacks were defeated.'

Without reinforcements or strong air support the ARVN survivors surrendered after thirty hours of siege. 'We basically wrapped up Ban Me Thuot by 10.30 am on 11 March 1975,' says Dung. He now received orders from Hanoi to swing quickly north and 'set up a blockade' of Pleiku province – the centerpiece of the Highlands which stretched half-way to the coast.

'Once Ban Me Thuot was abandoned,' says CIA analyst Frank Snepp, 'the Communists were in a position to sweep to the central coast and then in a right turn head south towards Saigon. And, in effect, that was the end of the war. The South Vietnamese army in the Highlands streamed toward the coast and was broken up along the way.'

Above: March 19, 1975—Cambodian refugees carry their belongings and move southward toward government lines 35 miles southwest of Saigon. They fled fighting along the Cambodian border.

Above: March 19, 1975—Refugees flee fighting along the Cambodian border and toward Saigon some 35 miles away.

In Saigon President Thieu appealed desperately to Washington for firm support. Instead, says Ambassador Martin, Thieu learned that 'not only was it highly unlikely that South Vietnam would receive any supplemental aid, it was unlikely that they would receive any aid at all in the next fiscal year, beginning that June.' In other words, Thieu faced an abrupt aid cut-off within three months.

Thieu decided on a drastic consolidating measure. On 15 March, only four days into the offensive, the South Vietnamese President informed his generals that the Central Highlands were to be abandoned. With this move he also abandoned Military Zones I and II, the provinces north of the Highlands. Almost overnight he had ceded half of his country. Ambassador Martin – who had no power or advice to offer – explains that Thieu felt the only wise course was 'to cut the military lines short and retain the great economic part of the country – the southern delta.'

Says Thieu, 'We had to take troops from the isolated areas, gather our forces to defend the more vital areas, because we judged that the United States would not help us again. If they wanted to help us they would have done so by then and we couldn't wait until it became too late. We had to take the calculated risk because withdrawal without mobility and great fire-power is a risk. But it was a must for us.'

So began what strategists have called the worst planned and worst executed withdrawal in military history. The ensuing panic fed on a rumor that a deal had been struck to give the North Vietnamese half of the country without resistance. The civilian exodus from the Highlands which began with the fall of Ban Me Thuot became an uncontrollable flood as Thieu announced his decision. Two days later the ARVN, accepting the orders, abandoned the province of Pleiku and the neighboring Highland province of Kontum – and now from this region 500,000 soldiers and civilians fled toward the coast in a pitiful and brutal procession remembered as the 'Convoy of Tears'.

The military authorities had chosen the little used – and almost unuseable – Highway 7 for the retreat. It was a narrow, winding pass banked by steep hills and was believed safe from ambush. But the North Vietnamese shelled the congested drawn-out convoy – and half a million people began pushing and fighting for the vanguard. Survivors told of old people and babies crushed and left to die as military vehicles bulldozed through the slowly trudging civilians, who still clutched at cartloads of lifetime possessions. In the stampede countless lost children died from the shells and from hunger. Only one in four of the vast human convoy reached the coast, with most of the civilians having fallen behind to await capture.

In the provinces to the north there was the same grim confusion as civilians and soldiers withdrew to the coastal enclaves preparing to evacuate by sea. Hanoi now ordered General Dung to prevent this, and he diverted his main force in a rapid thrust north against the two great cities of Hue and Danang. 'Hundreds of thousands of vehicles ran bumper to bumper day and night,' Dung records. His slogan was 'Lightning speed, daring and more daring'. Hue, the ancient capital, was a psychological prize; the port of Danang was the South's second largest city and the main escape route for a third of Thieu's army.

General Dung anticipated that he now faced a

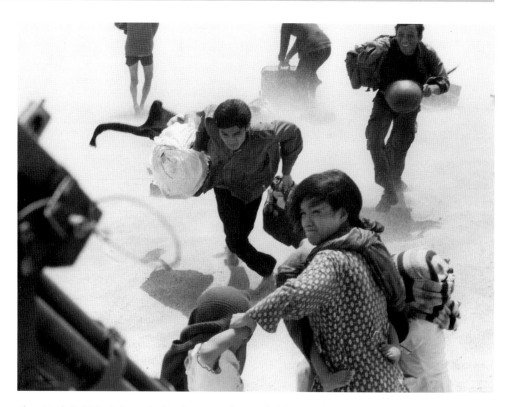

Above: March 23, 1975—Civilians and soldiers brave the windy storm of a helicopter to climb aboard the rescue craft in a threatened area near Tuy Hoa. Thousands of refugees left the highlands regional after a government decision not to defend the area against North Vietnamese forces.

drawn-out battle. Some 200,000 South Vietnamese troops remained in what Thieu called 'the isolated areas', including ARVN's crack 1st Infantry Division which had held its ground in Hue's Thua Thien province, guarding the approach from the Highlands to the northern coast. Dung had to overcome this force and also prevent its retreat. Dung spent a week planning his moves, then revealed how totally his army had adapted to modern conventional war. With three lightning pincer movements he encircled the ARVN 1st Division, and severed Highway 1 to block the sixty-mile escape road from Hue south to Danang.

'On 21 March,' as Dung describes it, 'our second Army Corps mounted a series of attacks from the North, West and South, leapfrogging enemy defense lines and forming many spearheads to encircle Hue.' For three days, heavy Soviet 130mm artillery hammered the outskirts of Hue. With the area commander abandoning the city, the officers and then the troops also fled, taking the only escape route by sea to Danang. On 25 March the city was occupied with hardly a shot fired. 'At exactly 10.30 am our flag was raised at the main gate of the Imperial city,' records Dung. It had flown there for twenty-eight days during the Tet Offensive of 1968. This time it would stay.

When he heard that Hue had fallen, Dung 'lit a cigarette. I had long sworn off tobacco but whenever I solve some thorny problem, or receive some news of outstanding conquest, I enjoy a smoke.'

Dung now sent 35,000 troops against Danang, where he faced an ARVN force of more than 100,000. The city's population had doubled with the refugee flow and now numbered three million. Hundreds of thousands besieged the boats, know-

ing only a few could escape. On 26 March, as Dung's army approached, the US State Department began a private airlift aimed at getting out 100,000 soldiers and key civilians. But the panic to board the first World Airways flight was so great that further air evacuation was canceled. Soldiers and civilians fought each other to reach the few remaining boats. People drowned, unhelped, with the newscameras equally dispassionately recording some of the worst scenes of television's first war.

The ARVN commander in Danang abandoned his men immediately after the fall of Hue. Other officers removed their uniforms and hid. On 30 March, only thirty-two hours after it had been surrounded, Danang capitulated. No fewer than 100,000 South Vietnamese soldiers, who had been left leaderless, surrendered.

Thieu says the people ran because they 'realized what was awaiting them when the Communists came'. But Thieu's Vice-President, Nguyen Cao Ky, says the people reacted to the soldiers – and he blames Thieu: 'The final debacle, I have to admit, was our own responsibility – or to be exact it was Mr Thieu's responsibility. At Ban Me Thuot, when it first started, commanding officers ran; everywhere commanding officers ran first, and all those commanding officers were appointed by Mr Thieu.' But Thieu counters that the morale of the army had rotted 'because everyone understood that military aid had been cut; there were many signs that America had abandoned us'.

Thieu was publicly saying that his army could fight harder now from more defendable lines and the South could be saved with American aid, but after Danang the Americans in Saigon doubted that anything could be salvaged. By the beginning of April the CIA's Frank Snepp assessed that with half the country occupied by the North

Vietnamese '150,000 South Vietnamese forces had been literally obliterated as fighting units, and what we were facing was an entirely new strategic equation'. Additionally, Dung's army had captured an estimated billion dollars worth of US military equipment – unused. On orders from President Ford the Joint Chiefs of Staff had urgently assessed Saigon's immediate replacement needs and had recommended an additional $700 million funding for an emergency airlift of supplies. But Ambassador Martin saw little prospect of Congressional approval, even though he cabled that Saigon – in his view – was displaying the resolve that the US had so long urged. 'While they were willing to fight,' says Martin, 'we made it clear that we would not give them additional ammunition, or supplies, without which any further resistance would be hopeless.'

But Embassy insider Frank Snepp charges that Martin all along 'wanted to convince Thieu he could still hold on', so that Thieu did not 'clean up his house' or 'pull in his defense lines' until too late. Snepp characterizes Martin as 'an extension of the Nixon White House, even after Nixon was gone,' saying he shared 'Kissinger's geopolitical perspective' and believed 'an American humiliation in Vietnam would affect our situation worldwide'. As a result Martin 'succumbed to another illusion in the final days. Martin came to believe that the military situation was retrievable.' ARVN could 'consolidate north of Saigon' and then negotiate.

Martin's counterpart in Washington, Ambassador Bui Diem, certainly had no illusions that any military stand would bring US support. He 'rushed back home but half the country was lost already, and I did say frankly to all my friends that there is no more hope from the US side. We have to think in terms of realities.'

The 'reality' now favored by Thieu's generals and encouraged by the US was to negotiate for a coalition government – the provision subverted after the 1954 Geneva Agreements, repudiated in favor of war in 1965, dismissed as a peace possibility in 1969 and again in the 1973 settlement when it *might* have brought a political resolution. On 31 March Hanoi announced that it was ready to confer with the Saigon government – but not with Thieu. The reality by then, as events would prove, was that Hanoi merely wanted the satisfaction of Thieu's dismissal by his own people, but with eleventh-hour hopes of salvaging some autonomy, the pressure began among Thieu's ministers for him to resign. He refused.

'I was very calm at that period,' he reflects. 'We had been overrun, but not all. One third of the army had been overrun, but not all. One half of the country had been overrun, but not all.' Thieu believed 'we still had the strength'.

The US press saw no evidence of this. 'The North Vietnamese are surging through the country and meeting only sporadic resistance; territory is being taken by virtual default,' reported *The New York Times* on 1 April. On that day, as ARVN troops abandoned the South's third largest city of Qui Nhon, Frank Snepp was assessing an alarming report from his informant on the other side: the Politburo had 'reconvened and made a new decision – they would go for total victory in 1975'. Whereas they had previously looked towards a two-year timetable, now they had 'stumbled on unforeseen victory'.

'Our intelligence as of 1 April', says Snepp, 'reflected this decision. On 4 April we got confirmation from our best agent inside the Communist high command. A week later we got further confirmation. I met with the agent myself and with his regular case officer. He said the North Vietnamese will be in Saigon for Ho Chi Minh's birthday, the 19th of May. And he added that in order to set up there for Ho's birthday they would have to take Saigon by the first of May. And in fact that is precisely what they did. The CIA called to the letter what Communist planning was at that particular time.'

General Van Tien Dung also had a personal reason for meeting this deadline, which would only be revealed on 1 May. Hanoi diplomat Ha Van Lau confirms that a precise date had been set for the take-over of South Vietnam. 'After the fall of Hue and Danang,' he says, 'our leadership decided to intensify the preparations to end the war before the rainy season. That is to say, in the month of April 1975.'

'At the beginning', says Wilfred Burchett, 'it was felt that in the first offensive season it would be good enough to get as far as Danang, dig in there, and consolidate. But it was the ease with which all these provincial capitals fell one after the other.' In the first week of April the coastal enclaves were falling like a domino a day: first Qui Nhon, then Tuy Hoa, Nha Trang and then – a long-term strategic loss for the US – the giant air and naval base at Cam Ranh Bay. Dung's army was racing down the coast. Explains Burchett: 'They didn't have to leave troops behind to mop up. The local people looked after the wounded, or whatever was left of the local Saigon forces. They insisted on that. It was an important ingredient in the success and speed of the operation.'

But all through the offensive General Dung felt that the advance could move faster. He recalls verbally whipping on his deputies: 'In these new, more demanding conditions, we were still caught up in the old style with many long drawn-out meetings.' He railed against some infantry units which 'had field radios but instead of using them were rattling around, stringing telephone wires. They had vehicles taken from the enemy, and prisoners who knew how to drive, but didn't dare use them – and instead just kept on walking.' Burchett says that at one field command meeting it was being debated 'whether they pushed on to take Saigon or not' and Dung said they had only to run for the capital: they had 'vast stocks of weapons hidden away in caches all along the route. . . . We have enough stocks there to make the enemy tremble for at least three generations.'

And now, recounts diplomat Ha Van Lau, 'the army units that had the mission of encircling and attacking Saigon only took with them what was necessary for the fight. Some advanced in convoys. Others advanced on foot and ran and made fifty kilometers a day. They didn't eat because their goal, their first preoccupation, was the taking of Saigon.' Says Dung, 'The whole land was on the march at top speed.'

At the US Embassy in Saigon Frank Snepp estimated that 'to defend Saigon now' the fragmented ARVN 'had no more than the equivalent of six divisions; the North had eighteen divisions; overwhelming superiority. What the South Vietnamese hoped to do was to establish a final defense line running from part of the Highlands to the central coast through the city of Xuan Loc – which was at the center of this defense line.' Xuan Loc was a small provincial capital only thirty-eight miles north-east of Saigon and 'it became the

Above: March 15, 1975—South Vietnamese troops prepare to board helicopters at Phuoc An to carry them to battle at Ban Me Thuot in the central highlands.

linchpin. If the Communists could take Xuan Loc they could move on to Saigon.'

Van Tien Dung records that 'the battle for Xuan Loc was fierce and cruel from the very first days'. The first North Vietnamese attack came on 9 April, and 5000 men of the ARVN 18th Division held their ground, repulsing 40,000 of Dung's troops. They were led by a one-star general, Le Minh Dao, 'a rarity who had worked his way from lieutenant by ability, not politics'. General Dung admits 'our divisions had to organize many assaults, striking and striking again to destroy each target and had to repel many enemy counter-attacks. Our artillery units had to use extra quantities of shells.' But still Xuan Loc held.

On 10 April, President Ford again appealed to Congress for one billion dollars in military and 'humanitarian' aid. Addressing a joint session of both Houses, Ford requested this aid 'without any delay' in order, he said, to give South Vietnam 'a chance to save itself'. In succeeding Nixon, Ford had declared: 'Our long national nightmare is over. Our constitution works. Our great republic is a government of laws and not of men.' But Ford had always supported the war – once attacking Lyndon Johnson in Congress by stating, 'Why are we pulling our best punches in Vietnam?' Ford had kept on Henry Kissinger as Secretary of State and the President used his twenty-five years of influence in Congress to keep pressing it to sustain US help for South Vietnam. The US, he told Congress, could buy time to arrange a political solution between Saigon and Hanoi – and evidently Ford and Kissinger still believed this was possible.

Kissinger, says CIA analyst Snepp, was deceived by the illusion that he had an understanding with the Soviets who 'lied to Kissinger' saying there was still 'a chance for a decent interval – perhaps a negotiated settlement'. And, says Snepp, Kissinger was fooled 'in particular by Soviet Ambassador Dobrynin' whom he had used so often to browbeat Hanoi. Ford, in turn, believed Kissinger – who in fact drafted Ford's speech to Congress. Ford then wanted the one billion dollars of aid delivered by 19 April – and at that time 'linchpin' Xuan Loc was still holding.

But from his Saigon perspective Frank Snepp thought that more military aid 'was utter nonsense. There was no aid which could have stabilized this situation.' Congress, anyhow, was in a mood to exert its long-stolen authority. It authorized only $200 million for the evacuation of American personnel – whose fate was now the overriding concern. On the 19th, instead of aid, the Saigon Embassy received orders to largely complete the evacuation within two weeks. On the same day the largest remaining air base at Bien Hoa near Saigon was abandoned after four days of saturation artillery fire. The avenues of escape were closing.

Now came the final political twist. Having, at great cost, fought extra years for an 'honorable' settlement predicated on Thieu's continuance in power, Washington concurred with the South Vietnamese generals that Thieu was a liability. Saigon itself, if not its political structure, might be saved if only Thieu would resign and accept voluntary exile. In effect, the South Vietnamese President was being asked to do what so many of his officers had done – abandon the people.

Ambassador Martin was the reluctant messenger: 'I simply went to Thieu and laid out as clearly

Left: Map shows the provinces lost to the enemy by April, 1973.

as I could the military situation – what the other side had, what we had, the political situation, the attitude of his own administration. I expressed the conviction that while I did not believe myself that there was any possibility of such a [coalition] transition, it was clear that some of his own generals wished to attempt it, but would not do so with him in position.' Thieu says that Martin 'never asked me to resign. He never suggested that.' He did not feel Martin was using him for purely American interests, rather 'I think he loved Vietnam.'

There was a further twist in that General Tran Van Don, the US contact ten years earlier in the ousting of President Diem which had led to Thieu's ascendancy, was again the go-between. General Don himself had been a victim of one of the numerous post-Diem coups; he had turned to the import-export business but in the past two years had become politically active again as deputy-premier. He believed that 'Vietnamization' should mean a Vietnamized peace – a government or 'concord' – and he says that in 1973 and 1974 when 'the military situation was good' he proposed

negotiations with the North. 'President Thieu was not against it – he thought it was a good proposal but I felt he was not free to decide. His entourage was against it. The Americans were against it. Why, I do not know.'

Don now quietly tried soundings through French channels and then 'in the last days,' he says, 'the French Ambassador told me that if you would like to save Saigon from long-range artillery, if you'd like to have a compromise solution to keep South Vietnam neutral, the only man who could do it was Big Minh. I asked the French Ambassador "Why Big Minh?" He said because Big Minh is the only one the other side would like to recognize as the new leader in South Vietnam. When I asked the American Ambassador. Graham Martin, he told me the same thing – maybe he got it from the French Ambassador.'

Says Snepp. 'The French bear a great responsibility for encouraging Martin.' He concedes that Martin's 'objective was humanitarian' but his 'focus on a negotiated ending' meant that 'he let our evacuation planning slide'.

696

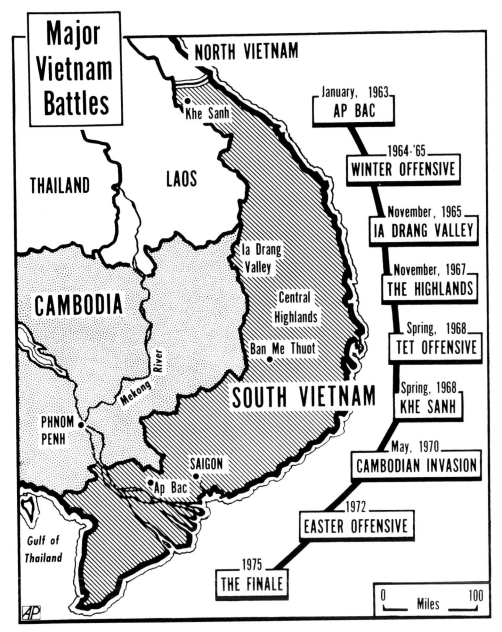

# Major Vietnam Battles

NORTH VIETNAM

Khe Sanh

THAILAND

LAOS

January, 1963
AP BAC

1964-'65
WINTER OFFENSIVE

Ia Drang
Valley

November, 1965
IA DRANG VALLEY

Central
Highlands

November, 1967
THE HIGHLANDS

CAMBODIA

Ban Me Thuot

Spring, 1968
TET OFFENSIVE

SOUTH VIETNAM

Spring, 1968
KHE SANH

PHNOM
PENH

May, 1970
CAMBODIAN INVASION

SAIGON

Ap Bac

1972
EASTER OFFENSIVE

Gulf of
Thailand

1975
THE FINALE

0 ⎿ Miles ⎿ 100

Above: Map locates the key battles in South Vietnam between 1963 and 1975.

The US support of General Duong Van Minh completed the twist: he was the 1963 anti-Diem coup leader whose 'neutralist' talk President Johnson wanted stopped 'by whatever means we can' – and the 'means' for the US had lasted a decade. Big Minh, so-called because he was six feet fall and weighed 200 pounds, 'called himself a member of the "Third Force",' says Frank Snepp. The CIA's dossier showed that Minh had 'a brother or a cousin – there was some debate over this – who was a high ranking North Vietnamese officer. So Big Minh was the last American hope. Thieu had to be gotten out of the way – and he had to be gotten out of Saigon.'

Thieu says he did not want his people 'accusing me of being an obstacle to peace, or to American aid'. But he did not believe a coalition was ever a reality: always Hanoi 'negotiated only when it was weakening'. On 21 April Thieu resigned, announcing his decision in a bitter anti-American speech over the national television network which the US had installed to help win

hearts and minds. Thieu stubbornly turned over the presidency not to neutralist General Minh but to his oldest minister, Tran Van Huong. On the same day Xuan Loc fell. For twelve days its defenders had displayed desperate last-ditch heroism, leaving at the end of the long alliance a better memory of the ARVN soldiers and suggesting a different fate had they been better trained and led years earlier.

The Americans undertook to get Thieu out of the country – safely. Embassy operative Frank Snepp was assigned to escort the President of the Republic of South Vietnam to Saigon's Tan Son Nhut airport within hours of his resignation: 'Several colleagues and myself from the CIA collected limousines. I was armed to the teeth', says Snepp, 'because I had visions of what happened to Diem in 1963: ordered out of the car, cut down by Young Turks.'

They drove, he says, to Thieu's villa and 'aides came running with suitcases and flung them into the back of my particular limousine and you could

hear the banging of metal upon metal. It was the last of Thieu's fortune. Actually he had already shipped most of his household belongings and his fortune out of the country in early April.' (*Time* magazine had then quoted unconfirmed reports that Thieu had shipped out between two and three tons of gold.) One of Snepp's colleagues asked Thieu ' "Where's your wife?" And Thieu said, "Oh, she went to Hong Kong to look at some pictures she wanted to buy." '

North Vietnamese artillery echoed on the city outskirts; the airport was coming under fire, and the Saigonese, who had been an island apart for thirty years, were engaging as usual in the ritual promenade of evening: the streets twice as packed with strollers, vendors and refugees, all oblivious to the black caravan of cars rushing away their leader.

'And what a night it was – a starlit night.' Snepp remembers, 'and there were tracers out along the perimeter of the airport. I looked in the rear-view mirror at Thieu's eyes and they were glistening with tears as we passed into the air base to the plane that was to whisk him out of the country. Thieu leaned over the seat and he said, "Thank you for all you've done." And it came to me: thank you for what, for the 56,000 American lives that had been given here in Vietnam? And I thought about saying that, but being the loyal bureaucrat that I was, I kept my mouth shut, and shook his hand. The man was crying. I guess he didn't need that final humiliation.

'He ran up to the airplane; the suitcases were whisked aboard, and there was Ambassador Martin, immaculately tailored, wearing horn-rimmed glasses, looking very much like a professor – nothing like an Ambassador bidding farewell to the last vestige of the American experiment in Vietnam.'

Thieu boarded his flight into exile carrying a lasting bitterness toward the Americans: 'They abandoned us,' he says. 'They sold us out. They stabbed us in the back. It is true – they betrayed us. A great ally failed a small ally.' Says Snepp, 'People lambasted Thieu rightly. Thieu was far too tolerant of corruption. He was a weak leader; he made countless military errors, for which many military men should have been drawn and quartered. But all that being said, he had been lied to by the US government.'

As Thieu flew out, the guns around Saigon seemed hopefully stilled and the city was 'very, very quiet' that next morning of 22 April, says Tran Van Don. He felt that life 'continued to be normal' – though by now almost all the rich and influential had already left and Van Tien Dung's legions formed an invincible ring around the capital. After only forty-four days of an offensive expected to last two years all forty-four of South Vietnam's provinces had fallen or were encircled. Saigon was alone – yet even now, says Don, 'people believed that something would happen – some political arrangement; maybe we could control again a part of South Vietnam. That's what people believed. I believed it, too.'

On the next day, with one week remaining to his 1 May deadline, General Dung informed the Politburo that Saigon was now 'like a snake without a head' and, in words that seemed to owe more to the ancient mandarins than to Marx, he reported that his forces were 'poised like a divine hammer held aloft'.

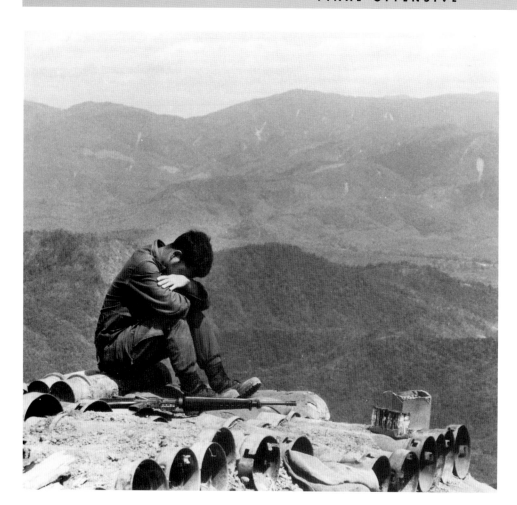

Left: March 24, 1974—A South Vietnamese soldier rests on a lonely hilltop outpost northeast of Kontum, overlooking a vital North Vietnamese supply road.

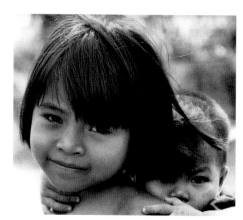

Above: January 1974—A girl and her younger brother pose for a picture in their village Northwest of Saigon.

Right: February 7, 1974— Viet Cong prisoners report to the camp at Loc Ninh, 75 miles north of Saigon, for a prisoner exchange, the first such exchange after a six month suspension.

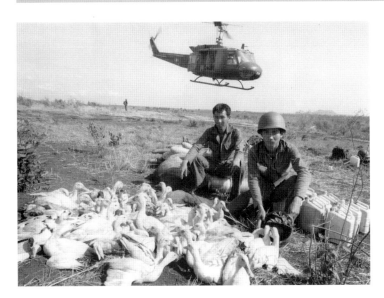

Above: April 10, 1974—South Vietnamese soldiers mind a flock of ducks brought in to their unit south of Pleiku in the central highlands. Far from any urban areas, the troops have their food flown in to boost their pre-packaged rations.

Above: April 12, 1974—A Vietnamese soldier helps a wounded buddy from the battle lines off Route 1 near Trang Bang.

Above: February 21, 1974—A South Vietnamese soldier waves the government flag at the Viet Cong in the central highlands province of Kontum. It was his answer to the Viet Cong flag flying in the distance.

Right: February 1974—The elaborate gate in the grounds of the Imperial Palace in the Citadel of Hue stands in partial ruins after allied troops recaptured the city from the Viet Cong and North Vietnamese.

Above: May 21, 1974—South Vietnamese infantrymen, backed by tanks and armored personnel carriers, charge toward Viet Cong and North Vietnamese positions in heavy fighting near Bo La, about 25 miles north of Saigon.

Above: July 12, 1974—Election posters go up in downtown Saigon as South Vietnamese prepare to go to the polls to select from more than 1,000 candidates running for the province and city councils.

Above: May 21, 1974—Smoke from South Vietnamese air strikes rises above the village of An Dien, 23 miles north of Saigon, as government forces hit Viet Cong and North Vietnamese positions.

Left: August 16, 1974—The cook of a South Vietnam unit on the move near Danang carries the food supply.

Left: August 9, 1974—On the day of his resignation, Richard M. Nixon, the first U.S. president to resign from office, waves good-bye from the steps of his helicopter as he leaves the White House following a farewell address to his staff.

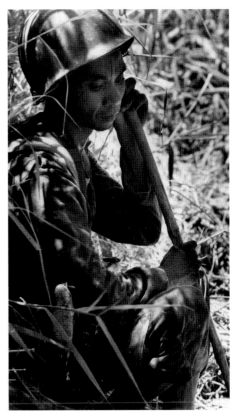

Above: August 24, 1974—A tired and wounded old soldier leans on a stick in a shady grove during fighting near the northern port city of Danang. His unit engaged a small band of Viet Cong who earlier cut vital Route 1.

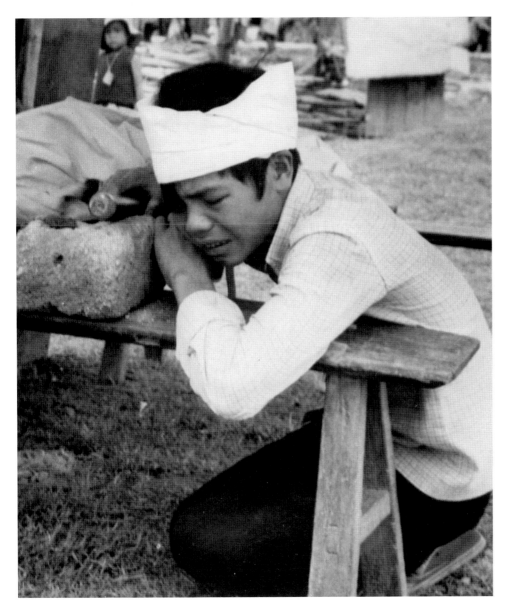

Left: August 1974—A South Vietnamese boy cries next to the body of his mother, killed during a North Vietnamese artillery attack on Loc Tan, a village southwest of the port city of Danang. Long-range artillery was driving many civilians to Route 1 and urban centers already overcrowded with refugees.

Left: October 20, 1974—Protesters, mainly Buddhists, attend a peaceful antigovernment rally at a Chinese temple near the imperial capital of Hue.

Right: October 20, 1974—Buddhist monks pray at the monument to Thuich (Venerable) Quang Duc, a monk who burned himself to death in 1963 to protest the political situation then prevailing in Vietnam. A protest march followed against the policies of current President Nguyen Van Thieu.

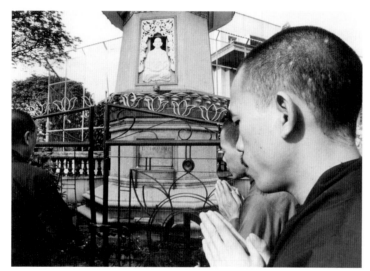

Above: October 20, 1974—Anti-government demonstrators occupy the steps of the National Assembly building in Saigon in growing dissent against President Thieu's government.

Right: September 5, 1974—A South Vietnamese soldier pauses to look at a battered village church caught in the crossfire with enemy troops in Thanh Huy, about 20 miles northeast of Saigon. Much of the damage was from government air and artillery strikes on the village after it was captured by the Viet Cong.

Left: October 31, 1974—Rock throwing demonstrators move toward police in a riot on the outskirts of Saigon.

Left: October 31, 1974—South Vietnamese riot police face angry protesters who wanted to move their anti-corruption rally from the suburbs to central Saigon. Smoke rises from a burning motorcycle.

Right: October 31, 1974—South Vietnamese police block antigovernment demonstrators from carrying their protest from the suburbs to downtown Saigon.

Left: October 31, 1974—Police use wicker shields to ward off the rocks thrown at them by demonstrators on the outskirts of Saigon.

Below: November 28, 1974—South Vietnamese riot troops armed with sticks and wicker shields close off a Saigon street to contain an antigovernment demonstration that protested a trial in which three newspapers were charged with slandering the government.

Above: November 1, 1974—Relatives gather at the grave of a soldier on Vietnamese National Day. He was killed in the war, one of many buried at Bien Hoa National Cemetery northwest of Saigon.

Left: November 2, 1974—A South Vietnamese policeman clears traffic from a Saigon street as flag bearers lead about 500 marchers to a memorial ceremony at the grave of Ngo Dinh Diem, South Vietnamese president slain in a coup 11 year earlier.

Above: January 22, 1975—A priest of the Cao Dai faith meditates in the sect's cathedral at Tay Ninh northwest of Saigon. Elements of Christianity, Buddhist, Confucianism, and Taoism combine to form the Cao Daist beliefs.

Left: December 17, 1974—Street urchins take a look at fully decorated artificial Christmas trees for sale in downtown Saigon as the country prepares for the holiday celebration.

Below: December 1974—A lone South Vietnamese militiaman drinks the milk from a coconut while sitting in the ruins of Phuoc Hoi village, 65 miles northwest of Saigon, where government reinforcements were sent in to combat North Vietnamese and Viet Cong troops. Ba Den, Black Virgin Mountain, is in the background.

Left: March 23, 1975—Overburdened trucks line the highway between Hue and Danang carrying refugees from north to south after government troops said they could no longer defend Hue.

Above: March 12, 1975—South Vietnamese infantrymen advance during operations to reopen Highway 12, which had been cut off the previous day by Communist forces about 40 miles northwest of Saigon. Without the highway, airlifts would be necessary to supply cities, towns and villages along the route.

Right: March 1975—South Vietnamese troops fill every available space on a ship evacuating them from Thuan An beach, near Hue, to Danang as Communist troops advanced.

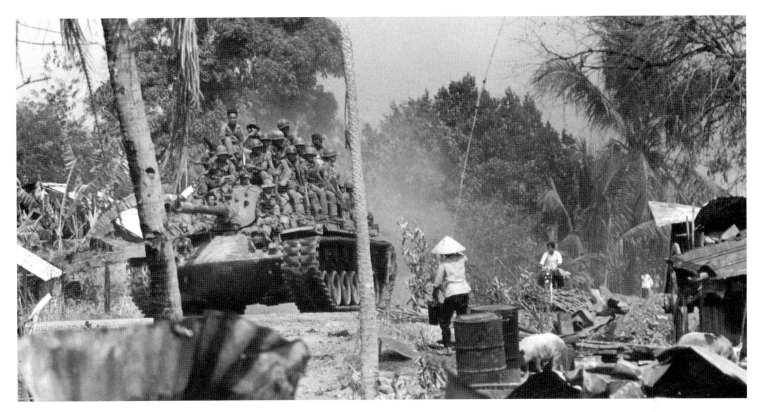

Above: March 1975—South Vietnamese troops sit atop a tank and roll through a Vietnamese village as they move away from the battlefront against the oncoming North Vietnamese army.

Above: March 13, 1975—A Vietnamese woman carries her wounded daughter as they flee heavy fighting near Huan Loc, about 35 miles north of Saigon.

Right: March 21, 1975—A South Vietnamese soldier on crutches leads other refugees ahead of advancing Communist forces near Nha Trang, along South Vietnam's central coast. The refugees had spent a week on the dirt trails from the highlands city of Ban Me Thuot after it fell to the North Vietnamese.

Above: March 29, 1975—South Vietnamese airborne medics tend to battle casualties following a clash with North Vietnamese troops in Tay Ninh province, northwest of Saigon.

Right: March 21, 1975—The highway is jammed with vehicles of all kinds as residents of Hue head south to Danang. Government troops said that Hue was no longer defensible, and they urged civilians to leave.

Above: March 9, 1975—Dead and wounded South Vietnamese soldiers await evacuation after fighting to reopen strategic Highway 19 east of Pleiku in the Central Highlands.

Left: April 1, 1975—Some 6,000 South Vietnamese Marines evacuate the northern port city of Danang from China beach as smoke rises from Viet Cong rockets.

Right: April 1, 1975—A cluster of South Vietnamese Marines, some of whom can't swim, holds onto inner tubes and plastic containers as a rescue line is thrown to them from a navy LST off China Beach as they fled Danang.

Above: April 3, 1975—Vietnamese orphans, some wrapped in blankets, sit on the floor of a World Airway DC8 jet as the plane stopped over at Yokata U.S. Air Force Base northwest of Tokyo. The children were the first South Vietnam refugees evacuated aboard an American airliner.

Left: April 1,1 975—A U.S. civilian pilot in the aircraft doorway tries to maintain order as panicking South Vietnamese civilians scramble to get aboard during evacuation of Nha Trang. Thousands of civilians and South Vietnamese soldiers fought for space on the aircraft to Saigon as Communist forces advanced following the fall of Qui Nhon, to the north.

Above: April 13, 1975—U.S. Marines evacuate American and other allied embassy personnel by helicopter in Phnom Penh, Cambodia. The Marines came under Khmer Rouge fire after they were on the ground near the U.S. embassy.

Above: April 11, 1975—Rifles are fired into a house in Thu Thua by a South Vietnamese field force looking for suspected Viet Cong in the building.

Right: April 9, 1975—The deck of a naval vessel is jammed with humanity as the ship docks at Vung Tau, a coastal town near Saigon. Refugees by the thousands crowded this ship and others to escape advancing North Vietnamese and Viet Cong forces farther up the coast.

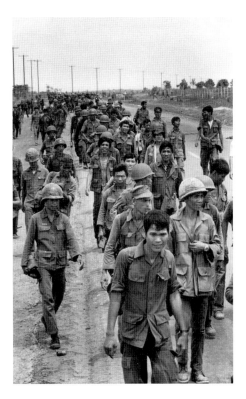

Above: April 23, 1975—A South Vietnamese father carries his son and a bag of household possessions as he leaves his village near Trang Bom on Route 1 northwest of Saigon. The area was becoming politically and militarily unstable as Communist forces advanced, just days before the fall of Saigon.

Below: April 28, 1975—Refugees fleeing the advance of Communist forces pour into Saigon, arriving in jammed vehicles and on foot from rural districts north of the capital.

Above: April 27, 1975—South Vietnamese troops, wounded in the final days of fighting near Saigon, make their way to an aid station after getting emergency care in the field. North Vietnamese and Viet Cong forces increased their attacks as they fought their way toward Saigon.

Above: April 28, 1975—A Vietnamese soldier attempts to comfort a boy wounded during fighting the outskirts of Saigon.

Left: April 13, 1975—A South Vietnamese army medic feeds a wounded North Vietnamese prisoner in Xuan Loc, about 40 miles east of Saigon, where there had been heavy fighting.

Right: April 30, 1975—Refugees fleeing the advance of Communist forces create a massive traffic jam on the northern outskirts of Saigon as South Vietnamese troops searched vehicles for communist infiltrators.

Right: April 28, 1975—A South Vietnamese woman and a boy push a cart with some food from the U.S. Embassy commissary in the Newport section of Saigon. Looting broke out as government troops fought Communist units in the final days before the fall of Saigon.

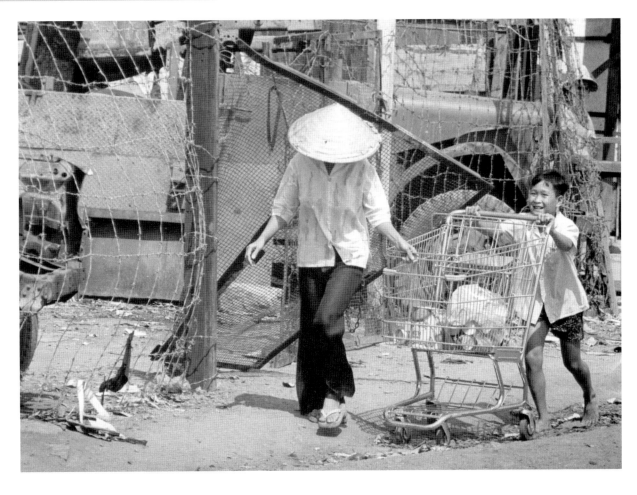

Left: April 28, 1975—South Vietnamese troops rush a wounded soldier to a motorcycle for transport to an aid station in Saigon after he was wounded in fighting around the Newport bridge on the outskirts of the capital.

Above: April 29, 1975—A Vietnamese soldier crosses a fence along with an American and South Vietnamese civilians during the evacuation of Saigon.

Right: April 29, 1975—A contingent of heavily armed Marines is on hand during the chaotic, last minute evacuation of authorized personnel and civilians from the U.S. embassy in Saigon.

Above: April 29, 1975—U.S. Marine helicopter crewmen carry Vietnamese civilians to safety aboard the USS *Blue Ridge* after their evacuation helicopter crashed on the deck of the amphibious command ship.

Above: April 29, 1975—Mobs of South Vietnamese civilians scale the 14-foot wall of the U.S. Embassy in Saigon, trying to reach evacuation helicopters as the last Americans departed from Vietnam.

Above: April 24, 1975—South Vietnamese seeking evacuation watch an Air American helicopter take off from the roof of the U.S. embassy building in Saigon.

Above: April 30, 1975—Desperate South Vietnamese try to get over the wall into the U.S. Embassy compound for evacuation on some of the last helicopters out of Saigon.

Left: April 29, 1975—Vietnamese clutch boxes of food looted from U.S. installations after the evacuation of Saigon.

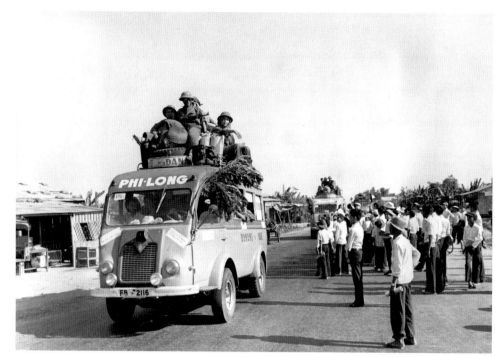

Above: April 10, 1975—North Vietnamese soldiers cheer from a government building in the final days before the fall of South Vietnam.

Right: April 30, 1975—A U.S. Marine helicopter lifts off from the landing pad atop the U.S. Embassy during the evacuation of Saigon.

Above: April 28, 1975—North Vietnamese troops ride past people on the highway at Danang en route to Saigon. Two days later, the South Vietnamese capital fell.

Below: U.S. Marines debark as evacuees load the CH-53 helicopter, known as the Jolly Green Giant, at the U.S. Embassy in Saigon. The Marines initiated the final stage of evacuation by air after a Communist victory in the Vietnam War.

Above: April 29, 1975—U.S. Navy personnel aboard the USS *Blue Ridge* push a helicopter into the sea off the coast of Vietnam in order to make room for more evacuation flights from Saigon. The helicopter had carried Vietamese fleeing Saigon as North Vietnamese forces closed in on the capital.

Right: April 30, 1975—Communist soldiers of the Provisional Revolutionary Government (PRG), celebrate the South Vietnamese surrender by driving captured tanks through Saigon.

Below: April 30, 1975—South Vietnamese officers sit dejectedly on a curb outside the Presidential Palace shortly after North Vietnamese troops captured the Palace in Saigon, ending the Vietnam War.

Above: April 24, 1975—South Vietnamese, some of who shield their faces from photographers, line up at the U.S. Embassy in Saigon, seeking evacuation in the last days before the fall of the capital.

Above: May 5, 1975—The U.S. embassy is looted on the day of the surrender of South Vietnam.

Left: April 24, 1975—As a helicopter takes off from the roof, South Vietnamese line up outside the U.S. Embassy in Saigon, seeking evacuation before the fall of Saigon.

Left: May 2, 1975—North Vietnamese gather on the square outside Hanoi's opera house to celebrate their victory over South Vietnam.

Below: April 29, 1975—A helicopter hovers over the asphalt as it prepares to evacuate personnel from the U.S. Embassy in Saigon in the last few days before North Vietnamese and Viet Cong troops entered the city.

Above: May 7, 1975—Saigon students carry a picture of the late North Vietnamese President Ho Chi Minh at a mass rally in front of Independence Palace where the Saigon Military Administrative Committee was introduced.

Right: May 15, 1975—A surface-to-air missile is paraded through Saigon at a rally marking the start of a three-day victory celebration for the provisional government troops.

Left: May 21, 1975—Abandoned and burned out tanks provide a playground for children of a village along Highway 1, 14 miles northwest of Saigon.

Above: May 7, 1975—An estimated 10,000 people, the biggest rally since the provisional government takeover, gather at Independence Palace where the Saigon Military Administrative Committee is introduced.

Right: May 4, 1975—Disarmed South Vietnamese military throw away their uniforms in front of Independence Palace in Saigon after President Duong Van Minh announced surrender and provincial government forces marched into the city.

Above: May 4, 1975—Troops of Vietnam's Provisional Revolutionary Government pass statues of South Vietnamese soldiers on Lam Son Square in Saigon.

Above: May 6, 1975—A war memorial to the South Vietnamese rangers near the Saigon police command is destroyed in a campaign to erase all signs of the old regime.

Below: May 4, 1975—Remains of tanks litter the edge of Saigon's Tan Son Nhut airbase after the last fighting before the South Vietnamese government announced its unconditional surrender.

Above: May 15, 1975—Girl student, wearing traditional Ao Dai dress and carrying portraits of Ho Chi Minh, wave North and South Vietnam flags at a victory celebration in Saigon.

Left: June 1, 1975—Picture-taking among the soldiers of the Provisional Revolutionary Government in Saigon became popular, especially for younger men who had never visited the south before. Cameras, which were looted from private homes and the American PX, are cheap in Saigon's street markets.

# SURRENDER

At his headquarters on the outskirts of Saigon General Van Tien Dung had gathered his senior officials around a large map of the capital and as he briefed them he sketched five red-ink arrows thrusting from every direction at the heart of the city. One arrow stabbed at the presidential palace and government quarters where returning Washington Ambassador Bui Diem found 'an unreal situation: people were still talking in terms of waiting for the Americans'. Another arrow knifed at the city's Tan Son Nhut airport where Ambassador Martin felt he had to 'juggle' the American evacuation to encourage Saigon's defense. A third arrow struck at the ARVN military headquarters where former Chief of Staff Tran Van Don was contending that Saigon had enough troops 'to hold the situation' and so negotiate a coalition government. A fourth arrow speared at the Directorate-General of Police where the vendors outside were doing a thriving trade in black pajamas. The fifth arrow sliced past the ever-surreal club *Cercle Sportif*, where champagne was being served as usual at the pool side, towards Embassy Row where, says Frank Snepp, 'we were facing Armageddon – the final reckoning'.

The divisions which General Dung held poised, and which had begun as a ragtag group of guerrillas in the caves of Tan Trao, were the elite of what was now the fifth largest army in the world. His sapper units would first take out the five nerve centers of the capital and then 100,000 men would be sent hurtling at Saigon, where ARVN also had 100,000 troops, of whom only 30,000 were in combat condition. Dung issued orders to 'use whatever force necessary', but he preferred an uncomplicated end with 'a minimum of blood-

> 'I listened to the radio and I heard people calling in – abandoned: "I am Mr Lon – I have served you for years – save me. I am Mr Hoa, save me." And there was no way to save them.'
>
> – CIA AGENT FRANK SNEPP

shed'. Hanoi had cabled Dung that 'the Americans and puppets are employing cunning diplomatic plans aimed at blocking our offensive on Saigon'. The Americans were to be given a little longer to get out and then Dung was to 'make the best use of each hour, each minute, for total victory'.

'Our intelligence told us precisely what was going to happen,' says Snepp. The CIA knew that Saigon was to be attacked from five directions and occupied within a week: 'We were facing a Communist onslaught – complete with strikes on the airfield; even an artillery bombardment.' As Snepp learned of this on 23 April, President Ford was declaring, 'Today America can regain a sense of pride that existed before Vietnam. But it cannot be achieved by refighting a war that is finished as far as America is concerned.'

Hearing this, Snepp could not understand why the evacuation was being slowed and endangered; Kissinger and Ambassador Martin, he felt, were still playing diplomacy. Martin 'wanted to save lives' through some kind of settlement; and as *Time* magazine noted: 'Kissinger's reputation and achievement in the Paris accords is in jeopardy.' It reported that 'for weeks' the evacuation had been 'stymied by Martin and Kissinger who feared such an operation might ignite retaliation'. A *New York Times* report said 'Kissinger was resisting proposals for a complete evacuation of all Americans'. A Defense Department official fumed that 'we're sending planes and they're coming back half and two-thirds empty'. After the Pentagon had publicly rebuked the State Department the air evacuation increased from about 500 to 5000 a day. Snepp's criticism that political miscalculations

Above: April 28, 1975—Retired Gen. Duong Van Minh assumes the presidency of the Republic of Vietnam at Independence Palace, two days before he surrendered his troops to the Provisional Revolutionary Government. He stands before a mural of legendary naval hero Tran Hung Dao.

Above: May 1, 1975—Tanks of the victorious Viet Cong and North Vietnamese forces enter the gates of the Presidential Palace in Saigon.

Above: Jolly Green Giant helicopter is loaded with evacuees on the grounds of the U.S. Embassy. Marines arrived on the chopper to maintain order in the embassy compound.

limited the evacuation and demeaned the US in the final days was therefore corroborated at the time.

Ambassador Martin contends that he could not 'pull out all the senior Vietnamese' or there would be no command for the Saigon forces who were 'still ready to fight, still with a considerable combat capability'. Similarly, the presence of the 5000 Americans then remaining was psychologically important, and Martin says he faced another dilemma: 'The Saigon police chief told one of our people that if you think you're going to march all the Americans to the airport and leave, you'll be fighting us on the way out.'

Snepp's concern was not for the senior Vietnamese who were fairly assured of a seat out, but for tens of thousands of middle-level Vietnamese officials who had served the United States. The State Department was not acting on the known deadline; Kissinger in the past had given so many ultimatums to the North Vietnamese, and now that the reverse situation applied the US could not adjust to it. Snepp's intelligence was that only one week remained. In the past few weeks 100,000 Vietnamese had bought their way out on commercial flights, but these had all but ceased. Another 140,000 Vietnamese were on the Embassy's 'endangered' list and Snepp now feared there was no hope for most of these.

The press reports described 'the rising terror' in the city, with thousands besieging the airport and others begging or bribing any American they could find to help them escape. A *New York Times* report on 24 April conveyed the desperation. It told of a young US-trained Vietnamese government economist who offered an American $10,000 to marry his wife, then three months pregnant, so that she could qualify for the official evacuation. And with government officials encouraging fears of a North Vietnamese bloodbath, the *Times* reported that 'others are buying up sleeping pills and tranquilizers for suicide if the worst should come'.

General Dung's forces had already crossed the rivers in the outer suburbs. On the 25th they began a massive mopping up of ARVN defenses within a thirty-mile radius of Saigon. An unending stream of soldiers and civilians were retreating into the capital, stampeding or shooting their way through the check-points. The Western Embassies began closing down, and watching the smoke rise as secret files were burned the Vietnamese saw hopes

Above: May 1975—South Vietnamese President Duong Van Minh looks up as directions are given at a Saigon radio station where he made his speech of surrender.

Right: April 28, 1975—A joint session of South Vietnam's National Assembly votes to ask President Than Van to turn over his office to Gen. Duong Van Minh.

turn to ashes. As one of them said, 'We know they're not burning incense for their ancestors.'

One by one the West Germans, Dutch, Thais, Japanese, Australians, British and Canadians departed. The British Ambassador was described as having left wearing a safari suit and driving a silver Jaguar. The Canadians, having sent their own air transport 13,000 miles, used it to bring out the Ambassador's car while leaving behind most of the Embassy's Vietnamese staff. Only the French and the Belgians – who had diplomatic relations with the North – remained. And, for a while longer, the Americans. At the US evacuation processing center, a one-time bowling alley, a large sign said; 'Turn off the lights when leaving.'

But it appeared that Henry Kissinger could still see a glimmer at the end of the tunnel. The total evacuation of the Americans had still not been approved, and Ambassador Martin says he was in constant touch with Kissinger: 'We tried to keep him fully informed on what was going on. I must say that I have no complaints about the kind of support that I was given. . . . Now we did play this sort of close to our chest, as we obviously had to. We could not say that there was not hope for negotiations.'

The go-between in these negotiations, Deputy-Premier Tran Van Don, says the French were still informing him that 'the other side would like to talk only with Big Minh and nobody else'. Don says that he met 'every day with either the French or the American Ambassador – and I met

Martin more than anyone.' On 26 April, five days after Thieu's departure, it was agreed that General Duong Van Minh should take over. In a new form of diplomatic nicety, the National Assembly informed Thieu's appointee, seventy-one-year-old President Huong, that it was granting him the power 'to select a man to replace himself'. General Minh was to be ceremonially installed on the 28th. But as Martin says, 'The North Vietnamese were convinced that the Americans were still sort of playing games in Saigon. Now this was not really the case, but they laid down a fairly heavy bombardment.'

In the early morning of the 28th Van Tien Dung signaled his impatience by firing several rockets into a slum area of the city, and the flames left 5000 homeless. Under darkness Dung's forces closed in on all sides, halting only one mile from the city limits. The Politburo was warning Dung that he must not risk being bogged down by the coming monsoon. He now seized the Newport Bridge, giving his main forces in the east direct access to the city center. Amazingly the ARVN had failed to dynamite the bridge and the North Vietnamese could be in Saigon within an hour. Instead, Dung broadcast a demand for Saigon's total surrender within twenty-four hours.

With this deadline Saigon's discipline completely broke. As General Minh was being installed as President, looting spread throughout the city. Thousands of civilians and deserting soldiers blitzed the main US commissary minutes after it had been abandoned in the Newport area. With North Vietnamese tanks only a short distance away, convoys of shopping carts came hurtling out of the PX, loaded with burgers and barbecue sauce and every edible Americana from chewing-gum to cocktail cherries. Within minutes the giant pantry was bare. It was the last of the old life, though at that moment at the presidential palace Tran Van Don and Ambassador Martin were talking hopefully about Big Minh's inauguration, and, says Don, 'It seemed to Martin and myself that we had reached our target to put in the right man to talk to the other side.'

'On the 28th,' says Frank Snepp, 'Big Minh stepped into power and the Ambassador thought this would bring about a negotiated settlement. Even at this last minute there was that illusion: a negotiated settlement.'

Big Minh, however, did have a surprise announcement. He had been a long-time advocate of what he called a Vietnamese 'Third Force' or coalition. He was a southerner born at My Tho, which had been leveled in the Tet Offensive, and in recent years he had been twice forced out of the country because of his conciliatory politics. Before assuming the presidency he had privately advised Ambassador Martin to get Americans out of Vietnam. Now, as his first act of office, Big Minh broadcast an order for all Americans to leave within twenty-four hours. Go-between Tran Van Don 'was very surprised'. He called the American

Embassy for its reaction and was told it was all over, and, 'If you want to leave, come to the Embassy before two o'clock tomorrow afternoon.'

Snepp recalls that he was on the top floor of the Embassy listening to Big Minh's speech and 'no sooner had he finished than the North Vietnamese flew an air strike against the city. It was about five or six o'clock. We heard the airplanes screaming in, and the thump of artillery. And from that point on we knew we were finished. The Ambassador called for a number of C-130 transports to complete the evacuation of high-risk Vietnamese. At this point he realized that even if there was a negotiated settlement we still had to get some of our allies out of the country. There were large numbers of Vietnamese lined up at the Embassy and at Tan Son Nhut airport. They realized better than we did that the show was over.'

But it was now too late for the full evacuation. After captured fighter-bombers with North Vietnamese pilots had strafed the city, General Dung unleashed his artillery. He had enough to level the capital if he chose. Instead, in a few hours before dawn on the 29th, he obliterated Tan Son Nhut airport. Snepp had returned to his apartment in one of the American buildings which had roof-top landing pads for an emergency helicopter evacuation. He remembers stumbling up the stairway full of waiting Vietnamese, then falling asleep: 'The bombardment threw me out of bed at four o'clock in the morning and I lay on the

floor thinking, "My God, what now?" I called the Embassy on my radio and was told we were taking heavy incoming. And one of the words that struck terror into the hearts of those who spent time in Vietnam is "incoming". It was just a massive artillery barrage directed at the airport and the outskirts. Rockets streaming in out of the darkness. I went up to the roof of my apartment building and the whole sky was lit up like miniature atomic explosions as Tan Son Nhut began to go up in flames.'

At daybreak Martin conferred with his military advisors and was told that a fixed-wing evacuation was now impossible. 'I visited Tan Son Nhut because I wanted to see for myself,' says Martin. Shells were still raining on the airport, but Martin had to be sure of 'my own judgement' because, he admits, the loss of Tan Son Nhut 'made a difference' to the extent of the evacuation. Full-scale evacuation only began, Snepp says, when 'Martin on the morning of the 29th went out to Tan Son Nhut by car, showing a great deal of courage, driving through check-points in a city in chaos. The Vietnamese were tearing like madmen around the city: it was like the Indy-500 gone crazy.' Back at the Embassy Martin 'picked up the phone and I told Secretary Kissinger to inform the President that I had decided to go to Option Four immediately – to the helicopter airlift.'

An hour later, says Snepp, the 'executive order was issued by the White House. Kissinger

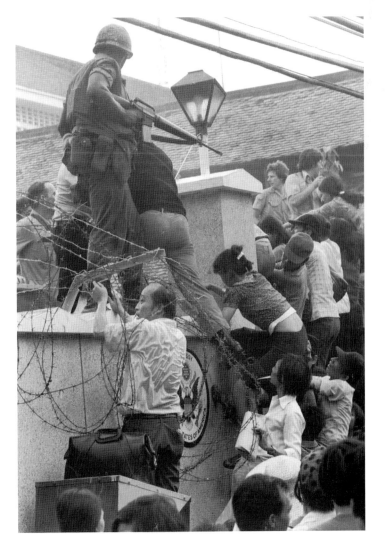

Left: April 30, 1975—U.S. Ambassador to South Vietnam Graham Martin speaks to reporters aboard the USS *Blue Ridge* after being evacuated from the U.S. embassy in Saigon.

Right: April 29, 1975—Vietnamese clamber over the wall of the U.S. Embassy as the seek evacuation on U.S. helicopters from Vietnam in the final days before the city fell to the North Vietnamese army.

Right: April 30, 1975—Vietnamese hopeful of obtaining a flight to freedom watch as a helicopter leaves the roof of the U.S. Embassy in Saigon just hours before North Vietnamese troops entered the city.

finally realized that the Soviets had lied to him. Martin realized that the illusions about a negotiated settlement were just that – illusions.'

An evacuation task force of forty ships was waiting 200 miles off the coast in the South China Sea. It included three aircraft carriers – the *Hancock, Okinawa* and *Midway* – with contingents of combat Marines. Sixty giant CH-53 ('Sea Knight') helicopters were standing by for 'Operation Frequent Wind' – a non-stop ferry between the ships and the 'LZs' or landing zones on Saigon roof-tops. There were thirteen of these. The remaining Americans, now numbering 1500, had been briefed to gather at particular roof-tops after a special signal to be broadcast over the US Armed Services radio.

At noon on the 29th the signal came – first a prearranged weather report: 'It is 105 degrees and rising,' said a solemn announcer; then a further code, Bing Crosby singing 'I'm Dreaming Of A White Christmas' – repeated every fifteen minutes. American officials, businessmen and journalists dropped everything and ran. Many had been in South Vietnam for years. They had only hours to get out. Senior Vietnamese officials were to report to the Embassy and be grouped for evacuation on a priority basis. Former Chief of Staff General Tran Van Don, who had helped form the latest – and last – government, now tried to find a way out of Vietnam: 'Nobody at the Embassy told me what to do – just go to the gate, they said.' Half of Saigon was clamoring at the locked Embassy gates. Only one day after his confident attendance at the palace, Tran Van Don was just one of the mob 'trying to find a way out'.

'Only one day to get out,' he reflects. 'Twenty-four hours in 1975 compared to what the French had arranged in 1954. Then we had one year to go South or North. In 1975 we had only one day.' People were shouting, 'That's General Don – follow him. He can leave. He knows the way out, for sure,' and Don led them from building to building until he was officially recognized.

The panic grew as the Americans assembled on the roof-tops but the helicopters did not come. Noon, 1 pm, 2 pm, and still no sight of the Sea Knights. Each helicopter would take an hour to reach the evacuation fleet and another hour to return. General Dung's ultimatum had another four hours to run. After weeks of planning, says Frank Snepp, 'Frequent Wind got confused somewhere between the fleet and Washington. The admiral running the evacuation did not get the helicopters off the decks and into Saigon before mid-afternoon. And meantime the North Vietnamese, as we know from intelligence, were becoming increasingly concerned. General Dung thought that the Americans were trying to pull a fast one, trying to hold up the evacuation to buy time. He had victory so close in his grasp. And he radioed his commanders and said, "If they're not out of Saigon by six o'clock we're going to blast the center of the city." And I can tell you that panic reigned at the Embassy at that point.'

General Dung says that 'up until the day he left Saigon, Martin felt certain that the quisling administration could be preserved, and that a cease-fire could be arranged, so he was half-hearted about the evacuation, waiting and watching'. As General Dung puts it, 'The Duong Van Minh card which they played far too late proved useless.'

Dung's long-range artillery began to fix positions and then, like the last reel of a B-movie, the Marines arrived. Once more, briefly, American soldiers returned to Vietnam as 130 armed Marines rushed from the first Sea Knights to secure the Embassy compound where thousands of Vietnamese were trying to climb the gates and walls. For years the symbol of 'unprecedented mobility' the helicopters could now only land on the Embassy roof. Other helicopters, says Snepp, 'were picking up people on roofs around the city. And the city itself was holding its breath. The Vietnamese knew that if the Americans didn't get out, nobody would. So they stood back and let us evacuate ourselves. That was one reason that the city didn't collapse around us on that final day.'

Says Snepp, 'There were young Embassy officers who risked their lives to get their Vietnamese friends on those helicopters. They went out among the crowd, pushing their way through. These are the heroes of that final day, and if the Americans salvaged anything of their honor from the last day of the war it is due to the young men who did the leg work during the evacuation.' Ambassador Martin describes how the last American soldiers died in Vietnam. 'Two Marines – members of the Embassy Marine guard – were on the edge of the Defense Attaché's compound when a shelling attack took place on the 29th, and they were killed by a direct hit.'

There were a lot of heroes that final day, notably the helicopter pilots who 'beyond all physical endurance', says Martin, 'just kept coming, kept coming, under very difficult landing circumstances'. The city was under sporadic shelling; it was like the 'hot LZs' of combat days, with ordinary Vietnamese instead of guerrillas just as determinedly assaulting the helicopters; General Dung observed how 'the number of these landing pads shrank gradually as tongues of fire from our advancing troops came closer'.

As Dung's deadline neared, the evacuation became a chaotic scramble to 'get Americans out and any Vietnamese that we could lay hands on,' says Snepp – and a Japanese journalist would bitterly complain about being swept up, whisked to the US evacuation fleet, thence to the refugee tent camps in Guam to wait weeks before he could identify himself. Out in the South China Sea, dozens of unscheduled helicopters ditched in the water alongside the boats or crash-landed on the decks of the carriers as South Vietnamese pilots arrived uninvited. The $250,000 machines had to be physically heaved overboard – 'discarded like pop-top beer cans to make room for later-arriving choppers,' as *Time* described it.

The last images were of two Saigons, of the fatalistic poor and the frantic official elite – and 'both seemed equally mad; dream-like, life went on in many parts of the city as though the North Vietnamese divisions were hundreds of miles away. Banners still proclaimed military victories in the province of Long Khanh, although the region was lost. Exotic aromas bubbled from hot food stalls in front of Saigon's cathedral. Young women crowded the lobby of the Mini Rex for a matinee performance of Brigitte Bardot in *Boulevard du Rhum*' while close by 'US Marines with rifle butts were pounding the fingers of Vietnamese who tried to claw their way into the Embassy compound'.

'Inside the Embassy,' says Frank Snepp, 'I saw CIA officers who had been solid to the last putting away bottles of cognac. Americans were breaking into the commissary behind the Embassy – drinking wine, guzzling wine. It was as if my friends were fiddling while Rome burned.

'I was sitting by the radios, on the top floor of the Embassy, monitoring the flow of intelligence as it continued to come in from various places. And I listened to the radio and I heard people calling in, agents and employees who had been abandoned at various evacuation points: "I'm Mr Lon – I have served you for years – save me. I'm Mr Hoa, save me." And there was no way to save them. They were cut off – we couldn't reach them. They were calling in to say that the CIA had abandoned them. And that, I believe, was the most tragic thing for me on that day: the voices over the radio.'

Ambassador Martin still sought to provide an 'aura of stability'. In the late afternoon he drove to his house to pick up his wife: 'The Marine Guard log showed that I was there for eleven minutes; she packed one bag and walked out.' The Ambassador had not packed anything in the preceding days because 'it would have been known all over Saigon'. He felt that his wife 'paid a sort of higher penalty than I did, in the sense of losing some of the treasured possessions of a lifetime'.

One hour remained. 'About five o'clock,' says Snepp, 'we got in touch with the Communist provisional government through Big Minh and he said, "The Americans are leaving – don't bombard Saigon." And I remember sitting in the Embassy at six o'clock wondering whether in the next few minutes General Dung's order to level the center of Saigon would be put into effect. Three minutes passed and there was an explosion outside the walls of the Embassy. I ran to the window. A car had been blown up outside. Somebody had dropped a match down the gas tank of one of the thousands of cars abandoned outside the Embassy. The bombardment didn't come.'

Snepp says his intelligence was that 'General Dung wanted to move on the city straight away. But there were those in Hanoi, particularly Le Duan – the Party's First Secretary – who argued that if Saigon was attacked and a lot of Americans were killed, the B-52s might be back. Rather than risk that they decided to give us a breathing spell on that final day.' The Americans knew they had until dawn the next day, 30 April.

The US base in Vietnam was now reduced to the few square feet of the Embassy roof – and from there the trickle of hopefuls stretched down the stair-well, and across the compound to the sea of faces beyond the gate. Every few minutes, through the night, the helicopters put down and the gate was inched open to admit a few more: then like as not it would suddenly slam back on the pressing crowd, separating husbands and wives, children and parents, whose screams were lost in the sheer volume of anguish. All those with priority got out. Former Vice-President and Air Marshall Nguyen Cao Ky decided that further resistance was futile: 'I landed on the *Midway* aircraft carrier and the admiral of the ship received me. He left his office with his staff and just left me alone. So I stood there for about fifteen or twenty minutes just crying by myself. I couldn't stop it. Even I said to myself, I'm a soldier, I never cry. But it happened.'

The tears for some would be life-long. Finally the Embassy gate remained closed: the crush was too great. 'One Vietnamese woman who was brought out was holding her child in her arms,' recalls Snepp. 'We managed to get her and her child over the wall of the Embassy but had failed to get her husband. Her life would be forever altered, and we had abandoned so many we should have rescued on the final day.'

Snepp himself 'got out with the last CIA contingent' late on the 30th: 'The helicopter began lifting off the roof of the Embassy and the tail gunner was crouched over his weapon. The helicopter arched up over the city and for a moment I could see framed in one of the windows Mimi's Bar, one of the most famous bars in Saigon where many an American soldier had lost his shirt and his innocence. And then the helicopter swung around and headed out toward the evacuation fleet: past Bien Hoa which was going up in flames – it had been the last South Vietnamese military position; and I could see snaking out beyond Bien Hoa, on the roads leading in, North Vietnamese convoys with their lights burning.' General Dung had begun his advance into the city and suddenly Snepp 'saw tracers coming up at us'. But the shots fell short and in a while there was the grey super-structure of an American carrier 'enveloping us like a giant metallic cocoon'.

Ambassador Martin was the last remaining US official. At 4.30 am he was at his desk, awaiting word from Washington on his pleas to extend the evacuation, when he received his final order: 'This young helicopter pilot came into my office with a scrawled message on a pad.' It was from the White House, transmitted via the naval task force, and said: 'The President of the United States directs that Ambassador Martin comes out on this helicopter. Well what do you do? Do you try to emulate Lord Nelson with the telescope and say you don't get it? For thirty-five years I had been a disciplined officer of the US government – and I wouldn't spoil it in the end by an act of disobedience. So I got on the helicopter and came out.'

Martin remembers that the helicopter they had sent for him was called the 'Lazy Ace'. Some 7000 Americans and Vietnamese got out on the last day; in all, about 50,000 had been air-evacuated since the siege of Saigon, three times as many had previously bought their way out and in the confusion of the next few days another 70,000 escaped by sea to the waiting fleet. Of the total that April about 190,000 would settle in the United States, 40,000 would go to Canada and as many more to Europe. The sentiment of all of them is probably expressed by their former Ambassador to Washington, Bui Diem, who then 'wanted to go back' because 'I am a Vietnamese deeply tied to the land'. He felt the manner of the ending was a distinct tragedy: 'Hundreds of thousands of families were completely dislocated.'

Ambassador Martin's feeling at the end was 'one of enormous relief'. And his sentiment was surely that of the great majority of Americans. At last, the war that was never officially called a war – though it was America's longest – was over. It was a 'conflict', an 'involvement', an 'experience' and its failure, historians may judge, was not a weakness but a strength of the American people. Quite simply, they had thought as they fought – or enough of them had. They had made their peace in Vietnam two years before, or so most of them felt: an 'honorable' peace they were told; now they watched with detached weariness, stunned yet really not at all surprised, as eight years of American combat was rendered meaningless in as many weeks.

Above: April 30, 1975—Conquering soldiers sit aboard their tanks outside the Independence Palace in Saigon moments after the government signed an unconditional surrender.

South Vietnam's survival had been equated with that of the Free World by five successive administrations spanning two decades: now this nation-cause had ceased to exist in just fifty-five days and the incredible suddenness had so totally validated what the majority of Americans had gradually come to realize – that honor begins at home, specifically in the White House. The needless wounds to the American psyche would bleed for unknown years to come, healed gradually by the fact – and it *is* a fact as important as any – that never before in the course of a great war had the people of one side judged themselves to be wrong and sought amends in withdrawal. But the honor, to paraphrase Dean Rusk, belonged to the folks in Cherokee County.

The unique nature of a television war had undoubtedly contributed a lot to that judgement, yet television had been very much a two-edged sword. While television measured the horrors of modern war, a democratic people measured what they saw against what they knew of themselves, and a great many would believe that the merciless nature of the war arose from that of the enemy. If the cameras denied the American cause, they also could not depict the cause of the faceless adversary who to the very end was generally 'pictured' by the press as a fanatical, pitiless ideologue who had to be brutally dealt with because the bloodbath would be far worse if and when the Americans left. In the end the huge American press contingent believed their own reports – all but a few scrambled to get out, abandoning the biggest story in American contemporary history. Only a handful of US-accredited journalists – most of them foreign-born – chose to stay. The very last American soldiers, eleven Marines bearing the Embassy flag, departed at 7.53 am, 30 April 1975. It had been thirty years almost to the day since the first American soldier, Major Archimedes Patti, had been assigned to Vietnam.

General Van Tien Dung's forces occupied the capital without resistance as columns of soldiers moved through the garbage-littered streets past a quiet, dazed population. At 11.00 am a single tank crashed through the half-open gates of Saigon's presidential palace. A lone soldier raced toward the palace balcony to raise the flag of the Provisional Revolutionary Government. And that, historically, was the end – but this was a television war and the foreign camera crews had missed the moment. The North Vietnamese obligingly re-enacted it.

At the palace South Vietnam's last President, General Duong Van Minh, broadcast an order to all ARVN troops to 'lay down your weapons and surrender unconditionally'. He was then arrested and led away. 'Big' Minh was the only senior general to remain in his native land and his one-time colleague, former Chief of Staff Tran Van Don, says Minh's 'personal sacrifice' spared Saigon from bloodshed and destruction. At least half of the ARVN's higher-rank officers had fled the country.

As General Dung heard that the victory flag had been raised, 'I lit a cigarette and smoked.' This last day of more than 10,000 days of war seemed to Dung to be 'so fresh and beautiful, so radiant, so clear and cool; a morning that made babes older than their years and made old men young again'. He got on the phone to Hanoi and could 'hear the sound of the fireworks going off; forests of people, seas of people, flooded the streets singing. I choked with emotion. The suffering of our separation had ended.'

'There was so much emotion at that moment,' recalls Ha Van Lau. 'Everyone could breathe again, the war was over, peace established. And above all we became the true masters of our own country, our own land. Independent.' For the first time since the French ships put into Da Nang in 1858, the Vietnamese were free of all foreign soldiers.

There were some who wished it otherwise. With the news that noon of Saigon's surrender, one of its former leaders made his way to the

Above: May 4, 1975—Saigon youths enthusiastically ride through the streets of the capital to celebrate the victory of the North Vietnamese army.

Above: May 30, 1975—A statue of a South Vietnamese soldier rests on its head at the entrance to a military cemetery at Bien Hoa, 12 miles northeast of Saigon. Soldiers of the Provisional Revolutionary Government pulled it over during their advance. Sign reads: 'Regret.'

White House and there presented President Ford with two letters, dated 1973, signed by Richard Nixon. The letters were addressed to former President Nguyen Van Thieu and pledged 'swift retaliatory' action by the United States against any North Vietnamese armed intervention. Thieu had given the letters to his former Planning Minister, Nguyen Van Hung, at a time when the US public was reacting adversely to the acceptance of Vietnamese refugees. The letters, says Hung, 'were to call attention to the conscience of America to help my people find some safe haven'.

In Saigon, Associated Press reporter Peter Arnett heard General Minh's surrender over the radio at the AP office and Arnett 'ran down six flights of stairs to Tu Do Street and I saw the first lumbering tanks roll past the Caravelle Hotel followed by six truck-loads of pith-helmeted soldiers staring up in wonder at the first tall buildings they had probably seen in their lives'. Arnett had been reporting from Saigon since 1962 and thought it 'worth the risk to be here at the end'. Says Arnett, 'There was no shooting at all, and the hundreds of Saigonese stood in open-mouthed wonder, as did I, as more and more Communist trucks came into town.'

The first hours and days were ones of total reprieve from war: Hanoi's soldiers mingled with the crowds; and for a brief while they succumbed to the temptation of the black market, marveling at the wonders of the PX – and politely paying.

Arnett ran back to his office to send this news by teleprinter to New York and 'a crowd of fright-ened Vietnamese rushed in behind me demanding asylum. There was nothing I could do to help them. Looking out the office window I watched North Vietnamese infantry teams maneuver in the small park near the town hall where American GIS used to sit with their Vietnamese girlfriends. A colleague came in the door and said the tanks had captured the presidential palace and arrested President Minh, all without a shot being fired.

'By noon it was all over and in thirteen years of covering the Vietnam war I never dreamed it would end that way. I had figured there might be a political deal similar to the one in Laos a decade earlier. Or even an Armageddon-type battle to the finish with the city left in ruins like World War II in Europe. A total surrender was what I did not expect and this was followed a short two hours later with a cordial meeting in the Associated Press office in Saigon with an armed and battle-garbed North Vietnamese intelligence officer and his aide who came in to say "hello". We served him a warm Coca-Cola and some stale pound cake as they described the battle plan that carried them in the last few days of the war into Saigon. We then sent his story on the teleprinter that still con-nected us to New York. I got the impression that the North Vietnamese wanted a neat, clean end-ing to the war and such it was.'

On 1 May at 'the Ho Chi Minh campaign headquarters' General Van Tien Dung was called by his officers and found a table set with 'candies, cake, soft drinks' and as a 'surprise', a bottle of liquor. But he was not really surprised: he had fully intended being in Saigon by 1 May because, as the officer who toasted him said, 'Today conveniently happens to be Van Tien Dung's birthday as well.' The General went for a drive around the city and 'there was no sea of blood, only a sea of people in high spirits'. He marveled at the 'vast enemy bases and storage depots; the banks, the American bil-lets, the hotels, many stories tall. We went into the headquarters of Saigon's General Staff. Here, as at the Directorate-General of Police, the files of the enemy commanders' top-secret documents remained. Their modern computers containing bio-data on each officer and soldier and civilian were still running. But American computers had not won in this war. The will of our nation had won completely.'

The victory parade, the Politburo decided, should symbolize the new physical coming of age. It was held in Saigon on 7 May – the twenty-first anniversary of the defeat of the French at Dien Bien Phu. Whatever the political judgement, whether it was a victory of Communism or of ancient nationalism, Vietnam was now one nation. The Vietnamese, South and North, had against all odds endured and fought the century's longest war, and before that a century of foreign rule – and history must judge them foremost in terms of human fortitude and courage, and con-clude that there was no greater example than that of a small Asian land which had emerged, once more, as one land.

# EPILOGUE

There remains what became of the cast in the long sorry drama, and why the wounds left by the war did not heal.

At first the peace seemed promising. Vietnam began by picking up the pieces – literally. Old US war material was melted down for reconstruction of towns and factories and there was said to be enough of it littering the countryside to feed the steel furnaces for a decade. The old regime was extensively purged, but no bloodbath was reported. An estimated 1.5 million former Saigon government officials and supporters were forcibly relocated in harsh rural development areas. Another 200,000 senior officials and military officers were sent to 're-education' camps for various periods – among them the last President of South Vietnam, General Duong Van 'Big' Minh. He then became, it was said, a government official representing minority groups.

Saigon itself ceased to exist on the new map of Vietnam. It became Ho Chi Minh City (though in everyday conversation the Vietnamese still called it Saigon), while in Hanoi, to symbolize the peace, the embalmed figure of Ho was placed in a great gray tomb in Ba Dinh Square where he had first declared the independence he did not live to see. After thirty years of battle the victor of the final offensive, General Van Tien Dung, became Acting Defense Minister, effectively replacing General Vo Nguyen Giap who took over 'long-range defense planning'. Both men assumed they could retire from the field; it was a rare miscalculation.

After two years South and North were officially united, becoming the Socialist Republic of Vietnam, which was admitted to the United Nations in September 1977 – almost twenty-one years after the Geneva deadline for reunification. In those years Vietnam suffered 'as many as fifteen million dead and wounded', says Ha Van Lau, the veteran of Dien Bien Phu who became his country's first – and continuing – Ambassador to the UN. 'There is at least one dead, or some wounded, in each Vietnamese family,' he reflects, adding: 'We absolutely needed peace to tend to our wounds and to reconstruct our devastated country.' But it was not to be.

The Soviet Union provided Vietnam with three billion dollars in reconstruction aid in the immediate postwar years. More than a hundred nations established diplomatic relations with Vietnam, and many Western countries – notably Scandinavia and Hanoi's old enemy, Australia – gave generous aid. The United States was the only major nation to withhold diplomatic representation. An American delegation visited Hanoi in 1977 to explore various ties, but nothing came of it. By then the US was increasingly siding with Peking against Moscow, and Vietnam was considered too much under Soviet influence. Though President Carter pledged America to forge a new

Vietminh soldier patrols the countryside in a flat-bottomed boat during the war against the French.

era of human rights the US was silent on China's armed support of the genocidal Khmer Rouge regime in Cambodia. After two years of border friction Vietnam invaded and largely occupied Cambodia in January 1979. At the time of writing – spring 1981 – the Vietnamese and Cambodians were still enmeshed in a debilitating Sino-Soviet proxy war. Ironically, South-east Asia – which the US had perceived as endangered by monolithic Communism – became the main arena for Communist rivalry.

In the preparation of this history the author was back in Vietnam in January 1979 and, as the cycle of ideological conflict resumed, was visiting Dien Bien Phu where the drama might have ended twenty-five years before. The old battleground provides a unique lesson – preserved like a physical textbook. Twisted tanks and rusting cannon still remain alongside the runway, where the same fog still seems to cling. Nearby, the command post of General de Castries is just as he left it that May day of 1954. On Eliane-I, where the French fought so hard so often, deep trenches reach like an underground maze to the crest where a giant billboard is a timeless advertisement, proclaiming simply E-1. Across the valley other huge hilltop letters spell out the Vietnamese attitude to time and events: this was their decisive victory and, they say, the next quarter of a century was what it took for others to acknowledge it.

On another of the Elianes the visitor stays in a comfortable brick 'guest house' adjoining trenches still blackened from the shells, and in the quiet of this small remote valley where birds sing where so many died even this one battle seems an inconceivable price for men to have paid. The memory of the extraordinary cast is vivid and close: the

young Giap who commanded from these hills; a lieutenant called Van Tien Dung who stormed this very slope; the indomitable one-time clerk 'Bruno' Bigeard who rallied the French, survived captivity and became a general and then a deputy in the French National Assembly; the aristocratic soldier's soldier Colonel Pierre Langlais who retired as a general to the peace of a French farm; the French commander General Henri Navarre who retreated to a small Paris apartment surrounded by the memorabilia of a war he knew he could not win; and the lady of legend, Genevieve, the lone French nurse at Dien Bien Phu who married a doctor and became a grandmother.

Twenty five years had passed; the United States had picked up the fallen Western banner specifically to contain Communist China; many millions of people were dead or scarred because of that, and now in a total turn-about the visitor at Dien Bien Phu heard on the radio that China had invaded Vietnam. Only days earlier the US had extravagantly welcomed China's new strongman, Deng Xiao-Ping, yet the new Chinese leadership was displaying the very territorial adventurism the US had once feared – and which in fact never occurred in the era of Mao Tse-tung. China called its action a 'punitive' response to the war in Cambodia and limited its invasion to six weeks of scorched-earth border warfare, but during that time the world feared Soviet intervention and perhaps nuclear war – a fear which remains as China and Russia compete in Asia, encouraged by the altered balance of detente.

In Hanoi the entire Politburo convened for the press in order to denounce Vietnam's thousand-year-old enemy, China. In private conversation General Van Tien Dung dismissively referred to the Chinese as 'an easier enemy than the Americans'. The average age of Vietnam's leaders was then seventy and some critics saw them as intransigent old warriors unable or unwilling to keep the peace. But Pham Van Dong – Prime Minister for twenty-seven years – still sought diplomatic relations with the United States 'to help stabilize the region'. Earlier talks had 'almost achieved good results', he confided, saying – as Ho Chi Minh had once said – that he wished for American 'friendship' and this would be 'treasured'. But the ensuing tragedy that year of the 'boat people' – the forced expulsion of some 400,000 Vietnamese, most of them ethnic-Chinese – brought international condemnation and served to delay the day of reconciliation. Yet there is little doubt that a US diplomatic presence would lessen tensions and perhaps influence Vietnam's political nature – which, but for the continuing conflict, appeared far from rigid.

With food and consumer goods scarce in the devastated North, officials in Hanoi found constant urgent matters requiring their presence in

Saigon – and it seemed far from settled as to whether South or North would socially prevail in the long run. Though Saigon's Presidential Palace became a museum to capitalist decadence, the refurbished Majestic Hotel still offered chateaubriand and lobster thermidor to the foreign businessmen and technicians who arrived each week in their hundreds on the Air France jumbo. The US Embassy had become the national petroleum exploration offices, but the black market in American products remained an important dollar earner – and at least for the Saigon street vendors bearing trays of Wrigleys, Winstons and 7-UP life was as ever. The girls of Mimi's Bar and thousands like it had long since taken up new positions in light machine-tool factories, but Saigon youth fashions of the late 1960s were being eagerly discovered by Hanoi's youth a decade later. The visitor left Vietnam feeling that some compromise was attainable, and that the US and Vietnam remained doctrinal enemies for no great reason.

The 230,000 South Vietnamese who left in 1975 to settle in North America are now citizens or eligible citizens of the US and Canada, and could safely revisit families in Vietnam if the diplomatic channels were opened. Tran Van Don says he has kept his Vietnamese citizenship and 'we have to hope that one day we'll be back – if not our children, our grandchildren'. The former Defense Minister opened several Vietnamese restaurants and then settled in Florida. Bui Diem also started a restaurant – in Washington where he was once Ambassador – and also feels the same. 'We thank the United States for welcoming us but deep in our heart we would like to go back,' he says, and 'looking back I cannot afford not to feel sad; all the sacrifices were in vain.' Former Vice-President Nguyen Cao Ky chose California and the liquor business and says if America was at fault it was 'in doing too much for us'. Ex-President Nguyen Van Thieu puts a different nuance on that: America wanted to control the Vietnamese but had not the patience to see it through. Thieu finally settled in a grand mansion outside London which he elected to call The White House. He preferred to be known by the alias 'Mr. Martin'.

Graham Martin, the last US Ambassador in Saigon, abandoned his dream farm in Tuscany – choosing a Tudor-style mansion in North Carolina. The envoys, all rich and venerable, retired sumptuously: Ellsworth Bunker to Vermont; Henry Cabot Lodge to the family estate at Beverly, Massachusetts; General Maxwell Davenport Taylor to a Washington apartment full of mementos of different wars. Bunker now feels that 'maybe in hindsight one would say that we shouldn't have been there'. Lodge believes 'we could have done something that cost less, took longer and would have had lasting results'. Taylor unequivocally regrets the war: 'We didn't know our ally. Secondly, we knew even less about the enemy. And the last, most inexcusable of our mistakes was not knowing our own people.'

The mistakes of the 1960s had hardly been addressed by the 1980s. The architects of the war had mostly retired or returned to law and business, some to write books of apology or conflicting analysis, others disdaining any explanation except for very large fees. The few who returned to power retained the old beliefs. Among them all, there was no shared understanding of the war's nature and purpose, and therefore no public coming to

terms. The continuing division is expressed by the two military intelligence officers who headed the first American missions in Hanoi and Saigon. Major Archimedes Patti, who believed in Ho Chi Minh, retired to Florida to write his own account and concludes that Vietnam was 'the putrefying albatross' which 'remains ever present on America's political scene – a scene dominated with an infantile optimism about world capitalist domination that, at best, could isolate the United States and, at worst, precipitate a new world war'. General Edward Lansdale, the prototype 'Quiet American' who helped establish Ngo Dinh Diem in power, still acts as a US government consultant from his Virginia home. Lansdale remembers South Vietnam as 'an open society, up against a closed society' and says that in future 'our political leaders have got to be hard enough and smart enough to fight the Communists'.

The advice of the Johnson people remains as contradictory as ever. William Colby, who became an attorney and author of *Honorable Men – My Life in the CIA*, still cautions that 'soldiers were not the right reaction'. But General William Westmoreland interprets the public as being 'quite aware that the war was not lost militarily'. Westmoreland is surrounded by an oriental garden at his home in South Carolina – where he ran for governor, and lost.

'If a situation of this sort should arise again,' says former Secretary of State Dean Rusk, 'I think the leadership of some future day would have to consider whether maximum force must not be used at the very beginning.' Rusk now presides at the Dean Rusk Center of International Law at the University of Georgia. 'One could make an argument', he says, that the US should have entered the war earlier: 'that President Kennedy should have put in a hundred thousand troops immediately – put in a stack of blue chips straight away'. As Rusk now analyzes war, past or future, the policy of 'gradual response also leaves it up to the other side to think that if they do a little more, you might not. These are far reaching questions we need to think about.'

Johnson's last Defense Secretary, lawyer Clark Clifford, conversely warns that the US 'didn't appraise it long enough' and that Americans must avoid military involvement 'unless we are very certain that the national security of the United States is at stake'. Says Clifford, 'What we thought was the spread of Communist aggression in my opinion now seems very clearly to have been a civil war in Vietnam,' and he adds: 'The domino theory proved to be erroneous, I believe.'

Secretary of State Alexander Haig expresses the continuing disagreement of the policy-makers. Haig, who was the Kissinger-Nixon military advisor when the US invaded neutral Cambodia, now rationalizes that 'the over-running of Cambodia by Vietnam confirms the heavy hand that Moscow has always had in the conduct of Hanoi's policy'. Haig describes himself as having 'always felt that this [Vietnam] was more of an East-West issue,' and: 'We should have dedicated the full range of our national power to bring about a successful outcome. That would have involved a number of military steps which were not approved at the time – mobilization and the total dedication of the American people.' He concludes that 'the war was eminently winnable'.

Against this argument Nixon's Defense

Secretary, lawyer Melvin Laird, provides an economic perspective. In inflated 1980s dollars, even the 'limited' Vietnam war cost the equivalent of $236 billion, he says. In other words, the real economic loss was $100 billion or sixty per cent greater than the official estimate – a sum that could have been available for improved Western defense. The critics who spoke out while holding political office generally stress the moral cost: 'The casualties, the sorrow, the reputation that we established in the world for misadventure – those were the really damaging things,' states historian John Kenneth Galbraith, who returned to Harvard. 'There are still great differences,' reflects lawyer William Fulbright. 'Americans just can't get away from the idea that we're big, and we wouldn't be so rich if we weren't wise: therefore we must be wise.'

Arthur Schlesinger Jr, who became Professor of Humanities at City University, New York, points out that during and since the war 'all the people whom we nominated for President and Vice-President were hawks on Vietnam' and 'it seems to me an odd way to vindicate our national honor'. Says Schlesinger, 'The people who were right on Vietnam have not received political rewards.' Fulbright, the most outspoken critic in government, lost his Senate seat. Eugene McCarthy, after his anti-war presidential candidacy, was left without any political base. He retired to a Virginia farm, but developed a new reputation as a writer of poetry.

Lesser known critics like the State Department's Roger Hilsman, who resigned in opposition to the ground war, turned or were turned away from political office. Hilsman became a teacher of political science at Columbia University, whereas his State Department successor William Bundy, who helped devise the bombing scenario and misjudged its effect, became editor of the magazine *Foreign Affairs*. Daniel Ellsberg who released the study of White House deceit, the *Pentagon Papers*, became a middle-income writer on defense politics, whereas Nixon aide John Ehrlichman who authorized White House illegalities in the Ellsberg case became a successful writer of political thrillers. CIA analyst Frank Snepp, who resigned to write a critical book (*Decent Interval*) about the bungled last days in Saigon, was successfully sued by the Agency which now receives all royalties from the publisher, whereas Henry Kissinger who was accused of mismanaging the evacuation received a very large advance for his memoirs, and Richard Nixon's brought him even more. In Eugene McCarthy's blank verse, 'Henry Kissinger got the Nobel Prize for watching the end of a war he'd advocated – and that's pretty high diplomacy.'

International jurist Professor Richard Falk considers that America's failure during and since Vietnam was in being unable to 'live by the rules it had set up for others'. The war, he says, was a 'violation' of the international standards of law which the US had itself established, and so the war leaders escaped being 'morally accountable'. As a result, the people have not had 'to face the truth; they don't understand and there is no way they could understand given what they have been told'.

Perhaps only the soldiers, who endured it, fully understand what happened in Vietnam and in their own society. 'The war is never going to be over for me,' says paraplegic Lou Carello, a self-styled 'hit-man' in Special Forces. 'Any man who fought there is going to go to his grave with that war.' Carello used his veteran's grant to resume post-graduate studies – but though seventy per cent of the combat veterans took such courses, few of them finished; they were unable to adjust psychologically to normal life, according to an official 1981 study by the Veterans Administration. Instead, the study found that twenty-four per cent of veterans who saw heavy combat had been arrested for criminal offenses.

'I still love America,' says Marine medic Jack McCloskey who fifteen years after his combat continued to organize self-help groups, 'and it's almost like Johnny Appleseed: I want to replant the seeds. Vietnam was a pesticide that we used and didn't know what damage it would cause to us until years later.' One of the most decorated soldiers, Special Forces Captain Dave Christian who became a government veterans' counselor, felt that an overall reconciliation was needed: 'We have problems within our country; we have to iron them out. And the world should be the same way. Vietnamese are human beings. Many of their families are suffering because they lost sons in something they believed in; we lost, and I think on all sides honor should be had.'

There remains what the uncertain supporting cast – the general public – felt at the time, and since. Bardstown, Kentucky, is the heartland of America, a town which has made and judged history since the Civil War, with a population of 5800, nine churches, three factories, one art gallery. A welcome sign proclaims that Bardstown is 'Bourbon Center of the World' and the inspiration for the song 'My Old Kentucky Home'. Along its broad avenues, lined with huge old trees and wood-framed homes a century or two old, are numerous plaques recalling historic places and events: where the slaves were sold, when emancipation came, and what happened to the town in each of America's ten wars. Ten? In Court House Square a newer plaque on the town cenotaph reads: 'World War I, World War II, the Korean War, the Vietnam Conflict.'

Fifteen sons of this small town died in Vietnam, four of them on one day on 19 June 1969, on a hilltop called Firebase Tomahawk north of Da Nang. All were reservists in the National Guard called up after the Tet Offensive – and even at that watershed period the Bardstown boys went without question. 'No qualms,' says the Mayor, 'we felt we were doing the right thing.' Recounts one survivor, 'We'd been taking the government's money as a reserve unit: it was time for us to do our thing. We were asked to go, so we went.' Says another, 'I felt that it was right. I was in that unit and I was willing to do my part.' One mother recalls her son leaving: 'He kept telling me, don't cry Mama – I'll be back. But when I last looked there were tears running down his eyes.' The families were comforted by the thought that their sons who had grown up together would be serving together.

The first four bodies came back in time for 4 July that year. Instead of banners and parades and picnics the Mayor ordered four days of mourning and a new honors list on the town cenotaph. As the inscriptions grew with the passing months, Bardstown changed. 'The town was shook – not only the families involved, everyone,' a citizen remembers. 'I really don't think it was worth the men that we lost there,' says one who returned. 'I don't think in any way, shape or form it was worth anything to the United States.' Says another survivor, 'It made me realize what life is about.'

'I felt like I had been cheated,' says a young Bardstown widow, whose daughter was only five days old when the government sent its telegram of regrets. 'And I felt she had been cheated out of a father – and I was scared.' Says a second mother, 'They were done wrong – all the boys.' Says a third, 'It just doesn't happen – but it happened.'

'It won't be forgotten here. It can't be – it's that simple,' says the Mayor, but though no one in Bardstown can forget the war none can say that they understand it. Well into the 1980s there had yet to be any national start toward an understanding and redressing of Vietnam – and perhaps it was too late. 'I was there, you know, for a year,' says a Bardstown veteran, 'and I never developed a love for those people. And maybe I should have, and this is something I need to search for. But I love this country and my country asked me to go. And that's the reason I went. And willingly. And I may have to do it again some place else. Who knows?

# BIBLIOGRAPHY

Baskir, L.M. and Strauss, W.A., *Chance and Circumstance* (Alfred A. Knopf, New York, 1978)

Blaufarb, Douglas S., *The Counter-Insurgency Era, US Doctrine and Performance* (Free Press, New York, 1977)

Bonds, Ray (ed), *The Vietnam War* (Crown Publishers, New York, 1979)

Braestrup, Peter, *Big Story* (Westview Press, Colorado, 1977)

Burchett, Wilfred, *Vietnam: Inside Story of the Guerrilla War* (International Publishers, New York, 1965)

Devillers, Philippe and Lacouture, Jean, *End of a War* (Praeger, New York, 1969)

Dickson, Paul, *The Electronic Battlefield* (Indiana University Press, 1976)

Dung, Van Tien, *Our Great Spring Victory* (Monthly Review Press, London, 1977)

Emerson, Gloria, *Winners and Losers* (Random House, New York, 1977)

Fall, Bernard, *The Two Vietnams* (Praeger, New York, 1963)

Gabriel, Richard A. and Savage, Paul L., *Crisis in Command* (Farrar, Straus & Giroux, New York, 1978)

Giap, Vo Nguyen, *Unforgettable Days* (2nd ed., Hanoi, 1978)

Halberstam, David, *The Best and the Brightest* (Random House, New York, 1972)

Haldeman, H.R., *The Ends of Power* (New York Times Book Co, 1978)

Hersh, Seymour, *My Lai 4: A Report on the Massacre and its Aftermath* (Random House, New York, 1970)

Kearns, Doris, *Lyndon Johnson and the American Dream* (Harper & Row, New York, 1976)

Kendrick, Alexander, *The Wound Within* (Little, Brown, Boston, 1974)

Kissinger, Henry, *The White House Years* (Little, Brown, Boston, 1975)

Lewy, Guenter, *America In Vietnam* (Oxford University Press, New York, 1978)

Littauer, R. and Uphoff, N. (eds), *The Airwar in Indochina* (Cornell University study, Beacon Press, 1971)

Nalty, Bernard C., *Airpower and the Fight for Khe Sanh* (USAF, History Branch, Washington, DC, 1973)

Nixon, Richard M., *The Memoirs of Richard Nixon* (Grosset & Dunlap, New York, 1978)

Patti, Archimedes L.A., *Why Vietnam? Prelude to America's Albatross* (University of California Press, 1980)

*The Pentagon Papers* (Gravel Edition; Beacon Press, Boston, 1972)

Porter, Gareth, *A Peace Denied* (University of Indiana Press, 1975)

Shawcross, William, *Sideshow: Kissinger, Nixon and the Destruction of Cambodia* (Simon and Schuster, New York, 1979)

Shore, Moyers S., *The Battle for Khe Sanh* (USMC, History Branch, Washington, DC, 1969)

Snepp, Frank, *Decent Interval* (Random House, New York, 1977)

Szulc, Tad, *The Illusion of Peace* (Viking Press, New York, 1978)

Walton, George, *The Tarnished Shield: A Report on Today's Army* (Dodd Publishers, New York, 1973)

Westmoreland, William C., *A Soldier Reports* (Doubleday, New York, 1976)

Westmoreland, William C., 'A War of Attrition', chapter in *The Lessons of Vietnam* edited by Frizzel, D.D. and Thompson, W.S. (Crane-Russak, New York, 1977)

Page numbers in boldface type indicate photos.